HENRY BRADLEY PLANT

HENRY BRADLEY PLANT

Gilded Age Dreams for Florida and a New South

Canter Brown Jr.

The University of Alabama Press
Tuscaloosa

The University of Alabama Press
Tuscaloosa, Alabama 35487-0380
uapress.ua.edu

Typeface: Minion

Cover image: Tampa Bay Hotel, 1898; courtesy of the Henry B. Plant Museum
Cover design: Cheri Marks

Library of Congress Cataloging -in -Publication Data

Names: Brown, Canter, Jr., 1948 - author.
Title: Henry Bradley Plant : gilded age dreams for Florida and a new South / Canter Brown Jr.
Description: Tuscaloosa : The University of Alabama Press, [2019] | Includes bibliographical references and index.
Identifiers: LCCN 2019013825| ISBN 9780817320379 (cloth) |
ISBN 9780817359669 (pbk.) | ISBN 9780817392666 (e book)
Subjects: LCSH: Plant, Henry Bradley, 1819 -1899. | Businessmen --Florida --Biography. | Florida --History --19th century. | Southern States --History --19th century.
Classification: LCC F315 .B87 2019 | DDC 975.9/04092 [B] --dc23 LC record available at https://lccn.loc.gov/2019013825

For my nephew Edgar Eugene Brown,
my niece Gwendolyn Brown Clark,
and their families, with love.

Contents

List of Illustrations ix

Introduction 1

1. Formative Years: 1819 to 1834 5

2. New Haven: 1834 to 1844 22

3. Recovery: 1844 to 1854 40

4. Southern Ways: 1854 to 1859 58

5. Unwanted Conflict: 1859 to 1863 75

6. A Work of Reconstruction: 1863 to 1868 95

7. Flush Times: 1868 to 1873 112

8. The Panic: 1873 to 1878 130

9. Florida and the Pearl of the Antilles: 1878 to 1882 147

10. Tampa: 1882 to 1886 166

11. Transportation and Tourism: 1886 to 1889 185

12. Unanticipated Outcomes: 1889 to 1893 203

13. In the Midst of Calamity: 1893 to 1896 223

14. War and Peace: 1896 to 1899 243

Afterword: The Ephemeral Nature of Legacies 266

Notes 269

Bibliography 315

Index 341

Illustrations

1. Branford Green 9

2. Erie Canal 14

3. DeWitt Clinton locomotive and train 20

4. Steamboat *New York* 29

5. Ellen Elizabeth Blackstone Plant 38

6. William Brown Dinsmore 45

7. City of New York, 1849 50

8. Henry Plant, "Expressman" 67

9. William Henry Seward 89

10. Havana, Cuba 121

11. Bust of Henry Plant 137

12. Bust of Mary Josephine Loughman Plant 142

13. Henry Morrison Flagler, 1870 152

14. The Plant System's *Margaret* 176

15. Havana's Grand Hotel Pasaje 181

16. Ponce de Leon Hotel 193

17. Henry B. Plant and President Grover Cleveland 201

18. Tampa Bay Hotel 214

19. Henry and Margaret Plant in rickshaws 230

20. Portrait of Margaret Plant 247

21. *La Grande Duchesse* 249

22. "Millionaire Plant" 259

HENRY BRADLEY PLANT

Introduction

The Gilded Age entrepreneur Henry Bradley Plant has been remembered since his 1899 death as a man who helped to invent modern Florida. The distinguished historian S. Walter Martin touched on this point in 1958, although he identified a greater—if regional—ambit for the magnate's influence. "To his credit was a great network of railroads, a well-developed express business, a growing system of hotels, and an increasing and expanding steamship line, in addition to directorships in several other enterprises," Martin asserted. "One of the best-known men in the South at the time of his death, he was loved and honored by some and thoroughly despised by others. He was a thrifty 'Southern Yankee' who had made his fortune in the South, unlike his contemporary Henry M. Flagler, who had made the bulk of his fortune in the North and had come South to spend it. There was neither a Standard Oil Company nor a John D. Rockefeller back of Plant. Through his own efforts he founded one successful enterprise after another. Though he never held a political office, he had a strong following among those who were elected to office in both Georgia and Florida." Martin added: "It was fairly well agreed that Henry B. Plant was a pioneer of the New South and a man who had faith in the future of Georgia and Florida. There were results to prove it."[1]

With respect to who have portrayed Plant in just such contexts, his vision and reach in fact ranged internationally, and his policies helped to pioneer modern corporate approaches in a variety of areas, including employee relations and benefits. By the 1890s the Plant System spanned over three thousand miles from Saint John, New Brunswick, to Kingston, Jamaica, and beyond. In piecing together his empire, the businessman had meanwhile blazed a path toward vertical integration of the tourism industry. Admittedly, he had reinvented a state. So successful had he proven in that endeavor that *Success* magazine in 1898 crowned him "King of Florida." Just as true, he linked New England to Canada's maritime provinces, while furnishing his home state of Connecticut with a model summer resort open to enjoyment by rich and poor alike. Plant's developmental passion rose highest, though, when it came to his perception of the intertwined—if still unresolved—destinies of Florida and Cuba. He loved the Pearl of the Antilles and dreamed of Havana's potential as a mecca for American travelers and investors. He tried repeatedly to forge inroads there. Time and again he faced frustrations as dynamics and personalities beyond his control stymied his actions.[2]

Even in the case of Sunshine State development, the magnitude of Plant's accomplishments has diminished over time. The subsequent achievements of Henry Morrison Flagler—who justly deserves credit for sparking the rise of the Atlantic coastal region from St. Augustine through Miami and, ultimately, Key West—have played a part in this. Collective memory can betray us, though. Plant stoked Flagler's developmental ambitions, guided him to Florida, taught him the complexities of the railroad industry, alerted him to the possibilities of remote Miami, expanded his vision to the Caribbean, and showed him how resorts and trains could be linked successfully and lucratively by luxurious steamships. The two men shared deep and abiding friendship while collaborating for years as business partners. Little wonder that upon Plant's death, Flagler stood at the forefront of his dear friend's pallbearers.

The glow of Plant's innovative approaches to Gilded Age management and employee relations has faded as well. His paternalistic approach today appears antiquated, if not sinister. Yet Plant pioneered health care and other benefits for his employees and did so without regard to race. He attempted to introduce corporate profit sharing and reached out a protective hand to black employees as the specter of Jim Crow increasingly shadowed the South. He desired to treat those who worked for him honestly and respectfully and often succeeded. Not that his record stands unblemished. He allowed—if he did not urge—the use of convict labor in the construction of Florida railroads; he permitted—if he did not order—dismissal of prounion activists; and for a brief time, he surrendered to local pressures and barred black service staff from his centerpiece hostelry, the Tampa Bay Hotel.

Through it all and despite his shortcomings, a large majority of those who gained their living from Plant's enterprises admired and remained loyal to him. He died taking immense pride that his businesses had never suffered from a major labor strike. Robert W. Davis, a Florida acquaintance, spoke to pertinent aspects of Plant's makeup at ceremonies marking the tenth anniversary of his death. "Horace Greeley said, 'Fame is a vapor; popularity an accident; riches take wings; those who cheer us today will curse us tomorrow; only one thing endures and that is character,'" Davis declared. "To character he might have added love for your fellowman. I glory in contemplating the man of peace. The man in whose heart burns the desire to uplift—to advance—to enlighten and to make better the condition of the people. The man who makes a blade of grass grow where none grew before. It has been said that peace hath her victories no less renowned than war, and it may be truly claimed that the victories of peace are the victories which have brought advancement and happiness and prosperity in their train."[3]

Why, then, has our collective memory of Henry Plant so disserved us? The simple answer is that he planned it that way, although he did not foresee all the consequences of his actions. Plant emerged from an express industry culture that prized secrecy in operations and administration, and he learned his lessons well. While his businesses were open to view by all comers, his business for the most part remained hidden from all but Plant and his partners. The entrepreneur applied the same principles to his personal life. He kept his confidences and his own counsel, rarely revealing a glimpse of his inner self or thoughts. As he aged and grew wealthier, he took the next step and sought to control his image insofar as the public and the future were concerned. He accomplished his goals through a variety of approaches, including his own behavior when in the public eye and the active labors of the Plant System public-relations staff. He also commissioned a laudatory, albeit flawed, biography that has influenced perception of him from 1898 to the present time. As a result, the blood, sinew, and humanity that were Henry Plant have been bleached from the record. An imperfect and ambitious man, he made serious mistakes but possessed the remarkable gift of learning from them. He accomplished much, and the respect and even affection that he earned in the process articulately underscored the nature of his humanity. Henry Flagler would have understood the point and agreed.

My attempt to realize the portrait of Henry Plant that follows could not have been accomplished without the support, encouragement, and assistance of numerous individuals and institutions. I first, as always, especially thank my wife and partner, Barbara Gray Brown, who for over twenty years has understood and encouraged my passion for history. Let me acknowledge as well that she has often shared with me key insights and information that I otherwise would not have seen. I have also benefited for decades from the friendship and collegiality of two outstanding scholars who have done their best to keep my work honest and have often improved on my attempts to reach that goal. I thank Larry Eugene Rivers, former president of Fort Valley State University and currently distinguished professor of history at Florida A&M University, and James M. Denham, professor of history and director of the Lawton Chiles Center for Florida History, Florida Southern College, Lakeland.

Very special thanks go as well to executive director Cynthia Gandee Zenober, curator/registrar Susan Carter, curator of education Heather Trubee, and the staff of the Henry B. Plant Museum, Tampa; George B. Howell III, Holland & Knight and Tampa Bay History Center, Tampa; the Honorable E. J. Salcines, Florida District Court of Appeals, Tampa (retired); president Ron Vaughn, University of Tampa; Arlene Royer, National Archives and Records Administration, Morrow, Georgia; Sherriley Strachan, Department of Archives, Nassau, Bahamas; Charles Tingley and Susan Parker, St. Augustine Historical Society, St. Augustine, Florida; Plant System historians Seth H. Bramson and Gregg M. Turner; Muriel Jackson, Washington Memorial Library, Macon, Georgia; Fred R. VanHartesveldt, Fort Valley State University, Fort Valley, Georgia; Andy Huse, special collections, University of South Florida Library, Tampa; Steven Engerrand, Georgia Archives, Morrow; Aisha Johnson, special collections and archives, University of North Florida Library, Jacksonville; LuAnn Mims, Lakeland Public Library, Lakeland, Florida; Daphne G. Hopson, Frances C. Gibson, and Nina Raeth, Augusta Genealogical Society, Augusta, Georgia; Al Langley, North Augusta, South Carolina; and Tina Monaco and Tina Rae Floyd, Augusta-Richmond County Public Library, Augusta, Georgia. I also relied on two excellent student researchers to complete necessary inquiries for me, and I thank Emily Yankowitz, Yale University, and Todd Ciardiello, University of South Florida. I would be remiss if I did not also credit the outstanding work of the University of Alabama Press staff, with particular thanks happily given to editor in chief Dan Waterman and copyeditor Laurel Anderton. Finally, my continuing debts of gratitude to the late Samuel Proctor, University of Florida history professor and *Florida Historical Quarterly* editor, and the late Leland M. Hawes of the *Tampa Tribune* remain, as ever, large indeed.

Incorrect spellings and usages in direct quotations have been left as they appear in the original, and the use of [*sic*] has been avoided. Responsibility for the interpretation of events and for errors of fact is mine alone.

1

Formative Years

1819 to 1834

"a liquid fire never to be quenched"

"I don't know much about Mr. H. B. Plant's religion or politics," humorist Charles Henry Smith—"Bill Arp" to readers—observed in 1896, "but I do know that he is a grand old gentleman of the olden time." Smith knew his subject well. Plant's perspectives, values, and judgment had been formed in the 1820s and 1830s when circumstances reflected little of the advanced industrial age that later propelled him to personal fame and immense wealth. Rather, the world for him then encompassed the badly misnamed "Era of Good Feelings" that followed the War of 1812 and its tumultuous successor the Jacksonian Age. To the child, titans of industry and captains of political parties offered few, if any, models for behavior. Instead, he sought worthy examples in cautionary tales born of youthful experiences and embellished stories of Revolutionary forebears. He lived in what he could truly call a home only sporadically. Still, he drew strength from family, friendship, religion, and heritage. As an all-too-human being, his mistakes created lasting pain for himself and others. He survived and prospered, though, by keenly observing his actions and surroundings and finding courage to follow truer paths forward. "I have taken note of him for nearly half a century, and if there is any bigger man in the line of public progress and public benefaction I don't know it," Smith commented. "Many other men have built on the foundations that others have laid and become notable on the wrecks of other people's fortunes, but Mr. Plant made his own plans in early life and has by slow and sure degrees expanded and matured them."[1]

Plant's life began in a moment infused with fear, which is to say a time when alarm bordering on panic prevailed. His parents, Anderson Plant and Betsey Bradley Plant of Branford, Connecticut, had married on December 23, 1818. Anderson was twenty-two, and Betsey had just turned nineteen.

The young couple quickly conceived their first child, but as the pregnancy evolved during 1819, distant reports increasingly stoked local concerns. Historic Branford lay on Long Island Sound less than eight miles east of New Haven and was thus tied to the sea and maritime commerce. As it happened, waves of "pestilential disorders" plagued the Atlantic seaboard that spring and summer. Yellow fever especially brought deadly consequences, striking from Boston to Savannah. Thirty-seven died in New York City despite a rigid quarantine. New Haven, in turn, blockaded against New York. On October 5 a local newspaper cautioned, "The citizens of New-Haven will have abundant cause for gratitude, if they escape the pestilence." They did not, and several cases appeared. This would not be the last occasion when disease threatened Henry Plant's survival.[2]

On October 27, with the fever persisting in its deadly course, Betsey gave birth to Henry Bradley Plant. Despite the perilous circumstances, he proved a healthy child, one fortunate enough to enter a usually stable world. Branford offered a locale where family and relations, even though not affluent, enjoyed respect and extensive networks of interconnections. Not that all the Plants lived in humble circumstances. Anderson's cousin David Plant served when Henry was born as speaker of the state house of representatives and, by 1827, sat in the US Congress. Still, David's example offered the exception rather than the family rule. "Mr. Plant was poor when young, his father being a worthy farmer of Branford," a local editor later observed. Anderson farmed land Plants had held since the seventeenth century. It lay "in a fertile little valley, a mile from the village, and [was] bounded on the west by the Branford Hills." Nearby in "Plantsville," Henry's grandparents Samuel and Sarah Frisbie Plant raised Anderson's younger siblings. Their son Samuel Orrin Plant, born four years before Henry and technically his uncle, came closest to being the older brother that Henry never had. They bonded as friends and, in time, married sisters.[3]

Beyond immediate family circles, Branford's Congregational Church offered focus for Henry's earliest years. Townspeople assembled at its sanctuary located strategically on the town green to find social as well as religious nourishment. Henry recalled that as a child, he sat "in the high galleries in the old church where the seats were arranged in slips, the boys on one side, and the girls on the other. Neither could see the minister, and it is very doubtful whether any of them heard him." Plant added: "There were no children's sermons in those days. The Babes, of whom Paul writes, were not fed on milk, but on strong meat, which even the rigid doctrinal appetites of the fathers sometimes found hard to digest."[4]

As with extended families, the Plants likely kept a "Sabbath-Day House" in a spot abutting the green. Such structures served as a center for activity on "the Lord's day" when congregants were not required in church. Religious leaders urged that available time be utilized for Bible reading or introspection, but the advice often went unheeded. "Possibly some one of less serious mood might talk with his neighbor of worldly matters, or the news of the day," one clergyman observed critically. Little wonder that many sought respite from faith's rigors. Congregationalists had moved past some "obnoxious" customs by the 1820s, but the times brought new and, in some respects, more frightful demands. No longer did members publicly confess "in detail, all of the[ir] particularly scandalous sins." Yet church fathers viewed the times as "dark ones from the standpoint of morality" and sanctioned a "committee of inspection and information" to investigate even wispy rumors of scandal. Church trials through the decade involved "drunkeness, theft, lasciviousness and adultery." In 1826, as Henry turned seven, congregation members felt themselves falling into ever-more-desperate straits. "The state of this church is such as imperiously to require discipline," they determined. A "new, and larger committee" resulted.[5]

Branford's Congregationalists might have suffered greater extremes of intolerance and poor judgment but for the steady, if hardfisted, hand of Pastor Timothy Phelps Gillett. "Blessed is the church which, in the days of stress and cleansing, has the gift of such a pastor," a church historian proclaimed. "Many another congregation was forever divided with hatred and schism in these same hard years, and we gladly ascribe to this shepherd's sanity and calm, forbearing judgment the praise for preserving his people in unity and concord." He added, "He was the last of those old New England pastors whose word was a law in the community and whose voice bore the authority of God." The historian conceded nonetheless, "The ministry of 'Father' Gillett was not spectacular, and will not measure up in dramatic incidents to that of his predecessors." The pastor baptized Henry on June 9, 1822. As Gillett also taught the local school, he instructed young Plant "for several terms." Biographer George Hutchinson Smyth reported Henry's memories: "[Gillett] was a sober, solemn, orthodox clergyman of the old school, scholarly and dignified both in and out of the pulpit. It is only a hint of the changes that time brings, and no reflection on this good man's charity to say that, had he seen one of the modern ministers visiting his flock on a bicycle, he would have had him deposed from the sacred office."[6]

While Father Gillett exercised significant influence on young Henry, the weight of his father's presence necessarily loomed even greater. Unfortunately for the child, Anderson Plant died young. Henry's mental images of him dimmed over time to two specific visions. "He can recall how his father once came in, with a friend, from a morning's duck shooting, and threw down half a dozen ducks on the floor," Smyth noted. "At another time, his father took him by the hand to see something that was happening in the town which had drawn out the people, but he does not remember what it was." That latter recollection surely concerned Branford's grandest day of the era. On August 21, 1824, Revolutionary hero the Marquis de Lafayette reached Branford while touring the United States. "He stopped but a short time, but long enough to receive and return the congratulations of many of the inhabitants," an account described. "The children far and near got a furlough for the forenoon—the afternoon is always unencumbered on that day—and they came pouring over the hill and valley for many a mile around, led on by their parents and grand-parents, their dames & patriarchs of the villages and hamlets." It added, "A crowd of people and two companies of foot [i.e., militia] awaited him at Branford, and they joined in loud acclamations at his approach." The dramatic nature of the day notwithstanding, Betsey Plant remained at home. Her responsibility lay in tending to her new daughter, Eliza Ann. Henry's baby sister had been born exactly three months earlier.[7]

While Henry's memories of his father faded with time, other ties forged in childhood endured with continuing impact. His relationships with his mother and grandparents proved crucial and will be examined shortly. Friendships supplemented those ties. No list of Plant's childhood friends has survived, but the identities of several key individuals are known. Samuel O. Plant, as noted, stood among them. Also close by were the Blackstone boys, sons of community leader James Blackstone. In politics a Federalist and later a Whig, Blackstone held numerous public offices. "He was a man of character and remarkable ability," a biographer observed, "and if his tastes had led him to a larger place for the exercise of his ability no field would have been so large that he would not have been a leader among men." Henry admired Blackstone, especially after Anderson Plant's death, while sharing friendship with his sons George, Lorenzo, John, and Timothy. Lorenzo, born four months before Henry, always ranked first. The Blackstone girls, too, factored heavily. Sam Plant in time married the eldest, Mary. That union left Ellen available for Henry.[8]

While the Plant boys eventually found love at the Blackstone home, they also gained considerably from Captain Asa Norton, who reigned at Branford as a larger-than-life figure. Admittedly, Norton meant more to Lorenzo—who married his daughter—than to Henry, but both boys grew enthralled. Unlike the farm-bound Plants and Blackstones, the captain looked to the sea for fortune and adventure. Best known as master of a packet line that ran from Branford to New York, he also helped tie New Haven businessmen to West Indian resources and markets. Norton's tropical tales intrigued Henry and Lorenzo on countless occasions, broadened their horizons, and

1. The Branford Green, Connecticut, c. 1914. Town of Branford, Connecticut.

in Henry's case, fixed his gaze toward the Antilles. Norton and his wife, Sophia Barker Norton, produced eight children. One son died in June 1826 at the outset of that year's sickly season, but other family members shared childhoods and adult friendships with Henry and Lorenzo. Daughter Emily, born in July 1820, eventually captured Lorenzo's heart.[9]

With family and friends available to enrich his days, Henry spent his first six years in relative stability and comfort. Farm work required exertion, a fact inherent in the family's circumstances. "His boyhood was spent principally on the farm assisting in matters which pertained to that type of life, which undoubtedly had an important bearing on his practical knowledge, as well as a beneficial influence on his health," future associate Franklin Q. Brown relayed. "The life of a New England boy in those days was not one of idleness in any sense." A solid work ethic originating in those tender years characterized the man as well as the boy. So, too, did a yearning for life and, especially, music. Betsey Plant's father, Levi Bradley, a community leader and sometimes a legislator, had taught a singing school and delighted in performing. Betsey, perhaps aided by her Episcopalian—rather than Congregationalist—heritage, took special pleasure of her own in music. She led the Congregational choir and filled the Plant home as well with mellifluous airs. "One of the first recollections I have of my mother," Henry recalled, "was on a Christmas Eve, when she dressed me up neatly, took me on her knees, talked affectionately to me, and sang that beautiful vesper hymn,

'Adeste Fideles'; even now, whenever I hear it, it brings tears to my eyes." Brown observed, "Mr. Plant always felt he had inherited a certain taste for music, particularly sacred, from his mother."[10]

Plant neglected to date the "Adeste Fideles" performance, but it probably came in December 1825. A mother's warmth and a beautiful Christmas carol then would have addressed a distraught six-year-old child's urgent need for comfort and reassurance as he faced a world that had tragically and abruptly turned upside down. Deadly fevers again beset Branford during summer and fall 1825. "It is well known," a New York newspaper had observed that June, "that in the warm season, agues and fevers, dysentery and typhus fever, frequently prevail." Rather than yellow fever, the problem now involved typhus syncopalis, or New England Spotted Fever. Today associated with meningitis and encephalitis, the typhus often proved deadly. "The disease had two notable elements," a researcher explained. "The first was described as 'an alarming or fatal sinking' or 'paroxysms of subsidentia' described by patients as a sensation of 'gastric sinking.' The second outstanding characteristic was the lack of response to, and indeed the danger of, the usual purging remedies usually employed in the treatment of fever." Headaches, vertigo, dizziness, and extreme exhaustion characterized early symptoms. Redness of the skin and "eruptions of all kinds" followed. "The patient often looked as if he or she was affected by poisoning or narcotics as well as stroke," the researcher advised. In cases involving the disease's "insidious form," a week or two of agony often preceded death.[11]

Typhus struck several Connecticut towns during the 1825 fever season, but Branford and the Plant household bore especially heavy losses. Postmaster Jonathan Barker became the first local casualty on August 12. Joel Ives succumbed two days later. Plant family relation Hannah Frisbie Hoadley, wife of farmer and blacksmith Orrin Hoadley, passed away after much torment on September 24. Henry's seventeen-year-old aunt, Mary R. Plant, followed on October 1. Soon, the pestilence invaded the Anderson Plant home. He fell ill, as did Henry and infant Eliza Ann. Anderson perished on October 29, aged only thirty. Eliza Ann lived a week or so longer. That Henry survived appeared miraculous. "[He] was so ill that he knew nothing of his loss," biographer Smyth explained, "until he was partially recovered from the dreadful disease."[12]

Betsey Plant strove as best she could to move beyond the tragedies, finding purpose in tending to her son's welfare. "[He] was brought up by his mother," Frank Brown commented, "to whom he was always devoted." Diminutive in size, she stood five feet, one inch tall but proved "a lady of strong personality." To help her surviving child cope with tragic loss, she enrolled him in Pastor Gillett's school, an event that Plant recollected vividly. Smyth preserved the memories, which probably arose in January 1826. "She had dressed him up in new clothes and talked to him about going to school and learning to read, and becoming a good scholar, and doubtlessly much more that her kindly mother-heart would suggest to awaken interest and stimulate ambition in the boy," he related. "Then she took him outside the gate, pointed out the schoolhouse, kissed him, and told him to go thither and give his name to the teacher as a scholar. His mother intuitively knew her child's sensitive disposition, and had her misgivings about his being able to carry out her instructions; so she concealed herself and watched him till he reached the school door. Here poor little Henry's courage failed him, and he came running back to his mother, not to be scolded but to be encouraged and helped over his childish timidity. His mother this time went with him to the schoolhouse, took him in, and made him acquainted with the lady teacher [an assistant to or substitute for Gillett]."[13]

Betsey quickly discovered that her need to keep the farm going infringed on her ability to keep Henry in school. While Anderson had not died a pauper, the means he passed on to his widow and son were modest. When estate distribution came in May 1827, she received personal possessions valued at less than $200. As Anderson's only surviving child, Henry inherited notes, cash, and personal property amounting in all to $383.59. The circumstances compelled mother and son to labor in order to make ends meet. That fact nearly led to Henry's demise. Alden Pardee Bryan, a Branford native and Plant protégé, related the tale: "When a boy of about eight or ten years of age [actually six or seven], he was one day riding a plow horse at work in the field. The horse became frightened and ran away, carrying plow, boy, and all with him. Barefooted and bareheaded, the brave lad clung to the horse until entirely exhausted, when he fell and was severely injured. He was found in the woods by friends who carried him into their house. After several hours' hard work by the doctor and others, he revived sufficiently to be taken to his home. The fight for life was severe and protracted, but he bore it heroically."[14]

Henry's second near-death experience changed Betsey's life and that of her son. "Some time after my father's death," he recollected, "my mother married again, a man by the name of Philemon Hoadley." At age twenty-nine, Hoadley had lost his wife on August 17, 1826, leaving a son named Henry Hodges Hoadley not yet three years old. A special-needs child, Henry Hoadley enjoyed excellent physical health but suffered from mental impairment that ultimately limited his employment to farm work and, eventually, fashioning walking canes. As a child, his conditioned called for special care. Philemon thus required a wife and caretaker at the same time as twenty-seven-year-old Betsey accepted that she needed a new husband. The Hoadley family maintained strong ties to New Haven and Branford; Philemon's cousin George Hoadley, for instance, presided as New Haven's mayor from 1822 to 1826. It took little effort, given extensive kinship and community networks, for the widower and widow to find each other.[15]

The marriage took place in Branford on May 8, 1827, and the occasion understandably presented a challenge of consequence for seven-year-old Henry, one on a par with his father's death. Fortunately, Philemon Hoadley strove to be a good man. Henry later praised him as "exceedingly kind to me" and especially cherished Hoadley's compliment that "I was the best boy he had ever seen." But the marriage obligated Betsey and her son to pull up stakes and relocate away from family and friends to a frontier-like region in New York. To cushion that break, Betsey devised a phased transition for the child. Henry temporarily remained with grandparents Samuel and Sarah, who kept him in school at Branford until time for his move. Afterward, they welcomed him home for occasional visits. The initial interlude afforded Sarah Frisbee (sometimes spelled Frisbie) Plant opportunity to verse her grandson in family heritage. Henry never forgot that she "had much to do with his 'bringing up,'" as a result of which "he held his Frisbee ancestors in high esteem." Ranking high among them was Sarah's father, Joseph Frisbee. "There has always been a tradition in our family," Henry later asserted, "that he was a major on Washington's staff at Valley Forge." However importantly that tradition weighed on Plant, it unfortunately was not true. Frisbee had served honorably, but only for two months late in the war as a private soldier in the Eighth Connecticut Regiment.[16]

At some time prior to 1830 and likely in 1827 or 1828, Henry's moment for relocation arrived. The journey demanded more than tear-filled goodbyes. It meant days of dangerous travel and required a variety of means. These were still pioneering days for steam boating, and risks abounded. First Henry would have steamed from Branford or New Haven to New York City. The boat's boiler thankfully not exploding and the vessel having avoided collision or grounding in a storm, he transferred to another steamer for a two-hundred-mile cruise up the Hudson River to Albany. Good fortune thereupon greeted him in the form of another recent transportation innovation. In 1825 the Erie Canal had opened, revolutionizing movement by providing a dependable water route from the Hudson westward 363 miles to Buffalo on Lake Erie. So, a canal packet boat could now carry Henry as far as Utica on the Mohawk River, about one hundred miles. A stagecoach or wagon then relayed him over the fifty-something tortuous miles northward through the Black River Valley to Martinsburg (then spelled Martinsburgh), seat of Lewis County. One area man described the stagecoach ride as "the hardest work ever done by travelers." As he recalled, "the perils of Deerfield dike in high water times" gave way to "the terrors of Trenton hill, the passage of which was enlivened by obedience to the driver, whose command, 'right' and 'left' was the signal for the passengers to lend the weight of their influence to the corresponding sides of the long square box wagon to keep it right side up." That ten-mile ordeal transitioned to "the tedium of Remsen mud," then seemingly endless stretches of sand and "an hour's drag over a road which stage drivers had declared was 'up-hill both ways'" in order for travelers to reach Boonville and the halfway point. A night at "Bagg's tavern" led the next day to a trek "through the Leyden and Houseville bottomless clay." The man insisted, "What dragging, what cramps in the legs, until Martinsburg, set upon a hill, welcomed the vision."[17]

Martinsburg presented in the late 1820s an unpretentious, if not rugged, appearance. A report stressed its location "upon a high and commanding site" and described the area as "surface undulating, soil fertile loam, resting on limestone, abundantly productive of wheat and other crops, drained easterly by Whetstone and Martin's creeks; settled in 1801 by Gen. Walter Martin and others." The Hoadley family, led by Philemon's father, Philemon Sr., numbered among the first to arrive in the county. Its members had traveled overland from Massachusetts. Philemon Jr. had moved away from his father's home, however, to make his own way nearby at Martinsburg. The Presbyterian Church, the first Christian sanctuary erected north of the Mohawk, particularly attracted him. The original Congregationalist fellowship had merged with the Presbyterians to form the church of the 1820s. Overall, 2,000 or so people shared the area with Philemon, plus about 2,000 head of cattle, nearly 1,000 horses, 8,000 sheep, and 4,000 pigs. Of particular interest, the magnificent Chimney Point chasm lay two miles southwesterly on Whetstone Creek. "The roar of the waterfall and the grandeur of the surrounding landscape add an interest to the scene rarely experienced," a state gazetteer advised.[18]

Although a few upscale houses graced Martinsburg, log cabins abounded in the late 1820s. L. L. Fairchild reminisced about conditions that Plant encountered. He had been born, Fairchild declared, "in the days of open-stone fire places with open fire, and tallow candles for lights." He explained: "Matches came into use about 1827. I was six or more years old before lo-co-fo-co matches were seen in our town. When the fire went out, many times I was sent to a neighbor to borrow fire, carrying a burning brand between two thick barks. When the wind blew, the little chap was quite apt to get his fingers burned." The pioneer continued: "Everybody dressed in homespun linen or wool. In a heavily timbered country, the flies and mosquitoes made a lively time for both man and beast. In hard winters of heavy snows the hungry wolves necessitated everything to be closely housed. If sheep were left in open sheds, a tin lantern was posted in front, to warn the

2. *View on the Erie Canal* by John William Hill, 1830–1832. Watercolor on paper, 9 ¾ × 13 ¾ in. From the New York Public Library, I. N. Phelps Stokes Collection of American Historical Prints.

wolves away." He added: "The earth is a Paradise and Heaven compared to eighty years ago[, with] angels of humanity occupying the land, with kindness, humanity, good will, and benevolence, abroad in the world and seeking the welfare of humanity."[19]

Martinsburg afforded young Henry two main centers for activity and interaction beyond the Hoadley farm. As at Branford these were school and church, although the rough-and-tumble Lewis County atmosphere considerably flavored his experiences. "The first school house in town was built on the west side of the road, on the brow of the hill South of the village," an account noted. An organized school committee supervised affairs, but Martinsburg rarely offered more than basic instruction. A more promising school named the Lowville Academy operated four miles north. Henry could have boarded at the nearby town, but his help was needed at home and the cost proved prohibitive. Accordingly, surviving academy enrollment lists from 1828 to 1830 omit mention of him.[20]

Church, given local circumstances, ranked even more importantly for Henry than had worship at Branford. As Henry observed of Philemon Hoadley, "He was a very religious man." An acquaintance added: "Mr. Hoadley was a Puritan in his religious principles and prejudices, and by his rigid sternness and tenacious adherence to his opinions, he sometimes made enemies, but those who knew him best, knew that he was a good man. He, like the patriarch Job, 'always called upon God,' and his Bible was his daily bread. He sympathized with the poor and the unfortunate, and manifested his devotion to their interests by kind attention and generous contributions." Hoadley's perspectives meshed with Martinsburg's religious conditions. L. L. Fairchild, for one, recalled the nature of religious service and discourse. "Dating back to youthful days, one of the disturbing elements of thought and happiness, was the persistent preaching of a revengeful God and devil, who were looking up and down the earth in wrath, for transgressors of divine laws, for which terrible penalties were to be meted out," he recorded. "A burning hell, a liquid fire never to be quenched, was promised to all who did not repent and be saved through faith. The devil, in disguise immemorial, was going up and down the earth for victims to cast into hell. One revivalist preacher said in the presence of our family: 'That he had no doubt hell was paved with infant skulls not a span long.'"[21]

The emotionalism that Fairchild underscored was something profoundly new and quite remarkable, especially for Presbyterian and Congregational churches. Credit went to the 1820s continuation of the Second Great Awakening. That term, experts explained, "refers to a period of intense religious activity in the history of the early republic, from about 1790 to 1840. It was marked by significant changes in the nature of the major Calvinist denominations—Methodism, Presbyterianism, and Congregationalism, and by new outreaches in social services and social reform." Hallmarks of the era included "enthusiastic revivalism," coupled with "camp meetings, devout prayer, and a high level of emotionalism." So intensely did the fires of awakening burn in a score of counties in northwest New York, including Lewis County, that the area famously took on the name "Burned-Over District." This derived from comments made in 1876 by revivalist Charles Grandison Finney that in this "burnt district," residents had experienced "a wild excitement passing through the region, which they called a revival of religion."[22]

An additional and key aspect of the Second Great Awakening particularly touched young Henry. This was known as the Benevolent Empire. The impulse for reform ran so strong as to call, at times, for complete purification. All of society's ills arguably demanded attention, whether prison reform through the opening of penitentiaries, operation of orphanages and mental asylums, or proliferation of public schools. Longtime ills such as "drunkenness, adultery, prostitution, and crime" offered especially popular targets, as Branford's 1820s Congregational experience had illustrated. The heart of many of the efforts pulsed in the work of a cadre of religious intellectuals. "At the very center of the Benevolent Empire was a small group of Congregationalists and Presbyterians educated at Princeton, Williams, Yale, and Andover Theological Seminary who were informally allied with members of the Baptist, Dutch Reformed, Episcopal, and Methodist churches," Steven Mintz observed. "During the antebellum years, the leaders of the Benevolent Empire struggled to create a wide range of cross-denominational missionary societies, Bible and tract societies, Sunday schools, and temperance societies—all aiming to reshape individual character and instill an ethic of self-control. In an era of convulsive social and economic transformations, of rapid urban growth and western expansion, prayer meetings, Sunday school classes, and benevolent societies not only held out the promise of a nation guided by evangelical principles, such institutions also provided many individual Protestants with a meaningful social identity as participants in a larger spiritual endeavor."[23]

At Martinsburg, Rev. David Kimball embodied the flowering of the Second Great Awakening and the Benevolent Empire. A New Hampshire native born in 1791, he graduated from Yale in 1818 and then the Andover seminary. Kimball took his ministry in 1822 to Martinsburg. "His labors were very onerous, as part of the time there was no other settled pastor in the county, and he was sent for far and near to perform pastoral duties, besides preaching three times regularly every Sabbath and holding meetings during the week." Despite the demands, Kimball nurtured a Sabbath School and expanded the Presbyterian ministry into Lowville. As the locality grew, he developed a county Sabbath School Union and, about the time in 1827 when Philemon Hoadley returned to town with bride Betsey, formed a Bible Society to provide free copies of the scriptures. He additionally formed a temperance society, and within three years the initiative—Kimball's own preference was for "total abstinence" as opposed to temperate use of ardent spirits—claimed a viable local network laboring within a statewide organizational framework. In 1830 alone, its seventy Martinsburg members closed two of the town's distilleries and cut "use of spirits" by one-eighth.[24]

The intersection of Reverend Kimball, the Martinsburg church, the Second Great Awakening, and the Benevolent Empire worked lasting impressions and consequences for Henry Plant. Kimball, for one thing, accepted special responsibility when it came to young people such as Henry. "He was a faithful pastor, and he seemed ever mindful of the direction of the good Shepherd, 'Feed my lambs,'" a biographer asserted. "He was very particular to notice children as he passed them in the street whether he was walking or riding." One time, Kimball "rode eleven miles through a dense forest to attend the funeral of a child." As the minister had been raised by a widowed mother, he took particular pains when it came to girls and boys who had lost fathers. In Henry's case Kimball enjoyed the opportunity to offer care firsthand because Philemon Hoadley acted as the pastor's strong right arm. Plant's stepfather supervised the Sabbath School and contributed to the Bible Society. He labored, as well, for the temperance cause and other church initiatives. Betsey, too, entered Kimball's close circle, in her case through music. "Mr. Kimball," the biographer added, "was extremely fond of singing, and possessed a melodious voice, a leader in the choir in college at Andover, sometimes also a teacher." The fact that the Hoadley family as a unit adhered closely to their church and its minister produced consequences for all. Henry, as one example, lived his life as a temperance man although not necessarily a teetotaler. His attempts in later life to demonstrate meaningful concern for fellow men also derived ultimately from Kimball and the teachings of the Benevolent Empire, a dynamic that often tempered Plant's adult judgment.[25]

Good works aside, the mostly congenial and beneficent state of Plant family affairs at Martinsburg eventually succumbed to critical misjudgments on Hoadley's part as well as Kimball's. Hoadley spent so much time on church causes that his farm and seasonal wool-carding business suffered. His capacity for making a living for his family diminished accordingly. Kimball meanwhile ventured too close to the all-consuming fires of rough-and-tumble politics, dragging Hoadley with him. Specifically, starting in 1828 Kimball backed the rising Anti-Masonic movement in battling supposed conspiracies emanating from Masonic lodges. This endeavor evolved into attacks on individuals called Republicans but who, as Andrew Jackson supporters, soon took the name Democrats.[26]

Kimball unfortunately allowed perceived support from the one hundred or so members of his congregation to cloud his assessment of prevailing county sentiment. He battled as if for God and country, but his misjudgment revealed itself in early 1830 at an Anti-Masonic convention held at his Martinsburg church. The surprise came when the event attracted only nineteen people, Kimball and Hoadley among them. "We suppose the usual cant and proscriptive measures were entered into, to stifle the peaceful sanctuary of the church and to girdle by way of politics, the true spirit and principles of our Republican institutions, and to palm them upon the unsuspecting public, as the proceedings of a numerous and *patriotic* society," an observer reported. The emperor having been revealed as wearing no clothes, even the Presbyterians turned against the pastor. By October Kimball had been urged to an unceremonious and hurried departure. The next month Anti-Masonic forces were swamped at the polls two to one, and Henry Plant at age eleven began to cultivate a permanent yearning to avoid politics and Freemasonry.[27]

Kimball's departure and the leadership void that followed produced unanticipated results that rocked Martinsburg, nearly incapacitated Hoadley, and soon ushered Plant and his mother back to Branford. These consequences came all the more unexpectedly because events of late 1830 and early 1831 had seemed to herald a happy new era in family affairs. Relieved of many church-related responsibilities by Kimball's leave-taking, Philemon for the time had concentrated on his farm and future. He and Betsey meanwhile conceived their first child together in January or February 1831. She remained in Martinsburg through the pregnancy, and on October 31 she and Philemon welcomed a son. They named Henry's half-brother George Anderson Hoadley.[28]

Unfortunately, before the birth Hoadley family circumstances had devolved toward chaos. Some locals traced the tenor of the Great Revival of 1831 to the demise of twenty-one-year-old teacher Mary Ann Waters, killed on June 20, 1829, in a fall from a horse during a storm. Her sudden death shocked young people such as Henry, and five hundred of them participated in her funeral. Kimball spoke, as did others. "The whole scene was said to be one of the most impressive ever witnessed in the county," an onlooker related. "Those who witnessed it probably never saw another such funeral." A wave of religious fervor ensued, although passions ebbed with time. Then, weeks after Kimball's departure small religious gatherings began to stir emotions once more. Finally, in April 1831, the dam that had restrained local passions broke completely. At Martinsburg and quickly through the region, revival meetings captured hearts and souls. "During the Winter and Spring of that year the whole region seemed overshadowed by the Holy Spirit," a resident recalled. "The church in all its branches was deeply humbled before God; confession and return to duty were the almost universal order of the day; individual christians were borne down by an overwhelming sense of the condition of the impenitent and also with a vehement desire for their salvation, accompanied with a wrestling and prevailing spirit of prayer."[29]

If Kimball had remained in favor, his reassuring presence and weight of authority might have held back—at least in Martinsburg—what in short order became religious excesses severe enough to spark bitter reaction. As it happened, no local leader proved capable of forestalling the clashes of summer and fall. Jefferson County adjoined Lewis to the northwest, and its local historian eloquently painted the picture. "In the summer of 1831 there occurred another series of religious revivals throughout the country, and 'protracted meetings' were held in nearly every village," he observed. "Great numbers professed conversion, and all the evangelical churches received accessions. These proceedings were strongly discountenanced by a portion of the citizens, and led to a convention at the court-house, July 2, 1831, at which addresses deprecating these excitements were made, and resolutions were published expressing their sentiments on this subject. In these a conscientious approval of pure religion was avowed, but the popular excitements of the day were denounced as whirlwinds of moral desolation."[30]

At Martinsburg and other places, residents found the fabric of their communities torn and tattered, while individuals such as Philemon Hoadley discovered their ability to deal with the stresses critically limited. Philemon's involvements can only be imagined, but the consequences appear clear. At about the time that Betsey gave birth to George, Philemon suffered mental or physical collapse. So severe did his condition prove that he sought relief in an expensive sojourn in the warm Antilles. He departed Martinsburg in early winter, leaving Betsey with two adolescents and an infant to cope as best she could. His ship *Plandome* sailed from New York City on January 7, 1832, and touched at Kingston, Jamaica, ten days later. Arrival brought surprise. A slave rebellion and acts of cruel repression ruled the day. "I assure you," he penned from Montego Bay on the twenty-third, "we found trouble enough." He later added: "The scene at Jamaica is indeed appalling, I never witnessed any thing of the kind before." Time passed while Hoadley healed and slowly began a personal transition toward becoming an ardent abolitionist. Travels ultimately brought him to Cuba by March. He then delayed his departure from Trinidad de Cuba for weeks. Meanwhile, Betsey and the children had endured terrible winter conditions. Their travail left her yearning for Branford. When the weather cleared sufficiently, she borrowed money from a local friend and took her leave of the Hoadley farm. Henry, now twelve, departed with his mother and half-brothers. He understandably carried with him several lessons learned. An apprehension of emotionalism and an abhorrence of religious extremism, traits that he carried for the remainder of his life, factored high among them.[31]

Betsey Hoadley presumably intended a return to Martinsburg, her husband, and the family farm soon after his reappearance, but a cholera epidemic held her at Branford through the summer. In early June the disease appeared at Quebec and Montreal. Within days cases broke out in New York, including on June 18 eighty miles north of Martinsburg at Ogdensburgh. Twelve days later New York City reported its first cases, and the death toll began to mount significantly. By July 2 panic was gripping New York City, among other places. "We understand that almost every steamboat which left New York yesterday was crowded with a dense mass of fugitives flying in alarm from the imaginary pestilence," an editor advised. "The roads, in all directions were lined with well filled stage coaches, livery coaches, private vehicles and equestrians, all panic struck, fleeing from the city, as we may suppose the inhabitants of Pompeii or of Reggio fled from those devoted places when the red lava shower poured down upon their houses, or the walls were shaken asunder by an earthquake." The death toll climbed as

3. DeWitt Clinton locomotive and train, c. 1904. Library of Congress.

the weeks merged into one another. Eventually, over 3,500 people died in New York City alone.[32]

The Hoadley family reunion finally occurred in late September or early October. If not on the journey to Branford earlier, the trip back to Martinsburg may have allowed Henry Plant—days before his thirteenth birthday—his first train ride, an event that embedded in him a lifelong fascination with railroads. The Mohawk & Hudson Rail Road, New York's first and one of the nation's earliest steam-driven lines, had debuted in September 1831, connecting Albany and Schenectady and allowing passengers to avoid slow and difficult Erie Canal passages. If nothing went wrong, the locomotive DeWitt Clinton pulled cars over the sixteen-mile course in less than an hour. In any event the party's homecoming proved a happy one, and by mid-October Betsey found herself pregnant once more. Her fourth pregnancy proceeded smoothly given one exception. Beginning on May 10, 1833, rains deluged the region. The *Martinsburgh Republican* advised that by Sunday night, the twelfth, "the streams were higher than they were ever known to have been but once, since this country was first settled. We have not been able to learn the extent of the ravages. But the destruction of bridges so far as we have heard seems to be general. Eleven bridges have been swept away in this town, besides other losses have been sustained to a considerable extent." The ravages notwithstanding, a healthy Horace Philemon Hoadley was born at Martinsburg on July 17. He and half-brother Henry Plant remained affectionately close until Horace's death in 1893.[33]

The Hoadleys quietly passed time through the first half of 1834. Philemon strove with mixed results to return the farm to profit, a task at which Henry Hoadley and Henry Plant assisted. Betsey worked alongside them while tending the two youngest children. Martinsburg's Anti-Masonic movement had been dealt another stinging electoral defeat in March 1832. Happily, with Andrew Jackson's White House arrival one year later, local political divisions eased. The same proved true at church. The Presbyterian congregation had regained sufficient cohesion to secure a new minister. Leicester Ambrose Sawyer was only twenty-five years old and a Lewis County native, and thus knowledgeable about local people and ways. He had graduated from New York's Hamilton College near Utica before attending Princeton Theological Seminary. The young pastor embraced most aspects of the Benevolent Empire but in certain respects went further than many of his older colleagues. He advocated biblical "higher criticism," questioned the inerrancy of the scriptures, and espoused the cause of abolition. Eventually, Hoadley rejected Sawyer's modernism for a more conservative path, but at Martinsburg he found encouragement in the minister's demand that slaves be freed.[34]

The Martinsburg era ended abruptly for Plant in summer 1834. Possibly he and his mother were already at Branford when word arrived of cholera at Prescott, Ontario, adjacent to Ogdensburgh. By mid-August, locations around New York State reported renewal of the dread disease. If not already in Connecticut, Betsey hurried her children to the state. This time she settled at New Haven, where Hoadley relations offered a haven. Good schooling also awaited Henry there, a fervent wish of his grandmother Plant. The fall term of the city's Lancastrian School commenced August 9, and by that time or soon afterward Betsey Hoadley and her children had settled in the city. Philemon followed once he had arranged his New York affairs. Henry rarely spoke thereafter of Martinsburg. His distaste for the place appeared starkly, though, in the fact that he never returned.[35]

2

New Haven

1834 to 1844

"too much pluck to quit"

When the Philemon Hoadley family arrived at New Haven, Connecticut, in the mid-1830s, fifteen-year-old Henry Plant entered a welcoming and diverse environment that allowed him for the first time to explore difference and possibility, a world that recognized broader horizons. There he also enjoyed access to enhanced schooling, a critically important factor given that his previous experiences had ranked modest at best and traumatic at worst. As had been his custom he embraced the warm comfort of family, friends, and relations. Beyond that he found that he also enjoyed discovering the acceptability of unfamiliar lifestyles and beliefs. "Henry was a very diffident child," biographer George H. Smyth noted. Now, life began to emerge for Henry first as less threatening, then as more adventurous, and ultimately as more exciting. In the process the boy slowly developed a willingness to venture out, to try new things and visit new places. At home his stepfather maintained influence while espousing hard attitudes, especially when it came to religious ideas and beliefs. Yet Henry forged a workable path away from Hoadley's strictures. As he did so, Plant commenced the process of learning to think for himself.[1]

New Haven in the mid-1830s presented a striking prospect. "If you were to set a poet to make a town, with *carte blanche* as to trees, gardens, and green blinds, he would probably turn out very much such a place as New Haven," sometime poet William Parker Willis waxed. "The first thought of the inventor of New Haven [the first planned city in the nation] was to lay out the streets in parallelograms, and the second was to plant them from suburb to water-side with the magnificent elms of the country. The result is, that at the end of fifty years, the town is buried in leaves. If it were not for the spires of the churches, a bird flying over on his autumn voyage to the Floridas would never mention having seen it in his travels." Willis added: "The houses are something between an Italian palace and an English cottage—built of wood, but, in the dim light of these overshadowing trees, as fair to the eye as marble with their triennial coats of paint; and each stands in the midst of its own encircling grass-plot, half buried in vines and flowers, and facing outward from a cluster of gardens divided by slender palings, and filling up with fruit-trees and summerhouses the square on whose limit it stands. Then, like the vari-colored parallelograms upon a chessboard, green openings are left throughout the town, fringed with triple and interweaving elm-rows, the long and weeping branches sweeping downward to the grass, and fair forms (it is the garden of American beauty—New Haven) flit about in the green light in primitive security and freedom."[2]

Day-to-day New Haven life failed for most people to reach the heights scaled in Willis's rosy prose, but the city unquestionably offered ambience far at odds with that of frontier Martinsburg. Perhaps twelve thousand to thirteen thousand people lived there. Where Branford held mostly white Congregationalists and Martinsburgh white Protestants of many sorts, different circumstances prevailed in New Haven. Particularly, African Americans had contributed to its urban life since near its founding. In 1835, six hundred or so black men, women, and children lived there, a figure notably including about thirty-five slaves. Many lived in New Guinea, an area east of downtown near Wooster Square. Nearby at Slineyville, Irish immigrants constituted a second significant minority. The founding in 1832 of Christ Church, the city's first Roman Catholic church, marked its progress, as did the opening two years later of its first parochial school.[3]

Yale College cast a giant shadow over community affairs. "Yale has brought to New Haven a scholastic atmosphere unfavorable to a normal political and social development, and a [traditional voting] population which has cared everything for the administration of the college, little or nothing for that in the City Hall," a resident explained. "Until a recent day, the best interests of the city have suffered because so many of its most intelligent residents were men who looked upon the affairs of the community as foreign to their world; who may have been profoundly interested in Roman politics of the time of Caesar, or even in national politics of their own day, but who overlooked the civic structure which immediately contained and concerned them."[4]

Alternatively, other factors ruled in the realms of commerce and the economy. New Haven's excellent harbor, where whalers had reaped profits for generations, counted heavily. Increasingly, though, maritime gains were derived from newly exploited sources. "A thriving trade with the West Indies sugar islands and the lucrative sugar boom brought sugar and molasses, which was then distilled into rum, back to New Haven in exchange for what the high-yield farms among the Connecticut hinterlands, despite relatively poor and rock soil except along the fertile Connecticut River Valley, produced—corn, pork, beef, and oats," observed historian Phillip Thomas Tucker. "By 1830, this lucrative West Indies trade was New Haven's very lifeblood that fueled the town's economy and general prosperity."[5]

Less noticed than the West Indies trade, a thriving industrial sector also contributed substantially. At New Haven, Eli Whitney had manufactured the first cotton gin in 1793, and two years following Plant's arrival, Samuel Colt would invent the first automatic revolver. Given Whitney's associations, close ties bound the community to the South and Cotton Kingdom slavery. "New Haven's economy touched the most remote corners of both America and the Caribbean," Tucker explained. "By the antebellum period, a good many slave-masters of sprawling cotton fields across the South drove fine wooden carriages made in New Haven. Gangs of slaves on Southern plantations used farm implements manufactured in New Haven. And slaves also drove teams of horses or mules with harnesses made in New Haven. This direct economic connection between New Haven manufacturers and merchants—and to a lesser degree the common farmers—to the South's plantation system and slave regimes, and the lucrative Caribbean sugar islands, thrived. Many aristocratic sons of leading Southern planter elites attended Yale College and brought their slave servants with them, as if they were yet in the sunny South."[6]

Within the bustling economy, Henry's stepfather set out to reclaim economic security. His local relations specialized in quality carriage making, but Philemon wanted to capitalize on his familiarity with horses. "Philimon Hoadley kept the up-to-date hack and livery stable in his time . . . on the north side of Court street," recalled Edward C. Beecher, whose father, Benjamin Beecher, in future times would aid Henry's entry into business. "Mr. Hoadley was an urbane, kindly spoken gentleman to everybody," he added. "He was a man of commanding physique and looked finely on a horse." Yale divinity students particularly appreciated Hoadley's operation. "Philemon Hoadley, a livery stable keeper in New Haven, never rented his horses out on Sunday, but gave the students free use of his teams during the revival [season]," one source related, "so that they could ride to churches in other towns and share the Gospel."[7]

The Hoadleys meanwhile lived at 19 Court Street. Their home was situated downtown on the corner with Orange Street. A block west was the New Haven Green with its historic churches and public buildings. Yale's "old campus" lay another block west beyond the Green. In the opposite direction from the Hoadleys, Court Street soon ended at Wooster Square, near where New Guinea and Slineyville sat. A half mile to the south the harbor and its hectic activity beckoned. Facing the Hoadley residence stood the Assembly House, a prominent tavern and hotel particularly popular with state legislators. Its ready hospitality, manifested in the form of ardent spirits served by black waiter Jim Cooper, must have enraged teetotaler Philemon, whose stables could be found immediately to the right. There was little that he could do about the situation, however. The family, chronically short of funds, necessarily had settled on property owned by Betsey's relations. The same house notably had served Captain Phineas Bradley when he helped to resist Great Britain's invasion of New Haven in 1779. Unfortunately, on April 8, 1836, it also witnessed the death of Henry's half-brother George Anderson Hoadley, not yet five years of age. The tragedy's cause was not reported.[8]

As Philemon slowly built his business, Henry pursued education. The Lancastrian School had operated to local acclaim since 1822. English-born John E. Lovell had guided its fortunes for three decades, earning the title, at least among New Haven's elite, "world's most famous teacher." Chronicler Everett G. Hill explained: "The feature of the Lancasterian system . . . was the employment of the older pupils to teach the younger. It seemed to work well under so excellent a master as Mr. Lovell, and appealed to some of the other educators of New Haven." He continued, "In those days of small numbers in the schools, when they were simply country schools on a little larger scale, it had some educational advantages." Locals felt greater enthusiasm for Lovell than did Hill. "Though a strict disciplinarian," an obituary read, "his old-time pupils about worshipped him." Even Hill admitted, "[Lovell's school] graduated many of the men who made the New Haven of their day."[9]

Henry left no account of his days at Lovell's school, but chances are that he looked on lessons and exercises there mostly as a chore. Biographer Smyth admitted, "Henry was not particularly fond of study." Although Plant acknowledged attendance at the Lovell school, he never claimed to have graduated. One source insisted that he did not. *Railroad Topics* reported: "He never went to college, but had to content his ambitious young spirit with a good academic course, supplemented by a brief term of finishing study under a thoroughly competent tutor. This, however, was only a theoretical disadvantage, from the fact that the termination of his school days was no interruption to his mental acquirements. He was born with an ambition for knowledge, and does not to this day feel himself too old, or too wise, to learn."[10]

The record fails to verify what, if any, ambition Henry displayed in the mid-1830s, but it does reveal preference for boyhood pursuits with friends who showed enterprise and determination. Plant's affinity for Lorenzo Blackstone and his brothers traced to childhood days. Lorenzo displayed solid intelligence but, as with Plant, little interest in formal schooling. At age sixteen, which is to say in 1835, he departed Branford for New Haven and a carriage-making apprenticeship. Three years of toil sufficed to convince him to acquire "a knowledge of accounts, and of general mercantile business." As will be seen, Lorenzo thereby identified a vocation that would launch him toward becoming a millionaire and standout success in mid-nineteenth-century trade and industry. James Edward English meanwhile embarked on his first venture in 1835, perhaps providing Plant some part-time work along the way. Descended from venerable New Haven forebears and seven years older than Henry and Lorenzo, he had "in boyhood exhibited singular self-reliance." English had learned the building trade in the 1820s rehabilitating the Lancastrian School building. Now "the possessor of a moderate capital," he set up on his own as an architect, contractor, and builder. English thereafter launched one successful project after another. Ultimately he branched out into the lumber business, shipping, and clock manufacture. He found time for politics as well. A New Haven selectman by 1836, the Democrat moved to the legislature in the 1850s, sat in Congress from 1861 to 1865, twice presided as governor, and later became a US senator. The three New Haven boys meanwhile remained friends and business associates until their deaths.[11]

The economic rise of English, Blackstone, and—eventually—Plant from humble 1830s beginnings owed much to opportunities created by fundamental changes in the nation's economy as it evolved, thanks to Industrial Revolution outflows, from an agrarian orientation to an ever-more-complex industrial one. T. J. Stiles examined those dynamics when considering the life of Cornelius Vanderbilt, himself a beneficiary of the changes and a future influence of significance to Plant. Stiles characterized the earlier era as functioning based on an "unspecialized, informal economy" that depended on "messy personal dealings." The system desperately required organization as times changed, ones in which institutions such as commercial banks flourished as did stock and securities markets. Credit came to be regularized, and corporate entities increasingly marked the financial and business landscapes. Economic cycles produced boom and bust conditions, but generally speaking, opportunity awaited those willing to take the risk. "These new institutions," Stiles concluded, "laid a foundation that was absolutely essential for the future."[12]

That Plant, Blackstone, and Edwards all gravitated toward the shipping industry suggests that their early years together in New Haven involved a great deal of time spent at the docks and on board ships. The waterfront throbbed with vital energy as exotic cargoes from the West Indies arrived to be handled by Irish and black stevedores and draymen. Unusual languages and accents punctuated noise-filled rooms in waterfront taverns. Tales of the open seas and strange places beguiled the young men; humor, deep-bellied and uninhibited laughter, swearing, collision, alcohol-fueled confrontation, and myriad other sensations and experiences assaulted them. A Plant biographer articulated the resulting attraction for deep water beautifully. "If the little harbor at Branford had set him dreaming of the sea," Kelly Reynolds observed, "the waterfront at New Haven would set his heart on it."[13]

The maritime industry then was benefiting from Industrial Revolution innovation, as were other segments of the economy. The steamboat, introduced by Robert Fulton on New York's Hudson River in 1807, had matured into a highly desirable, if still-dangerous, means of transportation by the time Henry departed the Lovell school. Bradley family relations early on had invested in the New Haven Steamship Company, which served routes between New Haven and New York City. In 1836 the firm introduced a new boat of cutting-edge design and technology, the *New York*. Running 250 feet in length with a twenty-three-foot beam, the vessel glided through water thanks to paddle wheels nearly twenty-five feet in diameter. It traveled, one onlooker observed, "with unprecedented dispatch" and overall was "a splendid boat." Novelist Charles Dickens agreed. "After a night's rest, we rose early, and in good time went down to the wharf, and on board the packet New York, *for* New York," he related. "This was the first American steamboat of any size that I had seen; and certainly to an English eye it was infinitely less like a steamboat than a huge floating-bath. I could hardly persuade myself, indeed, but that the bathing establishment off Westminster Bridge, which I left a baby, had suddenly grown to an enormous size; run away from home; and set up in foreign parts as a steamer. Being in America too, which our vagabonds do so particularly favor, it seemed the more probable." The *New York* commenced its regular run on April 4, 1836. Townsmen—likely including friends Plant, Blackstone, and English—cheered in excitement.[14]

The exact moment when Henry opted for a maritime career cannot be ascertained, but it came in 1837. His decision was based, beyond the question of adventure, on at least two major factors that emerged into the broad light of day that May. First, on the tenth, New York banks suspended specie payments, handing Democrat Martin Van Buren's new presidential administration the bill for Andrew Jackson's rash fiscal policies. A horrendous economic depression known as the Panic of 1837 followed. Although the panic proved devastating throughout the East, New Haven suffered particularly. Jim English's widow recalled: "When the commercial crisis of 1837 swept over the country Mr. English was twenty-five years old. In New Haven the suspension of banks was followed by the failure of merchants and manufacturers. Then ensued a general shrinkage of values and a temporary stoppage of traffic." Philemon Hoadley, along with others, sustained losses almost immediately.[15]

Coincidentally, the Presbyterian Church tore itself apart as religious "modernization" came under assault by influential individuals and groups espousing conservative values within the larger context of the growing national crisis over slavery. At Philadelphia from late May to early June, the "Old School" faction grasped denominational control. Its adherents repealed earlier measures designed to guarantee cooperation and eventual unity among Presbyterians, Congregationalists, Dutch Reformed Church members, and others. They also expelled four "New School" synods—including the Synod of Utica, to which the Martinsburg church belonged.[16]

The religious clash echoed at New Haven, where Yale's "New School" proponents faced increasing opposition from "Old School" adherents in town. Henry had experienced as a child how bitter and painful such confrontations could become. Now, he revisited the same pathetic scene as local Presbyterian and Congregationalist flocks reeled and split. Interestingly, Martinsburg pastor Leicester A. Sawyer was at hand, having relocated to New Haven shortly after the Hoadleys settled. He epitomized extreme "New School" sentiment at North Congregational Church (now United Church on the Green) until opposition compelled him in 1837 to found another church. On the other hand, Rev. Elisha Lord Cleaveland increasingly pressed the "Old School" cause at Third Congregational Church. A thirty-one-year-old graduate of Bowdoin College and Andover Theological Seminary, he also reeled from reaction. "The connection of the Third Church, through its pastor, with the opposition to what was called 'New Haven theology,' accelerated the process of disintegration," a memorialist commented, "and the result was that when the division came he and those who adhered to him were placed in circumstances of painful adversity." It took several years for Cleaveland and his followers, among them Philemon Hoadley, to find an acceptable new home. By the early 1840s the conservative breakaway faction worshipped in a Court Street building a short distance from the Hoadley home.[17]

Financial and religious stresses within the Hoadley family during spring and summer 1837 meanwhile reached painful levels, to the point of clashes between Henry and his stepfather. One clue: grandmother Sarah Plant invited Henry to move into her Branford home. Sarah's conditions, though, proved unacceptable. She planned for Henry to attend Yale and become a minister. He responded that he wanted "an active life." He apparently stumbled in that determination with several false starts or, as George Smyth put it, "attempted several things" that did not suit him. In fact, Henry had breathed ocean air and thrilled to dockside excitement too often. These things now represented escape from problems that he little understood and could not control. Probably through Bradley shareholders in the New Haven Steamship Company, he finally gained a position acceptable to him. By Henry's eighteenth birthday, on October 27, he was working aboard the *New York*.[18]

4. Steamboat *New York*. From C. Seymour Bullock, "Perilous Journeys of Some of the First Steamboats in American Waters," *Connecticut Magazine* 16 (October–December 1906).

Although life as a deckhand proved exacting for Plant, Henry never looked back. "I was employed on the side wheel steamer New York, which had for companion steamers the Splendid and Bunker Hill, on each one of which I served at one time or another," he reminisced. "It was on the New York, however, that I spent most of my apprenticeship. The deckhands slept below in the forecastle, an uncomfortably small space in the 'eyes' of the boat, and took our meals in the kitchen standing up. Take it all in all, it was rather rough on a fellow that had just left a good home, and when some of my towns people would come aboard and catch me with swab or broom in hand, I didn't feel altogether happy, but had too much pluck to quit."[19]

The eighteen months or so during which Henry initially labored on the *New York* and its sister vessels offered the young man years' worth of experience. Adventures ranged from rescues to setting speed records and from fun to fires. In February 1838, for instance, he aided the *New York*'s crew under Captain Solomon Bartlett Stone in rescuing survivors and freight from the *William H. Bunn*, a sloop that sank off Norwalk. Three weeks later the *New York* itself faced disaster when ice disabled its rudder in dangerous winter weather; once again, Stone's steady hand averted calamity. In April, nonplussed by the ice damage, the captain helmed the boat to an all-time speed record from New Haven to New York, covering the eighty-six miles in a breathtaking "4 hours 39 minutes." A New York newspaper exclaimed, "In consequence of this early arrival, passengers who breakfasted in New Haven, were enabled to arrive in Philadelphia via Trenton Rail Road, in time for supper." Henry also delighted in a gala celebration of the Fourth of July when the *New York* offered a patriotic daylong excursion from "the foot of Beekman street . . . down the Bay and up the North River."[20]

The *New York* tour of duty conversely ended for Plant in treachery and corporate intrigue, a dynamic with which he grew very familiar. The New Haven Steamship Company was nearing bankruptcy by spring 1839 for several reasons, including Panic of 1837 problems, competitor Cornelius Vanderbilt's desire to stifle competition, and endless complications connected with services provided for the US Post Office. "In April last, the [New Haven] company found it absolutely necessary to raise means to sustain their mail line, or sell out at a loss," Vanderbilt explained. "As they expected no aid from the [Post Office] Department, they had no alternative but to sell, even though it should be at a sacrifice: their property was in the market, and I bought their boats, wharves, &c. for one hundred thousand dollars." New Haven Steamship shareholders approved the sale on March 21. Hours later the *New York* erupted in flames as it lay tied to the New Haven wharf. "It is a gratifying circumstance that at the time of the fire, she had but a very small quantity of freight on board," a reporter commented dryly, "less than on any occasion for twelve months previous." Authorities blamed the "accident" on "carelessness in the fireman or watchman." Rumors pointed to arson. Although the boat had been "thoroughly burned out," Vanderbilt soon dispatched the hull to New York for rebuilding. "It is no small satisfaction that the model is preserved," commented the *New York Journal of Commerce*, "for the boat was not upon the whole surpassed by any boat in our harbor."[21]

Henry thus unwillingly found himself in spring 1839 working for cutthroat businessman Vanderbilt. The experience—a period that left Plant chafing—was not one that he later enjoyed discussing. Vanderbilt placed two boats on the New Haven to New York run, the *Bolivar* and the *Splendid*. A critic argued that "the Commodore" and his associates "seem disposed to try how far the feelings and interests of the public may be trampled upon with impunity." The *Bolivar*, the critic insisted, was an "old hulk" with "no accommodations,—the captain's office is kept in the bar,—she has no kitchen, except a temporary closet, with a common size cooking stove in it." A one-way trip now sometimes required eleven hours. As for the *Splendid*, it soon left service. "The steamboat Splendid, hence for New Haven, broke her shaft yesterday morning, near Throg's Point," a report noted on October 5.[22]

By early 1840 matters had improved little for the service or for Plant. The *New Haven* and *Bunker Hill* replaced the *Bolivar* and *Splendid*, and, to the good, average running time improved considerably. Henry manned the *Bunker Hill* under Captain Stone. Poor corporate management, though, meant continued problems and undependable service. The post office refused to patronize the boats. "Between New York and New Haven the mail is sent by land, lumbering along the shore of Long Island Sound in stages, while the steamboat passes in six hours, and often in a shorter time," a report observed. "A letter written at New Haven cannot be taken from the office in New York until the third day." As Vanderbilt and the post office battled over the slight, even the fledgling private express business turned its back on his vessels. Entrepreneur William Harnden announced that "owing to the existing state of the steamboat communication to New York," he had "determined to run his Package Express by land, via Springfield, Hartford, and New Haven." Harnden added that he proposed "to establish a regular Express, every other day, (Sundays excepted) to start simultaneously from New York and Boston." Extreme winter conditions thereupon prompted suspension of steamboat service.[23]

When the *Bunker Hill* returned to employment on March 1, 1840, scandal engulfed it. During the suspension Harnden had decided to begin utilizing the boat, but the post office persisted, at least publicly, in its refusal. Yet a mail contractor arranged with "one of the proprietors" to "smuggle" mail bags on board at New York. The contractor insisted that he acted "to relieve my horses during the excessive bad roads, caused by their early and sudden breaking up" and that "the bags did not contain any letters, but only a part of the newspaper matter." Stone smelled a rat. "This morning, very early, several bales of merchandise came down to the steamboat Bunker Hill, bound for New Haven," a New York newspaper informed readers. "The captain, a remarkably sly Yankee, having a curiosity to know what merchandise was shipped so early, and suspecting that some smuggling was going on in British goods, slipped his penknife cautiously in one of the bales, to have a peek, and discovered they were [Postmaster General] Amos Kendall's Letter Bags!! inside the bales. The worthy captain said to the agent 'Deliver this merchandise free; the poor devils at Washington have no money to pay their own way, and have to smuggle their mails.'" Stone then tipped newspapermen to the story. "Heaven deliver us," bemoaned an editor, "into what hands has our Government fallen!"[24]

Three weeks later disaster struck with near-fatal consequences for Plant. "The Steamer Bunker Hill left New York, on Tuesday afternoon [March 24], at 4 o'clock, during the storm, for New Haven, crowded with passengers," Harnden reported. "When one hour or more out, a squall struck her, split her amidships, and filled her with water to the depth of a foot over the cabin floors. To keep her from sinking, she was run ashore, and her passengers returned to the city the same night. She passed two sloops capsized." By the time Henry arrived in New York—cold, soaking wet, and still recovering from the narrow escape—he had begun to comprehend an important lesson. Earlier he had seen firsthand the value of quality service, solid product, and state-of-the-art equipment. As his future work would demonstrate, he now understood that he much preferred that state of affairs to any shoddy alternative that figures such as Vanderbilt might provide.[25]

Fortuitously, in tandem with the *Bunker Hill* debacle came word that the *New York* was readying to reenter service. "When she came out in the spring it was quite an event," Henry recollected. "She had two new copper boilers, one on each guard, the first to be placed on the guards." The vessel also had been lengthened, expanding available space considerably. The state-of-the-art boilers enabled it to achieve unheard-of speed (reportedly "up to twenty-five miles an hour"), a fact that had Vanderbilt excited that he could pull off a public-relations coup. The attempt came in mid-April and took the form of a race. A passenger, perhaps Harnden, promised Stone newspaper coverage "as soon as he got to Boston." As good as his word, the passenger passed on to the *Boston Journal* that "a steamboat race [was run] in [Long Island] Sound on Thursday last, between the steamer New York, bound to New Haven, and the Nimrod, bound to Bridgeport. The New York beat her antagonist." While the *Journal* chastised the parties for "such dangerous experiments," newspapers throughout New England and the Middle Atlantic states featured the report.[26]

The *New York*'s renewed tenure of service, with Plant aboard, proceeded well at first. New York newspaperman James Gordon Bennett, for one, loved the boat and crew. "From New York to New Haven, we came in the steamer New-York, Capt. Stone—a capital boat, and a capital Captain," Bennett declared. Another traveler attested: "We made a trip a short time since, to the beautiful city of New Haven, in the 'New York' under command of Capt. Stone, and have rarely enjoyed a more pleasant sail. Capt. Stone is very gentlemanly in his manner and agreeable in his deportment." Unfortunately, competition prompted Vanderbilt in September to cut fares down to one cent. This stunt attracted a problematic clientele and an epidemic of petty crime. The ensuing security problem, especially regarding packages and luggage, bedeviled Stone until he perceived a solution in the person of a now-seasoned though still-junior employee. Over the past three years, Stone had reportedly become "very fond of young Plant." Henry picked up the story from there. "Up to this time quite a considerable lot of package freight—express matter, as it were—began to be sent back and forth," he related. "This was stowed in different places about the boat and not properly cared for until one day the captain conceived the idea that a big double stateroom forward of the wheel could be used in which to store it, and I was assigned the duty of looking after it, and a berth put up there for me to sleep in. As I look back upon my career in those days the one on which I was transferred from the dingy forecastle to the express room was by far the happiest, and it was there that I took my first lesson in the express business." The date of the reassignment was not recorded, but it occurred in rough proximity to October 27, 1840, Henry's twenty-first birthday.[27]

As he took that first express business lesson, Plant found himself with an enviable perch from which to witness an industry's creation. The revolutionary developments then reshaping business and finance demanded fast, dependable, and confidential modes of communication that the post office simply could not, or at least did not, provide. Into the void in the late 1830s and early 1840s stepped not well-heeled corporate entities or industrial magnates but individuals of little means. "When we consider the vast extension of the Express service, both in area and importance," industry pioneer Alexander Lovett Stimson observed, "we cannot but wonder that so gigantic a growth should have sprung from the enterprise and persevering energy of a few men who began the good work, with neither capital nor rich relations, nor high social position to back them. Indeed, more than one of them had not enjoyed even the advantages of a first-rate common school education. Several of the most successful commenced their business with scarcely a dollar to their names, and all have to congratulate themselves that they have attained to their present standing, not by any adventitious aids, but solely by their own personal talents, united to the most indefatigable application to the work." William Harnden, with whom Henry was already acquainted, had labored among the earliest of the pioneers. Of considerable importance to Plant's future, in May 1840 Boston-based Alvin Adams, partnered with P. B. Burke as Burke & Co., launched himself into direct competition with Harnden. "After a few months of 'up-hill work,' Burke retired," Stimson commented, "and Mr. Adams executed all the 'opposition' himself." The efforts of such fledgling pioneers as Harnden and Adams eventually produced ties across regions and the nation of profound significance. They facilitated communication, trade, and long-distance financial transactions; meanwhile they overcame enormous obstacles of distance and government neglect.[28]

Whatever larger events were occurring around him, Henry passed the final months of 1840 and the first half of 1841 adjusting to his new station. He particularly grew close to Benjamin Beecher Jr., who had also set up a private express business. "Mr. Beecher started in with running an express to New York city and afterwards extended it to Boston," his son recalled. "He had a few cubic feet of storeroom in one end of the baggage room for his packages on the steamboats." Formerly a cabinetmaker and thirty-three years of age, Beecher proved an easy man for Henry to like. As their rapport developed, the older man enlisted Plant as his agent on board the *New York*. The arrangement permitted Henry to put aside the extra money and freed time for Beecher to expand his operations. It would not be the last time the two men found common ground for cooperation.[29]

Summer 1841, though, produced an unexpected turn of events. New Haven residents, appalled at Vanderbilt's continuing grip on their affairs, organized the "Citizen's Line." They purchased the *Belle*, said to be "a superior boat both in regard to accommodations and speed." The *New Haven Palladium* observed, "That she will receive almost the entire support of this city and the adjacent country, we do not entertain a doubt." The *Belle*'s new owners set passage fare at one dollar, in response to which Vanderbilt slashed his then-current rate from $1.50 to 12½ cents. "The consequence, as might be expected," one man advised, "was that the boat was crowded with all sorts and ranks of people, from a small jug of Day & Martin [bourbon whiskey], up to a four story dickey [high false shirtfront]." A New Haven resident commented, "Our city is flooded with loafers from New York, as they come now at a shilling a head." The turn of events exasperated Captain Stone. When delayed overnight in August on a Saturday departure, he dunned all aboard for the full dollar and a half, noting that the discount price had been quoted "for weekdays, Sundays excepted." Irritated, Vanderbilt transferred Stone to another line.[30]

Whether Plant remained in Stone's crew at the time of the captain's departure is not known. Henry's New Haven connections ran deep, and he likely preferred working on the *Belle* when it entered New Haven service as opposed to continuing in Vanderbilt's employment. In any event, on December 16 the *Belle* wrecked "under the lee of Hart's Island" in Long Island Sound with Henry aboard. "On account of the violence of the storm, the boat came to anchor at 6 o'clock," an onlooker described. "About ten it was discovered that the anchor dragged, and it was raised to cast in a new place. The cable soon parted, as did that of the second anchor.—The machinery was then set in motion, but owing to the violence of the wind and the roughness of the sea, the tiller ropes gave away, and the boat was driven at the mercy of the winds, and went ashore at half past ten. She continued to withstand a most furious sea until half past one, when she sprang a leak and soon filled with water." The onlooker added, "The passengers, crew, and freight, are all saved." Plant joined with others aboard in praising "the coolness, vigilance, and good conduct" of Captain Richard Peck for safeguarding their lives.[31]

Plant remained on board the *Belle* during the first nine or ten months of 1842. Following repairs and a brief suspension because of ice early in the year, it resumed runs with Henry handling consigned packages and luggage much as he had done on the *New York*. A bit of drama and a variety of new personalities appeared on the scene. Plant witnessed Benjamin Beecher, for instance, unsuccessfully attempting to stave off bankruptcy and then finding his way back into the express business. As the emergent express industry expanded overall, competition was heightening. Some one-man firms began to grow, bringing new people into Plant's daily life or else allowing growing acquaintance. He associated with several of them for much of his career. William Harnden created a good example by hiring eighteen-year-old Locke W. Winchester as his New York agent. That milestone, as will be seen, eventually carried special significance for Henry.[32]

More immediately important to Plant, Alvin Adams had discovered the need for New York help in his Boston to New York run. In summer 1841 he hired thirty-one-year-old Vermont-born William Brown Dinsmore, "a young harness maker." Dinsmore in turn forged links with onboard clerks such as Plant on whose discretion the industry relied. In the process Dinsmore encountered sixteen-year-old Irish delivery boy John Hoey. Possessed of immense charm and infectious humor, Hoey had already endeared himself to James Gordon Bennett. "I got in with a gang of boys, and in a short time we five made a corner in counting papers," Hoey recollected. "We counted, mailed, folded and shipped all the papers printed in the city. Mr. Bennett took a great fancy to us. . . . While I was doing this I made the acquaintance of an expressman named Beecher. He was running a little Connecticut express, and offered me four dollars a week and steady work. I accepted, and we took an office with Adams." The story, as related by a reporter, continued: "It was part of Hoey's duty to deliver papers to the New Haven steamer, which left New York every other day, and also at the office of Adams Express, a new venture. This express had just been started by Alvin Adams to run in opposition to Harnden's Express between New York and Boston via a steamer to Norwich, and thence by stage. Every other day a trunk was dispatched and one received. Hoey was taken into this office as an errand boy." By then Hoey and Plant had become firm friends. The ties held strong into the 1890s.[33]

Actually, express business ties served Plant well almost immediately. As it turned out, his days aboard the *Belle* were numbered. Vanderbilt seethed at the temerity of New Haven residents and ached to stymie the competition they had spawned. On June 9, 1842, the *Belle* lay close to the New Haven wharf. Vanderbilt took the occasion that night to fire a salvo in what some called the "steamboat war." According to a report: "[The *New Haven*] struck the Belle about midships, carrying away the wheel-house, wheel, &c., and otherwise damaging the boat. Had the blow been given a few feet after, the probability is that an explosion of the boiler, and a loss of life, would have been the consequence." The account added: "The affair has caused considerable excitement among the friends of the Belle, some of whom suspect she was designedly injured." Maritime historian C. Seymour Bullock concluded, "The 'Belle' . . . was deliberately run into by the 'New Haven.'"[34]

Whether Plant was aboard when the collision occurred remains uncertain, but if Vanderbilt was sending a signal, the stubborn persistence of the *Belle*'s New Haven owners decided him on sending another. "The steamers *Belle* and *Globe*, on their passage hence from New York, yesterday afternoon, came in contact in the Narrows, soon after passing Hellgate, the Globe running into the stern of the Belle, and afterwards crossing her bows, in which the anchor of the Belle ripped away a portion of her bulwarks," the *New*

Haven Herald related on August 6. "It would appear that there was a wanton attempt on the part of the Globe to injure the Belle, she having run into her stern when there was abundance of sea room for both," it added. "Passengers would naturally if possible, keep clear of them all." Within weeks the Citizen's Line's owners and Henry Plant, relieved to have survived his year on the *Belle*, communicated with clarity that all had understood Vanderbilt's message. "The Citizens' Line has sold the *Belle* to the Connecticut River Steamboat Company," an item published at New Haven on November 5 declared. "The citizens have now no defense against Vanderbilt."[35]

For his part, Henry left the water for a land-based job. When explaining his course he preferred not to mention Vanderbilt or the steamboat war. "Mr. Plant's position on the steamboat line plying between New York and New Haven, entailed a frequent absence from his home in New Haven, and he therefore decided to be more at home," biographer George Smyth recorded. "At this time he went into the express business of the line conducted by Beecher and Company. At first he had charge of the business at New Haven, but [several years] afterwards went to New York City, still keeping up his connection with the boats."[36]

Beecher had once more relaunched his express business and, since August 1842, had been working cooperatively with Alvin Adams on a New York to New Haven route. He operated out of Adams & Co.'s New York office at 7 Wall Street, while securing the New Haven end of his concern first at 40 Orange Street and then, beginning in May 1843, at 56 State Street. The latter site was a dry goods store operated by Washington Webb, a thirty-three-year-old merchant who had been acting since the previous summer as William Harnden's local agent. The change turned out well for Plant, as he and Webb found it easy to work together. The merchant, in fact, represented just the type of man Henry looked up to. "Mr. Webb was a native of Stamford, but came to this city when a young man, first as a clerk in the post-office, afterwards a merchant, and then attached to 'Harnden's,' afterwards to Adams' Express," a local man remembered. "Mr. W. was through life, an affable, kind-hearted, and popular business man—of generous impulses, and practical christian virtues. He had no enemies—but many friends."[37]

This transitional period proved a time of profound introspection and, ultimately, commitment to Plant. Certainly not least in importance, by age twenty-three he had decided on several basic standards and goals for his life. He later explained them to a Georgia editor. "He told [me] that sobriety and economy were the things he attributed his success to," Frank T. Reynolds recollected. "He said that at one time in his boyhood career he made up his mind to be rich and slept many a night on an express truck to save the 25 cents necessary to pay for his bed and this when his salary was $30 per month. When he was making $900 per annum his monthly expenses were not over $12 to $14 per month." Henry not only saved, but he saved wisely. "Young Plant was economical and saving," expressman A. L. Stimson confirmed. "He received his pay monthly, and instead of wasting it in folly and dissipation he gave his earnings to his mother, and she banked it for him. He then bought some stock in a New Haven bank which he still retains [in 1881]."[38]

Plant's economies and thrift served immediate purposes even if he continued to save for the future. For one thing, he yearned to enhance his position by investing in a business partnership that would not jeopardize his ties to Beecher. He and Webb conversed through much of 1843, as a result of which Webb & Plant debuted late that year or early in 1844. Webb wanted the capital in order to join an initiative then underway. It associated several express companies—including Harnden and Adams—in regular mail delivery in competition with the post office. Official rates ran so high that the companies could easily profit by cooperating, even with rate cuts and upgraded service. Accordingly, Webb & Co. Express commenced operations along with Webb & Plant. Henry continued to work with Beecher. Otherwise, Plant occupied himself with the partnership's dry goods and "West India Goods Business."[39]

The plans that Henry put in place in 1843 also included starting a family. Two years earlier, grandmother Sarah Plant had died, leaving a void in his life, and perhaps his thoughts of marriage arose at that time. Or, the 1839 wedding of Sam Plant to Lorenzo Blackstone's sister Mary may have sparked the idea. In any event, Henry and Ellen Elizabeth Blackstone had known each other since childhood. Ellen would have attended Sarah's funeral in August 1841. Henry likely also attended Ellen's twenty-first birthday celebration on February 21, 1842. Lorenzo's wedding to Branford's Emily Norton followed in October, with Plant's twenty-third birthday coming on the twenty-seventh. Regardless of the point at which the betrothal became official, the longtime friends had agreed by late 1842 to marry.[40]

Little personal information survives regarding Ellen. An image that Henry included in his biography portrays an intelligent, attractive, dark-haired young woman, if one somewhat severe in appearance as befitted a respectable Congregational maiden. The principal word portrait derives from an obituary. "Mrs. Plant . . . [shed] her sweet and gentle influences in every home and upon every heart that welcomed her cheerful presence," the piece observed. "As she lived, so she died—a calm, unobtrusive, consistent Christian." Twenty years earlier, though, Ellen flourished in the full blush of youth

5. Ellen Elizabeth Blackstone Plant. Collection of Henry B. Plant Museum.

and likely exercised less restraint and a greater yearning for passion, romance, and love. Sadly, as will be seen, causes were to arise to alter her attitudes. Her demeanor would grow severe with the pain of loss, and her religious devotion would intensify beyond the limits of her grief.[41]

For now, though, the young couple eagerly awaited the commencement of their lives together. The nuptials took place at Branford on Monday, September 25, 1843. No firsthand account of the event provides further detail. Willis Hemingway and Teresa Frieze had wed in the county a year or two earlier, and the circumstances of their rites were probably reflected in the Plant ceremony. "In those days the custom was in favor of quiet home weddings, and the marriage of '41 was at the home of the bride and was attended only by the near relatives of the contracting parties," an account related. "Not many newly-married couples took a bridal tour in those days, and Mr. and Mrs. Hemingway immediately started housekeeping." State senator James Blackstone surely hosted the occasion in his comfortable home. As Ellen's father, he would have proudly given the bride away. Rev. Timothy Gillett of the Branford Congregational Church, former teacher of both, performed the ceremony.[42]

In light of Henry's desire to economize in support of his business plans, the couple moved in with Philemon and Betsey Hoadley at New Haven. Plant's stepfather and mother had relocated across Court Street from their earlier home facing the Assembly Hotel and now occupied more modest quarters at No. 14 Court Street adjacent to Philemon's livery stable. A closer atmosphere allowed less space for privacy. Ellen did not conceive until mid-April 1844. She delivered a seemingly healthy son on January 13, 1845, likely at her parents' home in Branford. They named the child George Henry Plant. The middle name reflected George's father, while his first name honored Ellen's eldest brother, thirty-year-old George William Blackstone. His sudden death in 1861 would tragically and ironically set the stage for Ellen's own lamentable demise.[43]

3

Recovery

1844 to 1854

"failed in the grocery business in Connecticut"

The 1840s began promisingly for Henry Plant with a business partnership, marriage, and birth of a son; sadly, it quickly turned beyond disappointment to tragedy. A careful planner and fiscal conservative already determined in his early twenties to become rich, he had believed that sobriety, thrift, and hard work guaranteed him success so long as he persevered. As it turned out, he had not yet gained sufficient maturity to know that unexpected complications and impediments sooner or later confront every man. The vicissitudes of life, when they ultimately appeared, taught him important new lessons. He did not possess the means to go it alone in business, nor could he expect to control all the critical concerns that lay ahead as he doggedly traveled the road to wealth. At home, excesses of religious and reformist zeal revisited him, compounding challenges while facilitating and exacerbating debacle and heartache. Youthful dreams quashed, Plant located within himself reserves of strength sufficient to refuse an unacceptable status quo. Instead, he proved his mettle by pressing ahead. Henry meanwhile came to appreciate patience and empathy. He also learned that new dreams could be realized if they could be unshackled from the rigid embrace of the old.

When son George Henry Plant entered the world in January 1845, Henry and Ellen had been living at New Haven with stepfather and mother Philemon and Betsey Hoadley for well over a year. Henry had been managing the Webb & Plant dry goods store as well as independent expressman Benjamin Beecher's local operations. This combination of circumstances soon proved problematic. Philemon, now established in local business circles, increasingly delved into public affairs. His interest lay in long-held causes, including the antislavery crusade and the temperance movement. Hoadley's attitudes and advocacy, though, increasingly felt the influence of Rev. Elisha Lord

Cleaveland's reactionary views. The minister's physical and philosophical proximity to Hoadley had narrowed considerably in 1841 when the congregation occupied "a new house of worship in Court Street" near the Hoadley residence. There, Cleaveland had turned his energies ever more to pressing his priorities. The Washington Temperance Society of New Haven, formed in June 1841, was one of them. By late 1843 frustrated society members, having failed to work the impact they desired, resolved that "the indiscriminate sale of intoxicating liquors must be suppressed by law." A subsequent town meeting agreed, providing a spark that led to enactment of a compliant state law in June 1845. It read: "That from and after the second Monday in January next, no person shall sell any wine or spiritous Liquor, in any town in this state, except by license."[1]

The problem for Henry arose not from a personal failure of sobriety but from the fact that he and his partner sold rum. As did many local merchants, they advertised themselves as trading in "West India goods." This language effectively advertised West Indian liquors and other smuggled items. A government report shed light on the situation: "An old retired sea captain, who used to command a smart schooner plying between New Haven and the West Indies twenty years before the [Civil War], when asked what he knew about smuggling, seemed amused. "Smuggling, eh? Well, I've heard a good deal about it in my time, but of course don't know anything of my own experience, being as I was no smuggler myself and wasn't personally acquainted with anybody who was. But I've no objection to telling you what I've been told. When I was sailing out of New Haven the West Indies trade was pretty well concentrated there. One house had twenty-five vessels, most in that line, and there were several others pretty near as big. Then New Haven had big warehouses, did a rushing business, and everybody had plenty of money here, and felt jolly."[2]

Selling rum doubtlessly caused friction between Plant and his stepfather, but he and partner Washington Webb now dealt with a more critical concern. The new law imposed a strict deadline. If they could not obtain a license by January 12, 1846, they faced financial disaster, and the city refused to cooperate. In October 1845 a local temperance editor crowed: "The rumseller already droops his head before so many of his fellow men who have voted to eradicate from our midst this curse on the community. Already he feels the weight of public sentiment, bearing down upon him like a mighty river, moving slow but sure in its course, and which will soon sweep him and his business into oblivion." In the circumstances Webb & Plant in January 1846 sold out at distress prices. The firm had dissolved by April 1. Plant thereafter bore on his reputation a detested stain of failure that endured through life, past death, and into the twentieth century. As late as 1918 at

Augusta, Georgia—a place that Plant at times called home—a local newspaper would assert, "[Henry Plant] had failed in the grocery business in Connecticut."[3]

Barely had Plant begun to move past the firm's dissolution and loss of his investment before another calamity intervened. Intending to aid Henry in returning to the good graces of the community's "better part," Philemon had encouraged his stepson to purchase a pew in Reverend Cleaveland's nearby church. Plant did so and, if not earlier, he and Ellen began attending the pastor's services. In early June, inspired by Rembrandt Peale's painting *The Court of Death*, the pastor delivered a sermon with the same title that addressed sin and sexual pleasure. "The female form, representing the allurements of life, has such an expression of truthfulness, hope and innocence, that looking up at her countenance alone, one would hardly suspect any danger; and yet she is dipping the cup, the fatal consequences of which, are seen [in Peale's painting] in the wretched group behind her," he declared. "This is a most instructive part of the picture, and should be carefully studied. It shows where the real point of danger lies. It is not in the last stages of sin, but in the beginnings of evil. It is where pleasure first holds out her fascinations, that we must consider well where they will lead us. One of the most effectual safeguards of virtue, is an inflexible purpose to meet with a firm repulse, the solicitations of this powerful tempter." Cleaveland then thundered, "Death is the penalty of sin; and 'sin kills beyond the tomb.'"[4]

Days later, on June 17, 1846, son George suddenly died. With the minister's warning of penalty for sexual pleasure fresh in her mind, Ellen broke down. The couple rapidly departed New Haven and the Hoadley household. Instead, they stayed with relations at Branford, where they buried George's remains. Ellen essentially withdrew from society. Cleaveland's message haunted her. She had not been exposed as had her husband to any of the world outside New Haven County, nor had she closely observed other religions or belief systems. Her God and morals derived almost exclusively from the Congregational Church through Reverends Gillett and Cleaveland. Guilt seemingly overwhelmed her. Evidence for this resonated from the fact that Ellen did not conceive another child, so far as is known, for six years. When she did, she was not residing in Branford, New Haven, or for that matter, the state of Connecticut.[5]

Henry's reaction and how he handled the tragedy and its aftermath cannot be known with certainty. He preferred not to discuss his son's death. A hint of his pain is found in the Smyth biography's genealogical section. The listing for Henry's children begins simply, "I. A boy; ——; born ——; died June 17, 1846, age 17 mo., 4 days." The entry leaves the reader sensing that George Smyth, sensitive to his friend's personal agony, felt that he could not ask Plant the child's name and birth date. The text adds only, "One son was born to him, a promising child, who lived only eighteen months." Taught from birth, as boys were during Henry's day, to face tragedy stoically, he refrained from showing emotion. With no helpful alternative, he worked.[6]

Not that Henry faced his struggles entirely without support. He possessed kinship and friendship networks from Branford and New Haven to New York City. Childhood friend Lorenzo Blackstone had moved to Liverpool, England, soon after his 1842 marriage, but New Haven's Jim English was prospering nearby. Others remained also, and new faces enriched the mix. He interacted routinely, for instance, with business contacts. Webb and Beecher naturally were available to Plant, but so, too, were Adams & Co.'s Alvin Adams, William B. Dinsmore, and John Hoey. Plant's circle, of course, reached beyond the Adams people. Clapp Spooner, for one, was the twenty-two-year-old manager of Thompson & Co.'s express line at Hartford, where Plant's duties increasingly carried him. A onetime grocery clerk of modest means, he was newly married, hardworking, and ambitious. "Mr. Spooner's manner is affable and courteous," a biographer noted, "and his social personality is such that his friends are manifold." Elijah A. Johnson and William Lockwood "Locke" Crane counted as well. Johnson was a thirty-five-year-old Connecticut native. He had come to Plant's acquaintance in 1843 or 1844 as a Beecher employee, although he soon worked for Adams. Even younger than Spooner, Connecticut-born Locke Crane had labored with Johnson in New Haven at mid-decade, having begun work with Adams as a New York clerk. Before long, he rode the rails as an express messenger.[7]

However near Henry grew to these men, no one stood closer following his son's death than John Morton Freeman. A Nova Scotian by birth, Freeman was twenty in 1844 when Adams employed him as a driver. "The occupation demanded something more than the mere ability to drive a horse and handle freight," a fellow expressman recalled. "John was not very citified at the outset, but he had the material to make a smart business man, and he became finally one of the most popular and valuable agents that Adams & Co. ever had. After serving for a year or two as driver and messenger for Adams, he was promoted to a clerkship of great responsibility in Dinsmore's office in Wall Street. He was money clerk, and had charge of the Philadelphia desk in the office." Freeman and Plant probably met in 1845 or 1846. Plant interestingly shared nothing about his friend with George Smyth or in other interviews he gave. When he finally had another son, however, he took care to name the child Morton Freeman Plant.[8]

Freeman likely deserved credit for arranging work for Plant upon the collapse of Webb & Plant. In March 1845 the government had prohibited express companies from delivering letters in competition with the post office. The same month, Benjamin Beecher sold his company to a partnership that included Elijah Johnson and William Dinsmore. The new owners soon folded the operation into Adams & Co. Beecher worked for the firm before returning to New Haven and, in light of local political and legal upheavals, entering the grocery and liquor business. His departure set in motion a series of reassignments in Adams personnel. Those changes, in turn, recognized the need for a new express messenger on the New York to New Haven steamboat and sometimes on the train from New Haven to Hartford and Springfield, Massachusetts. Johnson managed route operations; Locke Crane held down the New Haven office. Henry returned to the steamboats and rode the rails. He lived again on wages.[9]

The job change occurred in early 1846 after the sale of the Webb & Plant store and involved serious responsibilities that sometimes brought personal peril. The messenger kept his safe and pouch under lock and key and carried a pistol. "The life of our express messenger is not an easy one," a veteran of the service explained. "With his little safe to hold his money he boards the train [or steamboat], and, regardless of hunger, heat, cold, robbery, accidents or fatigue, he is bound to deliver his packages or account in value for them. In case of a smash-up, his post is that of danger. There is nothing to prevent his being crushed beneath his own freight. Necessarily, he is exposed to all kinds of danger. And his work is never ended. He loses sleep, is cut off from social pleasure and even denied the pleasure of home, except at intervals. His work requires a clear head and frequently courage, for he not only delivers money packages, but collects bills, receives money for deeds and handles valuables generally." The man added, "It is a little singular that the force is always cheerful and apparently happy—a generous, whole souled set of fellows, caring nothing for danger and perfectly contented if the car does not leave the track."[10]

For nearly four years Henry shuttled between New York, New Haven, Hartford, and Springfield for Adams & Co. As mentioned, outside of contacts within business circles he lived "cut off from social pleasure and even denied the pleasure of home, except at intervals." This meant growing familiarity with men such as Dinsmore, Hoey, Johnson, Freeman, and Spooner, a process by which nearly indestructible bonds of trust and reliance developed. As importantly, the experience served Plant as a business and management school, one that allowed him to parse mistakes and develop needed skills to high degrees of proficiency. As Plant informed future protégé Matthew V. "Matt" O'Brien, "If you wish to know *how* the business is being conducted, ask the messenger." O'Brien explained: "The very nature of their business makes them watchful; makes them close observers of men and things. They are here to-day, and gone to-morrow; first in one office,

6. William Brown Dinsmore. From "The Railroad Men of America: W. B. Dinsmore," *Magazine of Western History* 10 (May 1889): 100–102.

then another; meeting this way agent, and that way agent; they are not supposed to note anything that is going on, they are 'so busy'; but they do see and hear many things, and know more of how the business is managed when the bosses are away than many would give them credit for; and while in their car [or express room], when they have nothing else to do, nothing to bother them but a cinder or two, then they *think*, they criticise, they compare the mode of doing business in one office, against the mode in another. They criticise the conduct of employes in one office against another." O'Brien added, "They are traveling all over the country, and they learn how the business is being conducted better than the 'bosses' could, for ye messenger has been heard to say—things are different when they are about—but us! they dismiss their fears as they see us, with the remark—'he's only a messenger!'"[11]

To his immense good fortune Plant entered the express business on a full-time basis at exactly the right moment. "Were you successful at first?" a reporter once queried John Hoey. "Not at all," he responded. "It was 1846 before we began even to see our way clear. It was a constant struggle. A three-dollar way bill was a wonder." Prosperity came for Adams & Co.—with due credit to Dinsmore's administrative genius—through consolidation with other companies and expansion into new territories. The firm had taken a huge step in 1843 when Dinsmore and Adams partnered with Samuel M. Shoemaker of Baltimore and Philadelphia's Edwards S. Sanford to interlink their cities with New York and Boston. Shoemaker within a few years pressed farther south to Richmond and Charleston. As already seen, the growing concern absorbed Beecher and Co. in 1845 and gained New Haven as an anchor for operations. The New Haven and Hartford Express followed in 1848. So, too, did service to New Orleans. Even John Hoey exploited the lucrative opportunities then enriching the company's partners. In 1850 he pioneered Hoey & Co.'s Charleston, Savannah, and Montgomery Express. As his experience indicated, it pleased Adams & Co. partners for key employees such as Hoey to share in the wealth, assuming they displayed initiative combined with good humor and hard work.[12]

Henry's tortuous climb out of the personal and financial doldrums into which he had plunged in 1846 unfortunately impeded his ability to display the kind of initiative that earned still-young Hoey a stake in the budding express industry. Ellen's fragile state of mind factored, as did Henry's need to rebuild financial good health. Into the late 1840s circumstances mandated that he bide his time. Meanwhile, Adams & Co. struck it rich. The story began in January 1848 when prospectors discovered gold near Sacramento, California. New York newspapers aired the news in August before President James K. Polk officially announced the strike to Congress on December 5. Twenty days later the long-awaited New York & New Haven Rail Road coincidentally opened for business. The line furnished rail connections between the two cities for the first time and alleviated the necessity for package transport between them by steamboat.[13]

The California Gold Rush did not impact Plant directly, but it set favorable changes in motion. For one thing, Morton Freeman yielded to the allure of untold wealth. By mid-December he had helped to organize the New York Mining Company, whose members aimed to secure a ship, travel together, and support each other's harvesting of golden riches. Company secretary Freeman hurried the project forward so that its fellows departed New York on February 3, 1849. One can imagine Plant on the wharf that day amid the fevered excitement, cheering his friend's departure while aching to be off to California, adventure, and riches.[14]

Dinsmore, for one, understood that personal travel to California was not required in order to harvest wealth from the gold rush. "Among the passengers for Chagres [Colombia, now Panama] in the Empire City next Saturday, on their way to California, will be D. H. Haskell, Esq., of this city, who goes out to establish a branch of the house of Adams & Co., the well-known express agents, at San Francisco," a New York report alerted in September 1849. Adams & Co. thereafter almost literally grabbed the goose that laid the golden eggs. Huge quantities of gold flowed from the Pacific coast to New York City, while the demand for package express exploded. Adams boomed, soon finding itself wildly prosperous. As John Hoey characterized matters, "Those were golden days." A reporter confirmed: "The California fever gave impetus to the express business. . . . The elder members of the organization became rich beyond the dream of avarice."[15]

Affairs for Plant meanwhile were turning rosier, if not yet golden. Before Morton Freeman sailed for California, tremendous excitement had attended the New York & New Haven Rail Road's opening. As it happened, Henry had been trapped in New York City by icy winter conditions at Christmastime 1848, so he and Morton found ample opportunity to discuss plans and, particularly, possibilities for Plant. At almost that very moment, the railroad offered Adams & Co. an exclusive contract for carrying money and small packages on its line. Accepting the deal represented a major gamble in the days before golden California rain fell on the company, but Dinsmore took the risk. "For this Adams & Co., contracted to pay, with fear and trembling in their boots, the enormous sum of $1,700 a month, but almost at the very start it proved a paying venture—indeed the venture which determined them to continue in their business," an account related. "The next step was to carry freight for merchants at either end of the line, and to establish agencies along the route as well, and in less than three years the whole custom of the country was changed, almost all the light freight and some of the heavier being sent by railroad express instead of on the boats as freight."[16]

Here, Plant's financial and commercial breakthroughs began. Freeman, who enjoyed the trust and respect of the high-level company leaders, pressed Henry's cause. Honest, dependable, and hardworking Plant, he argued, could be trusted with express messenger duties on the risky new rail line. Plant's supervisor Elijah Johnson concurred, as did Dinsmore. Beginning January 22, 1849, Adams & Co. manned the New York & New Haven Rail Road with express messengers, and Henry took up his new job. Ironically, Plant's old partner Washington Webb, now the local agent for Adams, greeted Henry in New Haven after each run, placing in high relief what a godsend the express business had become for both of them.[17]

Plant impressed his employers with his fidelity and reliability during the months he served in the express car on the New York & New Haven train. Unfortunately, events at New Haven meanwhile distressed him. Jonathan Harrington Green—who billed himself as "the Reformed Gambler"—had arrived during spring 1849. Strengthened by Reverend Cleaveland's support and that of the pastor's ally Philemon Hoadley, Green moved to rid the community of resurgent vice. He reached broadly, taking on billiard parlors, tenpin alleys, gambling, and lewd dancing. He poked into what a Yale student termed "dens of iniquity" at the city docks. "We saw plenty of Liquor & *nigger dances* & such like works of darkness," he reported. Soon enough, the inquisition turned toward the "traffic in intoxicating liquors." At that point affairs became problematic for Henry, because Green's antiliquor tirades stirred the ire of Plant's old employer Benjamin Beecher, now a liquor retailer. Clashes between Beecher and Green ran hot, with much "hard swearing." By August Green's backers had created a standing body "to labor for the removal of these evils by an exertion of moral influence, and by an appeal, when necessary, to the officers of the law." Hoadley's name unsurprisingly graced the sponsor list.[18]

Time spent in New Haven during the summer taxed Henry's reserves of emotion and patience and left him seeking a path away from constant reminders of his and Ellen's heartbreaks of three years previously. Events came to a head, coincidentally, just as Adams's New York & New Haven contract began to show success and also as D. H. Haskell was preparing to depart for California to launch the firm's coast-to-coast express. The demands of expanding business and personnel departures meant vacancies to fill in the New York headquarters. The situation proved a blessing for Henry. Industry historian A. L. Stimson put the circumstances of the deliverance simply: "[Elijah A. Johnson] wanted Plant to assist him in his office, and he became a clerk there." Accordingly, Henry celebrated his thirtieth birthday on October 27, 1849, as a brand-new resident of New York City.[19]

Released from what had become the stultifying atmosphere at New Haven, Plant experienced a metamorphosis in New York. He enjoyed life as he had not done in years, indulging in the wonders of the emerging metropolis. Dinsmore and Hoey especially abetted the efforts, providing companionship and introducing him to the theater, the arts, and other centers of entertainment and enlightenment. "He was a *bon vivant* and a wag, a noted man at table," a Dinsmore obituary advised, "and when surrounded, as he was on many occasions at his own festive board, by Vanderbilt, Sam Sloan, Chauncey Depew, Henry Hilton and hundreds of other men of note, he always kept the table in a roar." Another source added, "Mr. Dinsmore was particularly fond of music and of the drama, of flowers, of fruits and of pictures." Hoey, if anything, outpaced Dinsmore at social pleasures, and Plant often tagged along. "With usual good luck Hoey and [future stockbroker Frank] Work had managed to ingratiate themselves with the doorkeepers of the two or three theatres then in existence, and used to go deadhead to every play on," an account related. "Keen critics they were, too, and knew all the ins and outs of the stage and theatrical gossip at an age when most boys are in the school room. Henry [B.] Plant . . . had been employed on the New Haven boat to which Hoey delivered papers. The two kept their friendship and Plant finally came into the employ of Dinsmore & Adams and became the close intimate of young Hoey and Work."[20]

What a magnificent moment in city life for Plant to enjoy. "At the present time New York is uncommonly lively—presenting one vast whirl of business and pleasure," a resident declared in fall 1849. "No less thriving are the places of amusements than the stores and work shops.—Every set of entertainment, suited to different palates, is now in full tide. The theatres, circuses, dioramas, panoramas, &c, are all in full blast." Into the New Year city magic sparkled. "New York, at the present time, is full of life, and buildings of splendid architecture are rising fast in all directions, as signs of her wealth and prosperity," a spectator noted in March 1850. "New York is now the great city, the metropolis of this continent; and still her march is onward." From that time on Henry relished theater, opera, and art, and—his son Morton's unfortunate experiences in future years notwithstanding—he managed to avoid all unpleasantness in connection with some diversions. "Three females were arrested in New York a few nights since, while exhibiting as model artists *in puris naturalibus*," an October 1849 report indicated. "Some of the audience were arrested. They were taken before the Mayor next morning, when the women were held to bail and the others were permitted to depart."[21]

Ellen did not initially accompany Henry to the city. He roomed at Judson's Hotel, whose owner Curtiss Judson had known him in Hartford. "This establishment is delightfully situated at the lower end of Broadway, just below Trinity and old Grace Churches," a notice declared. The location required only a city block's walk up Broadway and then a short turn to the right on Wall Street for Plant to reach Adams & Co.'s offices. The New York Stock Exchange provides a handy locator for the site today. By summer 1850, however, Ellen had joined her husband. The couple settled briefly in a comfortable boardinghouse run by a young couple from Maine. Within months they leased an apartment in a home about a mile and a half farther north, what Henry described as "west of Broadway and below Broome-st." It was, he insisted, in "a very desirable and healthy location" and large enough to

7. City of New York, 1849, from the steeple of St. Paul's Church, with Brooklyn in the distance. Library of Congress.

allow "a very desirable residence for a small family." The suite of rooms required attention at first, but by spring 1852 he could point proudly to it being "newly painted and papered."[22]

The change of environment lifted Ellen's spirits, a fact that surely pleased Henry immensely. A second milestone in late summer or early fall aided her as well. Henry for the time being had continued to work as a New York and New Haven road messenger while also assisting in the New York office. Now his appointment as a full-time clerk came through. The promotion meant not only more income but also his routine presence in the city and at home. Then, in mid-November—as New York's crisp fall air stung cheeks and stirred passions—Henry and Ellen conceived another child. As the pregnancy progressed and with the coming of spring, Ellen journeyed to her parents' home at Branford. There, on August 18, 1851, she safely delivered a son. Henry named him Morton Freeman Plant.[23]

Ellen apparently avoided pregnancy problems; rather, her early departure from New York reflected further improvement in Henry's job status. Adams & Co.'s prosperity seemed to recognize no limits. "They have already made a fortune by their business of transporting, *dust* from the mines," an onlooker observed in January 1851. "It is astonishing how this Express business has increased. The upper part of Wall st. is full of Express offices, whence freight parcels &c. are *despatched* to every part of our wide-spread country. Every wide awake merchant sends by Express, in order to get his goods a few hours in advance of his duller neighbor, and is willing to pay about double freight in order to secure this despatch." The New York Custom House stood out as an increasingly lucrative center for profits. "Adams & Co., the Express people," one observer noted, "do a great business usually in rushing goods through the custom-house in advance of the regular custom-house brokers and importers."[24]

These circumstances created a new job for Henry after Adams & Co.'s familiarity with custom-house personnel and procedures led in April to a lucrative US government agreement. "One of the elements that spurred growth of the company in the Middle Atlantic was successful negotiation of a Treasury Department contract to take charge of government monies between the Custom House at New York and the Mint in Philadelphia," a company historian detailed. "Large sums of monies were involved and Henry Plant was assigned by Dinsmore to be the messenger." The *New York Times* added: "He alternated daily with another employe in carrying in two valises suspended from his shoulders by straps large sums of foreign gold, amounting in the total to millions of dollars, ordered from the New York Sub-Treasury to the Philadelphia mint for recoinage." Heavy responsibilities created unanticipated opportunities. Henry found himself often in Philadelphia during spring and summer 1851 and used the proximity to acquaint himself with local Adams partner Edwards Sewall Sanford. "He was a true friend, generous as he was honorable, a genial companion, full of wit, and covering many an unselfish good deed under the veil of a joke," an admirer recorded. Within a decade Sanford would become one of the most powerful men in a nation at war with itself, and Plant's early fidelity earned rewards in ways unimaginable ten years previously.[25]

The Philadelphia delivery schedule moreover allowed Henry free time in New York, and in Ellen's absence, he and John Hoey resumed their pursuit of city nightlife. This set the stage for one of the era's famous theater history moments, an incident that involved Hoey's crush on actress Josephine Shaw Russell. "Mrs. Russell, a charmingly pretty young English widow, was playing an engagement at Burton's old theatre in Chambers street," a correspondent recounted. "Mrs. Russell had been a Miss Shaw, of Liverpool, coming of a highly talented and respected family of theatrical people. She had married a Mr. William Russell. . . . Mr. Hoey fell madly in love with her, and one fine day married her without telling any one about it. When the time came to announce the marriage it was decided to do so from the stage of Burton's Theatre, which was also to be the announcement of Mrs. Hoey's retirement from the stage. Without telling his old friend Plant what was going to happen Hoey took Plant to the play with him, and they occupied their accustomed places in the orchestra. After the final curtain had been rung down and the house was still applauding the curtain was raised, the entire company, including John Lester Wallack and John Brougham, was mustered on the stage, and Burton himself advanced to the footlights and announced in a neat and witty speech that 'Mrs. Russell, if he might still call her so, had resolved to give up her part in the play and assume again the character of wife,' and then naming John Hoey as the happy man." The storyteller added, "Of course the funny incident was town talk for a number of days."[26]

Plant's 1851 rise continued apace. Elijah Johnson had run all company operations on the New York & New Haven Rail Road, but during the summer tuberculosis began to destroy his health. Johnson attempted to rest and gain strength for recuperation, but his efforts proved of no avail. He died at age forty-one on October 7. At Dinsmore's direction Plant was already filling in for Johnson by the fall. Henry now received the major administrative position on a permanent basis. Ensuing celebrations must have been impressive, especially after Morton Freeman's arrival for a visit on the eighteenth in plenty of time to meet his new godson. Nine days later Ellen and friends commemorated Henry's thirty-second birthday. After five years of trials, Plant was finally on his way to security.[27]

At the office, meanwhile, affairs grew livelier and livelier. Hoey took "charge of the Southern and Eastern steam line business," while Plant ran the vital New York & New Haven railroad service. With flush times at hand, Dinsmore in February 1852 bought a new headquarters building at No. 59 Broadway, next door to Judson's Hotel and near the splendid new Bank of the Republic "at the head of Wall street." A local man commented, "I don't know its precise dimensions, but of a similar lot, two or three doors nearer to Trinity Church and the Bank, (I allude to the mammoth dry goods and importing house of D. W. & J. T. Moore & Co.) . . . their building is 218 feet in depth, from the front in Broadway, to the rear in Trinity Alley. Reckoning Messrs. Moore & Co.'s front to be 40 feet, there are upwards of 8000 square feet." Adams was operating from the new facility by April 21.[28]

By then Morton Freeman was traveling back to California, and Ellen Plant had apparently returned to Branford with his namesake. The circumstances of Ellen's departure are not known, although her health concerns reemerged within only a short time and she may already have been suffering again after a cold and dreary winter. Henry moved back into the Judson. There in June, Captain Stone of New Haven steamboating days visited him. "Captain S. Bartlett Stone brought his son George to board at the Hotel, saying 'Henry, when you were a boy I took charge of you; now you do the same for my son.'" Stone and family soon departed for a two-year European tour. Henry meanwhile kept his new sixteen-year-old charge in tow.[29]

Henry's superintendence of George Stone's activities, as it turned out, came with interruptions. Plant had at long last recovered his financial health, yet all around he witnessed friends and business acquaintances such as Dinsmore, Hoey, and Freeman striking it rich. He coveted entry into the charmed circle and repeatedly explored possibilities with them. Childhood friend Lorenzo Blackstone, accumulating substantial wealth in England, joined the discussions during a visit from Liverpool beginning in April. Months passed and the only progress Henry tallied involved a modest beginning to an import business, undertaken assuredly at Blackstone's instigation. Wracked by his financial dreams, Plant meanwhile watched another acquaintance, James DeMartin of Bridgeport, head south to expand Harnden's Express operations out of Savannah in competition with Hoey's ongoing enterprise. Given that newspapers from across the nation flowed into Adams & Co. on a daily basis, Henry likely read the praise heaped on DeMartin just for making the effort. "Our Southern public have been thus far quite off the track of these useful purveyors," the *Savannah Daily Republican* declared in July. "Mr. DeMartin's recommendation for the agency which he has undertaken are found in his intelligence, promptness and fidelity as a business man."[30]

Words of that sort stoked fires of ambition, but they fueled only frustration for Plant until Dinsmore suggested an intriguing idea. He had ventured out in 1838 "to seek for business" in Florida but found the territory—Florida did not become a state until 1845—in the midst of the Second Seminole War. The Jacksonville area, where he resided, served as a supply center and administrative point distant from peninsular fighting. The town and its vicinity were prospering, but Dinsmore failed to take advantage. Within two years he had departed for Boston and a fortuitous encounter with Alvin Adams. Dinsmore had never forgotten Florida's potential, though, and in 1852 he suggested it to Plant as an untapped market. Years later Henry spoke with a Nashville reporter about the outcome. "Mr. Plant first came to the South as a representative of the Adams Express Company," the reporter observed, "which was then anxious to extend its territory Southward."[31]

A sense of personal and professional direction in hand, Henry by autumn prepared to act. His cousin Mary Elizabeth Plant wed William Tyler Norton, a friend of his youth, at Branford on November 9. Bidding goodbye there to Ellen and Morton, Plant boarded a New York steamer for Savannah. Interestingly, a unnamed correspondent who lived in New York City began writing the New Haven *Columbian Register*, with whose editors Henry was well acquainted. The subject involved an ongoing trip to Georgia and Florida. The author's unbounded enthusiasm, which is to say Plant's enthusiasm, came balanced with a degree of naiveté and a stroke of racist insensitivity. "This city is more of a Yankee town than I was prepared to see even in this State, and Georgia is not far behind some of her sister States in New England, in great enterprises and modern improvements," he reported from Savannah on November 27. "It is destined to be a great place: the energy, industry and high character of its citizens, as well as its geographical position, justifies me in saying this," he continued. "One word as to the Negroes, if my testimony can add anything to what has already been said by others. It is my candid opinion, made up after much reflection, and some little observation, that they are far better off here, as slaves, than the same number are or can be with us, free. The truth is, a great many of them are too lazy to ever wish to be free. Instead of the negroes being slaves to the whites, here, you may say, with nearly equal propriety, that the whites are slaves to the negroes. But I am not now about to spend my time concerning this subject; if I was, it would be to devise ways and means to get rid of them."[32]

In mid-December Plant reached Jacksonville, where, he marveled to an editor friend, "the thermometer stands at 70 degrees in the shade." Either traveling with him or joining him there were Henry's cousin Increase Cook Plant, his family, and his wealthy father-in-law, Robert Hazelhurst of Brunswick, Georgia. A Branford native, I. C. Plant had relocated to conduct brokerage businesses at Augusta and Columbus. A banking offer led him to Brunswick and then Macon, where he lived prominently when Henry arrived at Jacksonville. The two men were already close or, as I. C. later asserted, "especially warm." In fact, three years earlier the Macon Plants had named a newborn son George Henry Plant after Henry's deceased boy. The party explored the Jacksonville vicinity before Henry steamed on his own up the St. Johns River. He stopped at Palatka and Picolata and then continued upriver to Enterprise. A stay at St. Augustine followed, and the old Spanish town delighted him. "I believe St. Augustine would be the best place to be," he reported, "if I were to stop in one place." Henry planned to travel on to Georgia as soon as weather permitted, but "cold, dry, freezing weather, and plenty of ice" compelled him to bide his time in the sunshine rather than risk the overland journey. "I am going before long into Marion and Alachua counties, which are settled by respectable planters I am assured," he advised on January 23. "They raise the best kind of corn and other crops."[33]

By early March Georgia's weather picture had cleared considerably. "Peach trees are in bloom, and vegetation generally seems to be springing up," a resident gleefully reported. At the same time, L. W. Winchester and James DeMartin announced inauguration of Harden's Express service from Savannah to Macon, Oglethorpe, Columbus, and Montgomery. Plus, the Atlanta and LaGrange Railroad opened to connect those Georgia communities by rail. Travelers could now avail themselves of train service all the way from Montgomery to Charleston with only a seventeen-mile gap. The new state of affairs spelled revolution for southern transportation and immense possibilities for the express business.[34]

Plant aimed on the trip to assess locales as sites for potential Adams Express offices. I. C. either accompanied him or helped set his itinerary. Henry left little account of the journeys, but he would have seen Macon, Milledgeville (Georgia state capital), Columbus, Montgomery (Alabama state capital), Augusta, and Atlanta. At Augusta a railroad bridge across the Savannah River and new city train depots were nearing completion, milestones that facilitated transportation from Columbia, South Carolina, to Atlanta and points beyond. The concurrent completion of the Wilmington and Manchester Railroad allowed travel from Augusta to Fredericksburg, Virginia, where other connections carried passengers on to Philadelphia, New York, and Boston.[35]

While Plant then and later remained mostly silent about the trip, two sources permit relevant glimpses of the time and place. A passenger on the Macon-to-Atlanta train observed in late April 1853 what Henry had seen only a short while earlier. "We started from Macon to go by the cars to Atlanta, in the heart of Georgia," he recorded. "Railroad traveling here at the south is by no means what it is with us at the north. The trains stop all along the road, just as our omnibuses do, to take up passengers or set them down, consequently it takes a great while to go not a great ways. There are no pleasant villages either along the road to attract attention. Every thing looks new and rough and dirty. White men and negroes, children, cattle and dwellings, all seemed to wear the same untidy, uncomfortable look." At Atlanta the man acknowledged finding merely "the beginning of a town." Plant himself shared a few memories of the fledgling rail center in an interview given years later, suggesting that it left him little impressed as well. "The first time I ever came to Atlanta, was in 1853," he informed a reporter. "Then the little town was certainly in its infancy. The Georgia railroad had just been completed into the town and stage coaches were still running, with Atlanta as their center. What a difference do I find here this beautiful and bright morning, with locomotives steaming on every side, splendid trains crowding into the depot from every southern city and houses towering up to heights undreamed of in the days of 1853, when I first came."[36]

Plant departed the Deep South—taking advantage of the Wilmington and Manchester rail connection—ready to capitalize on ideas for a Jacksonville-based express operation. Beyond that, he carried to New York doubts about Adams & Co. investment in Georgia and Alabama because of competition from Harnden's Express. As one commentator put it, "Mr. Plant recognized the advantages which Florida offered to settlement and agricultural development." Another source observed similarly, "In 1853, when the delightful climate and fertility of Florida were as yet but poorly appreciated, Mr. Plant recognized the possibilities which that State opened up." Dinsmore and other Adams partners ultimately decided to limit extension of their Southern services for the immediate future. They agreed as well not to exclude the possibility of Plant's eventual engagement with Florida. "Adams & Co.'s Great Southern Express is now completely organized and in successful operation to the following places: Norfolk, Portsmouth, Alexandria, Fredericksburg, Richmond, Petersburg, Weldon, Raleigh, Warrenton, Wilmington, and by boats to Fayetteville, Charleston, etc. etc.," the company advertised in February 1854. "And Depots on the following railroads and connections: Seaboard and Roanoke railroad; Richmond and Fredericksburg; Orange and Alexandria; Petersburg and Weldon; Raleigh and Weldon; Wilmington and Weldon; Wilmington and Manchester, etc. Messengers accompany each train, to insure the safety of articles entrusted to us. Rates *economically low*."[37]

As the Adams principals considered Henry's recommendations in spring 1853, an interesting train of events highlighted the extent to which they were prepared to depend on him as well as his daring and personal courage. The story for Plant began upon his arrival at the Adams headquarters building in late April. He discovered that one month earlier a nineteen-year-old delivery clerk named Major Seth Damon had stolen money totaling $2,500. Coincidentally, Henry received word of the thief's whereabouts. "A few days since, Mr. Plant learned that the young man had located himself at Toledo; and Mr. Wm. B. Dinsmore, one of the firm of Adams & Co., went before Justice Bogart and preferred a complaint against him," a New York newspaper revealed. "A warrant for his arrest was issued, and Mr. Plant started with it to Toledo." Acting alone, Henry pursued Damon to Ohio, discovered his location, and confronted the accused. Plant convinced the young man to surrender the $2,250 that remained, confess his guilt, and return voluntarily to New York, where he received a two-year prison sentence. No one now questioned at Adams & Co. whether Henry Plant was a man to be reckoned with.[38]

Adams & Co.'s decision to delay southern expansion may have frustrated Plant, but Ellen's condition raised concerns that troubled him deeply. In his absence her health had deteriorated significantly at Branford. George Smyth, following Henry's wishes, commented simply, "It was in 1853 that Mrs. Plant was seized with congestion of the lungs, and Doctors Delafield and Marco advised that she at once be taken to Florida." The story bore a remarkable similarity to one that dated to fifteen years earlier and involved I. C. Plant's first wife. "The marriage was most happy except for the impaired health of the bride," a family history observed. "She had consumption and even the mild climate of Augusta was found ineffective to bring an improvement. It was thought wise to go further south and a journey was entered upon with the purpose of spending a few weeks of the winter in Cuba." That Ellen actually suffered from a problem other than "congestion of the lungs" appears from the fact that she and Henry consulted with Drs. Edward Delafield and Thomas M. Markoe. The partners ranked at the top of their profession and specialized in "diseases peculiar to females." In 1853, however, their interests lay in "cases of insanity" or, put another way, mental health issues of women.[39]

That Delafield and Markoe recommended a rest cure for Ellen appears evident, although Plant may have suggested Florida as the locale based on his personal observations. The decision to undertake the trip was reached in late winter 1854, about the time of Ellen's thirty-third birthday. It came on the heels of Captain Asa Norton's death at Branford on March 7. The Plants had looked up to him as children, and he was also father-in-law to her brother and Henry's friend Lorenzo Blackstone. Twelve days following the death, the couple departed New York on the steamship *Marion*. At Savannah by March 25, they reached Jacksonville on the twenty-seventh, eight days after leaving for the South. Barely had the couple settled in when a "great and disastrous conflagration" consumed "all the business portion of the town." Fortunately, Henry had found them a quiet haven in "a private house at Strawberry Mills, seven miles from Jacksonville, across the St. Johns River." They remained physically unharmed, but Henry's plans for a Jacksonville-based express operation actually went up in smoke. He quickly departed the scene of disaster for Georgia, leaving Ellen to her rest cure. His whereabouts for the next two weeks are not known, but in light of subsequent events, he presumably headed for Macon and discussions with I. C. Plant before making his way to Augusta to survey the situation there. On April 22 Plant boarded a steamer at Charleston for New York without Ellen. He arrived in the city four days later for consultations with Dinsmore, Hoey, and the other Adams & Co. principals. Ellen remained, presumably alone, at Strawberry Mills where, as time passed, she began to feel better. She returned to New York on June 7. Then came another painful death and the sudden redirection of her life and her husband's, ordeals that sorely tested the effectiveness of Florida's vaunted recuperative powers.[40]

4
Southern Ways
1854 to 1859

"the goose that lays the golden eggs"

Henry Plant turned thirty-five years of age in 1854 sensing that he stood on the verge of securing long-sought wealth. He had earned employers' respect and enjoyed the cooperation and good wishes of sympathetic friends. He accepted that—as good fortune's price—he must leave his cherished New York City haven. His powers of observation and intuition had meanwhile revealed business prospects in Georgia and Alabama sparked by railroad construction and town development. Beyond that, Florida's warmth promised the breakthrough necessary for a golden future. As the puzzle pieces fell into place, signs pointed to triumph. Still, frustrating obstacles slowed and had the potential to stall him. The principal one appeared in the form of a beloved heart that a child's death had broken. Earlier experience had introduced Henry to the beneficial nature of empathy and sacrifice. He yet lacked, though, all the skills needed to forge the delicate balance between one's own dreams and the need for sensitivity regarding the condition of others. He wanted to believe that he was affording care. The path he chose instead followed his dreams.

Plant's return from the South in late April 1854 occurred as the express industry reached a major turning point. Extended negotiations led by midyear to a major coalition. "The Harnden Express had never been in so prosperous a condition as it was at the time," A. L. Stimson observed, "when, by mutually advantageous arrangement between its proprietors (Thompson, Livingston & Co.) and the proprietors of Adams & Co.'s Express, Kinsley & Co.'s Express, Livingston's Philadelphia Express, Hoey & Co.'s Charleston Express, and Livingston, Winchester & Co.'s Savannah Express, the several interests were consolidated in one joint-stock, under the title 'The Adams Express Company.'" A Boston editor explained: "The Adams Express Company is a joint stock association, formed July 1, 1854, under the laws of New York, with some forty stockholders residing in Massachusetts, Rhode Island, Connecticut, New York, Pennsylvania, Maryland, Georgia and Ohio, and who are individually liable for all the losses of the company. The business is conducted by nine managers, who are large shareholders, and effects are vested in three Trustees." Alvin Adams presided, while Henry's friend William B. Dinsmore exercised day-to-day administrative power.[1]

The Adams Express organization reflected strategic choices, and its subsequent operations and dealings are difficult to comprehend or even justify absent an understanding of them. "All four express giants—The American, Adams, Wells Fargo and United States express companies—began as unincorporated joint stock associations, chartered under statutes of New York State," industry expert Peter Z. Grossman detailed. "Their stock, which traded like that of corporations, carried unlimited liability. But the joint stock organizational form still proved advantageous in other ways. Most important, the form allowed managers and directors to control the dissemination of information about their companies. This, in turn, permitted the firms, first, to reduce entry attempts, and, second, to gain advantages in contract negotiations with the railroads. Unincorporated status also allowed managers and directors special personal benefits."[2]

Put in simple terms, the company could operate in secret, refuse to disseminate balance sheets or profit reports, and decline to explain decision making. As to personal benefits, Grossman added: "Managers let large liquid funds accumulate that they could have distributed to themselves and other shareholders as dividends. Instead, they chose an indirect and less public method of distribution—a method that was possible only if the firms remained unincorporated. Specifically, officers and directors gave each other loans." The loans, in practice, could be shared with employees and "friends." Thus, if an employee such as Henry Plant desired to create his own express business connecting Florida to the nation, Adams and Dinsmore could loan him interest-free Adams Express money with minimal accounting or accountability. Once Plant's independent firm became operational—with Adams's cooperation, of course—he could sell it back to the parent company, extinguish his debt, and reap profits that would include cash and Adams Express shares. Friends helped friends. John Hoey had already proved that the scheme could work.[3]

Other quirks highlighted the company's administrative structure. Adams did not absorb other lines such as Harnden Express; rather, each operated under its own name within its geographic area of interest. The individual firms associated closely and collegially, but the public perceived them as maintaining an independent existence. The value of each brand name persisted. Within Adams Express itself, lines of authority flowed from controlling managers and officers down to New York staff to division directors. As far as Plant was concerned, the branch of greatest future significance was the Southeastern or Baltimore Division (Maryland, the District of Columbia, Virginia, North and South Carolina, and parts of Georgia and Tennessee). Samuel Moor Shoemaker—a Baltimorean two years younger than Henry and one of the company's principal managers and shareholders—superintended its activities.[4]

Normally, Adams executives Dinsmore, Hoey, E. S. Sanford, and Clapp Spooner would have faced long odds arranging an assignment for Plant that infringed on Shoemaker's authority. The year 1854, though, did not prove a normal one for Shoemaker. He had wed in 1853 and spent much of the next year's first six months honeymooning and settling into marriage. Subsequently, he contracted an ailment that required recuperation through summer and early fall. The other company managers took advantage of the distractions, naming Plant superintendent of Harnden Express southern operations. "He was placed in charge of all the interests then controlled by that company, and all that might be acquired by the company in the South under his management or through his efforts," biographer George Smyth explained. This move sounded grander than, in fact, it was. "Harnden Express . . . forwarded matter from New York by steamer to Savannah, and thence to Augusta, Macon, and Atlanta, by the Central, Macon, and Western Railroads," Smyth added, "and also in Charleston, of the Hoey Express, by which goods were forwarded from New York to Charleston and were then distributed through the interior by the South Carolina Railroad."[5]

Henry planned to assume his new duties by late summer or early fall. Unfortunately, relocation to an Augusta, Georgia, headquarters did not prove easy. Ellen's health presented one complication. A little over two weeks after she arrived in New York from her Jacksonville stay, her grandfather Timothy Blackstone died at Branford. Unfortunately, the death of anyone close to Ellen seemingly triggered episodes of depression. In the circumstances Henry preferred a change of scene as quickly as possible. His plans came to nothing. By the time son Morton reached his third birthday on August 18, catastrophe had intervened. Authorities had confirmed yellow fever at Savannah on the ninth. Hurricane winds and rains meanwhile devastated Savannah and Charleston. Officials soon declared the fever epidemic at Augusta, and weeks passed without relief. "Perhaps the utter desolation of Augusta," a visitor recorded in October, "may best be inferred from the fact, that this city of at least twenty thousand inhabitants, was estimated, when I entered it, to contain only from one hundred and fifty to two hundred whites, who were dying at the rate of six, eight, and ten a day!"[6]

The Plants bided their time into November. They likely resided in New York City at Judson's Hotel, convenient to Henry's work and Ellen's physicians. If so, trouble found them there. On November 20 the hotel burst into flames. "The fire spread with great rapidity," a report detailed. "The boarders and servants were compelled to make their escape in such haste that most of their clothing and personal baggage was lost. About one hundred and eighty guests were in the house when the fire broke out. Some of them were in bed at the time, and had to escape with barely sufficient clothing to protect them from the cold." Within two hours flames had reached toward other targets. "The next building south,—occupied on the lower floors by the offices of Adams & Co.'s Express and on the upper stories by J. C. Horn & Co. dry goods jobbers,—was at this time seriously threatened," the report continued. "The danger in this quarter, owing to the exertions of the firemen, was, after a great struggle, entirely subdued. At a later hour a portion of the wall of the hotel fell over on the dome of the rear office of Messrs. Adams & Co.'s Express Building, causing considerable damage."[7]

Five days later the couple—Ellen by then surely at wit's end—boarded ship for Savannah, leaving Morton behind. Upon arrival three days later, they learned to their relief that Augusta had been declared "perfectly healthy." Exercising caution, though, Henry escorted Ellen to Jacksonville and the same Strawberry Mills farm near where she had recuperated earlier. He returned to Savannah alone. Clapp Spooner also appeared in the region on Adams Express's behalf "for the purpose of establishing new agencies and points of delivery, and harmonizing and adjusting their whole system." The old friends teamed in travels that led them to Atlanta by mid-December as they examined major rail towns in Georgia and Alabama. Spooner headed north at Christmastime, satisfied that he had set Henry on a fast start. "Arrangements have been completed with all the Railroads that diverge into the interior from our Southern seaboard marts, and the Southern branch of this vast concern now includes Augusta, Atlanta, La Grange, Macon, Montgomery, Chattanooga, Knoxville, Nashville, &c.," the *Charleston Courier* advised, "in short, all towns or villages on the Roads now in operation throughout that whole region, as also the seaports from Charleston around to New Orleans, inclusive."[8]

Henry spent much of the next seven months shoring up the network that he and Spooner had mapped out and exploring new markets for Harnden and Adams Express. "Mr. Plant was busy organizing and developing the express business [and] was continuously on the road," Smyth confirmed. The job proved more difficult than anyone in New York had imagined. One issue arose in the person of Georgia-born Sterling Thomas Combs. Eleven years Henry's senior, Combs innately sensed the intensity of local resentments against Yankee businessmen and, in January, created "The Southern Express." The firm proudly proclaimed, "Our line has been established and is worked and owned by Southern men." Combs directly competed with Plant's operations, benefiting from the support of sympathetic southern newspapermen. "We would invite attention to the advertisement of Messrs. Combs & Co.'s Southern Express in another column," one editor commented. "The agents of this line are very courteous and obliging, and their punctuality and dispatch may be relied upon." Frustrated at his failure to gain ground, Henry reached a practical solution. He convinced Adams Express to buy out Combs and his partner Edward Mitchell. By the time the deal was consummated in October 1855, Plant had come to appreciate how valuable the friendship of potentially hostile editors could be. Courting them with free deliveries and other considerations became his standard practice.[9]

Henry had discovered meanwhile that others also resented his network-building attempts and that some of those men wielded extensive power. "Presidents and other representatives of all the railroads between Washington city and Montgomery, Ala." convened in March 1855 at Augusta. Richard R. Cuyler, head of the Central Railroad and Banking Company of Georgia, presided over debates that devolved into vitriol aimed at express companies. As the proceedings revealed, "it was resolved unanimously, that the system of private Expresses which at present prevails on the various railroad lines, is injurious to the interests of the companies, depriving them of the emoluments of a large and profitable portion of their business; and the companies present agreed to recommend to the executive boards not to enter into any new contracts, or extend existing ones beyond the first day of March next." Averting the looming disaster required much of Plant's time and energy during the year that followed. His exertions paid off, and he managed to keep contracts in place until the new Southern Railroad Association, which the Augusta meeting had sanctioned, convened at Richmond in July 1856. By then, Henry and his allies had won over enough railroad officials to stall adoption of any restriction. Instead, "it was argued that each company could control the matter to its own interest." The victory stood as a major one for Plant and Adams Express, but at the association's annual meetings thereafter the matter persistently bubbled to the surface in one form or another.[10]

Upheavals within Adams Express meanwhile jeopardized Plant's ability to deal with such challenges. Factions of shareholders enviously eyed the company's revenues and enormous financial reserves, craving the chance to grab control. Scandals involving the company's California operations created the opening they sought in early 1855. The insurgents forced suspension of services in the Golden State and, in April, prompted Alvin Adams's ouster as president. George W. Cass stepped into the power vacuum. The West

Point graduate, civil engineer, and Pittsburgh regional manager for Adams had developed express services from Baltimore to Pittsburgh. As Michigan senator Lewis Cass's nephew, he also possessed high-level political connections as well as support from shareholders excluded from decision making by Adams and Dinsmore. With some key players missing at an April called meeting held in New York, Cass bested Dinsmore for the presidency. Dinsmore found himself with little power as vice president and treasurer and was compelled to bide his time until Cass had moved on or been removed. E. S. Sanford filled in as secretary. The three men together served as the executive committee, known as the trustee managers.[11]

George Cass's tenure unexpectedly rebounded to Plant's favor, although this eventuality did not appear likely at the time. Adams Express attracted during his presidency a number of individuals who influenced Henry's career significantly in future years. Among the most prominent were J. Edgar Thomson, president of the vaunted Pennsylvania Railroad, and his associate Thomas Alexander Scott. In turn, Scott interested his twenty-year-old protégé Andrew Carnegie in the express company and loaned him money to purchase shares. These stocks constituted young Carnegie's first investment and proved their worth time and again. Along with his future friend Carnegie, Plant fully embraced the point of this lesson—to choose good investments and accept the risk. Tom Scott in due course helped Henry to capitalize on it.[12]

During the tumult of 1855, Plant made "frequent visits to the North" and witnessed much of the Adams Express drama firsthand. Dinsmore and his allies wanted to protect their friend's position as the California crisis built early in the year, and their sense of urgency heightened after Cass took over the company. They convinced S. M. Shoemaker that loyal worker Plant, already operating far away in Augusta, posed no threat to the Baltimore Division. Shoemaker subsequently agreed to concede to Henry those Deep South Adams operations below and to the west of North and South Carolina. Clapp Spooner particularly worked for this result, with his firsthand knowledge of Plant and of the area in which he was working proving essential. Details remain murky, but the pretense that Plant's authority extended only to Harden's express business ceased within months of his arrival at Savannah. "Our express service for Augusta, Atlanta, Chattanooga, Lagrange, Nashville, Macon, Columbus, Savannah, Montgomery and other points leaves daily at 8 A. M. and 4.15 P. M.," the company's Charleston agent advertised. "Have made arrangements to transmit, in the most safe and speedy manner, bank notes, specie, packages, and express freights of all description. Small packages at reduced rates."[13]

Henry lived mostly on the rails through summer 1855. Ellen probably stayed in Florida until spring. When the weather improved farther north, she likely took advantage of I. C. Plant's comfortable home in Macon. Sometime in spring, though, she settled in Henry's rooms at Augusta's Eagle and Phoenix Hotel. Situated on Broad Street in the heart of the downtown business district, the modest establishment had reasonable rates that fit well with Plant's ideas of thrift. Given Henry's frequent absences, the stay could easily have proved unbearable for Ellen. That it did not can be credited to the arrival of Captain William Williams—a seasoned sailor of Welsh descent—and his wife, Jane. The couple had previously covered the world and survived countless adventures, although in 1855 the captain commanded a Savannah River steamer. A few years younger than Henry and Ellen, the Williamses offered delightful company. They boarded at the Eagle and Phoenix, and the four outsiders to local society clung together. Jane especially supported and assisted Ellen. The arrangements and friendships pleased Henry enormously. The next year he hired Williams to work full time for Adams Express.[14]

Plant's Augusta attachment, as his routine absences demonstrated, did not run as deep as did his friendship with the Williamses. Later he often spoke of himself as a resident beginning "in 1854" and for decades thereafter, but for the most part, he sojourned in Augusta irregularly or not at all. Claiming the wealthy and elegant southern center as home served practical purposes, though. After the Southern Express experience, Plant often shrugged off the Yankee label and donned a southern guise. He did so even though he and his family passed a significant part of each year elsewhere than in Georgia. Most years during this period, the Plants spent weeks or months at Strawberry Mills in wintertime. They passed an equal or greater amount of time in the North. For example, Henry and Ellen checked out of the Eagle and Phoenix in mid-July 1855 upon receipt of word that his grandfather Levi Bradley had died at Branford. They arrived in New York from Charleston on the twenty-third. Henry made a quick August trip to Washington and, at the time of the Combs & Co. purchase, another to Charleston and Savannah in early fall. Otherwise, the family kept close to northern relations, friends, and the Adams Express headquarters until they stepped aboard a Charleston-bound steamer on November 14. With the year's travels they set two precedents. First, in November Henry and Ellen finally brought Morton, now four years old, to Augusta. They also routinely made it their practice thereafter to leave the South before the onset of the fever season and to return near year's end.[15]

Ellen in fact sometimes departed Augusta even earlier than did her husband, leaving him to his work. "Mr. Plant led a very busy life in Augusta,"

George Smyth wrote. "He lived with his wife at the hotel, and, when she was travelling in the North in the summer, he had his office, for convenience, on the same floor as his bedroom. It had been his habit to keep pad and pencil by his bedside, so that when there came to his mind a matter that called for attention he at once put it down on his memoranda. He was constantly receiving reports from his express offices all over the South. There came to him for adjustment, many questions of management that were perplexing and urgent, so that he was often on the road, called away at short notice, north, south, or southwest."[16]

Administrative issues figured prominently in Plant's southern schedule, and, importantly for his career, management techniques and deft personnel dealings emerged in time as hallmarks of his success. In the mid-1850s, of course, he was still studying how best to provide effective leadership and exercise good judgment in a steady and consistent manner. Understandably, he made mistakes. Beyond business affairs, his insights and wisdom relating to key matters concerning Ellen and her health also fell short in repeated instances. Still, when it came to a business context he possessed gifts of ability. Forty years later Plant praised one of his executives, Beverly Welford Wrenn. In doing so he effectively spoke of himself, qualities that he believed that he possessed, and approaches that he had learned to utilize. The comments harked back to his days as an express messenger and competencies that he had refined while riding the rails. "He is one of the most faithful and one of the most capable railroad men I know anywhere, ever vigilant, always awake to the situation and always making friends and helping somebody along," he commented. "Personally, he works his way into the kindest esteem of every man who comes to know him if it is but for five minutes. He sticks to his friends and makes new ones every day of the world. He is shrewd and capable and always doing something for the road for which he is working."[17]

Henry required those abilities from the start. In 1855 and immediately following, he faced two serious management concerns. Dinsmore had tasked him to maintain and expand territorial operations and additionally—at least in Plant's mind—to blaze his path to wealth by pioneering express service in Florida. His quest, when it came to the latter, at first glance might have appeared unrealistic to some. The Sunshine State in 1855 held only 110,000 residents, of whom nearly half were free blacks or slaves. The two largest towns contained populations of fewer than 3,000 each. Jacksonville accommodated about 1,500, while the state capital at Tallahassee boasted fewer than 1,000. Tampa claimed an even smaller number. Wealth or the potential for wealth existed in the Panhandle—the capital's Leon County and surrounding areas—where cotton plantations flourished. The peninsula, though, consisted mostly of poor white or "Cracker" homesteads, frontier outposts, and vast stretches occupied, if at all, by cattle or Seminole Indians and their allies.[18]

How could Plant have imagined generous profits flowing from an express business in such a place? Surprisingly, he had good reason to do so. For one thing, Florida was growing. Historians have tended to appraise the newborn state and its future potential through a Civil War prism, when it suffered devastating division, destruction, and dislocation. Prior to 1861, though, optimism about the future reigned supreme. Railroad development, as in Georgia and elsewhere, drove attitudes. A variety of 1850s schemes captured imaginations locally, regionally, and nationally. Among them, the Pensacola and Georgia Railroad anticipated construction eastward from Tallahassee toward Alligator (now Lake City). Its backers dreamed as well of connecting Pensacola with Tallahassee. Meanwhile, the Florida Atlantic and Gulf Central Railroad aimed to link Jacksonville to Alligator and beyond. Major excitement also stirred around a proposed Pensacola and Montgomery line. "Joy to Pensacola! Clear the track!—the Railroad's coming!" the *Pensacola Gazette* exclaimed on March 22, 1856. "Bright years will yet be thine, O Pensacola!"[19]

Other transportation and development schemes competed for attention and investments, but the Florida Railroad captured Henry's imagination. This initiative projected an Atlantic Ocean linkage with the Gulf of Mexico, eliminating a dangerous and time-consuming voyage around the peninsula and keys. Original plans connected Fernandina on Amelia Island in the northeast with Tampa Bay, but by 1855 a shorter run from Fernandina to Cedar Keys had won favor. If an express company already operating in the state managed to secure exclusive rights on Florida Railroad trains, it would reap riches. Plant meant to accomplish exactly that.[20]

Henry probably set his plans in motion during his 1853 Florida visit or soon afterward. "Within less than a year [after his first visit]," a reporter later observed, "he had again invaded the state and made some investments, which later turned out to have been judicious." This likely meant that he had purchased railroad shares when he and Ellen arrived in March 1854 before the Jacksonville fire. After their return to Georgia from New York that December, the Plants revisited Jacksonville. Interestingly, Florida Railroad president David Levy Yulee, a US senator, checked into a local hotel just as the Plants got to town. The length of their stay during the ensuing winter season is not known, but it may have extended into March 1856. By then, actual construction of the railroad was underway at Fernandina. Unfortunately for Plant's ambitions, Indian war exploded once more in the peninsula. The Third Seminole War, also called the Billy Bowlegs War, dragged

8. Henry Plant, "Expressman." Bramson Archive.

on until spring 1858. That conflict and other factors slowed construction to a crawl. Not until 1861 did cars run the entire 156 miles of the Florida Railroad's length. That moment, for Plant, came too late.[21]

In spring 1856, though, Henry's hopes remained bright, if results elusive. He found himself restricted as George Cass's presidency redirected Adams Express resources away from the Deep South and entrepreneurial projects there. Despite the resistance, Plant opened express service on the developing Memphis & Charleston Railroad to "Nashville, Tuscumbia, and intermediate stations." That was about all. Within a few weeks after the April announcement of the new route, he and Ellen left the South and, by June, resided at a New York hotel. Henry probably attended the next month's meeting of the Southern Railroad Association in Richmond and then continued on alone to Augusta, where he checked into the Globe Hotel. The hotel bears mention because Plant and owner Lucius Smith Morris, who had ties at New Haven to the Bradley family, became friends. Within three decades Morris's daughter Anne would marry Henry's New Haven friend Jim English. In the meantime Lucius had played a significant role in Plant's Civil War–era business affairs and, afterward, in the life of a teenage Morton Plant. For now, Morris struggled to pay his bills. With the coming of winter, he sold the Globe.[22]

At last matters improved for Henry, if only marginally, in early 1857. Having deposited Ellen at Strawberry Mills, he ventured to Baltimore in early January to meet twenty-nine-year-old James Shuter. Already a California gold-field veteran, Shuter had returned to Maryland only to see his home burn in December 1856. Morton Freeman or else Baltimore partner Sam Shoemaker had fortunately recommended him for Adams employment at a time when Plant needed a deputy to assist with expansion at the increasingly critical hub at Memphis, Tennessee. The two men were working there by January 16 preparing for completion of the Memphis & Charleston Railroad, an achievement that would tie Memphis closely to the southeastern rail network that Plant utilized. After daily express service commenced on April 1, 1857, Shuter with Plant's support turned to regularizing express deliveries between Memphis and the South's largest metropolis, New Orleans. This required steamboats. Michael J. "Mike" O'Brien, another young Baltimore native who soon joined Shuter's staff as a driver, explained the reason to a journalist: "Through [O'Brien's] devotion to the interests of his employers, the industry, energy and intelligence, he secured promotion to the then important position of shipping clerk. This was in 1858, before the railroad had been completed to New Orleans, and when all express was transferred to steamers at Memphis and transported thence to the South by the Mississippi river." Triweekly express service between Memphis and New Orleans commenced in October 1857. The Illinois Central Railroad, the line O'Brien mentioned, remained incomplete for decades.[23]

While spending a good deal of time facilitating the Memphis–New Orleans service during the first half of 1857, Plant maintained a watchful eye on the New York headquarters. There, corporate intrigue spun furiously as frictions between President Cass and his allies on the one hand and the Dinsmore faction on the other came to a boil. Cass in January 1856 had taken the Ohio and Pennsylvania Railroad's presidency but had refused to give up Adams Express control. Ensuing resentments incited the president to discipline one or more of the major corporate players. Specifically, in late August he relieved Shoemaker as Baltimore Division superintendent. This and other actions fueled opposition to the point that the dispossessed superintendent successfully wrenched control back from Cass's man in March 1857. The president's days by then were numbered. All parties nominally labeled his late-June departure a resignation. Whatever it was, as the *New*

York Tribune reported, "Wm. B. Dinsmore, then Treasurer of the Company, was unanimously elected President." He took office in July.[24]

Dinsmore's victory meant a win for Plant, Henry evidently having participated in events leading up to it. Ellen had rendezvoused with her husband at Augusta in the spring. The Southern Railroad Association met in the city during mid-May, after which he made for New York, leaving wife and son in Jane Williams's care. The journey positioned Henry to aid Dinsmore as the power struggle unfolded, and their ties of loyalty strengthened. Once Dinsmore had moved into the president's office, a happy Plant quickly made his way to Augusta and family. A few weeks later—on August 16—he, Ellen, and Morton departed together for New York. Neither Henry nor Ellen returned to Augusta until the following year.[25]

Notably, during their absence from the South Henry did not ignore or avoid the region entirely. As had been true earlier in 1857, his sights soon concentrated anew on New Orleans and Memphis, with his focus sharpened by necessity. On August 24, a few days after his arrival in the North, the Ohio Life Insurance & Trust Company failed. It was considered "one of the most highly respected financial institutions in New York City," and its fall initiated a major economic setback known as the Panic of 1857. The crash's disastrous consequences arrived in a rush. Major banks suspended specie payments, and manufacturers closed factories. Businesses failed in large numbers. Enterprises in southern towns such as Augusta followed suit. Summing up the catastrophe in mid-October, a Boston editor exclaimed, "We have now reached the height of financial calamity."[26]

With economic misery easily visible, Plant arrived in the Crescent City on Christmas Day. He had fulfilled his now-routine task of delivering Ellen and Morton to Florida for the winter. From a St. Louis hotel room he busied himself with all the details necessary to implement the new service from Memphis to New Orleans that Adams had inaugurated the previous October. "The extension of the line through to [New Orleans] . . . has been effected through the active and efficient agency of Mr. H. B. Plant, the Superintendent," a January 1858 report detailed. "This company, so well and favorably known throughout the U. States, is prepared to forward, in the most rapid and safe manner, bank notes, gold, silver, valuable packages, &c., from their office in [Charleston, SC] through to New Orleans, and thence to Natchez, Vicksburg, Memphis, Nashville, Cairo, St. Louis, Louisville, and all other points available by steamboats or railroads in the Union."[27]

As time passed, New Orleans captivated Plant. His future habits and preferences argued that he remained in the city until at least mid-February and Mardi Gras. Although the festival had not attained the heights of revelry and ribaldry that it later boasted, the holiday nonetheless offered a cornucopia of diversions. For Henry, the Orleans Opera stood at the forefront. The Crescent City, he soon believed, might cheer his long-afflicted wife and perhaps abet healing. Filled with enthusiasm, he traced his way back to Georgia to join Ellen and Morton, either at Augusta or at I. C. Plant's Macon home. William and Jane Williams had relocated to Atlanta a few weeks earlier, and the Plants dropped Morton off with those trusted friends. Henry and Ellen then made their way to New Orleans and the elegant St. Charles Hotel.[28]

The trip could well have relieved and comforted Ellen had chance not intervened. Four days after the Plants checked into the St. Charles, Nathan Maroney—whom Plant had appointed express agent in Montgomery one year earlier—stole $10,000 from a package in his care. The investigation raised myriad complications before the thief's identity was ascertained. Henry's judgment and management skills meanwhile came under close scrutiny, and he faced the possibility of ruin. The crisis eventually turned in Plant's favor chiefly because he received staunch support from President Dinsmore and E. S. Sanford, who had assumed general superintendence of all routes under the new administration. Had Cass remained president, a different outcome might have resulted. The affair historically carried importance because Sanford ultimately engaged detective Allan Pinkerton—then at the onset of his career—to track the culprit. For Henry, the incident's significance derived more from a new player that it introduced to his life. Dinsmore and Superintendent Sanford associated with the company a Bridgeport, Connecticut, attorney named Henry Sanford—not to be confused with Henry Shelton Sanford, the American diplomat and entrepreneur who founded Sanford, Florida—to handle special assignments that they preferred not to entrust to regular counsel William H. Seward or his partners. Plant and lawyer Sanford were already acquainted in 1858 in that they shared common friendships with Clapp Spooner and his close associate Phineas T. Barnum. Only now, through Sanford's work on the Maroney case, did they come to know each other well.[29]

That result lay months in the future in May 1858, however, with many actions and decisions coming beforehand. First, as the public learned of the theft the Plants hurried to Georgia, leaving E. S. Sanford in New Orleans to coordinate company follow-up. This allowed Henry to monitor a Georgia railroad convention held at Augusta from May 10 to 12. It also permitted him to post a $2,500 reward for information. A tense waiting period followed during what should have been a celebratory time. On May 22 dependable rail connections opened from New York to Memphis, allowing Adams Express, relatively speaking, to speed packages and freight from the Northeast to the Mississippi River. At almost the same time, the postmaster general declared "new mail arrangements" by which railways were to "convey the great southern mail, leaving New York in the morning, over the Central route, diverging from the seaboard route at Richmond, and then via the Virginia and Tennessee railroad, through Knoxville and Dalton, Georgia, to the grand junction fifty miles East of Memphis, and thence, via Jackson, to New Orleans." Effective July 1, this redirected major railroad subsidies away from routes that passed through Augusta and, instead, ushered Atlanta to greater prominence as a rail center.[30]

No sooner had the new mail route come into play than the Plants relocated to Atlanta. If Henry had not already concluded to move, then a yellow fever outbreak convinced him. The first deaths came at New Orleans and Charleston in mid-July. Casualties in coastal and river towns such as Galveston, Vicksburg, Mobile, and Savannah followed. The first Augusta fatality occurred on October 18 and involved a man who had passed through Charleston. Municipal authorities insisted, however, "Our city never was in a healthier condition than at the present time." Still, residents of potentially affected locales fled for safety. Atlanta meanwhile underwent an experience similar to that seen in other inland centers. "Many citizens of Mobile and New Orleans [have] congregated in the hotels here, deterred from going further south by the continued prevalence of yellow fever in those cities," a Montgomery correspondent advised on November 5. "These persons . . . have filled to overflowing the hotels and boarding houses. I notice many of the leading planters of Alabama,—men of wealth, of refinement, and of practical skill."[31]

Henry, Ellen, and Morton joined the Williamses at Atlanta's Trout House hotel. Sited on the northeast corner of Decatur Street at Pryor, it overlooked State Square and the Atlanta railroad depot to the southwest where Adams kept its offices. "It was the scene of many public gatherings and nearly all of the distinguished visitors in that day were entertained at this hotel in the most lavish hospitality," a townsman recalled. "The building was an ornamental structure four stories high, handsomely furnished and, for that day, was considered [at least by some Atlantans] as fine as any in the country." Doubtlessly to Henry's delight, a theater called the Athenaeum operated immediately across Pryor Street. Thompson's Atlanta Hotel, another leading hostelry, faced State Square and the depot as well, across Pryor Street from a perch southwest of the theater. Front views disappointed patrons at both hotels as an unsightly line of shacks masked the depot beyond. Later in the year, city fathers finally converted the area into Atlanta's first park. As State Square's status hints, Atlanta had not yet fully transitioned into a city. Only in summer 1858 did its leadership order plank sidewalks laid on Peachtree, Marietta, and Decatur Streets and insist, at the behest of property owners upset at "cows lying around their gates and Lots," that "cattle . . . be kept up at night." Moreover, the councilmen addressed Alabama Street's winter mud by ordering it filled "with broken rock." The atmosphere resonated with the frontier-town flavor that Plant had breathed there five years earlier, as evoked when "eight to ten thousand human beings" crowded into town in June 1858 for a hanging. The Trout House bar enjoyed land-office business.[32]

Its rough-hewn aspects to the contrary, Atlanta stood poised to transition into a closer approximation of a city or, more appropriately, a large town. Its population was growing toward an 1860 total of slightly fewer than 10,000, about three-quarters of whom were white. Augusta, by comparison, contained 12,500 inhabitants, only 4,200 of whom were white. "Atlanta, in [early 1859] was not at all city-like," writer Mary Edwards Bryan recalled. "It was a young, live, sociable town, where everybody knew everybody else, and neighbors took a friendly interest in each other's affairs. Of course, there was gossip—it is the bane of all towns—but it was rarely seasoned with scandal." She added proudly: "Atlanta had a literary set. In fact, literature was in high favor." City historian Franklin Garrett noted, "During 1858 nineteen substantial brick stores, some quite pretentious were erected." A scattering of nice homes, too, were replacing simple plank cottages and log cabins. Railroad executive Lemuel P. Grant's lovely house, remaining today near his namesake Grant Park, highlighted new construction during Plant's Atlanta sojourn. Whether it was completed in time for Grant to host Henry and Ellen is not known, but the future business associates necessarily became acquainted then if not before.[33]

How much Henry enjoyed Atlanta's 1858 social scene cannot be gauged, but in light of yellow fever concerns, the Montgomery theft situation, and the burden of his division's business generally he must have kept to the road almost constantly. He particularly needed to recruit personnel as the division expanded. He welcomed E. S. Sanford's recommendation of James Joseph McKeever to head the Memphis agency under James Shuter. McKeever proved so able that, within months, Plant transferred him to New Orleans. This was the year, too, when young Mike O'Brien came to Memphis from Baltimore with the enthusiastic encouragement of his friend John Hoey. O'Brien soon moved to New Orleans as well. Clapp Spooner could take credit for placing his brother Jacob as agent in Savannah. New Yorker Cyrus S. Plank arrived to clerk in Augusta, eventually to become cashier. Philadelphian Hugh Dempsey also found himself in Augusta, although he had come for health reasons. Henry met and liked the young man, and Dempsey went to work for him. These men—most of them, but not all, from the North—later occupied significant places in Plant's business affairs, and many in his personal life. Others of the same stripe responded as well to his entreaties in 1858 and the following year. From New York in 1859, for example, came Charles H. Phelps and Rufus Brown Bullock. President Dinsmore backed their assignments in order to press the company's growing interest in telegraphy. Meanwhile, Connecticut's Edward Hurlbert was working for the Atlanta and LaGrange Railroad when he impressed Henry with his cooperation in the Maroney investigation. He subsequently headed Plant's Central Division.[34]

Whatever activities their Atlanta sojourn involved, Henry and Ellen had moved on by the fall. They briefly returned to Augusta, this time frequenting the city's finest establishment, the Planters' Hotel. A few weeks later they entrained for New York. Morton Freeman had returned there from San Francisco for business and pleasure, as a consequence of which he rejoined Adams Express. He also proposed to Ellen's cousin Emily Francis "Fannie" Blackstone, daughter of New York City builder and financier Wyllis Blackstone. If Plant family custom serves as a guide, Henry and Ellen stayed on in the North enjoying Freeman's company and tending to business until December. Thereupon, they removed to Florida. "Mrs. Plant's health, which had been failing for some time, was rapidly growing worse," George Smyth observed.[35]

Henry stayed with his ailing wife at Strawberry Mills until the third week of January 1859, when he traveled to Montgomery. There, he blundered badly. Dinsmore and E. S. Sanford, reports from company detectives in hand, had instructed him to dismiss Agent Maroney. "The Superintendent of the Southern Division visited Montgomery on the twentieth of January 1859, but was anticipated in the matter of carrying out his instructions, by Maroney's tendering his resignation," Pinkerton recorded. "The resignation was accepted, but the superintendent [i.e., Plant] requested him to continue in charge of the office until his successor should arrive." Maroney explained: "The Superintendent had much suavity of manner, and it was hard for me to tell whether he considered me guilty or not. I rather thought he suspected me. When I found that my time with the company was to be so short I determined to make a good haul, as I knew I could never get a situation in the business again, for the Adams Express was the only express company in the South." Six days later Maroney took four packages containing $40,000 and disappeared. On January 31 authorities arrested him. Shock reverberated through the community. "Much sympathy is felt for this untoward event," a report asserted. Historian Daniel Stashower explained, "The local press rallied behind Maroney as a man of 'high character and Southern citizenship,' while the Adams Express Company—headquartered at that time in New York—was widely seen as a hostile northern concern launching a campaign of baseless persecution."[36]

Having stumbled in not showing Maroney the door when he resigned, Plant now discovered himself awash in an even bigger mess. Fortunately, Henry Sanford arrived to save the day. A preliminary examination ensued in a Montgomery court in early February with political winds blowing hot outside. Plant, among others, testified. Working with lawyer Sanford, he and E. S. Sanford also arranged for legal representation by the cream of the crop among Alabama lawyers, choices that within the next four years would work enormous consequences in Henry's life and career. Thomas Hill Watts had recently served in the Alabama legislature representing Montgomery, while his partner John A. Elmore—who possessed "a reputation for passionlessness and legal scholarship"—had sat in the state senate. A third team member, Elmore's former partner William Lowndes Yancey, had already earned fame through the South as a "firebrand" advocate for southern secession. Their presence on Adams Express's behalf telegraphed plainly that the company enjoyed powerful friends in high southern places.[37]

Events moved quickly. A legal shock wave stirred by Watts, Elmore, and Yancey temporarily overwhelmed local hostility to Adams Express as the lawyers fought off a dismissal attempt and managed to have Maroney bound over to the circuit court. "The friends of the accused (and their name is legion) are fully confident that the trial will result in a satisfactory showing of his perfect innocence," the *Montgomery Advertiser* boldly insisted, "if it should come to trial at all." Those holding such opinions failed to reckon with Adams Express clout. Maroney, though, understood his situation far better. In early April he absconded with his ill-gotten gains. Pinkerton operatives set out hot on his trail. Plant remained behind forlornly holding the empty bag.[38]

5
Unwanted Conflict
1859 to 1863

"a black cloud of more than common import"

The era that began for Henry Plant at Montgomery, Alabama, in February 1859 and ended with him fleeing the Confederacy at Wilmington, North Carolina, in September 1863 stands as one of the most fascinating but least understood periods of his life. Plant strove doggedly to make and keep it so. Those times nonetheless found him in key respects at his most brilliant in business and politics, if not in marriage and fatherhood. Secrecy and effrontery competed as elements of his story. Characters of national and international scope peopled the narrative. Themes of enduring significance illuminated the text. None of these factors, though, changed the day-to-day realities that Plant confronted: how deeply many white southerners detested northern businessmen and how important Yankee dollars and influence could be in holding back, at least briefly, the threatened flood.

The Nathan Maroney debacle had rendered Plant vulnerable at Montgomery in winter 1859 and left him searching for professional redemption. He possessed few options other than to take direction from Adams Express superiors. Fortunately, W. B. Dinsmore and E. S. Sanford also were friends, and—if the history of the express industry offered any lesson—personal loyalty to friends who worked with you counted for everything. As the partner on the scene and general superintendent, Sanford took charge. After Montgomery agent Maroney grabbed $40,000 on January 26, 1859, Sanford summoned Connecticut lawyer Henry Sanford to Alabama and also a telegraphed a detective he had not yet met: "ALLAN PINKERTON: Can you send me a man—half horse and half alligator? I have got 'bit' once more! When can you send him?" Thus, when Maroney fled Montgomery in April, Pinkerton's agents stood at the ready. Sanford personally aided the bail jumper's arrest at New York City on May 11.[1]

Meanwhile, Adams executives in Alabama—as well as lawyers Thomas Hill Watts, John A. Elmore, and William Lowndes Yancey—strove to soften and sweeten the company's northern image, especially in the minds of ardently prosouthern newspaper editors and politicians. If patterns illustrated elsewhere by the company and Plant ruled the day, "persuasion" involved "gifts" including cash and other considerations. The effort worked degrees of difference, and editorial reaction appeared subdued upon Mahoney's arrest. By October the *Montgomery Mail* exulted, "Recently, more than ever, we have observed the entire confidence of the country in the Adams Express." It added, "We could now no more get along without the Adams Express, than we could without rail roads and telegraphs.—May it 'wave,' while it continues now to discharge its multitudinous functions with perfect fidelity." These techniques of persuasion, fashioned in 1859 and given hardy polishing later on, proved of critical necessity to Plant in later times.[2]

Henry likely coped with aftereffects of the embarrassment at Montgomery before making his own way to New York, returning South in late April before the arrest. His subsequent itinerary vividly evidenced a need to bide time. He and Ellen took rooms at New Orleans's City Hotel on May 11, resuming the vacation interrupted by Maroney's original crime. Nine days later the couple arrived in Memphis, where Henry finalized arrangements for running freight over the Memphis and Ohio Railroad. Around June 1 they departed for New York and several easy days at Niagara Falls. They stayed at the posh Monteagle Hotel resort, famous for adjacent mineral springs and therapeutic baths. Henry Sanford meanwhile eased his fatigue at the nearby Clifton House. When Henry once more ventured South, Ellen remained behind. Before he resumed his journey, though, they stopped in New York City, where someone at Adams Express gave him "two Japanese coins, one gold, the other silver." The curious items fascinated Plant to the point of distraction. He proudly displayed the unusual money at Augusta on June 9. "They are both square, or rather parallelogramic in shape," an awestruck newspaperman related. Through June and July Plant awaited word from New York, where Pinkerton scrambled to recover stolen cash. Around August 1 the detective tricked the thief, and Henry made for company headquarters straightaway. He stayed a month. Parties, celebrations, and evenings out on the town followed. Immense relief resulted, and inadvertently a seed had been left to germinate that would propel Plant to Asia four decades later.[3]

As fall 1859 approached, Plant necessarily turned his mind to work. Prominent Alabamians, whose resentments of Adams Express had by no means been forgotten, had organized a "Southern Express Company" to keep lucrative profits from northern hands. "An Express Company has become a necessity at the South as well as at the North," expounded the Troy *Southern Advertiser*. "Their convenience is incalculable, as well as palpable, and yet as important as it has gotten to be of late years to every class of Southern people, the North has been permitted to enjoy an exclusive monopoly, when such an enterprise could have been as well carried on by Southern men and capital as Northern." Other editors concurred. The *Charleston Mercury* declared: "We rejoice to hear from the Montgomery *Mail* of the formation of a Southern Express Company. We are confident that a home company, knowing the wants and demands of our Southern public, would succeed to the exclusion of all others." In Charleston by September 19, Henry moved to shore up editorial support while looking into the proposal's feasibility. Soon convinced that backers would require a legislative charter before they could move ahead, he directed his Montgomery lawyers to frustrate any such effort.[4]

While the Southern Express problem occupied Plant's time, in October a radicalized abolitionist named John Brown and twenty-one followers seized the federal arsenal at Harper's Ferry, Virginia (later, West Virginia). Brown aimed to spark a slave rebellion. The ensuing explosion of sectional tensions had been building for a decade. Henry earlier in the year at Montgomery had already witnessed the southern white expression of the growing divide. Marines led by Colonel Robert E. Lee put down Brown's attack, but open flames of passion had been kindled in the North and the South. Typically, the *Daily Chronicle and Sentinel* at Augusta denounced "the effort of a few fanatics to produce an insurrection."[5]

In such circumstances and amid fanatical calls for confrontation, Henry Plant turned forty years of age on October 27. Augusta certainly housed numerous men with northern sympathies friendly to Plant, but he must have breathed a deep sigh of relief as he boarded the New York train in early November. W. B. Dinsmore, sensing the stress gnawing at his friend, attempted to divert him. The Adams Express president was involved with the Academy of Music, of which he would eventually become president. There on Thanksgiving night, Thursday, November 24, 1859, the singer Adelina Patti famously made her New York debut at age sixteen. The event constituted a triumph for Patti and launched her stellar career. The moment also struck Henry to the core. He had spent the year anguishing for a wife with declining health and ruing the possibility that his livelihood and chance for wealth—a dream he had compromised himself to pursue—were about to disappear. He now fixed on something beautiful and, to him, flawless. As time would tell, Plant's life had begun to change in unanticipated ways.[6]

The Plants stayed in New York through 1859 and into 1860, their Florida departure delayed for a wedding. On January 5 Morton Freeman married Ellen's cousin Fannie Blackstone. The Dinsmores and Plants, among others, naturally attended the rites. The three couples planned a honeymoon tour together in the Deep South with a mid-February departure. Events prompted Henry to head South in advance of the group, however, thanks to the skulduggery of a supposed ally. Lawyer William L. Yancey's partner William P. Chilton, one-time Alabama Supreme Court chief justice, had quietly maneuvered the Southern Express bill through the state legislature. Fervent discussions ensued among Plant, Yancey, and Chilton, and financial incentives were likely exchanged. In any event, although the measure received the governor's approval on February 23, Chilton undertook no immediate implementation steps.[7]

About one week prior to the Alabama governor's action, Henry rendezvoused with his wife and friends at Savannah. They called first at Fernandina or Jacksonville. Railroad projects were underway there, and the feasibility of a viable express operation was growing with each mile of track laid. The Plants and Dinsmores then passed on to St. Augustine in early March. However much the travelers enjoyed Henry's favorite Florida town, local attitudes stoked by the national crisis frustrated them all. "Let the South take her position," the *St. Augustine Examiner*'s editor proclaimed on the seventeenth, "that she will not buy goods of northern importation or manufacture, whether those goods are sold by Northern or Southern houses." Although that item reached publication soon after the Plants and Dinsmores departed, hostility to northern interests echoed around them nonetheless, created embarrassment, and convinced party members to spend their time and money elsewhere.[8]

Back at Savannah on March 13, the three couples set out in a leisurely manner for New Orleans. They registered at the St. Charles Hotel on the thirtieth. From there Dinsmore and Plant intended further explorations to a locale that offered hospitality where Florida had exuded hostility. "Col. W. B. Densmire, the President of Adams's Express Company, Mr. H. B. Plant, the Superintendent General of the same company, and J. M. Freeman, Esq., of Freeman & Co.'s California Express, have lately been on a visit to our city, in connection with a tour of inspection," the *Daily Picayune* reported on April 4. "It was the intention of the two former gentlemen to have made a trip to Cuba, on their return to New York: but the Spanish part of our city seems to have been so satisfactory to them, in the way of visiting foreign countries, that they abandoned their trip to Havana, and have returned North." The matter did not end there. Thoughts of Havana's tropical charms stuck with Henry, and he tucked away securely the idea of a Cuban alternative to a problematic Florida.[9]

Assuming that Henry returned North with the Dinsmores, the trip allowed but a brief respite from pressing southern concerns. Democrats had scheduled their presidential nominating convention for Charleston on April 23. Adams Express had prepared to work the event to curry favor with politicians and journalists. "The press were laid under renewed obligations to that truly National institution, the Adams Express Company, but when did it ever fail to give its best attention to the men who handle printer's ink?" an Augusta newspaperman intoned. "We desire to return our own especial thanks to [Charleston agent W. T. J.] Woodward, Mr. Plant, (the General Superintendent,) and [Deputy Superintendent Rufus] Bullock." Unfortunately for Democrats, in historian James M. McPherson's words, "In the fevered atmosphere of 1860, Charleston was the worst possible place for the convention." Plant thus commanded a front-row seat as the sections battled over slavery and the Democratic Party flung itself into chaos.[10]

Plant's activities during the two months that followed the catastrophic Charleston meeting reflected a man refusing to believe portentous signs all around him and, disregarding alarm bells, going about business as usual. After installing his family in an Augusta rental, Henry mulled not imminent national calamity but perishable crop transportation. "Mr. H. B. Plant, the superintendent of Adams's Southern Express, whose headquarters are at this city [Augusta], and who, by the way, is a most estimable gentleman and efficient officer, has informed me of a novel fact," a journalist reported. "He has been applied to by parties in Mississippi in regard to the shipping of fruit to Chicago. It is expected that the peach crop this year will be so large that the New Orleans market will be overrun, and it is proposed to ship by express peaches from Mississippi to Chicago, where they will arrive at least two months in advance of the season North." Henry got the shipments going before embarking on an inspection tour to Mobile and New Orleans. In the Crescent City on July 3 he announced that "large quantities of fruit—apples, peaches and pears—are now being shipped by express from the South to the Northwestern cities, thus giving them the benefit of fruit a month in advance of the season."[11]

In fairness, no one knew and few imagined in spring and early summer 1860 the terrible, blood-soaked national tragedy that lay ahead. Henry's thoughts were plainly elsewhere. In July, after the New Orleans visit, he hurried North, where he, Ellen, and Morton abided until almost year's end. In the meantime Republican candidate Abraham Lincoln won election as president, and South Carolina seceded from the Union. Family concerns explained the hurried departure from Georgia, not impending national calamity. Ellen's grandfather Asa Beach lay dying in Branford, Connecticut, and family members had summoned her home. The death came on July 31 and, it must be assumed, launched Ellen into depression. At Branford, the Plants exercised Henry's typical habits of economy and boarded with a local family.[12]

Whatever the degree of Ellen's condition, Henry did not stay in one place for long. He placed his wife and son in the care of relations, for instance, to attend an August 9 top-level Adams Express conference in New York. Dinsmore, E. S. Sanford, Spooner, and Henry Sanford attended, among others. The company executives braced for an uncertain future and planned how to profit, if possible. Coincidentally, Plant's top staffers convened at Lookout Mountain, Tennessee, for the same purpose. Policies regarding movement of guns and ammunition ranked high on the agenda, with those present opting to continue business as usual. "'Overt acts [of treason]' were everywhere visible throughout the South; while in the North, open and secret sales of arms and munitions were consummated during all the months of December, January and February—arms which the manufacturers and salesmen *knew* were to be used against the Government, and, beyond question, sold them so to be used," a resentful northerner recorded. "The Adams' Express was an accredited carrying agent for the transportation of arms to the South; and, during these months, almost daily transported packages which its agents *knew* to contain arms and munitions ordered by the revolutionary States for use against the Government." Henry comprehended the implications, as some of the military-oriented freight moved to Augusta and its volunteer Washington Artillery. "Resolved," the company's members declared on November 21, "that the Adams' Express Company will accept our thanks for delivering military equipments, free of charge, to our corps."[13]

Plant justified furnishing accoutrements of war to southern military organizations as a simple matter of business. Had he been asked the question on November 21, he additionally would have insisted that there would be no war. He held this attitude in common with many others. Lincoln had won the presidency, but South Carolina had not yet seceded. More than a few future Rebel leaders were meanwhile seeking compromise. Even within Plant's family evidence of optimism could be found. In November Henry's half-brother Horace P. Hoadley—who lived at New Haven with abolitionist father Philemon Hoadley—boarded his family on a steamer bound for the Gulf port of Lavaca, Texas. Railroad construction promised a bright economic future for that region, and Hoadley aimed to capitalize with a wholesale and retail carriage dealership. War appeared so unlikely that nothing deterred Horace from his goal. The Hoadleys accordingly debarked at Galveston on November 20. Within a week or two, though, the enormity of Horace's mistake became clear. "The lone star banner [in support of secession] has also been hoisted at Lavaca," an early December report declared. "Fifteen guns, one for each Southern State, were fired by the people of Lavaca."[14]

The bubble of optimism began to burst for many others about the same time as it did for Horace Hoadley. Once the process of disunion commenced, it bulldozed ahead at gradually increasing speed on a path toward war. South

Carolina abandoned the Union on December 20. Mississippi acted on January 9, 1861. In the next three weeks or so Florida, Alabama, Georgia, Louisiana, and Texas joined the parade toward national suicide. They all sent delegates to Montgomery in February to create a regional government. South Carolina's Christopher G. Memminger produced a draft constitution that, with a little editing, achieved approval and created the Confederate States of America. In short order Jefferson Davis of Mississippi and Georgia's Alexander H. Stevens had been selected, respectively, president and vice president.[15]

Plant watched these events unfold from near at hand. He reached Augusta in January or early February 1861 after leaving Ellen and Morton in Florida. The opening of the Confederate Congress soon pulled him to Montgomery, where he generously dispensed largesse. Plant knew Memminger from Charleston business dealings. The newly minted treasury secretary commented of one Adams perquisite, "They have brought free for every member of Congress everything sent during the whole session." An attempt to revive the nascent Southern Express Company especially commanded Henry's attention. William P. Chilton, now a Confederate congressman, chaired the post office committee and aimed to grab the postmaster generalship for a nephew. That accomplished, Chilton could have dominated the express business. As it turned out he miscalculated, either by overestimating his influence with President Davis or else underestimating that of Adams Express. The nephew fell to fellow Texan John H. Reagan. Congress adjourned on March 16 with Chilton's plans in shambles, but not before it prohibited express companies "from carrying any letters unless they were prepaid by being enclosed in a stamped envelope of the Confederacy." By then, though, Chilton and Plant had reached a deal.[16]

Henry actually reached numerous agreements in Montgomery. Several versions of events later circulated, although Plant's account contained at least elements of truth. "At that time I thought it was incumbent on me that my duties and opinions should be understood by President Davis and his advisers," he commented. "To that end I caused myself to be represented by counsel to Mr. Davis and his Cabinet, in order that my opinions and position might be clearly defined and known to the government, so that its wish might be expressed, as to whether I should continue to have charge of the express company without interference, or . . . take my departure with other citizens of the State of New York. I wished to know whether by remaining I would be required to abandon the express and its obligations." Memminger mediated the deliberations as treasury secretary. Thomas Hill Watts, lead attorney for Adams in the Maroney prosecution and Memminger's close friend, represented Plant. The combination sufficed to secure a favorable decision. "It was a great satisfaction to me to learn from my counsel that the Cabinet were unanimous in this decision expressed by the President, that I should remain and continue to conduct the business of my company, he having full confidence in whatever I might do."[17]

One or more direct meetings including Plant, Watts, and Davis occurred prior to Cabinet deliberations. Franklin Q. Brown, a close associate in Henry's last years, recalled pertinent conversations. "Mr. Plant told me about his interviews and understanding with Jefferson Davis, concerning the functioning of the Express Company which rendered valuable services in forwarding packages among other materials to the soldiers of both Armies," Brown related. "With the opening of hostilities, the Confederate Government Capital, being at Montgomery, Alabama, Mr. Plant was appointed by that Government collector of tariffs upon all goods consigned by the Express Company and given custody of the funds of the Confederacy that were to be transferred from one place to another." Plant hinted in a similar vein to a reporter in 1896: "President Jefferson Davis, of the Southern Confederacy, demonstrated his confidence in, and admiration of Henry Bradley Plant by giving him a pass entitling him to move hither and thither at will through army headquarters, or wherever he pleased, in the interest of the Adams Express Company, which he then represented, although Mr. Plant declared that he did not sympathize with the political movement which sought to rend the States."[18]

Whatever specifically was stated or agreed to during the encounters, Henry almost immediately after the Cabinet meeting headed for Louisville, Kentucky, where the Adams leadership convened. The Galt House hotel sessions found some participants fearing seizure of company assets by the new government. Plant countered with fresh intelligence and details of arrangements that he had concluded. "He cited access to powerful allies within the Confederate government, eager to sanction an essentially All-Southern transportation agency," biographer Kelly Reynolds explained. "But in time of war, did he think he could count on such allies, really, these rebel gentlemen?—Yes, he did. He was now more than an honorary southerner. He was a Confederate citizen, and he had the proof. He was carrying a Confederate passport."[19]

To sweeten his case, Plant offered to introduce Dinsmore to his "powerful allies." The Adams president then traveled with Henry back to Montgomery. They checked into the Exchange Hotel by April 4 and began rounding the correct bases. The two men got to Memminger on the fifth. "Both gentlemen are true friends of the South," the treasury secretary informed South Carolina governor F. W. Pickens, "and as you well know the company has proved itself." Plant and Dinsmore also concluded arrangements with Chilton for the absorption of the Southern Express Company. The congressman would advise as a director. Either Chilton or Memminger insisted on the involvement of Charleston businessman Edward Sebring, a New York native who presided over the State Bank of South Carolina. Furthermore, Memminger provided an introduction for the expressmen to Governor Pickens, suggesting that their upcoming visit reflected a "desire to see a little War and Camp Life."[20]

On the way to Charleston, Plant and Dinsmore stopped at Augusta to perfect the Southern Express organization. Aspects of the Alabama charter displeased them, and so they sought new authorization under Georgia law from the Richmond County superior court. Henry Sanford had either been traveling with them or met them in Augusta, and he drafted suitable documentation. "During [late April 1861] I met Henry Sanford on the cars between New York and Bridgeport," an Adams shareholder recorded. "He had attended to [Adams] affairs in the South, made its contracts there, &c.; he had lately returned from there and told me he had arranged things in the South, so that they were firmly fixed in the interest of the company." The man added, "The arrangement was made to keep the property from confiscation, he said." The idea was to transfer all assets of Adams Express within the Confederacy to the new company while spreading a cover story that Adams's southern stockholders had purchased everything. Actual ownership remained unchanged or virtually so. Plant would run the firm and receive stock. In line with express business custom, the principals wrote down little. Eight Richmond County residents, including Plant, filed a bare-bones charter petition. It requested authority not only to engage in providing express services but also to conduct "the business of telegraphy" and transact "custom house brokerage." Judge W. W. Holt approved the request on April 8 to become effective May 1, thus giving birth to the "Adams Southern Express Company."[21]

The task accomplished, Dinsmore and Plant moved on to Charleston. They found Edward Sebring amenable to their plans and extended Memminger's greetings to Pickens. President Lincoln, in office since March 4, had by then ordered the Navy to resupply the federal garrison at Fort Sumter in the city's harbor. Davis and his Cabinet had chosen to force its surrender. Confederate batteries opened fire at 4:30 A.M. on April 12. Dinsmore and Plant had arisen early to witness the unfolding drama and stood on the battery overlooking the harbor as the cannons erupted. "Bombardment of Sumter commenced this morning at daylight & continued with activity on both sides through the day," Dinsmore alerted his New York office. "Plant & I are looking on out of Harm's reach."[22]

Disruptions and dislocations following Fort Sumter's surrender contributed to delays in getting Adams' Southern Express officially up and running. After Lincoln called for volunteers to oppose southern belligerence, Arkansas, North Carolina, Virginia, and Tennessee joined the Confederacy. Its congress thereupon shifted the capital to Richmond. On his way to the Old Dominion State, President Davis briefly stopped in Augusta on May 26. Whether he and Plant spoke is not known, although communication appears likely. Henry otherwise grappled with the chaos swirling amid the new nation's creation. This included the loss of key agents and employees who fled North after the guns sounded at Fort Sumter. One tragic case troubled the Plants deeply. Clapp Spooner's brother Jacob resigned his Savannah agency in May. For three months he "ostensibly engaged in traveling to and from both sections of the country as the escort to ladies and children going from the North to the South, and *vice versa*." Spooner's travels led him in early August to Cincinnati. "Fearful if he went South they would impress him in the military service," Jacob killed himself. "It was one of the most determined acts of suicide it has been our province to record," a newspaperman lamented. Responsibility for Spooner's wife and daughter, still at Savannah, thereupon devolved upon Henry, Ellen, and other Spooner friends.[23]

The Southern Express Company formally coalesced in July, no doubt to Plant's enormous relief. It had become evident, however, that the new organization could not carry the reference to "Adams" without stirring southern fury. A second superior court petition was thus filed requesting a more detailed charter, one that recast the concern simply as the Southern Express Company. Judge Holt agreed on July 1. A "shareholders" meeting quickly selected a board of directors that included Plant, Chilton, and Sebring. The directors subsequently elected officers, naming Plant as president. Henry disingenuously insisted to the public—per previous plans—that "the Southern Stockholders of the Adams Express Company, have purchased from their late associates, all the property and interests of said Company in the Confederate States." He added to agents and messengers: "The business will be continued as heretofore and under the same rules and regulations, until otherwise ordered. It is hoped that all the employees will continue to take the same interest in serving the public under the present, as they have under the late, organization; and thereby best promote the interests of the Company."[24]

Plant followed up with a quick trip to Richmond and further meetings with Confederate authorities. From those first days as Southern Express president, he felt acute political heat. Postmaster General Reagan particularly proved no friend. On July 18 he banned express companies from carrying newspapers and periodicals "without the payment of postage," a potentially heavy blow if Southern Express had complied. Reagan's action represented the opening salvo in a war between the post office and the Southern Express that endured until the surrender. Neither Plant nor Reagan offered quarter. "From the very inception of the Confederate postal service, its monopoly rights were violated continually and with impunity by the express companies of the South," historian L. R. Garrison concluded, "the chief offender being that known as the Southern Express Company." Plant left Richmond a day before Reagan released his order to the press. Henry felt so happy to remove himself from the fray that he risked his life crossing the Cape Fear River to quicken his way home. "We were . . . favored with a copy of the Richmond *Dispatch* of the 17th, brought through by Mr. Plant, of the Express," advised an Augusta editor, "who managed to make the connection by crossing the river at Wilmington in a small boat, in advance of the ferry boat."[25]

No sooner had Plant reached Augusta than the war's first major clash ensued north of Richmond near Manassas Junction. Compared to later engagements, the First Battle of Bull Run proved a small and confused affair. Still, at day's end the Confederate Army remained on the field, Union survivors had fled to Washington, and most white southerners had found cause to exult. "The Fight at Manassas—Brilliant Victory—The Enemy Completely Routed" trumpeted the *Augusta Chronicle and Sentinel* on July 23. "Confederate invincibility" spread as the hour's theme, but a darker and more profound consequence evidenced itself with time. Previously, residents of both regions could believe that a war, if fighting actually occurred, would end almost as soon as it began. People spoke, for instance, of a "ninety days' war." The sections would then go their separate ways in peace. Now, personal and business decisions taken before the fighting appeared in starkly different light. The war would go on. For how long no one knew, but it would endure beyond almost everyone's pre–July 21 conception. War's realities were to become constant factors and pervasive challenges. Rules had changed. The stakes had been raised high.[26]

Plant at once endured consequences of intensified southern pride and Yankee hatred. In early August, for instance, the Columbus, Georgia, *Sun* condemned his company "for charging freight on packages sent to the soldiers." Others echoed the theme. "The Express Company *did*, at first, when only a few hundreds or thousands of soldiers were called out, deliver packages free of charge, but the business soon became too heavy," the *Chronicle and Sentinel* lamely offered in the company's defense. Not surprisingly, adamantly prosouthern newspapers questioned how "Southern" the Southern Express actually was. "For a week or two, we have noticed two or three newspapers making a war on the Southern Express Company—charging it with disloyalty to the Confederate States, in some cases, and in others for the transportation of packages to our soldiers, etc.," shrugged Atlanta's *Southern Confederacy*. "The war on the company is purely malicious."[27]

The most hurtful onslaught began August 9. The *Montgomery Weekly Confederation* commenced that day running letters that condemned Southern Express as nothing but the Yankee-owned Adams Express in false guise. Correspondence purportedly between Dinsmore and Plant condoned bribery and other "dirty work." The letters underscored hypocritical pretense and recourse to deception. The texts simulated the actual tone of dealings that Dinsmore and Plant had engaged in but otherwise constituted creative fiction. Plant shot back, slamming the "pretended correspondence" as "a *forgery*." The author, he insisted, was a "forger and culumniator." Henry then fell back on the deception that lay at the heart of his company's origins. "The Southern Express Company of Georgia is comprised solely of the Southern stockholders of the Adams Express Company," he declared, "who have purchased and are the sole owners of the property and interests lately owned by the Adams Express Company in the South."[28]

The affair unfortunately stung too deeply for Henry simply to let the matter play itself out. He ordered attorneys William P. Chilton and John A. Elmore to exact retribution. At Montgomery they brought charges against former Adams employees James E. McDaniel and James Simpson. So little evidence connected Simpson to the letters that authorities quickly dropped that complaint. McDaniel and Simpson then fled. Henry assigned Edward Hurlbert to pursue the men to New Orleans, where Hurlbert instigated charges against both for breach of trust. Tried in January 1862, McDaniel won an acquittal; Simpson beat the charges with a hung jury. Whereupon authorities indicted Hurlbert for "perjury, in making a false affidavit in October last, against Simpson & McDaniel, for embezzlement and absconding." Plant's local managers posted bond and hurried Hurlbert out of town. In February McDaniel and Simpson countered with printed circulars alleging "serious charges" against the company. The bottom line meant month after month of negative publicity that ultimately achieved no good end for Plant or Southern Express. The damage proved severe. Henry learned from his mistake, though, and avoided taking the same heavy-handed approach again.[29]

Beyond the Montgomery letter scandal, the late summer of 1861 brought happenings that heightened Henry's stress levels and dampened Ellen's spirits. Adding to business pressures with which Henry routinely dealt, word came in August that Jacob Spooner had suicided. On September 21, days after McDaniel's and Simpson's Montgomery hearings, Ellen's favorite brother—the brother after whom she and Henry had named their son George—apparently took his own life in Connecticut. "George Blackstone was killed on Saturday afternoon while walking on the track of the New Haven and New London railroad," a reporter described. "He was . . . 46 years old, and much esteemed." Little additional information reached the public about the death, although both alcohol and depression seemingly were involved. Then, on October 2 Horace Hoadley's twenty-five-year-old wife, Amelia, suddenly died in New Haven. Add a mother's concerns for ten-year-old Morton's safety and education in a wartime environment, and Plant family tensions neared the breaking point. Out of acceptable alternatives, Henry slipped Ellen and Morton out of Augusta and led them by way of Louisville and Cincinnati to New Haven and Branford. He and Ellen remained long enough to see their son enrolled in a Branford public school and for her to gain some consolation from loved ones. The Southern Express office at Charleston "burned to the ground" on December 12, and that event may have required their return. Henry had reached Augusta by the fifteenth.[30]

The decision to bring Ellen back to Georgia in the final weeks of 1861 perhaps loomed to Plant in retrospect as his most painful mistake. Her health dropped to regrettable lows with her brother's death and separation from her only child. As had become their custom, the Plants checked into Augusta's Planters' Hotel. In January 1862 Henry left Ellen there. He traveled to New Orleans to observe the renewed attempt to prosecute McDaniel and Simpson. A year earlier he had transferred their friend William Williams, with his wife, Jane, from the Atlanta express office to Athens, Georgia, to ensure that they were out of harm's way. Given Jane's absence from Augusta, Henry must have left Ellen in the care of local friends.[31]

Plant rejoined his wife by January 30. He brought with him a slave couple that he had purchased at Mobile. The two young people were well known to Ellen, as they had lived in Augusta until recently. The woman's name is not known. The man was Dennis Dorsey, whom Southern Express had rented the previous year to work as a porter. In subsequent times the fact that he had purchased slaves embarrassed Henry, and he took pains in the Smyth biography to paint the story in a favorable light. As he told the tale, Dorsey had come to him as the Plants prepared to depart for the North, bringing word that his owner intended to sell him. Dennis asked Henry to step in as buyer. Plant insisted that Dorsey told him the matter could wait until he returned. In the meantime, however, the owner sold Dennis and his companion to a Mobile resident. When Henry learned of this, he addressed the matter at first opportunity. How much of the story is true may never be known. The circumstances suggest that a distracted Plant might well have ignored pleas from Dorsey at a time when he was focused on his wife's distress. Upon his return he needed assistance for Ellen and thought of Dennis and his partner. The facts remain elusive.[32]

The Dorseys in any event now cared for Ellen full time, and Plant again found himself on the move. Federal forces under General Ulysses S. Grant captured Forts Henry and Donelson on the Tennessee River in early and mid-February. The Confederacy stood on the verge of losing Nashville and abandoning Middle Tennessee. The military threat to Southern Express assets drew Henry into the area to inspect damage and maximize the use of personnel and resources. In the tumultuous situation, this would have taken considerable time. Available evidence suggests that he was not again in Augusta until a few days before the twenty-eighth.[33]

Ellen Blackstone Plant passed away at Augusta's Planters' Hotel on Friday, February 28, 1862. Little information about her final days and hours survived. Identical, carefully crafted obituaries did appear in the city's two principal newspapers. No cause or circumstances of death were offered. "Two aged parents and an only son will mourn their great loss from a distant section of the country, as she too mourned the unhappy circumstances which prevented their presence in her dying hour, but it will be a source of consolation to them to know that she cheerfully resigned the present for the future, and trusted in God for a happy reunion hereafter," the text observed. "Providence, however, permitted the afflicted husband to be near her during the trying passage from time to eternity, and with kindest friends, soothed every want and smoothed the journey to the tomb." The obituary concluded, "She now is in that happy clime, and an eternal life has welcomed her to an abode where the weary soul has found rest, and whence as a guardian angel she can watch over those from whom she 'is not lost, but only gone before.'" The funeral was held on Sunday at Augusta's First Presbyterian Church. Presumably its pastor, Rev. Joseph R. Wilson, father of President Woodrow Wilson, presided.[34]

Henry tarried little at Augusta. He told biographer Smyth that he stayed at Athens with Captain and Mrs. Williams "for several weeks," but the truth was otherwise. Plant bore responsibility to tell Morton about his mother's death and provide him a father's support in a time of pain and trial. Henry's grandfather Samuel Plant, aged ninety, was also ailing and needed his grandson's presence. Beyond that, a bereft Henry required opportunity to grieve. He is not mentioned at Augusta again until June 14, from which fact a sojourn of three months or so in the North may be inferred. When traveling outside the Confederacy, he used the alias "Mr. Harris." President Lincoln's secretary of state, William H. Seward, probably arranged for his safe passage through Union lines. Seward had headed the New York City firm of Blatchford, Seward & Griswold in 1854 when Adams Express retained the lawyers as counsel. The lucrative connection bespoke personal ties for Seward, Dinsmore, John Hoey, E. S. Sanford, and Henry Sanford. Seward in February 1861, for instance, had involved Henry Sanford—along with Allan Pinkerton—in protecting Lincoln from assassination on his way through

9. William Henry Seward, between 1861 and 1863. Library of Congress.

Baltimore to the nation's capital. Pinkerton, before he knew it, headed the Army of the Potomac's "secret service."[35]

Meanwhile, E. S. Sanford's links to Seward and Secretary of War Edwin M. Stanton had led three days before Ellen's death to his appointment as "military supervisor of telegraphic messages throughout the United States." A newspaperman explained: "In this position Mr. Sanford exercised absolute censorship over all telegraph despatches sent over the lines for the army. Mr. Sanford not only gave complete satisfaction in the matter of keeping all order, but he furnished thorough service alike to the Government and the newspapers." Henry's friend wielded immense power. "Sanford's relations with the newspapers were always cordial and pleasant, notwithstanding the delicate and sometimes trying position of military censorship," historian David Homer Bates observed. "What his blue pencil erased from press reports had to be left out, and reporters frequently spent hours in procuring some choice bit of news which was never transmitted over the wires."[36]

All facts considered, arguments that the closely interwoven relationships between Adams Express top executives, Lincoln, the Department of State, the War Department, military intelligence, and military and newspaper censorship did not include Plant and Southern Express within their orbit beg credulity. Whatever misleading information his company distributed for public consumption, Plant worked for Dinsmore and E. S. Sanford and ultimately enjoyed only limited independence of action. Given Henry's access to top Confederate officials, back channels for communication were always available through him. Military and governmental secrets routinely passed through his hands and could be shared with ease. If any doubt existed about the importance of the Plant connection, Jefferson Davis erased it on March 18, 1862. That was the day he appointed Henry's lawyer Thomas Hill Watts as the Confederate States' attorney general. During the war everyone benefited from keeping the ties secret. The same state of affairs continued to apply for Henry after the peace. However, a variety of events to come—ones that will be considered carefully—evidenced plainly much of what these men endeavored to hide.[37]

The months that Plant spent in the North during winter and spring 1862 brought dramatic turns of fortune on the battlefield and in Southern Express accountings. Before Henry's return to Augusta in June, Nashville had been evacuated, Fernandina had been occupied, Georgia coastal ports had been raided, the Battle of Shiloh had taken place, New Orleans had surrendered, and Memphis had been captured. While Southern Express territory had shrunk with Confederate setbacks, the demand on its services had soared. The Confederate Post Office never operated efficiently, and a huge demand for reliable express service even at high prices mounted accordingly. The government knew these facts as well as the average southerner and demonstrated them emphatically. Loss had compelled the South to institute a military draft. On June 26 the secretary of war mandated, "All persons in the employ of the Southern Express Company, the services of whom the president of the company will certify to be indispensable, will be exempted from the operation of the conscript act so long as they continue in the said employment." More followed. "Since [receiving exemption of its employees from conscription] the claims of the company as an aid and adjunct to the Government have been vastly multiplied," the *Richmond Examiner* detailed at year's end. "At the time former exemptions were allowed it was chiefly serviceable in the transmission of funds under a contract with the Treasury Department.—Since then it has made contracts with nearly all the departments of the Government, and every branch of the public service is indebted to it for valuable and indispensible aid."[38]

Profits meanwhile flooded into Southern Express coffers and—for the first time in significant amounts—into Plant's pockets. Sources later reported that he began at this time to "invest heavily" in bonds of southern railroads at advantageous prices. In Augusta, Henry purchased the City Hotel for $20,000 and leased it to the Confederate government as a "general hospital." He also began speculating in cotton on a modest scale, storing bales that he purchased on his employee James Shuter's farm near town. There was simply not enough time to manage all the money that came in. In 1860 Plant had listed total assets of $3,000 when census takers asked him his worth. He voluntarily disclosed just under $240,000 in assets to Augusta tax officials as of January 1, 1863.[39]

So much money kept coming in that the need arose for Plant to distribute some of it to his northern partners. The opportunity came during September 1862 when General Lee invaded Maryland, a move that led to the Battle of Antietam. "The Confederate Government desired to send the General a large remittance of money, and shipped it through Mr. Plant's hands," the *New York Times* explained, "rather than trust to its own means of communication." Henry, once his mission to Lee was concluded, moved on to New York and Connecticut. Plant's Adams Express colleague and former employee Samuel Wilmot recalled seeing him at the time. "Mr. Clapp Spooner was president of the Pequonnoc National Bank, of which I was a director," he began. "Sometime during the war Mr. Spooner showed me an entry on the deposit accounts of the bank, to his credit, of $75,000; he gave me a significant look as he showed it to me; I said, 'Where did you get it?' he said, 'Oh, we've got it;' it was exciting times, when it wasn't safe always to speak out." Wilmot concluded, "Mr. H. B. Plant had come on here a few days before this from the South, under an assumed name, as Mr. Harris; I had seen him, and had heard he was staying with Mr. Spooner. . . . This was in the latter part of 1862, when I met Mr. Plant, which was in Bridgeport, and I think at my house; shortly before Mr. Spooner showed me this deposit entry. I asked him how the express business was getting along in the South; he replied that our interests were well protected; I had no doubt that the $75,000 deposit came from Plant, and that Mr. Spooner meant to have me understand it."[40]

Henry's intentions during fall 1862 about returning to the South remain difficult to discern. He had placed Rufus Bullock in charge of Southern Express operations, an action that allowed him flexibility. Grandfather Samuel Plant had died at Branford in late July 1862, and he doubtlessly found himself obligated with new family responsibilities. Morton's education and development, too, required attention. On the other hand, his partners, and probably Plant himself, wanted the flowing spring of money pouring from southern pockets to continue without interruption; plus, they and Seward wanted to maintain lines of communication and intelligence. The crucial factor, at least with the timing of his eventual return, may have been President

Davis's dismissal of Secretary of War George W. Randolph in mid-November and his replacement by James A. Seddon. Particularly, Seddon questioned the continued conscription exemptions for Southern Express employees. This had become personal to Plant because a recent change in the law had extended the draft to persons up to forty-five years of age. Henry turned forty-three on October 27. He obviously needed to address that matter seriously if he was to return South.[41]

Given the paucity of records, the timing of Henry's arrival in Richmond cannot be specified. An official response to an inquiry from the postmaster general put him at Augusta on December 9. Twenty days later, he inked an agreement in Richmond with Treasury Secretary Memminger vesting responsibility in Southern Express for transporting "all funds of the Treasury Department." With this strong show of support, Plant managed to conclude negotiations over draft exemptions with Seddon in a matter of days. Still at Richmond on January 6, 1863, he presented the secretary of war with a series of itemized lists of individuals he wanted exempted. He lingered in the Confederate capital nearly to month's end to ensure that he had covered all his bases.[42]

The pressures of war, responsibility, deceit, and fatigue meanwhile began to manifest themselves in the deterioration of Henry's health. Soon after Ellen's death he commenced suffering from "gastric fever," requiring Dennis Dorsey's careful ministrations when Plant was in the South. The problem intensified in 1863. For one thing, barely had Henry arrived at Augusta on January 28 or 29 when word came to him of the death of his stepfather, Philemon Hoadley, at New Haven on the twenty-eighth. Anxious for his mother's well-being, he retraced his steps of two months previously, making his way as quickly as he could to New Haven. Samuel Wilmot spoke with him there. "At a later period, during the war, I saw him again; this time at his mother's house in New Haven; he was, this time also, under the assumed name of Harris," Wilmot recorded. "I think it was in the winter of 1863." Henry remained for some time, possibly until June, tending to his mother and soon-to-be-adolescent son. Morton's education especially concerned him. Henry's half-brother Horace Hoadley had attended New Haven's Collegiate and Commercial Institute—also known as Russell's Military School—and, upon Horace's recommendation, Plant enrolled Morton there. Meanwhile, he faced a small degree of embarrassment when probate filings disclosed that he owed $1,400 to Philemon's estate. He hastily corrected the record to reflect an outstanding amount of only $1,072.75.[43]

If Plant had not made up his mind to abandon the South before he traveled back to Augusta in late spring or early summer 1863, he reached his decision quickly thereafter. Critics had excoriated Southern Express for months with claims of exploitation, profiteering, and corruption. The draft exemptions Henry had fought for in December and January factored, as did rumors of attempts to curry favor with Confederate officials at Richmond through routine bribes of hard-to-come-by "sugar, partridges, turkeys, etc." Postmaster General Reagan fumed at the company's "brazen effrontery" and insisted on prosecutions for "lawless acts." Attorney General Watts fended off Reagan's demands on Plant's behalf, but the attention they prompted served Henry and Southern Express poorly. Matters grew worse in late June and early July. The British parliament crushed Confederate officials' hopes by declining to formally recognize their government, and days later Union forces overpowered Rebel troops at Gettysburg and Vicksburg. At the same moment, Attorney General Watts himself upset Henry's plans when word circulated that he intended to quit his Confederate Cabinet post and instead run for governor of Alabama.[44]

Now committed to a new course, Plant snapped into action. He knew that he could count on a talented and loyal cadre of company managers whom he had nurtured over the years, a fact already proven during his wartime absences. James Shuter especially had matured into a competent leader. Having progressed from Memphis to New Orleans as local agent, he had emerged as superintendent of remaining central and western operations with headquarters in Atlanta. Plant tapped him acting president. Michael J. "Mike" O'Brien, too, came to the fore. A driver at Memphis in 1859 and later agent at New Orleans, he had served in the Confederate Navy for a time. Then, Memminger dispatched him to Southern Express in spring 1862, as O'Brien explained it, "in special charge of treasury shipments going from Richmond to points south." As the treasury secretary's personal liaison with Plant, O'Brien proved his ability and fidelity. In after times he liked to joke that his "splendid pensmanship attracted Mr. Plant's attention," but for Henry, entrusting power involved finding rarer and more precious skills. Confident in his man, Plant now turned to O'Brien as his personal representative in all Southern Express operations with the title of private secretary to the president.[45]

At which point Henry literally headed for the hills. In his case, this meant a mountain resort west of Richmond. He insisted to biographer Smyth that he was convalescing from gastric fever, and likely he was. He was also negotiating, through the intercession of a physician friend and Attorney General Watts, for an official Confederate passport that would allow him to depart for Europe. He succeeded on August 1. Sources later alleged President Davis's insistence that Henry serve as a courier for sensitive correspondence or, perhaps, monies to be used for secret purposes. Montreal and Liverpool, as will be seen, loomed as likely points of delivery. Whatever the case and whatever the cost, Henry's clout again prevailed. "Mr. Thomas H. Watts, attorney-general for the Southern Confederacy, had seen Mr. Plant's physician, who had advised a change of climate," Smyth informed his readers. "Mr. Watts sent Mr. Plant a passport, with an order from President Davis authorizing him to pass through the Confederate lines at any point." A Richmond diarist preserved a different version of events. "Mr. Plant, President of the Southern Express Company, was 'allowed' to leave the Confederate States to-day by the Assistant Secretary of War, subject to the discretion of Gen. Whiting at Wilmington," the man observed. "I suppose his fortune is made."[46]

Happy to leave behind what express historian Dudley Johnson characterized as "constant criticism," Plant wasted little time making his way to the blockade-running port of Wilmington, North Carolina. On or about September 4 he boarded the steamer *Hansa*, bound initially for Hamilton, Bermuda. Under cover of darkness, the gray-painted ship and its passengers quietly slipped out the mouth of the Cape Fear River and into the broad Atlantic Ocean. Surviving accounts reveal no regret or hesitation on Plant's part. Back in Augusta, though, word of his departure left many residents confused and more than a few angry. "We do not wish to be censorious," commented the usually friendly *Augusta Chronicle and Sentinel*. "We do not say that every man who leaves the Confederacy during the War is of questionable patriotism. Inexorable necessity, business, health may make it imperative. But the requisition ought to be so strong as to make the duty unquestionable." It came down to every individual's conception of where his or her duty lay. Henry Plant had made his decision.[47]

6

A Work of Reconstruction

1863 to 1868

"one of the deepest and foggiest of all mysteries"

The strains of civil war and personal loss collided in summer 1863 to catapult Henry Plant into exile. As the battered man departed the South, he stood aged through experience and altered in spirit and fortune. War times had gifted him with formidable wealth. The era had also confirmed the confidence placed in him by northern friends and business associates and cemented personal commitments of one friend to another. Still, the coins that he had reaped all came with two sides. Plant had faced bitter criticism and the threat of calumny. Events moreover had claimed a grievous human cost, with lessons of caution, tact, and sensitivity unfolding painfully and sometimes nonsensically. Politics, too, had proved a tricky monster. He had seen moods and loyalties shifting in a moment, that today's ally easily could morph into tomorrow's enemy. Hope of a happier future glimmered chimerically on the horizon, elusive and uncertain. If the exile believed, however, that fate would eventually allow him to resume the reins of business as before, surprises beyond comprehension awaited him. Henry had learned lessons, although not all the ones that he needed. At least he reassuringly understood one important thing. He could not continue or repeat ill-conceived mistakes.

Henry's absence from the South began September 4, 1863, and ran for nineteen months. That he found haven in Europe is a familiar story, although details about how he got there and his experiences along the way are less well known. One thing is for certain. His journey amounted to an expensive proposition. War's fortunes had forced him to leave behind assets such as stored cotton bales and Augusta's City Hotel. Yet, if a fellow Augustan can be believed, Plant had arranged carefully to meet his needs. "Thomas

Jackson, Augusta, Ga., writes that he can prove the president of the Southern Express Company, who recently obtained a passport to visit Europe, really embarked for the United States, taking a large sum in gold," a Confederate official noted on October 3, "that another of the same company (which is nothing more than a branch of Adams's Express Company of New York) will leave soon with more gold."[1]

Jackson correctly pinpointed Plant's immediate destination. Union advances had rendered travel northward through his traditional Louisville-Cincinnati corridor problematic; so, he took to the sea. This meant a stay at Hamilton, Bermuda, where he arrived on September 7. Henry remained for one month seeking out contacts. "The hotels are filled to overflowing with Southern men; and capitalists, who have an eye to the main chance, are talking of building another," a visitor explained. "Vessels come with coals to supply the blockade runners, and many a swift steamer that comes from Europe finds her most profitable venture in the direction of a Confederate port. Every project, and every venture looks toward the Southern coast." Not quite. Hamilton's Confederate-soaked atmosphere offered the ideal environment for intelligence gathering, and President Lincoln's secretary of state William H. Seward jumped to take advantage. "Bermuda and Nassau are overrun with the agents of Seward," a Richmond newspaper warned, "and these men will lose no opportunity of getting their hirelings on board Confederate vessels, agreeing to pay them enormous sums to betray the ship on which they take service into the hands of the blockaders."[2]

A curious series of occurrences underscored Plant's success at finding needed contacts. The events followed his departure from Bermuda on October 4 and arrival at Halifax, Nova Scotia, on the eighth. From the latter city Henry headed west for Montreal. Several motives directed him. The first likely involved an errand for Jefferson Davis, and the second related to undermining the same mission. Circumstantial—although highly suggestive—evidence suggests Plant's activities. Confederates then were planning raids from Canada on cities and facilities in upper New York State, Pennsylvania, and Ohio. The Davis mission seemingly involved delivery of money or messages to conspirators through native New Yorker Charles H. Haile and his brother-in-law James Simeon McCuaig. Plant was acquainted with Haile from prewar Memphis. When grander plans had failed to materialize, Haile and McCuaig had refocused on stealing an Adams Express safe to defer expenses and then freeing Rebel prisoners at Johnson's Island, Ohio, in Lake Erie. The unexpected appearance of a US warship off Johnson's Island slowed the raid. The plot collapsed completely when McCuaig tipped off Canadian authorities. Plant's complicity, as will be seen, evidenced itself months later.[3]

Another motive for Plant's Montreal visit, one related partially to the first two, involved contacts with the US government. "Some friends from New York came to see him [in Montreal]," biographer George Smyth detailed, "and brought his son Morton from school to him." Although Smyth insisted that Plant quickly went to New Haven to see his widowed mother, Betsy Hoadley, known facts suggest otherwise. For one thing, Henry's boyhood friend James E. English, now a congressman, returned to the United States from Europe on October 7 and promptly dropped from public notice. Although a Democrat, English had earnestly supported "the war measures of the Administration" and would soon sit on the committee that governed State Department expenditures. Ideally situated to intermediate between Plant and Seward, English was also the perfect choice to chaperone twelve-year-old Morton to Canada.[4]

Meanwhile, on October 31 Secretary Seward hurriedly departed Washington for his Auburn home in upstate New York, supposedly due to a son's "extreme illness." Auburn lies about three hundred miles by railroad below Montreal. Strangely, soon after the secretary's arrival an unexplained miracle healed the son sufficiently for the secretary to mount a campaign rally. There, Seward thundered about European conditions as if he had just been briefed on upsetting Confederate policies and contacts. "You have enemies in certain classes of society all over Europe," he roared. "They are fitting out a navy and privateers for the American insurgents. If the ballot-boxes could be opened at Laird's ship-yard in Liverpool, or in John Slidell's house in Paris, there would be a unanimous vote for [Democrats in the upcoming elections], and new iron-clads would escape from under the broad arrow, in armor impregnable, in array innumerable, and you would have superadded to this terrible struggle upon land, a more tremendous contest than the world has ever seen upon the high seas. The instinct of enemies is infallible." Seward later claimed that his remarks were extemporaneous, that they were given "by accident, and not by design." After the event he tarried only briefly before heading to New York City, where he visited the federal courthouse. It stood less than one mile from Adams Express headquarters, a concern with which Seward associated as counsel.[5]

The known facts may not prove that Plant and Seward rendezvoused in early November, but they at least illuminate the ease with which a meeting could have occurred. If it did, Henry's journey to New Haven happened soon afterward. Once again, he traveled quietly as "Mr. Harris," wanting to be in New Haven on November 20 when Morton marched in his first Russell's Military School parade and review. After the school term ended on December 23, they enjoyed time spent together. Through the holidays and into 1864 father and son shared each other's company. Finally, five days before Morton returned to classes on January 7, "Mr. Harris" boarded the *Edinburgh* in New York Harbor and steamed for England.[6]

Plant reached Liverpool on January 16, 1864, and his arrival proved a dismal one. "He was now a stranger in a strange land," George Smyth commented, "the weather was cold, and with impaired health his experience was rather depressing." If Plant had agreed to conduct Confederate business in Liverpool, he did so hastily. He at least alerted Southern agents to his presence, while exercising caution thereafter not to demonstrate too great a desire to distance himself from them. Still, Henry soon decamped for happier climes. "Mr. Plant has never been the man to despond, still less to despair, but to make the best even of discouraging circumstances," Smyth declared. "So, he went to Paris."[7]

Henry did indeed head for Paris. Once there, he found the City of Light changing profoundly before his eyes. "Building is going on in Paris with unexampled rapidity and on immense scale, and evidence of wealth and luxury meet the eye in every direction," a correspondent exulted. "[There are] signs on every side of a high state of material and political prosperity." For his patron Emperor Napoleon III, Baron George-Eugène Haussmann was transforming the city with magnificent urban redesigns and conceptualizations. "He who now runs in Paris may read the great glories of France in the designations of the splendid streets, gorgeous boulevards, and wonderful avenues which Napoleon III has caused to be erected," an onlooker exclaimed. The projects were many, but none impressed Plant more than the grandly conceived Opéra. Designed by Charles Garnier, the monumental edifice had begun to rise in 1861 on the Boulevard des Capucines. When it eventually opened in 1875, delighted Parisians exclaimed it the Opéra Garnier. "[The Emperor commands] that all the decorations of the new opera be in mosaic, marble, bronze and gilt bronze, which last forever without needing repair," an awed Frenchman advised. "He has ordered the architect of the new opera to build the theatre without regard to cost and with his eye fixed solely on durability."[8]

Art, architecture, and urban design highlighted change, but so, too, did politics and intrigue. Napoleon's attempt to meddle in Mexican affairs, for example, soon led to the appointment of Archduke Maximilian of Austria-Hungary as its emperor, a debacle in which Plant would become enmeshed before its disastrous collapse. Financial talk centered around the *Crédit Mobilier*, a Union Pacific Railroad funding scheme that also concluded ruinously. Foremost, though, was incessant discussion of America's civil war. "The tidings are that the North advances and the South retires; and so long as the movement continues in the right direction, so long will confidence in the Federal arms continue in the ascendant," a correspondent reported. "These tremendous incidents of the American conflict have occupied public attention more completely and exclusively from the total absence of its worth of interest in European affairs."[9]

Despite passions stirred in war conversations, Plant discovered a welcoming atmosphere. Former US senator William McKendree Gwin, who was in the city pursuing a Mexican mining project, attested to that fact. "Most educated Frenchmen spoke English fluently, that language being the current idiom of sport, dandyism, and high fashion," Gwin's biographer explained. "He found life in the glittering, light-hearted capital of Napoleon III's Second Empire brisk and pleasant; the colony of Confederates which he joined was popular with society as well as with the government." Henry found the situation further enhanced when W. B. Dinsmore and his wife, Augusta Snow Dinsmore, arrived. While affording well-appreciated company and social entrée, the couple possessed intimate familiarity with Paris. As a report noted of her January encounter with the emperor and empress, "Mrs. W. B. Dinsmore, of New York, a Boston lady by birth, was the most admired of the new faces at a recent presentation at the Tuileries."[10]

Plant grew to love Paris, but whatever the city's attractions in 1864 he looked forward especially to seeing one particular individual. He had attended Adelina Patti's triumphant New York debut in 1859. Four years later she glimmered as a European star, then performing in Paris at the Italian Opera. "The immortal 'Barbiere [*The Barber of Seville*],' with Patti and [Giuseppe] Mario, and [Enrico] Della-Sedie as Figaro, are enough to insure crowded houses," one critic assured. "To get a pretty young Rosina was most refreshing, after the fat middle-aged ladies who last year offended our associations and imaginations in this character." Patti's schedule contributed to Henry's speedy departure from Liverpool, as her Parisian engagement extended only through January. She planned to appear thereafter in Naples and, in summer, London.[11]

Little wonder that Plant set out in early February on an Italian opera tour. "He heard of some friends who were staying in Rome, and whom he would like to meet, so he determined to go there," Smyth related. When Patti changed her plans and temporarily remained in Paris, Henry continued on tour with the Dinsmores. When authorities questioned the serviceability of his Confederate passport in passing from French-occupied Rome to Naples in the Kingdom of Italy, he arranged through contacts—likely ones at the US embassy—to secure new documentation. Smyth continued: "A few days later he had the satisfaction of receiving a document which served as a passport, given in the name of the empire of France, and in which he was described as a citizen of the United States, resident at Augusta, Georgia, and all officers, civil, military, and naval, were commanded to protect this stranger. He . . . was received everywhere with great respect."[12]

Henry visited most major Italian cities before passing into the Austro-Hungarian Empire by rail from Venice on March 17. The Dinsmores had returned to the United States by then, and Plant had gained a new companion. One-time Rebel partisan Charles H. Haile had reached Italy from Montreal, a man happy to be an ocean away from angry Confederate raiders intent on exacting revenge. At Vienna, the men tasted the city's delights from the Archduke Karl Hotel. Opera, as always, offered Henry a singular attraction. "They are great on opera in Vienna," a visitor related, "during the last year there have been no less than three hundred and twenty-six performances at the Imperial Opera House at Vienna, in which Mozart, Beethoven, Meyerbeer, Halévy, Spohr, Adams, Boildieu, Bellini, Cherubini, Donizetti, Wagner, Gounod, Verdi, Flotow, Marschner, Doppler, David, Weber, Balfo, Rossini, Nicolai and Kreutzer were the composers represented, by thirty-eight different operas." Lulled by excellent music, Plant and Haile moved to Switzerland, where, Smyth noted, they "visited many places in that picturesque land, and returned to Paris by way of the Rhine."[13]

The French capital continued to throb with energy and excitement despite Patti's removal to London in mid-April. Marie-Caroline Miolan-Carvalho drew raves in debut performances of Charles Gounod's *Marveille*. Also, on May 1 the international fine arts exposition opened at the Palais des Beaux-Arts. So many paintings were displayed that one jaded critic moaned, "It is difficult indeed to discover genius among such heaps of mediocrity." Much of the genius, as Henry realized, had found haven at a *salon des refusés*. "There is, as last year, a special set of apartments for the rejected works of art," the critic commented. "But these, although quite as bad as before, are not so numerous." Fortunately, many art lovers—Plant included—could not so easily dismiss the birth of Impressionism.[14]

In June the Parisian social season finally closed, signaling time for Plant to venture on. Before departure, though, Henry gained yet another new companion. Connecticut native Daniel Hand Wilcox, now a refugee, had grown wealthy as an Augusta merchant and cotton broker. He, too, had found it advisable to remove himself from the scene of war. Now, Wilcox and Plant arrived in London during the second week of June, in time for a series of Patti operatic triumphs. On July 9, for instance, eight thousand listeners thrilled to her performance at the Crystal Palace. At a benefit six days later, she appeared as Margherita in *Faust e Margherita*. "Finer acting, more finished singing, were never heard," an onlooker commented. "Never did Adelina Patti's star shine more brightly in the London operatic firmament. Her popularity is at its zenith; and she is (as she well deserves to be) the idol of the public."[15]

Whether Plant's interest in Patti grew that summer from fascination into something more remains elusive. His attraction to beautiful stage performers would eventually command widespread attention, and he was clearly drawn to the diva. As for the nature of his feelings in 1864, the record reveals nothing. Or almost so. By August, Henry was purchasing expensive women's clothing and accessories. From London on the twenty-seventh he informed a middleman: "I have already written to you at Manchester, acknowledging receipt of the package with contents, as requested, excepting the parasol cover, which was not inclosed with others. If you should have received my note and have written to Mr. F. respecting the cover, all well. If you have not, please do so, and request him to send a cape (to be worn in the house) with it, together with the Bible, and I will leave the funds with you or remit to Paris, as may be desired. I think that the ladies call the cape I desire a pelerine."[16]

Whatever the bounds of his relationship with Adelina Patti, Henry did not want in London for male companionship. Wilcox, of course, remained near. Express pioneer Daniel Phillips also encountered Plant. "I met Mr. Plant in London, England, and enquired of him about the Adams Express interest in the South," Phillips recounted. "Plant said they were 'getting on very well,' were making money, and that the Southern Express would prove a valuable property for us after the war." Adams's general superintendent E. S. Sanford and Congressman English turned up in late July. English remained until late August, and Sanford held over until September 3. They brought news that immediately captured Plant's attention. Secretary Seward planned harsher rules on border crossings. "The Secretary of State has issued an order requiring passports hereafter from all travellers, except immigrant passengers, entering the United States from Foreign Countries," one newspaper explained. "The regulation is intended especially to apply to persons coming from British provinces." Plant's concern involved having to sign an "oath of allegiance." Confederate authorities would soon learn of such an act, prompting seizure of his assets and jeopardizing Southern Express.[17]

Henry took the only course realistically open to him; he discreetly returned to the United States before the rules barred him. On October 1 the *Europa* steamed from Liverpool for New York with "Mr. Harris" aboard. It made landfall at Halifax on the thirteenth and at Boston the next day. From one of the ports Plant made his way to New Haven. He arrived in time to celebrate President Lincoln's reelection victory on November 8. He learned not long thereafter of General William Tecumseh Sherman's departure from Atlanta and his army's subsequent March to the Sea. On December 21, the day that the general took Savannah, Morton finished his term at Russell's Military School. Father and son spent the holidays together, as Henry awaited further developments as unobtrusively as he could.[18]

The new year introduced change for Plant, but only slowly. Morton returned to school on January 5, 1865, allowing Henry to move to New York City. There, he received news from the South, although the fighting precluded a visit. Dinsmore, whose political and financial clout had snowballed with the war, observed no such restraints. In mid-March he joined a congressional delegation that visited Charleston and Savannah, returning to New York on the twenty-third. A week later Morton's winter term concluded, providing fresh opportunity for father and son to share company until the new session commenced April 20. They spent time especially in Connecticut, visiting—among others—Henry's longtime friend Clapp Spooner at Bridgeport, who had served as mayor and begun to see a grander future there. One aspect of his changed perspective involved rechartering the Pequonnock Bank, a state institution that he led as president, into the Pequonnock National Bank of Bridgeport. Accordingly, conversations between him and Plant included detailed banking discussions and Spooner's views as to how easy to obtain and lucrative in potential a federal charter could be.[19]

Even before Morton returned to classes, major events began to reshape national history and Henry's life. Robert E. Lee surrendered to Ulysses S. Grant at Appomattox, Virginia, on April 9. Six days later President Lincoln fell to an assassin's bullet, and Secretary of State Seward suffered grievous wounds. Vice President Andrew Johnson, a conservative Tennessean, entered the White House. Within days Henry's Southern Express subordinate Rufus B. Bullock, having surrendered to Union authorities at Richmond, arrived in New York to confer with Plant and Dinsmore. Bullock then journeyed to Washington to speak with E. S. Sanford. The men collectively charged the agent with a project that harked back to Henry's recent banking discussions with Spooner. From the nation's capital on May 4, Bullock wrote a friend that "he had obtained half a million dollars from Northern friends to organize a national bank." The National Bank of Augusta opened for business in December. Dinsmore served as president; he and Plant sat together on the board of directors. Given the paucity of capital and credit in the postwar South and the limited grant of national bank charters available for the region, the financial advantage gained by Plant and his associates was enormous.[20]

Meanwhile, the spring's momentous events tumbled one after another. On April 26 Joe Johnston capitulated to Sherman, obliging Rebel forces remaining in North Carolina, South Carolina, Georgia, and Florida to surrender. Augusta held out until May 3. Two days afterward and fifty miles to the northwest at Washington, Georgia, Jefferson Davis met with his Cabinet for the final time. His traveling party, including Henry's nemesis Postmaster General—now Acting Secretary of the Treasury—John H. Reagan, eluded capture until May 10, when federal soldiers seized its members near Irwinville, 175 miles southwest of Augusta.[21]

When on May 12 Davis's federal escort delivered him and his party to superiors at Macon, Plant was there consulting with military officials. He had returned to Georgia a few days earlier to find that the army controlled area railroads. Accordingly, Henry sought permission to use the lines for express purposes and mail carriage. General James H. Wilson agreed as a matter of public interest, and the company announced that it stood ready "to ship goods of all kinds to various points in this section of the Union." Its network included "Columbus, Eufala, Atlanta, West Point, Milledgeville, Augusta, and all intermediate points." One newspaper cautioned: "Owing to bushwhackers, guerillas, and such like growth who have an over-fondness for valuable packages, and who just now abound in uncomfortable numbers in outlying sections beyond railroad termini, business so far as this indefatigable company is concerned, is and remains suspended beyond those points until further orders."[22]

Henry also conducted banking business in Macon. He approached his cousin Increase C. Plant about establishment there of a national bank. Increase's biographer observed, "He readily obtained the substantial assistance of an old business acquaintance in New York and, with the cooperation of others, started the First National Bank of Macon." I. C. Plant carried the ball for the project in the same manner that Rufus Bullock had for the National Bank of Augusta. When the institution organized in November, the board consisted of the two Plants, Dinsmore, and a few others. I. C. Plant guided the institution as president for the remainder of his life.[23]

Henry thereupon turned to investing ready cash in the teetering southern economy. He had applied to authorities in Savannah to release cotton bales he had stored on James Shuter's farm near Augusta. They consented on May 24, and Henry headed up the Savannah River to reclaim his property. Once he had experienced the difficulties involved in a postwar passage of the Savannah, he decided to put a first-class river steamboat in service. Plant partnered with builder James Milliken. Using engines procured in New York, the two-hundred-ton *Eclipse* slid down the ways at Milliken's yard in mid-October. A month passed as it was fitted out and tested. On November 19, the *Eclipse* steamed for Savannah wharves packed high with cotton.[24]

Henry's remaining Augusta investment required no immediate attention. He had rented the City Hotel to the Confederate Army for hospital use. With the peace, occupancy transferred to the US Army to house a provost marshal's office and other government outposts. Merchants meanwhile continued to operate retail stores from its first floor facing Broad Street. In 1867 Plant conceived the idea of transforming the structure into a theater and opera house. "Magnificent and costly" plans were drawn, but they were "pretty liberally exposed to and criticized by the public." High costs and public opposition convinced Henry to drop the proposal. Before long he had lost interest in the hotel and, for that matter, the city of Augusta. Eventually, he transferred the hotel to Southern Express.[25]

As summer 1865 passed, Plant committed himself, as well, to kick-starting the revival of Southern Express. This naturally involved expanding service areas as railroads slowly came back into operation. "The surrender at Appomattox left the railroads in as wo[e]ful a condition as the country through which they had been built," Henry recalled. "In many instances the bridges and station buildings had been destroyed, the rails torn up, heated in fires fed with the crossties, and then twisted around the trunks of trees in fantastic forms known as 'Sherman ties.' The equipment had been gathered up by military officials, loaded with supplies and carried off in retreat, to be ultimately destroyed, abandoned or scattered. The roads that were in operation labored under all the difficulties consequent upon their dilapidated condition. The corporations, whose coffers were filled with Confederate money, were in default for their fixed charges due in gold. Destitute of credit and their property in ruins, but few of them escaped bankruptcy and reorganization." Even here, though, US government action ultimately benefited Plant. The military poured huge sums of money into many moribund lines, rehabilitating track and replacing equipment. When Plant and men like him eventually began snapping up properties, they seldom credited their government benefactors while bemoaning the earlier dilapidated status of their new possessions.[26]

Plant's greatest advantage, though, involved Adams Express backing. President Dinsmore had allocated a fortune from company reserves to support Southern Express. "Adams' & Co.'s Express Company has issued $2,000,000 of its accumulated capital to several of the Southern Railroads," a report detailed, "and has thus enabled them to resume operations." Not so fast. Plant and others approached individual lines on Southern Express's behalf with an offer. "[As you are] without the means to repair the road and make it safe for the transportation of passengers and freight," managers would be told, "[we can make you] a loan or advance [for a certain amount of money]." Plant promised the Western North Carolina Railroad, for example, $20,000 in December 1865. The catch required the line to grant Southern Express exclusive rights "for the transaction of all express business over the entire length of their road." The line also had to agree to carry Southern Express messengers, officers, and agents "free of charge" and perform other services for the company. The contract lasted for one year or until Southern Express had been reimbursed the payment with interest, whichever came last. Most railroads possessed no option but to accept the terms. The railroads gained a chance to survive and thrive; Henry meanwhile had protected railroad bonds he had purchased during the war from bankruptcy proceedings.[27]

The cash infusions set Southern Express back on the road to success, but other issues clouded its future. In 1865 it appeared questionable whether the company would continue as a distinct entity or whether Adams would absorb it. Adams partner Sam Shoemaker, who controlled southern operations, had never fully accepted the diminution of his territory in 1854 and 1861, and his men had moved with the advance of Union armies to reclaim lost business. On the day Lee surrendered, they "opened an office in Knoxville with perfect connections by Railroad." Shoemaker personally labored in Richmond during early May "on business connected with the re-establishment of the express line South." In early June he announced: "Steamship and Inland Express to all southern cities and towns [is] open to trade.—Adams Express Company forward their Expresses every Wednesday and Saturday by steamship to Richmond, Norfolk, Charleston, Savannah, New-Orleans, Newbern, Wilmington, Mobile, &c., &c." As of August 1, operations extended into Texas.[28]

Dinsmore once more stood by Plant. Henry had ridden the rails to New York City in late summer seriously concerned about Shoemaker's encroachments, as well as family matters. In the latter regard, either Morton had grown unhappy with military schooling once peace was declared or, quite possibly, Russell's Military School had grown unhappy with him. In the circumstances Plant enrolled his son in Deacon Edward Lucas Hart's English and Classical Family School for Boys at Farmington, Connecticut. The choice suggests that Henry believed Morton at age fourteen would benefit from an exacting moral environment. As to the clash between Shoemaker and Plant, Dinsmore proposed a simple, if arbitrary, solution. As Adams Express head, he would treat directly with Henry on behalf of Southern Express. A contract resulted. Signed in New York on October 3, its terms defined "a division of their territorial rights" that gifted Southern Express with exclusive rights, subject to some exceptions, "south of the Ohio river."[29]

The pact carried far-reaching implications. Previously, Adams shareholders had been assured that Southern Express existed as a fictive enterprise and that its assets would be returned to the parent company once Union forces had won the war. Adams partner E. S. Sanford, also American Telegraph Company president, had copied the 1861 Adams–Southern Express arrangement and created the Southern Telegraph Company. At war's end, its shareholders promptly turned the company back to American Telegraph. "In sum," one commentator concluded, "the record suggests that the Northern companies turned their lines over to Southern managers for use in the Confederate war effort, and then, at the war's end, the Northern companies quietly took their property back." Not so with Southern Express. Years of future litigation churned the question of why, inducing industry historian Alvin Harlow to brand the company "one of the deepest and foggiest of all mysteries." As questions arose, more deals were required to keep arrangements viable. After all was said and done Plant, Dinsmore, and their friends held most of the cards. They got away with grand theft.[30]

As Dinsmore and Plant inked their contract, businessmen all over New York schemed how to take advantage of postwar conditions and accumulated wealth. Henry joined other Adams associates, for instance, to exploit Mexican emperor Maximilian's need for "American capital and energy," not to mention key diplomatic and political contacts. They organized a Mexican Express Company headed by San Franciscan Eugene de Courcillon. Adams people active in the new company included Plant, Henry Sanford, L. W. Winchester, John Hoey, and Isaiah C. Babcock. Importantly, Adams's law firm spearheaded the initiative in the person of Clarence A. Seward, the secretary of state's nephew and acting secretary of state following the attack on William H. Seward in April 1865. Clarence's presence suggested the senior Seward's personal involvement. "The 'Imperial Mexican Express Company' . . . caused both Clarence Seward and Secretary Seward considerable embarrassment," the law firm's historian observed. The enterprise ultimately embarrassed all concerned as diplomatic and political complications exploded in the public press. "After Maximilian had been captured and executed by [Benito] Juarez [in 1867]," the historian added, "the Mexican Express Company venture was abandoned." Whatever else, the fiasco linked Henry Plant indelibly in the national consciousness with William H. Seward.[31]

That disastrous conclusion remained for the future in November 1865, when Plant returned South flush with Adams Express cash to pay railroads for agreements guaranteeing exclusive rights to Southern Express. Anticipating a December 25 withdrawal of Adams employees from regions where Shoemaker had advanced, Henry also reorganized his management team and began placing key personnel. Mike O'Brien emerged as Henry's strong right arm. Former acting president James Shuter became regional superintendent operating from Memphis. Plant even arranged to extend express service into Florida with offices in Jacksonville and Tallahassee. By year's end he boasted coverage—at least in theory—of virtually every principal town in the South as well as rights to carry packages and freight on most southern railroads. He pushed the work well into 1866, consolidating, improving, and expanding. Henry took special pride in the birth of the Texas Express in March. In April, in line with his newborn interest in Mexican affairs, he pressed for service between Texas and Mexico.[32]

The progress counted in a single year was breathtaking, but it had also raised hackles, provoked litigation, embroiled Adams in shareholder infighting, and encouraged jealous competitors to grab for a share of express business gold. Dinsmore's reaction focused on reorganization of Adams Express to protect early investors and company pioneers from Johnny-come-latelies. As of May 1, he split current assets apart from future earnings and acquisitions. These assets totaled $3.69 million, regarding which he distributed "certificates of interest" on a pro rata basis. Dinsmore also issued new company shares—ones effectively representing a 733 percent stock dividend—to create a property interest in income and profits accruing after the same date. Plant echoed Dinsmore's actions. On June 23 Henry and his allies increased Southern Express shares from five thousand to thirty thousand and distributed them pro rata among two dozen shareholders. Most prominent among recipients were Plant, Dinsmore, and Henry Sanford. "There is no existing record to show what was paid or subscribed by the original stockholders of the Southern Express Co.," an inquiry later found. "The existing records of the company do not show the disposition made of the proceeds of the original stock issued."[33]

His corporate finance and shareholder issues addressed, Plant in mid-1866 implemented another administrative reorganization. He divided Southern Express into four divisions: Virginia, North and South Carolina, much of Georgia, and Florida to be overseen from Augusta; west Georgia and Alabama, from Atlanta; Mississippi, Louisiana, and Texas, from New Orleans; and Tennessee and Kentucky, from Memphis. Henry relied on company veterans as superintendents, individuals whom he believed he could trust absolutely. They included Rufus B. Bullock, Edward Hurlbert, Alexander Benson Small, and James Shuter. Bullock, as of July 1, 1866, also assumed corporate secretary and general superintendent posts. Plant meanwhile depended ever more on Mike O'Brien, who carried the title of assistant superintendent but served as Plant's all-purpose troubleshooter. One newcomer graced the charmed circle. George Heath Tilley, a twenty-five-year-old Englishman, had worked for the Pennsylvania Railroad before coming South in 1865. George Smyth described him as "a gentleman of exceedingly modest and quiet ways, yet genial, and (with intimate friends) agreeable in conversation." Henry met Tilley, took his measure, and offered him the job of private secretary. Neither man ever regretted the decision.[34]

Convinced in August 1866 that he had set in place a dependable foundation for Southern Express's corporate health and successful operation,

Plant departed for New York. He rested there and in Connecticut through the year, spending time—when business did not occupy him—relaxing with Morton, relations, and friends or else conferring and socializing with Dinsmore and Adams partners. Not even the destruction of his river steamer *Eclipse* on December 30 with the loss of "seventeen souls"—the product of a boiler explosion—drew him back South. Rather, he watched from a distance as post–Civil War violence built to frightening levels and a furious northern electorate in November voted for congressional control by what some have called "Radical Republicans." With the new Congress scheduled to convene on March 4, 1867, all eyes peered toward Washington, where a momentous political struggle was expected between the Radicals and President Andrew Johnson.[35]

Not until February 27, 1867, did Plant again venture southward, to test the political waters and to join an Atlanta convention of railroad presidents and superintendents. The following weeks saw Republicans enact over presidential vetoes the Reconstruction Acts that placed most of the South under military control, mandated new state constitutions, and—for the first time—called for adult black male suffrage in elections for state constitutional convention delegates. Henry, though, dealt mostly with disaster control of a nonpolitical nature, problems so dire that Dinsmore rushed to the scene to assist. Incessant rains produced widespread flooding in Kentucky, Tennessee, Arkansas, Mississippi, and North Georgia, leading to "inconvenience and destruction of property in every direction." Enormous damage to railroads and freight carriers resulted. All transportation ceased for a time between Atlanta and Chattanooga. The havoc created even "greater privation" by cutting off food supplies to some areas.[36]

Circumstances did not permit Henry to ignore political matters completely, however. General John Pope had been appointed military governor of Alabama and Georgia, taking command at Montgomery on April 1. Plant, Dinsmore, and possibly Shuter spoke with him there, asking Pope to designate the rail center of Atlanta, rather than the state capital of Milledgeville, as his Georgia headquarters. The general soon acted, pursuant to numerous such requests, in Atlanta's favor. From Montgomery, Plant and Dinsmore headed to Nashville. The Adams Express president caught the train north for New York, and Henry moved south. He worked at Atlanta beginning on the eighth, fine-tuning company affairs in light of Pope's scheduled arrival and the advent of Military Reconstruction.[37]

Henry then vanished, and his disappearance loomed as no casual thing. Plant understood now that the closer he associated directly with volatile political affairs, the more he endangered himself and his business interests. Not that individuals close to him were not already deeply involved in politics;

they were. The deeper those involvements, though, the further he needed to appear separated from them. In the circumstances, Plant chose to enjoy Paris in springtime. The famed International Exposition opened April 1. Among sights to see, John Hoey had loaned Jean-Léon Gérôme's *L'Aimee*, a painting that Henry had first seen at the 1864 exposition and may have recommended to his friend. More significantly for Plant, Adelina Patti was performing through April 28, holding "reception parties" every Sunday at Madame Grisi's magnificent *hotel*. Debut performances of Jacques Offenbach's *La Grande-Duchesse de Gérolstein* meanwhile featured Hortense Schneider. "I saw it in Paris in 18[67]," Plant recollected, "and enjoyed it greatly." A reporter observed: "[On] a visit to Paris in 18[67] . . . he saw Schneider perform in it. She made it famous. He also later saw *La Grande Duchess* in New York with [Lucille] Tostee but felt that, while she was good, Schneider was the better singer." Plant commented, "The opera is much more enjoyable in French." Later accounts unfortunately transposed 1867 to 1876. In the latter year, though, *La Grande-Duchesse*—an antiwar opera—was banned from French performance in the aftermath of the Franco-Prussian War. "There will never be a Grande Duchesse like Schneider," Offenbach lamented in 1876. "There are no such artists in Paris as there were when it was produced." Whatever the case, *La Grande-Duchesse* arrived on the New York stage in September 1867 with Tostee singing the lead. Henry caught her performance at that time.[38]

Plant's return to the United States found him striving to avoid the South and its troubled political affairs. Although his managers had rewarded his trust with solid performances, business matters still necessitated a visit to Atlanta on May 21 and to Chattanooga on June 1. He then retreated to New York and Connecticut. This permitted his absence from Georgia in early July when Rufus Bullock, former Augusta mayor Foster Blodgett, and other associates of Henry's helped establish the Union Republican Party of Georgia. The same associates late in the month founded a newspaper, the *National Republican*, at Augusta amid rumors that Southern Express money was paying for everything. Plant, safe from requests for comment, instead concentrated on a different matter. He faced a quandary having to do with Morton. While Henry was enjoying Paris, his son—fifteen years old—had appeared at Savannah and Augusta, having walked away from Deacon Hart's school. Either Morton or Henry discussed the boy's education in Augusta with John Howard Brown, a young New York editor and graduate of Eastman National Business College at Poughkeepsie. Given Brown's endorsement, Henry arranged a six-month course at the school leading to graduation. Morton agreed to enroll in the fall.[39]

With the exception of a September 1867 railroad excursion from Chicago to St. Louis and back, Henry stayed close to his New York–Connecticut connections until Georgia held its constitutional convention elections in late October. He then dipped into the South to tend to affairs before making away once more before the Georgia state convention met in December. The business took him to Charleston, South Carolina, and to Memphis. He may have aided Bullock in securing election as Macon & Augusta Railroad president. In Memphis, Plant bought the Overton Hotel and installed Stephen B. Robbins, his friend from Augusta's Planters' Hotel, as its manager. "We speak advisedly in reference to the Overton Hotel at Memphis, when we say very few, if any, surpass or equal it as a first class house," a Cincinnati reporter declared that December. "The popular and experienced proprietors, assisted by their present corps of *attaches*, such as the young and gallant Robbins, the attentive and courteous M. D. Maine, and the good natured Barlow, or as he is termed 'Modest Billy,' is sufficient guarantee for a pleasant and satisfactory sojourn with them while in Memphis."[40]

Try as he might to avoid political stain, obligations compelled Plant's reappearance at Augusta in February 1868. Bullock appeared liable to sit soon in the governor's chair, and the general superintendent's political commitments and railroad presidency already limited his involvement with Southern Express. Mike O'Brien fortunately had picked up the slack, and Plant now elected to give him the proper title. Effective that month, O'Brien ran Southern Express, or as an informed onlooker put it, Plant "yielded the practical management of the business to the Gen. Superintendent." At roughly the same time, Plant abandoned for most purposes his claim to Georgia residence. He became, instead, a New York City man once more.[41]

Fortuitously, the change of residence occurred just in the nick of time. Bullock grasped the Republican nomination for Georgia governor on March 7, unleashing a torrent of passionate—not to say hate-driven—opposition from angry Rebels and assorted Democratic editors acting in tandem with them. Various claims were aired that the New Yorker had been a Union spy during the Civil War. These assertions escalated to charges that Southern Express had operated as a center for anti-Confederate intelligence gathering. The Macon *Journal & Messenger* quoted a former Union general to the effect that "the most efficient spies he had were among the employees of the Southern Express Company." It did not take long for the accusers to turn on Plant. On April 10 the Augusta *Daily Constitutionalist* declared: "It is generally believed that, under pretext of going to Canada for his health, the President of the Southern Express Company abandoned the Confederacy and kept snug quarters in Massachusetts. Did Mr. Bullock have any communication with the aforesaid President relative to matters progressing in this region? Did he furnish any information as to the movement of troops, etc. We ask, because it is popularly surmised that, during the years 1864-'65, our bullock was feeding upon a dangerous plant."[42]

Henry had already departed the state when Bullock achieved election as governor on April 20–23. Plant spent much of March and April with Mike O'Brien in South Carolina and Tennessee acclimating his new general superintendent to places, people, and management styles important to Southern Express. He took one quick trip to New York to borrow $50,000 from Dinsmore to upgrade and renovate the Overton Hotel. At April's end, Plant and O'Brien were finalizing that and other Memphis business. Henry thereupon quietly slipped away from the South as his protégé prepared to become Georgia's first Republican governor.[43]

After leaving Tennessee, Henry apparently pursued what was becoming a springtime tradition and boarded a steamer for Europe. Plant may have been pursuing rumors that Adelina Patti had agreed to marry. She had departed Paris after a final performance on April 30. In London the next month gossip dogged her that she already had wed. Whether Henry reached her in England may never be known. More certainly, Patti married Henri de Roger de Cahusac, Marquis of Caux, on July 29, 1868. "She looked, it need hardly be said, extremely pretty, and though very pale, she wore a smile on her face," a spectator recorded. "Among the not very numerous guests was Signor Mario," British journalist H. Sutherland Edwards recalled, "who, at the breakfast, whispered that the marquis, much as he might be attached to his fascinating bride, had never made love to her so much as he, her constant tenor, had done."[44]

7
Flush Times
1868 to 1873

"mark the richness of the express bonanza"

Entry to splendid homes on New York City's fashionable Fifth Avenue bespoke the beginning and end of a five-year epoch that began for Henry Plant in 1868. Fittingly, Henry's mentor and Adams Express Company president William B. Dinsmore bought the first of them. Plant, who accepted the second house's keys on behalf of a new bride of somewhat mysterious provenance, came after. Henry's life had by then altered beyond recognition from what it had previously been. He no longer resembled the untested thirty-three-year-old who had set out hopefully to explore Georgia and Florida in 1852, the adventurous young man who had sought metaphoric gold through pioneering express business routes. Living on a modest salary then and having the care of an ailing wife and infant son, he had possessed little more than a sound mind, eagerness for excitement, physical courage, a deep-rooted willingness to work hard, committed friends, and passionate ambition to become rich. Through trials, scandals, wartime intrigue, betrayals, hope, heartbreak, and hubris, he had matured into an aging gentleman of significant means who enjoyed the finer things of life. To his credit and despite mistakes, Plant along the way had demonstrated enduring substance while doggedly honing managerial talents and business skills to the point that his company almost ran itself. But what was he now to do? Henry turned forty-nine years of age in October 1868 coincident with the realization that, suddenly, he had become a man without purpose. He needed new worlds to conquer and triumphs to elevate him into the top ranks of a business elite whose membership he was coming to know. Of course, there were also the rewards. What he needed most, he sensed, were the right connections.

Two strands of news greeted Henry at New York City in August 1868. In the first, Dinsmore had paid $181,000 for an imposing home at the northwest corner of Fifth Avenue and Thirty-First Street, sounding the arrival of Adams Express entrepreneurs at the heart of Manhattan society. Avenue residence had exuded social cachet since the 1850s, when Astor family members sanctioned its special status. Meanwhile, Fifth Avenue had been extended in 1854 through Fifty-First Street, but growth had taken time to catch up. "Fifth Avenue, from Forty-third to Forty-fifth Street," a report specified, "was largely used for cattle yards." Beyond there, Columbia College was converting the old Botanical Gardens into residential tracts. The amount that Dinsmore paid for his home, it should be noted, sufficed to draw attention to the buyer, his wealth, and his relative business and social standing. "The sale was made for cash," one reporter noted. "[It] was attended by many persons of large means, and when the auctioneer—Mr. E. A. Lawrence—knocked down the property at the prices mentioned above, the result was received with applause."[1]

Plant could only have hoped that the second bit of news would prove as felicitous as the first, but facts suggested otherwise. His son, Morton, almost seventeen, had graduated from Eastman National Business College in April. When he arrived in Savannah on the nineteenth, Henry's Southern Express subordinate Rufus Bullock rested on the verge of election as governor. Plant was monitoring political developments from no closer than Memphis, where he and Southern Express general superintendent Mike O'Brien had taken refuge while avoiding Georgia and its political cauldron at all costs. Since Plant meant to leave the South as soon as possible, O'Brien agreed to look after the young man's well-being. He assigned Morton to a low-paying job in the auditor's office at Augusta's Southern Express headquarters. Henry seemingly hoped that a Yale education might follow for his son after a taste of practical experience, but he failed to reckon how much a son could reflect his father. That summer, Morton transferred instead to the Western Division auditor's office in Memphis. Henry acceded, however grudgingly. As events proved, he had blundered. Morton required adult supervision far more than he needed a new job.[2]

When Henry revisited the South in late November, Morton had already settled in at Memphis and father did not meet with son. Rather, the older man's trip involved consultations with O'Brien at Augusta. Similarly, in February 1869 Plant and O'Brien joined transportation executives in New Orleans "to enjoy Mardi Gras." Apparently, Henry returned to New York, again without seeing Morton, for an express company summit on the seventeenth. Those sessions aimed to establish agreements on distribution of territories after years of industry disorder that had seen corporate assaults and counterattacks undermine Adams Express. To protect Southern Express, Henry had stopped over in Washington on the way home in a fruitless effort to solicit the help of congressional friends to secure a national charter for his company.[3]

Although Plant ventured South several more times during 1869, he mostly remained in New York heading off trouble arising out of the 1866 contract that had saved Southern Express from takeover by Adams Express. Understandably, shareholders excluded from the Adams inner circle resented the loss of lucrative assets. Rumors of legal challenges abounded, in response to which inner circle members relied on Henry Sanford for counsel. Conveniently, the lawyer discovered a written agreement seemingly executed by Adams officers at the beginning of the Civil War that sold what became Southern Express to Plant. Dated April 8, 1861, the contract called for a payment of $300,000. When critics argued that the amount understated actual value, Sanford and Plant adroitly countered that the figure had really been $500,000. A court filing later noted, "The reasons given by Mr. Sanford [for the misrepresentation] being, that Mr. Plant said that in his judgment $500,000 was so large a sum that he did not think that the authorities of the Southern States would receive with credence the statement that that amount had been paid for the property purchased." Supposedly, Henry had executed five promissory notes to secure payment plus interest.[4]

Henry's 1869 goal involved crafting a viable scenario for arguing that the debt had been paid. A convoluted explanation resulted, one that incredibly called for Plant to receive a small reimbursement. Henry claimed that in 1861 he had asked Adams to withhold dividend payments on his company shares. By 1869 the amount due came to $395,000 including interest and stock dividends. He insisted also that he had paid Adams from Southern Express profits the amounts of $80,000 in 1867–1868 and about $308,000 in 1868–1869. Since his liability ran to $782,410.24, Adams owed him a refund of $506.42. No Adams or Southern Express records substantiated his claims, nor did any party proffer other supportive documentation. "The purchase money had been neither paid nor received, or even tendered to or accepted by the trustees implicated, until nine years after the pretended sale, and when the property and business with which they assumed to part for $500,000 had come to be worth 100 per cent. per annum upon $3,000,000," an opposition lawyer soon insisted. "The breach of trust in the sale of the property was still more flagrant in view of the undisputed fact that the [Adams] Trustees, upon their own concession, subsequently acquired individual interests to themselves in the very property which they claim to have sold, through the intervention of Plant, to the Southern Express Company, in which they are shareholders, and from which they are receiving one hundred per cent. yearly dividends." Historian Alvin Harlow exclaimed, "Mark the richness of the express bonanza."[5]

Confident that he had buttressed his company against attack, Plant celebrated his fiftieth birthday—October 27, 1869—in grand style. Business had kept him from a springtime trip to Paris, so he made up for the omission in late September or early October. Whether reports of infidelities within the marriage of the Marquis and Marchioness of Caux swayed his judgment cannot be determined. Regardless, Henry's favorite diva was singing in the City of Light to renewed acclaim. "Adelina Patti is again carrying everything before her in Paris," an observer noted. Late in October, however, Patti departed for Russia in the midst of reports that her marriage had proved resilient. A twenty-year-old fellow protégé of Maurice Strakosch, Mathilde Sessi, then claimed center stage as Amina in Vincenzo Bellini's *La Sonnambula*. Her triumph gifted Henry an excellent, if not fully satisfactory, birthday present.[6]

Plant, likely disappointed at the Caux marriage's health, returned to New York on December 12 to a significant turn of events concerning Pennsylvania Railroad vice president Thomas A. Scott. The railroad baron had been involved with Adams Express alongside his acolyte Andrew Carnegie since the mid-1850s. His association with Henry and, eventually, Southern Express was thus anchored by deep roots. During Reconstruction the ties had blossomed, especially when Governor Rufus Bullock's administration in Georgia was considered. While their relationship endured ups and downs, Scott and Bullock notoriously cooperated for years in their personal interests and that of Southern Express and the Pennsylvania Railroad. Whatever their dealings, the gist certainly came to Plant's attention. More probably, Henry quietly involved himself directly. Whether the cooperation involved convict leasing, funding initiatives, or other subjects, Henry and his Adams associates stood to benefit in the long run.[7]

As Georgia's political tumult mounted at decade's end, Scott's planning and that of his business associates gained a new dimension. Around New Year's 1870 he spent a good deal of time in New York. Events intimate that he, Dinsmore, and Plant discussed profits to be made from southern railroad consolidation. Scott possessed first-rate knowledge on the topic. A New York financial reporter explained in February 1870: "The Pennsylvania Railroad, which had only the three hundred and sixty miles from Philadelphia to Pittsburgh, now rules two thousand seven hundred miles of different railways. Most of this enormous extension has been acquired within a year or two. It is stretching out its arms now to embrace Omaha, the terminus of the Pacific Railroad, over thirteen hundred miles west of Philadelphia."[8]

Eager to capitalize on political and business connections then current in a devasted region whose day-to-day reconstruction had only just begun, Scott and his friends now fixed with renewed vigor on southern as well as western horizons. Corporate documentation summarized the vision: "The object and purpose . . . is to secure the control of such Southern railroads as may be essential to the formation of through lines between New-York, Philadelphia, Baltimore, Washington City, and the principal cities of the South, by ownership of the capital stock of said companies, by leases, and by contract relations." That is, the men sought to dominate southern rail transportation and associated northern connections. Reliance on a holding company as a mechanism for industry control pioneered twentieth-century approaches. Also, as one expert concluded, "[The implementation of the plan articulated by Scott] was to a large degree instrumental in establishing in the seventies a north and south trend of traffic, which has been an outstanding characteristic of the railroads of the South Atlantic States down to the present day."[9]

In early 1870 the ideas that Scott shared with Dinsmore and Plant were still maturing, and the New York discussions during January were mostly exploratory. A later Baltimore gathering fleshed them out. "On April 26, 1870, the members of the investment syndicate met again at Barnum's [Hotel], where Scott presented his ideas for widespread participation in the railroad network of the South," Albert J. Churella detailed. "The [Pennsylvania Railroad] needed traffic for its Baltimore & Potomac subsidiary, Scott explained, and the Wilmington & Weldon and other southern railroads could provide it. When connected to various Pennsylvania Railroad affiliates west of the Mississippi, those lines could also funnel PRR traffic to the southwest. Southern carriers required capital, and the PRR, with revenues on Lines East roughly thirty-five times those of the Wilmington & Weldon, could supply all that was required. Everyone would benefit, Scott argued persuasively, for the listless southern railroads, if adequately capitalized, managed, and coordinated, were certain to become profitable."[10]

Whether or not Plant attended the Baltimore meeting, he and Dinsmore understood that Scott envisioned a three-pronged southern rail network. According to Churella, the eastern prong ran down "the Atlantic seaboard, through Weldon and Wilmington to Charleston, with a branch continuing through South Carolina from Florence to Columbia and then to Augusta, Georgia." He continued, "A second truck route, often referred to as the Piedmont Air Line, connected Richmond and Atlanta by way of Danville, Greensboro, and Charlotte, North Carolina, with onward connections to Montgomery and Mobile, Alabama, as well as Pensacola, Florida." Dinsmore and, particularly, Plant held the key to desired expansion westward. Specifically, Scott wanted a third route "through Bristol, Knoxville, and Chattanooga, Tennessee, to Memphis," a line that also included connections between Chattanooga, Atlanta, and his other routes.[11]

Plant and Dinsmore figured so importantly in Scott's equation because the state of Georgia owned the Western and Atlantic Railroad, the line that connected Atlanta with Chattanooga. Further, Bullock had named one-time Southern Express division superintendent Edward Hurlbert as road superintendent. B. W. Wrenn, also a company veteran, served as general passenger agent. Southern Express thereby enjoyed extraordinary leverage with Georgia's government and the Western and Atlantic Railroad.[12]

As Henry's schedule through mid-1870 attested, a scheme as grandiose as the one presented by Scott required complex planning and preparation. Plant visited Philadelphia, Scott's home, in late January before spending a month in the South between mid-February and mid-March. En route to Columbia to begin his tour, he spoke with Bullock in Washington. If Henry's custom serves as a pointer, he enjoyed Mardi Gras on March 1, having arrived in New Orleans from Atlanta on Western and Atlantic connections. His return allowed renewed contact with Bullock at Atlanta and Washington. That Scott's Pennsylvania friend Senator Simon Cameron introduced a bill in March for a Southern Express federal charter highlighted Plant's presence in the capital on numerous occasions. A Senate committee approved the measure in May.[13]

Plant's travels, briefly interrupted in late March and early April, soon appeared frantic. He and Dinsmore journeyed to Charleston on April 8 and saw Bullock in Washington on their return. They thereafter conferred in New York with William H. Seward prior to Scott's syndicate meeting in Baltimore on the twenty-sixth. After the Senate committee charter vote on May 12, it was on to Mobile, New Orleans, and Galveston. Circumstances then drew Henry back to New York, although by then events were set for the fall that would allow Scott's puzzle pieces to fall into place to Plant's and Dinsmore's distinct advantage.[14]

Henry's New York return that May partly addressed the latest chapter in the continuing saga of the Southern Express ownership flap. Alienated shareholders, reacting to attempts by Dinsmore to ensure greater personal control of Southern Express shares owned by Adams, had demanded an accounting. Their pleas ignored, several shareholders sued, charging "that the pretense of a *bona fide* sale to Plant thus set up by the trustees was the result of a corrupt conspiracy and collusion between them and those managing the Southern Express Company, whereby they were seeking to deprive the certificate holders of that property and secure it for themselves." The plaintiffs also demanded the removal of the principal Adams officers as trustees and a receiver. Nonplussed, Dinsmore and associates sent the Seward law firm before a friendly judge on September 22 and procured a temporary injunction.[15]

Plant by late September thus looked to an immediate future fraught with several potentially embarrassing situations. For one thing, a New York judge could order his testimony under oath in open court about Southern Express origins and ownership, an ordeal that he had no desire to endure. Meanwhile, Bullock had maneuvered the Georgia legislature toward October approval of the Western and Atlantic Railroad lease subject to a bidding process. With so much money at stake, political clashes of the bluntest sort were guaranteed to appear. Henry had experienced how quickly attention could turn in volatile circumstances to Southern Express and himself. Civil War trials, as seen, had convinced him to absent himself on such occasions. Once more, he took his own advice.[16]

Henry essentially disappeared from late September 1870 until mid-December. "Mr. Harris" probably steamed to Europe, although he could not visit his beloved Paris. Franco-Prussian War fighting had erupted in July, and Germans were now besieging Paris. He apparently turned instead to London. Adelina Patti was there and spoke in chaotic times of retirement once she had completed a US visit. Her marriage teetered on dissolution. Moreover, she had earlier begun building "quite a palace in the Champs-Elysees . . . where her voice only will be heard" and wondered if she would be living there alone. Questions of fidelity had shifted to ones of infidelity. "The marriage produced no passion and no children," a biographer observed. "The major interest in her life, next to singing, was men."[17]

Whatever the specifics of the hiatus, mundane affairs pulled Plant back to a businessman's life in December. Cameron, aided by Connecticut's William Buckingham, managed on the sixteenth to bring the Southern Express bill before the Senate. The measure passed easily, but troubling problems surfaced. Thomas F. Bayard of Delaware argued that approval would lead "to endless legislation of a similar character" and amended the language to subject Southern Express to "taxation under State laws." Vermont's Justin S. Morrill inserted a second poison pill by "making corporators liable for the debts of the concern." The nature of the debate, unfortunately for Henry, shouted that Southern Express and its president were held in less than high esteem in some Washington political circles. "The bill . . . is the same concern the House committee on commerce reported against last session," one newspaper proclaimed. "There is a prospect that very few if any of these schemes will ever get through." The House Commerce Committee—despite the negative comments—favored the proposal in January 1871 only to see Louisianan Lionel A. Sheldon, a native New Yorker, table it on the twenty-seventh.[18]

However tarnished Henry's star may have appeared in Washington, it pulsed magnificently in Atlanta. The Western and Atlantic Railroad lease had moved forward. Upon its submission on December 24, the names of the twenty-three individuals backing the proposal stunned Georgia businessmen and politicians. Naturally, Plant, Dinsmore, and Scott numbered among them. Cameron's presence may have surprised some, while the participation of Atlanta hotel man and investor Hannibal I. Kimball—former New Haven carriage maker and friend of Henry's brother Horace Hoadley—probably did not. That Supreme Court chief justice Joseph E. Brown—Georgia's governor through the Civil War—headed the roll of investors launched reverberations through corridors of power, however. Had it not, the presence of Confederate vice president Alexander Stephens's name would have done so. Adding impact, Confederate States congressman and senator Benjamin Harvey Hill stood with them.[19]

Bullock processed the bids quickly and on Christmas Day announced that Brown's company had won. Whereupon Bullock granted the new Western and Atlantic Railroad Company a twenty-year lease for an annual payment of $25,000. The bidders themselves moved speedily, convening to organize on January 10, 1871, at Atlanta's Kimball House. Brown won election as president. He substituted his friend Edmund W. Cole as superintendent, but B. W. Wrenn remained as passenger ticket agent, preserving Henry's insider access. On his part Plant maintained a low profile. At day's end the "pleasant, private 'sociable'" that Kimball hosted permitted him to finally relax with his new partners.[20]

The Western and Atlantic lease gave Plant great satisfaction, while a new plaything that Bullock had acquired enhanced the pleasant nature of the moment. The plaything merits notice because a seed planted at that time later blossomed into a treasured facet of Henry's life. It was a railroad car named "The State of Georgia," and its story lay rooted in Bullock's birthplace of Albion, New York. He shared the hometown with George M. Pullman, who had begun during the Civil War to manufacture luxury railroad sleeping cars that eventually carried the name Pullman palace cars. Ultimately, H. I. Kimball and his brother Edwin N. Kimball joined in business with Pullman to establish "sleeping car lines in the Southern States." By 1870 Pullman headed the Pullman, Kimball & Ramsey Sleeping Car Company as its president. Directors included the Kimball brothers and Georgia chief justice Joseph E. Brown.[21]

The sleeping-car company's leadership sensibly wanted to promote the firm in Georgia and with its governor. Accordingly, Pullman, Kimball & Ramsey gifted Bullock with a car as he finalized preparatory plans for leasing the Western and Atlantic Railroad. Whether the company did so at its own expense or at the railroad's remains unclear. "I think about August, 1870, I met E. N. Kimball, who wished to purchase for the W. & A. R. R. a special car, to be used for the benefit of the Governor," recalled the president of the Jackson & Sharp Company. "Upon the statement of Mr. Kimball, that this car would be used on special occasions, and would be run over other Roads through the country, I agreed to sell at the cost of the manufacture [and] delivered it to the W. & A. R. R. in December, 1870." One admirer described the $12,000 coach as "the finest and handsomest car in the United States." Henry Plant never forgot it.[22]

On the other hand, within days of the Western and Atlantic Company's organization, Plant's prevailing state of satisfaction unexpectedly deflated in the face of chilling personal realities. From New York came word that Emily Frances Blackstone, wife of John Morton Freeman, Henry's friend and his son's namesake, had died suddenly one month prior to her thirty-seventh birthday. She left a widower and three daughters aged six to ten. The circumstances remain a mystery, although the family's silence harked back to the death nine years earlier of Emily's cousin Ellen Blackstone Plant. Three days after Henry learned the sad news, his former attorney and Confederate ally William P. Chilton succumbed in Alabama. The record does not reflect whether Henry attended funerals in either case. His presence with Mike O'Brien in New Orleans on January 23, 1871, though, raises the likelihood that they arrived from Montgomery, where Chilton's rites were held.[23]

These deaths—or Emily's, at least—cast a pall that, for the time being, Henry could not shake. From his New Orleans arrival until early April—as he was accustomed to doing when sad or embarrassed—he stepped into the shadows and away from public attention. Likely, he treated himself to a Havana visit. The "good, staunch, and swift-sailing" steamer *Bienville* maintained service between New Orleans and New York with stopovers at the Cuban capital. The vessel departed the Crescent City on February 4 and steamed into Havana days later. Passengers beheld in the harbor the US flagship *Severn*. Its appearance highlighted the ongoing Grito de Yara, an insurrection that had begun in 1868 and lasted for a decade. Henry could not have known at the time, but the *Severn*'s presence shone as a harbinger of US government involvement in Cuban affairs. It presaged, as well, the presence twenty-seven years later of the battleship *Maine*, the destruction of which was to play so great a role in Henry's career.[24]

Meanwhile, Governor Bullock's Western and Atlantic Railroad lease had afforded Tom Scott and partners the vital link they needed to move ahead with plans for domination of southern railroads. Scott fortified his own influence on March 8 by adding the presidency of the Union Pacific Railroad to his other professional responsibilities. Fourteen days later he goaded Pennsylvania's legislature to create the Overland Contract Company "to operate railroads as well as to own their securities." A charter clause enabled the company to change its name. This transpired at Philadelphia and New York in April and May when the corporators—including Plant at the initial session—first met. The businessmen called their enterprise the South-

10. Havana, Cuba, between 1880 and 1901. Library of Congress.

ern Railway Security Company (SRSC) and chose former Adams Express leader George W. Cass as president. Details of the meetings remain cloudy, although a board of directors plainly coalesced. Scott and Plant took seats, as did Cass. New York financiers D. Willis James, Morris K. Jessup, and James Roosevelt (future father of Franklin Delano Roosevelt) also joined the leadership. Plant grew close to Jessup, as he also did to Baltimore investors William T. Walters and Benjamin F. Newcomer. Those men controlled the vital Wilmington & Weldon Railroad. James Donald Cameron represented his father, Senator Cameron.[25]

Plant missed the second SRSC session—at New York—for personal reasons loosely related to Emily Blackstone Freeman's death. Henry and W. B. Dinsmore had concluded to spend time tending to personal feelings and needs. To some extent they were Plant's, although the men focused attention on Mary Blackstone Plant, who was the wife of Henry's uncle Samuel O. Plant, sister to Henry's late wife, Ellen, and Emily Freeman's cousin. The three individuals toured the Deep South so that Mary could visit her sister's Augusta gravesite and behold the southern locales that Ellen had particularly loved. The party arrived in Charleston on April 7, traveling directly from the first SRSC meeting at Philadelphia. Presumably a quick visit to Augusta followed on the eighth, allowing an overnight stay at Savannah on the ninth. Pursuing the path of Ellen's interests, they ventured next to Florida and Jacksonville, Strawberry Mills, and St. Augustine.[26]

Once the party's Florida visit neared its end in early May, Henry and Mary headed for Louisiana. The most direct route began with an eighty-five-mile ride westward from Jacksonville to Live Oak. In light of bold initiatives that he undertook a few years later, impressions of that ride and especially of the town and its depot must have stuck firmly in Plant's mind. Only at Live Oak could travelers make connections to Georgia and points west. The discomfort of stopovers there—indicative of the primitive nature of Florida's rail system generally—was already considered legendary. In any event, the travelers checked into the St. Charles Hotel in New Orleans on May 8. Morton Plant and Mike O'Brien awaited them, and they collectively enjoyed a pleasant few days' reunion. Henry and Mary seemingly then repeated his earlier New York voyage via Havana.[27]

At New York and again tending to business, Plant dealt with personal concerns for Rufus Bullock's well-being considered in light of intertwining SRSC priorities. Elections the previous December had returned overwhelming Democratic majorities to Georgia's legislature. The governor desperately stalled the convening of a new session until late 1871. Meanwhile, emboldened Ku Klux Klan members spawned widespread racial and political violence. "Throughout 1871, Bullock pondered what to do as Redeemer control of the legislature stared him in the face," biographer Russell Duncan related. "Bullock feared for his life and his liberty." Scott, Plant, and associates decided in the circumstances to pay respects and show support. The two men—with Secretary of the Interior Columbus Delano, Senator Cameron, General Horace Porter (secretary to President Ulysses S. Grant), and W. T. Walters—shared a private car to Atlanta. On June 6 they attended a "Governor's Reception" with other Bullock friends including Governor Brown and Senator Hill. "The reception given at the Executive Mansion last night in honor of our distinguished Northern visitors, was quite a *recherche* [exotic] affair," a newspaperman observed. "The reception was undoubtedly the most brilliant one of the season."[28]

However much the governor appreciated the gesture, it generated little gain for his political future. Instead, from then until he resigned under pressure on October 23 Bullock mostly stayed away from Georgia. He first traveled with the reception party to New York, although in his own car. An Academy of Music function on June 10 featured him among celebrities present. Plant and Dinsmore—Academy devotees—doubtlessly accompanied their friend. The governor returned North in mid-July. Dinsmore had developed an elaborate Hudson River estate near Staatsburg in Duchess County. President Grant visited him there on the nineteenth in company with Bullock and Adams Express grandees E. S. Sanford, Henry Sanford, and John Hoey. At various New York locales through August, H. I. Kimball served as Bullock's companion. "It is believed that neither Kimball nor Bullock dare return to Georgia," a correspondent asserted on August 21. During the month's last week ten friends joined the governor on "The State of Georgia" for an exciting ride to San Francisco, the driving of the "golden spike" having completed the first transcontinental railroad fifteen months previously. Bullock did not to return to New York City until October 4.[29]

Plant's name received no mention in accounts of Bullock's travels to the west, and for good reason. Subsequent to an appearance that he and Mike O'Brien made in Columbia on June 16, Henry once more slipped from public notice. He reappeared at Nashville only on October 10. His whereabouts during those four months are unknown, although the possibility of a European excursion cannot be discounted. Following a flurry of activity at Atlanta, New Orleans, and Memphis in October on behalf of Southern Express and SRSC, he again dropped from sight until nearly Christmastime. The pattern hints at a man struggling with a sense of loss and a measure of loneliness following the southern trip with Ellen's sister Mary. Extended periods of inattention to necessary business ran averse to his usual practice, although the reaction of friends and associates suggested understanding of trials that he endured.[30]

Perhaps fortunately, through the early months of 1872 circumstances allowed Plant little time to pine, as business commitments required close attention. Southern Express responsibilities appeared on his schedule repeatedly. They necessitated travels in the South, usually with Mike O'Brien. Henry initiated, as well, another attempt to secure a federal charter. Connecticut representative Henry H. Starkweather led the charge this time. Corporators named in the bill now reflected actual ownership rather than any pretense that southerners controlled the entity. Names other than Plant's listed in the measure included Dinsmore, Sam Shoemaker, Henry Sanford, John Hoey, Clapp Spooner, and I. C. Babcock. The Adams executives' political clout failed to move Congress, however. The measure died for the most part unmourned.[31]

Beyond Southern Express issues, expansion of the SRSC network also demanded Plant's attention. He, Scott, and others labored intently through winter and spring to extend the company's web through Texas, Tennessee, Mississippi, Louisiana, and Alabama. This activity necessitated Henry's personal presence at Memphis, New Orleans, Mobile, Vicksburg, Jackson, Atlanta, and other cities. "Colonel Scott and his associate capitalists are sweeping their lines through the South," a newspaperman helpfully remarked, "applying their energy and capital to the revival of old lines and the development of the resources of the country." By the time James Roosevelt succeeded George Cass as president in November, the SRSC—by whatever means its backers found appropriate—had stretched its tentacles through the South and seemed well on the road to unprecedented prosperity. "The present investments and future prospects of the Company are such as to warrant the Directors in paying seven per cent per annum upon the stock of the Company from date of investment," a report commented, "with the prospect of a large increase upon that amount when the objects of the managers are consummated, and the value of the lines now under control, and those to be controlled, are fully developed by efficient organization for through transportation."[32]

The SRSC work interestingly produced painful lessons for Henry while bringing untold rewards. Some of the boons were financial, of course, but others reflected the growing respect that Scott felt for Plant. After Scott clashed with Vanderbilt interests for Union Pacific Railroad control, for instance, he claimed the presidency of the Texas Pacific. At that line's annual stockholder meeting in May, Scott insisted that Plant join the board of directors along with other well-heeled associates. Proximity to Scott proved a mixed blessing, though. His reputation as a cutthroat businessman tainted his SRSC leadership. "Swindling the South" cried headlines in places such as Richmond and Savannah. "Remember, you cannot trust a man who sails under false colors—who uses more names than one," the *Richmond Whig* warned of Scott. "He may be very fair on the outside, but he is rotten within."[33]

Other aspects of Scott's persona emerged as even more problematic. To the extent that Plant intended to pursue business in the South and despite a questionable reputation earned in Confederate service, he required the loyal support of a predominantly black labor force. Scott, beyond habitual recourse to cutthroat methods, felt no compunction about cooperating with white politicians and others in the southern states who manifested in words and deeds vile degrees of racism and support for racial violence and oppression. "Scott may not have directly aided the Ku Klux Klan and other white supremacist groups," historian Albert Churella commented, "but he certainly tolerated them and facilitated their activities."[34]

For Scott and men like him, money and power constituted all. On January 11, 1872, black minister and Civil War veteran John W. Wyatt articulated to fellow Florida House of Representatives members the animus harbored by southern blacks against Scott and businessmen of his ilk. "Corporations are a dangerous power, especially large or consolidated corporations, and the American people fear them and view them with distrust," he expressed. "Take for instance, the Penn. Cen. R. R., which has and is daily encircling with extended arms the small roads and railway corporations throughout the Union. As a result of such consolidations, look what a fearful stretch of power and authority is placed within the hands of Thomas Scott, the President of that Railroad. We, who are here in Florida, cannot conceive of the vastness of his schemes. We are too far removed from his field of operations, but I am credibly informed that, by means of the power that he and his Board of Directors possess, they carry everything desired throughout the State of Pennsylvania." Wyatt concluded, "We want no *Tom Scotts, Jim Fisks* or *Vanderbilts* in this State to govern us, by means of which they would influence legislation tending to advance personal interests."[35]

Early in 1872 Henry additionally and necessarily reengaged the continuing dispute between Adams Express shareholders and company officers over Southern Express ownership. When the matter had blazed anew the previous spring, Dinsmore had attempted to quell the dispute by paying off the principal plaintiffs. One year later, though, litigation fires burned on. By June 1872 matters had flamed to white hot. Allegations of fraud screamed from the press as the parties fought ruthlessly in New York courtrooms. Suddenly, on June 25 the plaintiffs "abandoned" the case by failing "to appear in court." Rumors of ever-greater payoffs circulated in city legal and financial circles. Dinsmore, Plant, and allies breathed more easily, but they also remained wary as to whether the fight had yet reached its conclusion.[36]

The year's first half thus carried Plant at breakneck speed through a series of trips, tribulations, and endurance tests. The diversions demanded application of his talents to business affairs despite personal preoccupations. A clue to the state of affairs surfaced in July weeks after the plaintiffs abandoned the Southern Express litigation. Henry had been working in Memphis at midmonth on SRSC matters, but about the twentieth he and private secretary George Tilley checked into the Overlook Mountain House. Located in the Catskill Mountains near Kingston, New York, the new retreat sat only a few miles across the Hudson River from the Dinsmore estate at Staatsburg and James Roosevelt's nearby Hyde Park home. "The Overlook has already achieved a high reputation as a place of summer resort," an area guide proclaimed, "for its exceedingly elevated position (highest of any house in the mountains), the subsequent noble view it affords over the Hudson River Valley, and the admirable manner to which it has been conducted to meet the general requirements of tourists and resident summer visitors."[37]

The location—however magnificent the views—was not what offered special interest to Plant; rather, his sights aimed at the "Mrs. [M.] Birdsall" who checked in with him, presumably into separate accommodations. Margaret

Josephine Loughman Birdsall, age twenty-seven, was a widow of Irish heritage and Roman Catholic faith. By all accounts fifty-two-year-old Henry found her lovely in appearance; others later pointed to "her graceful tact and cordial hospitality." His biographer George Smyth praised her family background: "She is descended from an ancient and noble family, whose ancestral estate, eight miles long, in the Land of the Shamrock, is now occupied by Lord Dundrum," Smyth intoned. "[Her] great grandmother on her mother's side was Lady Mary Murphy, of Ballymore Castle, Ballymore. Her own mother was Miss Ellen O'Duyer, said to have been a woman of great beauty and to have been descended from the Kings of Munster."[38]

In future times Henry and Margaret made it their mission to muddle details of her past and, particularly, obliterate memory of her first marriage. They preferred softer and rosier recollections than the facts warranted. Actually, Margaret was the daughter of an Irish-born New York City liquor dealer who had bankrupted in 1850 and then made a small fortune during the Civil War supplying cattle to feed New York's voracious appetite for beef. Martin Loughman had risen in a rough-and-tumble immigrant world, and his personality and approach reflected his background. Margaret had never known her mother. Family sources asserted that the child had been born in the city on June 29, 1844. It appears more likely that she entered the world on or just before May 21, 1845, the day her mother died. Margaret preferred that no one know her birthday, an anniversary she did not celebrate.[39]

Margaret's childhood has stayed wrapped in mystery. It is known that an older brother named Simon, born in 1842, shared a close rapport. Also, she received her education primarily at New York City's Academy of the Sacred Heart. Dates of attendance must be estimated. Her father's financial situation likely precluded Margaret's matriculation before 1855, and records dating to that June do not mention her. Given the relative sophistication she later evidenced, a date within one or two years after June 1855 seems likely. The school operated west of Harlem at Manhattanville near the Hudson River. In the 1850s, the community comprised "one of the most flourishing localities, in a Catholic point of view, that can be found in the United States." The Society of the Sacred Heart had established the school. "The Ladies of the Sacred Heart are a French order," one account explained. "The mother house is in Paris." A French perspective understandably suffused the atmosphere. "We took every care to perfect our children in correctness of language and distinction of manner," an administrator observed. "And they were expected to be able to carry on a sensible conversation or to write a letter worth reading." A school historian added: "Students at the Academy were taught in French for half of the day. Courses in philosophy were the cornerstone of the Academy curriculum. Students also completed coursework in sciences, mathematics, literature, and musical performance."[40]

When Margaret graduated from the Academy in 1862 or thereabouts, her family had recently experienced tumultuous times. Her father had remarried in 1859, to Mary Jennings. They had a son in May 1860, whom they named Martin Francis Loughman. Shortly after Martin's first birthday, his mother died of causes that may have been associated with another pregnancy. The Civil War was on by then, and Ohio cattle operations increasingly occupied father Martin. Needing someone to care for his infant son, he married again in 1862, to twenty-two-year-old Pauline Coulon. Martin was senior to his new bride by about twenty-five years. The newlyweds with son Martin relocated to Ohio.[41]

Margaret and Simon meanwhile stayed in New York, and at some point after June 1863, she married. Like so many enigmas of her early life, the identity of her husband cannot be pinpointed with absolute certainty. Sources point, though, to George F. Birdsall, whose family resided in the same Lower Manhattan area where the Loughmans had also lived. Born in 1842 to Samuel and Susan Ann Birdsall, George by the early 1860s was clerking in the family grocery store at 299 Spring Street. Since the Birdsalls adhered to the Quaker faith and Margaret remained Roman Catholic for life, the young people must have eloped. Ill feelings resulted in both families, and the newlyweds lived apart from his parents at 71 Avenue C in the East Village. Unfortunately for Margaret, her husband's health deteriorated. On September 17, 1864, he died. She was left at age nineteen to fend for herself.[42]

Henry and Margaret perhaps first became acquainted soon afterward. A Plant biographer shared a rumor that, in light of Margaret's education and need for employment, may have contained elements of truth. "When he did return to Connecticut [from Europe in late 1864], he must have given serious thought to staying far longer than planned," Kelly Reynolds related. "For when he met the current housekeeper of the Branford home, Margaret Loughman, a young Irish woman, he formed a life-long attachment." Margaret could have served as companion to Henry's widowed mother, Betsey Hoadley, at New Haven. Her ability to converse easily and intelligently—coupled with a background in art, literature, and the workings of polite society—had prepared her well for such a position. Betsey certainly possessed the means to engage a young woman of Margaret's status. Possibly, the link that brought them together can be identified. Two sisters of Adams partner John Hoey, who had known Mrs. Hoadley since the early 1840s, became nuns. Sister Margaret Hoey, born in 1839, joined the faculty of the Academy of the Sacred Heart in the late 1850s. Known for a kindly interest in her students, Sister Margaret later served the Academy as mother superior. An attempt by her in 1864 to aid a widowed former pupil would have seemed completely in character.[43]

Little evidence suggests that Henry and Margaret, at ages forty-five and nineteen in 1864 and 1865, developed anything but a cordial relationship. John Hoey may not have forgotten the pretty young widow, however, so that—when he and W. B. Dinsmore grew concerned about Henry's state of mind seven years later—he thought of her. Margaret still lived close by, having returned to New York City about 1866 at roughly the time her father and his new family moved back as well. Margaret probably roomed with them until Martin briefly reestablished Ohio residence in 1868 or 1869. After that, she either boarded with other families or maintained her own apartment. Teaching music provided her some means for an independent life.[44]

Henry did not fall head over heels in love with Margaret during their 1872 Catskills sojourn, although he took interest enough to keep her in mind. He certainly did not rush things. His immediate reaction in fact was to repeat the previous year's pattern and absent himself from public sight through the rest of the year. Only vague references hint that he may have briefly visited South Carolina in October and, perhaps, lived for a time at Memphis's Overton Hotel that month or the next. Not until January 22, 1873, did he resume a customary business schedule. On that occasion he joined in Boston with Dinsmore, Hoey, Henry Sanford, Clapp Spooner, I. C. Babcock, and W. G. Fargo of Wells & Fargo's Express to discuss collaboration with Canadian officials. Plant then hosted the SRSC principals at Augusta in February before escorting SRSC president James Roosevelt and his wife, Rebecca Howland Roosevelt, to Mardi Gras. The party stopped by Memphis and the Overton Hotel on the way home.[45]

During the next two months Henry came to grips with his feelings for Margaret as well as his intentions toward her. By mid-April he was preparing for change. Collecting his mother and Henry Sanford, he journeyed to Memphis to rendezvous with son Morton and Mike O'Brien. There, he and Betsey enjoyed a performance of George Frideric Handel's *Esther* in which Morton sang as a chorus member. Henry also dissolved his Overton Hotel partnership preparatory to selling out. He arranged as well with Sanford for Morton's transfer to Adams Express in New York. O'Brien then escorted Plant and his mother to New Orleans and the St. Charles Hotel. By May 8 they had toured the sights and seen Betsey on board a steamer for the North. Henry returned home by rail, stopping in several places on express business. O'Brien stayed with him through Atlanta and to Augusta.[46]

Plant, Mrs. Hoadley, and O'Brien reunited eight weeks later at New York City's Episcopal Church of the Transfiguration. Known widely as the Little Church around the Corner, the picturesque sanctuary lay between Fifth and Madison Avenues at 1 East Twenty-Ninth Street. In its chapel on July 2, 1873, Henry wed Margaret Birdsall. The Right Reverend George H. Houghton performed the ceremony. Betsey looked on approvingly, offering a degree of substantiation to reports that Margaret had once served her as companion. The bride's father, Martin Loughman, attended, but his sentiments on the occasion are not known. Henry Sanford and Mike O'Brien signed as witnesses, while former congressman and governor Jim English delighted in his longtime friend's good fortune. A reception followed at friend Charles Delmonico's restaurant or, possibly, at the elegant townhouse Henry had purchased for Margaret at 586 Fifth Avenue (some sources specify 584 Fifth Avenue). The couple anticipated a European tour. Flush times were at hand. None could have known then how quickly they would end.[47]

8
The Panic
1873 to 1878

"the necessity of kissing the rod"

Newlyweds Henry and Margaret Plant anticipated a future virtually free of care. Henry at late middle age in early July 1873 had claimed a beautiful, young life partner at a time of good fortune and business success. Margaret, at last, could forever set aside anxieties about economic security and other worldly cares. They envisioned lives anchored amid plush surroundings set on the most fashionable residential street in the nation. Meanwhile, the couple enjoyed the good wishes of highly placed friends and looked to the future as monarchs of their own destinies. Sadly, success—however sweet—can skew perceptions of reality. As for every other man and woman, uncertainty lay ahead for the Plants even though confidence, wealth, and happiness buttressed them for trials to come. As it happened, their way forward soon faced scandal, endured family discord, and ended in a dear friend's suicide.

First, though, there were good times. The Plants organized their honeymoon as a grand European tour with Adams Express president William B. Dinsmore and his wife, Augusta. Plans called for a trans-Atlantic crossing on the steamship *Algeria*. On that point the generosity of magnate Thomas A. Scott, a power behind the Southern Railway Security Company (SRSC), with which Henry maintained intimately close ties, intervened. Scott's interests extended well beyond railroads. He had pressed the Pennsylvania Railroad, for instance, to create the American Steamship Company to furnish the world with luxurious transoceanic vessels reflecting state-of-the-art technology and design. This, Scott believed, would bolster passenger and freight business for the mother company. The first such ship to slip down the ways was the *Pennsylvania*. "There is great rejoicing in Philadelphia over the arrival there of the steamship Pennsylvania," a report advised on July 11.

"We have heretofore referred to this vessel as the solitary American steamship which crosses the Atlantic. It is but natural, therefore, that Philadelphia should be proud that she is the possessor of the craft, and perhaps her pride should be shared in by all Americans."[1]

Scott generously invited the newlyweds to enjoy their crossing on the *Pennsylvania*. He welcomed, as well, Henry's son, Morton, and mother, Betsey Hoadley. Subsequently, the unusual honeymoon party departed New York on July 23. The voyage proved a pleasant one. All told, the travelers were gone about three months, during which time Morton celebrated his twenty-second birthday and Henry his fifty-fourth. The itinerary commenced at Dublin, where, from the Shelbourne Hotel, Margaret reached out to explore her Irish heritage. A stopover at Harrogate—the beautiful English garden city near York—came next, allowing them to catch their breath before moving on to London in mid-August. There, the Plants and Mrs. Hoadley checked into the Midland Railway's brand-new Midland Grand Hotel near St. Pancras Station and eventually rendezvoused with the Dinsmores.[2]

Then, it was on to the Continent. Berlin hosted the party during September's first week. Dresden afforded relaxation during the second. Henry thereafter guided his family to more familiar locales. An international exposition was attracting widespread interest in Vienna that summer, and crowds of Americans flocked to the grounds to analyze its every aspect in anticipation of Philadelphia's planned Centennial Exposition in 1876. The Plants enjoyed the city's diversions toward midmonth. Paris came next, in late September or early October. The travelers lodged there at the elegant Grand Hotel de Londres. Located at 5 Rue Castiglione, the fashionable resort for Americans sat slightly more than one block across the Rue de Rivoli from the Tuileries Garden to the south and, beyond its elegant spaces, the Seine. The party's members reacted individually to what they discovered in the City of Light. Betsey, her proud Congregationalist spirit intact, found its attractions too, well, French and departed for London within a few days. Henry, Margaret, and Morton, though, delved energetically into Parisian sights and diversions for several weeks.[3]

Music naturally ranked highly as an object of interest. The Italian Opera's season commenced October 7. Marie Belval at age twenty and Louise Théo at nineteen drew "immense houses." However, eighteen-year-old Anna de Belloca, appearing as Rosina in *Il Barbiere*, counted as the season's sensation. "Not since the eventful night, twelve years ago, when Adelina Patti electrified the idle, careless, scattered *habitués*, who lounged into Covent Garden just to see 'a new girl from America' come out, have I been present at any such thoroughly hopeful *début*," one critic praised. "Mdlle. Belocca's success tonight has been, in one respect, even more remarkable; for, whereas Adelina

Patti had been accustomed to sing in public from the time that she could first toddle, the *débutante* of to-night has only been a very few months engaged in serious study, and has never before appeared on any stage." As for Madame Caux, reports suggested "that Adelina Patti is assuredly going to sing some time or other during the season." Worthy of note for Henry's future, the Théâtre de la Gaîté introduced a new chorine. Jeanne Granier by November had stepped into the spotlight as Louise Théo's understudy for Rose Michon in Offenbach's *La Jolie Parfumeuse*. "She is very young, very pretty, and has in her, we are inclined to believe, the making of a comédienne of the first order," one reviewer assured.[4]

Whatever delight the Plants drew from Paris, the mood of Americans then visiting the city darkened during their stay. The onset of financial troubles at home dampened spirits and suppressed enthusiasm for extravagant spending, a pastime at which Margaret soon excelled. "Mrs. H. B. Plant . . . is considered one of the handsomest brunettes of the Union," a reporter later commented. "Her costumes are rich, and in elegant taste." As the trip allowed twenty-eight-year-old Margaret her initial foray among the city's famed *couturiers* and *supermarchés*, the dismal economic developments lessened considerably her level of satisfaction. "The American ladies now in Paris are not much troubled about the political aspect [of the news], but they are in a great ferment over the financial news which reaches us from the United States. You see this is the most important moment of the year—to the estimation of ladies I mean," an onlooker observed. "They must prepare their toilettes for the fall and winter and must take cognizance now of what the busy brains of the men milliners have been concocting during the brief lecture afforded by the heated term. It is said that this summer, Worth, the great, the unrivaled, has surpassed himself, and the American ladies who are his most liberal patrons were in great glee and very busy when the news of [business] failures and suspension of payments at home burst over them like a tornado and made them dread that impending ruin would sadly interfere with the orders given or to be given the great dressmakers here." The onlooker concluded, "They know all about the best and the cheapest tradespeople in Paris, can state to a nicety the advantages offered by the [famed department stores] Bon Marche, the Petit St. Thomas, of the Grands Magasins du Louvre, but they have not had time to visit the galleries of the Luxembourg or the Musee of the Louvre, and have not even found leisure to visit Versailles."[5]

The financial troubles have come to be known as the Panic of 1873. An international tragedy reportedly ignited during spring in Germany and the Austro-Hungarian Empire, it evolved into one of the most severe economic depressions to strike the American economy. Some scholars have traced its

US origins to September 18, when New York bankers Jay Cooke & Company closed following the firm's failure to sell millions of dollars' worth of Northern Pacific Railroad bonds. "Within days, a financial panic engulfed the credit system," a historian explained. "Banks and brokerage houses failed, the stock market temporarily suspended operations, and factories began laying off workers. Throughout the western world, the Panic of 1873 ushered in what until the 1930s was known as the Great Depression, a downturn that lasted, with intermittent periods of recovery, nearly to the end of the century." Questionable financial issues associated with the railroad industry and companies such as the SRSC lay near the heart of the crisis: "In a way, it was fitting that the Northern Pacific's financial problems triggered the Panic, for if the railroad boom nourished postwar growth, the network's overexpansion, paid for by an outpouring of speculative credit, created a financial house of cards whose eventual collapse was only a matter of time. By 1876, over half the nation's railroads had defaulted on their bonds and were in the hands of receivers. And as track construction halted, the industries that had prospered from the railroad's growth suffered disastrous reverses."[6]

The financial calamity threatened Henry along with other magnates. His conduct demonstrated as much about October 21 when he abruptly and prematurely gathered his wife and son, sped to collect his mother in London, and rushed to Glasgow to meet the *Pennsylvania*. He either did not make it to the ship in time or else discovered suitable accommodations already booked. Plant instead secured passage on the slower British-owned *Georgia*, which steamed from Scotland on the twenty-fourth. Each day at sea witnessed further deterioration in the economy. When the vessel arrived at New York on November 7, the morning's newspapers and those of the next day brought chilling news and cautionary words. "The sermons in city churches to-morrow, as last Sunday, will, no doubt, if they are not preached altogether on the text of the panic and the hard times coming, administer a salutary warning by way of side issue thereupon," the *New York Tribune* admonished. "Resignation and the necessity of kissing the rod will be preached to Dives, who has lost millions, and Lazarus, who was working at a man's work last week, and this [week] is driven to his rich brother's gate for the crumbs that fall from his table. Something better than resignation, perhaps, awaits the New-York Dives who wakes this morning to find his money gone, but himself separated by no impossible gulf from his brothers. What that something is our reverend friends can tell to-morrow better than we."[7]

The cue for Plant's hurried European leave-taking probably originated with SRSC officials' attempts to gather company principals in emergency session. As they proceeded, a rattled James Roosevelt resigned as company president in favor of W. O. Hughart, who led the Pittsburgh and Connellsville Railroad. The emergency meeting—intended "to assess the full scope of the disaster"—subsequently convened in New York on November 21. "[Tom] Scott had made it clear that neither he nor the Pennsylvania Railroad would continue to participate in the syndicate," Albert Churella explained. "Absent the PRR's support, the remaining members had little choice other than to retrench. By the spring of 1874, the SRSC had either sold or else terminated the leases of many of its key assets." Desperate for cash, the SRSC quickly gave up the vital Atlanta and Richmond Air-Line to the Pennsylvania Railroad. As the slide continued, Plant joined those seeking to salvage viable prospects from the collapse. In March 1874 they reorganized the company under new president John B. Palmer, head of Central National Bank in Columbia, South Carolina. Vice president Henry B. Plant assisted him as the company's headquarters shifted to Columbia. "The Southern Railway Company is now emphatically a Southern institution," its publicity claimed. "The object of the organization [is] to secure the control of such Southern roads as might be essential to form through lines between the principal cities of the South and Baltimore and more northern cities, thus offering increased facilities for through freights and passengers, and at such rates as would tend to develop the sections traversed." At that point, the SRSC retained control of but 731 miles of road.[8]

Henry found himself dealing, as well, with problems at home stemming from Morton's years in Memphis. The young man, absent adult supervision, had circulated with a "fast crowd." While no one accused Morton of criminal behavior, a particularly ugly divorce case had dragged his name into the newspapers just as his father was preparing to marry. The New York litigation involved Elizabeth and Hugh L. Brinckley, who may or may not have been married during their Memphis stay. Perhaps fortunately, names far more prominent than Morton's also appeared. They included that of former Confederate general and Ku Klux Klan founder Nathan Bedford Forrest, who testified in early June. Morton appeared about the same time. "Her reputation," Forrest admitted of Mrs. Brinckley, "generally was bad." His information, it must be assumed, came firsthand. After a temporary adjournment, Henry ushered his son out of the country. This explained Morton's awkward presence on his father's honeymoon.[9]

Morton Plant's embarrassing plight presented in November an especially ticklish problem for Henry. More divorce-case hearings had been scheduled. Given the times and prevailing mores, that fact was bad enough in itself. Creating greater challenges, Margaret was yearning for high-society pleasures, or at least for the perquisites of a society wife. Arrayed against her were deeply ingrained prejudices against Roman Catholics, the shadowy circumstances of her first marriage and widowhood, and the rough reputation carried by her thrice-married Irish-born father. That Margaret's husband was almost twice her age paled by comparison as a subject of controversy. A family scandal coming as Henry was introducing her into Fifth Avenue circles could erect an insurmountable barrier. A curious thing then occurred. On November 10 the Brinckley hearing judge suddenly announced "that there was no marriage between them" and referred the matter to a jury "upon evidence embraced within a very limited compass." Morton, for the time being, had fortuitously dodged the proverbial bullet. To buttress his son's bruised reputation, Henry immediately set him to work at Adams Express headquarters. Six months later plaintiff Elizabeth Brinckley won her suit "on all the issues" after the judge brusquely informed jurors: "If your verdict is for the defendant, the plaintiff is sent away in disgrace, covered with infamy; if for the plaintiff, its effect[s] on the defendant are scarcely less disastrous. He is young, rich, and has brilliant prospects, and your verdict would be that a woman who can never be his wife shall hang like a millstone around his neck for the rest of his life." As it turned out, Morton should have heeded the judge's words carefully.[10]

Not all the news was bad. Henry yet controlled Southern Express, a dependable cash cow even in a poor economy. His biggest concerns there involved yellow fever and employee morale. Yellow jack spread through the South in fall 1873. Residents of Bainbridge, Pensacola, Montgomery, Louisville, New Orleans, Shreveport, and Corpus Christi particularly suffered. When Adams Express principals—the same men who stood behind Southern Express—convened late in the year, economics and disease headed their agenda. At Plant's urging and that of Adams executive Alfred Gaither, those present agreed to innovate. They backed the beginnings of a safety-net program for employees, starting with a mechanism for payment of death benefits. The initiative materialized in March with organization of the Expressmen's Mutual Benefit Association (EMBA), a collective often referred to as the Expressmen's Aid Society. Gaither emerged as president and Plant as vice president. Henry had apparently learned his lesson in the face of Tom Scott's autocratic behavior, and his continuing support for and pioneering efforts on behalf of employees earned him rarely seen levels of gratitude and loyalty. "One of the most earnest friends of this excellent institution [the EMBA] is its former president, Henry B. Plant, president of the Southern Express Co.," declared admittedly biased industry historian A. L. Stimson in 1881. "He believes that the fullest possible sympathy with all worthy employees, no matter what their position, is not only benevolent, but the best policy for the conservation and advancement of Express interests; and this, he thinks, is materially strengthened by the paternal feeling resulting from the mutual aid and benefit associations."[11]

Plant's financial position, while battered, thus allowed him to weather the Panic of 1873 storm better than many others. Reflecting that fact, Henry in April 1874 commissioned a bronze portrait bust for $150, an act that suggested a growing interest in collecting art in the manner of Dinsmore and John Hoey. The project's backstory traced to Henry's postwar efforts to reestablish Southern Express, including the telegraph system constructed earlier by Rufus Bullock. Young telegrapher Olin Levi Warner appeared in Augusta needing a job, and Plant obliged the Connecticut native and one-time resident of Bullock's New York hometown. Warner remained several years, saving toward the dream of studying art in Paris. He set out in 1869, remaining in France for three and a half years. "In the fall of 1872, he returned to New York and established a studio," a biographer explained. "[Unfortunately,] the art atmosphere of the New World was chilling to the man." Warner, desperate for income, reached out for help. "He made an application to Mr. Plant, president of the Southern Express company, for a position," the biographer related. "Plant heard his story and said it was a pity for him to give up art. But this was not all. He gave Warner a commission for a bust, which was very much to the purpose. The bust was so successful that Mr. Plant ordered one of his wife." Enabled by the contracts to endure as an artist, Warner in the late 1870s emerged as a recognized talent. By 1880, New York critics had heralded the arrival of artistic brilliance.[12]

However comfortable Plant remained in financial terms after 1874, he yet found himself ensnarled in prevailing economic doldrums that severely limited entrepreneurial initiatives that he might otherwise have pursued. The strictures curtailed his normally hectic travel schedule, leaving him considerable time in New York. It so happened that an elegant hotel had opened on Fifth Avenue in 1873. The mammoth Windsor arose on the avenue's east side, occupying the block between Forty-Sixth and Forty-Seventh Streets. Henry's townhouse sat cater-cornered across the avenue between Forty-Seventh and Forty-Eighth. The hotel quickly emerged as a fashionable place to meet and greet, including for Plant. "Its spacious lobbies were for a number of years the evening rendezvous of all the great financiers and railroad men," one report noted. "The Wall Street Club, it was commonly called, and the title had far more than a facetious significance. Occasionally it was, not inappropriately, spoken of as the 'Night Stock Exchange,' for every important Wall Street interest was represented in the unique nightly throngs." Plant encountered there many of the titans of industry and lions of commerce. William R. Vanderbilt and Henry's neighbor Jay Gould figured among them. Others whom he befriended or transacted business with included J. Pierpont Morgan, Collis P. Huntington, George M. Pullman,

11. Bronze bust of Henry Bradley Plant by Olin Levi Warner, 1874. Gift of the Henry Bradley Plant family. Metropolitan Museum of Art.

Andrew Carnegie, George Westinghouse, and Herman O. Armour. Adding interest, artists and performers mixed with the businessmen, some of them special favorites of Plant. "Adelina Patti's fondness for the Windsor was well-known," the report continued. "She always stopped there when in this city and occupied the same suite of rooms on the third floor looking out upon Forty-seventh Street."[13]

An April 1874 Windsor event, one that Plant may well have attended, deserves special mention. The occasion honored humorist Mark Twain (Samuel L. Clemens). "One of the events of my New York visit, was a dinner . . . with Mark Twain and the genial 'Dan' [Slote] of the *Innocents* [*Abroad*], whom everyone likes," an attendee recorded. "I almost forgot to eat, in my enjoyment of the conversation—what more could I say of its interest? The magnificence of the Windsor Hotel, which *we* honored by *our* presence, was a feast for the eyes as much as the dinner for the inner man, and words to describe the elegance of the furnishings at all adequately are hard to command and would sound so extravagant as to repel faith in them." Certain facts and circumstances notably lent the evening a fascinating topic of conversation. Twain had worked with Charles Dudley Warner on a recently published novel, a satire that dealt with materialism, greed, and political corruption. Twain and Warner called it *The Gilded Age: A Tale of To-day*. They thereby gifted the era with its name.[14]

Into 1875 Plant more or less patiently awaited improved business conditions, during which time his longtime friendship with James E. English commanded a good bit of attention. In October 1874 Caroline Fowler English, the wife of the former Connecticut congressman and governor, died. Three months later English moved into the Windsor, where he and Henry mapped out a southern trip. English left on the adventure in February with his son rather than with Plant. Henry had intended to meet his friend in New Orleans before March 24, 1875, but Southern Express business at Augusta detained him. Before he arrived in Louisiana, English had departed for Texas. Plant followed immediately in company with Southern Express superintendent Mike O'Brien and private secretary George H. Tilley. They expected W. B. Dinsmore to join them, but Adams Express affairs compelled his presence elsewhere.[15]

The friends came together at Galveston intent on mixing business and pleasure, aiming—among other things—to examine "the railroads of Texas" with an eye toward investment opportunities. Plant also consulted with Texas Express president A. B. Small. His company, in which Henry held a large stake, cooperated closely with Southern Express. First, though, came a relaxing cruise south as far as Matamoras, Mexico. Later, the men journeyed from Galveston to Austin and San Antonio, where they dined at the Alamo. Dallas followed, then Houston. "[They] have just made a tour of the State by rail, visiting all the principal towns and every section of the State," the *Houston Daily Age* reported. "These gentlemen express themselves enthusiastically in favor of Texas and its people. They regard it as great in all things and destined to be 'the' State of the Union. Its people they are delighted with and speak in eulogistic terms of the kindness, cordiality and hospitality they met with everywhere."[16]

With Texas and its potential for producing wealth in mind, Plant and English touched at Little Rock, Memphis, and Augusta before they parted company. Henry meanwhile pondered the trip's lessons as he tended in May to business at Cincinnati and Augusta. He continued the process into summer while he and Margaret enjoyed a fashionable getaway at the Ocean View Hotel on Block Island, an Atlantic retreat between the eastern tip of Long Island and Newport, Rhode Island. In August, they shifted to the lavish Grand Union Hotel at Saratoga Springs. One of the fabled Gilded Age resorts for the wealthy, Saratoga Springs and the hotel owed debts of gratitude to Jim English, "who helped to make the place the favorite resort of distinguished men from all parts of the United States." As his second wife, Anna Morris English, explained, "He had long experience of the Springs, visiting them year after year before the time of railroads, when the journey from Albany was made by stage-coach." She added: "Hundreds of men from all parts of the country will always remember the delightful 'rural breakfasts' which it was his custom to give at Saratoga, inviting twenty or thirty guests at a time. At these banquets nothing was spared which could give completeness to the entertainment, both in the way of menu and table appointments. But the impression best retained by all who enjoyed this hospitality is of the high spirits and animation of Governor English, who invariably showed special distinction as a host. The position seemed to give all his powers their freest play, and brought out almost unexpected elements of charm in his strong and individual character. He has been described on such occasions as 'the prince of good fellows.'" English's Saratoga Springs experiences offered an extremely useful model that Henry took well to heart, both as to resort development and how to behave as a resort host.[17]

In 1875 Plant's attention focused, though, on business opportunities in the midst of economic depression. Thoughts of Texas held center stage, and ideas began to gel by fall. His first project involved personal takeover of Texas Express and its closer integration with Southern Express. He convinced President Small to resign, citing for public consumption "[Small's] old malady, a disease of the bowels, contracted as he always believed in Mexico." At Galveston in late October Henry stepped into the presidency and designated Mike O'Brien superintendent, turning over to his trusted lieutenant operational control of Texas Express as well as Southern Express. Plant's interpersonal and business skills shone. He had removed a Texas company from seeming local control without ruffling feathers or stirring opposition. "In the names of Messrs. H. B. Plant, M. J. O'Brien and [cashier and auditor] C. L. Loup, we recognize the popular officers and successful managers of the Southern Express Company," a newspaperman observed. "While we part reluctantly with Col. Small we feel confident the management of the affairs of the Texas Express Company could not be placed in more able hands."[18]

The quiet coup revitalized Plant, propelling him to implement improvements at Southern Express, or at least upgrade its image in the eyes of the public and its employees. In December, for example, he transferred his New York offices from No. 59 Broadway to "a commodious suite of apartments" at 12 West Twenty-Third Street at the corner of Twenty-Third and Fifth Avenue near Madison Square. A February 11, 1876, ceremony finalized the move. "The offices are very elegantly furnished in black walnut," one report advised, "on the walls are hung choice engravings, and on the floor Axminster carpets that will warrant the use of snow shoes." New Yorkers knew the site as the Nathan Mansion. There, on July 29, 1870, assailants had brutally beaten banker Benjamin Nathan to death. Despite its reputation, the building offered significant advantages for Plant. For one thing, Adams Express offices there allowed for easy cooperation and communication. Not inconsequentially, the edifice also stood opposite the elegant Fifth Avenue Hotel across Twenty-Third Street. Where the Windsor drew businessmen, railroad executives, and financiers, the Fifth Avenue welcomed Republican power brokers in a continuous stream.[19]

Plant also took another step toward ensuring needed benefits for Southern Express employees. Where in 1874 he had aided creation of a mutual benefit association by which workers could secure death benefits, he now proposed that Southern Express directly make supplemental payments. "The Southern Express Company recognizing the benefits to its employees, and the advantages to be by them derived from a membership and support of the Expressman's Aid Society," Henry expressed, "proposes and agrees, in the event of death during the year 1875 [and the year 1876], of any of its members, who at the time of their death, were employees of the Southern Express Co., and not in the service of any other Express Co., to pay into the contribution fund, for the benefit of the families of such deceased members, in addition to what they may receive from said society by reason of their membership, a sum not exceeding $500 for each deceased member, and not exceeding $2,000 during the year." Plant's step, an insignificant one at first glance, takes on a somewhat different cast within the context of the times. The Panic of 1873 continued to suppress the economy and would do so for years. Unemployment dogged the workforce as many employers reduced labor costs by layoffs and wage reductions. Going against the grain, Plant kept his workers on the job and urged better conditions for them. The steps were small ones, but they set precedents, molded expectations, and could be expanded on in the future.[20]

Henry's prevailing sense of satisfaction received a further boost when Jim English returned from Europe in November. Having quickly touched bases in Connecticut, he checked into the Astor House near Plant's office at 59 Broadway bringing exciting news that the public learned on the twenty-seventh. "It seems that Governor [Charles Roberts] Ingersoll, of Connecticut, has appointed ex-Governor English to the place in the United States Senate made vacant by the death of Senator [Orris S.] Ferry," the *New York Herald* reported. The appointment ran for only six months, so English hurriedly prepared to assume senatorial duties. On December 4, though, he took rooms at the Windsor "on his way to Washington," affording the two friends renewed opportunity for a gleeful reunion. By the time English left the Senate in May 1876, some politicians were echoing his name as a potential Democratic presidential nominee.[21]

Henry's more demanding 1875 travel schedule, when combined with flurries of business activity, unfortunately meant that his surveillance of Morton's behavior—oversight that admittedly never posed a serious obstacle to the young man's inclinations—lapsed entirely and led to serious problems. Although living in his father's Fifth Avenue townhouse, Plant's son avidly pursued New York nightlife and enjoyed its temptations. In pursuit of pleasure he took cues from his cousin James de Trafford Blackstone. A Yale graduate four years Morton's senior, Traft was the son of Henry's childhood friend Lorenzo Blackstone, now a highly successful Norwich, Connecticut, manufacturer. Traft introduced Morton to the New York entertainment world, taking care not to overlook novice actresses impressed by wealthy young gentlemen. One of them, Sarah A. "Sadie" Whitaker, had arrived early in 1874. "[Sadie] was a charming conversationalist, and to this accomplishment added great personal beauty," a reporter recalled. "She was a blonde, with a remarkably clear skin and ruddy complexion. Her hair was her crowning glory, and hung in wavy abundance to her very ankles. She was neither robust nor slender, but her limbs were well molded and in perfect proportion with her figure of medium height." Sadie landed her first serious role in November, appearing in the obscure *Leffingwell on Hot Coals, or The Victim of Circumstances*.[22]

Morton and Traft shortly fell in love with the alluring Sadie, in which condition they by no means abided alone. As competition for Sadie's favors mounted, her acting and singing career escalated as well. By summer 1875, though, the heft of Blackstone's wealth outweighed the ardor pressed by Plant, and Sadie agreed to marry Traft. Devastated, Morton walked off his Adams Express job and onto a Liverpool steamer. The Blackstones eventually took vows in New York on September 1, two days prior to Morton's return. Fearful of his son's reaction, Henry hurried Morton to Block Island. Margaret went along for support, as did Henry's brother Horace Hoadley and his children. In their absence newly married Sadie debuted in her first starring role as "Libby dear" in *The Almighty Dollar*. Her performance received warm reviews. Afterward, the Blackstones relocated to Norwich, where in November 1876 they were blessed with a son, whom they named Lorenzo. Henry meanwhile had sought to stabilize Morton's life by arranging a return to Adams Express. Rather than assigning him to headquarters, however, company officials dispatched the truant to a new outpost at 636–

12. Bust of Mary Josephine Loughman Plant by Olin Levi Warner, 1874. Collection of Henry B. Plant Museum. Gift from Mt. Sinai St. Luke's Hospital, New York City, 2017.

38 Broadway. There, veteran expressman Asa S. Blake ruled with a tight fist. An ardent Episcopalian, Blake displayed little tolerance for the moral lapses of his men.[23]

The first ten months of 1876 then passed in an unremarkable fashion. Neither Henry's personal life nor his business engagements produced anywhere near the drama that the ongoing national contest to elect a new president was generating. During this period Plant spent close to two months in the South (February to April) looking after Southern and Texas Express interests and the SRSC's still-crumbling fortunes. He returned there briefly in June. Henry then remained a good part of the summer in New York City overseeing Southern Express from afar as Mike O'Brien toured Europe. He and Margaret enjoyed several vacations. In July they stayed at Long Branch, New Jersey, a coastal resort promoted by John Hoey and made fashionable by President Grant. August saw them at Saratoga Springs and the Grand Union Hotel. As the leaves changed color and the weather began to chill in October, Plant joined Henry Sanford on a rail excursion to Texas. They stopped in Chicago along the way to collect several other men of large means potentially interested in Lone Star investments. "The visit of H. B. Plant, President of the Southern Express, in company with other capitalists to Denison and Fort Worth and what they said about the immediate extension of the Red River and Rio Grande railway to Fort Worth and Austin, excited much interest in Denison, Sherman and Fort Worth," an Austin newspaperman related. The excitement proved premature, it turned out, and no investments resulted.[24]

As autumn evolved toward winter, the status quo abruptly shifted toward crisis. Plant watched from New York as yellow fever hit Charleston, Savannah, Brunswick, and Jacksonville. At least three expressmen died. Other residents of afflicted areas whom Henry had known for years succumbed as well. Plant refunded medical costs and paid burial expenses, but the actions little eased the loss. Violence meanwhile joined disease in wreaking injury and death. Politically related turmoil simmered, bubbled, and then boiled over through the southern region. The election on November 7 produced no clear winner in the presidential contest between Democrat Samuel J. Tilden and Republican Rutherford B. Hayes. The nation's fate hung in the balance with no path toward resolution evident to most Americans. As the national calamity intensified, Plant's financial position endured a further blow when the SRSC put its remaining assets up for sale. The shareholders agreed to take whatever price the properties, bonds, and shares could bring.[25]

Distracted by Texas investment schemes, yellow fever deaths, national calamity, and financial loss, Plant failed to note that Morton had resumed rakish habits. Before long, all New York learned ugly truths. "On the night of Dec. 8, Morton F. Plant, of No. 58[6] Fifth avenue, while under the influence of liquor, accompanied a woman named Nellie Osborne to a liquor store at the corner of Mercer and Prince streets," a report detailed. "Here Plant was robbed of his gold watch, locket, and scarf-pin by the bartender, Edward McLean, aided by Frederick S. Browne, alias Osborne, the woman's husband. Mr. Plant reported his loss at the Fifteenth Precinct Station-house, and Detective Edward Slevin, who was detailed by Capt. Byrne to work up the case, arrested Browne and the woman Osborne, McLean having fled."[26]

Understandably, complex tensions filled the Plant home in the New Year. They radiated from the father-and-son relationship and produced strains between stepmother and stepson as well as husband and wife. Given that Margaret was a family newcomer and Morton's senior by a mere six years, her place in affairs left her awkwardly positioned and ill equipped to act. Henry's business affairs only complicated matters. He had suffered public embarrassment and financial loss with the Southern Railway Securities collapse. He endured further ignominy through surprising criminal accusations, although the accusers' motives were admittedly political. The scandal grew out of the Western and Atlantic Railroad lease when Democratic investigators in Georgia alleged early in 1876 that bribery had corrupted the lease process. An Augusta newspaper had blared: "The Crooked Papers: The Bribery Charges against the State Road Lessees." When Plant visited Atlanta in mid-December, echoes of the charges rekindled anger and resentment in the wake of yellow fever deaths and his son's misconduct.[27]

An incident arose meanwhile out of Henry's Southern Express stewardship that showed the emotional and judgmental toll that internal tensions had begun to take by early 1877. A December 6, 1876, Florida event set the stage. When electors gathered at Tallahassee to cast electoral college ballots, Pensacola Southern Express agent Frederick C. Humphreys appeared to vote for Republican Rutherford B. Hayes. He did so despite the denial by superintendent Mike O'Brien, a Democrat and one-time Confederate officer, of a leave of absence. O'Brien subsequently suspended Humphreys. Sensitive not to offend Republican officialdom, Plant ordered Humphreys reinstated. What a difference three months then made in Plant's attitudes. Hayes eventually won—by the margin of Humphreys' vote—and took office March 4, 1877. Days later the hammer came down on the Pensacola agent. "A few days ago . . . he received a letter from Mr. Plant saying that a report had reached him that he (Mr. Humphreys) was very unpopular on account of his having been a Republican elector, and that the business of the company was suffering in consequence, and intimating that he would be glad to receive his resignation, it not being the policy of the company to keep men in its employ who are not in political sympathy with the people where the office is located," a report asserted. Plant's temerity infuriated Republicans, sentiments that Humphreys fanned in Washington. "He and his friends claim a Federal office in Florida, as vengeance for the 'political ostracism' which has banished him from the state," another man observed. Hayes obliged the expressman, making him collector of customs at Pensacola.[28]

Plant addressed the surrounding controversy as time-honored practice foretold. He essentially disappeared and did not again surface to public attention until midsummer. Mike O'Brien insisted that his president was ill "at home" in New York, and possibly this was so. On the other hand, he repeatedly feigned ailments in future years to mask trips that he quietly took during stressful times. The truth eludes discovery, although one bit of information vaguely hints that stress may well have made him sick. In mid-July, Henry and Margaret moved into Howland's Hotel at Long Branch, where they remained for a month or more. On August 19, the day after his twenty-sixth birthday, Morton arrived. He stayed, however, at the West End Hotel. The separation from his father foreshadowed persistent rancor and strained encounters. If Henry feared death or disability or had been otherwise sobered by illness to attempt a reconciliation, a reunion under such circumstances could be understood.[29]

A mentor's death ultimately pulled Henry back to public notice. Alvin Adams, the express industry pioneer who had launched the careers of Dinsmore, Hoey, Plant, and many others, died at Watertown, Massachusetts, on September 1, 1877. "Several hundred of the intimate friends of the deceased" attended services at Adams's Watertown home on the fifth. An outpouring of emotion marked the occasion as "old friends and former associates passed in and out, bestowing a farewell look upon his once familiar features." Many attendees followed the casket to the cemetery. "The funeral cortege was long," the *Boston Journal* observed. "First came the pall bearers—William B. Dinsmore, President of the Adams Express Company, E. S. Sanford, Vice President, Col. J. B. Thompson of Springfield, Secretary, ex-Governor James E. English of Connecticut, S. M. Shoemaker, John Hoey, Alfred Gaither, Henry Sanford and Clapp Spooner, managers of the Adams Express Co., and H. B. Plant, President of the Southern Express Company."[30]

The next month Plant turned fifty-eight years of age and resumed a business schedule. This time, he took Morton with him to spots such as Wilmington, Charleston, and Atlanta. Toward year's end, Henry commenced instructing his son on running a major enterprise. The optimistic tone carried through Christmas. He and Margaret had agreed to lend a new gallery Olin Warner's marble bust of her. "Messrs. Cottier & Co., in answer to numerous inquiries, beg to state that their second collection of exquisite chef d'oeuvres by the great modern masters will be on sight immediately after the holidays are over," the gallery advertised. The opening proved a solid success, with the bust drawing considerable attention. "I remember vividly the first piece of Warner's sculpture I ever saw," journalist William Crary Brownell recalled. "It was the bust of a lady shown at the opening of Cottier & Co.'s rooms in Fifth Avenue, seventeen or eighteen years ago. 'Just pass your hand over that back,' said Mr. [Daniel] Cottier to me. 'Did ye ever feel such modeling?' Certainly I never had. Cottier, who 'understood himself' remarkably in such matters, had indicated in his quaint way Warner's most obvious distinction. So far as technical expression is concerned, and in comparison with other sculptors—with all other American sculptors—the chief idiosyncrasy of his endowment is his modeling, pure and simple."[31]

The showing may well have pleased the Plants, but other developments did not. By the time the gallery welcomed invitees, Sadie Whitaker Blackstone had returned to their lives, dragging more scandal in her wake. As her pregnancy had matured, she and Traft bickered. Father Lorenzo sought to reconcile the couple, but matters grew worse. "There was no change in his conduct for the better," a later account detailed. "At times he remained away the greater part of the night, returning home only to beat and kick her. Not satisfied with this systematic cruelty, he bit her on the arms and turned her from the house, leaving her exposed to the cold and wet in the darkness." On January 1, 1878, Sadie fled with her child to refuge with Morton: "On New

Year's Day she visited this city and [was] received at the residence of her husband's uncle, Mr. H. B. Plant, President of the Southern Express Company, at his dwelling, no. 58[6] Fifth avenue." In Morton's absence, Henry and Margaret settled the young woman and counseled her to reconcile. "On the evening of her return to her husband at Norwich," the account continued, "he mistreated her so badly that her hip was permanently injured." Sadie again fled, this time to family in Massachusetts. Soon, she sued for divorce on grounds of cruelty.[32]

Barely had the hubbub of Sadie's visitation subsided than even more tragic news came to 586 Fifth Avenue. Henry's close friend John Morton Freeman had struggled for years with the early death, possibly suicide, of his wife, Emily Blackstone Freeman. He continued meanwhile to live in New York with his father-in-law, Wyllis Blackstone, who helped raise his three daughters. On Thursday morning, January 17, 1878—the seventh anniversary of Emily's demise—Morton Freeman died suddenly, arguably by his own hand, at fifty-five years of age. As had been the case with his wife and her cousin Ellen Blackstone Plant, circumstances of the death were held strictly confidential. Surviving accounts do not disclose Plant's reaction save for his avoidance of public appearances, with minimal exceptions, until late April. Henry left no eulogy or other comment to describe whatever pain he endured.[33]

9

Florida and the Pearl of the Antilles

1878 to 1882

"the cry of 'hard times' has for once been unheard"

"The modern Florida as a winter resort was largely developed by the late Henry B. Plant and Henry M. Flagler," the *New York Tribune* observed at the nineteenth century's end. "The two were great friends, and their rivalry, as a consequence, was always of the friendliest sort. To Flagler fell the east coast, with Miami as his southernmost point, from which a line of steamers ran to Cuba. Plant's southern terminus was Tampa, from which a similar line ran to Havana." In 1878, though, Miami existed mostly as a dot on a map, still called Fort Dallas by many. "People compared the Miami of those days to the Wild West," T. D. Allman reported. "In fact that understated its remoteness. By then the transcontinental railroads had brought the wilds of Wyoming within easy access of civilization. The mouth of the Miami River, in comparison, might have been the dark side of the moon." The same year a virtually abandoned Fort Brooke occupied much of Tampa, leaving plenty of room for its 722 residents. A local historian captured prevailing conditions with the words "When Tampa Slipped Backward." Cross-peninsular travel from Jacksonville and St. Augustine meant surviving an ordeal. "From Tampa to the St. Johns river is about 110 miles," one man explained that May. "I have met with visitors here who expect on going out into primeval country, away from the towns, to find beautiful houses, gardens, lawns and fruit orchards; to sit down to a table loaded with the choicest of viands, etc., and they seem disappointed to find the frontier house[, the] log hut, in all of its primeval nature, and to have to take epi-gastric exercise on pork and hominy." He added: "It is primeval country, and needs that development which has so quickly peopled the West, railroads, immigration, energy and capital."[1]

To claim that Florida received desperately needed railroads, immigration, energy, and capital because Henry Plant faced problems at home and needed a healthy release for his energies constitutes a gross exaggeration, but not a totally groundless one. In 1873 he had remarried to a bride half his age, expecting a satisfying—if not delightful—life anchored on New York City's elegant Fifth Avenue. His twenty-two-year-old son had also moved into Henry's new residence, perhaps with hopes of finding at last a comfortable family home. As it turned out, however, Morton pursued Gilded Age good life and a bon vivant's diversions. Particularly, he had fallen for actress Sadie Whitaker only to see his beloved snatched away by his cousin James de Trafford Blackstone. Periods of dissolution and unwelcome notoriety followed, leading in turn to unresolved tensions within the Plant home. Ultimately, the head of the house found himself floundering, whether from illness or a world spun out of control.

Morton Plant and Sadie Whitaker Blackstone's saga, unfortunately for Henry, had by no means ended with her surprise 1878 New Year's visit to the Plant home. Sadie pressed a highly publicized divorce against Traft on grounds of cruelty. She received her decree in June. Meanwhile, Morton dallied with the fetching "Miss M. Agnew," a budding actress. That he and his father had grown estranged showed itself when, in July, Morton escorted Miss Agnew to Branford, his father's conservative hometown. Within days Sadie had ingratiated herself with blond, blue-eyed cotton broker Samuel Sondheim during a vacation at the West End Hotel in Long Branch, New Jersey. Sadie married Sondheim sixteen months later, but not before kidnapping her son from Traft's custody in October 1878. Traft, father Lorenzo Blackstone, uncle Timothy B. Blackstone, and Plant were then enjoying a rail excursion to San Francisco. Traft and Lorenzo hurried back East but failed to recover his son until Sadie married Sondheim.[2]

Morton was not to be outdone in such antics. If Sadie defied Traft and cavorted with Sondheim, then young Plant would counter with marriage. When and where he met Ida Josephine Parsons is not known. Four years younger than Morton, she came from a respected Northampton, Massachusetts, family. Henry approved highly of Miss Parsons and endorsed the match. He and Margaret joined friends and family on May 5, 1879, to celebrate the nuptials in "the most notable society event that Northampton has enjoyed for many a day." A "very large" number of guests flocked to the First Congregational Church. Among them were ex-Governor and Mrs. Rufus Bullock, Southern Express superintendent Mike O'Brien, and Southern Express secretary and Mrs. George H. Tilley. From Adams Express came John Hoey, Sam Shoemaker, and their wives as well as James Shuter. "As the bride and groom left the house," a report detailed, "rice and the slipper were thrown after them, and the band escorted them to the depot, pleasing all with their music."[3]

The music, sadly, did not play on. Following a southern honeymoon tour, the couple settled in New York City. Before long Morton's behavior began echoing Traft's. Scandal resurfaced as the press revealed incidents of drinking, cavorting, and otherwise irresponsible behavior. Even the New York State Militia had enough. "Private Morton F. Plant having been expelled by Company C [Seventh Regiment] for neglect of duty, the action of said company is hereby confirmed," a notice advised in April 1880. Sometime between June and September that year, Ida left him. Morton quit his job and moved to Branford. He frolicked in September and again the following spring with New Haven's young Jennie Cramer, the dalliance coming to light following her murder in August 1881. He then spent the Christmas season and New Year's 1881 on a Hawaiian excursion. Having quietly obtained a speedy annulment or divorce, Ida remarried on August 17, 1881, to the son of a former Massachusetts lieutenant governor. Sadly, she died from childbirth complications on July 13, 1882.[4]

As this barrage of events played out from 1878 until 1882, Henry tried to cope as best he could with the ups and downs at home. As he did, tensions evident in previous years magnified with the days and months. Where the Plants earlier had traveled together often, they did so less and less as time progressed. They vacationed at Long Branch in summer 1878, for instance, but he then joined Henry Sanford without her at Cape May. They visited Savannah and Jacksonville in spring 1879 but only after Henry passed most of the month after Morton's wedding alone on a Bermuda jaunt. Then, in July he checked into a Brighton Beach resort without her. Records for 1880 omit any mention of them traveling together. Margaret had likely grown depressed. For one thing, if she and Henry had tried to have children, the effort had not succeeded. For another, she dealt with personal tragedies within the already problematic Loughman family. Her eighteen-year-old half-brother, Martin Francis Loughman, died on July 26, 1878. Sixteen months later, her youngest sibling—six-year-old Freddie Loughman—also succumbed. When these afflictions piled on top of Morton's embarrassments, the going for Margaret became very hard indeed.[5]

Henry meanwhile added disease to his cares. He did not so much fall ill as agonize over the consequences of pestilence borne by others. In 1878 and again in 1879 yellow fever afflicted large portions of the South, particularly Tennessee and the Mississippi Valley. Dozens of Southern Express employees died. Plant reached out to ensure that company benefits aided the families. Otherwise, he directed what he considered humane policy. Henry recalled in July 1879, to cite an example, "the fatal experience of last year, when the lives of twenty-eight heroic employees were lost in endeavors to maintain the express service intact, throughout the southwest, during the prevalence of yellow fever." He added: "It is to be hoped the fever will not spread, but should it do so and become epidemic, this company, for the safety of its employees, and the protection of the public health (by lessening the danger of contagion incident to intercourse with infected localities), will not undertake to operate its lines beyond the limits prescribed by quarantine regulations." The fever unfortunately attained epidemic proportions. Plant's gestures were not soon forgotten. "In those dark and unhappy days . . . many of you recall that, most of the banks being closed and business being entirely suspended, the Southern Express Company afforded about the only means of bringing into the city [of Memphis] the donations of money and supplies which came in unlimited quantities from every part of our broad land," a townsman testified. "And I may say that never a dollar was added to the treasury of the Southern Express Company for any such matter, addressed in those days to the Howard and other charitable associations at Memphis. It was all carried free."[6]

Plant regularly sought time away from his cares in the Windsor Hotel's public rooms. Unexpected benefits flowed as a result. In late 1877 or early 1878, to cite just one example, oil executive Henry Morrison Flagler began staying at the Windsor while he made initial arrangements to move his family from Cleveland to New York City. Aged forty-eight and an upstate New York native, Flagler had earned a large fortune in partnership with John D. Rockefeller at the Standard Oil Company. A lover of art, music, and other aspects of New York's cultural and social scenes, he looked forward to enjoying life at a Fifth Avenue home not far from Plant's own. Flagler's life was troubled, however. He feared for his wife, Mary Harkness Flagler, who suffered from tuberculosis. In late February 1878 he and Mary traveled to Jacksonville, Florida, for a rest cure. The two Henrys afterward found themselves well positioned to share insights and questions about Florida, its development, and its future prospects.[7]

Notably, Plant helped encourage the Flaglers to visit Florida and helped them plan and time their trip; moreover, he welcomed them to Savannah and spent time with them at Jacksonville. The story arose from a December 1877 visit to New York by Rufus Bullock, who also roomed at the Windsor. Bullock seemingly introduced Henry to high-powered Savannah attorney Walter Scott Chisholm. The one-time judge intimately knew the inside workings of Georgia's major business enterprises. He especially boasted influence with the Atlantic and Gulf Railroad, a line that tied Savannah with southern Georgia's rich agricultural regions and provided the sole existing rail connection from Georgia to East Florida. Chisholm wanted control of the line, and Plant owned a significant portion of its securities. The lawyer offered to buy out Henry's position. "Yes," Plant recalled telling him. "I will sell them to you. But if you do not accomplish what you wish, you can sell the whole of the property to me, I will take it."[8]

When he first talked with Chisholm, Henry's Florida views were in flux. His interest in the state had waned after 1860 because of hostilities to northerners that he and William B. Dinsmore had faced at St. Augustine. Plant's sights had shifted to Cuba and its cosmopolitan capital at Havana. The Ten Years' War that commenced on the island in 1868 unfortunately led to instability that forestalled initiatives there. Insofar as investment opportunities were concerned, the years after his 1875 Texas visit had seen him looking toward a Lone Star horizon. However, a highly influential member of Fifth Avenue society well known to Plant had become very interested in Florida. Whether in conversations at the Windsor or elegant gatherings of the famed "Four Hundred"—the New York social elite defined in size by the limits of his wife's ballroom—William Backhouse Astor Jr. proclaimed his intention to stir Florida from its prevailing stupor. As Plant and Chisholm argued the Atlantic and Gulf Railroad's future, Astor was confronting yellow fever fears to push his yacht *Ambassadress* up the St. Johns River to a Jacksonville wharf. In the next few months the millionaire spent $150,000 there on town improvements. They included a headquarters for the Florida Yacht Club, which he had founded and headed as commodore, and a four-story office building downtown. To Astor, the projects represented only a beginning. "Mr. William Astor, of New York," a correspondent emphasized, "is a Florida enthusiast."[9]

Henry found himself more open to changes in perspective than he had realized. As he dealt in January 1878 with fallout from Sadie Blackstone's flight from her husband, Morton's continuing problems, John Morton Freeman's death, and troubles at home, affairs in Savannah and Jacksonville piqued his curiosity. Coincidentally, business necessities required a Southern Express inspection tour with superintendent Mike O'Brien. Two significant gatherings caught Plant's attention, as well. The General Ticket and Passenger Agents Convention was slated for Jacksonville March 8 through 13, while the Expressmen's Aid Society planned to gather at New Orleans in April. Naturally, Henry had kept in touch with Sadie's father-in-law, Lorenzo Blackstone. The friends agreed that a Florida vacation might be just the balm needed to salve recent wounds. Flagler, of course, intended the same for his family. Plant left New York during February's first week without Margaret. His business at Nashville and Augusta concluded, he arrived at Savannah with O'Brien and Dinsmore about the twenty-fifth. Lorenzo and Emily Blackstone, with daughter Ella, joined the party three days later. The

13. Henry Morrison Flagler. 1870. Black and white photo print, 10 × 8 in. State Archives of Florida, Florida Memory.

Flaglers' private car rolled into the city about the same time. All parties, presumably together, thereupon set out for Jacksonville.[10]

From Plant's Savannah reappearance with Dinsmore on March 11 until he checked into a New Orleans hotel in mid-April, his whereabouts remain uncertain. Behavior patterns suggest that he quietly took a trip; the key to understanding where he went lies with the conclusion of the Ten Years' War in Cuba. "The Pearl of the Antilles," a headline trumpeted, "Peace Proclaimed in the Ever Faithful Isle." Although Henry was aiming to buy a railroad with connections to Florida, his object was establishment of transportation links to Havana. Checking out island conditions for himself seemed the logical next step. The means to make the visit were at hand in Savannah, where, on March 14, the steamer *San Jacinto* departed for the Cuban capital with stops at St. Augustine and Nassau. The trip led to a most fortuitous happenstance. Postmaster General David M. Key, a Chattanooga man whom Henry had known since the 1850s, planned to visit Cuba to assess southern postal needs and quality of service. The opportunity for the Southern Express president to entertain the postmaster general and identify what, if any, financial support he could expect for carrying mail on steamers between Cedar Key (its name changed from Cedar Keys about January 1878) and Havana stood out irresistibly. Key arrived in Cuba on April 11. He stayed two days before his party departed on the steamer *Emily B. Souder*. With stops at Key West and Cedar Key, that vessel steamed into New Orleans on April 19. The same day, Plant called for rooms at the St. Charles Hotel.[11]

Henry had remained apart from Margaret for three months when he ultimately arrived in New York during early May. On the twenty-first he traveled on his own to Branford for a family marriage. While in town, Plant began buying land for a bucolic haven. Then, given the approach of Sadie's divorce hearing, he dropped from sight until late July. Apparently, he traveled alone under an alias to London and Paris. The French that summer were holding a world's fair in answer to Philadelphia's 1876 Centennial Exposition, and it drew Americans such as Plant in large numbers. On June 1 alone, 522 "saloon passengers" left New York for Europe. William B. Astor, John Jacob Astor, and their families were among them. Henry's lawyer Clarence Seward also joined the eager throng. Paris, as usual, showed itself to good advantage. The Palais du Trocadéro, above the Seine on the hill of Chaillot, shone as the extravaganza's centerpiece.[12]

Henry's intentions differed from the typical affluent traveler's that season. The trip's focus, as far as he was concerned, centered on the stage, music, and leading ladies. Adelina Patti was singing at London's Theatre Royal, Covent Garden, in Meyerbeer's comic opera *L'Étoile du Nord*. One critic insisted that "the house was the most crowded, aristocratic, and brilliant of the season, and the performance one long triumph for the popular songstress, whose voice was in perfect order, and who was received with enthusiastic greetings." Another argued, though, that time and marital issues were taking their toll. "Patti is beginning to suffer, and has aged visibly during the past year," he wrote. "She is thin, and nervous; her splendid hair is turning gray, and going. At Covent Garden the *diva*, whose doors used to be heaped with flowers, got two miserable little bouquets and only one recall."[13]

In Paris, the opera drew Plant as well. Many of his favorites were performing, including Hortense Schneider, whom he had loved in *La Grande-Duchesse de Gérolstein* a decade earlier. Young Jeanne Granier, though, captured most hearts and suitors that summer, emerging as a "star of La Renaissance" theater. "Mlle. Jeanne Granier occupies in the world of operetta here somewhat the position of Miss [Emma] Abbott in the opera world of New York," a source explained. "She is a model girl. All her schoolmistresses and old boarding-school mates take the same deep interest in her success in all the parts she plays that the members of Dr. [Edwin Hubbell] Chapin's church feel in Miss Abbott. Moreover, she is Hippocrates in petticoats. The Artaxerxes who can get her to accept his presents has not yet seemed to be in the land of the living. The most beautiful lace can't attract 'Yes' to her lips. The most brilliant diamonds can win only 'No' from her." The man added: "She attracted more [admirers] than ever to the new operetta 'Le Petit Duc,' which she is playing, by appearing, for the first time wearing the breeches. She is irresistible in them."[14]

The year's final months passed agreeably for Henry in that he avoided major unpleasantries. Long Branch and Cape May vacations elapsed before, in October, he joined the already mentioned western rail excursion with Lorenzo, Timothy, and Traft Blackstone. Adams Express's Henry Sanford accompanied them. Mostly, Henry awaited resolution of the Atlantic and Gulf ownership question. In early 1879 the US Supreme Court delivered the road a major blow by ordering it to pay Georgia back taxes. Henry learned of the decision at Savannah. He returned there in March, with Margaret. The state's attorney general thereupon ruled that since the line could not pay the $74,000 it owed, it must "be offered for sale at public outcry about the first of July." A journalist noted, "The report is already rife that [Plant's associate] Mr. [Morris K.] Jesup and a New York Company are prepared to make the purchase and expect to get it at a bargain." The courts in June set the sale date for November 4 at Savannah. Plant's agents, with W. S. Chisholm, combed markets to grab the road's securities, especially its second mortgage bonds, so as to simplify the purchase path. As they moved ahead, Henry attended his son's marriage, visited Bermuda, vacationed at Brighton Beach, arranged financing, secured partners, and otherwise bided his time.[15]

Having done so, Plant in November 1879 celebrated the twenty-fifth anniversary of his 1854 move to Georgia by launching himself full scale into the railroad business. He arrived in Savannah on the third primed for the auction. At noon the next day the chief deputy US marshal in announcing the sale underscored that it would be subject to outstanding mortgages. "There could not have been less than six hundred persons around the custom house," a reporter observed. "In fact, attendance was larger than has ever been seen at a public sale in this city." Bids commenced at $50,000. At five times that amount only Plant and one other bidder remained. When Henry called $300,000, attorneys for creditors insisted that cash must be paid, prompting the marshal to suspend proceedings briefly. Only Plant came forward when bidding resumed, and the marshal gaveled the sale in his favor. Within one hour he had paid over $300,000 in cash. The poor lad from Branford had bought a railroad.[16]

Plant intended to assume control of his new line immediately, but legal niceties required attention. On November 19 the US Circuit Court finally directed that company organization could proceed. The shareholders rebranded their new concern as the Savannah, Florida and Western Railway Company (SF&W). Officers included Plant as president, Chisholm as vice president, and Tilley as secretary. Longtime general manager Henry Stephen

Haines assumed the position of general superintendent. A seven-member board of directors included Plant, Chisholm, Tilley, and four others. More legalities followed when the line's receivers balked at compliance. As a judge pondered the matter, Plant passed time riding the line to Thomasville and Albany, Georgia, and with a quick business trip to New Orleans. He had returned to Savannah by December 8, when the court ordered the receivers to immediately turn over "all the rights, franchises, and properties of said road." Plant obtained actual possession on the ninth and at once handed operational authority to Haines. "Mr. Plant will remain here until everything is satisfactorily adjusted, and will then return to New York, accompanied by Mr. George H. Tilley, the Secretary, where he will reside, but will come here again in February, and possibly divide his time between Savannah and Florida until the general meeting of the company in March," the *Savannah Morning News* related. Plant and Tilley celebrated with a leisurely cruise. They arrived at New York on the fifteenth.[17]

Henry's entrepreneurial forays had only just begun. Days after reaching New York he signaled the range of his newfound ambitions by aiding organization of the Southern Bell Telephone and Telegraph Company. Fellow shareholders named him a director. The Richmond-based enterprise aimed "to open telephone exchanges in all towns and cities where the population is large enough to support an exchange." Its agents reached Georgia within one month and introduced phones at Jacksonville in March. "Jacksonville has been talking to Lake City and Savannah," a source excitedly advised in mid-April, "through the medium of the telephone."[18]

Although the full breadth of his vision took years to mature, Plant had manifestly joined William Astor by December 1879 as "a Florida enthusiast." This fact appeared plainly at Christmastime when the SF&W "purchased a controlling interest in the steamboat line running on the Chattahoochee river from Apalachicola to Columbus and other points, connecting to Bainbridge." Three "excellent passenger and freight boats" came with the arrangement, affording the road a second gateway into Florida and access to fertile Panhandle cotton lands. "They will run hereafter in the interest of the Savannah, Florida and Western Railway, making close connection with the trains of that company at Bainbridge," a newspaper noted. "This movement will be of great benefit to the Railroad Company." A January letter brought word of even more developments. "Mr. H. B. Plant . . . has commenced arrangements to build a road from his road at Waycross direct to Jacksonville, which will obviate the necessity of the tedious roundabout trip up and down the elbow that is the terror of invalid passengers to Florida," it read. "This road will be finished as soon as possible, and will be a commanding line to Florida."[19]

Henry's connection to steamboats was soon elevated in the public mind, although not as a result of his own actions. On February 10, 1880, the steamer *H. B. Plant* slipped down the ways of a Delaware shipyard. Running 145 feet in length with a 24-foot beam, it drew 7 feet of water. "Her engines are of the most improved make and are below deck on an iron frame, and she has patent revolving wheels and patent balance rudder," a description detailed. "She has finely fitted up upper and lower saloons, with all modern conveniences, and plenty of open deck room, and was constructed under the personal supervision of Captain J. W. Fitzgerald, her commander and owner." Fitzgerald operated his new steamer out of Jacksonville through the remaining winter tourist season. One passenger called it "the handsomest, if not the largest steamer on the river." Soon, the captain switched to off-season runs from Savannah to Tybee Island. The vessel's story did not end there, however. The *H. B. Plant* earned fame and a closer connection with Plant steaming the alluring St. Johns River. Fitzgerald's compliment in naming his vessel had by then launched a friendship and eventually a business relationship with its namesake. The ties lasted through Henry's lifetime.[20]

Still, in early 1880 Plant kept his attention focused elsewhere than on the *H. B. Plant*. Specifically, he recognized the imperative need to forge a quicker and easier route from Savannah to Jacksonville. He believed a link to be critically important to please riders and encourage traffic from the North by rendering the infamous rail connection between Dupont, Georgia, and Live Oak, Florida, obsolete. Plant accordingly moved expeditiously to inaugurate construction of the Waycross Short Line. Although the seventy-mile stretch operated as one line with the SF&W, two companies stood behind it. The Waycross and Florida Railroad constructed thirty-three miles in Georgia to the state line, while the remaining thirty-seven miles to Jacksonville came under the aegis of the East Florida Railway Company (EFRC). H. S. Haines presided over both roads with orders from Plant to move construction along as fast as possible.[21]

These dynamics fostered an appalling situation bedeviling to Plant's legacy. Haines leased convict laborers for the EFRC from the state of Florida for fifteen dollars each annually plus expenses. Plant knew of Haines's move and agreed to it even though the action ran counter to attitudes and perspectives that Henry later lived by. "The state administered one of the most notorious penal systems in the world," historian Paul Ortiz observed, "[and convicts constituted] the state's newest slave laborers." Vivien M. L. Miller, a scholar of Florida's penal practices, agreed. She described leasing as "a dishonorable and anti-modern feature of the New South." For what it was worth, convict camp captain J. C. Powell defended the SF&W. The road attempted, Powell insisted, "to free the system, as far as possible, of the odium that then attached to it." He added: "The Plant Company managed their charge generously, the food was good and abundant, and no expense was spared to keep the standard of the camp at a first-class point." Actual conditions differed markedly from Powell's assertions, a reality that emerged when Haines moved to keep prying eyes away from the workers. "Among other things, the company gave me strict orders to allow no unauthorized person to pass on the grading," Powell acknowledged, "or to approach nearer than certain limits."[22]

As convicts pushed construction through snake- and alligator-infested morasses and across the streams and rivers of the Okefenokee Swamp region, Plant turned his sights northward. He needed to connect his system with the broad-rail networks in place above Charleston. The picture clarified on June 7 when Henry successfully bid $300,000 for the Charleston and Savannah Railroad. The syndicate that he represented contained familiar names. W. T. Walters and B. F. Newcomer went back to the Southern Railway Securities Company. Former Confederate secretary of the treasury Christopher G. Memminger, upon whose many kindnesses and helpful cooperation Plant and Southern Express had depended during the Civil War, stepped forward too. "Mr. Plant will be President of the Company," a report detailed. "The road will immediately be put in complete repair and thoroughly equipped. This, with the early completion of the road from Way Cross to Jacksonville, which is now being rapidly pushed forward, will establish a first-class coast line from Florida to New York."[23]

The idea of a "first-class line from Florida to New York" was exactly what Plant had in mind. Two days after the Charleston and Savannah purchase, the *New York Times* revealed that "a vast railroad combination, with the Richmond and Danville and the Richmond and York River Roads as the basis, has been formed in the South, negotiations for which have been in progress for 18 months." Prominent backers included Plant, Walters, and Newcomer. "This combination will seek to control all the through traffic to and from the sea-board, in the States of Virginia, North Carolina, South Carolina, Georgia, Tennessee, Northern Alabama, and Mississippi, striking deep water on the Chesapeake Bay at West Point and Norfolk," the *Times* explained. "This immense system of railroads is the counterpart of the Louisville and Nashville system, which reaches the seacoast at Charleston and Savannah, and covers a large extent of country." Newcomer, for one, insisted that nothing like the now-odious SRSC had been created. He disingenuously stressed that individual roads were not surrendering control to a holding company: "He stated that [the report] was incorrect so far as the formation of a syndicate or combination was concerned. There had been satisfactory arrangements made, he said, by himself, Mr. Walters and several other gentlemen of [Baltimore] and others in New York, Philadelphia and Richmond with the various railroads. Large amounts of stock had been purchased and controlling interests secured in all of the roads named, but not with the view of forming a syndicate, for that would be probably detrimental to trade, but on the contrary with the object of harmonizing the various companies, so that they would secure protection from close competition and establish a uniform rate of freight to the seaboard."[24]

This development came in the nick of time for Plant because the Louisville and Nashville network had taken umbrage at Southern Express's continuing success, not to mention Henry's entry into Savannah and Charleston railroad affairs. The L&N had shown its concerns in several ways, most notably by creating the Union Express to compete directly with Southern Express (and other express companies) and ejecting Plant's company from its lines. Already in February 1880 an Atlanta report had declared, "President H. B. Plant and General Superintendent M. J. O'Brien, of the Southern Express Company, have been flying about recently in a manner that would indicate a fixed purpose to make resistance to any attempt to drive that popular and liberal corporation from the railroads recently purchased by the Louisville and Nashville Railroad." Two months later Dinsmore and Adams Express aided Henry by obtaining a temporary injunction against L&N tactics. Plant also went on offense. Southern Express secured helpful court decisions as well, but none more important than a ruling by a Nashville federal judge on November 18. The jurist was former postmaster general David M. Key, whom Plant had engaged at Havana in April 1878. "The language is so plain and distinct, that there can be no misunderstanding or doubt about any portion of the decision," the express industry's leading publication declared. "It says emphatically, that the business of the Express companies has grown to be a public necessity and convenience, and that railroads will not be permitted to destroy it, either directly or indirectly; and takes a broad position on the question of equality, if a railroad also engages in the transaction of the Express business, which, however, says the Court, is no part of the duty of railroads."[25]

Plant's burst of activity and accomplishments in the ten months preceding June 1880 ranked as nothing short of phenomenal. Having set in motion so many different plans and ideas, Henry abruptly disappeared behind the curtains for four months beginning in late June. During those weeks Morton's marriage fell apart, and the twenty-nine-year-old man took up with Jennie Cramer. Henry's whereabouts, with one exception, remained locked in shadows. In early September he checked into the Manhattan Beach Hotel on Coney Island's eastern shore without Margaret. Instead, he joined W. B. Dinsmore's brother Clarence G. Dinsmore and his wife. The cartoonist Thomas Nast and his daughter filled out the party. The occasion offered the diversion of Brighton Beach fireworks, but for New York society it betokened greater significance. "The Lorillards, the Jeromes, the Heckschers, the Lawrences, and the Belmonts and other high-toned patrons of the turf paced the verandas of the Manhattan Beach Hotel last evening, and talked horses, in anticipation of the Coney Island Jockey Club races to-day," a Brooklyn newspaper detailed. "In the evening the club had a dinner party."[26]

Henry reemerged at Wilmington, North Carolina, on November 16, 1880, possessed of a rosier business outlook than he had taken away with him in June despite unresolved personal issues that dogged the family. Two weeks earlier, voters had selected James Abram Garfield of Ohio as president. The decision meant that—come March 4, 1881—Plant could count on a friendly, or at least neutral, greeting at the White House. True, he did not enjoy close relations with Garfield. Yet the hostility directed at Henry by incumbent Rutherford B. Hayes, who believed Plant had punished the Southern Express employee whose electoral vote arguably gave him the office, no longer stood as an impediment. Even better from Henry's perspective, Garfield's running mate Chester Alan Arthur was a New Yorker well known to Plant. When business matters touched on foreign countries and affairs—such as establishing steamer service between Florida and Cuba and winning contracts to carry the mails both ways—the importance of ties of such magnitude could not be underestimated.[27]

Matters took on a finer hue when Judge Key's decision came down while Henry in mid-November was touring the Southeast for Southern Express and the SF&W, including stops at Columbia, Brunswick, and Albany. In New York by month's end, Plant exploited his new advantage against the Louisville and Nashville. He did so adroitly, and by early January 1881, his antagonists had backed off. "The Southern Express Company . . . is now in charge of the express service on the Louisville and Nashville railroad lines," reports advised. Others declared, "The difficulty between the L. & N. and the Southern [has] been amicably adjusted." An Augusta newspaper pointed out that the L&N, given Plant's opposition, had "found the [express] business to be troublesome and unprofitable." It added: "Especially, too, does the South seem well satisfied with the business facilities of the Southern Express Company. Extending over thousands of miles and embracing the area of the South Atlantic and Gulf States, this corporation insures to the people of this section safe and speedy transportation of money and merchandise, with prompt and reliable delivery, and liberal allowance for loss or injury which may occur. The popularity of the company, which is so well conducted and so liberally managed, is not to be wondered at [as] it has grown up among the institutions of our country, and its officers are among our honored citizens."[28]

Matters kept getting better. The winter 1881 tourist season proved a boon to Florida. "The present is the most brilliant season Jacksonville has ever enjoyed," a resident asserted in March. "Not only has there been an unusual and remarkable influx of visitors, but there has been a most gratifying increase in all departments of business. Merchants, steamboats, railroads, hotels and the working classes have all shared in the general prosperity. There has been employment for all, and the cry of 'hard times' has for once been unheard." Having accepted the Expressmen's Aid Society's presidency in the aftermath of his victory over the L&N, Plant traveled South in February to assess the situation for himself. He discovered that reports did not exaggerate. "The biggest boom enjoyed just now by [Savannah] is the immense travel," a visitor recorded on March 12. "Every day crowds of strangers go surging through the streets, and fill to overflowing the extensive hotel accommodations, while thousands pass on to Florida or on their return to their Northern homes." Henry happened to visit Savannah's SF&W station that day. "The Savannah, Florida & Western railroad is doing more business than at any former season," the visitor continued. "As we passed off from the depot, I saw Col. H. B. Plant, the president, and Col. H. S. Haines standing on the platform, with the most complacent countenances and twinkling eyes as the overcrowded train and groaning engine moved away with its immense burdens. They ought to be satisfied."[29]

Henry might have been pleased, but he was not satisfied. While he stood on the depot's platform, his trains continued to make the laborious trek to Dupont and Live Oak as convict crews strained to complete the Waycross Short Line to Jacksonville. Plant pressed Haines to hurry the work so as not to waste the entire season. Finally, on Saturday, April 23, the last spike—"a solid silver one"—was driven in the East Florida Railway. A passenger train traversed the line at 3:42 that afternoon. Eighteen minutes later "the President's car" followed in a special train with Haines, construction superintendent Henry M. Drane, and guests on board. "The train left Savannah at 10 a. m. and arrived here at 6 p. m., making the run in eight hours," a rider related. "All expressed themselves as more than pleased with the trip." A second man remarked: "I venture the prediction that it will be pronounced one of the smoothest and best constructed routes in the entire country. No expense has been spared in the locomotives and rolling stock. The engines are by the best makers, of unusual power, and with all the latest improvements, while the passenger coaches and sleepers are said to be marvels of elegance and comfort."[30]

News of greater magnitude for Plant and Florida had diverted Henry's full attention from the thrill of his first trip over the Waycross Short Line. A new governor had taken office in Tallahassee in January 1881 determined to attract capital to the state on a scale grand enough to motivate widespread development. That goal in mind, William D. Bloxham had contacted Philadelphia businessman Hamilton Disston about draining "swamp and overflowed lands" in Central and South Florida, what newspapermen called "the Everglades." On February 18 newspapers broke word of an agreement. "An immense transaction, involving the reclamation of 12,000,000 acres of land, or one-third of one of the States of the Union, has been undertaken by a company of Philadelphia gentlemen with every prospect of success," the report declared. "Under the agreement already made with the State, the company is required to begin surveys within 60 days, and within six months to put a force equal to 100 men on the work, and continue as expeditiously as possible." Disston's reward for his efforts amounted to "one half of the land recovered."[31]

More followed. Bloxham perceived from Disston's willingness to undertake the drainage project that the Philadelphian might also be willing to eliminate the most formidable obstacle then blocking state-sponsored development. Called the Vose Injunction, the federal court order forbade the state—as historian Joe Knetsch described—"to sell or bargain away any State lands until Vose and friends had been paid in full" for debts owed from old Florida Railroad operations. By 1881 the total obligation stood at about $1 million. Bloxham in the circumstances made Disston an astounding offer. Florida would deed the businessman four million acres of land for only twenty-five cents an acre. Newspapers proclaimed the news in June. "What is claimed to be the largest purchase of land ever made by a single person in the world occurred today," a report of the seventeenth recounted. "It is Mr. Disston's intention to at once begin an emigration scheme which will result in a very large addition to the population of Florida."[32]

Suddenly, vast reserves of land held by the state of Florida became available to support and encourage railroad construction. Plant immediately perceived that the means had become available to accomplish his dream of a road into the peninsula and a steamer line from Cedar Key to Havana. He leapt at the opportunity. Already in February he had convinced the legislature to create the Live Oak and Rowland's Bluff Railroad Company to build from Live Oak twenty-three miles to the head of navigation on the Suwannee River near Rowland's Bluff, a locale that his employees eventually renamed New Branford. Crucially, section 8 of the act granted the company "alternate sections of the land . . . lying on each side and within six miles of the line of said railroad." Under Plant's orders, Haines commenced construction with dispatch.[33]

With a steamboat landing near Cedar Key soon to become available, Plant went searching for the partner he needed to realize his plans fully. Since the Florida Transit Railway (the reincarnated Florida Railroad) controlled access to Cedar Key, this meant David Levy Yulee. On May 11 Plant contacted the former US senator and suggested that, as historian Dudley S. Johnson put it, "the two cooperate in establishing a tri-weekly steamer service to Key West and Havana from Cedar Key." Yulee's team saw little advantage in aiding a competitor and either did not respond or else temporized. Henry tried again in August, this time "urging a meeting between officials of the two systems to make arrangements for the interchange of freight and passengers." Not until late October did a get-together occur. "The two met and agreed upon a friendly alliance permitting the two systems to exist side by side," Johnson explained. Yulee consented to Plant's road to Rowland's Bluff, although he did not encourage construction farther south.[34]

Plant had decided not to allow Yulee and the Florida Transit Railway to dictate his plans and had already moved to outflank his opposition. Once it had become clear that Yulee would not cooperate in a steamer service from Cedar Key, Plant cast his sights elsewhere. He settled quickly on Charlotte Harbor, a remote site but one in easy proximity to Key West and Havana. In July his agents incorporated the Live Oak, Tampa & Charlotte Harbor Railroad with a projected route from Rowland's Bluff direct to Charlotte Harbor. "Mr. [William Henry] Reynolds, engineer of the projected railroad from Rowland's Bluff to Tampa and Charlotte Harbor, made a preliminary survey of the route as far south as Bronson last week," the *Cedar Key Journal* soon reported. "Mr. Reynolds informed us that the Savannah, Florida & Western Railroad Company meant business, and as soon as a route was definitely determined upon dirt would be broken."[35]

Flaws in Henry's plans appeared almost immediately. Among them, several competing proposals threatened to create complications. Questions of distance, terrain, and whether Charlotte Harbor offered the best alternative to Cedar Key compounded matters. The *Palatka Herald*'s influential editor insightfully lent the weight of his opinion in late August. "It has always been a matter of surprise that nearly all the charters for railroads south on the peninsula should have for their terminus Charlotte Harbor, a place that is by no means inviting: a low, swampy place, infested with insects, and other causes not agreeable to the living," he opined. "Tampa ought to be the terminus for railroads. With the dredging of three miles, which would be at a small expense, ships could go to Tampa. Tampa Bay is one of the finest in the world, and presents unusual attractions and facilities. Even if Charlotte Harbor should become the terminus, it would be suicidal for any road to leave out Tampa. Tampa is bound to be the central outlet to the Gulf in that section; the place is healthy, one of the best places for invalids in Florida, and will, no doubt, become a great resort for pleasure seekers. Railroad facilities will bring the place up, and in a few years it may be counted one of the growing cities of the Gulf."[36]

Two independently occurring events meanwhile altered the dynamics of Plant's ambitions and plans. On July 2 crazed office seeker Charles Guiteau shot President Garfield at a Washington train depot. "I am a Stalwart [Republican], and Arthur will be president," the assassin yelled as officials hustled him from the station. Garfield lingered for weeks. After sixty-six agonizing days, his wish for a respite at Long Branch was granted. He died there on September 19, not yet fifty years of age. The next day Henry's friend Chet Arthur took the oath of office as president. "Charles Guiteau was a wildly successful assassin, not only from the standpoint of murdering a president, but also from the changes that his actions brought to the political area," biographer Ira Rutkow concluded. "None of America's other presidential assassinations so totally fulfilled the shooter's own wishes."[37]

A little more than one month following Arthur's ascension to the presidency, the second event occurred. An English parliamentarian named Sir Edward J. Reed walked off a steamer and into rooms at the Fifth Avenue Hotel, across the street from Plant's New York office. His intention in visiting the United States, he said, was "for the purpose of developing his interests in certain railways and lands in Florida." A newspaperman added, "He contemplates certain commercial improvements in the 'land of fruit and flowers,' provided he is met by a suitable public spirit commensurate with his capital and his progressive views for the expansion at least of one Southern State." Days later Plant and Yulee entered into their modest cooperative agreement, although the Florida Transit official neglected to mention any connection to Reed's interests.[38]

That a relationship did exist soon became plain. Reed first closeted himself with Disston, as a result of which the English investor committed in December to buy half of the Philadelphian's immense Florida purchase. The deal transferred two million acres to Reed. Following that announcement came word on the twenty-third that Reed was "negotiating for the Transit railroad from Fernandina to Cedar Keys." The notice continued, "This transfer gives Sir Edward Reed a controlling interest in the Florida Central Railway, of which he was today elected president." Four days later an updated advisory circulated. "Sir Edward J. Reed, the English capitalist who secured a controlling interest in the Florida Central Railroad last week," it read, "was to-day elected president of the Florida Transit Railroad." Jacksonville's *Florida Union* marveled at Reed's accomplishment: "By this transaction Sir Edward Reed's party completes a railroad combination of large proportions, even for these stirring times, involving the union of the Florida

Central, the Jacksonville, Pensacola and Mobile, the Transit and Peninsular, four roads with numerous branches, under one harmonious management, backed by abundant capital for development. This combination includes 484 miles of completed railroad, and 144 miles of proposed extension, making a total of 628 miles."[39]

Reed's Florida arrival found Plant pursuing numerous initiatives on a variety of fronts, the planning for which had taken no account of a need for urgency generated by the Englishman's bold moves. "The Savannah, Florida and Western Railroad Company—the H. B. Plant system—is extending one of its branches down through Florida in the direction of Tampa bay and Cedar Keys, and its main line from Bainbridge to Chattahoochie, on the Apalachicola river, there to connect with the Pensacola and Atlantic Railroad—now in the course of construction—and complete a continuous line of railway from Savannah to Pensacola, Mobile, New Orleans and Galveston," an editor explained on February 2, 1882. "Those works are being pushed by General Manager H.S. Haines, one of the most accomplished, energetic and capable railroad men in all the South, and, with a strong syndicate to back him, the success of his enterprises is only a question of time." But time was the very point. Henry's vision took time; now, literally, he needed to buy time.[40]

Almost at that moment a chance encounter on a Jacksonville street altered the equation decisively. On February 11 Henry and Margaret arrived at the city's Windsor Hotel. Within hours he chanced to meet Henry Shelton Sanford—former ambassador to Belgium and backer of Sanford, Florida (not to be confused with Adams Express executive and Plant's friend Henry Sanford). South Florida Railroad president James Edmundson Ingraham was present, as well. The South Florida—a line then under construction up the St. Johns River to Kissimmee and, ultimately, Tampa—was owned not by Sanford but by the Pulsifer family, proprietors of the *Boston Herald*. Ingraham told the story: "About this time I was walking down Bay Street in Jacksonville with General Sanford, when he remarked to me, 'You see that elderly gentleman on the other side of the street, the one wearing the long broadcloth coat and silk hat—that is a man I think you ought to know—Mr. Henry B. Plant, President of the Savannah, Florida and Western Railway Company, with whom I traveled on my last trip down from New York.' After saying I should like to meet him, I was introduced to Mr. Plant, who greeted me with 'So you are the young man who is building a railroad from Sanford to somewhere in the south of Florida.'" Ingraham continued: "'Yes, Mr. Plant, we have a little, narrow-gauge railroad there and we feel quite proud of it,' was my reply. 'We expect to open that railroad to Kissimmee shortly—sometime next week—and I should be more than glad to have you and your friends come down and be our guests at the opening.'"[41]

Intrigued by the overture, Plant continued the conversation. "Mr. Plant told of [recently] buying a steamer The Henry B. Plant, and with Captain Jim Fitzgerald thought of running to Sanford," Ingraham recalled. "Immediately I asked for a connection for our road. . . . Agreeing to this request, he said he would join our party on the proposed initial trip. Inquiring how many we could take care of, I told him to bring as many as he wished, and that there would be a special train to meet him on Tuesday morning, when the Henry B. Plant reached Sanford." Plant kept the appointment and, at Sanford, found himself deeply impressed by what he found. Upon returning from a countryside tour he inquired, "What can I do for you, Mr. Ingraham, on this railroad project?" Ingraham picked up his narrative: "'If you will give us connection with your river steamer, and secure for us through representation as to tickets and rates, I should be greatly obliged,' I replied. Continuing, I said that it was my ambition to extend the railroad to Tampa, and put on a line of steamers to Key West and Havana. 'Do you think that your stockholders would sell an interest in this property,' [Plant countered] to which I replied, 'If you can see your way to purchasing, say, a three-fifths interest in this property, extending it to Tampa, eventually putting on such a line of steamers, I am satisfied they would.'" Thus, James E. Ingraham in February 1882 gifted Henry Plant with the chance to buy time.[42]

10

Tampa

1882 to 1886

"giving new ideas and surprises to the world"

On February 14, 1882, workers completed the South Florida Railroad (SFR) line to Kissimmee, prompting Henry Plant to discuss the road's potential with its president, James E. Ingraham. Their conversations raised the possibility of Plant acquiring control, although Ingraham insisted on extension of the line's tracks to Tampa. Despite pressures created by Sir Edward J. Reed's takeover of several Florida railroads along with two million acres of the Disston Purchase, Plant merely promised to discuss the matter further. He yet questioned the wisdom of committing himself to Tampa and doubted whether he should limit his options so quickly. State promises of support for rail construction had meanwhile ignited a railroad boom, and several competitors had announced that they were vying for Tampa Bay access. Those actions rendered problematical whether Plant's crews could reach the remote town before his rivals. Above all, Plant believed that Reed's threat compelled him to first put his own financial house in order before extending himself further. For the time being, Henry took preliminary steps only. He concentrated instead on other matters, some of a personal nature. He undertook, as well, a trip not to be forgotten.[1]

Plant's steps included a series of meetings that led to crucial turning points. The most significant gatherings began with the organizational meeting of the Chattahoochee and East Pass Railroad at Jacksonville on February 24. As planned by Henry prior to Reed's arrival in Florida, his subordinates, led by H. S. Haines, W. S. Chisholm, and Henry M. Drane, prepped the new subsidiary to build a road "to run from Chattahoochee to some point on the Gulf of Mexico at or near that entrance to the Apalachicola bay known as East Pass." This effort extended an ongoing initiative that tied Bainbridge, Georgia, with Chattahoochee, Florida. Soon, annual meetings of all the lines within Plant's control were convened. Most importantly, Charleston and Savannah Railroad (C&S) shareholders and directors met at Charleston on February 27, and those of the Savannah, Florida and Western Railway (SF&W) March 1 at Savannah. The SFR proposal and Henry's financial plans necessarily ranked high on the agendas. As to his financial planning, matters clarified in late March and early April when the Connecticut legislature incorporated the Plant Investment Company (PICO). He intended the new entity to supersede a $2 million joint stock company he had previously organized in Connecticut to finance acquisitions. The corporate format ensured that when it came to the acquisitions and improvements within the volatile environments of Florida and its rail industry, investor liability would be limited to individual investments.[2]

In line with express industry practices, Plant kept secret as much as he could about PICO's internal affairs. This stress on confidentiality applied especially to the names of his investor-shareholders. The 1882 resolution that created the company actually named no individuals, not even Plant. The first public indication of identities came when PICO held its annual meeting at New Haven the next year. "The old directors were re-elected as follows," the *New Haven Evening Register* reported, "Henry B. Plant of New York, Morris K. Jesup of New York, Henry Sanford of Bridgeport, Lorenzo Blackstone of Norwich, G. H. Tilley of Darien, B. F. Newcomer of Baltimore, and W. T. Chisholm of Savannah." All were trusted associates, and many were longtime friends. Names of major investors not named likely included, among others, most principals of Adams Express and Southern Express: W. B. Dinsmore, John Hoey, E. S. Sanford, Clapp Spooner, Isaiah Babcock, Sam Shoemaker, Jim English, James Shuter, and Mike O'Brien. Henry M. Flagler of the Standard Oil Company, Henry's friend since the late 1870s and his near neighbor on Fifth Avenue, participated as well.[3]

Fittingly, as Connecticut's legislature mulled the investment company bill, Henry was combining business with matters of personal concern. The SF&W had allocated to him a "special car" from which to conduct business. On March 21 that car delivered him—along with wife Margaret, general superintendent Haines, George Tilley, and others to Bainbridge. The trip permitted passengers to assess work on the Chattahoochee extension as well as to examine a new steamer—the *Chattahoochee*—recently placed in service on the river of the same name. From Bainbridge several party members steamed to Columbus. "Last night Mr. H. B. Plant and lady and Mr. G. H. Tilly arrived in the city by the steamer Chattahoochee," a local newspaper reported on the twenty-fourth. "Mr. Plant's splendid palace car arrived from Savannah yesterday afternoon and he will leave for his home at 7 o'clock this morning."[4]

Perhaps most importantly to Henry, the southwest Georgia trip allowed him to visit the *Chattahoochee*'s "urbane clerk," his son, Morton. The thirty-year-old's presence on the vessel stemmed from Connecticut events months earlier when his Jennie Cramer dalliance became public knowledge. Henry, needing to remove his son from the glare of scandalous publicity, delivered a take-it-or-leave-it offer. Morton could get himself to Georgia and work quietly in a low-visibility steamboat job or else fend for himself. With the trial of Jennie's killer then pending, Morton acquiesced. Once he carried through, though, something akin to a miracle occurred as the change of scene transformed the former playboy. Away from New York and New Haven temptations, he thrived on river life. He also found that his affable personality endeared him to those whom he met, and that fact reinforced within him a desire to please. A Bainbridge newspaper observed on February 23: "Mr. Plant . . . is a new man on the river, but works as gracefully in harness as a veteran, young, handsome and attentive to his guests, and of pleasing address, he is bound to become popular. He has already captured Bainbridge." One week later the editor added: "Mr. [M. F.] Plant made us a pleasant call. In justice to himself and the girls we will state that he is not a married man; but one of the most genial and whole-souled fellows that ever walked the path of single blessedness." The remarkable metamorphosis happily proved a permanent one, and from March 1882 the relationship of father and son increasingly strengthened toward eventual intimate friendship and trust.[5]

Margaret's presence, too, held significance. The easing of home tensions in Morton's absence—coupled with the happy outcomes of Henry's recent business dealings and the healing that had occurred naturally with time's passage—had inspired him to work on his marriage. The Georgia trip and a Charleston stay set the stage for a second honeymoon. This time, the getaway involved only Henry and Margaret. The couple left New York on April 12 on the *State of Indiana*. At Glasgow thirteen days later they set out on an "extended tour of Europe." Itinerary details remain hazy, but at Paris particularly, they found conditions less than fully pleasing. A financial panic known as the Paris Bourse crash of 1882 had devastated the French economy. Some restaurants reportedly even featured "rat paté" on menus. Still, the École des Beaux-Arts featured inspiring works from the late Gustave Courbet, and Jeanne Granier drew crowds to the Renaissance Theater for *Madame le Diable*. "The little diva, who, by the by, has grown wonderfully buxom of late, has the stage to herself for a good half the evening, and appears in about fourteen different costumes," a critic observed. "She is charming in all."[6]

If Parisian conditions encouraged the Plants then to visit London, Henry found Adelina Patti awaiting at the Royal Italian Opera in Covent Garden. "Every frequenter of Italian opera has seen and admired her in a part which is almost identified with her," a reviewer commented. "Neither is it necessary to add that the reception of the favourite singer was such as she has for many years been accustomed to—a full house, the most agreeable compliment which the public can pay to an artist, being not wanting among other demonstrations of approval." Whatever diversions, entertainments, and sights they enjoyed in England, the Plants ultimately arrived at home in New York just under two weeks after their June 9 departure from Glasgow.[7]

Other than for routine business meetings and a brief vacation with Morton and Henry Sanford at Block Island, Plant spent much of his time during the following months quietly enjoying newfound family harmony. Four years earlier he had purchased property at Branford for a peaceful retreat, and there the Plants passed the days in relaxed comfort. Anxious to provide renewed support for his wife, he welcomed at least one Roman Catholic dignitary and facilitated publication of visit details. With Morton, Henry planned for a future that included added responsibilities. In mid-October the Live Oak and Rowland's Bluff Railroad began operations. Henry meanwhile wanted his son to explore the Suwannee River's navigability and assess the viability of steamboat operations from New Branford (as the Rowland's Bluff depot had been christened) to Cedar Key. This had become imperative after a hurricane devastated the region. Damages of $100,000 were reported at Cedar Key alone, involving "considerable destruction to the wharves, railroads &c." Henry needed conditions on the ground there and at Tampa examined with a critical eye, and Morton welcomed the adventure. The family returned to their Fifth Avenue townhouse about the time the new line opened for business. Following his father's sixty-third birthday on October 27, Henry's heir departed for Eufala, Alabama, the Chattahoochee River, and, ultimately, Florida.[8]

Morton's adventure played out mostly as planned. Immediately following his Jacksonville arrival on November 7, the exploratory party proceeded on its way. Two other men accompanied young Plant. James W. Fitzgerald, the *H. B. Plant*'s experienced captain, enjoyed Henry's trust and respect when it came to boats and navigation. Charles D. Owens, newly hired SF&W New York general agent, could relay information to Plant in an expeditious manner. At New Branford the men took over "a little steam yacht" called *May*. J. C. Powell, who superintended convict labor leased to the Rowland's Bluff railroad, recalled the moment. "[Morton] Plant proved to be as affable as he was unassuming, and he insisted on my accompanying the yachting party," Powell recorded. "He would not take no for an answer, and we had royal good time. There was no ceremony on board 'The May,' and as servants' room was limited every man took a hand at the work. Mr. Plant was wood chopper, Mr. [C.] D. Owens, a New York general manager, 'toted' water, and

Captain Fitzgerald was cook. The rest of us played the role of assistants. We went as far up the river as Troy and back again, past New Branford to the mouth of the Santa Fe River, a total trip of about fifty miles, through magnificent tropical scenery."[9]

Powell debarked, and the explorers proceeded sixty-five miles or so to Cedar Key. Fitzgerald left the group there, and longtime Florida railroad man Matthew R. Marks joined it. Posthurricane Cedar Key presented a miserable picture, however, as did the attitudes of Florida Transit and Peninsular Railroad officials. In the circumstances Morton decided to examine Anclote Key, north of Clearwater, as an alternative port of call. By November 21, the party had reached Tampa. "They visit our town for the purpose of making arrangements to have steamers of the Tampa Steamship Co., call in at Anclote; and they propose to put a light-draught boat on the route from that point to New Branford, the present terminus of the railroad, to connect with the boat of the Tampa S. S. Co.," a newspaperman explained. "The proposed line will be of vast benefit to the western portion of our country, and, in fact the entire Gulf Coast, in giving us a new and competing line, by which to forward our fruit and other products to market, and consequently reducing rates, which, at present, over the Railroad from Cedar Keys, are burdensome and oppressive."[10]

The exploratory party's members separated as word of their findings spread. Morton returned to Columbus, where he joined Capt. A. L. Rice of the *Caddo Belle*, the vessel assigned to the Suwannee River run. The boat left that city on January 11, 1883, and nine days later docked at New Branford. Meanwhile, Owens had hurried to brief his employer. Plant reacted poorly to Anclote Key's substitution for Cedar Key, though, and decided to see things for himself. He and Lorenzo Blackstone had already planned a Georgia trip in connection with the Atlanta Cotton Mills, a company run by Rufus Bullock. En route in early February, Henry arranged with Secretary of State Frederick Frelinghuysen for an introduction to the US consul general at Havana. Following two days in Atlanta during which purchase of the cotton mills was finalized, the friends left for Savannah on the thirteenth in Henry's private car. There, they inspected SF&W facilities, including its mile of riverfront wharves and warehouses. "Mr. Plant, the head man of this great railway enterprise, that is doing so much for Georgia, is a medium-sized, rather slender gentleman, with a fine, clear-eyed face and most attractive address," a reporter observed. "He has a pleasant voice, speaking with clearness and force, and a simple courtesy that wins one unconsciously. He has millions, which he uses with power. He is said to possess great administration ability, planning with consummate sagacity and executing with boldness and ability."[11]

On February 15 Plant and Blackstone quit Savannah on what became one of the most momentous journeys of Henry's career. They rolled through Dupont, Georgia, and Live Oak, Florida, to New Branford. This constituted Plant's first inspection of the completed Live Oak and Rowland's Bluff line. At New Branford, they boarded the *Caddo Belle* and, with Morton by his father's side, steamed down the Suwannee, into the Gulf of Mexico, and on to Cedar Key. Plant grasped Cedar Key's problems quickly. Having done so, he and Lorenzo boarded the Morgan Line steamer *Morgan* on February 17 and steamed for Havana via Key West. The vessel avoided Tampa Bay, but Henry by the eighteenth comprehended—however reluctantly—that the die had been cast for him in favor of Tampa. He and Lorenzo then enjoyed Havana business and pleasure. On February 28 they left the city on the Morgan Line's *Hutchinson* for Cedar Key and the future.[12]

Two months' hectic activity aimed at strategic expansion of the Plant lines followed, with Henry and his associates taking appropriate steps toward buying South Florida Railroad control. In his absence, most SF&W officials had gathered in Jacksonville. Henry's personal lawyer Judge Lynde Harrison of New Haven appeared as well. Plant and Blackstone joined them on March 3, whereupon the combined party made its way to Charleston and Savannah for annual meetings of the two principal roads. "Mr. H. B. Plant and his corps of railroad associates went Southward last night," the *Savannah Morning News* reported on the eighth. "If he and Colonel Haines keep on extending railroads much longer, it will soon be possible to breakfast in Savannah and sup in Havana." Now, leading PICO figures rendezvoused at Jacksonville. On the ninth alone Dinsmore, Hoey, J. Nelson Tupper, Charles Delmonico, and José M. Mora arrived together. B. F. Newcomer, D. T. Newcomer, R. R. Bridges, and Mike O'Brien had preceded them by a day. The thirteenth saw Dinsmore, Hoey, and Delmonico steam up the St. Johns on the *H. B. Plant* to see the country for themselves.[13]

All the while, former Georgia governor John B. Gordon—ambitious to capitalize on the prevailing Florida fever—hovered around Jacksonville adding an enhanced sense of urgency to the scene. The one-time Confederate general had managed to create the International Railroad and Steamship Co., a concern empowered, according to report, "to build a truck railroad down the backbone of the peninsula to Key West." The charter specified, though, a road from the "Georgia line to Key West and Tampa." Gordon underscored the connection March 11. Insisting also that construction would soon begin on a Jacksonville-to-Palatka link up the St. Johns, he added, "At the same time the work will be continued from Tampa to some point on the Peninsular Railroad, now finished to Wildwood."[14]

As these events transpired, Sir Edward Reed's agents pushed his plans and projects, further complicating Plant's situation. March rumors claimed that the English investor meant to consolidate his lines into one system, an end perhaps abetted ominously by one of Henry's Fifth Avenue neighbors. "It is a mistake to say that Mr. Jay Gould is going to Florida for the benefit of his health," an onlooker reported. "The fact is, he is going there for no other purpose than to look at some railroads which he will, in all probability, purchase." Within a week or two Gould, "with family and party of friends," was touring Northeast Florida under the care of a Reed official. By then reports had declared: "The Transit Road, on its trunk line extension, has reached Wildwood, within less than 100 miles of Tampa. From Wildwood the road has been graded southeasterly to Leesburg twenty miles." The Florida legislature contributed its own complication to the picture. "An exciting race will soon take place in Florida," an editor explained. "As the law now stands, the first road that is built to Tampa will get the lands granted, and at least five different managers are making preparations to come in ahead."[15]

Plant meanwhile contended with more than the question of the South Florida Railroad (SFR) and a line to Tampa. His plans to link the SF&W with the Gulf of Mexico at Apalachicola and with existing rail connections westward through North Florida were maturing rapidly. He aimed, in the latter instance, to forge a cooperative through route from New York to New Orleans. "The Savannah, Florida and Western operates the largest system of railroads in this section of the South, and will soon have in addition to new branches now extending in Florida, a straight and short connection with New Orleans," a Georgia newspaper explained in March. "This will give a swift schedule to the Crescent City, which will break into travel over the other great routes to the Southwest. The man known to the world as H. B. Plant is a bigger man than Jay Gould, and has a head on him as long as from New York to New Orleans. And he won't rest until his system gives the swiftest time between the two great cities. His network of railroads is developing Florida and South Georgia in a most remarkable degree, and he seems to have a brain able to lay off work for an indefinite number of men, and which is always giving new ideas and surprises to the world."[16]

Having spent precious time in New Orleans during late March and early April facilitating the westward expansion plans, Henry made his way back through Georgia to New York in time to read reports of Gould's southern explorations. "His recent trip South was not a mere pleasure trip as reported," one account declared. "It was the initial step of a great scheme—the connection of his Southwestern system with the southern ports of the Atlantic. The building of his yacht [the *Atalanta*] seems to have developed nautical dispositions in him. He wants to take hold of New Orleans, Brunswick, Savannah, and Norfolk as seaboard outlets for his southwestern system." Gould's intentions constituted fodder for rich conversations when he and Plant joined numerous other dignitaries at the Union League on the twenty-first to honor Mexico's ex-president Porfirio Díaz. Still, whatever threat Gould posed failed to materialize. Henry quietly spent time improving his Branford residence in the days leading up to May 4, when he purchased SFR control. "The road will be completed immediately to Tampa Bay," a notice asserted. "New York parties will run a line of steamships from Tampa to Havana."[17]

Plant's genius lay in recognizing that the SFR, insofar as its timely construction to Tampa was concerned, amounted in certain respects to a lost cause in that Reed, Gordon, or some other entrepreneur could reach Tampa and co-opt the state grant before he did. More importantly, the rewards for success—if he did succeed—came to far less than he preferred relative to the risks involved. The SFR's charter, whatever its benefits, authorized a grant of only 3,840 acres of land for each mile constructed. The Jacksonville, Tampa and Key West Railroad (JT&KW), already building from Tampa toward the St. Johns River, could claim the same basic grant plus an additional 10,000 acres per mile. On top of that, the road had already graded its route for fifteen miles east of Tampa. Its charter, on the other hand, required construction from Kissimmee to Tampa by January 25, 1884. Upon reflection, that opportunity proved too enticing for Plant to resist. Since the JT&KW had run out of money, $30,000 bought Henry "all its rights in the railroad built in and out of Tampa" and authority to use its land grant provisions for any track that he built under its charter. He had found a gamble that he was willing to accept.[18]

A headlong rush ensued as Plant railroad officials and crews raced to complete the Tampa line on time. Plant, though, remained away from Florida. Rather, he observed progress, issued instructions, and otherwise coordinated from New York and Connecticut. He watched, too, as Gordon's elusive dreams clouded in June and collapsed in July. One source believed "that Plant bought him off to eliminate competition." If so, the victor may have benefited from the advice of Mike O'Brien, who was drawing ever closer to his employer and friend as he spent "much of the time in New-York." A reporter captured his perspectives and admiration in mid-July: "I inquired about Mr. H. B. Plant, the president of the Southern Express Company, and Mr. O'Brien said: 'He . . . is one of the chief railroad builders in the South. He owns the railroad south of Savannah, not only to Jacksonville and the Appalachicola River, but he has built a line to Tampa Bay in South Florida, and will put on steamers next winter to make the run across to Havana in twenty-three hours, so that less than one day and night of sea voyage will divide the people in New-York from Cuba, which I think will become the most popular resort of Americans.'"[19]

Henry savored the passing months in the midst of summer pastimes and the company of friends. Branford offered sanctuary and relaxation, although he, Margaret, and Morton indulged in the pleasures of Saratoga Springs in August. Lorenzo and Emily Blackstone joined them there for the Mapleson Opera Festival. Among other events, several New York weddings also marked his calendar. To name one, on June 13 the Blackstones' son William Norton Blackstone united with Julia Squire at St. Thomas's Church. A reception followed at the fashionable Hotel Brunswick, located a few blocks from Henry's Twenty-Third Street office.[20]

A second wedding carried even greater portent for Plant's future. On June 5 widower Henry Flagler quietly married thirty-four-year-old Ida Alice Shourds, much—it must be said—to his family's chagrin. Historians for many years treated eccentric, red-haired, and eventually troubled Alice (or Alicia) poorly, reading into her shadowy past questionable activities and less-than-noble motivations. St. Augustine's Thomas Graham has recently elevated her image considerably, however, painting the new Mrs. Flagler in a clearer and kinder light. "Unlike Flagler's first marriage into the wealthy Harkness family, which had made sound economic sense, his marriage to Alice is a mystery," Graham conceded, "but it fits into what was becoming a pattern in Flagler's life: an attempt by a middle-aged man to recapture his youth." The story approximated Plant's own; only two or three years separated Margaret and Alice in age. Following a brief honeymoon, the Flaglers luxuriated with friends—the Plants likely among them—at their forty-room country home at Mamaroneck on Long Island Sound's northern shore. Locals called the estate Satanstoe (James Fenimore Cooper had named it years earlier) or else Lawn Beach. Flagler also purchased the "schooner yacht" *Columbia*, a winner of the America's Cup. Given time for refurbishment, the sleek vessel promised lazy interludes of pleasant diversion. As it turned out, public investigations of Flagler's potential involvement in alleged Standard Oil criminal activities left him late in the year needing such diversion, but *Columbia* yet remained in dry dock.[21]

Flagler notably chose instead to introduce his new bride to Florida and, especially, St. Augustine. The couple had not yet reached the Ancient City when Plant returned to New York from one of his greatest triumphs. The story commenced following PICO's annual meeting at New Haven on November 16 when Henry went to Savannah, where promoters wanted his sponsorship of an imposing new hotel. "Mr. Plant replied that it was not the business of railroads to put money in them, but that he knew good hotels induced people to travel, and travelers benefitted railroads, and for that reason he thought it very probable that the Savannah, Florida and Western Railway would contribute towards building the hotel," a reporter detailed, "but he was not prepared to say to what extent." At Jacksonville on the twenty-seventh, Henry announced plans to "go up the river to Sanford, then Kissimmee" to inspect the South Florida Railroad. Rumors circulated of schemes to expand PICO's holdings. "The road from Rowland's Bluff on the Suwannee River has obtained possession of the portion of the Florida Southern completed to [High Springs], between Gainesville and Newnansville, and will continue their broad gauge track to the former town, and the strong probability now is that trains will be in operation to that point by the end of January," an onlooker recorded. "The Plant syndicate is also to construct a branch road from the north bank of the Santa Fe river to Lake City, where connection will be made with the Florida Central and Western. Whatever the above company undertake they usually accomplish, and their contracts are carried out faithfully and in an expeditious manner. Before the close of another summer the Plant system will be extending their lines southward, opening up new country and greatly increasing present facilities."[22]

At Kissimmee, Plant set out with H. S. Haines, J. E. Ingraham, and several others on his first visit to Tampa. The party left at 5:00 A.M. on December 1, 1883, and required fifteen hours in transit. The eighteen miles between Auburndale and the nascent community of Plant City, a private initiative promoted by judge and future governor Henry L. Mitchell, were covered in a horse and buggy. "We had a day's journey to reach over the gap in the railway that was then being constructed, connecting Tampa and the St. John's River," Plant recalled. "It was an interesting trip. I think to the best of my recollection we passed not more than seven habitations on that journey, certainly not more than that while daylight lasted." Tampans understandably greeted the millionaire enthusiastically. "The party was royally entertained at the Orange Grove Hotel," a town historian related, "and on the following day taken on a Tampa Bay excursion on the *Capt. Miller*, a new steamer of the Tampa Steamship Line." Yet as visions of Havana's tropical splendors danced before his eyes, Plant felt little excitement about the village on Tampa Bay. "Well, when I first drove across the country from Sanford . . . I found Tampa slumbering as it had been for years," he recalled. Henry spotted potential, though. "It seemed to me that all South Florida needed for a successful future was a little spirit and energy, which could be fostered by transportation facilities," he confided. "I made a careful survey of the situation, calculated upon its prospects and concluded to take advantage of the opportunity."[23]

Nearly two months later—after stopping in Atlanta with Rufus Bullock before spending holidays at home in New York—Plant on January 25, 1884, retraced his December excursion on a celebratory train ride along his now-completed SFR link to Tampa. "The first train consisted merely of a crude engine, the president's private car, a coach, and a baggage car," a resident re-

14. The Plant System's *Margaret* is seen here at Tampa's Morgan Line docks in spring 1885, with the smaller vessel *Erie* at left. State Archives of Florida, Florida Memory.

called. "[It] made a tortuous journey from Sanford, and eventually parked at the foot of Twiggs street, where the union station now stands, to the huzzaing of a crowd of gaping villagers. The passengers were five: H. B. Plant, owner and builder of the road . . . ; J. E. Ingram, president of the line; H. S. Haynes, general superintendent; H. S. Drane, auditor; and John Mahoney, the auditor's chief clerk." Reporter William Drysdale recorded the scene: "Knots of men were down on their knees and haunches on the sidewalks, making diagrams of their 'property' and telling how much they had already been offered for their lots, and how much they expected to realize on them. There was a regular 'boom' in real estate as far as sellers were concerned, but I did not see any excited men rushing around looking for a chance to buy." Drysdale added, "I was in Tampa just five hours; next time I come I will not care to stay more than four hours and a half."[24]

Business affairs subsequently kept Plant occupied for weeks. He touched at Jacksonville, St. Augustine, Savannah, Augusta, New Orleans, Charleston, and other points. Distractions included duties as presiding officer at the Expressmen's Aid Society annual meeting held during mid-February at Jacksonville. His attention focused in good part, though, on Sir Edward Reed's move—concluded February 29—to consolidate his Florida lines into one operation to be known as the Florida Railway and Navigation Company. With Jay Gould a visible and irritating background presence, Plant step by step maneuvered his operations into position to compete effectively. Preliminary to taking final action, he gathered PICO investors for a grand tour of SFR holdings. From March 11 to 14 the party—including, among others, W. S. Chisholm of Savannah, R. M. Pulsifer of Boston, B. F. Newcomer and Harry Walters of Baltimore, Samuel O. Plant of Branford, and Mike O'Brien of Southern Express—viewed Sanford, Winter Park, Maitland, Orlando, and Kissimmee aboard "the special for Tampa."[25]

A reporter who accompanied the party left telling impressions of its leader. "Speaking of Mr. Plant reminded us that he is becoming the best known man in the Southeast," the man wrote. "I do not mean by name only, but personally. He is very affable and amiable, and makes friends wherever he goes. Most men in his position have something in their manners, or the people imagine they have, that repels friendly intercourse. Mr. Plant's quiet but hearty greeting invites confidence, and he thus enjoys direct intercourse with many people whom other capitalists could not, without the loss of considerable of their supposed dignity, do business with." He added: "He is very agreeable [and] very frank in the expression of his opinion but is considerate of those of others, and is not apt to say anything about business matters that he should not say, and therefore never has any explanation to make. He is, in a word, a very able and amiable gentleman."[26]

At Plant's direction, PICO countered Reed with a two-pronged assault. First, in March the corporation consolidated all its lines operating south of Savannah into the Savannah, Florida and Western Railway. Included were the Waycross and Florida Railroad; East Florida Railway; Live Oak and Rowland's Bluff Railroad; Live Oak, Tampa and Charlotte Harbor Railway; and the Chattahoochee and East Pass Railway. The SF&W's officers and directors assumed "full management and control." Second, on April 1 Plant mortgaged the new company to secure a $6.5 million loan from New York's Metropolitan Trust Company (MTC). "The mortgage is given to secure loans made to improve the road and its branches, and to equip and repair its increasing lines more thoroughly," a newspaperman explained. Henry's election to the bank's board of directors late the previous year, thanks to the influence of PICO backer and MTC director Morris K. Jesup, had made the loan possible.[27]

The enormous Metropolitan Trust financial package trumped the resources available to Reed and launched Plant into prominence as Florida's principal transportation baron. In New York he fine-tuned his vision and honed his program of initiatives. "Now, Mr. Plant sits in his office planning the continuation [of the new SF&W] through Gainesville, in Ala[chua]; through Marion County into Hernando, by the way of its county seat, Brook[s]-ville; on through Hernando into Polk to Charlotte Harbor, on the southern part of the gulf coast," an observer noted, "thus giving the inhabitants of the west coast of the State direct routes of travel and transportation, as well as those upon the St. Johns and the east coast, while those more centrally situated can choose between the two great routes." The observer waxed extravagantly: "It is . . . no more than reasonable to assert that coming generations, when they learn of the public spirit and mighty enterprise of H. B. Plant, as shown in the development of Florida, will rise up and pronounce him blessed, because of the great aid he had rendered Florida and all her people in the wonderous progress she has already made and is still making."[28]

Several Plant initiatives stood out. He quickly enhanced SFR service to Tampa by purchasing the *George R. Kelsey* for, as C. D. Owens described it, "the coasting trade to the south of Tampa." In this era of good feeling between Henry and his wife, he renamed the vessel *Margaret*. Running 170 feet in length with a beam of 43 feet, it commenced a Tampa-to-Manatee (i.e., Bradenton) run in June 1884. The system further announced future expansion: "The Plant Investment Company is having built North two large, swift, strictly first-class steamships, with splendid passenger accommodations and large freight capacity, to be placed on the line between Tampa and Key West. They will be here in readiness for next fall's business."[29]

Contemporaneously, Henry acted to erase past mistakes by building levels of trust and, eventually, loyalty within his African American workforce. He did not explain his motivations, so they remain hazy although not completely impossible to explore. On the one hand, Plant wanted to see himself as a decent man of conservative beliefs who had learned from the express business the benefits of farsighted management and positive employee treatment. As biographer George H. Smyth pointed out, "Kind and generous treatment of the deserving men in his employ have never been wanting." Since a deep-rooted sense of practicality ruled most of Plant's actions, he remained sensitive to the special kinds of worker issues faced in the South by racially antagonistic capitalists. Beyond that, Plant felt vulnerable to personal challenges of his own making. The fact of his ownership of slaves likely circulated within black leadership circles; more certainly, his recent willingness to lease convicts shouted a callous nature, whatever measures he might or might not have taken to ameliorate the harshest conditions. Most profoundly, in an era of rising labor turmoil and associated violence, Plant feared strikes. "There is a great waste of material from the destructive violence of infuriated mobs," Smyth admonished in 1898. "In 1877, the great railway strikes of the Baltimore and Ohio Railroad, and the Pennsylvania and Erie Systems, resulted in the destruction of sixteen hundred cars, one hundred and twenty-six locomotives, and five million dollars worth of property."[30]

Henry yearned to avoid labor confrontations at virtually all costs and prided himself that he managed to do so. "It is greatly to the credit of the Plant System, that the public has never suffered inconvenience in travel from strikes among its large working force, that the men have not suffered in person or estate, and the company has been saved losses and crosses from this hydra-headed monster, 'Conflict between labor and capital,'" Smyth insisted. "That these evils have been avoided, is due to the head of this great System, due to his sense of justice, to his personal knowledge of, and friendly interest in such a large number of the employees, and to a large-hearted consideration for the weaknesses of human nature."[31]

Plant's 1884 bridge-building efforts began with recognition that racial climates in Georgia and Florida were deteriorating. Growing economic discrimination generally meant lower pay and poorer working conditions for black employees. Meanwhile, spikes in race-based violence increasingly stained communities. Florida was already on its way to becoming—on a per capita basis—the South's leader in lynchings. Georgia fared little better. As to economic discrimination, Plant applied a relatively simple solution. He mandated payment of workers at standard rates without regard to race and insisted that all be treated respectfully. The dangerous hardening of race relations demanded greater creativity, though. Savannah's superintendent of wharves Robert LePage provided a partial answer. He suggested that the SF&W purchase property in nearby Brewton Hill for a company-sponsored all-black neighborhood. Within four years 35 houses out of a planned total of 108 had been completed in LePageville. Five remained under construction. At Waycross, where SF&W operations centered, a similar development occurred. Henry Wadsworth Reed, the line's roadmaster, urged Plant to create there what locals soon called Reedsville. Covering twenty-five acres, the "small suburb" within a few years "[had] been covered with neat cottages for the negro employees of the railroad companies." Also at Reed's behest, Plant soon erected a school and hired respected Republican leader and Congregational minister Floyd Snelson as its teacher. Snelson, in turn, provided Plant entrée into black leadership circles in both states. "Prof. Floyd Snelson is the arbiter and great medium which keeps the two races close together here," a local man later observed. "He is highly prized and honored by the Plant System people and stands high in their estimation."[32]

Through summer and into fall 1884 Plant mapped out future ventures while relaxing at Branford, where he added five acres to his estate. He mourned in June the death of Adams Express pioneer Sam Shoemaker of

Baltimore but watched with fascination the year's presidential contest between New York governor Grover Cleveland, a Democrat, and Republican James G. Blaine of Maine. He was probably flabbergasted when Blaine's electoral chances sustained a roundhouse blow on October 29 at his friend Charles Delmonico's Fifth Avenue restaurant. In what was called the "Millionaire's Banquet," several hundred leading citizens—including Henry M. Flagler, Jay Gould, and Plant's lawyer Clarence Seward—feted Blaine in anticipation of his expected win. But next-day headlines slammed "The Royal Feast of Belshazzar Blaine and the Money Kings." Nearby, Presbyterian minister S. D. Burchard—filled with the fire of a teetotaling Old Testament Protestant God—blasted Democrats as the party of "rum, Romanism, and rebellion." The evident slur on Irish Catholics, combined with disgust generated by accounts of the Millionaire's Banquet, swayed enough voters to throw New York and the presidency to Cleveland. Plant since the Civil War had avoided politics and political entanglements whenever he could. The choice had once again served him well.[33]

Summer and fall brought further surprises. In one of them, Henry grasped control of the Brunswick and Western Railway. "The purchase of this line inures to the benefit of Savannah," a Columbus editor explained, "as it gives a shorter line to the west via Montgomery and the Georgia Central to Albany." Another exclaimed: "The purchase . . . by Mr. H. B. Plant makes him one of the railroad kings of the south; now having 900 miles of road under his control. His roads are all located in Georgia, South Carolina and Florida, covering the orange and watermelon territory." A second surprise came with an ultimately unsuccessful November attempt by the Morgan Steamship Line to procure exclusive rights to steamer routes from Tampa to Havana. Finally, in December Henry's competition with Jay Gould peaked when Plant sued his Fifth Avenue neighbor over issues connected with the Missouri- and Arkansas-based St. Louis, Iron Mountain Railroad and Southern Railway. The New Year promised plenty of fireworks.[34]

Plant aimed for them to explode first over El Morro Castle in Havana harbor. He was not about to allow the Morgan Line to usurp his long-held Cuban dreams, nor, as events proved, was he now limiting his horizons to the Pearl of the Antilles. The litigation against Gould required his presence in Little Rock and St. Louis in January 1885, but as soon as Henry could, he and Margaret boarded his private car for the South. At Charleston by the twenty-ninth, they passed quickly through Savannah and Jacksonville, reaching their initial goal of Tampa on Tuesday, February 5. That Saturday night the Plants embarked on a Morgan Line steamer for Havana. "It is supposed," a report advised, "that his visit is in the interest of the establishment of the proposed short route between the United States, Cuba, and Central and South America via the Plant system of railroads through Carolina,

15. Havana's Grand Hotel Pasaje, seen here as it appeared in the early 1890s, often served as Henry Plant's headquarters when he visited Cuba. From J. C. Prince, *Cuba Illustrated* (New York: Napoléon Thompson, 1893).

Georgia and Florida." First stop came on Sunday at Key West, which was, Plant noticed, "growing rapidly, owing to the increase in the trade in cigars." As a reporter detailed, "Leaving Key West at sunset the gentleman arrived in Havana in time to see old Sol as he rose in the morning."[35]

The pleasant journey's magical qualities carried through the visit, which lasted two weeks. Beyond Old Havana sights, the Plants gauged prevailing economic realities by touring nearby sugar plantations. The couple especially examined influential magnate Don Pedro Fernandez de Castro's Nuestra Señora del Carmen, located twenty-six miles east of the capital. From de Castro and his son Rafael Fernandez de Castro, active in Cuban political affairs, Plant gleaned that the island teetered on the cusp of bankruptcy. "The low prices for agricultural products, the changing systems of labor [Cuba was transitioning away from slave labor] and high taxation has about ruined the country," he found. Only US tariff preferences could forestall collapse, Plant heard. At the capital he fortunately found better news and conditions. "Until recently Havana had no wharves or piers, and freight had to be loaded or landed in small boats," he explained after his return. "There are now three large iron piers, which will accommodate from eight to ten vessels. The largest vessels in the world can moor to them and have plenty of water under their keels. The piers are built over with an immense iron warehouse 66 meters in width and 155 meters in length, and two stories high."[36]

Plant returned to Florida interested in launching his steamship service as soon as practicable, as well as lobbying the Cleveland administration for West Indies mail contracts and tariff protections for Cuban sugar and related products. Henry knew Cleveland through New York business and social circles. He enjoyed, though, a secret key to access in his friend Jim English. The former governor, congressman, and senator commanded attention as one of the nation's leading Democrats and counted the new president as an intimate friend. So, while English forged headway in Washington, Plant busied himself with annual meetings at Kissimmee, Jacksonville, Savannah, and Charleston. Most reports reflected highly positive conditions, although discovery of a "defect in the title" disrupted transfer of the Brunswick and Western to the SF&W. Henry and Alice Flagler meanwhile had arrived at St. Augustine in mid-February, and Plant likely rendezvoused with them in the Ancient City or at Jacksonville. He also watched from afar as his lawyers pressed the case against Gould in St. Louis, only to see the US Circuit Court in late March dismiss his petitions. True to long-honored practice, Henry avoided answering awkward questions by disappearing for a month. One Jacksonville report had him and Margaret visiting Mexico, but more probably he had gone to Havana.[37]

At the very least, Havana dominated Plant's thoughts. Late April found him approaching the postmaster general "on the subject of the postal facilities between the United States and the West Indian Islands." He insisted: "The time has now nearly arrived when continuous railway service will be established as far south as Tampa, Fla., whence communication can be had with Havana in about thirty hours. By adopting this southern land route and the water communication between Tampa and Havana, the whole of the United States can be better served than is any section of it at present." Within two months he had also contracted on PICO's behalf with Philadelphia shipbuilders William Cramp & Sons for "a steamer to run between Tampa and Havana," one he wanted "fitted with all the modern improvements, and . . . lighted by electricity." Cleveland's administration before long signaled its cooperation regarding the mails. "The railroad from Pemberton's Ferry to Lakeland, Fla., has just been finished by the Plant Improvement Company," commented an item published on August 21. "This completes the all-rail route from Jacksonville to Tampa, and removes the only obstruction to the establishment of a fast mail to Cuba, which the postoffice department proposed putting into effect as soon as the uncompleted railroad between Palatka and Sanford had been finished."[38]

As these affairs played out, the Plants made time for an event that brought special pleasure. Jim English had been widowed in 1874 at sixty-two years of age, and he might have remained a bachelor had events turned out otherwise at Saratoga Springs in August 1885. At that time the Plants brought a family friend with them to the fashionable resort. Anna Robinson Morris, aged thirty-six, had known Henry since her childhood days at Augusta. Her father, Lucius S. Morris, had engaged prominently in business there and, during the Civil War, had invested in Southern Express. However, the postwar years had proved extremely difficult for Morris, personally and professionally. He separated from his wife and family, after which Henry aided him with a position in Memphis at the Overton Hotel. Morris's intimate friend S. B. Robbins left Augusta with him to manage the facility. Other hospitality-industry positions followed for both men, leading Morris to eventual prominence as culinary director during the 1880s at Washington's famed Metropolitan Hotel, which Robbins comanaged. Henry meanwhile had watched out for the Morris children, especially Anna. He had introduced his ward to English in the early 1880s at Branford, but not until August 1885 at Saratoga Springs "did it become evident that he entertained the deep feeling for the lady." Echoing Henry Flagler's experience, English's family reacted with trepidation. They quaked at the idea that such a distinguished man would marry a penniless woman half his age, much less one whose family story whispered of hidden scandal.[39]

Where Plant typically shied from public controversy and entanglements with political overtones, he did not hesitate when it came to the love match between Jim English and Anna Morris. Demonstrating deeply felt personal loyalty in the face of potential social ostracism, he opened his Fifth Avenue home to the couple. The wedding occurred there at noon on October 7. "The spacious parlors of the residence of Mr. Plant, who has been a father to Miss Morris since the death of his friend, her father [Lucius actually remained alive in Washington], were profusely decorated with flowers for the occasion," an account specified. "The bride entered leaning on the arm of Mr. Plant." Another account observed that "palms and ferns were displayed in the halls and the reception room, while in the drawing-room, where the ceremony took place, baskets of La France and Perle [d'Or] roses were distributed about." The occasion proved a happy one for all present: "The bride, who appeared very nervous, wore a handsome traveling costume; Gov. English was clad in a black suit, with a well-fitting Prince Albert. He looked at least thirty years younger than he really is." The party soon adjourned to Delmonico's, "where the wedding lunch was partaken of." The newlyweds then slipped away to the Windsor Hotel.[40]

The celebrations had only begun. Sixteen days following the wedding, Jim and Anna English traveled with the Plants to Philadelphia to launch Henry's new Havana steamer. Henry Sanford, Mike O'Brien, Hamilton Disston, and other familiars looked on as Margaret "broke a bottle of wine across the bows, and amid three hearty cheers, christened her the *Mascotte*." Running two hundred feet in length with a thirty-foot beam, the double-decker accommodated "seventy-five saloon passengers and is provided with a steam steering gear and all improvements known to modern naval architecture." Henry furnished the name, inaugurating a practice of utilizing the titles of operas he particularly enjoyed. *La Mascotte*, the most popular operetta composed by Edmond Audran, had debuted to audience acclaim at Paris in December 1880 and opened for the pleasure of New Yorkers less than six months later. The festivities thereafter adjourned to New Haven, where, on November 4, Anna with Margaret's help launched herself into Connecticut society with a reception for six hundred distinguished guests. Barely had the English servants put away the dinnerware when, on December 16, Henry led a group of PICO investors that included W. B. Dinsmore, Henry Sanford, Mike O'Brien, and Lynde Harrison on the *Mascotte*'s first water trials. "A few invited guests accompanied the excursionists," a Philadelphia newspaper observed, "and a pleasant and satisfactory trial trip was made to Bombay Hook and return."[41]

By then, the time had nearly arrived for Henry's vision of a steamer connection with Cuba to materialize. On December 27 he and "a party of personal friends" departed Philadelphia on the *Mascotte* for Nassau and Havana. In high spirits, he reported from Fortress Monroe, Virginia, that the steamer "behaved splendidly at sea." The vessel, proving its potential and having touched at Havana and Key West, reached its Florida destination by January 3, 1886. The voyage from Cuba took twenty-five hours, twenty-eight minutes, ranking it "the fastest trip on record between Havana and Tampa." As the *Mascotte* steamed up Tampa Bay, the *Margaret* saluted her with J. E. Ingraham, H. S. Haines, and C. D. Owens heading official greeters. "This steamship is unsurpassed in her interior decorations, comfortable staterooms, and sea-going qualities, and is considered the fastest steamship on the gulf," a correspondent enthused. "She will take her regular trip on Wednesday, Jan. 6, from Tampa to Havana, and will no doubt attract much of the Cuban travel by her superior accommodations."[42]

11

Transportation and Tourism

1886 to 1889

"Tampa is the one spot—the only spot—for your hotel"

The steamer *Mascotte*'s Florida arrival in January 1886 opened an era of entrepreneurial outreach during which Henry Plant's horizons expanded geographically and conceptually. His thinking at its onset basically conceived a transportation grid that stretched by rail from Charleston, South Carolina, to Tampa and Charlotte Harbor, with linkages northward to New York and Boston as well as westward to New Orleans and beyond. Other elements also adorned his emergent network. Plant had aided development of street railway systems, especially at Jacksonville. His priority, though, had been to complement his trains with comfortable and efficient steamboat service, whether for freight or passengers. Thus, by 1886 Plant vessels plied the St. Johns, Suwannee, and Chattahoochee/Apalachicola Rivers. At Tampa, the *Mascotte* afforded Key West access and a southern anchor at Havana, while the *Margaret* ferried people and cargo in season to and from the Manatee River. Henry, above all, believed that Havana offered the ultimate lure to draw travelers south. Just as surely, he thought responsibility lay primarily with others to house and entertain his customers wherever his trains and boats deposited them. That trend of thought, however, neared a metamorphosis.[1]

Appreciation of changes in Plant's business life during the late 1880s necessitates consideration of his relationship with Henry M. Flagler. Having been acquainted for about a decade, the men enjoyed an easy and complementary rapport that deepened eventually into intimate friendship and business partnership. Plant's priorities compelled him to focus attention on Central Florida and the Gulf Coast, while he and others encouraged Flagler to embrace St. Augustine, the Florida community that had been Plant's original favorite. The Ancient City, as it happened, captured Flagler as well. What he aimed to accomplish there differed significantly, though, from Plant's intentions elsewhere. Transportation then mattered to the oil executive primarily in terms of how visitors could reach St. Augustine. Instead, Flagler looked to furnish luxurious accommodations and pleasant diversions. In 1886, coincidentally, the two men forged a formal link that facilitated regular contact, interchange of ideas and influence, and mutual support. An investor in the Plant Investment Company (PICO) since its creation, Flagler joined the South Florida Railroad (SFR) board. Within two more years, he sat as a PICO director.[2]

The Florida development bug bit Flagler most profoundly in winter 1885, and when it did his vision for St. Augustine encompassed more than building and operating a hotel. He meant to transform a community into a tourist resort, a resort that catered only to a special clientele. "I used daily to take walks down St. George Street, around the plaza to the [yacht] club house, and back to the hotel again," he explained. "I found that all the other gentlemen did the same thing, with the same apparent regularity, and then, as now, that was all there was to do for recreation and amusement. But I liked the place and the climate, and it occurred to me very strongly that some one with sufficient means ought to provide accommodations for that class of people who are not sick, but who come here to enjoy the climate, have plenty of money, but can find no satisfactory way of spending it." Flagler later added: "It does seem singular that I, a busy man, who never had time for leisure trips or rest, should build a hotel practically for rich people alone. I thought at the time that somebody should consider and satisfy their wants to a winter home in Florida. I found it necessary, or at least desirable, that I should, with my family, spend a part of the winter South, and I studied and investigated the question of climate and location as I would a purely business matter. I found that St. Augustine filled every requirement, and so I invested here and built these hotels."[3]

Flagler's resort dreams had begun to take form by March 1885, but the brilliance of his concept stood out only when his grandest St. Augustine project rose from its foundations. "The hotels throughout Florida within range of Northern visitors are vastly better than the hotels of the prominent inland cities of Pennsylvania or New York or New England, and in the chief centres they rival the more pretentious hotels of Philadelphia and New York in the excellence of their table and the comfort of their rooms," an admirer recorded. "But even these hotels, which were deemed extravagant ventures only a few years ago, will now be eclipsed by the Ponce de Leon of St. Augustine, which will be comparable only with the hotel palaces of the Pacific coast in colossal proportions, grandeur and completeness in all appointments; and what shall now be done in St. Augustine will be speedily imitated, only on a lesser scale of expenditure, in the localities which are rapidly developing as permanent centres of Northern visitors. I hazard little in saying that the present generation will see scores of hotels in Florida far outstripping the most popular and costly watering-places of the North alike in number and elegance. There is only one Florida in North America. It was until lately far distant from the North, but now swift express trains with almost every comfort of home, and rapid coast steamers from every Northern commercial port, have brought the 'Land of Flowers' within easy reach of pleasure-seekers and invalids; and the prospect of profitable investments has turned a steadily growing tide of all classes of money-getters to Florida, from the conservative capitalist to the headlong speculator."[4]

As Flagler moved to rouse St. Augustine, Plant planned to concentrate on Havana, but circumstances forced him to delay his second 1886 visit until February. The intervening circumstances involved the loss of his mother. Word that she was "dying of paralysis" reached him at Savannah on his way north from Tampa after the initial January trip, and he sped to New Haven to offer the comfort of his presence. At age eighty-six, Betsey Bradley Plant Hoadley died on January 20. He buried her in Branford two days later. As the *New Haven Evening Register* observed, "There was a large attendance."[5]

Coincidental with his mother's death, Henry began gingerly testing the waters of the hospitality business. PICO required office facilities in Sanford, where St. Johns River steamer passengers offloaded before boarding SFR trains for points toward Tampa. As a result, he hired local architect William T. Cotter to draft plans, including for a suitable lodging. Now, Plant ordered the go-ahead on what became the PICO Hotel, located appropriately on the PICO Block, where in time he also erected an office complex. The red-brick structure's design revealed little flair other than an onion-shaped dome at one corner. "Henry Plant must have encouraged Cotter to take his inspiration from the new rage of the day, the mysterious 'Near East,'" biographer Kelly Reynolds advised. "For such inspirations surely piqued Plant's interest whenever he went to his office on 23rd Street in Manhattan. Close by, the Grand Masonic Lodge of New York had opened its portals. Its members, the Ancient Arabic Order of Nobles of the Mystic Shrine, regularly came marching up the street in red fezzes and flowing silk trousers."[6]

His Sanford business concluded, the Plants returned to Havana. Jim and Anna English and Miriam Florence Squier Leslie, *Leslie's Illustrated Newspaper* publisher and widow of its namesake, Frank Leslie, accompanied them. The party left Tampa February 3 on the *Mascotte*. It reached Cuba on the fifth. "The people of Havana accorded us a royal welcome and our stay in the city was one continued round of pleasure," Leslie recollected. "There was a grand reception tendered us, at which there were 1,500 persons present, the opera-house being used for the purpose, followed by a banquet, at which over 150 persons were present. Yes, they were very kind to us in Havana." Anna English agreed: "[We] were traveling with [the Plants] who were acquainted with many of the prominent people in Havana; they were accordingly much fêted, and enjoyed the charm of seeing a great deal of the private and social life of that city. Governor English found novelty and charm in this glimpse of the tropics, this new world, with its different civilization. . . . Everything, indeed, combined to add zest to this holiday experience; and while entering into the lively diversions offered, he sometimes said, 'I am only twenty-one.'"[7]

Careful preparation lay behind the elaborate reception. Henry had asked sugar planter Pedro Fernandez de Castro to make proper arrangements. The party headquartered at Plant's favorite Havana lodging, the Hotel Pasaje, so named for the covered passageway at its rear that led from the Paseo del Prado to Zulueta Street. The venerable establishment was situated across the Prado from Central Park and adjacent to the vaunted Tacon Theatre. The collapsed Payret Theatre stood abandoned nearby. Cafés dotted the park, and bands filled the air with music nearly every evening. The Pasaje's main drawing card, though, was its proprietor, P. M. Castro, who insisted to one and all that he was "alive to the comfort of his guests." Visitors appreciated his concern. "[Mr.] Castro was on hand, I assure you, bright, quick as lightning, and speaking English perfectly, his countenance radiant with joy because you have come," a tourist recorded in March 1886. "So efficient was Castro in proclaiming himself and his house that he nearly swept the board and took to his really good hotel the mass of the passengers."[8]

As with his guests, the Cuban stay lightened Plant's heart while illuminating Havana's magical qualities. He planned substantial investments, but nine months fraught with significant developments intervened. The first occurred one week after Tampans banqueted Henry as their deliverer, expressing "the warm feeling entertained by the business people towards the man who is so efficiently developing the transportation interests of Florida." That day—April 1—fire destroyed the heart of Key West, Florida's largest city. Two days later a correspondent lamented, "The recent conflagration here was the most appalling ever seen in this city." The destruction extended into the city's cigar district, notably consuming the Ybor & Co. factory.[9]

Key West's disaster foreshadowed Tampa's eventual emergence as an economic powerhouse. Already, Plant's railroad had kick-started processes of change. "When the first train on the South Florida Railroad rolled into Tampa about two years since, it found the city as dead as a fishing village on the bleak shores of Cape Cod," a February report had asserted. "The sidewalks were poor, the houses weather beaten and void of paint. The newspapers were printed on hand presses and an atmosphere of decay permeated everything. The waiters at the hotel would answer, 'I'll attend to it in an hour' instead of 'in a minute,' and things generally were rusting instead of wearing out." Such conditions no longer applied. "This order of things in this year of 1886 has rapidly disappeared," the report continued. "Trim vessels sail away by sea from new wharves. New sidewalks, new hotels, new railroads, water works, a Board of Trade, an Opera House, new manufactories, new business blocks, fast steam presses for the newspapers, are now the order of the day." Significantly, on April 26 "cigar making commenced at Ybor City, near Tampa." Key West manufacturers had signaled a willingness to relocate at least some facilities to the mainland and its railroad connections. Vicente Martinez Ybor purchased forty acres of land north of downtown to accommodate them. He christened the area Ybor City. Sanchez & Haya opened its doors first; Ybor & Co. quickly followed.[10]

Other peninsular areas prospered in the meantime thanks to improved transportation, justifying to Plant major investments in upgraded services. At Jacksonville in April he agreed with executives of the Jacksonville, Tampa and Key West Railroad (JT&KW)—a line that had recently opened tracks from Jacksonville through Sanford and Enterprise to the Atlantic coast at Titusville—to change from narrow to standard gauge by summer. The innovation would set both lines in compliance with regional and national standards while facilitating easy interchange of cars between lines. This step had been taken by mid-September. The advance eased Plant's way to securing an initial "contract for [mail] service between Tampa, Key West, and Havana by the new steamer *Mascotte*, and a consort of equal excellence from August 1, 1886, to June 30, 1887." Jim English's influence with Grover Cleveland had surely abetted the happy outcome. The lucrative government fee that Plant derived from the mail contract led him during August to order from Cramp & Sons another state-of-the-art steamer, one grander than the *Mascotte*. An unprecedented triweekly West Indian Fast Mail thereafter started up between Tampa and Havana on November 2, with the steamboat *Whitney* supplementing the *Mascotte* until Plant's new steamer came on line.[11]

Plant also took care at the time to fend off several competitors, including by purchase in November of the East Georgia and Florida Railroad "now being built." The road's backers had claimed that its tracks would shorten travel time from Georgia to Jacksonville "considerably." Henry in closing the deal frustrated the ambitions of a major corporate interest. "Mr. H. B. Plant made a bold movement to-day, which saves his Savannah, Florida and Western system from invasion," a report alerted. "The Richmond and Danville system has long looked eagerly to the Florida flesh-pots. They control a line to Mille[n], Ga., from which point certain parties are building a line direct to

Jessup, and from Jessup to Jacksonville. This projected line let the Richmond and Danville into the best passenger traffic in the country, and shortened the distance about a hundred miles." With control of the new road, Plant effectively blocked the Richmond and Danville. "Mr. Plant is autocrat below Albany and Augusta, and stoutly defends his territory," the report concluded. "This is the third time he has repelled invasion by a quiet purchase. He quaintly says: 'Florida is the railroaders' paradise. The people ship out every thing they raise, and ship in every thing they use. They all leave Florida in the summer, and the rest of the world comes to Florida in the winter.'"[12]

The results of opening the West Indian Fast Mail and his deft handling of industry rivals left Plant pleased as he undertook a ritual fall "tour of inspection." The only discordant note sounded at Charleston about November 21 as he surveyed damage wreaked by a deadly earthquake. "It had been with sorrow," an interviewer observed, "that he saw the desolation and destruction wrought here." Otherwise, Henry exulted in the new Cuban connections and the changes he believed the Fast Mail would work in Southerners' attitudes about the island. "He also said, speaking of the new rail route from Havana to New York, that it was a great advance in the economy of time made by the present National postoffice administration," a journalist recorded. "Formerly, he said, the Cuban mails from Charleston or any Southern city, except New Orleans, first went by the steamship line from Havana to New York, where the distribution for Southern points was made, and the mail sent South again. A similar delay was, of course, experienced in the transmission of the mails from Charleston to Cuba. All this, however, has now been changed and the mails come direct to all places along the route from Havana to Key West, Tampa, Savannah, Charleston and other points." The journalist added: "Under the old system, Mr. Plant said, the Southern trade and the merchants of the South were at a great disadvantage as compared with those of the North. They have now equally as good facilities as those of the North."[13]

At Savannah on November 23 Henry took his first major step to realize the substance of his Cuban vision. "He and Col. H. S. Haines, general manager of the Plant roads, left on the midday train yesterday in their private car for Tampa, from which place they will go to Havana," the *Savannah Morning News* advised. "They expect to spend several weeks in Cuba. Mr. Plant is in excellent health." Details of the trip have been lost, but rumors circulated upon his return of concrete developments. "It is reported in Key West," an account specified, "that Mr. H. B. Plant contemplates the erection of a fine hotel in Havana." As always Henry held his cards close to his chest, and at Savannah on December 9 he denied the rumors. Still, expectancy filled the air for those who followed his movements.[14]

Although Plant stayed in New York City through the holidays and into February 1887, he worked steadily on developing Havana hotel plans. An emerging relationship with architect John A. Wood, whose works dotted the Hudson River Valley, influenced him considerably. How Wood first came to Plant's attention remains cloudy, although his design for the Piney Woods Hotel in Thomasville, Georgia—local backers considered calling it the H. B. Plant Hotel—impressed Henry greatly when he toured the massive building late in 1884 just before it opened. "They were taken through the long corridors, capacious dining room and parlors, and beautiful suites of rooms in the Piney Woods Hotel," a local paper noted. "The gentlemen all expressed themselves more than pleased with the interior finish and outward appearance of the magnificent hotel." The *New York Times* described the impressive wooden structure as "the finest hotel in the state." It rose three stories in "the Italian style of architecture." A visitor added: "It will be situated in the centre of a block of land handsomely laid out in gardens on three sides of the building. The main building will be 40 feet in width, with extensions containing the parlors, dining-rooms, and guest rooms. The south front of the building will be 400 feet long, 28 feet wide, and 24 feet high, and is designed to be the favorite lounging-place." Modern conveniences including private bathrooms, gas light, electric bells, wood-burning fireplaces, hot and cold running water, laundries, bowling alleys, and more set the facility apart as far from ordinary.[15]

Henry felt prepared to implement the Havana plans by March 1887. He had begun a routine tour of inspection following the launch February 16 in Philadelphia of his new steamer. He called her *Olivette* after Edmond Audran's 1879 opera *Les noces d'Olivette*. He prided himself on the sleek design and the fact that it was "probably the fastest commercial ship, which carries the flag of the United States into a foreign port." Inspections and annual meetings that followed brought him to Sanford on March 9, where SFR stockholders and directors convened at the PICO Hotel. There Plant procured the last nod of approval required for Havana construction. His party departed Tampa on March 12 under cover of hosting a Cuban tour for presidential hopeful Senator John Sherman of Ohio. As one public event after another acclaimed Sherman, Plant quietly worked out of the Hotel Pasaje to solidify plans. "Mr. H. B. Plant, of New York, who had previously conceived the idea of building an immense American hotel in the city of Havana, Cuba, went over to that city from Port Tampa on one of his own ships, accompanied by General Manager [Haines] of the Savannah, Florida and Western railway, and Mr. J. A. Wood, the well-known architect of New York," the *Atlanta Constitution* later detailed. "Their object was to look the ground over in Havana for hotel purposes, some inquiry about sites and other matters having already been set on foot there. Mr. Plant had in view particularly the purchase of the Payette [Payret] theater property, around the corner to the left from the Hotel Inglaterra."[16]

Henry's Cuban hotel scheme unfortunately ran awry. "Well, Messrs. Plant, Haines and Wood spent a long time in Havana looking into the matter," the *Constitution* continued. "The result was that the Payrette theater site appeared to be the most available property to be had, and the price asked for it was not unreasonable. But when it came to the matter of titles it was discovered that a legal transfer of the property could not be made for some years to come, the ownership being in dispute, the titles obscured and the testimony necessary to an untangling of the matter not easily procurable." Haines, long opposed to the Havana project, "could not conceal his satisfaction at the outcome." Plant, on the other hand, understandably "was disappointed—very naturally so." Bad weather plagued the *Mascotte*'s return voyage to Tampa, necessitating a Key West layover on March 18. The interlude and subsequent voyage allowed Wood to pose alternative possibilities. "'Now, I've got an idea,' broke in Architect Wood," the newspaper related. "'Why build a hotel in Havana any way? Let somebody else try the experiment and build up the business of the railroads and steamships for you? Old Tampa, in my opinion, is the ideal place for your palace hotel.'" Haines concurred. "There now, that's good sense," the railroad superintendent urged. "I'm with you on that proposition. That's business. I believe that Tampa is the one spot—the only spot—for your hotel, Mr. Plant. Don't you think so?"[17]

Whatever influence Wood and Haines brought to bear on Plant to favor Tampa failed to extinguish his hopes for a Cuban hotel; still, the Tampa scene quickly echoed with renewed commitment from Plant interests. One portent of what was to come involved the arrival of news that his lobbying efforts had prompted Congress to declare Tampa a port of entry. "Vessels may now go direct to Tampa," a journalist explained, "without stopping, as heretofore, at Key West." On March 21 Wood spoke at "a mass meeting." A notice of the proceedings declared, "Among many wants Tampa needs a big hotel worst." Plant as yet was not committed to the idea, certainly not on Flagler's St. Augustine scale. So, Henry played for time by airing a proposal likely to fail. "H. B. Plant seems determined that Tampa shall have a big hotel, and with that object in view he has sent his architect, Mr. Wood, to this place to raise subscription stock to the amount of $50,000, and select the location," a local man noted in late March. "Mr. Plant will see the remaining $100,000. The present hotels are clearly insufficient to accommodate or attract the tourist."[18]

As Plant had expected, local fundraising efforts floundered. The practical workings of his mind had meanwhile refocused his attention away from

16. Ponce de Leon Hotel, St. Augustine, Florida, c. 1902. Library of Congress.

the town itself. To improve steamship service and mail delivery to Cuba and other Caribbean spots, he required a deepwater port. Engineers had determined that the needed dredging of Hillsborough Bay and the Hillsborough River was not feasible relative to costs; so, Henry's agents had sought a location where deep water could be assured. The spot lay on the southwestern shore of the Interbay Peninsula at a place called Brushy Point (or Black Point), some nine or ten miles southwest from town. "The Plant Investment Company . . . in a few weeks will have the Hillsborough river bridged and their road extended some six or eight miles down the western shore of the bay to 'Brushy Point,' where they will build a dock for their steamships and establish a quarantine station," a correspondent mentioned in March. "By doing this, they have deep water right at their wharf."[19]

Port Tampa construction progressed through spring and summer. "The grading of the Brushy Point extension of the South Florida is nearly completed, and on Monday [August 29, 1887] work was begun on the bridge over the Hillsborough River," a Tampan recorded. "Trains will be running to Deep Water by November at the furthest, at which date the tri-weekly schedule of the Tampa and Havana Steamship Line (Plant Steamship Company) will go into effect." Among other concerns yellow fever caused delays, but Plant nonetheless invested huge sums over the next several years in his port. “The extension of the railway system to Port Tampa, 10 miles below Tampa, brings the trains to a depth of water of 25 to 30 feet, where these large and substantial wharves, recently erected at great expense, offer every facility for the convenience of commerce,” he boasted three years after construction began. “The bay is admirably located for defense in case of war, and with the adequate railroad facilities diverging from Tampa, is the most convenient and safe rendezvous for shipping on the eastern shore of the Gulf of Mexico.”[20]

Plant entrusted PICO Hotel architect W. T. Cotter with responsibility for conceptualizing and designing the facilities at Port Tampa, including a suitable hotel. Manifesting creative inspiration not readily apparent in his Sanford design, he capitalized on the mile-long pier required to reach deep water. “The new town, if I may call it a town, is built over the water, a mile out from shore, and the railroad track runs out to it over a long causeway of piles,” a visitor described. “About a [half] mile out the train runs first past The Inn, then past a restaurant connected with it, and then, last of all, up to the steamship dock, where lay on one side the Mascotte and on the other the Olivette, the former looming up in the night like a great, gloomy house, and the Olivette a blaze of light, for she was the ship to go out.”[21]

One visitor preserved his impressions. “The beautiful and picturesque ‘Inn’ and restaurant are situated about half way from the shore and end of the pier,” he recorded. “‘The Inn’ is constructed somewhat after the old English style of architecture. The rooms are all cool and airy, and furnished in the most artistic and comfortable manner. The reception or general sitting-room is exquisitely furnished. The interior finish is of the native Florida pine in all its natural beauty; all the furniture, including the piano, is of the same shade; easy chairs, couches and lounges offer tempting resting places for the lazy or tired, and rugs which harmonize and give the requisite touch of color, are scattered over the hard-wood floors. The walls are covered with engravings, etchings and graceful water-color sketches.” The man added: “No spot on earth can offer more alluring bathing facilities. You don a bathing suit, and if expert, dive from your window! If not so venturesome you can run down the steps from the piazza, and float off in the seductive water, which embraces one with warm caresses.”[22]

The Port Tampa Inn opened in stages. The small St. Elmo’s Inn (“the annex”), capable of hosting fourteen guests, debuted in June 1888. Yellow fever delayed the main building’s availability until January 30, 1889. To mark the occasion Henry and Margaret hosted a “free supper and ball” that admittedly “was rather impromptu, and was not intended for an elaborate affair.” The facility proved immediately successful. “‘The Inn’ is fast becoming a favorite resort of both commercial and railroad men," a visitor noted on June 2. "No matter where they may be during the early part of the week, Saturday or Sunday finds them at the Port partaking of the good cheer and ample hospitality, lounging, sailing, bathing, flirting, fishing and all other innocent amusement." Given demand, Plant ordered expansion. "'The Inn' has already been found too small to accommodate the increasing throngs who flock to this popular place of resort," a local man related. "A large addition is almost completed. It is a sort of demi-semi-Colonial and Queen Anne style of architecture. There are over twenty guest chambers in the new addition, three immense dining-rooms and a large kitchen."[23]

Henry had spent little time in the area as construction of Port Tampa first progressed in summer and fall 1887. He and Margaret enjoyed the *Olivette*'s premier voyage from Philadelphia to Cuba and Florida in April, followed by a brief interlude of mackerel fishing in Tampa Bay, but afterward the couple kept mostly to New Jersey and New York resorts when they were not at Branford or in their Fifth Avenue home. Two exceptions, beyond annual meetings and business conferences, deserve special mention. In mid-May they toured California and "the West" with J. E. Ingraham, probably to examine firsthand the "hotel palaces of the Pacific coast" that Flagler's Ponce de Leon reputedly rivaled "in colossal proportions, grandeur and completeness in all appointments." They had originally expected to be away "about two months," but son Morton's June 23 wedding to Nellie B. Capron at Baltimore drew them back. The event marked the culmination of Morton's recovery from his dark period of the late 1870s and early 1880s. Now a trusted Southern Express executive, he held office as well in several other Plant enterprises. Morton resided at Fort Gates on the St. Johns River, where, on his father's behalf, he maintained an orange grove and residence. Following a honeymoon trip to Canada, though, the newlyweds made Jacksonville their principal home.[24]

Through 1887 and into 1888 Plant's thoughts concerning a possible grand hotel at Tampa gradually evolved. J. A. Wood scouted sites and prepared more detailed plans in his absence, although the architect also pursued other projects. His Oglethorpe Hotel, for instance, which echoed Thomasville's Piney Woods Hotel with long porches and corner towers adorned with spires, opened for customers at Brunswick on January 9, 1888. At Tampa, Wood pressed a particular site, arguing aesthetic values and land prices. It lay on the Hillsborough River's western side immediately facing downtown. Plant toyed with other possibilities, though, as a March 1889 conversation with Grover Cleveland highlighted. "[The former president] was pleased with the view of the bay from the site of old Fort Brooke, and asked Mr. Plant why he hadn't built his hotel at the foot of Franklin street," a townsman recalled. "Mr. Plant explained that he had wanted to erect it there but was unable to get a clear title to the land." Given that impediment, Plant accepted Wood's choice but not before visiting Havana in late January 1888 to make renewed inquiries. Whatever he discovered failed to slow impetus for Tampa action. On February 1 Henry's agents purchased a large parcel "immediately opposite the South Florida Railway depot." A correspondent boasted: "Tampa's grand hotel is now assured . . . and work will be commenced immediately. The location is beautiful and commands a fine view of the river and bay." A second report soon noted: "Mr. J. A. Wood, a New York architect of large experience, is already on the ground and preparations are being made for the early commencement of work. The house will contain nearly or quite two hundred rooms and will be fitted with every comfort and convenience skill and money can secure. To make it unique of its kind the architecture will be Moorish and attendants will be dressed in Spanish costume."[25]

In the meantime, during early 1888 the usually steady and easygoing Plant interestingly confounded observers with a somewhat frenetic and otherwise atypical manner. The change came after a January 12 gala event, the grand opening of Flagler's Ponce de Leon. Whether Henry attended is not known. He definitely enjoyed Flagler's hospitality within weeks, though. Henry temporized meanwhile on a final decision about Tampa. Remaining at a distance, he and Margaret headquartered during much of the period at Winter Park's Seminole Hotel with friends, including the George Westinghouse family and Mrs. George M. Pullman. There, he undertook excursions, consulted with Wood and other visiting associates, and prepared to greet President Cleveland on February 24. Annual meetings and a tour of inspection occupied March, although he and Flagler traveled to Tampa on the thirty-first to discuss "building of the grand hotel." One local newspaperman assured that "an understanding will be reached." No such result came to pass. From Tampa the Plants, lawyer W. S. Chisholm, and several others embarked on another "delightful trip to Havana." Henry steadfastly clung to his Cuban dreams.[26]

Freshly restored to Florida from the Havana visit, Henry, Margaret, and their party then traveled to St. Augustine, arriving at the Ponce de Leon on April 8. Flagler's accomplishments, which now included a second hotel—the Alcazar—clearly astounded Plant. "I have studied it closely, and it is the greatest individual enterprise I have any record of," he told the *Atlanta Constitution*'s Henry W. Grady. "It is amazing that any man should have had the courage to spend millions so lavishly in an old and dead city." Flagler returned the compliment. He also hosted Plant, Grady, Elias Cornelius Benedict (his daughter Jennie Louise's father-in-law), and writer Thomas Bailey Aldrich for a day's sail on Benedict's yacht *Oneida*. On the night of the ninth

Flagler also sponsored "a grand illumination" in the Plants' honor. "The fairy lamps numbering 3,000 with the beautiful electrical display, will exceed even that of last Wednesday night [the anniversary of Ponce de Leon's landing in Florida]," a correspondent observed. "From each of the [nearby] towns will be rendered concert solos, and after this they are to play in concert a most beautiful duet."[27]

Within days thereafter several developments struck Plant that additionally influenced his future course. Blunt realities of political conflict and trials of emotional stress factored among them. In the first case, in mid-April the governor general of Cuba declared martial law in "the provinces of Havana, Pinar, Del Rio, Matanzas and Santa Clara." He justified his action due to "brigandage in those sections," but persistent rumors insisted that a war for independence might have begun. Word then reached Plant late on April 20 that one of his mentors and a longtime supporter, Adams Express president William B. Dinsmore, had died. "Mr. Dinsmore's career from the day he came to New York to represent [Alvin] Adams," the *New York Herald* proclaimed, "proved what skill, vim and industry could accomplish by building up from a carpet bag as a foundation, with the assistance of the lad he termed 'his boy Hoey,' an organization unequalled in the world in its responsibility to the public and the government as the greatest carriers of this generation." The funeral took place on the twenty-third at New York's Calvary Episcopal Church with Plant in attendance. Longtime colleagues George Tilley, W. S. Chisholm, and Henry Sanford looked on with him as John Hoey, Clarence Seward, Clapp Spooner, and Jim English, among others, carried the coffin. The occasion's intensity ran extraordinarily high for the aging men. Some relief from the pain of loss was happily afforded to Plant in May when Hoey succeeded Dinsmore as Adams Express president.[28]

On the day of Hoey's selection—May 10, 1888—Plant finally, if reluctantly, offered to begin construction of a large hotel at Tampa. Continuing hesitation echoed when he announced conditions. Historian James W. Covington explained that they included "concessions concerning a [Hillsborough River] bridge and real estate taxes." Henry then finalized arrangements for the *Olivette* to spend the summer running between Boston and Bar Harbor, Maine. That accomplished, he and Margaret hurriedly turned local affairs over to Wood, Ingraham, and Haines. In New York by the thirteenth, Henry did not return to Tampa until January 1889. Troubling reports circulated in the interim about his general dissatisfaction with business affairs and possible infighting among Plant System executives. A particular concern, they declared, involved a huge investment Henry had made in the mammoth Richmond and West Point Terminal Company, predecessor to the Southern Railway Company. "H. B. Plant wants to sell out his immense system of railroads and steamships, reaching from Charleston to Havana, says one report," a Savannah correspondent insisted, "and it is a true one." Others described a power struggle for control of the system should Plant opt to retire rather than sell out. "For some years it was a question who would succeed Mr. Plant when he abdicates—Judge Chisholm or Col. H. S. Haines, the general manager of the system," a Charleston newspaper advised. "Every one believes now that Mr. Plant has picked out Judge Chisholm for that distinction."[29]

Whatever his true feelings, Plant strove to gainsay the reports. He and Margaret energetically "led a large party of guests" on the *Olivette*'s first cruise to Bar Harbor in mid-June, insisting that the group board in media-friendly New York rather than at Boston. Henry Sanford stood by him, as did his brother Horace P. Hoadley, now PICO secretary, and New Haven attorney Lynde Harrison. Chisholm also figured among the guests; Haines did not. Plant's agents ensured their employer a warm arrival at the *Olivette*'s northernmost destination. "The ship was greeted by the turn out of nearly the entire populace, and, much to their satisfaction, the ship was thrown open for their inspection," a Bar Harbor man related. Friendly newspapermen, too, buttressed Plant's position. "Nothing that Mr. Plant has said or is doing justifies such a report," one argued. "He is going right ahead developing his great railway and steamship system with his accustomed energy and judgment, and his plans reach years into the future." Still, it could not be denied that when celebrants laid the Tampa Bay Hotel's cornerstone on July 28, its backer remained 1,200 miles away in the comfort of his Branford estate. "The honor must be ascribed to Mr. H. B. Plant," a speaker insisted despite the absence. "It was his gigantic brain that conceived the project of giving Tampa a hotel second to none in the Union, and it is to his liberality and his faith in our city's future that we are indebted for this great stroke of fortune."[30]

Henry's appreciation that his hotel plans would not, in fact, furnish Tampa with "a hotel second to none in the Union" offered one basis for misgivings. A prevailing sense of lassitude complicated the picture. He and Margaret had scheduled a European vacation into early fall that would have allowed him distance to mull his desires and intentions. Unfortunately, one catastrophe after another altered the plans. Foremost among them, yellow fever—which had attacked Tampa in fall 1887—returned in July 1888 to infect hundreds of residents while spreading its vicious grasp to other peninsular locales. The yellow jack particularly devastated Jacksonville. Henry ordered Southern Express to carry relief supplies and medicines to Florida without cost. He also beseeched state authorities in the face of general panic to assume responsibility after counties needlessly quarantined themselves against each other. When his effort failed, he appealed "to President Cleveland to send national troops to Florida and establish a Government quarantine." As his representative D. H. Elliott underscored, "The present state of affairs in Florida is described as terrible." Doubts in Plant's mind redoubled about the viability and responsibility of a state government run by white conservatives, many of them former Rebels and now known as Bourbons. As Henry's frustrations mounted, the bad news kept coming. On October 21 his SFR associate Royal M. Pulsifer suicided in Massachusetts. Less than one month later, lifelong friend Lorenzo Blackstone succumbed in Connecticut. Henry helped bury him at Norwich on November 17.[31]

Amid these personal crises and calamities, Plant somehow managed to right himself, and the decisive and committed entrepreneur reappeared. During the year's final two months Henry summoned key subordinates to New York and reinforced to them his aspirations for the Plant System and for Florida. "Mr. Plant is undismayed by the fever, and is going right ahead with the erection of his new hotel at Tampa," Haines explained. Henry instructed architect Wood to dream bigger dreams. "After a conference with Plant in New York City, Wood returned to Tampa in November, 1888, with plans for a much larger hotel which included 50 more rooms, 16 private parlor suites and a large dining room added to the planned structure," James W. Covington related. "In his initial projections Wood planned the erection of a $200,000 wooden building to serve as dining hall, but when plans were changed to erect the hotel in the Ponce de Leon resort hotel style, additional land had to be purchased to accommodate a larger building." Haines commented, "Next to the Ponce de Leon at St. Augustine it will be the largest hotel in Florida." Boldly underscoring the reach of newfound ambition, Plant in December added Flagler to the PICO board in Blackstone's stead.[32]

The PICO annual meeting at which Flagler accepted a director's chair met at New York in early December, and within days Plant set out to South Carolina and Georgia on a tour of inspection. He boasted about speedier trains, including a Monday, Wednesday, and Friday "New York and Florida Special" with a running time between New York and Jacksonville of "less than thirty-six hours." He promised even more. "At Havana connections will be made for the West Indies, South America and other foreign countries and connections will be made with the American ship for Vera Cruz once a week," a newspaper detailed. "In fact, Mr. Plant said that he is now perfecting arrangements for the sale of through tickets to the City of Mexico all along the coast over the Plant system, via Havana and Vera Cruz." On January 1, 1889, he presided at the opening of the SF&W's new Savannah depot. He then touched base at Tampa and Port Tampa. "He seemed pleased at the marked improvement made in the city since his last visit," an editor remarked. A night at Winter Park's Seminole Hotel followed before business meetings at Savannah and Augusta on the way to New York. At Charleston by the twenty-eighth, he hastened through Jacksonville to the Port Tampa Inn's opening on the thirtieth.[33]

The pace that Plant set in January 1889 intensified over the next few months as he resolved problems with competitors, assured continued alliances, and reassured the nation as to the safety and desirability of winter travel to Florida. Having touched at Montgomery and Mobile in early February, he accepted accolades at a New Orleans banquet on the eighth. From there he, Margaret, and Mike O'Brien set out "in their private car for a tour of Mexico." A Charleston newspaper recapped the one-week outing. "He had just returned from a trip to the City of Mexico, which city he visited partly on business and partly for pleasure," it detailed. "As a result of the trip he has about completed arrangements for a delightful tourist route to Mexico, or by rail to Tampa and thence by the Plant steamers via Havana and Vera Cruz. The Plant System has about arranged for satisfactory connections, and the basis is now being laid for a more-extended travel to Mexico and Cuba next winter by way of Florida."[34]

A fabulous present awaited Henry at New Orleans, one that quickly gained renown of its own. George Pullman had built his friend a "palace car." Some believed "Car No. 100" to be "the handsomest private palace car that has ever been turned out of shop," and its creator glowed with pride when presenting it to Plant. "Mr. Pullman declared that the car was the most thoroughly equipped and by far the finest that had ever left his works," a report observed. "Every convenience that modern demand for comfort could suggest is to be found within. The interior is of handsome oiled wood, magnificently carved and turned and relieved on all sides with heavy mirrors. The upholstery is of blue and salmon plush, and the ceiling is artistically frescoed. The furniture is of mahogany and the floor is heavily carpeted. In the rear is the kitchen, refrigerators, pantries, lavatories and closets. The middle section of the car is used as a reception and dining-room. The sleeping apartments, richly upholstered, are near by, and immediately next to them is a lavatory and bath-room. An extra apartment, comfortably furnished and used by Mrs. Plant's maid, adjoins, and the front end is a smoking and sitting-room. The car is steam-heated and is complete in all its apartments, being the first of its kind that has been seen South and the latest that Mr. Pullman has made." A friend exulted, "Col. Plant is delighted with it."[35]

Henry utilized the car immediately for business advantage as well as personal comfort. It carried him in the two or three weeks after he departed New Orleans to annual meetings and business conferences in various southern locales. He looked especially to March 12, though, and the Flagler-sponsored

17. Henry B. Plant and President Grover Cleveland aboard the SS *Olivette* on the way to Cuba, in March 1889. Collection of Henry B. Plant Museum.

national tropical tennis championship at the Ponce de Leon. The occasion offered the two friends a chance to finalize plans for Grover Cleveland's upcoming Florida visit. The president had lost his reelection bid the previous November to Republican Benjamin Harrison and departed the presidency on March 4, 1889. His Florida trip, billed as a vacation following years in the national spotlight, carried great meaning for Plant and Flagler. The agenda included a Plant-guided tour of Havana with introductions to the cream of Cuban political and social life. Rumor had it meanwhile that Cleveland traveled informally as Harrison's emissary, in one reporter's words, "to recommend to the new administration at Washington the purchase of the island from Spain by the United States."[36]

The Plants slipped away from St. Augustine before Cleveland's stay there and in time to reach Tampa to ready final preparations for his visit. Henry arrived on the fifteenth to a hero's welcome. "The party consists of Messrs. Plant and Ingraham, Judge Chisholm and ladies," a correspondent related. "The party was enthusiastically received, and the locomotive was handsomely decorated with flowers, flags and bunting, and the gentlemen were visited to-day by the leading citizens of Tampa. The city realizes and appreciates the vast benefit derived from the Plant System, and especially honors its distinguished head." Four days later Flagler escorted the former president from St. Augustine's new depot to the Ponce de Leon. His guests departed the next day for Port Tampa and the *Olivette*, which Plant's officials had "decorated from stem to stern with flags and bunting." The "grandest demonstration ever witnessed on this island" greeted them at Key West during a stopover on the twenty-second before the steamer reached Havana harbor the following morning. "Crowds of people thronged the wharf since early morning and gave the distinguished travelers an enthusiastic welcome," a report advised. "The party took carriages, and were driven to the Hotel Pasaje, where an aide, in the name of the Governor-General, welcomed them to the island."[37]

Thanks in good part to the hospitality of Cuba's governor general Don Manuel Salamanca y Negrete, the five-day Cleveland visit passed triumphantly. The new governor general impressed Plant and the former president. "During ex-President Cleveland's recent visit to Havana he was shown marked attention by Capt. Gen. Salamanca," a reporter commented. "The freedom of the city was tendered to him and the Captain General's palace placed at his disposal." The final evening Governor Fitzhugh Lee of Virginia—whose Cuban ties proved of enormous value to Henry in the future—accompanied Cleveland, Plant, and others to a Salamanca-hosted palace banquet before adjourning to the Albion Theatre, where they "warmly applauded" the "noted singer and dancer" Amelia Rodriguez. Back at Tampa on March 29, Plant honored his guest with "an informal reception" at the Port Tampa Inn. During a brief tour of Tampa and Tampa Bay Hotel construction, Cleveland recommended that Plant purchase additional land for expansion. Henry accordingly picked up nine more acres and ordered erection of an additional three-hundred-foot-long wing "to be of glass, fitted up with parlors, sitting and reading rooms, and promenades, so that in case of a cold snap the guests can have the benefit of light and sunshine without being exposed to the sharp winds or cold." Then all moved by rail to Jupiter on the Atlantic coast. There, Margaret Plant landed a ninety-four-pound tarpon with the ex-president's assistance. The publicity value, Plant quietly relished, could not have been counted.[38]

12

Unanticipated Outcomes

1889 to 1893

"Mr. Plant, that is right across the Everglades of Florida"

The *H. B. Plant* was steaming down the St. Johns River on the morning of April 3, 1889, when it halted a short distance above Palatka to allow passengers to sightsee at tiny Fort Gates. Morton Plant, son of the vessel's namesake, maintained a home there and an orange grove. With others, ex-President Grover Cleveland—fresh from vacationing with Henry and Margaret Plant at Tampa, Havana, and Jupiter—stepped ashore. A brief but quietly enjoyable interlude followed before the party resumed the journey North toward almost-certain national notoriety. The passengers believed that reverberations of their island visit would produce closer ties to Cuba and, possibly, its purchase by the United States. The visit meanwhile also recognized the onset of an interregnum in Cleveland's presidency. Sidelined from power the previous month by Republican Benjamin Harrison, Cleveland now bided his time in anticipation of the return to office that he achieved four years later. At Fort Gates, though, it was excitement about Florida and Cuba that filled the air. A reporter related, "Regarding their trip to South Florida Mr. Cleveland was very enthusiastic and said that he had one of the most pleasant trips of his life, and the only trouble was that it had been too short, as it had not given him the amount of sport that he desired when he found himself in such an angler's paradise as Indian River." Meanwhile, Plant's vision of the tropical paradise that was Havana surpassed Cleveland's ardor for Florida. At that moment the developer ached to sell the world on Cuban dreams. And he knew where and how to begin doing so. "H. B. Plant, president of the Savannah, Florida and Western Railway Company, and owner of a line of steamers to Tampa," a Washington newspaper observed on April 10, "passed through this city yesterday with his wife, en route to New York and the Paris Exposition."[1]

Looking toward a mid-May departure for the new world's fair at Paris, Plant had readied for an extended absence. Site preparations for his grand Tampa hotel had moved ahead steadily, aided by the laying of two special railroad tracks to deliver sixteen or more carloads of material daily. Cleveland, upon gazing at the progress, had exclaimed, "What an immense structure!" Architect J. A. Wood credited workers for the gains. "Speaking of the colored laborers on the work," a report observed, "[he] says they cannot be equaled by any body of laborers, white, black, native or foreign [of] any state or country." Plant's commitment to the hotel had also raised the stakes of his commitment to Tampa. To build its economy, he had visited Mobile to assess the viability of steamer service between the two cities. "The condition of affairs seems to him satisfactory and he has no doubt the steamers will get good business, especially in Alabama coal to Tampa and Key West," one newspaper observed. "It is intimated also that a line of steamers will be established to Central American ports." Beyond that, Florida's economy as a whole necessarily factored in calculations by Plant and his friend and partner Henry M. Flagler. "If low [railroad] rates [have] any virtue," one-time Tennessee governor John Calvin Brown quoted Plant as declaring, "he and Mr. Flagler were going to fill Florida chock-a-block with tourists and settlers next winter."[2]

Henry and Margaret ultimately left the United States May 15 on the magnificent new steamer *City of Paris*, traveling with an elite company that included, among others, friends Miriam Squire Leslie, George M. Pullman, and Andrew Carnegie. Arriving at London in early June, Plant began attending to the challenge of finding elegant furnishings and accoutrements for the Tampa hotel. He had entrusted Margaret with principal responsibility for selecting and securing appropriate purchases, a task she pursued enthusiastically in England and on the Continent. Credit for the forty-one boxcars of acquisitions that arrived at Tampa in October belonged for the most part to her, although Henry assisted the buying spree with items that particularly appealed to him. The "great orchestrion" ranked as a favorite. "We are informed that during the world's fair at Paris, Mr. Plant secured something new in a large music-box which is operated by steam and excels in sweetness and softness of its music anything of the kind that has ever been heard," the *Tampa Tribune* explained. "This will be an attraction that no other hotel in the world has."[3]

Following a short London sojourn, the Plants availed themselves of the convenient boat train to Paris and the world's fair. Historian James W. Covington explained: "When the United States was invited by the Republic of France to send people and exhibits to the Paris Universal Exposition of 1889, the governor of Florida requested the legislature to provide adequate funds for a Florida display but the legislature did not act. Realizing that this was a good opportunity to display Florida products, the Plant Investment Company spent $15,000 to display samples and a selection of southern resources." Henry had enlisted public-relations expert David H. Elliott to accompany him. Elliott's duties included overseeing transportation and erection of the display, promoting travel between Florida and Cuba, and—importantly—countering mounting criticisms within Florida of Plant and his focus on Cuba and other places outside the Sunshine State. "Colonel Elliott, one of the best men in the world for such work, goes to attend this display," an Orlando newspaper advised. "It has been said that Mr. Plant is greedy, avaricious and illiberal toward the people of Florida," the item continued. "This is not true. He has done much, and is doing more to develop her resources and populate her untilled acres." A well-informed Parisian correspondent commented on June 29, "With Mr. and Mrs. Plant came Col. Elliott who is making himself conspicuously useful, and if there is not a very large increase in Florida and Cuba travel via the new overland and short sea route, it will not be his fault."[4]

Elliott's contributions proved beneficial. To maximize utilization of his time, Henry engaged "Professor" Arthur C. Jackson, a "popular member of the American Exposition colony," to deal with the Florida exhibits and furnish Floridians a steady flow of complimentary prose about Plant's labors on their behalf. Henry's age (he reached seventy on October 27) had unfortunately begun to tell on him. "The weight of years prevents Mr. P. from following all his kindly impulses," Jackson reported, "but no one is working more actively or successfully for Florida's interests than he, and it is certain that Florida owes more of its industrial development and commercial prospects to him than to any other living man." Fortunately, from a publicity standpoint, the US commissioner general for the exposition invited Henry to serve as a juror. Honored, Henry carried out the responsibility with relish.[5]

Plant's attention, though, never strayed far from his main task. "Much credit is heartily given by American visitors to the Exposition to the handsome way in which Florida has distinguished herself at the Exposition," a visitor exclaimed. "Not only has Florida the only separate State exhibit at the Exposition, but she really has two separate exhibits. In the agricultural department of the United States section there is an attractive pavilion, bearing 'Florida' on its four facades, and with its specimens of woods, cotton, wines, moss, fruits and general agricultural products forming really one of the most attractive spots in the whole section." He added: "The second Florida exhibit is in a conspicuous location in the United States section of the Palace of Liberal Arts. It has besides various specimens of Florida sea island and other cotton, a fine case of native woods, handsomely displayed, and a collection of Florida manufactured products." Having detailed specific categories of items displayed, a second onlooker added: "There is a splendid collection of . . . paintings of the magnificent hotels of St. Augustine built by Mr. Flagler, the one partially erected at Tampa, and the steamships of the Plant line." The onlooker commented, "Mr. Plant's efforts will probably attract tourists of the future from Europe, who hitherto have held the idea that Florida is a wild swamp, half Okeefeenokee and the rest Everglade."[6]

Thanks to Elliott and Jackson, Plant enjoyed plenty of time for pleasant diversions despite advanced age and heavy responsibilities. William F. Cody's "Wild West show" thrilled Parisians that summer. Elliott had known him for years and brought Henry and Buffalo Bill together. A warm friendship emerged. Henry's delight reached another peak on July 4 when, as the *New York Times* reported, "by special favor of M. Eiffel, Colonel Plant ascended the famous Eiffel Tower and planted the American flag on its apex, that being the only flag except the French tricolor that has floated from that point." The *Times* added, "The flag remained on the tower until after the exercise of unveiling the [Parisian] Statue of Liberty [replica] had been finished, when it was taken down by Col. Plant." Elliott actually "waved the American flag from the top of the Eiffel tower at noon," but that fact little diminished Henry's joy.[7]

Not everything, as it turned out, went according to plan. In the midst of the summer's activities, alarming word from home suddenly compelled Plant to cut short his French visit. "Mr. Plant was called back earlier than expected," a newspaperman soon advised, "owing to the serious illness of Judge W. T. Chisholm, vice president of the Plant Investment company." Henry and Margaret hurriedly left France in order to reach the *City of Paris* prior to its Liverpool departure. Their return to New York on July 31, 1889—despite Chisholm's plight—proved a gala occasion. "It was a quick trip that the Inman steamship City of Paris ended when she arrived in port yesterday—five days, twenty-three hours and ten minutes from Queenstown," a local report noted. "Coming up the bay she bore at the foremast head a small American flag which was first unfurled to the breeze on the top of the Eiffel Tower, in Paris, by Colonel H. B. Plant, of Florida, a passenger on the vessel."[8]

Fortunately, Chisholm averted catastrophe and his condition improved. As a result, the Plants observed an easy schedule for several months, during which time they enjoyed the comforts of Branford, Saratoga Springs, and Bar Harbor before resuming residence on Fifth Avenue in mid-September. Henry managed in the process to conduct needed business, including purchase of the "fine steamer" *Juniata* to service the regular run he proposed from Mobile to Port Tampa. Moreover, at New Haven on October 10 he found himself suddenly inspired. The occasion involved a dinner honoring delegates to an International Conference of American states that had convened at Washington on October 2 preparatory to its members beginning "a 7000 mile tour of the country." The effort aimed to strengthen Western Hemisphere ties while promoting trade and prosperity. Conversations that evening spurred Plant to press John Inman of the massive Richmond Terminal Railroad to join in making Port Tampa "the great shipping place for all or nearly all the export freight from the Southwest and Northwest to Europe, South and Central America." The plan, according to published accounts, specified: "The Plant Steamship Lines and several new lines of steamers, which are to be established by these companies at once, will take the export shipments to foreign markets. The harbor will be improved and new wharves built and other terminal facilities arranged." A report added, "Besides this, it is given out that Messrs. Inman and Plant will build an independent line of their own from Tampa northward and westward to Mobile and New Orleans, to be better able to handle the big influx of Western freights from the Southern Pacific and other lines centering at New Orleans from the West."[9]

The Richmond Terminal arrangement, sadly for Port Tampa, fell through. A frustrated Plant consequently tacked while maintaining the broader course. Now, he aimed to capitalize on his new Mobile connection to channel the trade of the Midwest and its great metropolis of Chicago through Tampa Bay. At Tampa on November 12, he undertook the *Juniata*'s inaugural voyage to Mobile. A two-day trip led to spirited festivities upon arrival. From Mobile, Car No. 100 then transported him to St. Louis, Chicago, Cincinnati, Indianapolis, and other points. He preached the merits of "a direct line of rail and steamship communication from Chicago to South and Central America." More particularly, he urged business interests "to subsidize a line of steamers from Florida to Rio [de] Janeiro, Brazil."[10]

The effort quickly stalled with only limited progress tallied. "[Mr. Plant] came down to Port Tampa to meet the steamer that is to go on the South American line," the *Tampa Tribune* advised on December 14. The *Charles Morand* steamed into Port Tampa the next day from Jamaica and Honduras carrying thousands of bananas and 141 bags of coconuts consigned to the Central American and Tampa Fruit Co., a new concern over which Henry presided. The milestone afforded sufficient encouragement for him to build grander "steamship offices" at Port Tampa. They opened for business in April 1890. Coincidentally, a "banana train" began running to Chicago. "The banana train is a coup on the part of Mr. H. B. Plant," the *Atlanta Constitution* credited. "The fruit from Central America to Chicago has heretofore gone by steamer to New Orleans, and thence by the Illinois Central to Chicago. Mr. Plant conceived the idea of diverting it by steamer to Port Tampa and thence by his lines and the East Tennessee to Chicago. The bananas went without a break to Chicago, where they arrived in excellent condition."[11]

Whatever disappointments Plant felt when his international plans faltered paled in early 1890 by comparison to other setbacks. He had counted, for instance, on the grand opening of the Tampa Bay Hotel for the winter 1890 tourist season. As one man put it, the facility was "intended to be the connecting link between the Plant Railroad system and the Plant Steamships" while "rival[ing] in magnificence the Ponce de Leon at St. Augustine." Henry meanwhile had recruited George H. Carter, manager of Bar Harbor's posh Malvern Hotel, to organize staff and services. Plant had traveled with Carter in early November 1889 to Tampa, where they discovered, to their dismay, that construction lagged expectations. "The owners have decided not to open the new Plant Hotel at Tampa, Fla., until next season," the *New York Times* ultimately reported in mid-January. "The manager and most of the principal employees are now on the ground, but the building is not entirely finished, and only a part of it could be opened to the public this Winter. Mr. Plant said yesterday that he had determined not to open it till it is complete in every part, and it is impossible to have it thoroughly ready this Winter."[12]

Plant delayed returning to Tampa from his usual New York holidays until late January 1890. He arrived with Margaret, a "party of friends," and new private secretary Francis de Chantal Sullivan to be greeted by homegrown attempts to rally spirits that had sagged with disappointment. "Flags were flying from all the towers on the Tampa Bay Hotel yesterday," an account observed, "in honor of Mr. H. B. Plant's presence in the city." Henry's thoughts centered not on Tampa, though, but on Cuba. If the Tampa Bay Hotel could not operate for another year, he considered, there might be time to conjure a counterpart in Havana. His optimism about island conditions remained strong. The previous March he had befriended the new governor general, Don Manuel Salamanca y Negrete. He had shared with Salamanca his chagrin at widespread corruption, especially in the customs services, and detailed how the dismal situation impeded investments crucial to economic stimulation. Salamanca had subsequently launched an assault on official misconduct that resulted by New Year's Day 1890 in disruptions of many improper practices and flight of some key malefactors.[13]

In these circumstances Henry yearned to reach the island to explore lucrative possibilities. He took with him Tampa Bay Hotel architect J. A. Wood. They left Port Tampa February 5 on the *Olivette*. "Mr. Plant has gone South on an important trip, the results of which will appear later on," a correspondent related. "The International highway opened up, by which Tampa is to become mistress of the south seas, and the entrepot of trade between North and South America, is already calling here capital from all parts of the world. There is no power on earth that can stop Tampa's progress now." To the contrary, disastrous tidings greeted the travelers upon arrival at Havana. Governor Salamanca died suddenly on the sixth "after a short illness." Local dignitaries reassured the American millionaire with courtesies and soothing words, but the news left Henry shaken. He quickly scrubbed his planned ten-day to two-week stay and steamed back to Florida on the *Mascotte*, reaching Port Tampa on the eleventh. Weeks later, an interviewer noted, his thoughts remained on Salamanca and the promise that had died with him. "While in Havana he attended the funeral of Gen. Salamanca," the man wrote, "whose death, he said, is to be deplored, for he was doing much for the island."[14]

A disheartened Plant pondered next steps while confiding his thoughts to few. Rumors of railroad acquisitions and combinations circulated broadly, yet he remained silent. "Mr. Plant keeps his own counsels," a Savannah man affirmed in mid-March, "and does not unveil his plans." Henry diverted himself meanwhile with his usual March tour of inspection before hosting longtime New York friends vice president and Mrs. Levi Morton at Port Tampa during the middle of the month. President Harrison's wife, Mary Dimmick Harrison, followed within a few days. By then Henry's New Haven attorney Lynde Harrison—the key figure in Plant's entrée to the presidential circle through kinship as well as friendship—had joined the party. Henry thereafter slipped back to Havana and remained there until April 6. Whatever he learned in Cuba evidently confirmed the unsettled nature of things and convinced him to suspend initiatives there for the time being. Operational issues during the trip also reinforced in him a growing inclination to take personal control of the Plant Steamship Line. He did so. Henry then quietly eased out of New York at month's end for Paris.[15]

The spring 1890 visit to France remains a mysterious one. Plant for years had escaped stress and confrontation through solitary travel. Tampa Bay Hotel construction delays, Salamanca's death, and frustration of his international plans furnished—in Henry's perspective—adequate justification for strategic absence. Only one piece of contemporary evidence even denotes his European presence. On June 5 the New York *World* published items drawn from recent Continental occurrences. "Mr. H. B. Plant, President of the Southern Express Company of the Plant Investment Company and of the Plant Steamship line, is one of the shrewdest and most successful organizers of business enterprises in the South," the last item declared. "He is somewhere about fifty [*sic*], white-haired, with a grizzly mustache and shrewd eyes. His nose is straight, and so is his talk. If he makes a statement it is compact, terse and to the point. His steamers—the Mascot and Olivette—which play between Havana, Key West and Tampa, are as fast as ocean steamers, and make the round trip in three days or less. His hand has the Midas touch. It turns everything it touches into gold."[16]

Future events clearly highlighted Henry's presence in Paris that spring, however, and they heralded a crucial turning point in his personal life. The happenings traced to May 12 and the revival of *La Grande-Duchesse de Gérolstein* at the Théâtre des Variétés. Hortense Schneider had risen to fame in the late 1860s thanks to her performances in the lead. Now, acclaimed diva Jeanne Granier grasped the grand duchess's mantle for her own, perhaps capturing Henry's heart as well. Even the role's originator acknowledged the power of her rival's interpretation. "Schneider, on being interviewed as to what she thought of this her latest emulator," a critic advised, "declared Granier's performance to be the best she has seen."[17]

Reverberations of Plant's temporary escape and Granier's artistic triumph would resound as time passed, but indications of changing conditions and circumstances showed themselves immediately in Henry's attitudes and temperament. Having inaugurated the *Olivette*'s annual summer service to Bar Harbor in late June, he turned quickly to Florida, where he made "arrangements for the opening of the Plant Hotel next season." He had arrived in Tampa excited about prospects, a fact that he celebrated by raising the Eiffel Tower flag over the construction site. Closer inspection unfortunately revealed disturbing problems. "Mr. Plant is reported to have said the other day that the Tampa Bay hotel would at all hazards be opened for the reception of guests next winter," a local editor reported. "As a great quantity of work yet remains to be done, it will be necessary to at once increase the force of workmen and to push things to the utmost from now on." Atypically, Henry lost his temper and suspended J. A. Wood as construction superintendent. David Elliott put out word that the architect had gone North "for rest and recreation," yet the local rumor mill insisted that Wood "had severed his connection with the enterprise." Plant abruptly left the scene for a tour of nearby Manatee River settlements. Then he hurried to Alabama to finalize purchase of the Alabama Midland Railroad, a necessary element of his outreach to Mobile and the Midwest. Wood's replacement, Port Tampa Inn designer W. T. Cotter, substantially enlarged the Tampa Bay Hotel workforce. His manner proved so high-handed, however, that the efficient workers Wood had praised earlier now reacted furiously. "The negro laborers on the Tampa Bay hotel struck yesterday, because the superintendent imported some [other] colored laborers and put them to work," a Tampa newspaper advised on July 15. "The strikers sent some threatening notices to the new hands warning them to leave. The police were appealed to for protection."[18]

As a man who abhorred worker discontent and intently dreaded strikes, Plant was likely fearing Tampa clashes when more distressing news of a personal nature reached him in Alabama on July 13. That day his brother-in-law Simon Loughman, a New York businessman, died suddenly at forty-nine years of age. Coming on the heels of her husband's Parisian interlude, her dearly beloved brother's death prostrated Margaret. Henry rushed to her side. When her condition permitted, he moved her to Saratoga Springs and, within a few days, to the more tranquil environs of the Hotel Kaaterskill in New York's Catskill Mountains. South Florida Railroad president James E. Ingraham, who saw them there in early August, detailed Margaret's suffering. "Mrs. Plant is very much broken down by her brother's death," he recorded. "They were devoted to each other." Half a month at Kaaterskill produced modest improvement in Margaret's well-being, allowing the Plants in mid-August to return to Saratoga Springs.[19]

Marital issues may well have contributed to Margaret's illness, and her convalescence apparently suffered when those issues could not be resolved. Henry soon left his grieving wife either at Saratoga Springs or else at their Branford, Connecticut, country home to pursue business concerns. He spent a week or more in Boston and Bar Harbor, much of the time involved in discussions with executives of the Boston Fruit Company, a large concern with heavy investments in Jamaica. He had decided that since Cuban conditions discouraged investments, he would build ties with the English-speaking island to the south. "It is the intention of the Plant Steamship Company to put a line of steamships in service between Port Tampa and Kingston, Ja., for passengers, making a weekly line from New York over the 'fast mail route,'" a Boston newspaper alerted readers on September 7. Henry also expanded his Florida hospitality holdings. Francis B. Knowles, principal owner of Winter Park's Seminole Hotel, had died in May, and his heirs desired to sell the property. Plant quietly negotiated a purchase for "about $100,000." Word of the change in ownership began to circulate in early November, although Henry maintained his customary silence well into 1891.[20]

In the meantime Plant followed up on his Jamaican scheme. On October 24 the *Olivette* steamed out of Port Tampa with Henry, Morton, a State Department official, Boston Fruit Company representatives, and Plant System administrators bound for Kingston, where they received a warm welcome. "Ah, this is the first time we have been here, and it surpasses all that I imagined it to be," Henry exclaimed. "It is wonderfully beautiful, that magnificent range of Blue Hills in the background; the city among the trees and the tropical brilliancy of everything. That should delight the visitors who will come from the States." He added: "I think there is a great field for enterprise here, and the development of new industries would be an easy and safe matter. I have been much pleased indeed with my visit." Ever the cautious investor, though, he resisted temptation to rash action. "Nothing has been arranged conclusively, this trip being merely a tentative one—a prospecting tour in fact," he informed a reporter. "I expect, however, to be back in Jamaica in February, to make a thorough tour of the island, and to settle things permanently. Meanwhile the service will run from Port Tampa."[21]

Barely had Henry reached New York before calamity again struck. Walter S. Chisholm had emerged as his principal aide for the Plant System, and most observers believed that Chisholm—who had moved to New York to better assist his employer—would inherit company leadership upon Henry's death or retirement. But on December 5 the fifty-four-year-old man succumbed to a heart attack. "His body was carried to the State he loved so well last night," the *World* informed readers on the sixth, "accompanied by his widow, four sons and H. B. Plant, of the Plant Investment Company, of which Judge Chisholm was Vice-President." The Savannah funeral drew a large crowd of mourners, including former governor Rufus Bullock, who remained closely associated with Chisholm and Plant. Henry ordered Southern Express and Plant System offices everywhere to be "draped in mourning" to honor the departed. "He was Mr. Plant's right arm in the management of the great Plant System," a Georgia newspaper observed, "and it will be a difficult thing to find a man who will fill the place as he filled it."[22]

Chisholm's death understandably necessitated a Plant System reorganization, with further adjustments as circumstances required. The changes began in New York on January 7, 1891, when the Plant Investment Company (PICO) board convened in special session. Its members ratified Henry's decision to elevate Chisholm's one-time rival H. S. Haines to the vice presidency while continuing his responsibilities as general manager of the Savannah, Florida and Western (SF&W). Haines additionally received a seat on the board. Morton Plant emerged as assistant manager, with Doctor F. Jack—former Southern Express manager for Florida and general manager of the Jacksonville, Tampa and Key West Railroad—accepting designation as auditor. Either at the same meeting or else not long afterward, Chisholm's Savannah law firm was selected as general counsel "for the entire Plant system of railroads and steamships, and of the Southern Express." It operated thereafter as Erwin, duBignon and Chisholm. One partner, thirty-six-year-old Robert Gallaudet Erwin, increasingly represented the firm in its business with the Plant interests. As time passed, he provided advice and counsel to Plant personally in the same manner as Chisholm had done.[23]

That Plant remained PICO chairman after the board meeting surprised some people because Chisholm's death had proved far from easy for him to endure. While heralded for his attention to company matters, Plant had depended on the deceased man for day-to-day management of railroad affairs. This relieved the businessman from time-consuming chores and allowed plausible deniability when it came to unpleasant aspects of ongoing affairs. Now, Plant claimed to be unaware of resentments against Chisholm's policies and treatment of workers and appeared shocked to learn that SF&W workers—many of them black—had refused orders to attend Chisholm's funeral. He found or else was compelled to recognize that seeds of the discontent had been planted over a decade earlier with Chisholm's sharp practices in facilitating Plant's SF&W purchase. A reporter addressed the issue within the context of the Alabama Midland purchase. "Wall street men in this matter are forcibly reminded of the methods originally used by the Plant syndicate to secure possession of the Savannah, Florida and Western Railway, of which the Alabama Midland is a branch," he related. "There are scores of creditors of the old Savannah, Florida and Western road, both in [New York] and Savannah who to-day declare that they were 'euchred' by the Plant people when they organized the line. Brakemen, workmen and small tradespeople were ruined during the financial operation which resulted in that road coming into the possession of Mr. Plant." That at least some of the revelations unsettled Plant appears from rumors published in December. The reports insisted, although events proved them unfounded, that Henry planned to retire as Southern Express president in Mike O'Brien's favor to spend more time on SF&W affairs.[24]

Thus, a weary Plant hosted the Tampa Bay Hotel's launch in early 1891. The formal opening came in Margaret's absence on January 31. "Mr. H. B. Plant, the noted railroad magnate, in the presence of an immense crowd, to the accompaniment of booming cannon and the music of several bands, hoisted the stars and stripes to the top of the monster flagstaff on the grounds," a report described. "The flag used for the occasion is the same which President Plant threw to the breeze from the famous Eiffel Tower." Henry received "hearty congratulations on the completion of his elegant hostelry," but glittery celebration awaited the grand opening ball on February 5.[25]

Hotel chronicler James W. Covington captured the scene as Henry, Margaret, elite guests, and friends partied into the wee hours at the grand ball in celebration of Henry's splendid feat. "Just prior to nine o'clock in the evening of February 5, 1891, crowds began moving toward the building that was illuminated with electric lights, Chinese lanterns and 'fairy candles,'" he related. "Those coming in carriages entered through the horseshoe arches on the west porch and those who walked entered through the eastern porch. The guests, dressed in formal attire, moved into the rotunda; those fortunate enough to obtain seats were able to listen to a concert given by the sixteen piece Tampa Bay Hotel Orchestra recruited from Boston and conducted by Henry Stubbeline, which featured a duet from *Martha* presented by artists in the yet unfinished music room. Those who could not crowd into the

18. Tampa Bay Hotel [photo], 1898. Collection of Henry B. Plant Museum.

music room listened to the concert from the rotunda and porches. After the concert was concluded, Mr. and Mrs. Plant and Mayor Herman Glogowski led a grand march to the dining room . . . , newly decorated with flags of South American countries where a reception was held and, at its conclusion, dancing began. The twelve dance numbers included waltzes, lancers, schottische and the featured lively dance, 'Tampa Bay Hotel Galop.' From eleven to one a buffet meal was available in the nearby breakfast room . . . which included oysters, fish, cold meats, salads and a dessert." Covington concluded, "The list of guests was impressive but could have contained more celebrities had the hotel been on the lower east coast of Florida or in coastal New England."[26]

The Plants spent much of the next two months at their sumptuous new hotel. Margaret stayed in place to a greater extent than her husband, finding purpose that helped lift the pall that had lain so heavily upon her. As a reporter noted in July 1892, "During the past two winters she has remained in Tampa personally superintending the domestic arrangements of the great house." Henry meanwhile in February surveyed the Charlotte Harbor area including Fort Myers, Punta Gorda, and Pine Island. "Mr. Plant will now run the steamer Margaret every Saturday from Tampa to the island," a passenger observed, "a trip which the most delicate woman can make." A tour of inspection then followed in late February and early March 1891, allowing Henry and Morton to spend a night in Winter Park at Plant's new Seminole Hotel. The highlight of the season occurred when the Navy's "White

Squadron" visited Tampa Bay. Weeks of festivities surrounded the occasion, including a ball held at the Tampa Bay Hotel on March 30 in honor of Admiral John Grimes Walker and his officers. Following a farewell reception aboard the *Chicago* on April 1, Henry and Mike O'Brien joined the fleet for a cruise to Havana.[27]

Following the season's close in April, the Plants returned to New York and resided there or at Branford through late August. Alabama Midland complexities and controversies occupied a considerable amount of Henry's time, although he managed a week or two in the South during July. Savannah—where an incipient dock-worker strike threatened—particularly challenged him, and he networked there within local black leadership and labor circles to ensure protections for his interests before moving on to Florida. "He has spent most of his time in Tampa, inspecting his large interests there, and it is likely that the matter of the ship canal and docks at St. Petersburg will be pressed to completion," a local report advised. "The Plant Investment Company has in contemplation the establishment of a steamship line between Tampa and Colon (Aspinwall), and Mr. Plant is now making inquiries relative to the building of two fine iron steamships, with a large carrying capacity, for the South American trade, and is not at all unlikely to be one of the bidders for the carriage of the South American mails." On the issue of shipbuilding, Henry consulted in Wilmington, Delaware, and Philadelphia. In the former case, he discussed with Pusey and Jones Company the rebuilding of the *H. B. Plant*, which had burned in the St. Johns River during his stay in Paris the previous year.[28]

Then, purportedly to aid resolution of Alabama Midland bondholder issues, Plant headed for Europe. He left New York on the *Normandie* on August 27 and arrived at Southampton on September 4. His business apparently went well because he was soon spending time, along with John Hoey and Mike O'Brien, in consultations with Britain's "nitrate king," John T. North. Large deposits of phosphates had been discovered two years earlier near Tampa, giving rise by 1890 to an economic boom that augured well for that city's port and the Plant System. The men easily discovered common ground for serious business discussions while enjoying North's lavish country estate Avery Hill at Eltham in Kent. While in England, Henry found time to promote Florida and his various operations there. "Since the tourists have been coming in such increasing numbers we have built costly hotels to meet their demands at all the most attractive parts of the state," he informed the *Financial Times*. "We have just erected a very fine one at Tampa, and have also extended our road ten miles below [the city to] Port Tampa to deep water, where ships now load for American, continental and English ports."[29]

Plant and O'Brien then left London for Paris on September 11. During the next two weeks he scoured the City of Light for sculptures to adorn his Tampa hotel and its grounds. The period allowed both men to indulge in the full range of Parisian life and entertainment, including the opera. Jeanne Granier was sojourning at Aix-les-Bains and St. Petersburg, but enthralling performances by other artists provided sufficient diversion with, surprisingly, an element of danger. The presentation of Wagner's *Lohengrin* at the Opéra especially stirred passions. Resentments from the Franco-Prussian War remained hot among Parisians, and hundreds—if not thousands—turned out to protest what they considered an insult to French dignity and pride. At the second performance alone, police arrested 160 "rioters." As they did, protesters interrupted the presentation. "During the second act of the opera a number of globules containing a fetid chemical substance were thrown from the gallery to the orchestra," a report advised. "The police commissary gave warning that if this was repeated the galleries would be cleared."[30]

Plant and O'Brien escaped the Parisian excitement without injury or harm and joined John Hoey, Henry Flagler, and journalist Richard Harding Davis by September 30 in time to board the *City of Paris* for New York. Their October 8 arrival made headlines when Margaret Plant and Josephine Shaw Russell Hoey greeted them in New York Harbor from the *Olivette*'s deck. Bolder headlines followed when Adams Express suddenly found itself engulfed in tumult and scandal. Its directors on October 12 abruptly fired Hoey as president and compelled vice president Clapp Spooner's resignation. The actions came at lawyer Henry Sanford's instigation, and he ascended to executive power. Sanford justified the coup by alleging financial irregularity, although eventual disclosures revealed mostly the kinds of loose practices that Adams executives had indulged in for half a century. Still, the company sued Hoey for over $700,000, at which point Plant found himself ensnarled in the legal maneuvering. "The Adams Express Company's officers had reason to believe that Hoey owned, in all, about 5000 shares of the Southern Express Company, which is operated in connection with the H. B. Plant Railway, Steamship and Hotel System," an October 17 report explained. "At the office of the Southern Express Company access to President H. B. Plant was sought in vain. The clerks said that Mr. Plant was closely engaged." Mostly, the fury amounted to a show for public consumption. Within two months Sanford and Hoey had settled matters more or less amicably after the former president transferred certain properties to the company.[31]

As scandal's odor filled the air that October, Plant quit New York. "Mr. and Mrs. H. B. Plant are expected to return to Tampa this month, where they will look after things in general and enjoy the beauties of Tampa Bay," the *Tampa Tribune* revealed on the fifteenth. Henry and Margaret finally reached that destination in early November after stopovers at Charleston,

Savannah, Brunswick, Jacksonville, Sanford, and Winter Park. Plant gave Savannah special attention. The feared dock-worker strike had recently taken place, fortunately without damage to the Plant System. Now, Henry toured the city, including the SF&W's wharves, where he chatted with laborers and officials. His representative to the local black community—journalist and businessman Milton J. Christopher—accompanied him. Coincident with the visit Christopher established—likely with Plant financing—a newspaper called the *Labor Union Recorder* that emerged as a strong community voice and an ardent friend of Plant interests. Relieved, Henry turned his attention to Florida. At Jacksonville he announced a desire "to see what [is] necessary to be done to encourage business and to help out the orange and vegetable growers and phosphate producers." He projected reenergized support for Tampa. "Mr. Plant referred with pride to the excellent manner in which the hotel grounds had been kept and said that while in France he purchased a number of iron figures to be placed inside the hotel and in the grounds," a local reporter observed. Plant added: "My only wish is that the city may continue to grow and expand until she becomes the metropolis of the Gulf states, and the gateway for the commerce of that vast country to our south. Tampa has only reached the surface of her greatness. Her future is aglow with promise."[32]

The Tampa stay lasted for ten days before the Plants extended their tour of inspection through Georgia, Alabama, South Carolina, and North Carolina. Henry bubbled to reporters about rosy business prospects and tourism forecasts. "Mr. Plant said that there was every indication that there would be a very large travel to the South this winter," one newspaperman expressed. "'It will be accommodated to the best of our ability,' said he, 'and when I say our ability I mean all of the lines forming the system making up the line between the North and South. The hotels will be in readiness for business whenever the public desire it. The hotel at Tampa is being brightened up with beautiful grounds. Business in Tampa is very encouraging, and since the opening of the big hotel there the place has grown very much.'"[33]

Unfortunately, after Henry's return to New York in mid-November, the optimistic aura turned sour. He and Margaret had apparently quarreled, prompting her essentially to withdraw from society. "Notwithstanding all reports to the contrary Mrs. Henry B. Plant will not give any social entertainments in New York this winter, but will close her town house, No. 586 Fifth avenue, late in January and go to Florida," a city newspaper reported in mid-December. "Mrs. Plant has a large house and it seems a pity such a splendid home should remain closed all winter. The Plants are among the wealthiest New Yorkers and in the past have entertained delightfully." Henry returned South without his wife about the time the item appeared. "He is en route to Port Tampa," the *Savannah Morning News* related, "where he is preparing for extensive improvements to the harbor."[34]

Henry and Margaret stayed apart during the first weeks of January 1892, a fact that he attributed to her indisposition from a lingering fever. He opened the Tampa Bay Hotel season on January 10 and 11. In the days following he positioned statuary brought from Paris and toured Polk County, located east of Tampa, where rich vegetable farms and expanding phosphate mines thrived. A night followed at the Seminole Hotel before the party traveled to Jacksonville on the nineteenth. "Mr. Plant goes back to New York, after his estimable wife, who has been ill for several weeks," a report announced. "Their return for the winter at the Tampa Bay hotel will be hailed with genuine pleasure by a host of warm friends and admirers."[35]

The Plants had reestablished themselves amid the hotel's comforts by February 1. Margaret, now rid of her "low fever," resumed responsibilities "superintending the domestic arrangements." Henry remained with her for several weeks, spending his time developing ideas for business expansion. The plans appeared on PICO and South Florida Railroad board-meeting agendas ten days or so after his arrival. Henry Flagler, George Pullman, and Henry Sanford, among others, joined SFR directors to consider as well extending the road to remote Miami on the lower Atlantic coast. "'Mr. Ingraham, could we build a line from here to there?' being from Fort Myers to Miami," SFR president James E. Ingraham recalled Plant asking. "I said in reply, 'Mr. Plant, that is right across the Everglades of Florida.' 'Well,' he said, 'what of it?' I said, 'So far as I know only two white men ever made that trip, and they were accompanied by Indians, and I doubt if there is any record of their experience but I would be very glad to run a line across there and go in person.'" The PICO and SFR directors asked Ingraham to do exactly that. Additionally, they approved plans submitted by Plant for "extensive improvements to Tampa Bay." Noted an onlooker, "This includes dredging the harbor and new docks."[36]

As Ingraham organized his exploratory party, Plant launched a tour of inspection and parade of annual meetings with a group of directors that included Flagler. Morton Plant meanwhile had been promoting the Tampa Bay Lawn Tennis Tournament to be held in late March and early April at the hotel. Partially to generate publicity, Henry diverted his private car to New Haven, where he and Henry Sanford made headlines on March 12 by picking up several of the players for a luxurious journey to Tampa. For the most part, Plant's interest in the tournament ended there. While Tampa reports touted little but tennis, he and Mike O'Brien quietly slipped off to Havana. At Henry's direction, John A. Wood had spent much of the winter searching out an appropriate hotel site and arranging for its purchase. Plant arrived on April 2 to discover that another buyer had snatched the property. Still, Henry yearned "to build a big hotel in Havana." He, O'Brien, and Wood resumed their search and apparently succeeded. "Mr. H. B. Plant, of the Plant System, and Col. O'Brien have just selected in Havana a site for a great American hotel," the *New Orleans Item* announced on the eighteenth.[37]

A thrilled Plant returned to Tampa to be greeted by distressing business news. Ingraham had reached Miami in early April after an arduous trek. As the Tampa Bay Hotel season closed at midmonth, the exhausted traveler quickly reached out to Plant to report that "a railroad through the Everglades was impracticable." Within a short time Henry, though disappointed, had accepted the conclusion and turned his attention elsewhere. Flagler took a different tack. Now aiming to build his rail lines down the Atlantic coast, he saw potential. By late summer the oil magnate had lured Ingraham to his side. Beginning October 1 the former railroad president was taking first steps on Flagler's behalf that would eventually would lead directly to Miami.[38]

The distressing tidings additionally touched Plant's marriage. Once he and Margaret had settled at Branford in May, her health failed. "She was taken down . . . with a low fever, which finally developed into typhoid fever," a New Haven journal advised. Another source asserted, "Mrs. Plant is supposed to have contracted typhoid fever in Florida last Spring." Authorities reported no such outbreak at the Tampa Bay Hotel that season, so Margaret had likely slipped into the previous year's malaise. Whether from fever's effects or otherwise, physicians deemed her condition critical as of July 20. Her favorite priest, Father Thomas J. Ducey of New York City's St. Leo's Church, hurried to her side "to give her the sacraments of the Church." Anxious days passed before signs of improvement appeared. By the twenty-eighth the crisis had eased, yet chronic problems lingered for years. "She is suffering with spinal troubles," a correspondent would remark late in 1893, "with which she has been afflicted ever since she had the typhoid fever two years ago." A tendency to weight gain complicated matters. Margaret—a beauty of elfin dimensions when she married in 1873—had become two decades later "a lady of . . . stately and ample proportions." That her appearance had changed accorded with the realities of aging for many, but the matronly trend still factored as an element in the Plant marriage equation.[39]

Henry's behavior underscored the likelihood that marital problems had become a driving force when it came to Margaret's health. Atypically for summer months, he occupied himself with business affairs, accepting numerous engagements that separated him from his ailing spouse. His work aimed especially at warding off competition in Florida. "A recent special from Jacksonville says: H. M. Flagler, of New York, and H. B. Plant, president of the Plant system of railways and steamships, have formed a close alliance, by which, it is said, they hope to control all the Florida railroad business and 'freeze out' all competitors," a June publication related. Henry reorganized aspects of the Plant System, combining passenger services on all lines under Charles D. Owens as general passenger agent. "Mr. H. B. Plant owns or controls all the lines of the system that bears his name," a report observed, "and the present action of the officials would seem to indicate an ultimate consolidation of all the roads under one management." Henry also implemented regular steamship service between Boston and Halifax. In late June and early July he joined investors and officials on the *Olivette*'s inaugural run to the Canadian port. "Gen. Plant, as well as the whole party, was delighted with the trip," a Halifax correspondent declared.[40]

Conversely, although expected in Florida during the "critical" time of Margaret's malady, Henry remained at Branford. Within days, though, the system president was in New York City handling matters preparatory to another trip South. Over two weeks he visited Charleston, Savannah, Waycross, Jacksonville, and Tampa before resettling at month's end at Branford. A relatively quiet time followed until October 8, when Henry's "intimate" financier friend Otis Greye leapt from a steamer into frigid waters off Massachusetts. The disappearance prompted major publications to reveal Greye's deep involvement in Florida land frauds, activities in which he associated closely with Plant's public-relations man David Elliott. Henry consequently kept a low profile through the month. He finally ventured out in early November for the wedding of veteran aide George H. Tilley's daughter at Noroton, Connecticut. Morton and his wife lent their support to Plant and Tilley, joining at the event with John Hoey, Henry Sanford, Lynde Harrison, Mike O'Brien, H. S. Haines, R. G. Erwin, and D. F. Jack.[41]

A suddenly beleaguered Henry surely yearned to believe that the joyous Tilley wedding signaled an upturn toward better times. At first, that seemed the case. The year's presidential race had witnessed Democrat Grover Cleveland besting Republican Benjamin Harrison. With his friend set to reoccupy the White House on the following March 4, a reviving Plant traveled to New York and the Fifth Avenue Hotel on November 14, 1892, to preside at a gathering of southern railroad men convened to force higher freight rates. As the discussions persisted Plant met with more personal setbacks. That evening, after Father Ducey administered last rights, John Hoey died at Delmonico's Restaurant, where he maintained rooms. Barely two days later Henry's cousin and business associate Increase C. Plant passed away at Macon, Georgia. A distraught Henry Plant the next day stood with Mike O'Brien and others to serve their friend Hoey as pallbearers at the St. Leo's Church funeral. "Among those who sent cards of condolence," the New York *World* advised, "were Mr. and Mrs. Grover Cleveland."[42]

True to form, Henry buried his grief in activity. One week after Hoey's funeral he set off to inspect facilities and operations in Georgia, Alabama, and Florida. He presented to business associates and the public a surprising countenance given recent events. "It is a pleasure to his friends to see Mr. Plant looking so well," a Savannah resident observed, "[and] in fact he looks scarcely a day older than he did twenty-five years ago, his many cares seemingly only having the effect of making him younger and more energetic." Henry's actions demonstrated a remarkable facility for creative engagement while stressed. Having become more sensitive to worker attitudes after the fallout from Walter Chisholm's death and the Savannah dock strike, he proposed an experimental program of employee profit sharing. "The scheme is Mr. Plant's, and his wonderful success as a railroad manager and as the manager of the complicated affairs of the Southern Express Company is an assurance that if the plan of profit-sharing and co-operation has any merit in it, he will bring it out," the *Atlanta Constitution* remarked. "Indeed, the fact that so successful a business man has taken the matter up for the purpose of applying its principles to his own affairs is an evidence that he sees his way clear to successful application of the plan; for Mr. Plant is, above all things, a practical man, and he is not likely, at his time of life, and in the face of all his experience, to enter upon a doubtful experiment. He has taken up this scheme because he is convinced that profit-sharing is at once a wise and liberal policy."[43]

Henry additionally acted to ensure that his black employees felt his particular concern for their interests. He stressed the point in a number of ways, but an action that he took relative to the Tampa Bay Hotel carried special, if arguably mostly symbolic, meaning. The previous year Plant had blundered badly by caving to local pressures from Tampa white leaders to exclude black waiters from the hotel's dining room. Now, he reversed himself. In doing so he employed as the new headwaiter fifty-year-old Wilson Percival, then living with his family at Babylon, New York. A South Carolina native, the veteran headwaiter had distinguished himself at many premier northern resorts, including the Grand Union Hotel at Saratoga Springs. Percival's work at Tampa thereafter ranked as outstanding as he remained respected and in place through the decade. Following Henry's death, Percival served in Henry Flagler's employ as headwaiter at Palm Beach's Breakers Hotel.[44]

A week's stay in Havana capped the December tour. If Henry sought fresh reassurances about Cuban conditions, he failed to get them. Instead, he planned monthly Jamaican excursions beginning in early 1893. Those arrangements set, Plant conferred with counsel R. G. Erwin about compelling personal issues. He then headed North to spend the New Year's holidays with Margaret and several of her friends at the new Laurel-in-the-Pines Hotel at

Lakewood, New Jersey. Plant soon afterward executed a will that dramatically altered his wife's future prospects and thereby set in play personal and legal dynamics that would not be resolved until after his death. He did so by drastically restricting Margaret's and Morton's shares in his estate in favor principally of grandchildren then unborn. In addition to certain other benefits, Margaret was to receive "for her natural life the sum thirty thousand dollars ($30,000) per annum in equal quarterly payments in advance." Counsel Erwin drafted the will. Henry signed it on January 23, 1893.[45]

Having recognized marital woes through reorientation of his estate plans, Plant hurried to Florida, where he joined Henry Flagler in touring the state before moving on to Savannah for a businessman's banquet. "He gives an encouraging report of the condition of affairs [in Florida]," a local man related in early February. "He says the travel southward this year has been very satisfactory, especially that which travels 'first class' and pays the highest prices at the hotels." Margaret, who may not have known yet about the will amendments, met her husband in Savannah. Rufus Bullock joined them. The Plants then traveled with Flagler on February 9 to St. Augustine, where the hotel proprietor and his wife lavishly hosted the party at the Ponce de Leon. Six days later the two Henrys stepped aboard the *Halifax* at Port Tampa to enjoy the first of the season's Jamaica cruises. Having enjoyed a Nassau stopover, the men entered Kingston on the twentieth to be "particularly struck with the magnificent view obtained on entering the harbour." The same day, the Pennsylvania and Reading Railroad bankrupted. "The first waves of economic disaster hit the nation," one historian declared, "forerunners of the upcoming Panic of 1893." As the nation propelled itself toward economic collapse, best-laid plans conceived by men such as Plant and Flagler suddenly began to shatter.[46]

13
In the Midst of Calamity

1893 to 1896

"Everyone is in a blue fit of terror"

Days before Grover Cleveland succeeded Benjamin Harrison as US president on March 4, 1893, the nation began to slide into a disastrous economic depression. The Panic of 1893 saw the stock market collapse by May; spurred bankruptcies, business failures, and unemployment across the country; and spread misery generally through the president's second term. By any measure the calamity stood out as one of enormous proportions. "The panic of 1893 and its accompanying depression marks one of the decisive crises in American history," historians Douglas Steeples and David O. Whitten concluded. "Henry Adams reflected its crushing impact when he wrote, 'Everyone is in a blue fit of terror, and each individual thinks himself more ruined than his neighbor.' Hard times provided a lurid setting for sullen outbursts of the unemployed, violent strikes, the climax of the Populist and silver crusades, the creation of a new political balance, the continuing transformation of the country's economy, significant changes in national policy, and far-reaching social and intellectual developments. At the center of events, the business contraction was the crucial force shaping the tumultuous decade that ushered out the nineteenth century."[1]

As the era opened Plant was enjoying the luxurious surroundings and moneyed clientele of the Tampa Bay Hotel. March 1893 in fact witnessed an influx of well-heeled visitors. "While the famous Ponce de Leon and other hostelries in St. Augustine are taxed to their capacity," a report observed, "the tide of tourists this winter is directed to Tampa where the magnificent Tampa Bay Hotel, built by that progressive gentleman, H. B. Plant, Esq., has been scarcely able to accommodate the great influx seeking the luxuries and comforts which that palatial establishment offers." A banquet honoring the new president opened the month's festivities on March 4, while Morton

Plant's annual Tampa Bay Tennis Tournament closed the lunar cycle. Famous names graced the guest roster, including sleeping car manufacturer George Pullman, meat baron Philip Armour, and railroad magnate George Gould. *Atlanta Journal* writer Homer Reed happened upon some of these men at their leisure. "I heard, or rather overheard, a conversation in the wine room of the Tampa Bay Hotel," he recorded. "Everything is served buffet, and seated at the dainty tables were numerous parties of ladies and gentlemen discussing their wines or liquors, as their tastes (or exchequer) might dictate. At the adjoining table were the great Chicago pork-packer, Armour, George Gould and four others. The jest and the wine went round, and finally the conversation turned to the great deal in meat which the Armour Company consummated in 1886. I listened with all my ears. Mr. A. signed the waiter and, feeling in his fob, produced his fold of bills and peeled off one. I eyed him closely, and I am certain that he never noticed the denomination, but he placed it on the tray, and the party gave their orders."[2]

Isolated from catastrophe elsewhere, Plant and his friends enjoyed the wherewithal to ignore for the time being realities that bedeviled the less fortunate. Henry's behavior, though, signaled anxieties. Tampa Bay fishing trips for friends such as one-time Georgia governor Rufus Bullock offered diversion, but a sense of restlessness beset him. By mid-March he had summoned several guests and system executives for an impromptu and aimless rail jaunt through Central Florida. "When a man who scarcely has time to sleep starts out for three days of fishing, it is usually safe to look for something else than fish at the end of the line," *New York Times* reporter William Drysdale reflected. "But in this case the only other object was sightseeing, and as sightseeing is a legitimate part of fishing, the real object was not interfered with." By the end of March, Henry had abandoned Tampa for an inspection tour. On April 11 a local newspaper announced the hotel's season early end. Its editor asked, "What is the Future?"[3]

An immediate basis for Plant's anxieties, one other than the onset of economic depression, soon revealed itself in a major Plant System reorganization. Thanks to Morton's labors, Henry was already expanding his steamship line and eliminating competition through merger with a Canadian rival. The Canada-Atlantic and Plant Steamship Company resulted. In the Southeast, competition threatened rail ridership and freight revenues as well. The particular villains in his eyes were the newly minted Florida Central and Peninsular Railroad (FC&P), a successor to Sir Edward Reed's 1880s-era interests, and the lines with which it associated. The *Atlanta Constitution* reviewed matters in 1895. "Until a year ago the Plant system had practically a monopoly of the business coming into and going out of Florida," it explained. "The season of two years ago ended the exclusive control by the Plant system of the trunk line business into Florida. The next season saw its active competitor in the field for business, not only between interior Florida points, but for the whole country.[4]

The threat materializing from this emerging combination compelled broad and long-term strategies, as well as innovative implementation. Plant began by embarking "on a vigorous aggressive policy" that in time placed "the entire system under a general superintendent, he wiping out . . . some division superintendencies, and [mandating] a general concentration of power." The first steps came in late April 1893 after the Plant Investment Company (PICO) president had considered outright purchase of the FC&P network. He decided instead to consolidate the Savannah, Florida and Western (SF&W) with the South Florida Railroad (SFR). He announced the new Savannah, Florida and Western Railway Company on April 27. Plant did not alert the public nor his own employees that more steps necessarily were to follow. Neither did he disclose his decision to borrow an astounding $20 million to refinance outstanding SF&W obligations, undertake repairs and improvements, and purchase new properties.[5]

Banking-industry volatility delayed for months Henry's attempt to secure the massive loan, although elapsed time helpfully afforded opportunity for a financial reorganization in light of the revised will that he had signed in January. His goal was to arrange control of his financial assets to permit their efficient management and smooth transfer. The solution came in the form of the South Eastern Investment Company. An approach likely recommended by New Haven attorney Lynde Harrison, the corporation received the Connecticut legislature's approved in May and the governor's endorsement the following month. Henry, Morton, Henry's brother Horace P. Hoadley, Morris K. Jesup, George Tilley, E. B. Haskell, H. S. Haines, and R. G. Erwin served on its board. A broad grant of powers permitted proactive participation in all business areas in which Plant was invested as well as allowing the corporation's use as a holding company. By action of the directors, the capital stock could be raised as high as $20 million.[6]

As fallout from the Panic worsened from May to August, Henry remained for the most part at Branford, mixing work with personal matters and relaxation. "Notwithstanding his large business responsibilities Mr. Plant finds time to see every one who has anything of importance to talk about," a reporter advised, "and a chat with a friend is always a pleasure to him if that friend knows when to stop." A few business trips interrupted the routine. He and counsel R. G. Erwin negotiated steamship business at Boston in May before Henry traveled with Mike O'Brien to Chattanooga in June to celebrate transfer of Southern Express headquarters from Augusta. The dip into the South also allowed stopovers at Montgomery, Savannah, Winter

Park, Tampa, and Waycross. Finally, Plant and Capt. J. W. Fitzgerald visited Galveston in late July and early August on other business connected with the steamship line. At every stop and in every interview, Henry boosted Florida and its prospects, Panic and depression notwithstanding. "Take him all in all, he is one of the most remarkable men I ever met," an impressed correspondent observed. "He is an enthusiastic believer in the future of Florida, not alone as a winter resort, but as a great commercial center. He points with pride to the prosperity and growth of Tampa, that in a few years has grown from a straggling village to a large and prosperous town."[7]

Despite the business interludes, personal matters eclipsed relaxation at Branford, and subsequent events signaled that his marriage ranked chief among them. On that subject, a new influence had appeared in the person of Dr. Ghislani Durant. A few years older than Margaret and trained in French medical schools, Durant had built a reputation in New York as an eccentric opponent of saltwater swimming ("sea-bathing"). He also claimed expertise at cancer care and family medicine. The doctor later insisted that he had treated Henry since 1879, a possibility given an interest in "hygiene of the voice" and strong connections in city show business circles. His close association with Margaret, though, came after his 1890 purchase of a West Forty-Sixth Street townhouse not far from the Plant home. Her indisposition following her brother Simon's death that year and Henry's subsequent French sojourns saw her draw Ghislani closer. By 1892, in his words, he "practically lived in their house." Now, Ghislani posed as a healer of a different sort, urging his patient and her husband to reconcile as the nation tumbled into economic chaos.[8]

Ghislani's ministrations produced positive short-term results when the Plants decided to share a long trip beginning in late August. "H. B. Plant, the veteran railroad manager, left Branford, Ct., on Thursday [the twenty-fourth], in his private car, for a six weeks' trip to the Pacific coast through Canada, and home by way of Chicago," a notice advised. "He is accompanied by Mrs. Plant, Mr. [Frederick Roblin], passenger agent of the Plant system, and Mr. [E. C.] Richardson, Boston agent of the Plant Line of Halifax steamers." To permit examination of Canadian Maritimes steamship opportunities, the party—after passing through Boston and Portland—visited St. John, New Brunswick; Halifax, Nova Scotia; and Cape Breton Island. Quebec, Montreal, and Ottawa followed. A Saratoga Springs stopover in early September allowed a pleasant interlude with friend Andrew Carnegie. From there Car No. 100 ventured west to Buffalo and, by midmonth, had reached Chicago and the 1893 World's Columbian Exposition. Henry's brother Horace P. Hoadley awaited the Plants there. The fair's "Railroad Day" fell on the sixteenth, and Henry attended a ringing presentation by H. S.

Haines delivered partly on the Plant System's behalf. Meanwhile, the Plants shopped. Henry selected two electric launches for use by Tampa Bay Hotel guests, as well as a "monster" locomotive. Together, they sought interesting furniture and furnishings, which they obtained in bulk and at advantageous prices for shipment to Florida.[9]

The Plant traveling party returned to New York in early October for the America's Cup races. Henry had arranged for the *Olivette* to join the "following fleet," carrying passengers at five dollars each per day. "The vessel was fitted up specially for the occasion with restaurant and bar, and supplied with a band of music," a correspondent informed Jamaica's *Daily Gleaner*. "It was stated to accommodate 600 passengers and this number were on board including Col. H. B. Plant and his specially invited guests. The Jamaicans in New York appear to have marked their appreciation of the 'Olivette's' visit to Jamaica by joining her party." The "industrious band" gained renown during the races for its punctuation of critical turning points. "As the cutter [*Valkyrie*] sailed away on the homestretch, the never weary band on the Olivette played 'Home, Sweet Home!'" a New York reporter recorded. "When the Vigilant rounded the mark, half an hour later, the same symphony in steam [from the 'following fleet'] was executed, and the band, in its effort to furnish something appropriate played 'The Girl I Left Behind Me.'"[10]

Matters of more serious import also commanded Henry's attention. Yellow fever raged in a number of southern locales, most virulently at Brunswick, Georgia. Compounding that crisis, a massive hurricane had swept through Savannah and adjacent coastal areas in late August. Plant responded typically by arranging free shipment of food and supplies, including a special "relief train" intended to furnish critically needed commodities to Brunswick. He confronted, as well, his brother's sudden death. At Boston on October 20 while preparing plans for regular Maritimes steamship service, Henry suddenly received word that Horace was "sinking rapidly." He hurried to New Haven and arrived just in time. The death occurred that afternoon. "Mr. Hoadley had been at the World's fair and returned with a severe cold, which developed into pneumonia," a New Haven report detailed. "He also had a severe attack of typhoid fever." The funeral took place at Horace's Crown Street home on the twenty-third.[11]

Henry's usual manner of dealing with grief involved immersing himself in business affairs, and he behaved true to form following the Hoadley funeral. Most significantly, he joined Henry Flagler at Washington during November's first week for meetings to align and adjust winter train schedules. While in the capital, the men conversed in depth about Florida political affairs, where race-based lynchings had become common and politics had turned ever meaner in spirit. This tragic state of affairs had worsened with the election as governor in November 1892 of Tampa lawyer and judge Henry L. Mitchell, the founder some years earlier of Plant City. Plant abhorred the one-time Confederate officer and the circle of Tampa businessmen with whom he associated. Their preferred local newspaper, the *Tampa Tribune*, meanwhile undermined PICO projects and frustrated Henry personally. At Washington, Plant and Flagler decided to appeal to their friend the president for assistance. Flagler took the lead, writing to Cleveland on the ninth. "Help us redeem the state" from "a miserable set of demagogues," the magnate pleaded, urging use of presidential patronage powers to force change.[12]

When it came to his business interests, Plant had been quietly exerting his own pressure within state government for years. He utilized lobbyists but—as the *Tribune* gleefully pointed out—he increasingly positioned loyal men in public office. "The Atlanta Constitution in slapping over on Mr. H. B. Plant has the monumental gall to say that 'he has avoided politics and speculation,'" it declared in October 1895. "We don't know about the speculation, but the political part of this remarkable assertion will prove highly edifying to those who know anything of the inside history of Florida politics." Plant System contractor William Henry Reynolds offered a case in point. A Georgia native, he had dabbled in Florida Democratic politics for a decade before work with Plant on railroad construction. In the mid-1880s Reynolds had settled at Lakeland in Polk County, the heart of Florida's lucrative cattle industry and a growing economic center grounded increasingly in citrus groves, vegetable farms, and phosphate mines. Reynolds parlayed the county's economic clout and Plant's resources to achieve appointment as secretary to the Florida Constitutional Convention of 1885. The same year, he won election as clerk of the house of representatives, a position he held for two biennial sessions. In 1892 the Plant man claimed a state senate seat, gaining the body's presidency during its 1895 meetings. By 1896 Reynolds had anchored himself even more firmly in the Democratic hierarchy by winning office as state comptroller. Along the way, Plant knew that he could count on his man's influence to advance his perspectives and secure his wants.[13]

After Plant and Flagler parted company in November 1893, Henry returned to New York to prepare for his customary late-year round of annual meetings and inspections. Beginning at midmonth, the circuit took him through the Southeast, with Flagler eventually joining the tour. The PICO president never stopped spreading optimism about Florida. "I am not yet posted on Florida affairs," he informed a Savannah reporter in one example. "The hope, however, is father to the thought, and I am of the opinion that the season will be a good one." Plant ended up at Tampa for a brief stay on December 5. The Tampa Bay Hotel had opened its season the previous day, and he deftly sparked national publicity by insinuating himself and the hotel into coverage of the upcoming Jacksonville championship fight between "Gentleman Jim" Corbett and Englishman Charles Mitchell, a controversial bout that Governor Mitchell adamantly opposed. Henry enjoyed the public-relations gambit immensely. Meanwhile, he served as chief greeter for arriving guests. He delighted as well in finalizing paperwork for the $20 million loan he had sought for months. "I found Mr. Plant in high spirits and despite his 70 odd years, evidently in the best of health," a visitor commented. "Firm of grip and clear of eye and strong of voice, few men have impressed me more forcibly or given a deeper sense of restrained power."[14]

New Year 1894 found Henry in motion early, although when he ventured South he did so without Margaret. "Spinal troubles" justified her absence, although the failure of reconciliation efforts likely figured as a greater factor. For whatever reason, she remained in New York into the summer. Henry, though, showed excellent spirits. Asked about tourism prospects at Savannah on January 10, 1894, he offered a rosy forecast: "We hope for a very large business this year and a fashionable season. The northern people are not spending their money so freely just now, but this is not owing so much to the lack of money as to the uncertainty as to what legislation will be enacted by congress [in light of the depression]. I think we can reasonably expect a very large travel, however." Stopovers here and there kept him from Tampa until around the twentieth. Once at the hotel, he again indulged happily in hosting duties, especially enjoying the company of North Carolina senator and former governor Zebulon B. Vance. A highlight came in February when Plant and Mike O'Brien took the relatively new Plant Line steamer *Florida* for Kingston. "Mr. Plant and Mr. O'Brien were the guests of the governor, Sir Arthur Blake, and Lady Blake at the King's House," an onlooker advised. "They were royally entertained while at his majesty's home, and speak in highest terms of their hospitality and with the friendship of the inhabitants of that beautiful little island." Convinced from the "pleasant trip" that sufficient demand existed for Jamaican cruises, Plant ordered the service continued despite the depression.[15]

Whatever his feelings about Jamaica, Havana remained fixed in Plant's mind. He spent the winter's remainder, in fact, preparing to enlarge his Cuban commitments in light of a respite in recent turbulence encouraged by liberal US trade concessions. "A few days ago we placed a new steamship line in operation between Tampa and Havana," Henry declared in April. "The number of vessels will be increased as the business grows. Cubans are taking more of the product of American mills than ever, and it will only be a short time until the trade between Florida ports and Havana will be very important." He made the comments after having slipped away to the Pearl of the Antilles in March. Earlier, at Kingston, he had remarked, "When we com-

19. Henry and Margaret Plant in rickshaws being pulled by Tampa Bay Hotel porters, 1891. Collection of Henry B. Plant Museum.

menced that service [to Havana] very few people traveled by steamer, but now the hotels in Cuba are unable to accommodate all the people we take down." In the circumstances the idea of building a Havana hotel reappeared as a subject for his renewed consideration. Unfortunately, economic conditions on the island remained volatile as the US Congress pondered tariff changes that could affect investments there. So Henry bided his time.[16]

Cuban and Jamaican prospects still appeared to Henry that spring as far more desirable than those prevailing in the United States. Florida tourism, doubtlessly to Plant's relief, proved disappointing rather than disastrous. "It is safe to say that on the whole the tourist travel has been about one-fourth less this year than last," an April 9 report declared. "The Florida hotel season for the winter of 1893–4 is practically at an end, and by the middle of the month nearly every large hotel in the State that has not already closed its doors will be preparing to do so. Several of these hotels, the Seminole, at Winter Park, Tampa Bay Hotel, at Tampa, and the Indian River and Plaza Hotels are already closed to tourists and have sent their help North." As the times did not encourage major expenditures, Plant husbanded the proceeds of his $20 million loan.[17]

Given prevailing economic lassitude, Henry used much of April to generate trade to and from Florida, taking opportunity to also address a personal matter. Coincident with the opening of Henry Flagler's railroad to Palm Beach, Plant visited Cincinnati, Pittsburgh, and other midwestern locales to boost Sunshine State growth. "Railroads are doing wonders in developing the resources of the sunny south," he bragged at Pittsburgh. "This is particularly true of Florida. We have already built a road down the eastern coast and through the central part of the state, and are now building another line along the western coast. When this has been completed Florida will be pretty well supplied with railroads. Seven years ago, when we went into Tampa it was a struggling village of 700 people. Now it has 12,000 inhabitants, and has become quite a commercial center. Cubans ship tobacco to this point and make it into cigars, thus [under current tariff law] escaping the duty." He added, "The railroads [also] have made it possible to develop the phosphate beds of Florida, and now thousands of tons are shipped annually where a short time ago nothing whatsoever was done." Plant appeared at times, it should be noted, almost as if his mind was focused elsewhere. An Augusta, Georgia, correspondent may have illuminated the cause on May 1: "The remains of Mrs. H. B. Plant, who died in this city thirty-two years ago, were disinterred at the cemetery today. She was the wife of Mr. H. B. Plant, the railroad magnate. The remains, which were enclosed in a metallic casket, were taken to Savannah and thence to [Branford, Connecticut] on a special train."[18]

Plant—after tending to additional business matters at Washington, New Haven, and Branford—then discreetly left for France. He enjoyed Parisian lights through most of May and June. The art world likely filled him with nationalistic pride even though the city's traditional annual exhibition, now referred to as the Old Salon, lacked the flair and weight of previous spectacles. French enthusiasts expressed little more than disgust. "It's only foreigners!" one exclaimed. Meanwhile, Plant found plenty of excitement on the stage. Jeanne Granier had opened at the Théâtre des Variétés on April 12 in *Satan-Revue*. "[She now] burlesques the fair Diane de Pougy, the much-jewelled demi-mondaine, who nightly does a few feeble conjuring tricks on the Folies Bergere stage, amidst tremendous applause from *Decadents* and club men," a reviewer explained. The show proved what one Parisian newspaper called "*un très grand succès*." It added, "Never has the charming diva been more witty and more acclaimed."[19]

Plant, once returned to American shores, resumed the mantles of southern economic boosterism and entrepreneurial initiative. His attempt to bring northern businessmen together to support their southern counterparts sadly generated lukewarm results. A less-than-enthusiastic turnout at a Fifth Avenue Hotel conference on June 22 produced a "permanent Committee on Organization" and little else. Meanwhile, plans Henry had set in motion earlier materialized in July at New Haven and Branford. He had leased Double Beach on Long Island Sound for a seasonal resort and amusement park. He dubbed the enterprise Pico Park and scheduled the *Margaret* to ferry excursionists back and forth. Dedication ceremonies took place on July 4. "A native of Branford Mr. Plant himself raised the silken flag that July day to dedicate Pico Park as a vacation Eden," a newspaper detailed, "while Branford's Military Band played a medley of national airs and 700 stepped ashore as the Margaret made her first landing." Henry thereafter welcomed Cuban friends Pedro and Rafael Fernandez de Castro to New York before departing in early August with Morton, J. W. Fitzgerald, and others for Boston and Halifax to attend the Canada-Atlantic and Plant Steamship Company annual meeting.[20]

No sooner had Henry landed back on US soil on August 13, 1894, than his marital woes resurfaced. Margaret had suffered a relapse in the aftermath of his Parisian jaunt. Dr. Durant advised a rest cure in the Pennsylvania mountains, and the three of them made their way to Cresson Springs "for a few weeks." As a report advised, "Mrs. Plant, who has been ill for a long time, is slowly recovering her health, and when winter comes she may be able to do a little entertaining." Henry felt comfortable enough within a few days to leave Margaret for a Southern Railway and Steamship Association gathering at Coney Island. His absence worsened her condition. On the thirtieth he hurried his wife and her physician back to New York, where, presumably, she might be stabilized.[21]

Henry's fevered return to New York also highlighted recent events that had generated a serious emergency as far as his business plans were concerned. On August 28 a new tariff act had become law without the president's approval. Intended as a modest reform measure aimed at reducing levies, the final product imposed formidable rates on imported sugar and sparked devastating consequences for the Cuban economy. "By establishing a new duty of 40 percent *ad valorem* on all sugar entering the United States, the Wilson-Gorman Tariff Act of 1894 dismantled the cornerstone of previous reciprocal trade arrangements between Washington and Madrid," Louis A. Pérez explained. "Spanish authorities responded swiftly . . . and canceled duty concessions extended earlier to American imports. An impenetrable protectionist wall reappeared around the island in mid-1894, reviving memories of the worst features of Spanish commercial exclusiveness. The sudden disengagement of Cuba from its prosperous but brief privileged participation in international trade had jolting consequences on the island. Cuba lost preferential access to the only market with the capacity to absorb its sugar exports and insulate the island from the uncertainties of world competition. The restoration of Spanish tariffs, further, raised the spectre that the United States would retaliate by banning Cuban sugar from American markets altogether. Profits declined immediately. Production followed."[22]

The rapid turnaround in Cuban affairs breathed new life into the island's revolutionary movement. Leaders such as José Martí, Antonio Maceo, Máximo Gómez, and Manuel García moved to prepare for open warfare. García acted first. On September 21 he attacked Pedro Fernandez de Castro's showplace sugar plantation Nuestra Señora del Carmen, a retreat Plant had often enjoyed. The raiders aimed to kidnap one of de Castro's sons, the politically powerful but absent Rafael Fernandez de Castro. Instead, they snatched his brother Antonio, who had volunteered to surrender in order to save his father "deep pain and discomfort." Antonio, too, eventually escaped unharmed, but only after the family paid the revolutionaries a reward of 15,000 pesos, or about $20,000.[23]

More bad news came to the fore as Plant lamented his wife's struggles, fretted disruption of his Cuban plans, and feared for the welfare of his de Castro friends. A "big West Indian hurricane" plowed ashore on Florida's Gulf Coast in late September, leaving misery in its wake. "The hurricane of Sept. 24th to 26th did considerable damage to the orange and vegetable crops and caused the destruction of much property of all kinds," a report conveyed. Plant learned details of the storm's impact at Branford on the twenty-sixth. "Mr. Plant's despatches said there had been washouts all long his lines in Southern Florida, and that railroad traffic has been suspended," a correspondent related. Henry had already learned that Tampa had not been spared: "At Tampa several large cigar factories were destroyed. The First Presbyterian Church and the palatial Tampa Bay Hotel were badly damaged. Several smaller structures were also demolished. The total loss on buildings at Tampa is estimated at $50,000."[24]

All such considerations aside, Henry concentrated in fall 1894 on seizing control of Florida railroad affairs as his competitors ramped up their confrontation with the Plant System. "Mr. Plant is left with no northern outlet," newspapers announced in mid-October. Rumors also suggested that his direct competitor, the FC&P, had swallowed up the "Orange Belt" line from Sanford to St. Petersburg, denying Plant's hopes to secure the road and jeopardizing his Havana-run mail contracts. Plant quietly moved to negate that acquisition's value. In early October he purchased the Florida Southern Railway (FSR), an artery that stretched down the peninsula from Palatka on the St. Johns River to the seat of Polk County at Bartow on the Peace River, and on south to Punta Gorda and Charlotte Harbor. The maneuver offered closer access to Havana than did St. Petersburg and essentially mooted the mail-contract issue. Plus, it added the Hotel Punta Gorda to Henry's hotel chain and, given the facility's 1,200-foot pier, access to deep water.[25]

Those arrangements made, Plant headed South to assess hurricane damage and calculate further moves. Henry took advantage of stops along the way—Charleston, Savannah, and elsewhere—to cheer Florida prospects. "The influx from the North this winter will be simply immense," he insisted at Jacksonville. "I find more enthusiasm now relative to Florida than ever before. In fact, one is almost led to believe that everybody in the North is coming to Florida this winter." At Tampa on October 27—his seventy-fifth birthday—he discovered to the good that most Tampa Bay Hotel repairs could be completed by the season's opening on December 3. Less pleasantly, he faced dissension from irate businessmen who had heard rumors of the FSR purchase and feared Plant's priorities shifting from Tampa to Punta Gorda. "The facts in their entirety will have to come out sooner or later," one man observed. "But as to results there is no question. The Plant system is in control of the Florida Southern; if not in actual control, possession in a strictly legal sense, and the Florida Central and Peninsular has declared open warfare on its opponent. It is an open secret in this part of the state that all the friendly arrangements for the exchange of traffic and schedule conditions heretofore existing between the two companies in Florida are now declared off."[26]

Within about one month, Plant, buttressed by the FSR success, had crafted further plans to address competition, ones that required action in concert with Flagler. He formulated the basic approach at New York in early November. Having attended PICO partner W. T. Walters's Baltimore funeral, he joined Flagler in Savannah on November 26 to begin their regular inspection and annual meeting circle. Over the next ten days the party covered Georgia, Alabama, and Florida, ultimately reaching Punta Gorda about December 5. Meanwhile, the two Henrys had called railroad executives to meet at Flagler's Royal Poinciana Hotel in Palm Beach three days later, thereby hoping to forestall a "traffic war." Among the roughly two dozen people at the meetings were Boston's Frank Quincy Brown, FSR president and a future Plant intimate, and FC&P chief executive Hanson Reiman Duval. Enough progress resulted to justify a follow-up session in Savannah on December 11 that included traffic managers. Observers reported "acknowledged friction between the Plant system and the Florida Central and Peninsular company," and hard compromises proved elusive. Eventually, attendees accepted the general premise of pooling traffic while announcing that they did not possess "sufficient information" to resolve particular traffic issues. Instead, they created a commission to seek common ground. The truce appeared shaky, but it temporarily averted a railroad war.[27]

Henry left Savannah for Tampa, where the tourist season progressed. Doubtlessly he seethed at Christmastime when Governor Henry Mitchell, enforcing retribution for Flagler's political assaults, tried to extradite the developer from Florida pursuant to a Texas indictment against Standard Oil executives. Flagler laughed off the matter from New York. "I shall leave for the South in January," he retorted, "and shall make no attempt to evade the serving of papers." Mitchell's *Tampa Tribune* allies meanwhile praised their favorite governor, demanding to know "Who Is Mr. Flagler?" Better outcomes in other matters fortunately allowed Plant "a very contented state of mind." He announced plans for a huge new steamship "of such speed that only a few of the trans-Atlantic liners like the City of Paris, etc., can show their heels to her." He thrilled that "[Tampa Bay Hotel] guests this season are far more numerous than at any period in December of previous years" and voiced cautious optimism about the economy. "So far as the business on our roads and ships is concerned, it is improving every day," he commented. As 1894 closed he also implemented expanded reorganization plans aimed at girding the SF&W for eventual clashes with the FC&P. Specifically, Henry created the system-wide position of traffic manager. He filled the key post with a trusted post–Civil War Southern Express employee, Beverly W. Wrenn, who had become a nationally regarded railroad traffic executive.[28]

Satisfied with progress made, Plant rang in the New Year at Palm Beach. Flagler's Royal Poinciana opened to the public on December 28 with a "grand affair" to which many of Henry's friends had been invited. Among them, Rufus Bullock attended the celebration with an Atlanta delegation. Its members invited Henry to sponsor a Florida display for the upcoming Cotton States and International Exposition, and he did not disappoint them. "Mr. Plant was much impressed by what the committee told him," a delegate related, "and promised to make a handsome exhibit." The occasion marked decided advances and nurtured future dreams. Sparkling champagne, moonlight glittering over Lake Worth, and laughter echoing off the corridors of "the largest hotel in the world" should have set a magnificent stage, all other things being equal, for the welcoming of better and more prosperous times ahead.[29]

Sad to say, the night of the twenty-eighth began turning an otherwise enjoyable holiday into a harbinger of disaster as a killer freeze blanketed the peninsula. "The great 'freeze' on the 28th, wrought fearful havoc here," a Royal Poinciana guest recorded. "It lasted but six hours, but when again the sun was warm and the breeze soft the country looked as if it had been swept by fire. Oranges were frozen on the trees, flowers and vegetables, and even the great trees were scorched and withered and the appearance of the whole landscape was changed." Plant hurried to survey his own properties. At Winter Park's Seminole Hotel on New Year's Day, he found only thirty guests and widespread damage. At Tampa, where temperatures had plunged to eighteen degrees, the scene staggered beholders. Nearly three years later a reporter reminded Plant of their encounter "at the Tampa Bay Hotel, January 2, 1895, when we looked over the desolation in the park, wrought by the freeze." Henry lamented in response: "So it was. That was a sad sight."[30]

Plant, not unexpectedly, attempted after the December freeze to project a more hopeful vision than stark reality strictly dictated. After meeting with Flagler at St. Augustine during the Ponce de Leon's season opener in mid-January, he enlisted Jacksonville journalists to spread encouraging words. "The doctors tell us that the state needs some cold weather every few years to keep everything healthy, and the cold weather has doubtless done a great deal of good in this way, even though it has done a great deal of harm to the oranges and vegetables," he argued. "By careful investigation I have discovered that the cold was not so disastrous as it had been pictured. . . . You know the people thought at first that the trees were killed, but from what I have seen I feel pretty sure that there will be a good crop of oranges next year. In a good many places the oranges were not frozen, and some that dropped from the trees, on account of the cold, have not soured, but are edible. I am getting quite hopeful of the future outlook."[31]

The enthusiasm endured for less than three weeks. Henry used the time to fine-tune system-wide reorganization and to bring Margaret to Florida after prolonged absence. "Mr. and Mrs. H. B. Plant arrived at the Tampa Bay Hotel last evening," the *Tribune* noted on January 24. "Mrs. Plant looks in the best of health, and Mr. Plant seems to be as young today as he was ten years ago." Then, beginning on February 7 a hard freeze blanketed much of the peninsula for four consecutive days. "Yesterday morning the thermometer was down to 22 degrees, and the weather was cloudy," an onlooker noted on the ninth. "Snow fell thick and fast up to noon, and the weather cleared up in the evening. The mercury kept going down, and at midnight had reached the 20 mark." Days passed as "the Great Freeze of 1895" ravaged crops and destroyed livelihoods. "We saw the statement made by some newspaper correspondents to the effect that 'if fire had consumed every house in the State the night of the frost, the loss would not have been equal to the loss of property resulting from this death frost,' and we thought the statement extravagant," a tourist noted in March 1896. "Now that we have seen for ourselves the destruction wrought, we are prepared to believe that the 'half has not been told.'" B. W. Wrenn recalled "Mr. Plant's expression of opinion made to me just after the freeze." He continued: "We were walking through these very [Tampa Bay Hotel] grounds, where in a single night $50,000 worth of rare exotica had been destroyed. I spoke of the heavy loss sustained. 'All that' said Mr. Plant, quietly, 'can be replaced, but what is to become of the orange-growers?' This is by no means idle talk with him."[32]

Many businessmen by then—if they did not give up entirely—counted their losses, retrenched, and awaited better days. Not so with Plant. "Mr. Plant is still here; his great hotel is open and well filled with guests who find in the admirable management . . . new reasons for continuing their winter residence in Florida," a tourist had observed on the freeze's second day. "The great railroad man mingles freely with the guests of the house, and in conversation dwells with pardonable enthusiasm upon the future of a state which no man has done more to develop than himself." Almost immediately after icy conditions lifted, Henry doubled down on his belief in Florida and its future by taking a specific public action that echoed his larger message. At Sanford on February 12 the entrepreneur captured the first reporter that he could find, who related their conversation with the headline "Mr. Plant Not Disheartened." The report detailed: "Instead of crying over spilt milk and reducing the size and expenses of his proposed exhibit at the Cotton States and International Exposition in Atlanta, with a liberality of unbounded praise, he today gives orders to enlarge the space already agreed upon and increase the display to be made by the Plant system." Henry's traffic agents meanwhile urgently gathered with their opposites in Atlanta "to harmonize the differences." The resulting contract amazed industry experts. "Dixie's Railroad Row Ended," the *Atlanta Constitution* proclaimed. The Plant System coincidentally announced that "it would reach out its arms and make a bid for European business direct." Agent A. H. Groover, system sources alerted, was "already established in Paris."[33]

The flurry of activity had only just begun. Henry's ongoing reorganization took a crucial turn on February 16, for instance, with his designation of Alabama Midland Railroad superintendent Bradford Dunham as "superintendent and general manager of the entire Plant system." With the placement of the veteran railroad man in the newly created and powerful job, industry insiders truly began to understand the breadth of changes that Plant meant to impose. "There can be no mistake about the significance of these appointments," an observer asserted. "The Plant managers find it necessary to immediately assume a more aggressive and vigorous policy in order to overcome the inroads of their rivals." Further personnel changes soon diminished chronic complacency issues. The *Constitution* commented, "Since Mr. Dunham's appointment, all the employes are momentarily expecting to have their heads lopped off."[34]

The pace of Plant's personal movements matched those of Plant System changes. With son Morton and others he toured FSR-served communities in Northeast Florida before heading to Savannah, Macon, Atlanta, Memphis, and—for Mardi Gras—New Orleans. Presenting a relaxed and composed manner apparently free from dread about Florida conditions, he grasped opportunities to evidence confidence in his future and that of Florida. He also hinted vaguely at expanding his international ties to Venezuela. Quietly, though, Henry moved decisively against his competition. In early March he snatched the Orange Belt Railroad (Sanford and St. Petersburg Railroad) from the FC&P, whose takeover attempts had stalled. Public announcement came on March 15. "As the Plant System now owns or controls the Florida Southern Railway, from Palatka to Punta Gorda, this system has practically shut out any possible competition for its West Indies and Gulf business," the *New York Tribune* commented. "It owns or controls all the railway terminals on the Florida Gulf Coast, except Cedar Keys and Apalachicola, and these are too far north to give President Plant any concern."[35]

Whereupon Plant turned his attention to Caribbean affairs. The long-awaited Cuban Revolution had broken out on February 24, and initial reports had suggested quick rebel gains. The conflict jeopardized, among other interests, an investment Henry had been considering in a "new railway running from Havana to Pinar del Rio" on the island's western tip. Havana consultations in early March led him to better understand prevailing conditions. At Tampa he convened top executives at midmonth to gauge follow-up moves in Cuba and Florida and then ventured with Margaret to Jamaica on the twentieth. The Cuban Revolution punctuated their departure as three suspected "revolutionists" were "forcibly thrown" from the *Mascotte* before it left Port Tampa. "It is known that these three men had $50,000 for the revolutionists in Cuba, and important papers for the patriots," a correspondent declared. Eleven days later the Plants returned to the *Mascotte*'s home port with up-to-date intelligence. Five "prominent Cuban leaders" had escaped Spanish agents and ridden the steamer to Kingston with "money and dispatches." A source also indicated that "revolutionist clubs throughout Jamaica are thoroughly organized, and the leaders are only awaiting an opportunity to join the insurgents in Cuba." Furthermore, Henry had directed his captain to reconnoiter the island to assess coastal defenses. "She almost circled the Island of Cuba, going south to Cape Maysi and returning by Cape San Antonio, but at no time was a Spanish war ship sighted," the *New York Herald* advised. "They report the Cuban coast very poorly guarded and that nothing like a cordon or blockade is being maintained."[36]

The Caribbean voyages sobered Plant about new Cuban investments and turned his attention elsewhere. As the Tampa Bay Hotel closed out its 1895 season on April 3, he launched short inspection trips to Punta Gorda and several Tampa Bay–area communities before he set out at month's end for Virginia. There, he made all-but-final arrangements with Collis P. Huntington's Newport News Ship Building & Dry Dock Co. for the construction of his grand steamship announced the previous December. At New York in early May, he inked the construction contracts and then reportedly took ill with a "congestive chill." Notably, though, Henry's only grandchild, Henry Bradley Plant II, entered the world at Baltimore on May 18, and, perhaps, a proud grandfather quietly traveled to see his legacy and principal heir. The May interlude may have reflected, as well, ongoing troubles within the Plant empire. Henry's reorganizational steps had impinged on many system executives, and some seethed at what they considered personal slights. Among others, longtime aides Bolling R. Swoope and Charles D. Owens resigned. Vice president Henry D. Haines, according to reports, attempted to leave the system as well. Plant rejected the resignation, leaving a disgruntled Haines to represent the system at a London railroad conference.[37]

PICO's president preceded Haines in crossing the Atlantic even though the system's office persisted in assertions that Plant was ailing in New York. On June 5 even Margaret supported the tale by informing reporters that upon Durant's orders, she had relocated him "to his farm at Branford, Conn." She added, "He made the journey without fatigue, and was told by his physician that in the course of a few days he might return to business." Unfortunately, insider sources had already revealed Henry's intentions. On May 31 a Thomasville, Georgia, newspaper had reported: "President H. B. Plant of the Plant System sailed for Europe from New York yesterday. He goes for rest and recreation." A delay of a week or so apparently kept Plant in New York, however, for on June 4 the Charleston City Council was striving to complete business requested by Henry "before his early departure for Europe." Meanwhile, Margaret tactfully withdrew from social affairs. Particularly, she absented herself from a committee preparing New York's exhibit for the Cotton States Exposition. Public appearances notwithstanding, trouble brewed at home for the Plants.[38]

During Henry's six-week absence from New York the platform upon which significant elements of his future life were to play out began to take form. Jeanne Granier was enchanting Théâtre des Variétés audiences in Jacques Offenbach's *La Perichole*. Despite her success, the diva yearned for a change in direction. "The popular light operatic artist, Mlle. Jeanne Granier . . . is about to quit the lyric for the dramatic stage," a London critic observed. Whatever their relationship previously, Granier now enthralled Henry. "He displayed the gallantry of the South," the *Washington Post* observed years later. "It was quite the fashion in Paris then to profess devotion to the comic opera star. Just to show that when in Paris he thought best to do as Parisians did, Millionaire Plant sent the most magnificent bouquet his money could buy to the dressing room of the pretty Mlle. Jeanne. There were many dinner parties afterward—for what successful actress would not be flattered by the notice of such a noted multimillionaire, the owner of railroads, steamships and such great hotels as the Tampa Bay Hotel."[39]

Before long, Henry had fashioned plans for the diva. "He would enjoy, he said, making it possible for Mlle. Granier to give his country such a treat, for instance, as her delectable interpretation of La Grande Duchesse—her most captivating role," the *Post* continued. New York's Metropolitan Opera, he believed, should welcome the diva, and he would build "a beautiful, marvelous, boat worthy of a queen" to transport her there. The latter task proved more easily accomplished than the former. Upon his mid-July return to the United States, Henry immediately "inspected work on the new ship." Within days he and J. W. Fitzgerald had closeted themselves at Shelter Island across Long Island Sound from Branford. Rumors circulated that Plant intended to retire. Fitzgerald left Shelter Island in early August, though, for Newport News. Morton joined him there. Plant's son thereafter reported to his father at the Hotel Edgemore on that Atlantic shore of Queens on the twentieth. From that resort Plant moved back to Branford, where Fitzgerald rendezvoused at month's end. Existing plans for the new steamer had been upgraded, and construction was moving ahead.[40]

The passing months came with highs and lows for Henry. H. S. Haines resigned in August. This time, Plant acquiesced and D. F. Jack became vice president. Mike O'Brien and R. G. Erwin gathered with their employer and Henry Flagler the next month aboard Flagler's *Alicia* for the America's Cup races in New York Harbor. A few weeks later the *Margaret* wrecked in a storm off Cape Henry, Virginia. Its owner indicated that he would rebuild it "as a floating palace" but kept his attention glued on the vessel already underway. Also, on October 7 Plant's agent purchased the Ocala House at Ocala, Florida, to complement his hotel chain. Henry soon visited the new acquisition along with other system locations. The circuit led to Atlanta on the twenty-fifth, where the Cotton States Exposition adorned what today is called Piedmont Park. History has remembered the fair mostly as the setting for Booker T. Washington's famed "Cast down your bucket where you are" speech on September 18. For Henry and the Plant System, though, the high point arrived October 28, when system employees gathered on Plant Day to celebrate, if belatedly, their employer's seventy-sixth birthday. On that occasion, Plant shared with those present his current perspective of their mutual core mission: "Be sure that we are not all for ourselves. We are public servants and we must serve with the rights of recognition of our patrons. We must never take a customer's money without giving him his money's worth. All this is very easy to say, but it is very difficult, in the human mind, to carry it out. We must recognize them and we must school ourselves in the effort to learn how all these things are accomplished."[41]

Margaret had joined Henry for the Plant Day festivities, but when he took to the road again in mid-November she remained behind. A continuing cycle of inspections and annual meetings brought Plant to Montgomery on November 29, where news reached him that his father-in-law, Martin Loughman, had died in New York. Suggesting the state of his relations with father and daughter, Plant did not to interrupt the tour to attend funeral services. Instead, he pressed on to Ocala and Jacksonville en route to the Tampa Bay Hotel's season opening on December 7. Lawyer Lynde Harrison served him as companion. From Tampa the party crossed the peninsula to Palm Beach, where its members enjoyed Flagler's hospitality and a personally guided tour of his newly completed east coast railroad. Still, Henry found reasons not to return to New York. By the eighteenth he was in Atlanta, where for several days he toured the fairgrounds and pressed the causes of Florida tourism and growth from what seemed by then an almost preposterous perspective. "I believe that this cold wave will serve as a blessing in disguise to many of the farmers of Florida," he insisted. "Perhaps they may never have such a killer frost again, but at the same time they are making money on other crops and are not dependent on the orange groves and sunshine entirely." Disbelieving, the *Atlanta Constitution* blared, "Mr. H. B. Plant Is More Hopeful Than Many Who Have Viewed the Groves."[42]

The Branford holidays barely interrupted Henry's travel regimen, and when he rode the rails again his wife still did not accompany him. He and J. W. Fitzgerald met at Newport News on January 8, 1896, to examine the nearly completed steamship and confirm to the builders his selection of its name. Satisfied that progress was well advanced, he now contracted for a new vessel to replace the *Margaret*. At Savannah soon afterward, Caribbean tidings preyed on his mind. Among other incidents, rebels had burned de Castro fields on the second and would return seventeen days later to raid the Nuestra Señora del Carmen plantation. "Mr. Plant said last night that the war in Cuba is affecting the travel on the line between Tampa and Havana," the *Morning News* reported. "Many people who would otherwise visit the island do not care to do so in the present uncertain state of affairs there. As a trade-off to this, he said, the line to Jamaica, which was put on last winter, will be resumed this winter, with a sailing every two weeks." Plant understood initially that Margaret would accompany him on the season's first Jamaican cruise on January 18. She did not. Instead, he traveled with George

Hutchinson Smyth, his longtime New York minister. They returned to Port Tampa on the twenty-eighth, allowing Henry to reach Savannah two days later, where he had promised to treat with railroad engineers about outstanding grievances. There, Plant received a telegram. *La Grande Duchesse* had been ceremoniously launched that day. Neither Henry nor his wife had attended the momentous event.[43]

14
War and Peace
1896 to 1899

"a case of root hog or die"

With many Americans still suffering in 1896 from the Panic of 1893, Henry Plant found himself confronted as well by painful and abiding reminders of previous years' adversities. The continuing threat of Cuba's revolutionary struggle had halted his island expansion plans, while he grappled fitfully with a Florida economy staggering from Great Freeze of 1895 devastation. Closer to home, Henry's relations with wife Margaret pulsed weakly as he expended energies favoring the career of a Parisian diva. Many entrepreneurs reacted to contemporary challenges cautiously, if not with retrenchment or bankruptcy. Backed by the might of the Plant Investment Company (PICO) and its ability to borrow money, however, Henry took an alternate course. No typical businessman, he chose levels of engagement at age seventy-six that many younger men would have found daunting. He pressed past commitments to unprecedented levels as he sought new and innovative routes toward goals otherwise denied to him. He factored almost everything except unexpected consequences.

Plant's approach during winter and spring 1896 involved several facets, with his efforts proving more successful in some than in others. Cuba's difficulties, for instance, inspired him to refocus on Jamaica. He announced six excursions for the winter season. During a January visit, he also approached the colonial government, as one source put it, "with a view to developing that earthly paradise upon the go-ahead American plan." Specifically, Henry believed Kingston's tourist accommodations to be insufficient. The Myrtle Bank Hotel, as a respected guidebook declared, was then "the largest and best hotel in Kingston." The guide added: "It is situated on Harbor Street, the principal business street of the city, and about five minutes' walk from the post-office and stores. Situated as it is upon the seashore, with a beautiful tropical garden between it and the shore, in the centre of which is the band-stand, it has all the advantages of a city, country, and seashore residence combined." Henry proposed to run the facility "as a winter resort in connection with other of his hotel enterprises." Unfortunately, he failed to consider Jamaican sentiments and found in March that the colonial governor had "coldly rejected" his plans. The PICO president, with childhood friend and Chicago railroad magnate Timothy Blackstone, thereupon hurried to the island on the *Mascotte*'s mid-March voyage. Plant and Blackstone implored Governor Henry Arthur Blake to reverse his stance but left Jamaica with little to show for their exertions.[1]

Desperate Floridians proved more willing than Jamaicans to accept Plant's leadership. Unable to create a world-class resort at Kingston, he pressed expansion of Sunshine State hotel and transportation holdings. "Florida is coming out," one newspaper asserted, "and Mr. Plant will lend her a helping hand." Plant's initiatives involved purchase and construction. He quietly acquired Kissimmee's Tropical Hotel, for instance. He soon renamed it "The Kissimmee." Also in spring he leapt across Tampa Bay, extending his reach to Clearwater on the Pinellas Peninsula's Gulf side. He selected a site for a resort hotel that he named the Belleview. Moreover, he envisioned an entirely new community eventually called Belleair. Plant also began looking farther south down to Charlotte Harbor and the Caloosahatchee River. His 1894 Florida Southern Railway acquisition had brought the Punta Gorda Hotel within his ambit. Now, he mulled extending rails to Fort Myers. Preparing the way for expansion, he secured control in fall 1896 of the Fort Myers Steamboat Company, which ran routes from Punta Gorda to Punta Rassa and Sanibel Island. As Henry observed, "Sanibel Island is a beautiful gem of the Gulf."[2]

Facility upgrades also commanded Plant's creative energies, with special attention paid to his most prized hotel. "Vast improvements are being made at the famous Tampa Bay Hotel in Florida," a visitor remarked in October. "This hotel, which stands for all that splendor and comfort could possibly signify in the great world of hostelries of America, will open in December, 1896, with increased temptations and charms for the winter tourists." Various enhancements adorned the plans, including a golf course and race track as well as "a large bathing pool 50x70 feet, a double bowling alley, and a shuffle-board room." None stood out more than an exposition building designed to house the system's 1895 Cotton States world fair collection and an impressive opera house and theater called "the Casino." At its gala opening on December 3, Tampa's mayor lavished praise: "He thanked Mr. Plant for the enterprise he has shown in providing the city with a playhouse of which any city might be proud. After expressing the hope that this grand old man might live to witness many anniversaries of the present brilliant occasion he proposed three cheers for the president of the Plant System which was given with great enthusiasm by two thousand people."[3]

The Tampa Bay Hotel Casino's construction perhaps reflected more of Plant's intentions than the public knew. Since the previous year the millionaire had tried to attract Parisian diva Jeanne Granier to the United States. He had reworked steamship construction plans to produce a suitable state-of-the-art vessel that was launched in January but not yet completed. He ordered it christened after one of Jeanne's great roles as *La Grande Duchesse*. On the other hand, New York's Metropolitan Opera and presumably other venues had declined his overtures, leaving him at a loss. The casino theoretically could offer an alternative. A report later alleged that he envisioned steaming *La Grande Duchesse* across the Atlantic and returning with the diva ensconced "in the sumptuous 'grand suite.'" While visiting his old colleague Rufus Bullock in Atlanta during April, Henry revealed that "he expects to put the new ship, 'The Grand Duchess,' in commission in June." If so, a stop at Newport News a few days later brought shock as his forward progress ground to a halt. He learned that final work on the ship was running months behind schedule and that it would be steaming nowhere during summer 1896.[4]

At Newport News, Plant had intended to return to New York, having concluded exhausting rounds of planning sessions, annual meetings, and inspection visits. Appearances suggested that he was bearing the exertions well. As late as his Atlanta visit, a reporter had insisted, "Mr. Plant is in very good health." By the time Henry reached New York following the Newport News revelations and "a few days" in Washington, the situation had altered significantly. "He was taken violently ill and was constantly under the doctor's care for four or five months," biographer George H. Smyth detailed. Previous illnesses had sometimes masked quiet trips abroad, but this time proved different. Henry fared so poorly that he could not travel to Newport News in late May to see the new *Margaret* christened by her namesake, nor could he leave the comforts of his Fifth Avenue townhouse for his country home at Branford in early June. That relocation came several weeks later, and then only when Henry Flagler personally conveyed Plant and his physician Dr. Ghislani Durant to Connecticut on his yacht *Alicia*. Henry recuperated there through early September. Other than for son Morton, the aging entrepreneur received no business visitors until mid-July. He did so sparingly even then. When ready to return to New York, he depended on Flagler to transport him on *Alicia*.[5]

The close brush with death entailed consequences for Plant, including an accelerated desire to mold or cement his image insofar as public attention was concerned. Perhaps as early as the Kingston trip in January, Henry had engaged George H. Smyth to pen a friendly biography. The project came to notice in May with a story that quoted Plant's comments to the novice author: "I will be gratified, and am sure my friends will be, to give you any and all information obtainable that you may desire, in order that you may have it completed at as early a day as possible." While Smyth labored, his subject strove mightily to establish claims to distinguished heritage through genealogical investigation and organizational memberships. Even during his illness, he had received family historian Oliver Libby Frisbie of New Hampshire. He returned the visit in mid-September. "It is stated that President H. B. Plant will soon adorn the corridors of the Tampa Bay hotel, Tampa, with the beautiful and interesting diplomas of a number of different patriotic societies of which he is a member," a January 1898 notice advised. "He is descended from Colonial and Puritan stock for eight generations, his ancestors having defended the cross of St. George in all wars of the British colonies, and have been on the side of 'Old Glory' since it first floated. They were among the founders of America, and have helped to build, stone by stone, this temple of liberty and equality from the very foundation."[6]

Coincident with Henry's illness, the Plant System enhanced employee health care provisions. He had dealt earlier in the year with labor troubles among railroad engineers, forestalling a strike. Henry had departed a February 7 Waycross summit, though, after an unusual display of pique at the temerity of demands for a union contract in the face of his paternalistic attention to worker needs. "He deprecated the fact that they should join a society which would compel them upon the say so of a majority or even two thirds of their number to give up the work upon which they are dependent," an observer explained. Savannah, Florida and Western Railway superintendent Bradford Dunham's subsequent dismissal of key union activists exacerbated residual ill feelings, and Plant refused to intercede. Instead, he responded typically by courting worker favor through voluntary expansion of benefits. The new policy applied without regard to race. An early 1897 report concisely described the results. "The Plant System Relief and Hospital Department was established July 1, 1896, modeled after the relief feature of the Baltimore & Ohio's department," it detailed. "The plant system and its employes maintained a hospital for fifteen years. Up to 1895 only one hospital was maintained; then a second one was erected. It was necessary to add two more in the spring of 1896. Then Mr. Plant decided to establish a relief department, to be managed conjointly with the four hospitals, under the name of the Relief and Hospital Department. Membership was made voluntary for all employes in the service of the company July 1, 1896, and obligatory upon all persons entering the service or receiving promotion in the service subsequent to that time. Ninety-five per cent. of the

20. Margaret Josephine Loughman Plant. Portrait by Richard Hall, 1902. Collection of Henry B. Plant Museum. Gift from Mt. Sinai St. Luke's Hospital, New York City, 2017.

employes have joined the departments." The report added, "The Relief and Hospital Department comprises the employes of both the steamship and railway companies."[7]

Held in check by illness in summer 1896, Henry yearned to assess progress on current projects. "The new steamer La Grand Duchesse that is being built at Newport News is nearly completed, and Mr. Plant expects to go there and witness her trial trip," a New Haven report related on September 2. "He is also very much interested in the large and beautiful casino, which he is building at Tampa Bay, and is obliged to be in New York to look after matters pertaining to this. Mr. Plant is also interested greatly in what is called in the south, Plant's New Paradise, the Belleview Hotel, on the west shore, now in course of erection, and which when completed will be one of the grandest in the world." The first inspections came September 17. "The first trial of La Grande Duchesse, the elegant and most gorgeously finished vessel ever built in America, proved satisfactory to all parties concerned," a Newport News correspondent observed.[8]

As he pursued business in New York, Plant received word on September 29 that a hurricane had devastated Cedar Key before sweeping across the peninsula to Jacksonville and Savannah. Widespread damage resulted, including flooding of the Tampa Bay Hotel's grounds. Plant rapidly departed to inspect damage, especially concerned about the Belleview. He touched at Charleston, Savannah, Sanford, Kissimmee, and Tampa before assuring himself that the new resort had survived the tempest and could open in January. While at Clearwater, Henry learned that a tidal wave had unexpectedly swamped Brunswick and Savannah. He quickly turned northward in a steady progress through Ocala, Gainesville, High Springs, and Waycross, arriving at Savannah on October 14. Then, for a month stretching through November 18, he rested in New York and Branford while the titanic national political clash that was the presidential election of 1896 resulted in Republican William McKinley's defeat of Democrat William Jennings Bryan. Like Bryan, Plant had by then endured failure. Given his health crisis and with at least some consideration for Margaret's care, he had forgone hopes of steaming *La Grande Duchesse* across the Atlantic for Jeanne Granier. Instead, he leased his dream vessel to another steamship company for runs between Savannah and New York. Still, Henry returned to Newport News on the nineteenth to again view his new ship. "Mr. Plant highly complimented the work of the Newport News Dry-Dock and Ship-Building Company," a visitor noted, "and said that the Grande Duchesse was in every way satisfactory to him."[9]

The weeks following the Newport News visit found Henry frequenting annual meetings and inspecting facilities through the Southeast. He reached Tampa in late November in plenty of time for the casino's December 3 opening in the absence of Mlle Granier. Other than for quick trips to Punta Gorda and Fort Myers, plus a Savannah stopover that again allowed a tour of *La Grande Duchesse*, he remained at the Tampa Bay Hotel into the New Year. The Belleview debuted in mid-January 1897 to acclaim, although Henry spent the day in Polk County at Winter Haven and Florence Villa discussing investment opportunities with "three wealthy Cubans" and "several other wealthy men from New York." He then made his way to Savannah to meet Margaret, whom he escorted back to Tampa. Together, they hosted a South Atlantic and Gulf States Harbor Defense and Improvement Convention at the Tampa Bay Hotel that drew dignitaries from around the nation, including Florida governor William D. Bloxham and former Michigan governor Russell A. Alger. Henry led delegates on a Tampa Bay tour to select sites for fortifications in case of war with Spain over Cuba and participated with Alger in the organization of a "permanent" National Coast Defense Association. The opportunities proved especially fortuitous for Plant when in March newly inaugurated President McKinley named Alger as secretary of war.[10]

Plant maintained a hectic travel schedule in the months that followed aimed mostly at assessing conditions in Cuba and possible projects in Jamaica. He began with a quiet Havana journey. He seemingly intended to

21. SS *La Grande Duchesse*, Plant Line, c. 1901. Library of Congress.

calm fevered waters to avoid war. Instead, he angered *New York Journal* owner William Randolph Hearst, who as of January had determined to provoke conflict. "You furnish the pictures," the publisher had reportedly cabled artist Frederic Remington, "and I'll furnish the war." Hearst's reporter Richard Harding Davis seized on a routine search by Spanish authorities aboard the *Olivette* to create a fictional outrage wherein "three young girls" were "undressed and searched." Davis falsely accused the ship's captain of complicity before turning his vitriolic pen against Plant: "A person named Plant, who owns what there is of Florida that is not owned by Mr. Flagler, and who paints his half a hideous yellow [Plant System stations and other buildings were painted "Plant yellow" at Margaret's suggestion], so that there will be no confusion between the two, also owns the Olivette, and he does not wish his contract with the Spanish Government to be jeopardized by any disputes with Spanish officials who may please to come on board and search passengers and threaten them, and walk over them, and treat the flag at the stern which should protect them with such contempt that it hangs its folds in shame. His employees know his wishes, and will sacrifice any one passenger sooner than lose their wages, and they hold their breath when the officers and detectives take possession of the ship."[11]

On February 12, the day Hearst published the attack, Henry and Morton left Port Tampa on the *Olivette* for Kingston. They learned of the article eight days later upon returning with a load of tropical plants. Plant handled the matter by releasing a detailed account from the *Olivette*'s captain. "I have only to say that [Davis] appears to have a loose method of expressing himself," Henry added, "and his terms with reference to the captain, myself and others appear to be specially unguarded." The *Lakeland Sun*, among other organs, rejected Davis's smear attempt. "The Journal might have, with more truthfulness, added that this same 'Person Plant' has peopled 'his half' with thousands of happy and prosperous toilers, who have with his help made the one time forest blossom like a rose," its editor observed. "He has converted his 'half' from a howling wilderness fifteen years ago into what is today one of the most important commercial sections in the United States. He has built a railway system through the uninhabited forests of Florida that is second to none on this continent. He has, while 'painting his half yellow,' developed the sandy wastes of the Gulf into what is now the finest port in Florida, and what is destined, within a few years, to be the gateway of the Nicaragua Canal. He has made the western half of Florida a household word in every country in the world where civilization abides. He has brought sails from every sea to take the mineral wealth of 'his half' to the four corners of the earth. He has made the people of 'his half' love and respect him and quick to resent any wrong that is done him. The only pity is that there are not more 'Persons named Plant' in Florida."[12]

The outrage calmed as the facts reached wider audiences, allowing Henry to resume his travels. In mid-March he joined Flagler at Palm Beach before they rode together to Miami, where the East Coast developer's Royal Palm Hotel had opened in January. The sojourn served as prelude to Henry's second Jamaican voyage of the season, this time utilizing the new Plant System steamship *Florida*. "Mr. H. B. Plant is in most excellent health, having stood the trip splendidly," a fellow passenger recorded. "He was the centre of attraction during the entire journey. Besides being a man of great financial prominence, he is possessed of many charming social qualities that is admired by a host of personal friends everywhere." In early April Henry explored tobacco cultivation in Polk County at Bartow and Fort Meade. Days later he joined the Florida Southern's Franklin Q. Brown at Punta Gorda and Fort Myers to discuss regional rail construction and support for a Captiva Island hotel. Capping the occasion, Henry landed "a monster tarpon" on the Caloosahatchee River. At midmonth Havana once more hosted the American millionaire for several days. A tour of inspection then consumed much of the rest of the month before Henry left Tampa on the twenty-ninth for Savannah and New York.[13]

Certain implications of Plant's Punta Gorda and Fort Myers visits merit further attention. He and Brown had been growing closer since the Florida Southern Railway (FSR) purchase three years earlier. The time spent together that April at Charlotte Harbor and on the Caloosahatchee cemented ties, particularly after Henry agreed to invest in Brown's Captiva Island development. The men enjoyed each other's company, but Henry's motivations entailed complexities. William McKinley had taken the presidential oath on March 4, and, as a friend later recorded of Brown, "he was an intimate friend of the late President McKinley." Given Plant's close association with Grover Cleveland, the level of access to the new administration afforded by Brown's friendship could and did prove invaluable. In recognition of that fact, Henry in May arranged for the PICO board to elect Brown in place of D. F. Jack as a vice president with authority over "the hotels and lands of the company." Brown retained the FSR presidency as well.[14]

Not that the nation's new president was completely unknown to Plant. As noted, Henry often spent time and forged relationships at a famed New York City gathering spot. "Henry B. Plant . . . visits The Windsor [Hotel] when he is in town," an Ohio visitor bluntly observed in February 1897. The Ohioan mentioned as well that "among those seen in the lobby of The Windsor" was the president's brother Abner McKinley. A businessman always in search of opportunity, Abner lived at the hotel. With his brother's inauguration, he emerged as, in one political columnist's words, "a 'big Injun' with the Administration." Meanwhile, the president and his mentor Ohio senator Mark Hanna frequented a second oasis, a Republican mecca sited directly across the street from Plant's office. "We often met Theodore Roosevelt, who[se mother] lived near by on East Twentieth street, on his way to meet [New York senator] Tom Platt, McKinley, or 'Boss' Mark Hanna, at the Fifth Avenue Hotel, opposite—and how they rushed Teddy around 'Amen Corner,'" Plant secretary John Stuart Thomson recalled. "But he 'out-vociferated' them and, in addition, added his teeth."[15]

In spring 1897 Henry increasingly appreciated the extent to which he and the Plant System needed the administration's support and assistance. He found deteriorating conditions in Cuba, continued official resistance in Jamaica, slackening rates of tourism, and a stubbornly anemic Florida economy. His mood, already problematic, darkened further with word that on April 9 *La Grande Duchesse* had collided with another vessel off the New Jersey coast, sinking the other ship, leaving five dead, and wreaking extensive damage to the pride of the Plant fleet. Henry's habitual optimism now deserted him, and he ordered costs cut across the system. "In speaking of the immediate business outlook, he did not seem very hopeful," an April 29 report observed. "He anticipates an extremely dull summer season, and it was in the expectation of decreased receipts that certain changes among the employes were ordered." Plant amplified his thoughts a few weeks later: "It is dull in Florida. The orange crop was so seriously hurt by frost two years ago and since then that about two-thirds of the trees died. We will have to wait until they grow up again. Many of the Northern and Eastern people who came there went back home to wait, and with the others it has been a case of root hog or die. It is quiet all over and I don't expect it will be better right away."[16]

Plant's angst revealed itself in his movements over the next five months. He indicated first that he and Margaret would "spend their time traveling in Europe." The possibility sparked a spirited difference of opinion, for reports shortly declared that they would "pass the summer on the Pacific coast." The couple set out about May 20 for Asheville, North Carolina, where they toured George Washington Vanderbilt II's Biltmore estate. They stopped next in Nashville for the city's then-ongoing exposition, where the Plant System exhibit featured Henry's Caloosahatchee tarpon. The party reached California's Hotel del Coronado on the Pacific coast near San Diego on the thirty-first. The trip had seemingly generated further familial disputes. At San Francisco by June 5, he declared surprising new plans, ones that he intended to pursue without Margaret. "I am here to get away from business," he announced, "and intend to leave in a few days for Japan." Twelve days later Henry steamed alone for Yokohama. July found him first in Japan, then voyaging on to Shanghai and Hong Kong. August he spent back in Japan. He had secured from Governor Bloxham a commission, as Plant described, "to invite Japan to send commissioners to the national fish convention to be held at Tampa next year." As Henry recalled, "I had the pleasure of meeting the Prime Minister of the Mikado's realm and other members of the Japanese Ministry, and we had many interesting chats together." He also toured "the entire railroad system of Japan during his stay." An interviewer related: "Mr. Plant said it is like looking at a picture to travel through the country and see the farms which are cultivated entirely by hand. The fields reminded him of well-kept flower gardens at home."[17]

So profoundly did Japan intrigue Henry that he delayed his departure until early September. Even then he interrupted his return with a visit to Honolulu so that he might "see, for a couple of hours, the venerable lady [Mrs. Mary Parker], whose marriage he had attended when a child." He also paid a call on "his old friend" former Confederate general and Alabama senator John Tyler Morgan, who was in Honolulu in connection with Hawaiian annexation by the United States. Henry discovered, in fact, that annexation talk had stirred turmoil in the islands, with rumors circulating that "the Japanese were gradually and quietly building up a strong military establishment in Hawaii" and that Japanese troops had secretly arrived on his ship in the guise of steerage passengers. Having made his personal calls, Plant cautiously kept to the ship until it continued on its way. He landed at San Francisco on the twenty-third to be "extend[ed] the courtesies of the port" by the secretary of the treasury's orders. Margaret, who had passed the summer in Branford mulling their differences, awaited him on the dock. At Chicago six days later, Morton and Southern Express executive Mike O'Brien joined them. The party reached New York on September 30.[18]

His marital quandary produced no alarms that autumn, but the news from elsewhere brought ominous tidings. On October 3 the Spanish-backed Cuban government fell, introducing a heightened level of uncertainty and insecurity. Revolutionary leaders insisted that a change of government meant little. "Generals [Máximo] Gomez and [Manuel] Garcia take the stand that they will not lay down their arms until Cuba is free," a correspondent emphasized. Action by the United States appeared possible if not imminent. Intervention furor served as backdrop for a meeting Plant held with the president on October 25 shortly after a McKinley conference with Secretary of War Alger. Whatever Henry's input, McKinley resisted entreaties for action. A few weeks later, rebels again burned the de Castro family plantation Nuestra Señora del Carmen. They returned on December 3 to destroy the town of Jaruco in another vain attempt to kidnap Plant's friend Rafael Fernandez de Castro. In the meantime, yellow fever plagued Jamaica. Officials warned that "all Caucasians going to Jamaica at this season, not being acclimated are liable to take fever of some kind, whether it be yellow, typhoid, malarial or other." The pestilence persisted into late December. Fears persisted for months thereafter.[19]

Still, the Pacific trip worked wonders when it came to Henry's attitude about Florida business affairs. He spent much of October in the state seeing to various interests and came away with a distinctly altered perspective. "I have seen and heard enough to convince me that business is picking up," he told associates. "Men are beginning to believe in themselves again. That is a great thing, you know—belief in one's self. I think idle labor is going to be employed, because capital will seek channels for sensible investment. I feel sure there will be a steady return to good times." Plant's restored optimism even identified positive aspects to Caribbean troubles. "Others' misfortunes are pretty sure to work for the good of some," he expressed, "and so when Jamaica and Cuba are practically cut off as tourist points, on account of the war and the sickness, which have made both of those points unpleasant for travellers, Florida will have a better chance." Plant added, "The railroads and hotels [will] be ready to do as big a business as could possibly be hoped for, and [we will] have finer trains, quicker schedules and more accommodating officials, if that [is] possible, than during the year past."[20]

Mid-November found the PICO president once more engaged in customary annual meetings and inspections. The Tampa Bay Hotel opened for the season on December 8 without him, however, as he had quietly boarded the *Olivette* two days earlier for Havana. "One could scarcely see any signs of the war," he remarked. "The only war like scenes I found was the customary parade of volunteers on the parade [ground] with a concert by the regimental band in front of the Hotel Pasaje. All of the hotels in the city, the Pasaje, Ingleterra, Roma, Telegrafo and Mascotte, the leading ones, are all open for business and are giving their same excellent service." Henry, encouraged by his findings, held extensive but unreported discussions with the managers of the Payret Opera House and the Tacon Theatre. Plant declared only, "My observation is that Havana is going to be a gay place this winter." He thereafter passed the remainder of the year mostly at Tampa, where he enjoyed the company of his son, daughter-in-law, and grandson.[21]

The holiday spirit carried into 1898. Word reached Tampa from Havana that the Spanish government had lifted its embargo on tobacco shipments to the United States—giving Tampa's economy a boost—and that a "home rule government" would take office January 1. In Florida, Henry busied himself preparing to launch a new Fort Myers hotel, a project that he had undertaken with Frank Brown the previous spring. Happily, as it turned out, he and Margaret reunited in Charleston at midmonth. Onlookers noticed that the couple appeared to have passed some positive turning point after their separation for most of the summer and fall. "Mrs. Plant is in excellent health and is delighted to be at the Tampa Bay again," a local reporter related, "and says she will probably spend the winter in Florida." Together, they welcomed delegates to the International Fisheries Congress that Henry had promoted in Japan. They followed by entertaining a group of congressmen from the House Committee on Rivers and Harbors, an event punctuated by a "grand banquet" at the Tampa Bay Hotel. The month closed with Henry and Margaret at Belleair. There, they attended "the first grand ball and reception of the season at the Hotel Belleview."[22]

February similarly, if temporarily, brought felicitous tidings as Plant authorized resumption of Jamaican steamship service, greeted South and West Commercial Congress attendees at the Tampa Bay Hotel and Casino, conducted the delegates on a Tampa Bay tour, and then inaugurated steamer connections to Honduras by joining Margaret on board the *Mascotte* for the initial voyage. "Mr. Plant said yesterday," the *Tribune* observed on the twentieth, "that the tourists who failed to take advantage of the future trips to Honduras during the present season would miss a rich treat." By then, though, Cuban affairs were spinning out of control. Recent ominous reports had caused Henry to send Frank Brown to Havana to assess conditions. The PICO vice president returned on the thirteenth. Two days later the USS *Maine* exploded in Havana Harbor, triggering calls for war from, among others, Henry's nemesis William Randolph Hearst. The state of affairs that greeted the Plants at Port Tampa on the twentieth had thus altered perilously. Henry refused to join calls to war and treated matters lightly. "[The Plants] were glad that war had not been declared," an interviewer related, "for they might have been picked up at sea by a Spanish war ship." Further evidencing his freedom from war fever, he and Margaret left Tampa to enjoy Mardi Gras at New Orleans. Asked for insights there, Henry observed: "I can but quote that gallant [*Maine*] Capt. [Charles Dwight] Sigsbee, who said: 'It is better to know than to think,' and let us await the investigations that are being made before we reach a conclusion. I share in the hope of all peace-loving citizens that there will be no break in the harmonious relations now existing between the States and foreign nations. The trouble in Cuba has certainly had disastrous effects upon business generally, and we can but trust that it may have an early termination."[23]

Through mid-March, as war's drumbeat mounted, Plant passed time enjoying himself. On March 3, for example, he, Margaret, Morton, Frank Brown, and other associates ventured to Lakeland for the Polk County Fair's "H. B. Plant Day." Henry aimed his remarks not at the international crisis but on agriculture and prosperity. "He spoke in the highest terms of the magnificent exhibits of the products of Polk county, displayed in the exhibition buildings," an onlooker related. Henry and Margaret then departed Port Tampa on the *Mascotte* for Kingston. They spent four days "visiting the points of interest on the island" before leaving from Montego Bay. Meanwhile, "active preparations for war" prompted Plant upon return to Tampa to urge Secretary of War Alger to see to port defenses. "In case of hostilities, it would seemingly be an attractive object of attack by the enemy," he insisted. Alger assured him that "Tampa will not be overlooked." Heartened, the Plants headed for a rendezvous with Henry Flagler. After a short stay at Palm Beach, their party steamed from Miami to Nassau, where Flagler was considering erecting what became the Colonial Hotel. "In the harbor of Nassau Mr. Flagler entertained on board the steamer the governor of the Bahamas [Sir Gilbert Carter] and his staff," an account noted. A leisurely cruise with the governor led them to Governor's Harbor, where guests partied into the night. A slow-paced return brought the Plants back to Nassau, Miami, Key West, and Tampa. "They . . . expressed themselves as being greatly pleased with their visit to the East coast and the Bahamas," the *Tribune* announced.[24]

By then Plant could no longer ignore war fever. He frantically planned evacuation of Americans from Cuba, while also protecting his corporate interests. Captain James W. Fitzgerald, his longtime maritime adviser, reported that Plant "was using every effort in his power to prevent the government from taking charge of the company's ships." Fitzgerald added, "Mr. Plant looks a long ways ahead, and he thinks that after the war with Spain the shipyards of this country would be so busy that it would take a long time to replace a first-class merchant ship." Henry likely also conducted his own assessment at Havana. At least, he disappeared for nearly one week while he and Margaret supposedly amused themselves at Fort Myers fishing for tarpon. She claimed headlines in his absence by landing a prize catch.[25]

Frank Brown meanwhile hurried to Washington, where he met with McKinley, Alger, and others on Plant's behalf to "extol the use of Port Tampa . . . as a point of embarkation in the event of war with Spain." Army adjutant general Henry C. Corbin detailed the results. "Mr. Plant, of the railroad system bearing his name, persuaded the Secretary of War that Tampa was the place [to organize the expedition] and that his railroad was competent to handle that army and all its supplies," he explained. "Secretary Alger had all confidence in his judgement and ability[, and] when one had Alger's confidence he relied on him implicitly." Events moved quickly as Congress authorized war against Spain on April 19, and McKinley issued a declaration of war five days later. Major General James F. Wade had already arrived at Tampa to Brown's warm greetings. Wade quickly selected the Tampa Bay Hotel "as general headquarters." Henry and Margaret feted him there at month's end with "a full dress hop in the ball room." As an onlooker pronounced, "Never has any of the social events that have taken place at the magnificent Tampa Bay Hotel, equalled the brilliancy of the hop in honor of the general commanding the Tampa division of the army, and officers of his division."[26]

Plant now immersed himself in the details of hosting, supporting, and transporting an army, including leasing his ships to the government. His performance at first drew plaudits. "The troops, officers and men are enthusiastic in praising Mr. Henry B. Plant, president of the railways, steamships and hotels comprising the Plant system, and his wife, for there is nothing left undone by these delightful people in making all happily comfortable," an officer informed the *Army and Navy Journal* in early May. "Mrs. Plant lends her sweet womanly ways to her husband in receiving the officers, every one of whom have been most cordially received and extended warm hospitalities." As the military presence swelled, though, tensions arose as supply lines clogged, heat and humidity elevated, and tempers flared. Theodore Roosevelt, well known to Plant from Fifth Avenue Hotel encounters, lodged at the Tampa Bay Hotel for several days in early June to allow private time with wife Edith Kermit Roosevelt. He exercised little restraint in voicing criticisms. "No words can paint the confusion," Teddy recorded. "No *head*; a breakdown of both railroad and military system of the country."[27]

By then, influential voices had targeted Plant as the individual most responsible for the mess. "Who Is Plant?" a prominent national magazine demanded rhetorically. "Plant is king of Florida and owner of nearly all the South. He is an old man with brains still young. Into his pocket go ninety-nine cents out of every dollar spent by the army of soldiers and visitors in Florida. Everything in sight belongs to Plant. Plant is a happy man. He permits no competition, and insists upon double prices. The soldiers, and, in fact, all of us, must ride on Plant railroads, eat in Plant restaurants, sleep in Plant hotels, use the Plant telegraph, ship goods via Plant express, drink Plant beer, smoke Plant tobacco, and have your linen washed in a Plant laundry." The magazine added, "The Government is paying Mr. Plant twice as much per diem for the use of his possessions as we pay the President of the United States per annum for the use of his brains." The New York *Press*, among other organs, joined the chorus. "The Plant System is the greatest thing that ever happened—for H. B. Plant," it asserted. "It beats any faro bank or black and red system that ever came over the pike. It's as sure a winner for anybody but Plant as the eagle bird down at Key West is for the suckers who try to pull the feathers out of his tail. You talk about playing both ends against the middle!"[28]

Mounting frustrations erupted on June 8, when Plant and Major General William R. Shafter, the Cuban expedition commander, quarreled at Port Tampa about delays and confusion during embarkation of troops. Henry at the time, as a soldier observed, "was directing the whole clogged system." As he labored, Shafter confronted the PICO president. One account insisted that the general "swore at him until the air became oppressive." Henry walked away. Within a day or two he had set out for Washington, where he knew that critics were aching to relocate the base of supplies from Tampa. For nearly one week he successfully lobbied in the halls of government, offering the president assurances that fault for the problems lay with the military. On June 19 he uncharacteristically vented his sentiments to a *New York Herald* reporter, who quoted him extensively the following day. "It was unfortunate that many of the army quartermasters were young and inexperienced in the shipment of large quantities of supplies and the transportation of men," he declared. "They lacked the knowledge of cars and railroad equipment which would have fitted them for this work. There was, therefore, considerable confusion upon their arrival." As to Plant System liability, he insisted that "railway and steamship facilities at Port Tampa are all that could be desired." Believing that the president sympathized with his position, Plant mailed him the *Herald* article. "I rather expect to start South again within a few days time," he noted, "and, should it be your pleasure to see me, I shall be glad to call on you the day I am in Washington."[29]

Henry returned to Tampa on June 25. "He will remain here for some time," a local account related, "and says that he is greatly pleased to find it really cooler here than in the cities of the North." Plant encountered animosities from some remaining military and government officials, however, and took leave of Florida three days later. His public justification asserted that his wife had "been indisposed for several days [in New York]." He spoke with the president on his way home, but otherwise, Henry looked on from the Empire State as Cuban fighting continued during July and operations moved to Puerto Rico. His absence from the scene of action weighed heavily on him, and he fell sick. He and Margaret spent a few days at a Catskill Mountains resort, and Henry additionally passed a day or two at Branford and Long Branch. He occasionally shared newspaper clippings and advice with the president. "I have not been quite well for the past three weeks, nor since I was last in Washington, and contemplate a sea voyage that will keep me away from here for three or four weeks from Saturday next," he mentioned to McKinley on the twenty-fifth. "I hope to return in time to render any aid possible in the way of transportation whenever my services in that line shall be desired."[30]

Transportation issues, as time's passage proved, stood foremost in Plant's thinking during the weeks consumed by his subsequent European voyage. He departed New York for Liverpool on July 30 and arrived in London before mid-August. He scoured markets there for Cuban railroad bonds and conferred with other investors about postwar opportunities on that island. On August 25 the *Savannah Morning News* articulated its surmise of his goal: "Rumor has had it for some time that Mr. Plant, while abroad, is either organizing a syndicate to take hold of all the railroads in Cuba, or is quietly maneuvering a movement to secure control of them for himself and American associates. Large English investments are said to have been made in Cuban railroad properties, and this lends a touch of credibility to the story that this is the secret of Mr. Plant's trip across the ocean." His inquiries in England and on the Continent, in any event, kept Henry away from the United States nearly twice as long as he had anticipated, and he did not return to New York until September 15.[31]

Two key events had taken place that influenced Plant's course once at

22. "Millionaire Plant," from the *San Francisco Call*, June 10, 1897.

home. Critically, wartime hostilities had ceased, with McKinley on August 12 declaring an immediate cease-fire "on all fronts." The president anticipated the convening of a formal peace conference at Paris on October 1. Less happily, the *Olivette* sank nineteen days later. Serving as a hospital ship, it had returned to Fernandina from delivering returning troops to Montauk and Boston. "The Olivette went down in about thirty feet of water, her main deck being submerged," the *New York Tribune* explained. "No one apparently knows how the accident could have occurred." The Navy quickly disclaimed "liability for damages resulting from the sinking of the ship" and stopped "payment of the per diem compensation the moment the vessel became unserviceable." Engineers raised the ship on September 28 and initiated the laborious task of towing her to a Philadelphia shipyard.[32]

Fortunately, Plant's smoothly functioning shipping line staff—guided by F. Q. Brown, Morton Plant, and Captain J. W. Fitzgerald—capably addressed the *Olivette*'s restoration with interior design help from Margaret Plant, thus allowing Henry to concentrate on Cuban plans. He joined island railroad executives and Southern Express vice president Mike O'Brien at Delmonico's Restaurant on October 4 to honor General Fitzhugh Lee, a longtime Plant acquaintance about to assume command of the army of occupation at

Havana. Henry's consultations and planning, despite a brief renewed bout of illness, had advanced sufficiently by his seventy-ninth birthday on the twenty-seventh to permit him to launch two weeks of inspections through the Southeast. At Tampa on November 1, he appeared to be "enjoying good health" and declared that "it is a relief to get back to Tampa." He touched at Port Tampa and Belleair but, within days, had headed north to Alabama to continue the customary circuit. Congressional elections, held on the eighth as he headed north from Savannah, cheered him because Republican Senate wins promised easy confirmation of a McKinley-negotiated peace treaty. The pieces required for his plans to gel were falling into place handily.[33]

At that point, limits of endurance imposed themselves. At Jersey City, New Jersey, on November 10 fatigue brought temporary incapacitation as Henry stepped from his private railroad car. "While preparing to leave the car he complained of dizziness and sat down a moment," the *New York Times* related. "When he tried to get up he found he could not do so, and was put to bed by his son and an attendant." Summoned to the scene, physician Ghislani Durant watched through the day before announcing in the evening that "all danger had passed." Transferred to his Fifth Avenue townhouse, Plant for days remained shaken and restricted to limited activity.[34]

Henry fortunately had recovered sufficiently by midmonth to prepare for a voyage to England in pursuit of his Cuban railroad plans. By then, according to the Parisian journal *Le Matin*, he had become fascinated—beyond mere interest in Cuban railroads—with a scheme to ferry "trains and their locomotives" from Tampa to Havana via Key West. Chance intervened, though, before he could board ship. "While alighting from a cable car in New York," Plant fell, hurting himself severely and sparking "an attack of kidney trouble from which he has suffered for years." Confined to bed for days, he suffered "a slight setback" in early December. George H. Smyth's biography, which was released that month to a distinctly tepid reception, could not have helped his disposition. "A book such as G. Hutchinson Smyth, D. D., has written partakes of something of the character of an advertisement for the Plant Line," the Philadelphia *Times* opined. "If it be free of that smirch in fact it cannot escape suspicion on that ground. It goes without saying that the book is written in the most eulogistic vein." In any event, circumstances kept Henry homebound into the New Year. "Further advices from the Hon. Henry Plant report his condition gradually improving," a report advised on January 5, 1899. "Mr. Plant will leave New York for the South, as soon as his physician considers him able to travel."[35]

That moment arrived on January 16 when Henry, Margaret, Dr. Durant, and attorney Lynde Harrison rolled from the New York station toward

Tampa with the PICO president primed for new advances. "It was said that if Mr. Plant soon recovers his strength," the *New York Times* commented, "he will go from there to the West Indies to further a plan for steamship lines between Cuba, Puerto Rico, and Jamaica, which has been under consideration for several months." The freshly renovated *Olivette* arrived at Port Tampa to a jubilant reception at month's end, and Henry announced a schedule of "five sailings per week" by the Plant System to Havana. "This places Tampa at the head of any Southern port so far as Cuban service is concerned," the *Tribune* boasted, "giving almost a daily service." Margaret then joined Henry, who was "feeling much better," on the *Olivette*'s first Cuban voyage of the season. They returned on the *Yarmouth* February 3. Rumors and reports whirled about his intentions now that Spain had ceded control of the island to the United States and Fitzhugh Lee had taken charge as governor of Havana Province. "Messrs. Flagler and Plant are now striving to form closer relations than ever with Cuba, the former by building a great hotel in Havana, and the other by improving the steamship service between Tampa and the Cuban capital," a Chicago newspaper observed. "A few years of peace in Cuba not only will cause that island to be transformed by American brains and capital, but will result in increasing many fold the importance of Florida as a maritime state." The *New York Times* added, "[Plant] is now cogitating plans for the erection of a magnificent Winter resort of palatial proportions and furnishings in Havana."[36]

Whatever the talk about steamships and resorts, Henry's plans now focused in good part on railroads. To some extent his thinking centered on Florida competitors, but hopes for Cuban projects stirred his deepest passion. Morton had sailed his new yacht *Ingomar* to Port Tampa in late February. On March 1 Henry, his son, Durant, and several others left Port Tampa for an "extended cruise." The voyage took them quietly to Havana, where Henry rendezvoused with President McKinley's now-infamous brother. "While Abner McKinley denies that his visit to Cuba is more than a mere pleasure trip there appears to be little doubt that he has a two-fold mission, political and business," an observer asserted from Havana on March 7. "Officials here say he has private instructions from the president to investigate the situation, sound the sentiment of business men and thoroughly gauge the Cuban feeling toward the American administration. He will look after the interests of an express company, with which he is connected, and a railroad enterprise will have his attention." One editorialist referred to a McKinley connection with "that projected railroad which was to run from one end to the other of an island we do not own." Another assailed his promotion of the issuance of Cuban bonds for American-inspired capital projects. "After

Brother Abner and the Wall street sharks get through with their schemes to 'finance' Cuba and bond the island to a stand-still, how much more 'free' will the Cubans be than they were under Spanish bondage?" the critic asked.[37]

Whatever particulars were discussed or acted on, Plant soon retraced the route to Tampa. McKinley within a few days made the same journey. Once they had conferred at the Tampa Bay Hotel, Plant arranged for Abner's party to enjoy a Tampa Bay excursion to St. Petersburg on the eleventh, after which McKinley left for Washington and a meeting with his brother. Curiously, six days later at New York fire totally destroyed the Windsor Hotel, where Abner resided. The conflagration apparently began "immediately over the rooms occupied by President McKinley's brother." Abner and his family "lost everything except the clothes they wore." Firemen later discovered in the building's ashes a memento of his confidential dealings. It consisted of "a smashed metal box containing a lot of scorched telegrams to Abner McKinley."[38]

As the Windsor collapsed in flames, Henry, Morton, and Plant System general manager Bradford Dunham forged connections and pursued business arrangements in Havana. "Mr. Plant, the railroad and hotel magnate of Florida, has bought a piece of land in a desirable location at a cost of $250,000, and will erect a magnificent hotel," a visiting businessman related. "Havana is destined to become a great winter resort for rich Americans." Henry was not feeling well. He had expected to remain for two weeks but instead returned to Tampa on the twenty-sixth. His motivation related not so much to his health, though, as to urgent calls for a smallpox quarantine against Havana and other Cuban ports due to an outbreak in Tampa's black community. Henry quickly suspended direct steamship service between the two cities. Still, his outlook continued rosy. "He stood the trip exceedingly well and feels much improved in health," the *Tribune* observed. "He will remain at the hotel until after the close of the season." Even the shock of a "disastrous fire" at St. Petersburg that consumed "the entire Plant system dock and three large freight buildings" failed to diminish his ardor for the coming Cuban expansion.[39]

Springtime sparkle shone warmly for Henry as March progressed into April. On the third his agents scored a major coup by acquiring for $600,000 his longtime Florida competitor the Jacksonville, Tampa and Key West Railroad. When the Plant System took control on the twenty-second, Henry renamed it the Jacksonville and St. Johns River Railroad. He meanwhile embarked on a brief tour that took him, Margaret, and Durant to Ocala, Jacksonville, Savannah, and Charleston. From the latter city they journeyed on April 7 to Washington, where ongoing festivities marked official peace ceremonies observed on the eleventh at the White House. Rather than return to Tampa, the party proceeded on to New York. Through the period

Henry's stamina and demeanor commanded attention. "My health is much better at present than it has been for the past few months, I am pleased to say," he had informed the president on April 3, "and I hope to be in Washington for a day or so within the next week to ten days, and if able when in that city will endeavor to call upon you at your leisure." A *Tribune* reporter concurred with Plant's assessment. "The aged railroad promoter was feeling in splendid health when he departed," the man advised. A Charleston colleague agreed: "Mr. Plant is looking remarkably well for a man of his years and has recovered from his late illness."[40]

As his representatives fine-tuned plans to implement his projects for Florida and Cuba, Plant consumed his time at home handling business and personal details. At Tampa in January he and Lynde Harrison had discussed a wish to "perpetuate his name under the title of the Henry Bradley Plant Company." Harrison suggested simply changing the name of the existing Plant-controlled South Eastern Investment Company, a transition they finalized in Connecticut during late April. Henry then commenced transferring properties into his namesake concern. Harrison meanwhile discovered a defect in Plant's 1893 will. That document, executed in New York but prepared by Georgia lawyer Robert G. Erwin, had effectively limited benefits to Margaret and Morton in favor of Henry's grandson, Henry Bradley Plant II. The arrangement it contemplated contradicted New York law but was permissible in Connecticut. On May 25 at New York City Henry executed a codicil that updated bequests and administrative provisions. He then took steps to establish Connecticut residence, including the execution of an additional codicil at New Haven on June 20. To what degree Margaret was made aware of the details is not known, but she knew the will's contents by then and understood her husband's intent to adopt a new legal residence for estate purposes. Early in June with Morton they had greeted *La Grande Duchesse* at Boston following her extensive rehabilitation. From there, the couple traveled to Connecticut, where they passed the tenth with Harrison "[driving] around New Haven looking at various houses from the outside." During the tour, Margaret "pointed out . . . among others the Hotchkiss house . . . as an apparently desirable location."[41]

When not in New York, Henry spent much of the next two weeks at New Haven and Branford. On the twentieth he toured the Hotchkiss house. "Mr. Plant examined up to the third floor, looking at closets, stairs, and cellar," Mrs. Hotchkiss recalled, "[and] inquired whether an elevator could be placed where the back stairs came up from the basement to the first floor." The homeowner added, "He made some statements to the effect that he wanted to use the basement exclusively for an office; [when] the suggestion was made that he did not need the back stairs from his office to the first floor . . . Mr. Plant replied, 'It is my residence, sir.'" Plant agreed to pay $85,000 but, as Harrison later attested, "No papers were drawn up, no memorandum was signed, nor was any time set or fixed for concluding the transaction or reducing the contract." Through the period he appeared healthy, if not robust. "Mr. Plant met numerous friends while here, to all of whom he expressed himself as feeling very well," a Branford man recollected, "and said he had almost entirely recovered from his recent severe illness."[42]

Henry Plant died unexpectedly at his New York home on Friday, June 23, 1899, a few months shy of his eightieth birthday. He had visited his West Twenty-Third Street office the previous afternoon, remarking to associates "that he felt very well indeed." He and George H. Tilley left together for "a series of business calls through the down-town district." Returning to the office, "Mr. Plant left for his home in his usual spirits." He was not seen again in public. Upon reaching home he reportedly "complained of feeling ill." Dr. Durant spent the night overseeing his patient "as a matter of precaution" but departed the next morning, "not considering the case serious." Tilley dropped by a little later, finding his longtime employer and friend "cheerful." The *New York Times* provided further details: "At 1 o'clock Dr. Durant called. At that time no apprehension whatever was felt by the physician or Mrs. Plant, but at 2 o'clock the patient began to show signs of exhaustion and sank rapidly until the end came." Bereaved relations joined his widow and son, veteran friends, and longtime colleagues at his funeral. The services, held at home the following Monday, were conducted by his biographer the Reverend Smyth. "There was a charm in the calm, quiet sweetness of Mr. Plant's nature, and honesty was one of his most conspicuous traits," Smyth declared. "He was not a man who promised rashly but having given his promise its performance was assured." A five-car train transported the funeral party to Branford. There, on Tuesday morning, Plant was buried "in a highly polished mahogany casket with silver trimmings." The pallbearers included Henry M. Flagler, Senator Thomas C. Platt, former Georgia governor Rufus B. Bullock, Benjamin F. Newcomer, Robert G. Erwin, Franklin Q. Brown, Henry S. Haines, Lynde Harrison, Benjamin W. Wrenn, Bradford Dunham, George H. Tilley, Hugh Dempsey, Doctor F. Jack, and Father Thomas J. Ducey.[43]

Many attempts were offered in the wake of Smyth's eulogy to capture what their authors saw as the essence of Henry Plant. They understandably tended toward hyperbole but occasionally sounded telling insights. A North Georgia editor, for one, stated the case bluntly. "He has done more to develop the south, and particularly Florida, than any dozen men living," F. T. Reynolds wrote, "He was an honest and pleasant gentleman. He always had the interest of his employees at heart and was the staunch friend of the young men." Reynolds added, "His life is a model for all young men to pattern after." The southern writer Charles Henry Smith, known more familiarly as Bill Arp, took a more personal tack. "Always dignified, always self-poised and earnest, he seemed as much concerned for others as for himself," Smith reflected. "He was frank but careful in speech, genial, uncomplaining and never worried over business cares or disappointments." Smith continued: "I have taken note of him for nearly half a century and know of no greater man in the line of public progress and public benefaction. Many millionaires have acquired fortunes from speculations—speculation that robbed others. Many have built on the foundations that others laid and some have wrecked railroads and private enterprises on purpose for their own profit, but Mr. Plant made honest plans in early life and has by slow and sure degrees expanded and matured them. He has added to values not only of his own property, but to that of communities and states. He has proved himself an unselfish friend to the south and won the love and admiration of our people."[44]

Afterword

The Ephemeral Nature of Legacies

"I have been grossly misrepresented"

The business behemoth constructed by Henry Plant did not long survive his demise, at least in the form its creator left behind. Absent his energy, inspiration, and guiding hand, the Plant System and its various allied enterprises drifted and soon stalled. Considerable blame can be attributed to a fight over money. He had attempted through his will, signed in 1893 and updated as late as the week of his death, to pass on the greater portion of his financial legacy to his grandson, Henry Bradley Plant II. Annual payments of $30,000, among other considerations, were allotted to his widow and son. At first, the arrangement appeared acceptable to all principal parties. Plant and attorneys Robert G. Erwin and Lynde Harrison had reckoned, though, without the influence of Margaret Plant's friend Mary A. Wood and Plant family physician Ghislani Durant. Wood, the widow of New York physician Dr. William G. Wood, had faced a similar situation in 1890. Mrs. Wood had sued to set Dr. Wood's will aside as violating New York law and, in 1891, had prevailed. That precedent now served as template. Dr. Durant exercised his influence with the widow Plant following Henry's death to pursue the same legal course as had her friend. Rumors that spread by early October from the Plant household, perhaps amplified by Durant, suggested a contest based partly on the physician's opinion that Plant "acted while his mind was partially unbalanced." Two months later Margaret sued estate trustees Lynde Harrison, Morton Plant, George Tilley, and Robert Erwin. She alleged that her late husband had acted "with fraudulent intentions."[1]

The estate litigation dragged on for slightly more than two years. Morton Plant, the once truant son who had become his father's trusted ally and adviser, raged at his stepmother's temerity in challenging Henry's wishes. "All through the affair I have been grossly misrepresented," he declared in May

1900. "In the first place, so it appears to me, some one thought it would be judicious to misrepresent me to the extent of asserting that I had joined with Mrs. Margaret Plant in contesting the will of my father. Such has never been my intention, either implied or expressed. The provisions in the codicils in no manner changed the main document as far as Mrs. Plant and I were concerned. At various times when the will was being read in the presence of those who were to be executors, and who are now executors, Mrs. Margaret J. Plant and I expressed our satisfaction with the provisions made for us." As Morton's expressions intimated, the legal fight generated bitter divisions. At one point, the trustees even ceased to pay Margaret's annuity under the will. Negotiations ensued but failed. New York Supreme Court judge David Leventritt ultimately heard the issues. In January 1902, he ruled in Margaret's favor and awarded her a dower right valued at $7 million. The trustees opted not to appeal the decision and, following recalculation of estate valuation, eventually paid over to her in excess of $8.5 million.[2]

The victory assured Margaret enormous wealth, but she managed to enjoy it for only a few years. On January 18, 1904, before she received final payment, she quietly remarried to New York wallpaper manufacturer Robert Graves at 586 Fifth Avenue, the Plant townhouse. The couple spent much of their time together in Europe. At Paris, in August 1908, she collapsed. Quickly returned to New York, Margaret underwent extensive care at St. Luke's Hospital before being relocated to her Edgemere, Long Island, summer home. Fall chills prompted her transfer to her new townhouse at 7 West Fifty-First Street. She died there May 30, 1909. Her physician and confidant Dr. Ghislani Durant was not present during the final illness. Having found his reward in Margaret's generosity, he had departed New York several years earlier to reside on the French Riviera at Villa Yaddo in Menton.[3]

Already by the time Margaret won her lawsuit, the Plant System's days were numbered. On July 1, 1902, its rail lines were consumed by the Atlantic Coast Line Railroad. "Gradually, the old name will vanish over the entire system," the *Tampa Tribune* observed, "and the Plant System of Railways will be but a memory." Despite Margaret's effort to transfer ownership of the Tampa Bay Hotel to the Jesuit Order, Morton continued to try without success to find a buyer. Eventually, he agreed to sell the facility to the city of Tampa. Transfer of ownership took place June 22, 1905. On the other hand, Morton kept the Belleview and nurtured it with care as a world-class golf destination. It proved successful and remained so into the twenty-first century. Most of the steamship line ended up, also with Morton's assistance, in Henry Flagler's hands as the Peninsular & Occidental Steamship Company. Henry probably would have been pleased. The Southern Express Company held out the longest, operating independently until its World War I consolidation into the Railway Express Agency. Credit goes in greatest part to the gifted administration of its new president, Mike O'Brien. Perhaps more than anyone he had absorbed the values his mentor Henry Plant had professed to honor. "In manner he was always genial, unpretentious, cordial and possessed of a frankness, sincerity and courtliness that made him well liked by all who knew him," an obituary noted upon O'Brien's death in September 1909. It added, "He was always generous."[4]

Notes

ABBREVIATIONS

AC	*Atlanta Constitution*
ACh	*Augusta (GA) Chronicle*
ADC	*Augusta (GA) Daily Constitutionalist*
ADI	*Atlanta Daily Intelligencer*
AWNA	*Weekly News and Advertiser* (Albany, GA)
BDA	*Boston Daily Advertiser*
BDE	*Brooklyn (NY) Daily Eagle*
BH	*Boston Herald*
BHR	*Bar Harbor (ME) Record*
BJ	*Boston Journal*
BO	*Branford (CT) Opinion*
BP	*Boston Post*
BS	*Baltimore Sun*
CC	*Charleston (SC) Courier*
CDE	*Columbus (GA) Daily Enquirer*
CDES	*Columbus (GA) Daily Enquirer-Sun*
CDG	*Cincinnati Daily Gazette*
CDN	*Charleston (SC) Daily News*
CDP	*Daily Phoenix* (Columbia, SC)
CDT	*Chicago Daily Tribune*
CE	*Cincinnati Enquirer*
CEP	*Evening Post* (Charleston, SC)
CIO	*Inter Ocean* (Chicago, IL)
CM	*Charleston (SC) Mercury*
CNC	*Charleston (SC) News and Courier*
CO	*Charlotte (NC) Observer*
CtC	*Connecticut Courant* (Hartford, CT)
DS	*Daily Saratogian* (Saratoga Springs, NY)
FLIN	*Frank Leslie's Illustrated Newspaper* (New York, NY)
FM	*Florida Mirror* (Fernandina, FL)

FTU	*Florida Times-Union* (Jacksonville, FL)
GDN	*Galveston (TX) Daily News*
KDG	*Daily Gleaner* (Kingston, Jamaica)
LAR	*London American Register* (London, England)
LBRG	*Black River Gazette* (Lowville, NY)
LC	Library of Congress
LCJ	*Courier-Journal* (Louisville, KY)
LJR	*Journal and Republican* (Lowville, NY)
MDA	*Memphis Daily Appeal*
MH	*Miami Herald*
MT	*Macon (GA) Telegraph*
MWT	*Macon (GA) Weekly Telegraph*
NA	National Archives
NHCR	*Columbian Register* (New Haven, CT)
NHDH	*Daily Herald* (New Haven, CT)
NHER	*New Haven (CT) Evening Register*
NODP	*Daily Picayune* (New Orleans, LA)
NOTD	*Times-Democrat* (New Orleans, LA)
NT	*Tennessean* (Nashville, TN)
NUA	*Nashville (TN) Union and American*
NV	*Norfolk Virginian*
NYCA	*Commercial Advertiser* (New York, NY)
NYDG	*New York Daily Graphic*
NYEE	*New York Evening Express*
NYEP	*Evening Post* (New York, NY)
NYET	*Evening Telegram* (New York, NY)
NYH	*New York Herald*
NYMC	*Morning Courier and New York Enquirer*
NYP	*Press* (New York, NY)
NYS	*New York Sun*
NYSp	*New York Spectator*
NYT	*New York Times*
NYTr	*New York Tribune*
NYW	*World* (New York, NY)
OES	*Ocala (FL) Evening Star*
PDN	*Palatka (FL) Daily News*
PI	*Philadelphia Inquirer*
PT	*Times* (Philadelphia, PA)
RD	*Richmond (VA) Dispatch*
RG	*Royal Gazette* (Hamilton, Bermuda)
RNO	*News and Observer* (Raleigh, NC)
SDMN	*Daily Morning News* (Savannah, GA)
SDNH	*Savannah Daily News & Herald*
SDR	*Savannah Daily Republican*
SFC	*San Francisco Call*
SFCh	*San Francisco Chronicle*
SLPD	*St. Louis Post-Dispatch*
SMN	*Savannah Morning News*
SR	*Springfield (MA) Republican*
TDJ	*Tampa Daily Journal*
TDTE	*Thomasville (GA) Daily Times-Enterprise*
TIRA	*Indian River Advocate* (Titusville, FL)
TJ	*Tampa Journal*

TT	*Thomasville (GA) Times*
TTr	*Tampa Tribune*
TWT	*Tampa Weekly Tribune*
WD	*Weekly Democrat* (Bainbridge, GA)
WDNI	*Daily National Intelligencer* (Washington, DC)
WES	*Evening Star* (Washington, DC)
WH	*Waycross (GA) Herald*
WMS	*Wilmington (NC) Morning Star*

INTRODUCTION

1. Martin, "Henry Bradley Plant," 276.
2. "Henry B. Plant, the King of Florida," 5–6.
3. "Henry B. Plant Is Paid Tribute," *TTr*, February 16, 1910.

CHAPTER 1

1. "Leisure Hours in Florida, on the West Coast Short Line, Plant System," *AC*, January 13, 1896. Principal biographical works on Henry Bradley Plant include: Smyth, *Life of Henry Bradley Plant*; Martin, "Henry Bradley Plant"; Johnson, "Henry Plant and Florida"; Reynolds, *Henry Plant, Pioneer Empire Builder*; and Brown, *Henry Bradley Plant: The Nineteenth Century "King of Florida."* On Charles Henry Smith, see Parker, *Alias Bill Arp*.
2. Smyth, *Life of Henry Bradley Plant*, 335; Plant, *Descendants of John Plant*, 27; *Annual Report of the Supervising Surgeon-General*, 434; *Connecticut Herald* (New Haven, CT), September 21, 1819, 3; "Yellow Fever," *Connecticut Journal* (New Haven, CT), October 5, 1819.
3. Smyth, *Life of Henry Bradley Plant*, 35, 335; Plant, *Descendants of John Plant*, 36; "H. B. Plant's Success," *NHER*, October 30, 1895; Rockey, *History of New Haven County*, II, 68.
4. Smyth, *Life of Henry Bradley Plant*, 17–18.
5. Simonds, *History of the First Church*, 129–35.
6. Simonds, 136, 147; Smyth, *Life of Henry Bradley Plant*, 19; *Connecticut Church Records*, II, 295.
7. Smyth, *Life of Henry Bradley Plant*, 35–36; "From the Correspondent of the Daily Advertiser, New Haven, Aug. 21," *Saratoga (NY) Sentinel*, September 1, 1824; Eliza Ann Plant headstone inscription, Old Branford Center Cemetery, Branford, CT.
8. Harrison, "James Blackstone and His Family," 19–26; *Genealogical and Biographical Record of New London County, Connecticut*, 4–7; Van Slyck, *New England Manufacturers and Manufactories*, 101–4.
9. *Genealogical and Biographical Record of New London County, Connecticut*, 8–11; Van Slyck, *New England Manufacturers and Manufactories*, 104; "From the N. York Commercial Advertiser," *Geneva (NY) Gazette*, March 26, 1819; "Died," *NYEP*, March 10, 1854.
10. Franklin Q. Brown to A. J. Hanna, January 24, 1938, notebook: Henry Plant, Part One, Henry Bradley Plant Collection, Henry B. Plant Museum Archives; Smyth, *Life of Henry Bradley Plant*, 36–37.
11. "Mr. Coleman," *NYEP*, June 22, 1825; Leng, "Typhus Syncopalis," 555–59.
12. "Died," *Connecticut Herald* (New Haven, CT), September 13, 1825; "Died," *CtC*, October 11, 1825; "Connecticut Cemetery Inscriptions, 1629–1934," XIV, 364, 366, Charles R. Hale Collection, Connecticut State Library, Hartford; Trowbridge, *Hoadley Genealogy*, 66–67; Smyth, *Life of Henry Bradley Plant*, 36, 324–25.
13. Brown to Hanna, January 24, 1938; Betsey Hoadley passport application, July 26, 1873, US Passport Applications, 1795–1925, Microfilm Publication M1372, roll 197, NA; "Henry B. Plant Dead," *NYT*, June 24, 1899; Smyth, *Life of Henry Bradley Plant*, 38–39.
14. Anderson Plant will and probate record, 1827, Guilford Probate District, Connec-

ticut State Archives, Hartford; Smyth, *Life of Henry Bradley Plant*, 40–41; "In Memoriam: Alden Pardee Bryant," *News and Observer* (Raleigh, NC), December 9, 1900.

15. Trowbridge, *Hoadley Genealogy*, 52–53, 88; entry for Harry Hoadley, 1850 federal census manuscript, Martinsburg, NY, Lewis County, 10; entry for Harry H. Hoadley, 1860 federal census manuscript, Meriden, CT, New Haven County, 78; "Branford News," *BO*, March 3, 1900; "Branford," *NHER*, December 25, 1900, April 6, 1905.

16. Smyth, *Life of Henry Bradley Plant*, 13–14, 40; Trowbridge, *Hoadley Genealogy*, 88; Anderson Plant will and probate record; Henry Bradley Plant membership application, September 12, 1896, National Society of the Sons of the American Revolution, Louisville, KY.

17. "Reminiscence of Travel," *Black River Herald* (Boonville, NY), December 10, 1868; "Stage Coach and Plank Road Days in Northern New York," *Watertown (NY) Daily Times*, May 19, 1928. Among works on the Erie Canal, see Bernstein, *Wedding of the Waters*; and Shaw, *Erie Waters West*.

18. Entry for Philemon Hoadley, 1830 federal census manuscript, Martinsburg, NY, Lewis County, 392; Gordon, *Gazetteer of the State of New York*, 502–3; Barber and Howe, *Historical Collections of the State of New York*, 240–41; "Reminiscences of Collinsville," *LJR*, August 29, 1901; "Collinsville," *LJR*, June 4, 1908.

19. "Memories of 80 Years," *LJR*, September 26, 1907.

20. *LJR*, July 15, 1886, 2; Lowville Academy advertisement, *LBRG*, September 24, 1828, September 16, 1829, September 15, 1830. On Lowville Academy, see *Lowville Academy Semi-Centennial Anniversary*; "History of Lowville Academy by Walter S. Keen, for Degree," *Black River Democrat* (Lowville, NY), June 16, 1938.

21. Smyth, *Life of Henry Bradley Plant*, 40; "Death of Philemon Hoadley," *New Haven (CT) Palladium*, January 29, 1863; "Memories of 80 Years," *LJR*, September 26, 1907.

22. Findling and Thackery, *What Happened?*, 1; Cross, *Burned-Over District*, 3; Finney, *Memoirs of Rev. Charles G. Finney*, 78. See Johnson, *Shopkeeper's Millenium*, for an excellent review of early nineteenth-century religious and social changes in western New York.

23. Henretta, Edwards, and Self, *America's History*, 293–94; Mintz, *Moralists and Modernizers*, 53–54.

24. *Minutes of the Thirty-Third Annual Meeting*, 77; "Congregational Necrology," 67–68; Hough, *History of Lewis County*, 189–91; "Sabbath School Union," *LBRG*, August 7, 1827; "Lewis County Bible Society," *LBRG*, February 25, 1829; *Second Annual Report of the New-York State Society*, 31; "Mr. Webster," *New Hampshire Patriot and State Gazette* (Concord, NH), March 13, 1839.

25. *Minutes of the Thirty-Third Annual Meeting*, 78; "Congregational Necrology," 68; *Connecticut Church Records*, I, 189; "Inside View of the Country Church, or Steps That Led to the Revival of 1831 in Martinsburgh," *LJR*, July 4, 1877; "Lewis County Bible Society."

26. "Wool Carding," *LBRG*, June 4, 1828; *Minutes of the Thirty-Third Annual Meeting*, 78; Kimball, "Rev. Charles Finney."

27. *Minutes of the General Assembly of the Presbyterian Church*, 272; "Correspondent from Martinsburgh," *Oneida Observer* (Utica, NY), March 2, 1830; "Election Returns," *New York Morning Courier*, November 9, 1830.

28. Trowbridge, *Hoadley Genealogy*, 88.

29. "Inside View of the Country Church, or Steps That Led to the Revival of 1891 in Martinsburgh," *LJR*, July 4, 11, 1877; "Sudden Death," *LBRG*, June 24, 1829.

30. *History of Jefferson County*, 108.

31. *Emancipator* (New York, NY), October 3, 1839, 90; "By the Evening Mail," *BDA*, February 17, 1832; "Arrived," *Baltimore Gazette and Daily Advertiser*, March 16, 1832; Hoadley, "Jamaica Persecutions"; Brig *Ontario*, April 6, 1832, Registers of Vessels Arriving at the Port of New York from Foreign Ports, 1789–1919, Microfilm Publication M237, roll 16, NA; "Passengers," *NYSp*, April 10, 1832; "Death of Henry B. Plant," *LJR*, June 29, 1899.

32. Beck, "Report on Cholera"; "Cholera in New York," *LBRG*, July 25, 1832; *NYEP*, July 3, 1832, 2. On the 1832 cholera outbreak generally, see also Rosenberg, *Cholera Years*.

33. "All on Rail Roads," *NYCA*, September 24, 1831; "Rail Road Excursion," *NYCA*,

September 28, 1831; Greene, *History of the Mohawk Valley*, II, 1288–1306; "Great Freshet," *Martinsburgh (NY) Republican*, quoted in *CtC*, May 27, 1833.

34. "Lewis County," *Daily Albany (NY) Argus*, March 10, 1832; *Necrological Reports and Annual Proceedings*, 507–8; Shook, *Dictionary of Early American Philosophers*, 924–25; Sawyer, *Dissertation on Servitude*, 87, 93.

35. "Cholera in Canada," *Plattsburgh (NY) Republican*, August 2, 1834; "Cholera in Montreal," *Plattsburgh (NY) Republican*, August 9, 1834; "Cholera," *Plattsburgh (NY) Republican*, August 16, 1834; Smyth, *Life of Henry Bradley Plant*, 41–42; "List of Letters," *NHCR*, March 14, 1835; "Messrs. Editors," *NHCR*, August 9, 1834; Trowbridge, *Hoadley Genealogy*, 149; *Commemorative Biographical Record of New Haven County*, 436.

CHAPTER 2

1. Smyth, *Life of Henry Bradley Plant*, 39.

2. Willis, *Dashes at Life with a Free Pencil*, Part III, "Inkling of Adventure," 39.

3. "Ethnic History of New Haven," Ethnic Heritage Center, accessed July 16, 2016, connecticuthistory.org/wp-content/uploads/2013/04/AnEthnicHistoryofNewHaven2/pdf; "Canal Worker's Legacy," 1–3.

4. Levermore, *Republic of New Haven*, 280.

5. Tucker, *Emily D. West*, 28.

6. "Ethnic History of New Haven"; Tucker, *Emily D. West*, 28.

7. "George E. Hoadley Dead," *NHER*, March 11, 1893; Beecher, "Reminiscences of Three Quarters of a Century in New Haven," 686, 688; Mouheb, *Yale under God*, 151.

8. *Patten's New Haven Directory, for the Year 1840*, 6, 48; "Died," *NHCR*, April 23, 1836; "Stafford Suicide," *NHCR*, November 17, 1860; Beecher, "Reminiscences of Three Quarters of a Century in New Haven," 686; Goodrich, "Invasion of New Haven," 69–70.

9. Smyth, *Life of Henry Bradley Plant*, 42; Hill, *Modern History of New Haven*, I, 137; "The World's Most Famous Teacher," *Pittsburgh Dispatch*, May 8, 1892.

10. Smyth, *Life of Henry Bradley Plant*, 41–42, 129.

11. Van Slyke, *New England Manufacturers and Manufactories*, 101–4; *Genealogical and Biographical Record of New London County, Connecticut*, 4–6; Hill, *Modern History of New Haven*, 122–26; "Notable Wedding," *AC*, October 10, 1885.

12. Stiles, *First Tycoon*, 15–19. On the evolution and increasing sophistication of the economy and financial institutions serving it, see also, among others, Olegario, *Culture of Credit*; and Sandage, *Born Losers*.

13. Reynolds, *Henry Plant*, 30.

14. Bullock, "Perilous Journeys," 695–701; Morrison, *History of American Steam Navigation*, 341–42; "Sound Navigation," *NHCR*, October 30, 1869; *NYCA*, March 30, 1836, 6; Dickens, *American Notes*, I, 183–84; Reynolds, *Henry Plant*, 31–32.

15. English, *In Memoriam*, 12. On the Panic of 1837 generally, see Lepler, "1837: Anatomy of a Panic."

16. Balmer and Fitzmier, *Presbyterians*, 66; Borchert, "Exscinded!," 186–242.

17. Borchert, "Exscinded!," 186–242; *Necrological Reports and Annual Proceedings*, 507; Bacon, *Memorial*, 1–16.

18. Smyth, *Life of Henry Bradley Plant*, 41–42.

19. "Interesting Reminiscence," 331.

20. "On Board the Steam Boat New York," *CtC*, February 17, 1838; *NYSp*, March 1, 1838, 1; *NYCA*, April 27, 1838, 2; "Fourth of July Excursions," *NYEP*, July 2, 1838.

21. "Steamboat Burnt," *Daily Herald* (New Haven, CT), March 22, 1839; "Steamboat New-York," *NHDH*, March 23, 1839; "Steamboat New York Burnt," *Hampshire Gazette* (Northampton, MA), March 27, 1839; "New York and New Haven Mail," *NYEP*, January 14, 1840; *New York Journal of Commerce* quoted in *Weekly Messenger* (Boston), April 3, 1839, 1.

22. "Beware of Imposition," *NHDH*, June 3, 1839; *NYCA*, October 5, 1839, 2.

23. *North American* (Philadelphia), January 9, 1840, 2; "New York and New Haven Mail," *NYCA*, January 21, 1840, 2; "For Albany, via New Haven and Hartford," *NYEP*, January 22, 1840; "Harnden's Express," *Boston Commercial Gazette*, January 23, 1840.

24. "Loss of the Steamer Bunker Hill," *Liberator* (Boston), April 17, 1840; *NYEP*, March 2, 1840, 2; "To the Editors of the Commercial Advertiser," *Newark (NJ) Daily Advertiser*, March 6, 1840; "Smuggling Mails," *Auburn (NY) Journal and Advertiser*, March 11, 1840.

25. "Another Steamer Lost," *Nantucket (RI) Inquirer*, April 2, 1840; "Loss of the Steamer Bunker Hill," *Liberator* (Boston), April 17, 1840.

26. "Interesting Reminiscence," 331; "Steamboats," *Morning Herald* (New York, NY), August 6, 1840; *BJ* quoted in "Steamboat Racing," *NYSp*, April 20, 1840.

27. "Mr. Bennett's Letters," *Morning Herald* (New York, NY), September 7, 1840; "New York and New Haven Steamboats," *Troy (NY) Daily Whig*, August 27, 1840; "Traveling Cheap," *BP*, September 24, 1840; "Stealing from a Steamboat," *New York Express*, September 1, 1840; "Interesting Reminiscence," 331.

28. Stimson, *History of the Express Companies*, 90–92. See also, among others, Olegario, *Culture of Credit*; and Sandage, *Born Losers*.

29. Beecher, "Reminiscences," 688; "William B. Dinsmore Dead," *NYH*, April 21, 1888; "Death of an Aged Citizen," *NHER*, July 17, 1890.

30. "Steamboat Belle," *CtC*, July 24, 1841; *Newburyport (MA) Herald*, August 3, 1841; "Real Yankee Trick," *NYSp*, August 11, 1841; "For New Haven," *NYS*, August 18, 1841; "New Haven and Sag Harbor, Steam Boat Line," *Norwich (CT) Courier*, August 18, 1841.

31. *Newark (NJ) Daily Advertiser*, December 18, 1841, 2; "Steamboat Belle," *CtC*, December 25, 1841.

32. "District of Connecticut," *CtC*, February 26, 1842; *NYCA*, May 28, 1842, 2, June 14, 1842, 2; "Acknowledgements," *NYEP*, May 31, 1842; Hotchkiss, *Winchester Notes*, 271–72.

33. Hahn, "Adams' Express and Independent Mail," 181–88; "Death of John Hoey," *PT*, November 15, 1892; "Alvin Adams, the Expressman," *NYS*, September 4, 1877.

34. Osterweis, *Three Centuries of New Haven*, 240–42; *New Haven Palladium* quoted in "Collision," *Norwich (CT) Courier*, June 22, 1842; "From the New Haven Herald of Yesterday," *NYSp*, July 9, 1842; Bullock, "Perilous Journeys," 712.

35. Osterweis, *Three Centuries of New Haven*, 240–42; *New Haven Herald* quoted in "Steamboat Collision," *Norwich (CT) Courier*, August 10, 1842; Stiles, *First Tycoon*, 133–41.

36. Smyth, *Life of Henry Bradley Plant*, 45.

37. "Washington Webb," *NHCR*, April 5, 1873; "Casualty," *CtC*, December 17, 1842.

38. "Hon. H. B. Plant Dead," *North Georgia Citizen* (Dalton, GA), June 29, 1899; Stimson, *History of the Express Business*, 46.

39. Hahn, "Adams' Express and Independent Mail," 190–97, 201; Stimmell, "Independent Mails."

40. Smyth, *Life of Henry Bradley Plant*, 324–25, 336; Van Slyck, *New England Manufacturers and Manufactories*, 104; "Death of Mary E. Plant," *NHER*, April 12, 1900; Reynolds, *Henry Plant*, 49.

41. "Died," *ADC*, March 4, 1862.

42. Smyth, *Life of Henry Bradley Plant*, 45, 335–36; "Their Golden Jubilee," *NHER*, December 31, 1890; "Married," *NHDH*, September 27, 1843; Harrison, "James Blackstone and His Family," 23.

43. Patten, *Patten's New Haven Directory, for the Year 1840*, 48, *Patten's New Haven Directory for 1844–5*, 53, 77, *Patten's New Haven City Directory for 1845–6*, 71, 97; Patten, *Benham's New Haven City Directory for 1846–7*, 76, 102; George Henry Plant tombstone inscription, Branford Center Cemetery, Branford, CT.

CHAPTER 3

1. "Connecticut: Call for a State Convention," *Emancipator* (New York, NY), February 4, 1841; *Memorial of Elisha Lord Cleaveland*, 16, 67; "First Annual Report of the Washing-

ton Temperance Society, of New Haven, Ct."; "Washington State Temperance Society of Connecticut"; "Adjourned Town Meeting," *NHDH*, December 27, 1843; "New Haven Town Meeting"; "No. 10: An Act to Regulate and Restrain the Sale of Wines and Spiritous Liquors," *Morning News* (New London, CT), June 28, 1845.

2. Hahn, "Adams' Express and Independent Mail," 201; "Smuggling of Dutiable Goods"; "The Rum-Selling Grocery," *NYT*, April 25, 1854.

3. "No. 10: An Act to Regulate and Restrain the Sale of Wines and Spiritous Liquors"; "The Crest-Fallen"; "New Grocery and Provision Store," *NHDH*, January 15, 1846; "Dissolution," *NHDH*, April 2, 1846; "Talking It Over," *ACh*, November 8, 1918.

4. Smyth, *Life of Henry Bradley Plant*," 46; "The Court of Death," *Boston Recorder*, June 18, 1846.

5. George Henry Plant tombstone inscription, Branford Center Cemetery, Branford, CT; "Died," *NHDH*, June 17, 1846.

6. Smyth, *Life of Henry Bradley Plant*, 45, 336.

7. Van Slyck, *New England Manufacturers and Manufactories*, 102; Hall, *America's Successful Men of Affairs*, II, 742–44; "Thompson & Co.'s New Express Line," *Vermont Phoenix* (Brattleboro, VT), June 11, 1846; Stimson, *History of the Express Business*, 57, 106; "Married," *People's Advocate* (New London, CT), July 30, 1845; entry for Elijah A. Johnson, 1850 federal census manuscript, Brooklyn, NY, King's County, 420; "Explanation," *Times* (Hartford, CT), July 26, 1845; "General Sessions—Tuesday," *NYSp*, August 13, 1845; entry for William L. Crane, 1875 state census manuscript, Brooklyn, NY, King's County, 45; William Lockwood Crane tombstone inscription, Spring Grove Cemetery, Hartford, CT; Patten, *Patten's New Haven Directory for 1845–6*, 52; Poore, *Conspiracy Trial*, 472.

8. Stimson, *History of the Express Companies*, 103; "Died," *NYH*, January 19, 1878; "Travelers' Record," *NYSp*, March 23, 1848.

9. Stimson, *History of the Express Companies*, 106; Stimmell, "Independent Mails"; "From Our New York Correspondent," *Boston Daily Bee*, March 21, 1845; "Explanation," *Times* (Hartford, CT), July 26, 1845; "Death of an Aged Citizen," *NHER*, July 17, 1890; Green, *Twelve Days in the Tombs*, 57.

10. Stimson, *History of the Express Companies*, 159; "To the Subscribers and Customers of the Albany Courier, and the Public Generally," *Albany (GA) Patriot*, November 19, 1845; "John K. Stimson," *NYH*, August 19, 1886; "Express Business," *MT*, July 9, 1881.

11. O'Brien, "Only a Messenger," 295.

12. "Alvin Adams, the Expressman," *NYS*, September 4, 1877; "Adams Express Co. and the Baltimore & Ohio Railroad," 277; "Express to Charleston, S. C.," *Boston Evening Transcript*, July 7, 1846; "Adams & Co.'s Express," *Boston Evening Transcript*, July 22, 1848; "Hoey's Package and Parcel Express for Charleston, S. C., and Savannah, Geo.," *CC*, October 3, 1850; "Correspondence of the Commercial, New York, Oct. 1," *Tri-Weekly Commercial* (Wilmington, NC), October 1, 1851.

13. Starr, *California*, 78–83; "New York and New Haven Road," *NYMC*, December 23, 1848.

14. Sullivan, *Early Days in California*, 115; "Ho! For California," *NYMC*, December 23, 1848; "California Emigrants," *NYTr*, February 7, 1849.

15. "For California," *Boston Evening Transcript*, September 8, 1849; "Alvin Adams, the Expressman," *NYS*, September 4, 1877; "John Hoey," *Daily Inter Ocean* (Chicago, IL), October 19, 1891.

16. "New York and New Haven Road," *NYMC*, December 23, 1848; "Alvin Adams, the Expressman," *NYS*, September 4, 1877.

17. "Special Express Notice," *NYMC*, January 22, 1849; Hahn, "Adams' Express and Independent Mail," 205.

18. Green, *Twelve Days in the Tombs*, 47–57, 257–59; Vaill, "Letters from an Old Hair Trunk," 702–3.

19. Stimson, *History of the Express Companies*, 106; *Transactions of the American Art-Union, for the Year 1849*, 92, 97.

20. "William B. Dinsmore Dead," *NYH*, April 21, 1888; "William B. Dinsmore of New York," *Boston Weekly Globe*, April 25, 1888; *Transactions of the American Art-Union, for the Year 1849*, 92, 97; "Death of John Hoey," *PT*, November 15, 1892.

21. "Communicated," *McGrawville (NY) Express*, October 11, 1849; "Letter from New York," *Christian Watchman* (Boston, MA), March 14, 1850; "Model Artists," *Louisville (KY) Daily Courier*, October 27, 1849.

22. Smyth, *Life of Henry Bradley Plant*, 51; "Judson's Hotel in New York," *NYEP*, March 20, 1846; entry for Henry and Ellen Plant, 1850 federal census manuscript, New York, NY, New York County, 290B; "Part of a House to Let," *NYTr*, April 28, 1852.

23. Stimson, *History of the Express Companies*, 106; entry for Henry and Ellen Plant, 1850 federal census manuscript, New York, NY, New York County, 290B; Morton F. Plant passport application, January 23, 1905, US Passport Applications, 1795–1925, Microfilm Publication M1372, roll 668, NA; "'Branford House' Up for Auction," *Branford Review and East Haven News* (Branford, CT), September 21, 1939.

24. "Correspondence of the Register," *Salem (MA) Register*, January 27, 1851; "New York Correspondence," *WDNI*, May 21, 1851.

25. Hahn, "Adams' Express and Independent Mail," 214–15; "Henry B. Plant Dead," *NYT*, June 24, 1899; *NYT*, September 13, 1882, 4.

26. "Death of John Hoey," *PT*, November 15, 1892.

27. "Arrivals at the Hotels," *New London (CT) Daily Chronicle*, July 12, 1851; Elijah A. Johnson death record, Massachusetts Vital Records, 1840–1911, New England Historic Genealogical Society, Boston, MA; Hahn, "Adams' Express and Independent Mail," 215; "Passengers Arrived," *NYEP*, October 18, 1851.

28. "Death of John Hoey," *PT*, November 15, 1892; "Things in General," *Boston Courier*, February 16, 1852; "Correspondence of the Register," *Salem (MA) Register*, March 22, 1852; "Conflagration in Broadway," *NYEP*, November 20, 1854; "Express Removal!," *NYEP*, May 1, 1852.

29. "Part of a House to Let"; Smyth, *Life of Henry Plant*, 51; entry for Solomon B. Stone family, 1850 federal census manuscript, New York, NY, New York County, 20; *Supreme Court [for the City and County of New York], General Term*, 92, 96; passenger manifest, ship *Pacific*, June 10, 1854, Passenger Lists of Vessels Arriving at New York, New York, 1820–1897, Microfilm Publication 237, roll 141, NA.

30. Passenger manifest, ship *Arctic*, April 19, 1852, Passenger Lists of Vessels Arriving at New York, NY, 1820–1897, Microfilm Publication 237, roll 141; "Foreign Importations," *NYMC*, November 2, 1852; "Passengers Sailed," *Weekly Herald* (New York, NY), July 10, 1852; "Harnden's Express," *SDR*, July 17, 1852.

31. "William B. Dinsmore Dead," *NYH*, April 21, 1888; "Express Business," *NYTr*, October 10, 1857; "Administrator's Sale," *Florida Herald and Southern Democrat* (St. Augustine, FL), November 15, 1838; "President of Plant System," *Tennessean* (Nashville, TN), December 27, 1897.

32. *Genealogical and Biographical Record of New London County, Connecticut*, 10; "Correspondence of the Register," *NHCR*, December 11, 1852.

33. *Constitution* (Middletown, CT), December 29, 1852, 2; "Passengers" and "Arrivals at the Hotels," *SDMN*, January 24, 1853; Plant, "Increase Cook Plant," 42–43; Dickerman, *House of Plant*, 43, 180; "Correspondence of the Register," *Ancient City* (St. Augustine, FL), March 19, 1853; *NODP*, February 5, 1853, 1.

34. "Weather in Georgia," *NODP*, March 14, 1853; "West Point and Atlanta Railroad," *NODP*, February 22, 1853; "Harden's Express," *SDMN*, February 22, 1853.

35. "South Carolina Bridge across the Savannah River to Augusta," *SDMN*, March 8, 1853; "Stages on the Wilmington and Manchester Rail Road" and "New Arrangement," *Sumter (SC) Banner*, April 19, 1853; Thompson, *Railway Library*, 16.

36. "Mr. Plant Was Here," *AC*, February 23, 1895; "Atlanta, Ga.," *NODP*, March 25, 1853; *CC*, March 28, 1853, 2; "Correspondence of the Boston Post," *BP*, May 13, 1853.

37. "Notable People of the Day.—No. 8," 251; "Mr. Henry B. Plant," *MT*, December 2, 1886; "Adams & Co.'s Great Southern Express," *BS*, February 16, 1854.

38. "Robbery of Adams' Express Company," *NYTr*, May 7, 1853; *NYTr*, May 9, 1853, 3; "Court of General Sessions," *NYTr*, May 21, 1853; "Alleged Robbery of Adams & Co.'s Express," *NYT*, May 10, 1853.

39. Smyth, *Life of Henry Bradley Plant*, 46; Dickerman, *House of Plant*, 17–18; "Dr. E. Delafield," *FLIN*, February 9, 1856; Gallaudet, "Dr. Thomas M. Markoe," 47–50; "Dr. Simson Female Hospitals," *NYEP*, May 19, 1854.

40. Smyth, *Life of Henry Bradley Plant*, 47–50; *Genealogical and Biographical Record of New London County, Connecticut*, 9; "Passengers Sailed," *NYT*, March 20, 1854; "Passengers," *Savannah Daily Georgian*, March 26, 1854; Davis, *History of Jacksonville, Florida*, 100–101; "Ship News," *CC*, April 24, 1854; "Arrivals," *NYH*, April 27, 1854; "Passengers Arrived," *NYEP*, June 11, 1854.

CHAPTER 4

1. Stimson, *History of the Express Companies*, 85; "New President of Adams' Express Company," *CC*, April 20, 1855; Smyth, *Life of Henry Bradley Plant*, 52.

2. Grossman, "Golden Silence," 300.

3. Grossman, 301–6.

4. "The Middle States," 345; "William H. Trego," *BS*, November 20, 1899; *National Cyclopaedia of American Biography*, 524.

5. "Married," *BS*, January 2, 1854; "Lists of Arrivals at the Hotels," *WES*, March 30, 1854; *Washington Sentinel*, October 5, 1854, 3; "Arrivals at the Principal Hotels," *RD*, September 29, 1854; Smyth, *Life of Henry Bradley Plant*, 51–52.

6. Timothy Blackstone tombstone inscription, Branford Center Cemetery, Branford, CT; Smyth, *Life of Henry Bradley Plant*, 51; Fraser, *Savannah in the Old South*, 297–98; "Dreadful Storm," *Savannah Daily Georgian*, September 9, 1854; "Great Gale at Savannah," *NODP*, September 14, 1854; Jones and Dutcher, *Memorial History of Augusta, Georgia*, 261; "Yellow Fever in Augusta," *CC*, September 25, 1854; Redpath, *Roving Editor*, 117.

7. "New York City," *Rockland County Messenger* (Haverstraw, NY), November 23, 1854; "Conflagration in Broadway," *NYEP*, November 20, 1854.

8. "Passengers Sailed," *NYMC*, November 27, 1854; "Churches Opened in Savannah" and "Our City," *Atlanta Weekly Intelligencer*, November 25, 1854; "Arrivals at the Trout House," *Atlanta Weekly Intelligencer*, December 16, 1854; Smyth, *Life of Henry Bradley Plant*, 47–48; "Plant of the Plant System," 156; "Adams & Co.'s Great Express," *CC*, December 25, 1854.

9. Entry for Sterling T. Combs, 1860 federal census manuscript, Augusta, GA, Richmond County, 847; *CC*, January 12, 1855, 2; "Southern Express," *CC*, January 23, 1855; "Dissolution of Co-Partnership," *CC*, November 1, 1855.

10. *SDR*, March 17, 1855, 2; "Southern Railroad Convention," *SDMN*, March 24, 1855; "Southern Railroad Convention at Augusta," *ACh*, March 24, 1855; "Local Matters," *RD*, July 10, 1856.

11. Winther, *Express and Stagecoach Days in California*, 44–51; Cullum, *Biographical Register*, I, 499–500; "Obituary Record," *CDT*, May 22, 1888; "Adams & Co.'s Express," *Washington (PA) Reporter*, March 8, 1854; "Adams Express Company," *RD*, April 9, 1855.

12. Bostaph, *Andrew Carnegie*, 28–29.

13. Smyth, *Life of Henry Bradley Plant*, 63; "Adams Express Co.," *CC*, January 23, 1855.

14. Smyth, *Life of Henry Bradley Plant*, 63–65; "Southern Express Veteran," 151; entry for William and Jane Williams, 1880 federal census manuscript, Athens, GA, Clarke County, 53; "Captain William Williams," *AC*, March 8, 1896.

15. Smyth, *Life of Henry Bradley Plant*, 63; "Plant of the Plant System," 156; "Died," *Constitution* (Middletown, CT), July 25, 1855; "Passengers Arrived," *NYMC*, July 24, 1855;

"Kirkwood House," *WES*, August 23, 1855; "Passengers," *SDMN*, September 24, 1855; "Passengers Sailed," *NYMC*, November 15, 1855.

16. Smyth, *Life of Henry Bradley Plant*, 62.

17. "Mr. Plant Was Here," *AC*, February 23, 1895.

18. Walker, *Ninth Census*, 18–19, 97–99; Brown, *Florida's Peace River Frontier*, 63–105. On Florida's Panhandle cotton belt, see particularly Rivers, *Slavery in Florida*; and Baptist, *Creating an Old South*. On Florida's antebellum frontier atmosphere and its pervasive violence, see particularly Denham, "*A Rogue's Paradise*."

19. Johnson, "Railroads of Florida," 26–30; "Central Railroad," *Florida News* (Jacksonville, FL), March 15, 1856; *Pensacola Gazette*, March 22, 1856, quoted in "Pensacola and Montgomery Railroad," *Florida News* (Jacksonville, FL), April 5, 1856; Brown, "Florida, Atlantic and Gulf Central Railroad," 411–20. On Florida during the Civil War, see particularly Johns, *Florida during the Civil War*; and Brown, "Civil War, 1861–1865."

20. Johnson, "Railroads of Florida," 30–32.

21. "Henry B. Plant Dies Suddenly: Heart Failure Cause of Death," *AC*, June 24, 1899; "Plant of the Plant System," 156; "Departure of Steamers," *SDMN*, November 30, 1854; "Arrivals at the Hotels," *Florida Republican* (Jacksonville, FL), December 7, 1854; "Consignees," *SDR*, January 17, 1856; "Florida Railroad," *Florida News* (Jacksonville, FL), March 15, 1856; "Indian War Inevitable," *Florida Republican* (Jacksonville, FL), January 3, 1856. On the Third Seminole War, see particularly Covington, *Billy Bowlegs War*; and Knetsch, Missall, and Missall, *History of the Third Seminole War*.

22. "Express Notice," *ACh*, July 22, 1856; "A Card," *ACh*, May 9, 1851; "Globe Hotel for Sale," *ACh*, December 23, 1856; Smyth, *Life of Henry Bradley Plant*, 63; "Arrivals at the City Hotels," *NYEE*, June 4, 10, 1856; "Passengers Arrived," *NYEE*, June 5, 1856; Hart, *Memoranda of the Descendants of Amos Morris*, 24, 28–30; "Globe Hotel, Augusta, Ga.," *SDR*, June 16, 1857.

23. "Obituary Notes," *NYT*, October 23, 1890; entry for James Shuter, 1880 federal census manuscript, Baltimore, MD, Baltimore County, 337D; "Fire," *BS*, December 17, 1856; "Arrivals at the Principal Hotels," *Memphis Daily Eagle and Enquirer*, January 17, 1857; "Adams Express Company," *MDA*, April 18, 1857; Stimson, *History of the Express Companies*, 128; "Col. M. J. O'Brien Dies in New York," *Tampa Tribune*, September 13, 1909; "M. J. O'Brien of Express Co. Popular Here," *Atlanta Georgian and News*, September 13, 1909.

24. Cullum, *Biographical Register*, I, 499–500; "The Obituary Record: Gen. George W. Cass," *Chicago Daily Tribune*, May 22, 1888; "Ohio and Pennsylvania Railroad," *BS*, August 23, 1856; "Fall and Winter Arrangements, the Adams' Express Company," *BS*, January 28, 1856; "Special Notice," *BS*, April 2, 1857; "Special Notice," *Daily Dispatch* (Richmond, VA), November 5, 1856; "Express Business: Its Founders, Present Conductors, Routes and Extent," *NYTr*, October 10, 1857.

25. "Railroad Convention," *SDMN*, May 25, 1857; *SDMN*, July 11, 1857, 2; "Passengers," *SDMN*, August 17, 1857.

26. Stampp, *America in 1857*, 223–30; "Financial Panic in Georgia," *CC*, October 16, 1857.

27. "Arrivals at Principal Hotels Yesterday," *NODP*, December 26, 1857; "Adams' Express Company," *SDMN*, January 23, 1858.

28. "Home Department," *Daily True Delta* (New Orleans, LA), February 18, 1858; Smyth, *Life of Henry Bradley Plant*, 63; "Arrivals at Principal Hotels, Yesterday," *NODP*, April 22, 1858.

29. "U. S. Circuit Court," *NYMC*, December 9, 1859; "Express Companies," 283; "Late Henry Sanford," 229; Stashower, *Hour of Peril*, 110–14. Allan Pinkerton's version of the Maroney affair is contained in Pinkerton, *Expressman and the Detective*.

30. "Passengers to Arrive," *NYCA*, June 19, 1858; "Georgia Railroad Convention," *SDMN*, May 14, 1858; "$10,000 Paid by Adams' Express Company," *SDMN*, May 17, 1858; "Great

Southern Route to New York," *SDMN*, May 26, 1858; "Railroad Convention," *SDMN*, May 27, 1858; "New Mail Arrangements," *SDMN*, May 31, 1858.

31. Arnold, "Identity of Dengue," 314; Strickland, "Nativists and Strangers," 148–50; "Health of Augusta," *CC*, August 26, 1858; "Health of Augusta," *SDMN*, September 22, 1858; "Report of the Board of Health," *Atlanta Weekly Intelligencer*, October 28, 1858; "For the Mercury: Exchange Hotel, Montgomery, Ala.," *CM*, November 8, 1858.

32. Smyth, *Life of Henry Bradley Plant*, 63; Garrett, *Atlanta and Environs*, 237, 374–75, 437–38; "Park," *Atlanta Weekly Intelligencer*, December 30, 1858; "Thirty Years Ago," *AC*, April 8, 1894; "Execution of Radford J. Crockett," *NYEE*, June 24, 1858.

33. Kennedy, *Population of the United States in 1860*, 74; Garrett, *Atlanta and Environs*, 435, 438; Mary E. Bryan, "Literary Reception When Writers Held Sway," *AC*, October 7, 1906; Brown and Rivers, *Mary Edwards Bryan*, 145.

34. *MDA*, April 17, 1858, 2; "Death of a Prominent and Esteemed Citizen," *Houston Post*, July 20, 1900; "John Hoey Lies Close to Death," *NYH*, November 13, 1892; *SDMN*, October 7, 1858, 2; "Death of Mr. Spooner," *SDR*, August 12, 1861; "Death of Mr. C. S. Plank," *Charleston (SC) News and Courier*, November 15, 1886; *ACh*, May 11, 1899, 4; "Hugh Dempsey Cross River," *AC*, July 17, 1904; "One of the Latest," *AC*, October 22, 1873; Duncan, *Entrepreneur for Equality*, 9; entry for C. H. Phelps, 1860 federal census manuscript, Augusta, GA, Richmond County, 36.

35. Smyth, *Life of Henry Bradley Plant*, 63; "For the East," *Daily Alta California* (San Francisco, CA), July 19, 1858; "Personal," *Daily Alta California* (San Francisco, CA), January 30, 1859; "Important from Mexico," *NYH*, August 12, 1858; "Married," *NYEE*, January 5, 1860; "Plant of the Plant System," 156.

36. Pinkerton, *Expressman and the Detective*, 15, 236; Stashower, *Hour of Peril*, 52; "$40,000 Stolen from Adams Express," *MWT*, January 28, 1859; "Robbery," *Daily Confederation* (Montgomery, AL), February 1, 1859.

37. "Express Case Robbery," *Daily Confederation* (Montgomery, AL), February 5, 1859; "Governor Watts Dead," *AC*, September 17, 1892; "Thomas H. Watts Dead," *Dallas Morning News*, September 17, 1892; "Chit-Chat," *St. Louis (MO) Republic*, August 10, 1889; Walther, *William Lowndes Yancey*, 149.

38. "Adams Express Embezzlement Case," *NODP*, February 12, 1859; *Montgomery Advertiser* quoted in "The Express Robbery Case," *Atlanta Weekly Intelligencer*, February 17, 1859; Pinkerton, *Expressman and the Detective*, 48–82.

CHAPTER 5

1. Pinkerton, *Expressman and the Detective*, 17–133; *Daily Nashville (TN) Patriot*, May 12, 1859; "Arrest of Nate Maroney," *NUA*, May 12, 1859; "Pursuit of the Supposed Robber of Adams' Express Co.," *Press & Tribune* (Chicago, IL), May 13, 1859; "Arrest of an Express Employee," *Daily Confederation* (Montgomery, AL), May 20, 1859.

2. "Arrest of an Express Employee"; *Montgomery Mail* quoted in "Adams Express—An Institution," *ACh*, October 25, 1859.

3. "Passengers," *SDMN*, April 23, 1859; "Arrivals, Yesterday, at Principal Hotels," *NODP*, May 11, 1859; "Arrivals," *MDA*, May 21, 1859; "Adams Express," *MDA*, June 1, 1859; "Hotel Arrivals," *Daily Gazette* (Niagara Falls, NY), June 2, 1859; "Niagara Discoveries: Monteagle Hotel, Niagara Falls' Forgotten Resort," *Lockport (NY) Union-Sun & Journal*, February 13, 2016; "Japanese Coins," *ACh*, June 9, 1859; Pinkerton, *Expressman and the Detective*, 131–270; "Arrivals at Principal Hotels," *WES*, August 10, 1859.

4. *Southern Advertiser* (Troy, AL) quoted in *Daily Confederation* (Montgomery, AL), September 28, 1859; *ADC* quoted in "Southern Express Company," *Daily Confederation* (Montgomery, AL), September 16, 1859; *CM*, September 5, 1859; "Passengers," *CC*, September 19, 1859.

5. "Harper's Ferry Insurrection" and "Insurrection at Harper's Ferry—Authentic Details," *ACh*, October 22, 1859. On John Brown and the Harper's Ferry raid, see also Villard, *John Brown*; Nelson, *Old Man*; Scott and Scott, *John Brown of Harper's Ferry*; Reynolds, *John Brown, Abolitionist*; and Horwitz, *Midnight Rising*.

6. "St. Nicholas Hotel," *NYEE*, November 8, 1859; "Academy of Music—Adelina Patti," *NYT*, November 24, 1859; "Academy of Music: Debut of Miss Patti," *NYTr*, November 25, 1859; "Adelina Patti, the Youthful Prima Donna," *FLIN*, January 7, 1860; "W. B. Dinsmore's Death," *NYT*, April 21, 1888.

7. "Hotel Arrivals," *MT*, February 9, 1860; *Acts of the Seventh Biennial Session of the General Assembly of Alabama*, 480–81.

8. "List of Letters," *SDMN*, February 16, 1860; "South" and "Arrivals at the Magnolia House," *St. Augustine (FL) Examiner*, March 17, 1860.

9. "Passengers," *SDMN*, March 14, 1860; "Arrivals at Principal Hotels, Yesterday," *NODP*, March 31, 1860; *NODP*, April 4, 1860, 1.

10. "Our Late Trip to Charleston," *ACh*, May 10, 1860; McPherson, *Battle Cry of Freedom*, 214; Craven, *Coming of the Civil War*, 412–16.

11. Entry for H. B. Plant family, 1860 federal census manuscript, Augusta, GA, Richmond County, 761; "Returning from Charleston," *NODP*, May 20, 1860; "H. B. Plant, Esq.," *NODP*, July 3, 1860.

12. Entry for H. B. Plant family, 1860 federal census manuscript, Branford, CT, New Haven County, 926; McPherson, *Battle Cry of Freedom*, 213–35; "Deaths," *NHCR*, August 11, 1860.

13. "St. Nicholas Hotel" and "Fifth Avenue Hotel," *NYEE*, August 9, 1860; "Letters from a Tourist.—No. 6," *CM*, September 29, 1860; Victor, *Comprehensive History of the Southern Rebellion*, 220–21; "Washington Artillery Drill Room, Augusta, Ga., Nov. 21, 1860," *ADC*, November 25, 1860.

14. McPherson, *Battle Cry of Freedom*, 234–73; *Commemorative Biographical Record of New Haven County*, 436; "Lavaca," *NODP*, February 26, 1860; entry for Philemon Hoadley family, 1860 federal census manuscript, New Haven, CT, New Haven County, 382; *Civilian and Gazette* (Galveston, TX), November 20, 1860, 1; *Texas Almanac for 1861*, 268; "Texas Intelligence," *MDA*, December 11, 1860; "Texas," *NODP*, December 26, 1860.

15. McPherson, *Battle Cry of Freedom*, 234–35; Rable, *Confederate Republic*, 49–67.

16. "Plant of the Plant System," 156; C. G. Memminger to F. W. Pickens, April 5, 1861, accessed June 4, 2015, www.stampauctionnetwork.com/f/f1347.cfm; *Acts of the Called Session of the General Assembly of Alabama*, 123; *Journal of the Congress of the Confederate States of America*, 61–62; Keehn, *Knights of the Golden Circle*, 140–41; Garrison, "Administrative Problems," 243–44; McCaleb, "Organization of the Post-Office Department," 66–69.

17. Smyth, *Life of Henry Bradley Plant*, 56–57; Memminger to Pickens, April 5, 1861; "Southern Congress," *Liberator* (Boston, MA), March 22, 1861.

18. Franklin Q. Brown to A. J. Hanna, January 24, 1938, notebook volume: Henry Plant, Part One, Henry Bradley Plant Collection, Henry B. Plant Museum Archives; Smyth, *Life of Henry Bradley Plant*, 138–39.

19. Reynolds, *Henry Plant*, 81–82.

20. "Special Correspondence, Montgomery, Ala., April 4, 1861," *ADC*, April 6, 1861; Memminger to Pickens, April 5, 1861; "Southern Express Company," *ACh*, July 11, 1861; "The Sebrings: Information about Edward Sebring," accessed June 16, 2016, http://www.genealogy.com/ftm/s/e/b/Richard-A-Sebring-MO/WEBSITE-0001/UHP-1082.html.

21. Reynolds, *Henry Plant*, 83; "Argument of William D. Shipman," 14, in *N. Y. Supreme Court, William B. Dinsmore et al., Trustees &c., against Alvin Adams et al.*; "Henry Sanford," *New York Times Illustrated Weekly Magazine*, February 27, 1898; "Southern Express Company," *ACh*, May 17, 1861; Thomas, *Digest of the Railroad Laws of Georgia*, 428–29.

22. "Southern Express Company," *ACh*, July 11, 1861; Memminger to Pickens, April 5, 1861; McPherson, *Battle Cry of Freedom*, 273; Stimson, *History of the Express Companies*,

160; W. B. Dinsmore to I. C. Babcock, telegram, April 12, 1861, accessed October 25, 2015, http://catalogues.lesliehindman.com/files/SALE_253.pdf; "Descendant of Eli Yale," *BDE*, February 14, 1897.

23. McPherson, *Battle Cry of Freedom*, 276–307; Rable, *Confederate Republic*, 77–79; "Arrival of President Davis," *ADC*, May 27, 1861; "Journey of the President," *CM*, June 1, 1861; "Argument of William D. Shipman," 14, in *N. Y. Supreme Court, William B. Dinsmore et al., Trustees &c., against Alvin Adams et al.*; "Singular Suicide at the Burnet House," *Cincinnati Daily Enquirer*, August 11, 1861.

24. Johnson, "Southern Express Company," 225–26; Interstate Commerce Commission, *First Annual Report on the Statistics of Express Companies*, 44; "Southern Express Company," *ACh*, July 11, 1861.

25. "Decision of Postmaster General," *Louisville (KY) Daily Courier*, August 6, 1861; *ACh*, July 19, 1861, 3; "Southern Express Company," *ACh*, August 3, 1861; Garrison, "Administrative Problems," 243.

26. McPherson, *Battle Cry of Freedom*, 331–61; "The Fight at Manassas—Brilliant Victory—The Enemy Completely Routed," *ACh*, July 23, 1861.

27. "Adams Express Company," *ACh*, August 4, 1861; "Southern Express Company," *CC*, August 6, 1861; "Express Company," *Southern Confederacy* (Atlanta, GA), August 9, 1861.

28. Johnson, "Southern Express Company," 227–29; "Express Company Again," *Southern Confederacy* (Atlanta, GA), August 10, 1861; "Express Company," *Southern Confederacy* (Atlanta, GA), August 11, 1861; "Office Southern Express Company, Augusta, Ga., August 10, 1861," *ACh*, August 16, 1861; "Southern Express," *ACh*, August 23, 1861; "Southern Express Company," *MT*, August 20, 1861.

29. Johnson, "Southern Express Company," 228–30; "Southern Express Company," *Georgia Weekly Telegraph* (Macon, GA), August 10, 1861; "Southern Express Company," *CM*, August 20, 1861; "Southern Express," *ADC*, August 22, 1861; "Southern Express Company," *SDMN*, September 21, 1861; "Express Case," *MT*, September 21, 1861; "Southern Express—Suit for Libel," *Daily True Delta* (New Orleans, LA), September 22, 1861; "Southern Express Company," *SDR*, October 14, 1861; "First District Court," *New Orleans Daily Crescent*, December 19, 1861; "City," *NODP*, January 14, 1862; "Great Breach of Trust Case," *New Orleans Daily Crescent*, January 16, 1862; "Card," *NODP*, February 23, 1862.

30. "Singular Suicide at the Burnet House" and "Connecticut Items," *New London (CT) Weekly Chronicle*, September 26, 1861; "Deaths," *NHCR*, October 5, 1861; "Died," *ADC*, March 4, 1862; Society of Colonial Wars in the State of New Hampshire, *List of Officers, Committees and Members*, 55–56; Herndon, *Men of Progress*, 458; "Further Particulars of the Great Fire in Charleston," *SDMN*, December 14, 1861; "Contributions to Aid Sufferers by Fire in Charleston," *ACh*, December 15, 1861.

31. "Died," *ADC*, March 4, 1862; "Southern Express Veteran," 151; Smyth, *Life of Henry Bradley Plant*, 58–59, 64; Adams Express Company cover, franked "H. B. Plant, Jany 30, 1862" at Augusta, GA, accessed November 28, 2015, http://www.rumseyauctions.com/auctions/chapter/34/116.

32. "H. B. Plant," 1863 Richmond County (GA) tax digest, no pagination (available at Georgia State Archives); Smyth, *Life of Henry Bradley Plant*, 58–59.

33. McPherson, *Battle Cry of Freedom*, 396–405.

34. "Died," *ADC*, March 4, 1862; "Funeral Notices," *ADC*, March 4, 1862; "Obituary," *ACh*, March 3, 1862; Baker, *Woodrow Wilson*, 28–55.

35. Smyth, *Life of Henry Bradley Plant*, 64; "Deaths," *NHCR*, August 2, 1862; "Argument of William D. Shipman," 14, in *N. Y. Supreme Court, William B. Dinsmore et al., Trustees &c., against Alvin Adams et al.*; Swaine, *Cravath Firm*, I, 1–2; "Late Henry Sanford," 229; McPherson, *Battle Cry of Freedom*, 361.

36. "Censorship of the Press," *NYW*, March 25, 1862; "Edwards Sewall Sanford," *Brooklyn (NY) Union-Argus*, September 11, 1882; Bates, *Lincoln in the Telegraph Office*, 108–9.

37. "President's Cabinet Organized," *ADC*, March 19, 1862.

38. McPherson, *Battle Cry of Freedom*, 406–76; Johnson, "Southern Express Company," 230–31; *War of the Rebellion*, series IV, vol. I, 1174; *Richmond (VA) Examiner*, December 23, 1862, 2.

39. Henry B. Plant Dead," *NYT*, June 24, 1899; Hillery B. Fraser to Henry B. Plant, August 18, 1862, Richmond County (GA) Deed Records, Book RR, 266 (available on microfilm at Georgia State Archives); "H. B. Plant," Confederate Papers Relating to Citizens or Business Firms, 1861–65, M346, roll 0805, NA; "H. B. Plant," Union Provost Marshals' File of Paper Relating to Individual Civilians, M345, roll 0219, NA; entry for H. B. Plant, 1860 federal census manuscript, Branford, CT, New Haven County, 926; "H. B. Plant," 1863 Richmond County (GA) tax digest, no pagination. A helpful and interesting discussion of cotton speculation and smuggling is found in Johnson, *Red River Campaign*.

40. Henry B. Plant Dead," *NYT*, June 24, 1899; "Argument of William D. Shipman," 14, in *N. Y. Supreme Court, William B. Dinsmore et al., Trustees &c., against Alvin Adams et al.*

41. "Express Notice," *SDR*, September 25, October 24, 1862; "Deaths," *NHCR*, August 2, 1862; Rable, *Confederate Republic*, 171; *Richmond (VA) Examiner*, December 23, 1862, 2; "Express Company and the War," *CM*, December 29, 1862.

42. *Report of the Postmaster General in Answer to the Resolution of the House of Representatives*, 40–41; "Contract made this twenty ninth day of December 1862, between the Southern Express Company of the first part and the Confederate States of American of the second part," and H. B. Plant correspondence, January 6, 1863, Confederate Papers Relating to Citizens or Business Firms, M345, roll 0965, NA; *ADC*, January 30, 1863, 1.

43. Smyth, *Life of Henry Bradley Plant*, 58–59; "Death of Philemon Hoadley," *New Haven (CT) Palladium*, January 29, 1863; "Argument of William D. Shipman," 15, in *N. Y. Supreme Court, William B. Dinsmore et al., Trustees &c., against Alvin Adams et al.*; Herndon, *Men of Progress*, 458; *Catalogue of the Officers, Teachers and Students in the Collegiate and Commercial Institute, New Haven, 1876*, 28; *Catalogue of the Officers and Students in the Collegiate and Commercial Institute, New Haven, Conn., for the Term Ending December 23d, 1863*, 11; Philemon Hoadley probate records, No. 19,659, Wills and Probate Records, 1609–1999, Connecticut State Library, Hartford.

44. Johnson, "Southern Express Company," 230–34; Garrison, "Administrative Problems," 246; Jones, *Rebel War Clerk's Diary*, I, 257–58; Bradlee, "Blockade Running during the Civil War," 43; Monaghan, *Diplomat in Carpet Slippers*, 316–17; McPherson, *Battle Cry of Freedom*, 626–65; Rable, *Confederate Republic*, 220–21.

45. "Col. Shuter Resigns," *News* (Frederick, MD), June 2, 1888; "James Shuter," Confederate Papers Relating to Citizens or Business Firms, 1861–65, roll 0932, NA; Stimson, *History of the Express Companies*, 1881; Marden, *Talks with Great Workers*, 77–80; "To Resign," *CE*, December 6, 1890; "Patriotic Offer," *ADC*, August 8, 1863.

46. Smyth, *Life of Henry Bradley Plant*, 59; Bradlee, "Blockade Running during the Civil War," 42; Jones, *Rebel War Clerk's Diary*, II, 4.

47. Smyth, *Life of Henry Bradley Plant*, 59; Johnson, "Southern Express Company," 232; "Nassau to Wilmington—A Trip between These Two Secession Cities—Life and High Prices at Wilmington—How the City Is Defended—Testimony by an Eye Witness," *Wilmington (NC) Journal*, November 19, 1863; "Arrived," *RG*, September 8, 1863; Martin, "Henry Bradley Plant," 261–76.

CHAPTER 6

1. Jones, *Rebel War Clerk's Diary*, II, 60–61.

2. "Arrivals," *RG*, September 8, 1863; "Passengers Sailed," *RG*, October 6, 1863; "Bermuda and the Blockade," *Liverpool (NS) Transcript*, November 19, 1863; "Perfidy among the Blockade Runners," *RD*, November 19, 1863.

3. "Passengers Sailed," *RG*, October 6, 1863; *Halifax (NS) Morning Sun*, October 9,

1863; Bell, *Rebels on the Great Lakes*, 25–37; Crist and Williams, *Papers of Jefferson Davis*, 86; "Death of Charles H. Haile," *MDA*, October 21, 1868.

4. Smyth, *Life of Henry Bradley Plant*, 59; "Mr. J. E. English," ship *Persia*, October 7, 1863, Passenger Lists of Vessels Arriving at New York, NY, 1820–1897, Microfilm Publication M237, roll 234, NA; "Returned," *New Haven (CT) Palladium*, October 10, 1863; "Congressman English," *Indiana Herald* (Huntington, IN), May 6, 1863; "Standing and Joint Committees of the U. S. Senate and House of Representatives," *National Republican* (Washington, DC), December 14, 1863.

5. "From Washington," *Pittsburgh Daily Commercial*, November 4, 1863; *Providence (RI) Evening Press*, November 3, 1863, 2; "Secretary Seward at Auburn," *NYT*, November 5, 1863; "Secretary Seward's Auburn Speech—Issues Involved in War and Peace," *NYH*, November 6, 1863; "Personal Intelligence," *NYH*, November 8, 1863; Wilson, *Trow's New York City Directory* [1865], 5–6.

6. Smyth, *Life of Henry Bradley Plant*, 59; *New Haven (CT) Palladium*, November 20, 1863, 3; *Catalogue of the Officers and Students of the Collegiate and Commercial Institute, New Haven, Conn., for the Two Terms Ending July 27th, 1864*, 11, 33; *Catalogue of the Officers and Students of the Collegiate and Commercial Institute, New Haven, Conn., for the Term Ending December 23d, 1863*, title page, 34; "Sailing of the 'Edinburgh,'" *PI*, January 2, 1864; "Passengers Sailed," *NYT*, January 2, 1864.

7. "Latest, Liverpool, Jan. 15," *NYTr*, January 29, 1864; Smyth, *Life of Henry Bradley Plant*, 59–60; *War of the Rebellion*, series IV, vol. III, 210; "Last Roll," 438–39.

8. Chadych and LeBorgne, *Paris*, 107–16; "Our Paris Correspondence," *WDNI*, June 3, 1864; "History in Stones," *Irish Times* (Dublin, Ireland), March 25, 1864; "Letter from Gamma," *NODP*, June 28, 1863.

9. "Our Paris Correspondence," *WDNI*, April 26, May 27, 1864.

10. Thomas, "Operator and the Emperors," 4–5; Reynolds, *Genealogical and Family History*, III, 1258; "Personal," *Daily National Republican* (Washington, DC), February 3, 1864.

11. Klein, *Reign of Patti*, 111; "Patti, Della-Sedie, and Mario," *Irish Times* (Dublin, Ireland), February 3, 1864.

12. Smyth, *Life of Henry Bradley Plant*, 60; "Erzherzog Karl," *Fremden-Blatt* (Vienna, Austria), March 18, 1864; "Music and Musicians," *SR*, March 9, 1864; "Theatrical," *Plain Dealer* (Cleveland, OH), March 9, 1864.

13. Smyth, *Life of Henry Bradley Plant*, 60–61; "Erzherzog Karl," *Fremden-Blatt* (Vienna, Austria), March 18, 1864; "The Stage," *NODP*, March 6, 1864.

14. "Our Paris Correspondence," *WDNI*, May 20, 1864; "Town Gossip," *FLIN*, June 3, 1865; "Le Theatre a Paris," *Courrier des États-Unis* (New York, NY), April 16, 1864; Hollengreen et al., *Meet Me at the Fair*, 170; "European News," *NYT*, May 15, 1864.

15. "Our Paris Correspondence," *WDNI*, June 3, 1864; "Daniel Hand Wilcox," *NYTr*, October 15, 1890; "D. H. Wilcox Dead," *ACh*, October 15, 1890; *NYEP*, July 2, 1864, 2; "Adelina Patti at the Crystal Palace" and "Royal Italian Opera," *Musical World* (London, England), July 23, 1864.

16. "Tragedy of the Ill-fated Carolina," *Washington Post*, July 21, 1918; "Last Roll," 439.

17. "Argument of William D. Shipman," 18, in *N. Y. Supreme Court, William B. Dinsmore et al., Trustees &c., against Alvin Adams et al.*; "Personal," *NYT*, July 31, October 2, 1864; "Passengers Arrived," *NYTr*, September 7, 1864; Passenger manifest, ship *Scotia*, September 7, 1864, Passenger Lists of Vessels Arriving at New York, NY, M237, roll 245, NA; *BS*, September 16, 1864, 4; "Passengers," *BDA*, September 17, 1864; "Savannah Hemmed by Sherman; General Dix's Order Modified; Travellers to Have Passports," *Sun and Advertiser* (Halifax, NS), December 19, 1864; "Passport Regulations; Important Instructions from Washington," *NYT*, January 11, 1865.

18. "Passengers," *Sun and Advertiser* (Halifax, NS), October 14, 1864; "Ship News," *Boston Traveler*, October 15, 1864; McPherson, *Battle Cry of Freedom*, 803–11; *Catalogue of*

the Officers and Students in the Collegiate and Commercial Institute, New Haven, Conn., for the Two Terms Ending Dec. 21st, 1864, title page, 11.

19. "Distinguished Visitors," *CC*, March 21, 1865; "Arrival of Distinguished Visitors," *Savannah Daily Herald*, March 21, 1865; "Departure of the Congressional Party," *Savannah Daily Herald*, March 22, 1865; "Arrived," *NYTr*, March 27, 1865; *Catalogue of the Officers and Students in the Collegiate and Commercial Institute, New Haven, Conn., for the Two Terms Ending July 27th, 1864*, 33; Hall, *America's Successful Men of Affairs*, II, 742; "Died," *Republican Farmer* (Bridgeport, CT), June 2, 1865; "Treasury Department, Office of Comptroller of the Currency, Washington, March 23, 1865," *Republican Farmer* (Bridgeport, CT), April 28, 1865.

20. McPherson, *Battle Cry of Freedom*, 848–51; Foner, *Reconstruction*, 74–75, 176–77; Duncan, *Entrepreneur for Equality*, 16–17; "Rufus Brown Bullock," *ACh*, April 30, 1907; "Talking It Over," *ACh*, November 8, 1918; "Varied Career Closed by the Death of Bullock," *AC*, April 28, 1907; Jones and Dutcher, *Memorial History of Augusta*, 359; "National Bank," *ADC*, December 19, 1865; "National Bank of Augusta," *ADC*, December 20, 1865. For an insightful review of southern financial conditions at the Civil War's end and the significance of national banking charters, see Carter, *When the War Was Over*, 99–103.

21. Connelly, *Autumn of Glory*, 515–36. On Jefferson Davis's last days as Confederate president, see, among many fine works, Hanna, *Flight into Oblivion*.

22. "Express Company and the Mails," *Macon (GA) Daily Telegraph*, May 13, 1865; "Southern Express Company," *Macon (GA) Daily Telegraph*, May 18, 1865; "Southern Express Company," *Savannah Daily Herald*, May 13, 1865.

23. Dickerman, *House of Plant*, 20; "Interesting Items," *ACh*, December 6, 1865.

24. "H. B. Plant," Union Provost Marshals' File of Paper Relating to Individual Civilians, M345, roll 0219, NA; "At Home," *MT*, May 31, 1865; "Launching of the Steamer Eclipse," *MT*, October 20, 1865; "Ship Building in Augusta," *ADC*, June 27, 1865; "Launching of the Steamer Eclipse," *ADC*, October 17, 1865; "River News," *ADC*, November 18, 19, 1865; Hammond, *Reports of Cases in Law and Equity, Argued and Determined in the Supreme Court of Georgia, at Atlanta, Parts of December Term, 1869, and June Term, 1870*, 85–86.

25. "Directory," *ADC*, May 24, 1865; "Communicated," *ADC*, August 15, 1867; "New Theatre," *ADC*, May 7, 1869; "Old City Hotel," *ACh*, July 14, 1872.

26. Plant, "Great Railway Systems," 681. For discussions of the condition of southern railroads at the Civil War's conclusion and US government efforts to rehabilitate and maintain them, see Wilson, *Business of Civil War*, and Angevine, *Railroads and the State*.

27. "Interesting Items," *ACh*, December 6, 1865; Otto, *United States Reports, Supreme Court*, 191–92.

28. "Adams' Express Company," *Brownlow's Knoxville (TN) Whig*, April 26, 1865; "Latest from Richmond," *WES*, May 6, 1865; "Richmond, Petersburg, Lynchburg," *NYTr*, May 12, 1865; "Express Companies," *NYTr*, June 2, 1865; "Texas," *NYTr*, August 3, 1865.

29. Andrews, *Genealogical History of Deacon Stephen Hart*, 329; "Instruction," *NYTr*, August 12, 1854; "Mr. Edward L. Hart," *Hartford (CT) Daily Courant*, August 9, 1869; "Obituary," *CtC*, June 1, 1876; Hammond, *Reports of Cases in Law and Equity, Argued and Determined in the Supreme Court of Georgia, at Milledgeville, Parts of December Term, 1868, and June Term, 1869*, 522–23.

30. "Argument of William D. Shipman," 18, in *N. Y. Supreme Court, William B. Dinsmore et al., Trustees &c., Against Alvin Adams et al.*; Woolf, *Western Union*, 62–63, 82; Andrews, "Southern Telegraph Company," 320, 343; Harlow, *Old Waybills*, 288.

31. "Message of the President of the United States," 565–69; Swaine, *Cravath Firm*, 213–14; Schoonover, *Mexican Lobby*, 99–112.

32. "Express Companies," *CDP*, November 16, 1865; "Southern Express Company," *Flake's Bulletin* (Galveston, TX), December 29, 1865; *Florida Union* (Jacksonville, FL), December 30, 1865, 3; "Adams Express Company," *Tri-Weekly Sentinel* (Tallahassee, FL),

January 2, 1866; "Southern Express Company," *CC*, January 17, 1866; "Southern Express Company, No. 147 Meeting-Street," *CC*, March 8, 1866; "Texas," *LCJ*, March 1, 1866; "The Southern Express Company," *SDNH*, March 3, 1866; "Express for Mexico," *NODP*, April 19, 1866.

33. *Annual Report of the Public Utilities Commission of the District of Columbia, 1913*, 149, 151; Interstate Commerce Commission, *Report No. 4302, Memphis Freight Bureau et al. v. Adams Express Company et al.*, 437.

34. "Southern Express Company," *SDNH*, March 8, 1866; *Testimony Taken by Committee Appointed to Investigate the Official Conduct of Rufus B. Bullock, Late Governor*, 143; Pughe, *Pughe's Directory for the City of Augusta and Its Vicinity*, 12; "Personal," *MDA*, April 29, 1866; "Southern Express Company, Augusta, Ga., July 28," *Commemorative Biographical Record of Fairfield County, Connecticut*, 518–19; Smyth, *Life of Henry Bradley Plant*, 165.

35. "St. Nicholas Hotel," *NYCA*, August 17, 1866; "St. Nicholas Hotel," *NYEE*, September 8, October 30, 1866; "Argument of William D. Shipman," 15, in *N. Y. Supreme Court, William B. Dinsmore et al., Trustees &c., Against Alvin Adams et al.*; Foner, *Reconstruction*, 261–77.

36. "National Hotel," *ADI*, February 28, March 16, 1867; "Meeting of Railroad Officials," *ADI*, March 1, 1867; "Meetings Yesterday," *ADI*, March 5, 1867; "Memphis Correspondence," *ADI*, March 20, 1867; "Railroad Communications in Tennessee," *ADI*, March 22, 1867; "Great Flood," *ADI*, March 28, 1867; "Flood in Middle Tennessee," *MWT*, March 22, 1867.

37. *CDE*, April 2, 1867, 2; "General John Pope," *ADI*, April 2, 1867; "Hotel Arrivals," *ADI*, April 9, 1867; "Montgomery, Ala.," *Memphis Daily Avalanche*, April 3, 1867; "Arrival of General Pope at Atlanta, Ga.," *NYEP*, April 5, 1867; "Hotel Arrivals," *NT*, April 5, 1867; "General Orders from General Pope on Assuming Command of the Third Military District," *MWT*, April 5, 1867.

38. Andrew Clements, "Offenbach: La Grande-Duchesse de Gérolstein, Lott/Piau/Beuron/Le Roux/Les Musiciens du Louvre-Grenoble/Minowski," *Guardian* (London, England), October 13, 2005; "Fine Arts," *NYEP*, January 11, 1867; "A Masterpiece of Art," *NYEP*, December 3, 1864; "Fine Arts," *NYH*, March 31, 1865; "Town Gossip," *FLIN*, April 15, June 3, 1865; Lauw, *Fourteen Years with Adelina Patti*, 25; "Nouvelles Diverses," *Le Menestrel* (Paris, France), April 21, 1867; "News in Brief," *BS*, April 23, 1867; Offenbach, *Offenbach's Songs from the Great Operettas*, xiii, xvi; Bonami, *La Diva d'Offenbach*, 112–14; "To Meet with the Engineers," *SMN*, January 31, 1896; "Under the Post's Eyes," *CEP*, February 5, 1896; "All Sorts," *BP*, May 10, 1876; "French Theatre," *BDE*, September 14, 1867; "Amusements," *NYCA*, September 25, 1867.

39. "Hotel Arrivals," *ADI*, May 31, 1867; "State News," *MDA*, June 4, 1867; Currie-McDaniel, *Carpetbagger of Conscience*, 80; Duncan, *Entrepreneur for Equality*, 23–26; "Newspaper Changes in Augusta," *SDNH*, July 29, 1867; "Arrivals at the Hotels," *SDNH*, May 1, 1867; "Southern Express Company," *SDNH*, August 1, 1867; "A Georgia Black Republican Newspaper Arrangement," *MWT*, August 2, 1867; Brown, *Lamb's Biographical Dictionary*, I, 447; "Talking It Over," *ACh*, April 30, 1917; Herndon, *Men of Progress*, 458; Eastman National Business College, *Start in Business Life*, no pagination.

40. Avery, *History of the State of Georgia*, 373; Duncan, *Entrepreneur for Equality*, 27–36; "Hotel Arrivals," *CDN*, November 4, 27, 1867; "Locals in Brief," *Public Ledger* (Memphis, TN), November 16, 1867; "Railroad Election," *NYTr*, November 7, 1867; *Reports of Cases Argued and Determined in the Supreme Court of Tennessee*, 537–38.

41. "Southern Express Company, Memphis, Tenn., December 5, 1870," 241–42; Stimson, *History of the Express Companies*, 164; "Col. M. J. O'Brien Dies in New York," *TTr*, September 13, 1909.

42. Duncan, *Entrepreneur for Equality*, 37–49; "Tough Question," *ADC*, April 8, 1868; "Bullock as a Spy," *Rome (GA) Courier*, April 14, 1868.

43. "Locals in Brief," *Public Ledger* (Memphis, TN), March 3, 1868; "Hotel Arrivals," *CDN*, March 20, 1868; "News in Brief," *Memphis Daily Avalanche*, April 29, 1868; *Reports of Cases Argued and Determined in the Supreme Court of Tennessee*, 539.

44. "Patti in Paris," *NYCA*, May 18, 1868; "Letters from Paris," *American Traveller* (Boston, MA), May 23, 1868; "The Drama Abroad," *NYT*, May 24, 1868; "Musical Matters," *NYT*, May 31, 1868; *BDA*, August 13, 1868, 2; "Personal Intelligence," *BDA*, August 14, 1868; Edwards, "Prima Donna," 158.

CHAPTER 7

1. "Good Sale," *NYEP*, June 27, 1868; "Columbia Property Sale," *NYEP*, January 16, 1904; Homberger, *Mrs. Astor's New York*, 258.

2. Herndon, *Men of Progress*, 458; "Hotel Arrivals," *SDNH*, April 20, 1868.

3. "Personal," *ADC*, November 28, 1868; "Distinguished Arrivals" and "Arrivals at the Principal Hotels Sunday and Monday," *New Orleans Crescent*, February 9, 1869; "Fortieth Congress," *NYH*, February 26, 1869; "House of Representatives," *Evening Telegraph* (Philadelphia, PA), March 22, 1869.

4. Reynolds, *Henry Plant*, 109–10; Harlow, *Old Waybills*, 301–3; "Points for Plaintiffs," 6–7, in *N. Y. Supreme Court, William B. Dinsmore et al., Trustees &c., against Alvin Adams et al.*; "Financial and Commercial," *NYH*, July 10, 1869; "Cases—Other Investigations," *CDG*, July 10, 1869.

5. Reynolds, *Henry Plant*, 110; Harlow, *Old Waybills*, 301–2; "The Adams Express Case," *NYT*, June 25, 1872.

6. Musical and Theatrical Notes," *NYH*, October 30, 1869; "The Opera," *NYH*, November 26, 1869.

7. Nelson, *Iron Confederacies*, 90–94; Nathans, *Losing the Peace*, 206–7. See also Duncan, *Entrepreneur for Equality*.

8. "Prominent Departures Yesterday," *NYH*, January 1, 1870; "Personal," *NYTr*, January 5, 1870; "New York, January 15," *NYW*, January 17, 1870; "Railroads and Railroad Kings—The New Power in the World," *NYH*, February 28, 1870.

9. Brown, "Southern Railway Security Company," 158, 160.

10. Churella, *Pennsylvania Railroad*, 439.

11. Churella, 440–41.

12. "Winter Arrangement," *CDE*, March 4, 1870; Duncan, *Entrepreneur for Equality*, 112; "Georgia," *NYS*, August 10, 1868; "Beverly Welford Wrenn," 26; "Western & Atlantic Railroad," *Weekly Atlanta Intelligencer*, April 28, 1869.

13. "Personal," *NYTr*, January 27, 1870; "Prominent Departures," *NYH*, January 30, 1870; "Personal Intelligence," *NYH*, February 2, March 16, 1870; "Hotel Arrivals," *CDP*, February 12, 1870; "Personal," *Daily National Republican* (Washington, DC), February 7, 1870. "Western & Atlantic R. R.," *Weekly New Era* (Atlanta, Ga.), February 2, 1870; "Opera House," *NODP*, March 1, 1870; "Washington," *NYTr*, March 16, 1870; "Congress," *Evening Telegraph* (Philadelphia, Pa.), March 23, 1870; *Alexandria Gazette* (Alexandria, Va.), May 13, 1870, 2; "Domestic News," *CDP*, May 18, 1870.

14. "Personal," *CDN*, April 9, 1870; "Washington," *NYTr*, April 20, 1870; "Personal Intelligence," *NYH*, April 22, 1870; "Domestic News," *CDP*, May 18, 1870; "Prominent Arrivals," *NYTr*, April 4, 14, 1870.

15. "Argument of William D. Shipman," 21, in *N. Y. Supreme Court, William B. Dinsmore et al., Trustees &c., against Alvin Adams et al.*; Swaine, *Cravath Firm*, I, 287; "Adams Express in Trouble," *NYT*, October 27, 1870; "Adams Express Company in Court—Application for a Receiver," *CDG*, October 29, 1870.

16. Duncan, *Entrepreneur for Equality*, 112.

17. Lauw, *Fourteen Years with Adelina Patti*, 53–55; "Personal Intelligence," *NT*, January 15, 1870; "General News," *Pittsburgh Weekly Gazette*, February 28, 1870; "All Sorts and

Sizes," *Bangor (ME) Daily Whig and Courier*, May 7, 10, 1870; "Miscellaneous," *Titusville (PA) Herald*, July 26, 1870. On the Franco-Prussian War see, for example, Howard, *Franco-Prussian War*.

18. "Senate," *NYH*, December 16, 1870; "XLI Congress—Short Session," *Syracuse (NY) Daily Journal*, December 17, 1870; *SR*, December 22, 1870, 4; "Forty-first Congress, (Third Session)," *New National Era* (Washington, DC), December 22, 1870; "Reconstruction," *NYW*, January 27, 1871; "House," *NUA*, January 28, 1871.

19. *Report of the Joint Committee of the General Assembly of Georgia*, 162–65; Parks, *Joseph E. Brown of Georgia*, 451–57; "State Road Lease," *AC*, January 12, 1871.

20. "State Road Lease" and "Meeting of the Lessees," *AC*, January 12, 1871; "Railway Lease," *PI*, December 29, 1870; "Lease of the Western and Atlantic Railroad," *WES*, December 29, 1870; "Lease of the State Road," *Southern Watchman* (Athens, GA), January 4, 1871; Reed, *History of Atlanta*, 162–69; "Georgia Press," *MWT*, January 17, 1871; *ADI*, January 11, 1871, 3; "State Road," *ADI*, January 12, 1871; Nathans, *Losing the Peace*, 207–11 .

21. Duncan, *Entrepreneur for Equality*, 3, 57; Reed, *History of Atlanta*, 162–63; *Weekly Constitution* (Atlanta, GA), June 14, 1870, 3.

22. *Evidence Taken by the Joint Committee of the Legislature of the State of Georgia*, 121–22; "Notable Party," *NUA*, June 9, 1871.

23. "Died," *NYT*, January 18, 1871; "Mrs. Fanny Blackstone Seaman," *NYT*, April 23, 1895; entry for Willis Blackstone household, 1870 federal census manuscript, New York, NY, New York County, 6; *Northern Alabama, Historical and Biographical*, 631; Garrett, *Reminiscences*, 117–18; "Arrivals at the Principal Hotels," *NODP*, January 24, 1871.

24. "From New York via Havana," *NODP*, February 2, 1871; "Miscellaneous," *NODP*, February 14, 1871; *Reports of the Secretary of the Navy and of the Postmaster General*, 21; Ziegler, "Revolt of 'the Ever-faithful Isle,'" 16–17, 208; "General News Items," *SR*, February 15, 1871.

25. "Organization of the Union Pacific R. R.," *CDG*, March 9, 1871; Brown, "Southern Railway Security Company," 159–60; Churella, *Pennsylvania Railroad*, 439–41; Stover, "Pennsylvania Railroad's Southern Rail Empire," 30–31.

26. "Hotel Arrivals—April 7," *CDN*, Saturday, April 8, 1871; "Hotel Arrivals," *SMN*, April 10, 1871.

27. Martin, "Henry Bradley Plant," 271; Rivers, Mathews, and Brown, *John Willis Menard*, 15, 84; "Arrivals at the Principal Hotels," *NODP*, May 9, 1871; "For New York via Havana," *NODP*, May 18, 1871.

28. Duncan, *Entrepreneur for Equality*, 133–35; "Nashville," *Atchison (KS) Daily Champion*, June 6, 1871; "Hotel Arrivals," *AC*, June 7, 1871; "Governor's Reception," *Southern Banner* (Athens, GA), June 8, 1871.

29. Duncan, *Entrepreneur for Equality*, 135–36; "Notable Party," *NUA*, June 9, 1871; "Unveiling the Statue," *PI*, June 12, 1871; "Washington News and Gossip," *WES*, July 19, 1871; "Personal," *NYEE*, July 20, 1871; "The President on the Hudson," *Poughkeepsie (NY) Eagle-News*, July 21, 1871; "Personal Intelligence," *NYH*, August 3, 1871; "Albion News," *Medina (NY) Tribune*, August 17, 1871; "By Telegraph," *Savannah Daily Advertiser*, August 22, 1871; "Prominent Arrivals," *NYTr*, August 22, 1871; "Personal Intelligence," *NYS*, September 1, 1871; "Westward Bound Passengers," *Daily Alta California* (San Francisco, CA), September 5, 1871; "Arrived," *Sacramento Daily Union*, September 6, 1871; "Where Is Bullock?" *Union and Advertiser* (Rochester, NY), September 13, 1871; "Washington Intelligence," *Sacramento Daily Union*, September 13, 1871; "Miscellaneous Items," *Geneva (NY) Gazette*, September 15, 1871; "State Matters," *Savannah Daily Advertiser*, September 20, 1871; "Prominent Arrivals," *NYTr*, October 5, 1871. On the building and completion of the transcontinental railroad see, for example, Ambrose, *Nothing Like It in the World*.

30. "Hotel Arrivals, June 16," *CDP*, June 17, 1871; *Bonds of the State of Tennessee*, 64–65; "Arrivals at the Principal Hotels," *NODP*, October 24, 1871; "Personal," *MDA*, October 26, 1871; "Personal Intelligence," *NYH*, December 22, 1871.

31. "Hotel Arrivals, January 15," *CDP*, January 16, 1872; "Arrivals at the Principal Hotels," *NODP*, January 28, 1872; "Worthy Compliment to a Worthy Man," *NODP*, February 14, 1872; "Hotel Arrivals—March 22," *CDN*, March 23, 1872; "Southern Express Company," *WES*, January 15, 1872.

32. "Lease," *MDA*, January 21, 1872; "Memphis and Charleston Railroad," *Knoxville (TN) Daily Chronicle*, January 27, 1872; "Arrivals at the Principal Hotels," *NODP*, January 28, February 15, 1872; "Tom Scott's Project," *Savannah Daily Advertiser*, February 2, 1872; "Fast Railroad Times," *NODP*, February 2, 1872; *Daily Sun* (Atlanta, GA), March 5, 1872, 3; "Railroad Magnates—What's Up!," *GDN*, February 3, 1872; "By Rail to Mobile," *New Orleans Republican*, February 3, 1872; "From New Orleans to Mobile by Rail," *Donaldsonville (LA) Chief*, February 10, 1872; "A Worthy Compliment to a Worthy Man," *NODP*, February 14, 1872; "Railroad Lease," *NUA*, February 25, 1872; "Hotel Arrivals," *AC*, February 25, 1872; "Alabama and Chattanooga Railroad," *NODP*, May 24, 1872; "Financial Affairs," *NYT*, November 30, 1872; "Colonel Thomas A. Scott," *NYDG*, April 17, 1873; "Southern Railway Security Company," *Charlotte (NC) Democrat*, February 18, 1873.

33. "Vanderbilt versus Scott," *Providence (RI) Evening Press*, March 8, 1872; "War of the Giants—The Republic Ruled by Railway Kings—Government Control of the Railways," *NYH*, March 11, 1872; *American Railroad Journal* 28 (May 25, 1872): 675; Poor, *Manual of the Railroads*, 638; "Swindling the South," *SMN*, February 7, 1872.

34. Churella, *Pennsylvania Railroad*, 444.

35. Brown, *Florida's Black Public Officials*, 142; *Journal of the Proceedings of the Assembly of the State of Florida*, 90.

36. "Argument of William D. Shipman," 49, in *N. Y. Supreme Court, William B. Dinsmore et al., Trustees &c., against Alvin Adams et al.*; "Suit against Adams' Express Company," *NYH*, June 6, 1872; "Adams Express Co. Litigation," *NYCA*, June 24, 1872; "Adams Express Case," *NYT*, June 25, 1872; "New York, June 25, 1872," *BDA*, June 26, 1872.

37. "Personal," *MDA*, July 18, 1872; "Arrivals at Overlook," *Daily Freeman* (Kingston, NY), July 21, 1872; "New Summer Resort," *Hudson (NY) Evening Register*, July 6, 1872; Morford, *Short-Trip Guide to America*, 316.

38. "Arrivals at Overlook," *Daily Freeman* (Kingston, NY), July 21, 1872; *Tampa Daily Journal*, March 22, 1890, 2; Smyth, *Life of Henry Bradley Plant*, 66–67.

39. Edward J. Loughman affidavit, July 1909, Henry B. Plant Collection, Henry B. Plant Museum Archives; "Notice," *Albany (NY) Argus*, February 22, 1850; Wilson, *Trow's New York City Directory for 1853–54*, 421; Wilson, *Trow's New York City Directory for the Year Ending May 1, 1857*, 500; "Ellen Loughman, May 21, 1845" in "New York Deaths and Burials, 1795–1952," index, accessed February 15, 2014, https://familysearch.org/pal:/MM9.1.1/FD16-23Y; "New York Cattle Market," *NYTr*, November 23, 1864; "Transactions," *NYW*, July 28, 1865; "List of Persons in Division No. 9th, of Collection District No. 12th, of the District of New York," August 1865, Internal Revenue Service Tax Assessment lists, Record Group 58, NA; "New York Live Stock Market," *NYW*, September 22, 1865; Wilson, *Trow's New York City Directory for the Year Ending May 1, 1868*, 626; entry for Martin Loughman family, 1870 federal census manuscript, 9th District and 20th Ward, New York, NY, New York County, 46.

40. Edward J. Loughman affidavit, July 1909; "Mrs. Robert Graves Dead," *NYS*, May 31, 1909; entry for Sacred Heart Institution, 1855 state census manuscript, 4th Election District, 12th Ward, New York, NY, County of New York, no pagination; "New Religious Order in the United States," *NYEP*, April 5, 1855; "Manhattan College Marks 125th Anniversary," *Yonkers (NY) Herald-Statesman*, December 14, 1978; "The Academy of the Sacred Heart: 1841–1917," accessed February 15, 2014, http://www.mville.edu/undergraduate/academics/library/special-collections/manhattanville-timeline.html#AcademyofSacredHeart.

41. "Marriages," *Brooklyn (NY) Evening Star*, June 7, 1859; "Loughman," *NYH*, July 28, 1878; Martin Loughman birth record, May 29, 1860, Birth Records, 1846–1909, and Martin

Francis Loughman death record, July 26, 1878, and Pauline Loughman death record, June 14, 1929, Death Records, 1795–1949, New York Municipal Archives; "Died," *NYH*, June 28, 1861; "New York Cattle Market," *NYTr*, April 4, 1861; entry for Martin Loughman family, 1870 federal census manuscript, 9th District and 20th Ward, New York, NY, New York County, 46.

42. Wilson, *Trow's New York City Directory for the Year Ending May 1, 1874*, 108; entry for "Geo. F. Birdsall" on "Consolidated List of all persons of Class I, subject to do military duty in the Fourth (4th Ward) Congressional District, consisting of part of the County of New York, State of New York, enumerated during the month of June 1863," Consolidated Enrollment Lists, 1863–1865, Records of the Provost Marshal General's Bureau (Civil War), NA; entry for Samuel Birdsall family, 1860 federal census manuscript, 4th District, 8th Ward, New York, NY, County of New York, 86; Hinshaw, *Encyclopedia of American Quaker Genealogy*, III, 36; Wilson, *Trow's New York City Directory for the Year Ending May 1, 1865*, 82; "Died," *NYT*, September 19, 1864.

43. Reynolds, *Henry Plant*, 99; entry for Academy of the Sacred Heart, 1860 federal census manuscript, 3rd District, 12th Ward, Manhattanville, NY, County of New York, 121; "Catholic World," *New Zealand Tablet* (Dunedin, New Zealand), September 6, 1917; "Croker's Firm Sued," *NYP*, December 13, 1895.

44. Wilson, *Trow's New York City Directory for the Year Ending May 1, 1868*, 626; Harris, Jacobs, and O'Keefe, *Search for Missing Friends*, 282; "New York Live Stock Market," *CDG*, December 17, 1867; "Live Stock Markets," *NYW*, October 26, 1869; entry for Martin Loughman family, 1870 federal census manuscript, 9th District, 20th Ward, New York, NY, New York County, 46; Wilson, *Trow's New York Directory for the Year Ending May 1, 1871*, 103; entry for Margaret Birdsall, 1870 federal census manuscript, 13th District, 22nd Ward, New York, NY, New York County, 34; Wilson, *Trow's New York Directory for the Year Ending May 1, 1872*, 9.

45. "Election of Officers," *CDN*, October 17, 1872; *Boyle & Chapman's Memphis City Directory*, 17, 274; "Local and Suburban," *Boston Traveler*, January 23, 1873; "Railroad Men in the City," *BP*, January 23, 1873; "Personal," *Daily Sun* (Atlanta, GA), February 6, 1873; "Convention of Railroad Magnates," *ACh*, February 9, 1873; "Arrivals at the Principal Hotels," *NODP*, February 15, 1873; "Personal," *MDA*, February 19, 1873.

46. "Personal," *MDA*, April 25, 29, 1873; "Amusements," *MDA*, May 1, 1873; "Arrivals at the Principal Hotels," *NODP*, May 5, 1873; "Personal Intelligence," *Atlanta Daily Herald*, May 9, 1873; "Personal," *ACh*, May 11, 1873.

47. Church of the Transfiguration Marriage Records, 1873–1877, vol. 8, 400–401; Dunlap, *From Abyssinian to Zion*, 131; "Dr. G. H. Houghton Dead," *NYT*, November 18, 1897; "Prominent Arrivals," *NYTr*, July 2, 1873; "Married," *NYH*, July 16, 1873; "Local News," *NYET*, July 23, 1873.

CHAPTER 8

1. "Local Notes," *Evening Telegram* (New York, NY), July 23, 1873; Flayhart, *American Line*, 33–38; Moore, *History of the Five o'Clock Club*, 275; "Rejoicing," *Detroit Free Press*, July 11, 1873.

2. Henry B. Plant passport application, July 21, 1873; Morton F. Plant passport application, July 21, 1873; Betsey Hoadley passport application, July 18, 1873, US Passport Applications, 1795–1925, M1372, rolls 197 and 425, NA; "Steamship Pennsylvania," *Liverpool Mail* (Merseyside, England), June 28, 1873; "Harrogate on Thursday," *Morning Post* (London, England), August 8, 1873; "Americans Registered in Dublin," *Anglo-American Times* (London, England), August 9, 1873; "Americans Recently Registered in London," *LAR*, August 23, 1873; Denby, *Grand Hotels*, 51–52; "Americans Recently Registered in London and Paris," *LAR*, August 16, 1873.

3. "Germany," *LAR*, September 6, 13, 1873; "Austria," *LAR*, September 20, 1873; "Vienna Exhibition," *NYW*, May 2, 1873; "Paris," *LAR*, October 18, 1873; Geoffrey and Sibley, *Going Abroad*, 15.

4. "Sardon and Strakosch at Work," *Columbus (IN) Republican*, October 23, 1873; "European Stage Gossip," *Sunday Times* (Chicago, IL), October 12, 1873; "New Operatic Stars," *NYEP*, October 25, 1873; Barker, *France of the French*, 186; *Who Was Who in the Theater*, II, 979; "Our Muscial and Theatrical Review," *LAR*, November 21, 1874.

5. "Blondes and Brunettes," *Saratoga Sentinel* (Saratoga Springs, NY), August 16, 1883; "Paris, Oct. 3," *Boston Evening Journal*, October 20, 1873.

6. Foner, *Reconstruction*, 512. For provocative insights into the Panic of 1873 and its origins, see Nelson, *Nation of Deadbeats.*

7. "Foreign Ports," *NYH*, October 25, 1873; "Steamship 'Pennsylvania,'" *PI*, November 5, 1873; "Passengers Arrived," *NYT*, November 6, 1873; "City Intelligence," *NYCA*, November 7, 1873; "Our Saturday's Sermon," *NYTr*, November 8, 1873; "Arrivals," *NYH*, November 8, 1873.

8. "Roosevelt," *NYEE*, November 13, 1873; Churella, *Pennsylvania Railroad*, 441; "Important Railroad Purchase," *Richmond (VA) Whig*, December 23, 1873; "Southern Security Company," *WMS*, November 29, 1874.

9. "Courts," *NYTr*, June 4, 1873; "Brinckley Divorce Suit," *NYTr*, June 10, 1873.

10. "Brinckley Divorce Suit," *NYTr*, November 11, 1873; Herndon, *Men of Progress*, 458; "Mrs. Brinckley's Triumph," *NYTr*, May 23, 1874.

11. Keating, *Yellow Fever Epidemic of 1878*, 92; "Continental," *PI*, December 30, 1873; "Local Paragraphs," *MDA*, March 23, 1874; "Delegates Arriving," *Boston Daily Globe*, July 15, 1884; Stimson, *History of the Express Business*, 294.

12. Mitchell, "Connecticut's Contribution to Art," 127; "Olin L. Warner," *Fitchburg (MA) Sentinel*, June 9, 1884; O'Neill, *American Sculpture*, 203–5; Eckford, "Olin Warner, Sculptor," 392–95; Caffin, *American Masters of Sculpture*, 135–37.

13. "New Fifth Avenue Palace," *NYS*, September 23, 1873; Bruce, *Hudson River by Daylight*, inside cover; "Windsor's History" and "Windsor a Noted Resort," *NYT*, March 18, 1899.

14. Frank and Smith, *Mark Twain's Letters*, 109; *NYTr*, April 23, 1873, 4; Twain and Warner, *Gilded Age*.

15. English, *In Memoriam*, 27–28; "Deaths," *NHCR*, October 31, 1874; "Personal Intelligence," *NYH*, January 28, 1875; "Arrivals at the Hotels," *NYT*, February 5, 1875; *GDN*, March 25, 1875, 1; "Arrivals at the Hotels," *New Orleans Bulletin*, March 30, 1875; "A Munificent Donation," *ACh*, March 16, 1875; "Personal," *New Orleans Times*, March 25, 1875; "From Houston," *GDN*, March 26, 1875.

16. *GDN*, March 25, 1875, 1; "Morgan and the Ship Channel," *GDN*, March 26, 1875; *Austin (TX) Weekly Statesman*, April 1, 1875, 1; "From the Capital," *GDN*, April 6, 1875; *Denison (TX) Daily Cresset*, April 7, 1875, 4; "Express Magnates," *Denison (TX) Daily News*, April 7, 1875; "Gov. English, H. B. Plant, Mr. J. Durand—The Distinguished Visitors—What They Did and Said, and Who They Are," *Austin (TX) Weekly Statesman*, April 8, 1875; "Texas Facts and Fancies," *Weekly Democratic Statesman* (Austin, TX), April 8, 1875; "Right Spirit in Texas," *BS*, April 9, 1875; *Dallas Weekly Herald*, April 10, 1875, 1; *Houston Daily Age* quoted in "Distinguished Visitors," *ACh*, April 20, 1875.

17. "Personal," *MDA*, April 13, 1875; "Ledger Lines," *Public Ledger* (Memphis, TN), April 13, 1875; "Distinguished Visitors," *ACh*, April 20, 1875; English, *In Memoriam*, 28, 30–32; "Hotel Arrivals, April 29," *Charleston (SC) Daily News and Courier*, April 21, 1875; "Hotel Personals," *CE*, May 5, 1875; "Hotel Arrivals," *CDG*, May 5, 1875; "Watering Place Notes," *NYH*, July 24, 1875; "Grand Union Hotel," *DS*, August 12, 1875.

18. "Personal," *GDN*, October 29, November 2, 1875; "Death of A. B. Small," *Waco (TX) Daily Examiner*, November 2, 1875.

19. Stimson, *History of the Express Business*, 127; "News Notes," *NYCA*, March 31, 1875;

"Adams Express Company," *NYDG*, April 21, 1875; "Important Notice," *NYT*, May 29, 1875; "Southern Express Co.," 86; McCabe, *Lights and Shadows of New York Life*, 359–64; Mendelsohn, *Touring the Flatiron*, 16–17.

20. "Expressman's Aid Society," *Cincinnati Daily Times*, November 9, 1875; "Proceedings of the Second Annual Convention of the Expressman's Aid Society," 138.

21. *AC*, October 30, 1875, 2; "City and Suburban News," *NYT*, November 4, 1875; "Prominent Arrivals," *NYTr*, November 11, 1875, January 5, 1876; "New Connecticut Senator," *NYH*, November 28, 1875; "Personal Intelligence," *NYH*, December 5, 1875; "Connecticut Senatorship," *NYT*, May 17, 1876; "Would Refuse a Nomination," *NYH*, May 22, 1876.

22. Van Slyck, *New England Manufacturers and Manufactories*, 103–4; "Romances of Two Lives Still Increase," *Evening Telegram* (New York, NY), February 20, 1897; "Son Reunites Them," *NYH*, February 21, 1897; "Turned from Home by the Son She Kidnapped," *NYW*, February 25, 1900; "Gossip of the Stage," *NYDG*, June 23, 1874; "City Summary," *New York Clipper*, November 21, 1874.

23. "Wood's Museum," *NYT*, January 17, 1875; "City Summary," *New York Clipper*, April 17, May 15, 1875; "Amusements," *NYDG*, May 20, 1875; "Personalities," *NYDG*, June 7, July 16, 1875; "Passengers Sailed," *NYTr*, July 29, 1875; "Amusement Notes," *NYDG*, August 19, 1875; "Park Theater," *NYTr*, September 2, 1875; "Park Theater," *Evening Telegram* (New York, NY), September 8, 1875; "State Items," *Daily Constitution* (Middletown, CT), September 20, 1875; "Passengers Arrived," *NYTr*, September 4, 1875; "Ocean View Hotel, Block Island," *Newport (RI) Daily News*, September 11, 1875; "Akron-ic Epidemic," 157; Herndon, *Men of Progress*, 458; "Important Notice," *NYT*, May 29, 1875.

24. "Texas Express Company's Annual Meeting," *NODP*, March 2, 1876; "Kimball House Arrivals," *AC*, March 4, June 11, 1876; "Texas Express Company," 86; "Proceedings of the Second Annual Convention of the Expressmen's Aid Society," 139; "South Carolina," *ACh*, April 8, 1876; "Visitors at Long Branch," *NYH*, July 23, 1876; Hazard, *Long Branch in the Golden Age*, 31, 46, 56, 84, 86; "On the Beach at Long Beach," *NYS*, July 23, 1876; "Hotel Arrivals" and "Personal Mention," *DS*, August 12, 1876; "Saratoga Leisure," *NYTr*, August 19, 1876; "Return of Major O'Brien," 310; "Hotel Arrivals," *CDT*, October 9, 1876; "City Personals," *Daily Inter Ocean* (Chicago, IL), October 9, 1876; "Personal Mention," *SLPD*, October 21, 1876; "Local Matter," *Indian Journal* (Muskogee, OK), October 26, 1876.

25. Keating, *Yellow Fever Epidemic of 1878*, 92; "Death of Mr. W. H. Phillips," *SMN*, October 31, 1876; "Death of an Expressman," *SMN*, November 8, 1876; "Death of Another Expressman," *SMN*, November 11, 1876; "Obituary," *SMN*, November 23, 1876; "Commendable," *SMN*, January 31, 1877; Foner, *Reconstruction*, 564–79; "Public Notice," *WMS*, December 8, 1876.

26. "A Bar-Room Robbery," *NYT*, February 21, 1877.

27. "Evidence," *AC*, February 26, 1876; "Crooked Papers," *ACh*, February 29, March 4, 1876.

28. "Current Topics at the Capital," *NYTr*, March 27, 1877; "Humphreys, of Florida—What It Costs to be a Republican Elector," *Record of the Times* (Wilkes-Barre, PA), March 27, 1877; "Reform in Civil Service," *Observer* (Raleigh, NC), March 30, 1877; "Presidential Elector in Luck," *Helena (MT) Daily Herald*, April 3, 1877.

29. "Proceedings of the Third Annual Convention of the Expressmen's Aid Society," 156; "Long Branch," *NYH*, July 19, 1877; "Summer Leisure," *NYTr*, August 1, 1877; "Long Branch," *NYTr*, August 20, 1877.

30. "Obituary Notes," *NYT*, September 2, 1877; "Funeral of the Late Alvin Adams," *BJ*, September 6, 1877; "Alvin Adams," *NYH*, September 6, 1877.

31. "Hotel Arrivals," *Daily Review* (Wilmington, NC), November 19, 1877; "Hotel Arrivals, November 21," *CNC*, November 22, 1877; "Personal," *ACh*, December 1, 1877; Mitchell, "Connecticut's Contribution to Art," 127; "A Card," *NYTr*, December 31, 1877; Brownell, "Sculpture of Olin Warner," 429–41.

32. "Mrs. Blackstone's Story," *NYDG*, October 24, 1878.

33. "Died," *NYT*, January 18, 1871, *NYH*, January 19, 1878.

CHAPTER 9

1. "Passing Throng," *NYTr*, April 1, 1900; Allman, *Miami*, 120–21; Brown, *Tampa in Civil War and Reconstruction*, 167–68; Grismer, *Tampa*, 168–69, 178; "South Florida Letter," *Ashtabula (OH) Weekly Telegraph*, May 31, 1878.

2. "Mrs. Blackstone's Story," *NYDG*, October 24, 1878; "Watering Place Gossip," *NYDG*, July 22, 1878; "Hotel Arrivals," *Branford (CT) Gleaner*, July 10, 1878; "Amusements," *NYEE*, January 22, 1879; "Elopement in High Life," *Jersey Journal* (Jersey City, NJ), February 2, 1881; "Divorced Wife's Theft," *NYT*, October 24, 1878; "Excitement over an Abduction," *NYW*, October 25, 1878; "Abducting Her Own Child," *National Police Gazette* (New York, NY), November 2, 1878; "Railroad Magnates," *Daily Tribune* (Salt Lake City, UT), October 24, 1878; "Passengers Passing Carlin for California," *Sacramento Daily Union*, October 26, 1878; "Recovered His Child," *NYH*, November 8, 1879.

3. Parsons, *Parsons Family*, 251–52; "Elegant Wedding at Northampton," 182–84; "Good Society," *Branford (CT) Gleaner*, May 5, 1879.

4. "Elegant Wedding at Northampton," 184; "In the City," *Observer* (Raleigh, NC), May 20, 1879; "Military," *NYEE*, April 17, 1880; entry for Morton and Ida Plant, 1880 federal census manuscript, New York City, NY, New York County, 442; "Jennie Cramer's Death," *NHER*, August 14, 1881; "A Cross-Examination," *NHER*, September 8, 1881; "Dramatic Court Scene," *NYS*, September 9, 1881; "Recent Hotel Arrivals," *Pacific Commercial Advertiser* (Honolulu, HI), December 25, 1880; Parsons, *Parson Family*, 252; Ida Josephine Parson Hayden tombstone inscription, Bridge Street Cemetery, Northampton, MA; "Northampton," *SR*, July 14, 1882.

5. "Season at Its Height" and "West End Hotel," *NYT*, July 29, 1878; "Watering-Place Gossip," *NYDG*, July 29, 1878; "From Our Summer Resorts," *PT*, August 7, 1878; "Hotel Arrivals," *SMN*, March 15, 1879; "Our Florida Letter," *SMN*, March 24, 1879; "Passengers Sailed," *NYEP*, June 6, 1879; "Passengers Arrived," *RG*, June 10, 1879; "Passengers Arrived," *NYTr*, June 30, 1879; "Passengers Sailed," *RG*, July 1, 1879; "Brighton Beach," *BDE*, July 21, 1879; "Died," *NYH*, July 28, 1878, November 27, 1879.

6. Keating, *Yellow Fever Epidemic of 1878*, 92–94; "Southern Express Company, Augusta, Ga., July 28," 236; "Memphis, Tenn.," 266.

7. Martin, *Florida's Flagler*, 76–78; Akin, *Flagler*, 3, 71–73; "Union League Ladies' Reception," *NYH*, January 27, 1882.

8. "Hotel Arrivals," *NYH*, December 4, 1877; "Local Personal," *SMN*, December 8, 1890; "Death of Judge Chisholm," *SMN*, December 6, 1890; "Gath," *CE*, April 6, 1889.

9. Vanderbilt, *Fortune's Children*, 98; "Mr. Astor's Big Yacht," *SMN*, February 14, 1878; Martin, *City Makers*, 116; "Notes about Town," *North American* (Philadelphia, PA), April 16, 1878; "Jacksonville, Florida," *CDES*, June 20, 1878.

10. "Personal," *NT*, February 9, 1878; "Personal," *ACh*, February 16, 1878; Akin, *Flagler*, 72; "Hotel Arrivals," *SMN*, March 1, 1878.

11. "Hotel Arrivals," *SMN*, March 12, 1878, and *New Orleans Daily Democrat*, April 21, 1878; "Cuban Affairs," *SMN*, March 1, 1878; "Late Cuban Rebellion," *SMN*, March 5, 1878; "Pearl of the Antilles," *ACh*, March 1, 1878; "Passengers," *SMN*, March 15, 1878; "Bahamas," *FLIN*, March 2, 1878; "Scenes from Sun-Lands," *FLIN*, May 4, July 6, 1878; "Peace in Cuba," *FLIN*, July 6, 1878; "Postal Excursion to Havana," *BDE*, April 1, 1878; "Postal Excursion to Cuba," *WES*, April 26, May 2, 1878; "Postal Excursion to Havana," *WES*, April 29, 1878; "On to Havana," *Cleveland (OH) Leader*, May 1, 1878; Fishburne, *Cedar Keys in the 19th Century*, 102; "Marine News," *New Orleans Daily Democrat*, April 19, 1878.

12. "President of the Express Company," *ACh*, May 4, 1878; "Hotel Arrivals," *Daily Review* (Wilmington, NC), May 6, 1878; "Locals," *Branford (CT) Gleaner*, May 29, 1878; "Bran-

ford Briefly Chronicled," *NHER*, June 28, 1903; "The European Exodus," *NYTr*, June 1, 1878; Bird, "Aucune Usine au Monde," 299–310.

13. "Varieties," *CDG*, June 13, 1878; "Poor Patti," *San Francisco Bulletin*, July 13, 1878.

14. "Paris Theatrical Inklings," *NODP*, March 10, 1878; "Glimpses of Life in Paris," *NODP*, May 12, 1878; *SLPD*, June 25, 1878, 2.

15. "Matters and Things Laconically Noted," *SMN*, January 25, 1879; "Associated Press Dispatch," *AC*, January 28, 1879; "Hotel Arrivals," *SMN*, March 15, 1879; "Our Florida Letter," *SMN*, March 24, 1879; "Probable Sale of the Atlantic and Gulf Railroad," *MWT*, March 25, 1879; "Gulf Railroad to be Sold," *SMN*, June 24, 1879; "Sale of the Atlantic and Gulf Railroad," *SMN*, September 2, 1879; "Mr. H. B. Plant Buys the Atlantic and Gulf Railroad," 302–3.

16. "Mr. H. B. Plant Buys the Atlantic and Gulf Railroad," 302–3; "Sale of a Railroad" and "Matters and Things Laconically Noted," *SMN*, November 5, 1879.

17. "Successor of the Gulf Railroad Company," *SMN*, November 27, 1879; "Savannah, Ga.," *NODP*, November 27, 1879; "H. B. Plant," *TT*, November 29, 1879; "Elections and Official Changes," 1135; "Arrivals at the Principal Hotels," *NODP*, December 1, 1879; "Personal," *Albany (GA) News*, December 4, 1879; "Personal" and "Possession to Be Given Immediately," *SMN*, December 9, 1879; "Savannah, Florida and Western Railway Company," *SMN*, December 11, 1879; "Matters and Things Laconically Noted," *SMN*, December 12, 1879; "Passengers Arrived," *NYT*, December 16, 1879.

18. "Telephone Line," *PI*, December 18, 1879; "Grand Scheme for the Benefit of the South," *SMN*, January 13, 1880; Therrell, "Division One Has Fine Record," 2, 4; Webb, *Webb's Jacksonville and Consolidated Directory*, 17; "State News," *FM*, March 10, 1880; "Florida Affairs," *SMN*, April 14, 1880.

19. "Savannah, Florida and Western Railway," *SMN*, December 25, 1879; "Railroad Combination," *AC*, January 11, 1880.

20. "American Ports," *NYH*, February 16, 1880; "Departed Yesterday," *SMN*, February 25, 1880; "Our Seaside," *SMN*, April 21, 1880; "Orange Grove Notes," *SMN*, March 8, 1880.

21. Pettengill, *Story of the Florida Railroads*, 63–65; "Legislature," *SMN*, October 9, 1879; "Our Jacksonville Letter," *SMN*, November 10, 1879; "Waycross and Florida Railroad Company," *SMN*, March 5, 1880; "Florida Extension," *AC*, March 9, 1880; "Jacksonville and Savannah Short Line," *SMN*, March 16, 1880; "Waycross and Florida Railroad Co.," *SMN*, April 2, 1880.

22. Mancini, *One Dies, Get Another*, 187; Powell, *American Siberia*, 5–6, 138–51; Ortiz, *Emancipation Betrayed*, 54; Miller, *Crime, Sexual Violence, and Clemency*, 22–23.

23. "Union Times," *Intelligencer* (Anderson, SC), April 15, 1880; "Greenville and Columbia Railroad," *Daily Review* (Wilmington, NC), April 15, 1880; "Greenville and Columbia," *ACh*, April 16, 1880; "Railroad Management," *NYT*, June 8, 1880; "Sale of the Savannah and Charleston Railroad," *SMN*, June 8, 1880; "New Coast Railroad Line," *Dallas Daily Herald*, June 8, 1880; "Railway Projects," 589.

24. "New Railroad Syndicate," *NYT*, June 16, 1880; "Gigantic Railroad Enterprise," *SMN*, June 19, 1880.

25. "Rival Express Companies," *NT*, August 21, 1879; "What Colonel Cole Has to Say of the Business," *AC*, January 20, 1880; "Our Atlanta Letter," *SMN*, February 16, 1880; "Railway Matters," *Detroit Free Press*, March 12, 1880; "Railroad Matters," *NT*, March 25, 1880; "War of the Express—Adams vs. Union," 74–76; "Selma Branch Lease," *AC*, April 18, 1880; "General Railway Notes," *NYT*, April 25, 1880; "Railroad Items," *SMN*, April 28, 1880; "Mississippi Valley Express Co.," *SLPD*, May 1, 1880; "St. Louis Letter," *Dallas Daily Herald*, May 28, 1880; "Express-Railroad War," *SLPD*, May 27, 1880; "Express Company's Rights," *NYT*, November 19, 1880; "Another Important Decision—Southern Express Company vs. Louisville & Nashville Railroad Company," 229–30.

26. "Coney Island," *Brooklyn (NY) Union-Argus*, September 4, 1880.

27. "Personal," *WMS*, November 16, 1880. On James A. Garfield see, among other works, Doak, *James A. Garfield*, and on Chester A. Arthur, Reeves, *Gentleman Boss*; and Dehler, *Chester Alan Arthur*.

28. "Personal," *WMS*, November 16, 1880; "Greenville Railroad," *News and Herald* (Winnsboro, SC), November 30, 1880; "South Carolina News," *Yorkville (SC) Enquirer*, December 2, 1880; "Albany News and Advertiser," *MWT*, December 3, 1880; "From High Bridge to Brewster's," *NYS*, December 4, 1880; "Railroad Men Take a Holiday," *NYT*, December 4, 1880; "News Items," *MT*, January 12, 1881; "Among the Railroads," *CDG*, January 22, 1881; "Southern Express," *ACh*, January 21, 1881.

29. "Our Jacksonville Letter," *SMN*, March 23, 1881; "The Forest City," *SMN*, March 18, 1881.

30. Hoffman, *Building a Great Railroad*, 57–58; Reynolds, *Henry Plant*, 134–35; "New Georgia Road," *AC*, April 26, 1881; "The First Train" and "Opening of the Waycross & Jacksonville Railroad," *FM*, April 30, 1881.

31. Knetsch, "Hamilton Disston and the Development of Florida," 5–9; "Draining the Everglades," *NYW*, February 18, 1881; Williamson, *Florida Politics in the Gilded Age*, 72–74.

32. Knetsch, "Hamilton Disston and the Development of Florida," 8–10; "Huge Land Purchase," *Harrisburg (PA) Telegraph*, June 17, 1881.

33. Pettengill, *Story of the Florida Railroads*, 66; *Acts and Resolutions Adopted by the Legislature of Florida, at Its Eleventh Session*, 145–47.

34. Johnson, "Florida Railroad after the Civil War," 297, 299–300; H. B. Plant to D. L. Yulee, May 11, August 21, 1881, David Levy Yulee Papers, P. K. Yonge Library of Florida History, University of Florida, Gainesville.

35. Pettengill, *Story of the Florida Railroads*, 66; *Sunland Tribune* (Tampa, FL), July 30, 1881, 2; "Flank Movement from Georgia," *FM*, August 6, 1881; *Cedar Key Journal* quoted in "Railroad Notes," *FM*, August 6, 1881; "Some of the Men Identified with Lakeland's Prosperity," *FTU*, December 27, 1896.

36. *Palatka Herald* quoted in "Railroad Notes," *FM*, September 3, 1881.

37. Rutkow, *James A. Garfield*, 82–130; "Assassination," *WES*, July 2, 1881.

38. "Personal Intelligence," *NYH*, October 30, 1881; *BS*, November 7, 1881, Supplement 1; "Two Million Acres," *Buffalo (NY) Express*, December 23, 1881.

39. "Florida Railways," *PI*, December 28, 1881; "Florida English Capital," *Columbus (GA) Daily Enquirer*, December 29, 1881; *Florida Union* (Jacksonville, FL) quoted in "Florida Railroad Developments," *Columbus (GA) Daily Enquirer*, December 31, 1881.

40. *Galveston (TX) Weekly News*, February 2, 1882, 2.

41. "Personal," *Florida Daily Times* (Jacksonville, FL), February 12, 1882; Ingraham, "Sketch of the Life of Mr. Henry Plant," 28.

42. Ingraham, "Sketch of the Life of Mr. Henry Plant," 28.

CHAPTER 10

1. "Kissimmee City" and "New Railroad," undated and unattributed clippings, Ammidown Holmes Scrapbook, 1880–1882 (St. Augustine, Everglades, etc.), St. Augustine Historical Society, St. Augustine, FL; "State News," *Weekly Floridian* (Tallahassee, FL), January 31, 1882.

2. "Chattahoochee & East Pass Railroad—A Visit to Jacksonville," *WD*, March 2, 1882; "Railroad Reports," *ACh*, March 1, 1882; "Savannah, Florida and Western Railway," *SMN*, March 2, 1882; "Waycross and Florida Railroad Company," *SMN*, March 3, 1882; "Savannah, Florida and Western," *AC*, March 8, 1882; *Special Acts and Resolutions Passed by the General Assembly of the State of Connecticut, at the January Session, 1882*, 546–49.

3. *Special Acts and Resolutions Passed by the General Assembly of the State of Connecticut, at the January Session, 1882*, 546–49; "Plant Investment Co.," *NHER*, November 17, 1883; Graham, *Mr. Flagler's St. Augustine*, 37.

4. "Distinguished Visitors," *WD*, March 23, 1882; "Personal" and "River News," *CDES*, March 27, 1882.

5. Herndon, *Men of Progress*, 458; "The Cramer Murder," *PT*, January 22, 1882; "River News," *NOTD*, January 30, 1882; "Notes from Our Exchanges," *NOTD*, February 11, 1882; "Chattahoochee," *WD*, February 23, 1882; "Local Odds and Ends," *WD*, March 2, 1882.

6. "Brevities," *AC*, March 29, 1882; "Passengers Sailed," *NYT*, April 13, 1882; "Steamers Arrived," *BJ*, April 26, 1882; "Personal," *ACh*, September 9, 1882; Sharpley-Whiting, *Bricktop's Paris*, 156; "Transatlantic Notes," *NYH*, April 29, 1882; "Easter in Paris," *NYH*, April 10, 1882.

7. "Royal Italian Opera," *Times* (London, England), May 20, 1882; "Arrived," *NYT*, June 23, 1882; "Mr. Plant" and "Mrs. Plant," *State of Florida*, June 23, 1882, Passenger Lists of Vessels Arriving at New York, NY, 1820–1897, M237, Roll 453, NA.

8. "Chattahoochee Extension—To Be Built from Climax," *WD*, July 6, 1882; "R. T. Committees," *NYS*, August 10, 1882; "Newport, Aug. 15," *NYTr*, August 16, 1882; "State Correspondence: Branford," *NHER*, August 14, 1882; "Florida Affairs," *Sunland Tribune* (Tampa, FL), September 21, October 19, 1882; "Various Matters," *NHER*, October 5, 1882; "Branford," *NHER*, October 19, 1882; "Personal Points," *MT*, November 3, 1882.

9. "Personal," *Florida Daily Times* (Jacksonville, FL), November 8, 1882; "All Rail," *Florida Dispatch* (Jacksonville, FL), November 6, 1882; "Angel of Death," *NV*, January 17, 1897; "Florida News," *CDES*, November 22, 1882; "Florida," *NOTD*, November 24, 1882; Powell, *American Siberia*, 268–69.

10. "Florida News," *CDES*, November 22, 1882; "Florida," *NOTD*, November 24, 1882; *Sunland Tribune* (Tampa, FL), November 23, 1882, 2; "Marks, Matthew Robertson," *FTU*, April 14, 1893.

11. "Caddo Belle," *CDES*, January 11, 1883; "Apalachicola (Fla.) Items," *CDES*, January 24, 1883; "Savannah, Florida and Western Railway," *AC*, January 24, 1883; "Suwannee River," *FTU*, March 13, 24, 1883; Frederick Frelinghuysen to Adam Badeau, February 8, 1883, "Summer 2014 Auction, Part II, Alexander Historical Auctions," accessed April 28, 2016, https://auctionzip.com/auction-lot/FREDERICK-FRELINGHUYSEN; "Augusta," *AC*, February 11, 1883; "Only a Majority Vote," *NHER*, February 13, 1883; "Cotton Mill's Future," *AC*, February 14, 1883; "Atlanta Cotton Mills," *AC*, February 16, 1883; "Gate City Gossip," *SMN*, February 21, 1883; "Savannah Salad," *ACh*, February 18, 1883.

12. "Personal," *FTU*, February 16, March 4, 1883; "Cleared Yesterday," *NODP*, February 15, 1883; "Connections," *FM*, February 17, 1883; "Nautical Notes," *NODP*, February 23, 1883.

13. "Personal" and "Hotel Arrivals," *FTU*, February 18, March 4, 16, 1883; "Matters and Things Laconically Noted," *SMN*, March 7, 8, 1883; "Personal," *FTU*, March 9, 10, 1883; "Railroad Affairs," *FTU*, March 13, 1883.

14. "Personal," *FTU*, March 11, 13, 1883; "General Gordon's Railway," *FTU*, March 11, 1883; "Georgia and Florida," *SMN*, March 13, 14, 1883; "Florida Legislature," *AWNA*, March 3, 1883; *Acts and Resolutions Adopted by the Legislature of Florida, at Its Twelfth Session*, 117–20; Eckert, *John Brown Gordon*, 248–49.

15. "Our Railways," *FTU*, March 14, 1883; *CDES*, March 23, 1883, 3; "Railroad Extension," *FM*, March 24, 1883; "Editorial Notes," *WD*, April 26, 1883.

16. *Augusta (GA) Evening News* quoted in "Magnificent Railway System," *NODP*, March 6, 1883.

17. "Personal and General Notes" and "Railroad Notes," *NODP*, March 31, 1883; "At Home," *AWNA*, March 31, 1883; "Personal," *ACh*, April 8, 1883; "Railway Time Standards," *NYT*, April 19, 1883; "Mid-Week Echoes," *NYS*, April 5, 1883; Crandall, *Season*, 352–53; "Dined by a Millionaire," *NYT*, April 22, 1883; "Branford," *NHER*, April 24, 1883; "New York, May 4th," *TT*, May 12, 1883.

18. Grismer, *Tampa*, 172–73; Brown, "Tampa and the Coming of the Railroad," 14, 16; Spann, "South Florida Railroad," 1–2; McClellan, *Digest of the Laws of the State of Florida*,

1984–86; Johnson, "Railroads of Florida," 149–50; Pettengill, *Story of the Florida Railroads*, 76; "Sale of the South Florida Railroad," *FM*, May 19, 1883; "Stirring Railroad News," *Bartow (FL) Informant*, June 2, 1883; "State News," *Weekly Bee* (Gainesville, FL), June 23, 1883.

19. Reynolds, *Henry Plant*, 147–57; Grismer, *Tampa*, 172–75; Spann, "South Florida Railroad," 1–3, 7; Pettengill, *Story of the Florida Railroads*, 76–77; Brown, "Tampa and the Coming of the Railroad," 16–17; Nolan, *Fifty Feet in Paradise*, 82–83; J. B. Gordon to Charles T. Smith, May 17, 1883, Gordon to John T. Lesley, June 18, 1883, resolution of shareholders of the International Railroad and Steamship Co., June 20, 1883, Gordon to H. B. Plant, June 29, 1883, John Brown Gordon Records, Georgia State Archives, Morrow; "Railroad Obligations," *Advertiser and Appeal* (Brunswick, GA), June 30, 1883; "Broadway Note-Book," *NYTr*, July 15, 1883.

20. "Branford," *NHER*, August 15, 1883; "Mapleson Opera Festival" and "Grand Union Hotel," *DS*, August 3, 1883; "Victims of Cupid's Darts," *NYW*, June 14, 1883; King, *King's Handbook of the City of New York*, 209.

21. Akin, *Flagler*, 116–17; Graham, *Mr. Flagler's St. Augustine*, 34–41; "Yachting Notes," *NYH*, July 19, 1883; "How Patterson Struck Oil," *National Republican* (Washington, DC), November 17, 1883.

22. "Plant Investment Co.," *NHER*, November 17, 1883; "New Hotel," *SMN*, November 27, 1883; "Mr. Plant's Arrival," *FTU*, November 28, 1883; "Rousing News!," *FTU*, November 30, 1883; "In the Land of Flowers," *SMN*, December 6, 1883.

23. Grismer, *Tampa*, 174; Smyth, *Life of Henry Bradley Plant*, 70; Bruton and Bailey, *Plant City*, 72–73; "Growth of Tampa," *NYTr*, December 11, 1891.

24. "Tampa's First Train Came Forty Years Ago Today," *Tampa Daily Times*, January 24, 1924; "Lost on Terra Ceia Bay," *NYT*, April 27, 1884.

25. "Henry B. Plant," *ACh*, February 8, 1884; "National Bank of Augusta," *ACh*, February 9, 1884; "By Rail to Tampa," *FTU*, February 12, 1884; "The Man about Town," *AC*, February 24, 1884; "Expressmen's Aid Society," 49–60; "Southern Florida: Railroad and Express Notes," 35; *Southern Reporter*, 906; "Jay Gould in Southern Waters," *NYT*, March 2, 1884; "Four Lines Made One," *NYT*, March 2, 1884; "S. F. & W. Railway," *SMN*, March 6, 1884; "What Young Expressmen Should Do," 102; "Steam-Yacht 'Atalanta,'" *FM*, March 8, 1884; "Georgetown Railroad," *AC*, March 11, 1884; "Another of Jay Gould's Schemes," *National Republican* (Washington, DC), March 14, 1884; "Reflections," *FM*, March 15, 1884; "Financial and Industrial," *National Tribune* (Washington, DC), March 20, 1884.

26. "Way Down South," *SMN*, March 21, 1884.

27. "S. F. & W. Railway," *SMN*, March 6, 1884; "Heaviest Mortgage on Record," *Union and Recorder* (Milledgeville, GA), June 10, 1884; "Railroads Consolidation," *MWT*, March 7, 1884; "Savannah, Florida and Western," *AC*, March 8, 1884; "Metropolitan Trust Company of New York in New Quarters," 168–70; "Legislature's Work," *NYT*, March 15, 1881; "Metropolitan Trust Co., the City of New York," *NYT*, February 8, 1882; "Financial: Metropolitan Trust Company, of the City of New York," *NYT*, October 8, 23, 1883; "Sudden Death of M. E. S. Sanford," *PT*, September 10, 1882.

28. "Florida—The Means of Entering and Traveling Her Sunny Clime," 103–104.

29. Mueller, *Steamships of the Two Henrys*, 143–44; "Man about Town," *AC*, February 24, 1884; "Off for Florida," *NHER*, March 21, 1884; "State Press," *PDN*, June 8, 1884.

30. Smyth, *Life of Henry Bradley Plant*, 150, 153.

31. Smyth, 151–54.

32. Ortiz, *Emancipation Betrayed*, 33–84; Brown, *Florida's Black Public Officials*, 43–69; Brundage, *Lynching in the New South*, 103–39; 191–207; Jolly, *Founding of LePageville*, 2–3; "Over the Plant System," *SMN*, March 16, 1890; "In Memoriam: Henry Wadsworth Reed," *Waycross (GA) Herald*, December 22, 1900; *Savannah Tribune*, June 22, 1889, 2, August 31, 1889, 3; "Colored School at Waycross Dedicated," *Savannah Tribune*, September 7, 1889; "R. and H. D. Meeting," *Savannah Tribune*, September 8, 1900.

33. "Branford," *NHER*, May 27, June 18, 1884; "Local Matters," *BS*, June 4, 1884; Cum-

mins, *Anything for a Vote*, 130–35; "Blaine in New York," *PI*, October 30, 1884; "Belshazzar Blaine's Feast," *SLPD*, November 5, 1884.

34. "Morning News," *Evening Critic* (Washington, DC), August 28, 1884; *CDES*, August 29, 1884; "B. & W. Sold or Leased," *Advertiser and Appeal* (Brunswick, GA), August 30, 1884; *Americus (GA) Recorder*, September 3, 1884, 1; "New Line to Cuba," *SMN*, November 29, 1884, 4; "Railroad Notes," *NYH*, December 31, 1884.

35. "Opposed to Railroad Consolidation," *PT*, January 5, 1885; "Wabash and Iron Mountain," *CIO*, January 6, 1885; "Personal," *CNC*, January 30, 1885; "President Plant Gone to Cuba," *MT*, February 5, 1885; *SMN*, February 12, 1885, 1; "People vs. Jay Gould," *NYH*, February 17, 1885; "Personal," *FTU*, February 24, 1885; "Voyage to Cuba," *SMN*, February 26, 1885.

36. "Voyage to Cuba," *SMN*, February 26, 1885; "Two Great Sugar Plantations," 277, 280.

37. "Personal," *FTU*, February 24, March 5, 1885; "Voyage to Cuba," *SMN*, February 26, 1885; "Notable Wedding," *ACh*, October 10, 1885; "Personal," *CNC*, February 27, 1885; "At the Hotels," *CNC*, February 28, 1885; "B. & W. Railroad," *AWNA*, February 28, 1885; Akin, *Flagler*, 117; "Gould's Western Roads," *PT*, March 2, 1885; "Railroad Intelligence," *SMN*, March 5, 1885; "State and the South," *CNC*, March 7, 1885; "Notes of Various Interests," *NYT*, March 13, 1885; "Colonel Whitfield's Death Song," *NYH*, March 20, 1885; "Items," *CDT*, March 22, 1885; "On the Wing," *CIO*, March 29, 1885; "Plant Downed," *CE*, March 30, 1885; "Florida Gossip," *CIO*, April 29, 1885.

38. *Annual Report of the Postmaster General*, 114–16; "Gotham Gleanings," *CDT*, June 29, 1885; "William Cramp & Sons," *MT*, July 4, 1885; "Daily Mail to Cuba," *CNC*, July 8, 1885; "Fast Mail to Cuba," *CNC*, August 21, 1885.

39. "Saratoga Crowded," *NYH*, August 23, 1885; "Only a Frequent Visitor," *BDE*, September 22, 1885; "Notable Wedding," *ACh*, October 10, 1885; Carhart, *Genealogy of the Morris Family*, 317–18; "Notice," *NHDH*, March 9, 1837; "Card," *ACh*, May 9, 1851; "Office of Southern Express Company," *CC*, January 6, 1865; "Letter from Hot Springs, Ark.," *ADC*, October 20, 1868; "Ocean House!," *Stamford (CT) Advocate*, August 11, 1876; Barton, *Historical and Commercial Sketches*, 121; "At the Altar," *BDE*, October 7, 1885.

40. "At the Altar," *BDE*, October 7, 1885; "Connecticut—Georgia," *LCJ*, October 8, 1885; "Ex-Governor English Married," *NYH*, October 8, 1885.

41. Mueller, *Steamships of the Two Henrys*, 21–23; "Fast Mail Steamship Launched," *NYT*, October 23, 1885; "Marine Notes," *BP*, October 24, 1885; "Mascotte Launched," *FM*, October 31, 1885; Mesa, *Opera*, 168; "'La Mascotte' at the Bijou Opera House," *NYH*, May 6, 1881; "Brilliant Reception at New Haven," *NYW*, November 5, 1885; "Ex-Gov. English at Home," *NYT*, November 5, 1885; "New Haven (Conn.) Notes," *NYW*, November 8, 1885; "Mascotte," *ACh*, December 3, 1885; "Testing a New Iron Steamship," *NYT*, December 17, 1885; "Trying a New Steamship," *MWT*, December 22, 1885.

42. Mueller, *Steamships of the Two Henrys*, 23–24; "News in Brief," *NHER*, December 28, 1885; "Steamer to Cuba," *CNC*, December 30, 1885; "Plant's Steamers," *AC*, January 4, 1886; "Ocean Palace," *SMN*, January 4, 1886.

CHAPTER 11

1. Reynolds, *Henry Plant*, 132.

2. Graham, *Mr. Flagler's St. Augustine*, 43–45; Akin, *Flagler*, 116–18; Ingraham, "Sketch," 29; *TT*, December 15, 1888, 2.

3. Graham, *Mr. Flagler's St. Augustine*, 44–45.

4. "Land of Flowers," *PT*, March 22, 1886.

5. Reynolds, *Henry Plant*, 163; "News about Town," *NHER*, January 18, 1886; "Funeral of Mrs. H. P. Hoadley," *NHER*, January 22, 1886.

6. Reynolds, *Henry Plant*, 163.

7. "In the Land of Flowers," *NYW*, January 31, 1886; "American Ports," *NYH*, Feb-

ruary 5, 1886; "Viajero Distinguido," *NHER*, February 14, 1886; "Mrs. Frank Leslie," *CNC*, February 28, 1886; English, *In Memoriam*, 34. Mrs. Leslie presented a fuller account of the 1886 Cuban trip in Leslie, "Cuban Bygones."

8. "Cuba for Annexation," *MT*, September 29, 1887; "Two Great Sugar Plantations," 277; Prince, *Cuba Illustrated*, 50–51, 103; "Beautiful Island of Cuba," *PT*, April 4, 1886; "On the Island of Cuba," *Weekly Wisconsin* (Milwaukee, WI), March 37, 1886.

9. "Local News" and "Board of Trade Meeting," *Tampa Guardian*, March 24, 1886; *AC*, March 27, 1886, 5; Ogle, *Key West*, 97; "Key West Destroyed," *South Florida Courier* (Plant City, FL), April 3, 1886; "Blaze at Key West," *SMN*, April 11, 1886.

10. "Tampa: The Metropolis of the Gulf," *Tampa Guardian*, February 17, 1886; "Floridiana," *FTU*, May 6, 1886; Grismer, *Tampa*, 182–83.

11. "Jacksonville, Tampa and Key West R. R.," *SMN*, April 7, 1886; "Florida's Metropolis," *SMN*, April 11, 1886; "South Florida," 681; Curtis, *Trade and Transportation*, 343–45; *PT*, August 27, 1886, 4; "West India Fast Mail," *TT*, November 6, 1886; "Mr. Plant and His Railroads," *CNC*, November 22, 1886.

12. "Miscellaneous Railway Intelligence," *NYTr*, November 18, 1886; "H. B. Plant's Scoop," *CE*, November 30, 1886.

13. "W. and W. R. R. Co. Fifty-first Annual Meeting," *RNO*, November 21, 1886; "Mr. Plant and His Railroads," *CNC*, November 22, 1886; "Ruler over Many Things," *CNC*, November 20, 1897; "General Railway News," *SMN*, November 24, 1886.

14. "General Railway News," *SMN*, November 24, December 10, 1886; "Georgia, Alabama and Florida," *CDES*, December 15, 1886.

15. Covington, *Plant's Palace*, 59; "Well-Known Architect Dead," *Poughkeepsie (NY) Eagle-News*, December 22, 1910; "Which Way Will They Go," *AWNA*, September 29, 1883; "Piney Woods Hotel" and "Rising Anew from Its Ashes," *TT*, October 13, 1883; *TT*, December 27, 1884, 1.

16. Mueller, *Steamships of the Two Henrys*, 24–25; "Maritime Miscellany," *NYH*, February 17, 1887; Curtis, *Trade and Transportation*, 352; "Atlanta Personals," *MT*, February 25, 1887; "General Railway News," *SMN*, February 26, 28, 1887; "Railway Notes," *CNC*, February 27, 1887; "Local Personal," "Six Per Cent. Increase," and "Hotel," *SMN*, March 2, 1887; "Open Letter Discussion," *ACh*, March 2, 1887; "Local Personal," *SMN*, March 3, 1887; "Forest City Notes," *CNC*, March 3, 1887; "Savannah, Ga., March 2," *NYT*, March 3, 1887; "Savannah," *MT*, March 4, 1887; "Proposed New Southern Railroad," *NYH*, March 5, 1887; "Sherman as a Reorganizer," *Kansas City (MO) Times*, March 12, 1887; "Railroad Magnates," *TTr*, March 11, 1887; "Senator Sherman in Florida," *PDN*, March 11, 1887; "Junketing Senators," *NYH*, March 11, 1887; "Senators in Cuba," *Olean (NY) Democrat*, March 31, 1887; "Story of a Hotel," *AC*, December 22, 1893.

17. "Story of a Hotel," *AC*, December 22, 1893; "Wild Winds," *PDN*, March 19, 1887; "Senator Sherman's Party," *Cleveland (OH) Leader*, March 20, 1887; "Sherman's Return," *CDT*, March 20, 1887; "Notes from Florida," *FTU*, March 22, 1887.

18. "Great South," *Sunny South* (Atlanta, GA), March 26, 18878; "Notes from Tampa," *FTU*, March 22, 1887; "Tampa," *PDN*, March 30, 1887.

19. Grismer, *Tampa*, 186–87; Covington, *Plant's Palace*, 56–57; "Tampa on a Boom," *FTU*, March 16, 1887.

20. "Tampa Twistings," *FTU*, September 2, 1887.

21. Covington, *Plant's Palace*, 57; William Drysdale, "A Flying Trip to Cuba," *NYT*, July 14, 1889.

22. "Venice of the South," *FTU*, June 23, 1889.

23. Covington, *Plant's Palace*, 57; "Port Tampa Hotel Opening," *TJ*, January 31, 1889; "Floridiana," *FTU*, February 3, 1889; "Gath," *CE*, April 6, 1889; "Sporting at Port O'Tampa," *FTU*, June 6, 1889; "Venice of the South," *FTU*, June 23, 1889.

24. "American Ports," *NYH*, April 20, 1887; "Foreign Ports," *NYH*, April 27, 1887; "Olivette at Key West," *PDN*, April 28, 1887; "New Steamer Olivette," *NODP*, April 28,

1887; "Olivette," *TTr*, April 29, 1887; "Personal Points," *TTr*, May 6, 20, 1887; "Jacksonville, May 5," *PDN*, May 6, 1887; "Local Personal," *SMN*, May 11, 1887; "Long Branch Wide Awake," *NYT*, June 6, 1887; "Loiterers at Long Branch," *NYT*, June 27, 1887; "Will Preach in Branford Sunday," *NHER*, July 22, 1887; "Notes from Richfield Springs," *Utica (NY) Daily Press*, August 26, 1887; "Society News," *Richfield Mercury* (Richfield Springs, NY), September 1, 1887; "For the International Yacht Races," *NYT*, September 23, 1887; "Olivette's First Trip," *NYT*, September 25, 1887; "Democratic Devotees," *NYH*, October 1, 1887; "New York to the South," *CNC*, November 19, 1887; "Mobile and Ohio," *Daily Inter Ocean* (Chicago, IL), November 22, 1887; "Northeastern Railroad," *CNC*, November 26, 1887; "Railroad Chess Moves," *BH*, December 21, 1887; "Great Railroad Alliance," *CNC*, December 22, 1887; "Passing Events in Society," *Evening World* (New York, NY), December 30, 1887; "State Items," *Florida Dispatch* (Jacksonville, FL), June 7, 1886; "Personals," *PDN*, February 27, May 19, 1887; "Local Personal," *SMN*, May 6, 1887; "Plant-Capron," *BS*, June 24, 1887; "Plant-Capron," *SMN*, June 26, 1887; "At the Hotels," *Ottawa (ON) Journey*, July 14, 1887; "Hotel Arrivals," *Victoria (BC) Daily Colonist*, August 8, 1887; "Local Briefs," *Charlotte (NC) Observer*, October 20, 1887; "Personal," *PDN*, February 9, 1888.

25. Covington, *Plant's Palace*, 58–59; "J. A. Wood," no pagination, in Thomas, *Lapham-Patterson House*; "The Oglethorpe," *Weekly Advertiser-Appeal* (Brunswick, GA), January 13, 1888; "Hotel," *SMN*, March 2, 1887; "Tampans Once Went Dry by Local Option," *TTr*, October 20, 1929; "City News," *Tampa Weekly Journal*, January 26, 1888; "Big Hotel for Tampa," *FTU*, February 3, 1888; "Tampa's Prosperity," *FTU*, February 8, 1888.

26. Graham, *Mr. Flagler's St. Augustine*, 27; "Personal," *CNC*, January 11, 1888; miscellaneous newspaper clippings, Loring Chase Scrapbooks, vol. 1, 261, 263–65, 268–69, Rollins College Archives and Special Collections, Winter Park, FL; "Glances Here and There," *NYTr*, February 2, 1888; "In Delightful Florida," *BH*, February 24, 1888; "President's Tour," *PI*, February 27, 1888; "City News," *Tampa Weekly Journal*, March 1, 1888; "Florida's Metropolis," *SMN*, March 2, 1888; "Junction in the Pines," *CNC*, March 4, 1888; "Charleston and Savannah," *CNC*, March 6, 1888; "Local Personal," *SMN*, March 6, 1888; "At Winter Park," *Critic* (Washington, DC), March 7, 1888; "Plant System," *SMN*, March 8, 1888; "S. F. & W. Railroad," *ACh*, March 8, 1888; *Weekly Advertiser-Appeal* (Brunswick, GA), March 9, 1888, 6; "Hotel," *Tampa Weekly Journal*, March 29, 1888; "News from St. Augustine," *Daily News Herald* (Jacksonville, FL), April 10, 1888.

27. "New from St. Augustine," *Daily News Herald* (Jacksonville, FL), April 10, 1888; "Millions in a Hotel," *AC*, April 29, 1888; "Celebrating in Florida," *Auburn (NY) Bulletin*, April 2, 1888.

28. "Sparks from the Cable," *NYH*, April 18, 1889; "Cubans Want Independence," *NYH*, April 21, 1888; "William B. Dinsmore Dead," *NYH*, April 21, 1888; "W. B. Dinsmore's Funeral," *NYTr*, April 24, 1888; "Personal," *BJ*, May 15, 1888.

29. Covington, *Plant's Palace*, 58; Reynolds, *Henry Plant*, 166; "New Steamboat Line," *BH*, June 16, 1888; "World of Society," *NYW*, May 13, 1888; "Plant Party," *TJ*, January 3, 1889; "Will Savannah Suffer?," *CNC*, June 4, 1888; "It Doesn't Look That Way," *TT*, June 9, 1888; "Plant's Programme," *CNC*, June 11, 1888.

30. "Olivette," *BH*, June 23, 1888; "New Line to Bar Harbor," *BH*, June 25, 1888; "Of Local Interest," *BHR*, June 28, August 9, 1888; "It Doesn't Look That Way," *TT*, June 9, 1888; "Tampa's Big Hotel," *FTU*, July 27, 31, 1888; "Society Notes," *BP*, July 12, 1888; "Society Notes," *BHR*, August 2, 1888; "News about Town," *NHER*, August 3, 1888; "Mt. Desert Canoe Club," *BP*, August 4, 1888.

31. "Summer," *New York Amusement Gazette*, June 25, 1888; "Society," *New York Amusement Gazette*, August 13, 1888; Eirlys, "Sneaky, Cowardly Enemy," 6–19; Davis, *History of Jacksonville*, 180–86; Brown, *In the Midst of All*, 163–65; "Articles for Jacksonville, Fla.," *Hickory (NC) Press*, September 20, 1888; "Colonel Elliott's Views," *Evening Bulletin* (Maysville, KY), September 16, 1898; "Mr. Plant Wants Federal Troops," *CNC*, September 17, 1888; "Pulsifer Is Dead," *AC*, October 22, 1888; "Col. Pulsifer's Death," *SR*, October 22,

1888; "Around the State," *Stamford (CT) Advocate*, November 23, 1888; "Lorenzo Blackstone's Funeral," *BH*, November 18, 1888.

32. "Tramp of the Tourist," *CNC*, November 11, 1888; Covington, *Plant's Palace*, 61; *TT*, December 15, 1888, 2.

33. "From Ty-Ty," *CDES*, December 20, 1888; "Georgia and Florida," *SMN*, December 22, 1888; "Plant System," *CNC*, December 25, 1888; "H. B. Plant's Plans" and "To Open the New Depot," *SMN*, January 1, 1889; "Plant Party," *TJ*, January 3, 1889; clipping dated January 11, 1889, Loring Chase Scrapbooks, vol. 1, 304, Rollins College Archives and Special Collections, Winter Park, FL; "Florida on the Move," *SMN*, January 7, 1889; "Augusta National Bank," *SMN*, January 9, 1889; "National Banks," *ACh*, January 9, 1889; "Railroad Magnates in Augusta," *CNC*, January 9, 1889; "Head of the Plant System," *CNC*, January 29, 1889; "On Rail and Crosstie," *SMN*, January 30, 1889; "Florida Travel," *AC*, January 30, 1889; "Port Tampa Hotel Opening," *TJ*, January 31, 1889.

34. "Fair Fountain City," *CNC*, February 5, 1889; "Mr. Plant and Party Arrive in Montgomery, Ala.," *NODP*, February 7, 1889; "Personal and General Notes," *NODP*, February 8, 1889; "Railroads," *NODP*, February 9, 1889; "Dinner at the St. Charles" and "Society," *NODP*, February 10, 1889; "Railroad Racket," *NODP*, February 25, 1889; "Plant Party" and "Railroad Magnates," *NODP*, February 26, 1889; "Capt. H. B. Plant's Palatial Car," *Memphis Appeal*, February 28, 1889; "Arrivals at Thomasville," *SMN*, February 28, 1889; "House on Wheels," *CNC*, March 3, 1889.

35. "Capt. H. B. Plant's Palatial Car," *Memphis Appeal*, February 28, 1889; "Plant Party," *NODP*, February 26, 1889; "House on Wheels," *CNC*, March 3, 1889; Drysdale, "Number 100," 622–24.

36. "Capt. H. B. Plant's Palatial Car," *Memphis Appeal*, February 28, 1889; "House on Wheels," *CNC*, March 3, 1889; "S. F. & W.'s Tenth Year," "Southern Express Company," and "Made Vice President," *SMN*, March 7, 1889; "Forest City Notes," *CNC*, March 7, 1889; "Items in Three States," *SMN*, March 11, 1889; "Sports Well Patronized," *NYH*, March 13, 1889; "Florida's Metropolis," *SMN*, March 13, 1889; "S. F. & W.'s Tenth Year" and "Distinguished Visitors," *Bainbridge (GA) Democrat*, March 14, 1889; "Mr. Cleveland's Trip to Cuba," *Plain Dealer* (Cleveland, OH), March 14, 1889; "Cuba," *NODP*, April 2, 1889.

37. "Touches from Tampa," *FTU*, March 19, 1889; "Rail and Crosstie," *SMN*, March 21, 1889; "At St. Augustine," *St. Louis (MO) Republic*, March 21, 1889; "Mr. Cleveland's Trip," *NYH*, March 21, 1889; "Grover in His Glory," *SMN*, March 22, 1889; "Cleveland at Key West," *SMN*, March 23, 1889; "Cleveland in Havana," *SMN*, March 24, 1889; "Arrival of President Cleveland—His Reception by the People and Departure for Havana," *NODP*, March 23, 1889; "Mr. Cleveland and Party at Havana," *BS*, March 25, 1889; *NODP*, April 2, 1889, 4 ; "El General Salamanca y Mr. Cleveland," *Novedades* (New York, NY), April 4, 1889.

38. "Cleveland in Havana," *SMN*, March 24, 1889; "Mr. Cleveland and Party at Havana," *BS*, March 25, 1889; "Cleveland's Jaunt," *NYH*, March 26, 1889; "Cleveland Comes Back," *NYH*, March 28, 1889; "Cleveland's Return," *SMN*, March 28, 1889; "Tampans Once Went Dry by Local Option," *TT*, March 29, 1889; "Cleveland in Florida," *NYH*, March 29, 1889; "Cleveland Party at Tampa, Fla.," *Cincinnati Commercial Tribune*, March 29, 1889; "Tampa News," *FTU*, April 2, 1889; "Floridiana," *FTU*, April 9, 1889; "Cleveland Goes Fishing," *BH*, March 30, 1889; "Ex-President Cleveland and Party Catches Speckled Beauties," *Pittsburgh Daily Post*, March 30, 1889; "Monster Tarpon," *Pittsburgh Daily Post*, April 3, 1889; "Local Laconics," *Florida Star* (Titusville, FL), April 4, 1889.

CHAPTER 12

1. "Monster Tarpon," *Pittsburgh Daily Post*, April 3, 1889; "Homeward Bound," *NYT*, April 5, 1889; "Cleveland Party," *Buffalo (NY) Courier*, April 5, 1889; "Grover Speeding Home," *MT*, April 5, 1889; "City and Suburban," *Daily Critic* (Washington, DC), April 10, 1889.

2. "Poughkeepsians in Florida," *Poughkeepsie (NY) Daily Eagle*, March 1, 1889; "Cleveland in Florida," *NYH*, March 29, 1889; "President Plant's Plans," *AC*, May 10, 1889; "City News," *TJ*, May 9, 1889; "State News," *Florida Star* (Titusville, FL), July 10, 1889.

3. "City News," *TJ*, May 9, 1889; "Crossing the Atlantic," *NYTr*, May 16, 1889; "List of Visitors Registered at 'Low's Exchange,' 44 Charing Cross, Trafalgar Square, London, up to Date," *New York Amusement Gazette*, June 10, 1889; Covington, *Plant's Palace*, 62; "Fruits and Fancies of a Short Trip through Florida," *NYH*, April 6, 1890; "Hotel Notes," *TJ*, October 31, 1889; *BDA*, April 14, 1891, 4; *TTr* quoted in "Music-Box Run by Steam," *Albany (NY) Times*, October 2, 1890.

4. Covington, *Plant's Palace*, 62; *Orange County Reporter* (Orlando, FL) quoted in "H. B. Plant in Paris," *TJ*, May 30, 1889; *Biographical Souvenir of the States of Georgia and Florida*, 193–94; "Paris Exposition," *TJ*, July 18, 1889.

5. Smyth, *Henry Bradley Plant*, 61–62; "Paris Exposition," *TJ*, July 18, 1889; "Carolinian Abroad," *CNC*, July 31, 1889.

6. "Carolinian Abroad," *CNC*, July 31, 1889; "Our Florida Letter," *Columbia Republican* (Hudson, NY), August 29, 1889.

7. *Biographical Souvenir of the States of Georgia and Florida*, 193; "Buffalo Bill's Parisian Opening," *BDE*, May 19, 1889; "Les Gaillards de Paris," *NYH*, July 28, 1889; "Very Close to the Record," *NYT*, August 1, 1889; "Things and Other Things," 389.

8. "Mr. Plant at the French Exposition," *NHER*, August 6, 1889; "Halstead Interviewed," *NYH*, July 21, 1889; "Fashion and Varieties," *Freeman's Journal* (Dublin, Ireland), July 23, 1889; "Latest by Cable," *BH*, July 26, 1889; "Very Close to the Record," *NYT*, August 1, 1889; "Nearly Four Minutes Late," *NYH*, August 1, 1889.

9. "Arrivals," *DS*, August 8, 1889; "Summer Notes from New Haven," *NYTr*, August 11, 1889; "New Haven," *NYP*, August 11, 1889; "In Old Connecticut," *NYET*, August 17, 1889; "Table Gossip," *Boston Sunday Globe*, August 18, 1889; "Corridor and Piazza," *DS*, August 24, 1889; "Society Notes," *NYET*, August 26, 1889; "Steamship Juniata," *PI*, August 28, 1889; "Of Local Interest," *BHR*, August 29, 1889; "String of Saratoga Pearls," *NYH*, September 1, 1889; "Cheap Excursion Rates," *TJ*, October 3, 1889; "International Congress," *Worchester (MA) Daily Spy*, September 2, 1889; "American Congress," *NODP*, October 11, 1889; "Congressional Delegates," *Wilkes-Barre (PA) Times Leader*, October 11, 1889; Plant, *Reply of H. B. Plant*, 1; "Tampa to Be a Great Port," *NYTr*, October 17, 1889.

10. "About People We Know," *CNC*, November 3, 1889; "Plant Party," *TJ*, November 7, 1889; "Alabama," *NODP*, November 12, 1889; "Handsome Coach," *TDTE*, November 14, 1889; "Mobile Commerce" and "Mobile," *NODP*, November 15, 1889; "Short Lines," *St. Louis (MO) Republic*, November 17, 1889; "Speculative World," *CIO*, November 19, 1889; "Direct to South America," *Indianapolis Journal*, November 20, 1889; "Projected Line of Steamers," *NODP*, November 21, 1889; "Plant Party" and "Men and Things about Town," *CE*, November 21, 1889.

11. "Local and General News" and "The Ship Comes In," *TTr*, December 19, 1889; "Scene of Enchantment," *TDJ*, April 14, 1890; "Banana Train," *AC*, April 13, 1890.

12. "Of Local Interest," *BHR*, August 29, 1889; "Hotel Notes" and "City News," *TJ*, October 31, 1889; "New Hotel at Tampa, Fla.," *NYT*, January 17, 1890.

13. "City in Brief," *TDJ*, January 29, 31, 1890; "Society," *New York Amusement Gazette*, February 3, 1890; "Mr. Plant in Macon," *MT*, February 27, 1890; "Plant Will Fight Closing," *NHER*, February 6, 1901; "Cuba," *NODP*, April 2, 1889; "Caught in New York," *SLPD*, January 3, 1890; "Heavy Defalcation," *Topeka (KS) Daily Capital*, January 8, 1890.

14. "City in Brief," *TDJ*, February 5, 7, 12, 1890; "Salvation Moving Tampa," *FTU*, February 11, 1890; "Salamanca Dead," *Evening World* (New York, NY), February 7, 1890; "H. B. Plant's Trip South," *SMN*, February 26, 1890.

15. "Playing a Big Game," *CDES*, March 21, 1890; "Mobile and Ohio," *NODP*, February 20, 1890; "Local Personal," *SMN*, February 25, 1890; "H. B. Plant's Trip South," *SMN*, February 26, 1890; "Mr. Plant in Macon" and "H. B. Plant in Atlanta," *MT*, February 27, 1890; "St. Louis Exporting Flour via Mobile," *NODP*, March 2, 1890; "Snow in the Fountain City"

and "Our Distinguished Visitors," *CNC*, March 3, 1890; "Plant Directors' Trip," *SMN*, March 3, 1890; "Plant Directors," *SMN*, March 4, 1890; "Off for the Land of Flowers," "Forest City Notes," and "Charleston and Savannah," *CNC*, March 4, 1890; "Vice President Morton in Savannah," *Pittsburgh Dispatch*, March 4, 1890; "Vice President Morton," *AC*, March 5, 1890; "Columbus Southern," *AC*, March 8, 1890; "To Chautauqua Directors," *AWNA*, March 8, 1890; "Vice Presidential Party," *TDJ*, March 14, 1890; "Over the Plant System," *SMN*, March 16, 1890; "'Doing' Florida," *ACh*, March 15, 1890; "Winter in Florida," *New York Age*, March 15, 1890; "To Meet the Harrison Party," *BH*, March 16, 1890; "Vice President's Southern Trip," *NYP*, March 17, 1890; "City in Brief," *TDJ*, March 19, 24, 26, April 7, 1890; "From Monday's Daily Journal" and "Interview with H. B. Plant," *TJ*, March 20, 1890; "Call on Mrs. Harrison," *TDJ*, March 21, 1890; *TDJ*, March 22, 1890, 2; Judd, *Affection*, I, 170–75; "Charmed with the South," *Charlotte (NC) News*, March 24, 1890; "Off They Go for Florida," *NYH*, March 30, 1890; "Idling in Florida," *CIO*, April 2, 1890; "Affairs in Augusta," *CNC*, April 23, 1890; "Society News and Chat," *Sunday Herald* (Washington, DC), April 27, 1890; "Personal and Pertinent," *NYW*, June 5, 1890.

16. "Personal and Pertinent," *NYW*, June 5, 1890.

17. Noël and Stoullig, *Les annales du théatre et de la musique avec une préface par M. Ludovic Halévy*, 250–52; "Grand Duchess," *PI*, June 1, 1890; "Dramatic Notes," *SLPD*, June 1, 1890.

18. "Of Local Interest," *BHR*, June 26, 1890; "Another Ponce de Leon," *CNC*, July 3, 1890; North, "Building of the New Tampa Bay Hotel," 33–34; "Only a Summer Trip" and "Tampa Topics," *TTr*, July 10, 1890; "Alabama Road Sold," *Brooklyn (NY) Daily Eagle*, July 10, 1890; "Sale Perfected," *TDTE*, July 11, 1890; *TDTE*, July 11, 1890, 1; "There Will Be No Changes," *AC*, July 12, 1890; "Local Paragraphs," *Manatee River Journal* (Bradenton, FL), July 17, 1890; "Floridiana," *FTU*, July 17, 1890.

19. "Died," *NYH*, July 16, 1890; "Arrivals," *DS*, July 24, August 14, 1890; J. E. Ingraham to My Darling Wife, August 1, 1890, James Edmundson Ingraham Papers, P. K. Yonge Library of Florida History, University of Florida, Gainesville.

20. "Table Gossip," *Boston Sunday Globe*, August 31, 1890; "Of Local Interest," *BHR*, September 4, November 20, 1890; "Work on the Tampa Bay Hotel," *BH*, September 7, 1890; "Extension of Trade," *BH*, November 9, 1890; "Death of F. B. Knowles," *Worchester (MA) Daily Spy*, May 16, 1890; "Sale of a Florida Hotel," *Worchester (MA) Daily Spy*, January 23, 1891; "Floridiana," *FTU*, November 13, 1890.

21. "New Line to Jamaica," *KDG*, October 22, 1890; "Fast Time to the West Indies," *NYW*, October 24, 1890; "Arrival of the Olivette," *KDG*, October 29, 1890; "Departure of the 'Olivette,'" *KDG*, October 30, 1890; "Plant's Line to Jamaica," *SMN*, November 3, 1890; "Extension of Trade," *BH*, November 9, 1890; "Trip to Jamaica," *AC*, November 10, 1890.

22. "Walter Chisholm," *NYH*, December 6, 1890; "Ex-Judge Walter Scott Chisholm Dead," *NYTr*, December 6, 1890; "Death of Judge Chisholm," *SMN*, December 6, 1890; "In Honor of the Dead," *SMN*, December 7, 1890; "At Rest under the Oaks" and "Local Personal," *SMN*, December 8, 1890; "Death of Judge Chisholm," *NYW*, December 6, 1890; *TDTE*, December 6, 1890.

23. "Plant Investment Co.," xxx; "Col. Haines the Man," *TDTE*, January 15, 1891; "Will Move to New York," *Bainbridge (GA) Democrat*, January 29, 1891; Mesic, *Cobb's Legion Cavalry*, 245; "General Manager Jack Resigns," *NYTr*, July 2, 1890; "Robert Gallaudet Erwin," *Trinity Tripod* (Hartford, CT), January 16, 1906; "Firm Reorganized," *AC*, March 16, 1891.

24. "Comment on the Plant Plan for Grabbing the Alabama Midland," *NYH*, May 3, 1891; "Railroads," *NODP*, December 16, 1890; "Among the Railroads," *AC*, December 17, 1890.

25. *NOTD*, February 5, 1891, 4; "About People We Know," *CNC*, January 20, 1891; "En Route for Tampa," *CNC*, February 5, 1891.

26. Covington, *Plant's Palace*, 65. See also McKay, *Pioneer Florida*, II, 428–29.

27. "Mrs. H. B. Plant Critically Ill," *NHER*, July 20, 1892; "Sweet Palace of Rest," *CDT*,

February 14, 1891; "Mobile Matters," *NOTD*, February 19, 1891; "Lie in Bed and Fish," *CIO*, February 26, 1891; "Plant Officials," *AC*, March 1, 1891; "To Divide the Money," *CNC*, March 2, 1891; "Millionaires in It," *CNC*, March 3, 1891; "Sweet Palace of Rest," *FTU*, March 3, 1891; "S. F. and W.'s Annual Meeting," *SMN*, March 5, 1891; *TDTE*, March 7, 1891, 1; Johnson, "Early History of the Alabama Midland Railroad Company," 286; "Annual Tour," *AWNA*, March 7, 1891; newspaper clippings, Loring Chase Scrapbooks, vol. 2, 370–71, Rollins College Archives and Special Collections, Winter Park, FL; "Alabama Midland Meeting," *AC*, March 7, 1891; "White Squadron," *WES*, March 12, 1891; "White Squadron," *AC*, March 14, 1891; "Entertained on the Dolphin," *BH*, March 19, 1891; "Notables in St. Augustine," *CNC*, March 26, 1891; "Facts from Florida," *AC*, March 29, 1891; "Squadron's Cruise," *BS*, April 1, 1891; "Distractions of Southern Travel," *NYEP*, April 4, 1891; "Roman in Florida," *Rome (NY) Daily Sentinel*, April 6, 1891; "On to Tampa," *Marion (OH) Star*, April 7, 1891; "White Squadron," *Marion (OH) Star*, April 9, 1891; "Tampa Topics" and "Reception on the Chicago," *TTr*, April 9, 1891; "Pleasures in Cuba," *BDE*, April 19, 1891.

28. Newspaper clippings, Loring Chase Scrapbooks, vol. 2, 376, 380, Rollins College Archives and Special Collections, Winter Park, FL; Johnson, "Early History of the Alabama Midland Railroad Company," 286–87; "To Scale Down the Interest," *CDT*, May 2, 1891; "'Hanky-Panky' Played on the Bondholders," *NYH*, May 2, 1891; "Comment on the Plant Plan for Grabbing the Alabama Midland," *NYH*, May 3, 1891; "About People We Know," *CNC*, May 5, 1891; "May Interest on Midland Bonds," *NOTD*, June 1, 1891; "Millionaire Visitor," *State* (Columbia, SC), July 7, 1891; "Three Coast Line Magnates," *CNC*, July 8, 1891; "Around in Alabama," *CDE*, July 8, 1891; "Looking at the Terminals," *SMN*, July 8, 1891; "To See the Harbor," *SMN*, July 9, 1891; "Plant Sees the Harbor," *SMN*, July 10, 1891; "Central Deal," *CNC*, July 15, 1891; "Mr. Plant's Movements," *AC*, July 17, 1891; "Delaware Breakwater," *NYH*, July 18, 1891; "Local Personals," *Morning News* (Wilmington, DE), July 24, 1891; "Vacation Season," *NHER*, August 3, 1891.

29. "Yesterday in London," *NYW*, September 13, 1891; "Hamburg-Amerikanische Packetfahrt-Actien-Gesellschaft," *Fremden-Blatt* (Karlsbad, Austria), September 15, 1891; "Mail and Ship News," *Bristol Mercury* (Bristol, England), September 4, 1891; "With Nitrate's King," *SLPD*, November 8, 1891; Brown, *Florida's Peace River Frontier*, 312–15; *Financial Times* (London, England) quoted in "Chamber: The Proceedings at Yesterday's Meeting," *Los Angeles Herald*, December 12, 1891.

30. "Yesterday in London," *NYW*, September 13, 1891; "Tampa of Today," *TTr*, November 12, 1891; "Choses de Paris," *Gil Blas* (Paris, France), August 6, 1891; "'Lohengrin' in Paris," *Times* (London, England), September 17, 1891; "Opera House Rioters," *NYH*, September 19, 1891.

31. "Americans in Europe," *SLPD*, September 27, 1891; "On the City of Paris," *NYT*, October 8, 1891; "New York City," *NYTr*, October 8, 1891; "Shipping News," *NYTr*, October 9, 1891; "Henry Sanford in John Hoey's Shoes," *NYH*, October 14, 1891; "Action against John Hoey," *NYT*, October 17, 1891; "Gotham Gossip," *NODP*, October 19, 1891; "Legal Action," *NODP*, October 21, 1891; "Hoey Gave Up Half a Million," *NYH*, December 21, 1891.

32. "Tampa Topics," *TTr*, October 15, 1891; "Good Morning, Gentlemen," *CNC*, November 1, 1891; "H. B. Plant and M. J. O'Brien and Party in This City," *SMN*, November 1, 1891; "Mr. Plant on a Tour of Inspection," *AC*, November 8, 1891; "Mr. Plant Arrives," *TTr*, November 5, 1891; "Tampa's Friend Mr. H. B. Plant Talks Briefly to a Tribune Reporter" and "Tampa of Today," *TTr*, November 12, 1891.

33. "Looking over the Road," *AC*, November 14, 1891; "Investigating the Road," *AC*, November 15, 1891; "Railway World," *AC*, November 17, 1891; "Mr. Plant Is Pleased," *CNC*, November 19, 1891; "Wilmington and Weldon Railroad," *BS*, November 24, 1891.

34. *TDTE*, November 17, 1891, 2; "Vanity Fair," *NYP*, December 13, 1891; "Richmond Terminal Crisis," *CNC*, December 16, 1891; "Inspecting the Property," *CNC*, December 31, 1891; "Rail and Crosstie," *SMN*, January 1, 1892.

35. "Cuban Party," *RNO*, January 14, 1892; "Opening of the Tampa Bay Hotel," *LCJ*,

January 16, 1892; "Georgia and Florida," *SMN*, January 17, 1892; "Personals," *Evening Telegram* (Jacksonville, FL), January 18, 1892; "Jaunt in South Florida," *NYT*, May 16, 1892; "Etched and Sketched," *AC*, January 22, 1892.

36. "Scrap Heap," *AC*, February 2, 1892; "Mrs. H. B. Plant Critically Ill," *NHER*, July 20, 1892; "Georgia and Florida," *SMN*, February 16, 1892; "Plant Planned a Railroad across the Peninsula," *MH*, January 3, 1922; "Tampa Palace," *SMN*, March 15, 1892; Edward F. Flanner, "Romance of Miami and the Miami Section, Where Sunshine Turns to Gold: Period XVII," *MH*, January 22, 1925.

37. "Brunswick's Depot," *MWT*, February 24, 1892; "Local Personal," *SMN*, February 26, 1892; "To Keep the Fast Mail," *SMN*, February 27, 1892; "All around Town," *CNC*, February 28, 1892; "Plant System," *CNC*, March 1, 1892; "Trio of Millionaires," *SMN*, March 2, 1892; "City by the Sea," *State* (Columbia, SC), March 2, 1892; "S., F. & W.'s Annual Meeting," *SMN*, March 3, 1892; "Director's Train," *TDTE*, March 5, 1892; "Plans Here," *AWNA*, March 5, 1892; "Tennis in the South," *NYT*, February 13, 1892; "Tennis Players to Go South," *NHER*, March 3, 1892; "In the Field of Sports," *NYEP*, March 14, 1892; "Tampa Palace," *SMN*, March 15, 1892; "Tennis Finals at Tampa," *NYW*, April 3, 1892; "Plant's Project," *NODP*, April 10, 1892; "Wayside Notes," *New Orleans Item*, April 18, 1892; "News from Cuba," *KDG*, April 26, 1892.

38. Telegram, H. B. Plant to Mrs. J. E. Ingraham, April 11, 1892, Ingraham Papers; "Local Brevities," unidentified clipping dated April 16, 1892, Loring Chase Scrapbooks, vol. 2, 402, Rollins College Archives and Special Collections, Winter Park, FL; "In a Reminiscent Mood J. E. Ingraham Tells St. Augustine Record of Early Days," *MH*, June 17, 1915; "Memory of Late Henry M. Flagler Honored at Unveiling of Bronze Table Yesterday," *MH*, November 13, 1920; "Plant Planned a Railroad across the Peninsula," *MH*, January 3, 1922; "J. E. Ingraham's Career in Florida Full of Achievement for the State; A Developer," *MH*, February 12, 1922; "Ingraham Funeral Is Set for Tuesday," *MH*, October 27, 1924; Flanner, "Romance of Miami and the Miami Section," *MH*, January 22, 1925. On Ingraham's journey of exploration, see Marchman, "Ingraham Everglades Exploring Expedition."

39. "Mrs. H. B. Plant Critically Ill," *NHER*, July 20, 1892; "Mrs. Henry B. Plant Very Ill," *NYT*, July 26, 1892; "Georgia and Florida," *SMN*, December 20, 1893; "Mrs. Plant Recovering," *NYT*, July 28, 1892; "White Squadron," *Marion (OH) Star*, April 9, 1891.

40. "Florida Project," 617; "New Line to Florida," *TDTE*, June 22, 1892; "New Railroad Deal," *CNC*, July 6, 1892; "Between Boston and Halifax," *BH*, June 28, 1892; "Newspapermen at Halifax," *BH*, June 30, 1892.

41. "Winter Park Whisperings," unidentified clipping, Loring Chase Scrapbooks, vol. 2, 408, Rollins College Archives and Special Collections, Winter Park, FL; "Railroads," *NODP*, July 19, 1892; "R. T. Committees," *NYS*, August 10, 1892; "Travelers and Others," *CNC*, August 16, 25, 1892; "Lease of the South Bound," *TDTE*, August 19, 1892; "Personal Mention," *Waycross (GA) Herald*, August 20, 1892; "Doing Little Building Now," *SMN*, August 24, 1892; "New Richard Peck," *NHER*, September 10, 1892; "Railway Traffic," *AC*, September 21, 1892; "No Trace of Greye," *NYP*, October 17, 1892; "Missing Otis Greye's Florida Land Schemes," *NYH*, October 18, 1892; "Otis Greye's Frauds," *St. Louis (MO) Republic*, October 24, 1892; "Autumn Diversions of Our Society," *NYH*, November 6, 1892.

42. Ayers, *Promise of the New South*, 274–75; "Southern Railroads Mean Business," *NYH*, November 15, 1892; "John Hoey Lies Close to Death," *NYH*, November 13, 1892; "Death of John Hoey," *PT*, November 15, 1892; "Obituary," *NYTr*, November 15, 1892; "I. C. Plant's Death," *CDE*, November 17, 1892; "Funeral of John Hoey," *BDE*, November 17, 1892; "Tributes to John Hoey," *NYW*, November 17, 1892.

43. "Railroad Magnates," *Watchman and Southron* (Sumter, SC), November 23, 1892; "Charleston and Savannah Railway," *CNC*, November 26, 1892; "Election of Officers," *RNO*, November 26, 1892; "Charleston & Savannah Railroad," *Charlotte (NC) Observer*, November 27, 1892; "Southern Express Company" and "Carries His Years Lightly," *SMN*, November 29, 1892; "Southern Express Company," *NT*, November 29, 1892; "Meeting of the Sa-

vannah, Florida and Western Railroad," *Roanoke (VA) Times*, November 30, 1892; "Annual Tour," *TDTE*, December 1, 1892; "Railroads," *Weekly Star* (Washington, DC), December 2, 1892; "Alabama Midland," *NT*, December 3, 1892; "Robbing the Express," *NODP*, December 4, 1892; "No Trouble on the S. F. & W. Ry.," *TDTE*, December 11, 1892; "Local Personal," *SMN*, December 12, 1892; "Southern Express Company," *AC*, February 16, 1893.

44. "Floridiana," *FTU*, October 29, 1891; "Babylon Local Record," *South Side Signal* (Babylon, NY), April 23, 1892, January 14, March 18, December 2, 1893, January 5, November 30, 1895, April 25, 1896, March 13, December 4, 1897; Wilson Percival entry, 1900 federal census manuscript, Babylon, NY, Suffolk County, 13; "Local," *Weekly Saratogian* (Saratoga Springs, NY), August 12, 1875; "Lelands," *Kalamazoo (MI) Gazette*, September 12, 1877; "Moral Show," *Lowell Daily Courier* (Lowell, MA), April 1, 1881; "From New York," *Freeman* (Indianapolis, IN), April 5, 1902; "Leading Head Waiters," *Freeman* (Indianapolis, IN), December 27, 1902; "Waiter," *Freeman* (Indianapolis, IN), December 12, 1902.

45. "Local Personal," *SMN*, Monday, December 12, 1892; "Excursions to Jamaica," *CDE*, January 17, 1893; "New Winter Resort Trip," *Buffalo (NY) Express*, January 21, 1893; "Jollity at Lakewood," *NYH*, January 1, 1893; "South Land!," *Daily Plainsman* (Huron, SD), January 5, 1893; Henry B. Plant wills, Polk County, FL, Will Records, Wills, 1883–1912, vol. 1–2, 164–74.

46. "Passing Throng," *AC*, February 3, 1893; "Mr. Plant in Savannah," *SMN*, February 6, 1893; "Florida Travel and Crops," *BS*, February 11, 1893; "Plant's Big Interests," *SMN*, February 7, 1893; "To-Night's Banquet," *SMN*, February 8, 1893; "Trade Men Dined," *SMN*, February 9, 1893; "Editorial Correspondence," *LJR*, February 23, 1893; "Excursion to Jamaica," *CNC*, February 17, 1893; "Halifax," *KDG*, February 22, 1893; Clark, *Gilded Age*, 151; Dobson, *Bulls, Bears, Boom, and Bust*, 181–82.

CHAPTER 13

1. White, *America's Fiscal Constitution*, 131; Wicker, *Banking Panics of the Gilded Age*, 58; Steeples and Whitten, *Democracy in Desperation*, 1.

2. Telegram, Mr. and Mrs. H. B. Plant to Hon. Grover Cleveland, March 5, 1893, Grover Cleveland Papers, LC; "Object Lesson," *New Orleans Item*, March 12, 1893; "How Proud Was Our Society at Washington," *NYH*, March 12, 1893; "Mrs. Logan's Fishing Luck in Florida," *NYS*, March 20, 1893; "Tennis Players at Tampa," *BDE*, March 22, 1893; "Tennis Tournament Ended," *Boston Sunday Globe*, March 26, 1893; Homer Reed, "Well-Groomed Yankees," quoted from *Atlanta Journal* in *Keowee Courier* (Pickens, SC), April 27, 1893.

3. "Just from Jamaica," *AC*, March 17, 1893; "Mrs. Logan's Fishing Luck in Florida," *NYS*, March 20, 1893; William Drysdale, "Fishing by Special Train," *NYT*, April 16, 1893; Drysdale, "Sport on Florida Waters," *NYT*, May 7, 1893; "Editorial Briefs," *TDTE*, April 1, 1893; "What Is the Future?" *TWT*, April 11, 1893.

4. "New Steamer Line," *BP*, February 9, 1893; "Gen. Plant President," *BH*, April 19, 1993; "Go to Halifax," *BDE*, July 8, 1894; "Midwinter Glimpse of Florida," *AC*, March 17, 1895.

5. "Haines to Go," *TDTE*, May 22, 1893; *TDTE*, April 20, 1893, 3; "Florida News," *Evening Telegram* (Jacksonville, FL), May 11, 1893; "Savannah, Florida and Western," 325; "Making Progress," *NYW*, December 9, 1893.

6. "Day at Hartford," *NHER*, May 23, 1893; *Special Acts and Resolutions Passed by the General Assembly of the State of Connecticut, at the January Session, 1893*, 658–61; *New York Supplement*, 417.

7. "Our Washington Letter," *BDE*, May 7, 1893; *BH*, May 12, 1893, 7; "Tribute to Mr. Plant," *TDTE*, May 16, 1893; *NOTD*, June 12, 1893, 4; "Local Happenings," *TDTE*, June 13, 1893; unidentified clipping dated June 18, 1893, Loring Chase Scrapbooks, vol. 2, 433, Rollins College Archives and Special Collections, Winter Park, FL; "Georgia Glimpses," *CDE*, June 24, 1893; "Elections and Appointments," 312; "Hotel Arrivals," *GDN*, July 31, 1893.

8. Entry for G. Durant in Henry Van Schaict household, 1880 federal census manuscript, New York, NY, New York County, 282A; Durant, *Hygiene of the Voice*; Durant, *Sea-Bathing*; Durant, *Family Physician*; "Hygiene of the Voice," *NYH*, October 21, 1879; "Personal," *NYTr*, August 16, 1884; "Real Estate in Demand," *NYH*, November 8, 1890; "May Contest Plant Will," *NYTr*, November 14, 1893; "Contest over Plant Will," *NYT*, November 15, 1899.

9. "Personal and General Notes," *NODP*, August 30, 1893; "Saratoga," *Albany (NY) Evening Journal*, September 8, 1893; "Railroad Monarch," *Buffalo (NY) Express*, September 10, 1893; "September Days at the Spa," *NYT*, September 10, 1893; "One More Million," *CIO*, September 17, 1893; "World's Fair Notes," *CDT*, November 12, 1893; "S. F. & W.'s Big Locomotive," *TDTE*, January 12, 1894; Covington, *Plant's Palace*, 66; Covington, "Tampa Bay Hotel," 10; "Death of H. P. Hoadley," *NHER*, October 21, 1893.

10. "America's Cup Races, Steamship Olivette," *NYTr*, October 1, 1893; "On the Following Fleet," *NYTr*, October 6, 1893; "Cup Stays Here," *NYTr*, October 14, 1893; "Jamaicans at the Great Yacht Race," *KDG*, October 17, 1893.

11. "Battling the Fever Scourge," *NYT*, August 24, 1893; "Relief Train," *NYW*, October 18, 1893; "Much Damage in Savannah," *NYT*, August 30, 1893; "Along the Waterfront," *BP*, October 20, 1893; "H. P. Hoadley Very Low," *NHER*, October 20, 1893; "Death of H. P. Hoadley," *NHER*, October 21, 1893; "Funeral of Horace P. Hoadley," *NHER*, October 23, 1893.

12. "Flagler's Latest Scheme," *Charlotte (NC) News*, November 2, 1893; Brown, *Florida's Black Public Officials*, 55–56; Ortiz, *Emancipation Betrayed*, 33–78; Woodward, *Origins of the New South*, 279; Henry M. Flagler to Daniel S. Lamont, November 9, 1893, Cleveland Papers.

13. *TTr*, October 31, 1895, 2; Brown, *Florida's Peace River Frontier*, 308; Brown, *In the Midst of All*, 150–54; "Democratic Meeting in Hamilton County, Florida," *SMN*, August 8, 1872; "Personal," *FTU*, December 27, 1896; "Our Tallahassee Representative," *Courier-Informant* (Bartow, FL), April 3, 1895.

14. "Sullivan-Kennedy," *BDE*, November 12, 1893; "Mr. H. B. Plant," *Wilmington (NC) Messenger*, November 22, 1893; "Annual Meeting," *WMS*, November 23, 1893; "After the P. R. & A.," *State* (Columbia, SC), November 24, 1893; "Notable Gathering," *CNC*, November 24, 1893; "Kingly Gathering," *CNC*, November 25, 1893; "Prosperous Prosperity," *CNC*, November 26, 1893; "President Plant Here," *SMN*, November 27, 1893; "S. F. & W. Railway," *SMN*, November 28, 1893; "Doesn't Want It" and "Plant System," *CNC*, November 29, 1893; *TDTE*, November 29, 1893; "S. F. & W.'s Big Year," *SMN*, November 29, 1893; "H. B. Plant at Thomasville," *SMN*, November 30, 1893; "Alabama Midland," *NT*, December 2, 1893; "R. R. Officials," *Waycross (GA) Herald*, December 2, 1893; "Plant System" and "Distinguished Visitors," *TDTE*, December 2, 1893; "Railroad Officials," *Albany (GA) Weekly Herald*, December 2, 1893; "Alabama Midland" and "Abbeville Southern," *CDE*, December 2, 1893; Davis, *History of Jacksonville, Florida*, 199–200; "Five-Ounce Gloves," *AC*, December 6, 1893; "Opening of the Tampa Hotel" and "Georgia and Florida," *SMN*, December 6, 1893; "Lawful to Fight in Florida," *NYH*, December 6, 1893; "Bonded for $20,000,000," *SMN*, December 8, 1893; "Making Progress," *NYW*, December 9, 1893; "Mortgage for $20,000,000," *MT*, December 9, 1893; "Mr. Plant's Reply," *TDTE*, December 12, 1893; "Growing Port Tampa," *SMN*, December 19, 1893.

15. "Mr. Plant on the Fight," *AC*, January 11, 1894; *SMN* quoted in "Tourist Travel," *Thomasville (GA) Weekly Times-Enterprise*, January 13, 1894; "Day Fixed," *TDTE*, January 17, 1894; "Council Proceedings," *TDTE*, January 24, 1894; "No Material Effect," *WES*, January 26, 1894; "Plant System's Annual Excursions to Kingston and Jamaica," *CNC*, February 5, 1894; "Tour of Jamaica," *AC*, February 6, 1894; "Vance in Florida," *Fayetteville (NC) Weekly Observer*, February 8, 1894; "Plant Line Steamers in the Mobile Trade," *NODP*, March 29, 1893; "Drawing People," *TWT*, February 16, 1894; "Just from Jamaica," *TWT*, March 2, 1894.

16. "Southern Enterprises," *Pittsburgh Press*, April 23, 1894; "Jamaica," 66.

17. "Florida Tourist Season," *BS*, April 10, 1894.

18. "Ingraham Funeral Is Set for Tuesday," *MH*, October 27, 1924; *TDTE*, April 20, 1894, 1; "Notes of the Railways," *NT*, April 22, 1894; "Southern Enterprises," *Pittsburgh Press*, April 23, 1894; "Death Roll," *AC*, May 2, 1894.

19. "Summer Schedule on the Coast Line," *CO*, May 2, 1894; "To Open Double Beach to the Public," *NHER*, June 5, 1894; "Old Paris Salon," *NYT*, June 17, 1894; Noël and Stoullig, *Les annales du théatre et de la musique avec une préface par Francisque Sarcey*, 308–9; "Music and the Drama," *LAR*, May 5, 1894; "Courrier des Spectacles," *Le Gaulois* (Paris, France), May 15, 27, 1894; *London Man of the World* (London, England), May 16, 1894.

20. "Shabby Treatment of Southrons," *CDT*, June 23, 1894; "Correspondence," *New York Dramatic Mirror*, June 23, July 21, 1894; "Sacred Concert at Double Beach," *NHER*, June 30, 1894; "Pico Park Was Favorite Amusement Spot," *Branford (CT) Review*, August 20, 1942; "Day on the Water," *NHER*, July 4, 1894; "Go to Halifax," *BDE*, July 8, 1894; "Going to Pico Park," *NHER*, July 23, 1894; list of passengers, steamship *Cienfuegos*, July 17, 1894, M237, Roll 629, Passenger Lists of Vessels Arriving at New York, NY, 1820–1897, NA; "Saratoga Springs," *BH*, July 28, 1889; "Halifax Decorated," *BP*, August 8, 1894; "Entertained at Halifax," *NHER*, August 14, 1894.

21. "Cresson Springs," *PI*, August 19, 1894; "Railroad News," *AC*, August 23, 1894; "Affairs of the Railroads," *NYH*, August 23, 1894; "Table Gossip," *Boston Daily Globe*, August 26, 1894.

22. "New Tariff Law," *NYT*, August 28, 1894; Pérez, *Cuba between Empires*, 31–33; Gibson, *Empire's Crossroads*, 222–23.

23. Gibson, *Empire's Crossroads*, 222–23; Pérez, *Cuba between Empires*, 35–36; Vesa y Fillart, *Voluntarios de la isla de Cuba*, 158–59; "Living under a Reign of Terror," *NYH*, November 2, 1894.

24. Barnes, *Florida's Hurricane History*, 75; "Washouts along Railway Lines Cause a Suspension of Traffic," *NYH*, September 27, 1894; "Damage by the Storm," *NHER*, September 29, 1894; "Storm in Florida," *PI*, September 29, 1894.

25. "Railroad Situation," *Watchman and Southron* (Sumter, SC), October 17, 1894; "Battle of the Rail," *AC*, November 5, 1894; Brown, *Florida's Peace River Frontier*, 290; Peeples, *Punta Gorda*, 26.

26. "Plant System Magnates," *CNC*, October 24, 1894; *Waycross (GA) Herald*, October 27, 1894, 4; "Here and There," *Tropical Sun* (Juno, FL), November 22, 1894; *TDTE*, October 27, 1894; "Notes from Waycross," *CDE*, October 30, 1894; "Battle of the Rail," *AC*, November 5, 1894; "Mr. Plant's Movements," *AC*, November 9, 1894.

27. H. B. Plant to Grover Cleveland, November 17, 1894, Cleveland Papers; "Funeral of W. T. Walters," *RNO*, November 25, 1894; "Annual Meetings," *WMS*, November 22, 1894; "Annual Meetings Held," *AC*, November 25, 1894; "Southern Express Co.," *SMN*, November 26, 1894; "Southern Express Co.'s Year" and "Never Answer Rumors," *SMN*, November 27, 1894; "S. F. & W. Annual Meeting," *SMN*, November 28, 1894; "Old Officers Re-Elected," *AC*, November 28, 1894; "Distinguished Party," *TDTE*, November 29, 1894; "Plant System," *Age-Herald* (Birmingham, AL), December 1, 1894; "Two Annual Elections," *AC*, December 1, 1894; "Plant System Officials Here," *Waycross (GA) Herald*, December 1, 1894; "Hill Down South," *WH*, December 1, 1894; "In the Rotunda," *AC*, December 2, 1894; "Distinguished Visitors," *Bainbridge (GA) Democrat*, December 6, 1894; "From Winter Haven," *TWT*, December 14, 1894; "Railroad Men Talk Politics," *NYW*, December 9, 1894; "Railroads," *NODP*, December 9, 1894; "Railway Men to Meet," *AC*, December 11, 1894; "To Talk Florida Traffic," *SMN*, December 11, 1894; "Fears of a Railroad Fight" and "Big Guns in Session," *SMN*, December 12, 1894; "Florida's Traffic War," *AC*, December 12, 1894; "Southern Railroads Arranging to Pool All Freight Traffic," *NYH*, December 12, 1894.

28. "Nicaragua Canal," *NODP*, December 20, 1894; "Will Deliver Up H. M. Flagler," *NYH*, December 26, 1894; "To Arrest Flagler" and "Flagler Surprised but Polite," *CIO*, December 26, 1894; "Mr. Flagler Not Alarmed," *NYH*, December 27, 1894; "Gov. Mitchell Did His Duty," *TTr*, January 4, 1895; "Plant's New Ship," *TWT*, December 21, 1894; "Their New

Steamship," *AC*, December 26, 1894; "Mr. H. B. Plant's Innovation" and "B. W. Wrenn Is In It," *AC*, December 29, 1894.

29. "Society Event," *AC*, December 17, 1890; "Personal Pickings," *Tropical Sun* (Juno, FL), January 3, 1895; "Cotton States Exposition," *St. Andrews (FL) Buoy*, January 17, 1895; Culberson, *Images*, 100.

30. Martin, *Florida's Flagler*, 153; Brown, *Florida's Peace River Frontier*, 321; "From Florida," *Morganton (NC) Herald*, January 10, 1895; "Seminole Opened," *TTr*, January 2, 1895; "Business Prospects," *WES*, October 26, 1897.

31. "Florida in Mid-Winter," *AC*, January 23, 1895; "Silver Living," *NODP*, January 23, 1895.

32. Brown, *Florida's Peace River Frontier*, 322; Covington, *Story of Southwestern Florida*, I, 194–95, 343–45; Covington, *Plant's Palace*, 67; "Snow Balls in Tampa," *TTr*, February 9, 1895; "Orange Crop Destroyed," *Wilkes-Barre (PA) Record*, March 25, 1896; "Wrenn's Weighty Words," *TTr*, February 26, 1895.

33. "Interesting Letter from Florida," *WH*, February 16, 1895; "Mr. Plant Not Disheartened," *SMN*, February 13, 1895; "Dixie's Railroad Row Ended," *SMN*, February 14, 1895; "Plant Railway System in Europe," *Bainbridge (GA) Democrat*, February 14, 1895; "It May Be Superintendent Haines," *Savannah Morning News*, March 3, 1895.

34. "New Superintendent of the Plant System," *Daily Picayune* (New Orleans, LA), February 17, 1895; "Dunham in Savannah," *Atlanta Constitution*, February 18, 1895; "Railroads," *Cincinnati Enquirer*, February 18, 1895; "General Superintendent," *Bainbridge (GA) Democrat*, February 21, 1895; "Official Order," *TDTE*, February 21, 1895.

35. "Alexandrians in Florida," *Alexandria (VA) Gazette*, February 19, 1895; "Day in Macon," *AC*, February 21, 1895; "Mr. Plant Was Here," *AC*, February 23, 1895; "Rail and Crosstie," *SMN*, February 24, 1895; "President Plant," *NODP*, February 26, 1895; "King Rex," *Sandusky (OH) Register*, February 27, 1895; "Close of Mardi Gras Carnival," *Westville (IN) Indicator*, February 28, 1895; "Local Happenings," *TDTE*, March 1, 1895; "President Plant Visits," *SMN*, March 1, 1895; "It May Be Superintendent Haines," *SMN*, March 3, 1895; *TTr*, March 15, 1895, 1; "Deal Consummated," *TTr*, March 16, 1895; "Added to the Plant System," *NYTr*, March 16, 1895.

36. "Expedition from Tampa," *NYH*, March 8, 1895; "Is the Year of the Sugar Trust," *NYW*, May 12, 1895; "City Brieflets," *TTr*, March 21, 1895; "Detained at Tampa," *Knoxville (TN) Journal*, March 21, 1895; *TTr*, March 31, 1895, 1; "Progress of the Rebellion," *BH*, March 31, 1895; "Cuban Rebels Gaining Ground," *NYH*, April 1, 1895.

37. "Tampa Bay to Close," *TTr*, March 31, 1895; "Cuban Rebels Gaining Ground," *NYH*, April 1, 1895; "Port Tampa!," *TTr*, April 9, 1895; "City Brieflets," *TTr*, April 12, 28, 1895; Reynolds, *Henry Plant*, 179; *TTr*, April 18, 1895, 4; "As to Ashley Junction," *CNC*, April 26, 1895; "H. B. Plant Reaching Out," *SMN*, April 30, 1895; "Mr. Plant in Charleston," *CEP*, April 30, 1895; "Receiving at Railway King," *CNC*, May 1, 1895; "Great Ship Yard," 12, 22–23; "Superintendent Swoope Resigned," unidentified clipping dated May 2, 1895, Loring Chase Scrapbooks, vol. 2, 475, Rollins College Archives and Special Collections, Winter Park, FL; "Promise of Better Things," *CNC*, May 3, 1895; "Superintendent Swoope Resigns," *AC*, May 4, 1895; "New Steamer for the Plant Line," *NODP*, May 7, 1895; "Plant's Enterprise," *BDA*, May 8, 1895; "Plant's New Vessel," *AC*, May 9, 1895; "Have You Heard This?," *CEP*, May 31, 1895; "More Plant System Changes," *TDTE*, May 21, 1895; "Haines to Go," *TDTE*, May 22, 1895; "Resignation of Capt. Owens," *CNC*, May 29, 1895.

38. "State News," *NHER*, May 27, 1895; "Henry B. Plant Better," *NYT*, June 6, 1895; *TDTE*, May 31, 1895; "Right of Way Granted," *CEP*, June 4, 1895; "Atlanta Exposition," *NYT*, July 3, 1895.

39. "To-Day's Topics in France," *PT*, June 9, 1895; "Notes," *BH*, August 18, 1895; "Strange Romance and Tragedy of the Ill-Fated Carolina," *Washington Post*, July 21, 1918.

40. "Strange Romance and Tragedy of the Ill-Fated Carolina," *Washington Post*, July 21, 1918; "Colonel Wrenn Away Up North," *AC*; "Week at Long Island," *NYT*, August 4, 1895.

41. "Colonel Haines Resigns," *NYH*, September 7, 1895; "With the Visitors," *NYH*, September 8, 1895; "Heavy Travel by Rail," *NHER*, September 9, 1895; "Put in Col. Haines's Place," *AC*, September 22, 1895; "Southern News," 259; "Ocala House to Be Sold," *NYH*, October 2, 1895; "To Replace the Margaret," *NHER*, October 7, 1895; Mueller, *Steamships of the Two Henrys*, 145; "Sidewheeler Wrecked," *GDN*, October 7, 1895; "H. B. Plant's Birthday Party," *WH*, October 12, 1895; "What President Plant Said," *RNO*, October 12, 1895; "Mr. H. B. Plant Here," *AC*, October 14, 1895; "Made a Quiet Visit," *AC*, October 15, 1895; "Distinguished Visitors," *TDTE*, October 16, 1895; "Mr. Plant's Views," *OES*, October 16, 1895; *TTr*, October 16, 1895, 1; "Men of Mark," *TTr*, October 17, 1895; "Plant Buys a Hotel," *Bradford County Telegraph* (Starke, FL), October 18, 1895; "Mr. Plant Is in the City," *OES*, October 21, 1895; "President Plant's Birthday," *SMN*, October 24, 1895; "Hammond Elected," *AC*, October 26, 1895; Perdue, *Race and the Atlanta Cotton States Exposition*, 26–28; "Mr. Plant Toasted," *AC*, October 29, 1895; "President Plant Happy," *NYT*, October 29, 1895.

42. "Our Own People," *CEP*, November 23, 1895; "C. and S. Stockholders," *CNC*, November 24, *1895*; "Plant System Officials," *SMN*, November 25, 1895; "Southern Express Company," *CO*, November 26, 1895; "S. F. & W.'s Year's Earnings," *SMN*, November 27, 1895; "Miner-Blum," *NYH*, November 27, 1895; "Plant System Officials," *TDTE*, November 28, 1895; "From the State Capital," *Age-Herald* (Birmingham, AL), November 30, 1895; "Plant People Held a Meeting," *AC*, December 1, 1895; "Deaths" and "Obituary Notes," *NYH*, November 30, 1895; "Additional Locals," *OES*, December 2, 1895; *TTr*, December 3, 1895, 6; "All Aboard!," *TTr*, December 3, 1895; "Season Started," *TTr*, December 7, 1895; "Railway Magnates in Titusville," *TIRA*, December 13, 1895; "President Plant Here," *TTr*, December 13, 1895; *OES*, December 16, 1895, 8; "Local Personal," *SMN*, December 18, 1895; "Sanford and Florida," *SMN*, December 19, 1895; "Prominent Railroaders Here," *AC*, December 19, 1895; "City in Brief," *RNO*, December 19, 1895; "Mr. H. B. Plant Here," *AC*, December 20, 1895; "Etched and Sketched," *AC*, December 21, 1895; "Orange Traffic," *AC*, December 25, 1895.

43. "Leaves for Augusta" and "Jamaica Line of Steamers," *AC*, January 1, 1896; "Strike Talk on the Plant System," *SR*, January 2, 1896; "Florida Orange Crop Good," *TTr*, January 3, 1896; "Newport News Nuggets," *NV*, January 7, 1896; "Newport News," *RD*, January 9, 1896; "President Plant," *CEP*, January 10, 1896; "Hearing to Be Had," *CNC*, January 11, 1896; "Margaret's Successor" and "Plant to See the Engineers," *SMN*, January 11, 1896; *OES*, January 11, 1896; "Plant's Acceptance" and "Six Winter Excursions," *OES*, January 13, 1896; *TTr*, January 14, 1896, 1; "Late Shipping News," *NODP*, January 28, 1896; "Jamaica Ginger," *TTr*, January 28, 1896; "No Date Has Yet Been Set," *SMN*, January 28, 1896; "War and Peace Are Sisters," *CEP*, January 30, 1896; "Star of the Sea," *TTr*, January 31, 1896; "Succesfully Launched," *NV*, January 31, 1896; "Plant's New Steamer" and "To Meet with the Engineers," *SMN*, January 31, 1896.

CHAPTER 14

1. "Six Winter Excursions," *OES*, January 13, 1896; *TTr*, March 13, 1896, 2; Stark, *Stark's Jamaica Guide*, 55–56; "Wheelmen Back from Jamaica," *BS*, March 13, 1896; "Col. Plant in Kingston," *KDG*, March 20, 1890; "Jamaica Journey," *TTr*, March 21, 1896; *TTr*, March 24, 1896, 4.

2. *OES*, February 26, 1896; "Under the Post's Eyes," *CEP*, March 18, 1896; "Plant Buys Another Hotel," *AC*, October 15, 1896; *OES*, August 17, 1896, 1; "Plant's Latest Purchase," *SMN*, October 15, 1896; "What Col. B. W. Wrenn Has to Say about the Tourists," *TTr*, October 15, 1896; "Plant System Plans," *TTr*, May 5, 1896; "Plant's New Paradise," *TTr*, August 23, 1896; "It Is Belleair," *TTr*, November 19, 1896; *TTr*, April 12, 1896, 2.

3. "Improvement the Order," *Indian Chieftain* (Vinita, OK), October 15, 1896; "Charmed at the Casino," *TTr*, December 4, 1896; Covington, *Plant's Palace*, 68–69.

4. "Strange Romance and Tragedy of the Ill-Fated Carolina," *Washington Post*, July

21, 1918; "Mr. H. B. Plant Here," *AC*, April 23, 1896; "Large Docket," *NV*, April 28, 1896; "Grande Duchesse," *NV*, September 18, 1896.

5. "Mr. H. B. Plant Here," *AC*, April 23, 1896; "Miss Andrade's Will Be a Very Venezuelan Wedding," *Washington Times*, April 1, 1896; Smyth, *Life of Henry Bradley Plant*, 294; "New Steamer Margaret," *NHER*, June 4, 1896; "Branford News," *BO*, June 5, 12, 27, July 18, August 1, 15, 22, 1896; "Branford Budget," *NHER*, June 26, 1896; "Branford," *NHER*, July 23, 31, September 2, 1896; "Margaret Is Not Coming," *NHER*, July 29, 1896.

6. "Life of H. B. Plant," *OES*, May 11, 1896; "Branford News," *BO*, August 22, 1896; Henry Bradley Plant application, Sons of the American Revolution Membership Applications, 1889–1970, National Society of the Sons of the American Revolution, Louisville, KY; "Among the Hotels," *Indian River Advocate* (Titusville, FL), January 28, 1898.

7. "To Meet with the Engineers," *SMN*, January 31, 1896; "Engineers Conference," *CEP*, February 1, 1896; "Met Them at Waycross," *SMN*, February 3, 1896; "Plant and His Men," *AC*, February 3, 1896; "Engineers' Meeting," *WH*, February 8, 1896; "Engineer Futch Is Out," *WH*, February 15, 1896; "Railway Notes," *AC*, March 5, 1896; "Plant System," *Indianapolis News*, January 19, 1897; Caldwell, "Relief and Hospital Department," 22–27; "Plant System Relief Fund," *WH*, July 5, 1896; "Plant System R. & H. Department," *WH*, May 15, 1897.

8. "Branford," *NHER*, September 2, 1896; "Newport News," *NV*, September 18, 19, 1896.

9. Barnes, *Florida's Hurricane History*, 77; "Raging Storm" and "Storm at Tampa," *TTr*, September 30, 1896; "Great Loss of Life in Florida," *Americus (GA) Times-Recorder*, October 3, 1896; "Terrific Storm," *WH*, October 3, 1896; "Our Own People," *CEP*, October 5, 1896; "Grand Duchess to Run Here," *SMN*, October 6, 1896; "Local News," *Kissimmee (FL) Valley*, October 7, 1896; "Mr. Plant and Party Arrives," *TTr*, October 7, 1896; *TTr*, October 8, 1896, 1; "Grande Duchesse," *BS*, October 8, 1896; "Day of Crime and Disaster," *MT*, October 10, 1896; "First, Minnie M. Fisk," *TTr*, October 11, 1896; "Mr. Plant's Party," *OES*, October 13, 1896; "Plant's Latest Purchase," *SMN*, October 15, 1896; "Plant Buys Another Hotel," *AC*, October 15, 1896; "Plant's New Purchase," *TTr*, October 17, 1896; unidentified clipping, dated October 17, 1896, Loring Chase Scrapbooks, vol. 2, 438, Rollins College Archives and Special Collections, Winter Park, FL; "Branford News," *BO*, October 17, 24, 1896; "Mr. Plant Is in the City," *WH*, October 17, 1896; "Not Coercing His Men," *AC*, October 20, 1896; "Branford," *NHER*, October 21, 1896; "Concluded with a Trip," *Times* (Richmond, VA), November 20, 1896.

10. "Railroad Earnings," *CNC*, November 22, 1896; "Plant System Officials," *SMN*, November 23, 1896; "Southern Express Officers," *SMN*, November 24, 1896; "H. B. Plant Re-Elected," *RNO*, November 24, 1896; "Distinguished Visitors," *TDTE*, November 26, 1896; *TDTE*, November 28, 1896, 1; "Plant Party," *TTr*, November 29, 1896; "Charmed at the Casino," *TTr*, December 4, 1896; "To Meet the Grand Duchess," *SMN*, December 11, 1896; "New Casino at Tampa," *New York Dramatic Mirror*, December 12, 1896; "Viewed the Grand Duchess," *SMN*, December 12, 1896; *TTr*, December 13, 23, 24, 1896, 1; "Tampa Bay Hotel Topics," *TTr*, December 18, 25, 1896; "Epitome of Spicy Events," *TTr*, December 20, 1896, January 6, 7, 15, 1897; "Confederates Convene," *TTr*, December 29, 1896; Sterling, *Marion County, Alabama, Newspaper Clippings*, 11–12; "Security for Uncle Sam," *TTr*, January 20, 1897; "Delegates Inspect Proposed Fort Sites," *NODP*, January 22, 1897; "Branford News," *BO*, January 23, 1897; "Tampa, Fla., January 22," *PT*, January 23, 1897; Cosmas, *Army for Empire*, 47, 51–53.

11. McCullough, *Brave Companions*, 80–81; Dyal, *Historical Dictionary*, 17–18; "Stain on the Flag," *CDT*, February 12, 1897; "Lakes on Every Hand," *NYT*, February 21, 1892; "Seeing the Sights in Florida," *Elyria (OH) Reporter*, March 4, 1902.

12. "Truth Is Clearly Told," *TTr*, February 23, 1897; *Lakeland (FL) Sun* quoted in "A Person Named Plant," *Hopkinsville Kentuckian*, March 30, 1897.

13. "Local News," *TIRA*, March 12, 19, 1897; "Tribune Timely Topics," *TTr*, March 16,

1897; Dern, "Recollections," 50; "Tampa Bay Tourists," *TTr*, March 20, 1897; "Inflow of Tourists," *KDG*, March 26, 1897; "Florida's First Trip," *TTr*, March 31, 1897; "H. B. Plant's Tarpon," *Fort Myers (FL) Press*, April 15, 1897; "Mr. Plant Writes about His Tarpon Catch," *Fort Myers (FL) Press*, April 22, 1897; "Road to Fort Myers," *Fort Myers (FL) Press*, May 13, 1897; "Plant Visits Ft. Meade," *FTU*, April 8, 1897; "Mr. H. B. Plant," *TTr*, April 9, 1897; "Commencing to Close," *TTr*, April 13, 1897; "Local Happenings," *TDTE*, April 24, 1897; "West Coast Will Win," *TTr*, April 28, 1897; "Plant System Notes," *TTr*, April 29, 1897.

14. "West Coast Will Win," *TTr*, April 28, 1897; xerographic copy, Franklin Q. Brown to A. J. Hanna, January 24, 1938, notebook volume: Henry Plant, Part One, Henry B. Plant Museum Archives, Tampa; Johnson, "Plant's Lieutenants," 385–87; "Col. F. Q. Brown" in De Groff, *Heart of the American Rhine*, no pagination; "Railroad Men and Matters," *NYT*, May 25, 1897.

15. "Ohio Man," *Plain Dealer* (Cleveland, OH), February 21, 1897; "Bill Snort Letters," *Tammany Times* (New York, NY), July 4, 1898; "Chelsea History," *NYS*, August 5, 1944.

16. "Five Lives Lost at Sea," *NYT*, April 11, 1897; "Loss of the Nellie Smith," *CO*, April 12, 1897; "Plant System Notes," *TTr*, April 29, 1897; "He Owns the Plant System," *San Francisco Call*, June 6, 1897.

17. "Branford News," *BO*, May 22, 1897; "Incidents in Society," *NYW*, May 18, 1897; "H. B. Plant Here," *Asheville (NC) Citizen-Times*, May 22, 1897; "President Plant Here," *NT*, May 24, 1897; "Society," *NT*, May 25, 30, 1897; "Immense Tarpon Captured by Mr. H. B. Plant," *NT*, May 31, 1897; "Personal Notes," *Evening Tribune* (San Diego, CA), June 1, 1897; "Local Intelligence," *San Diego Union* (San Diego, CA), June 3, 1897; "He Owns the Plant System" and "Coronado," *SFC*, June 6, 1897; "Millionaire Plant and His Big Fish from Florida," *SFC*, June 10, 1897; "Mr. Plant on His Way to Japan," *TTr*, June 12, 1897; "Hotel Arrivals," *SFCh*, June 12, 1897; "Plant Tells of the Coming Fish Congress," *SFCh*, June 13, 1897; "Personal," *SFC*, June 13, 1897; "Under the Post's Eyes," *CEP*, June 14, 1897; "Movement of Steamers," *SFCh*, June 17, 1897; "Departure of the China Steamer," *SFCh*, June 18, 1897; *North China Herald* (Shanghai, China), July 9, 1897, 6; "Mail and Steamship News," *London Standard* (London, England), July 15, 1897; "Summary of News," *North China Herald* (Shanghai, China), July 16, 1897; "Export of Tea to the United States and Canada," *North China Herald* (Shanghai, China), August 6, 1897; "Foreign Ports," *SFC*, August 6, 1897; "Has Been Training with the Ministry," *SFCh*, September 23, 1897; "In the Land of the Mikado," *SMN*, November 22, 1897; Smyth, *Life of Henry Bradley Plant*, 295.

18. "Passengers" and "Wharf and Wave," *Hawaii Gazette* (Honolulu, HI), September 17, 1897; "Commissioner Plant Coming," *SFCh*, September 21, 1897; "Annexation," *BDA*, September 23, 1897; "Active Politics in Hawaii," *SR*, September 23, 1897; "China-Japan," *BDA*, September 24, 1897; "Has Been Training with the Ministry," *SFCh*, September 23, 1897; "Hotel Arrivals," *SFC*, September 23, 1897; "Young Old Man," *ACh*, October 14, 1897; "Quiet Visit," *Pacific Commercial Advertiser* (Honolulu, HI), October 7, 1897; Smyth, *Life of Henry Bradley Plant*, 295.

19. "Cuba Wants Only Freedom," *Democrat and Chronicle* (Rochester, NY), October 4, 1897; "White House Callers," *Evening Times* (Washington, DC), October 25, 1897; "Business Prospects," *WES*, October 26, 1897; "Cuba's New President," *NYS*, November 22, 1897; "Cuban Planters Want Money," *NYS*, December 10, 1897; "Fever Spreads in Jamaica," *NYS*, October 23, 1897; "Business Bad in Jamaica," *NYT*, December 22, 1897.

20. "Business Prospects," *WES*, October 26, 1897; "Ruler over Many Things," *CNC*, November 20, 1897.

21. "President Plant in Charleston," *CEP*, November 19, 1897; "Ruler over Many Things," *CNC*, November 20, 1897; "Successful Year," *CNC*, November 21, 1897; "Taking Their Yearly Trip," *SMN*, November 21, 1897; "In the Land of the Mikado," *SMN*, November 22, 1897; "Southern Express Co.," *BS*, November 23, 1897; "S. F. & W. Annual Meeting," *ACh*, November 24, 1897; "Brunswick and President Plant," *AC*, November 24, 1897; "Plant Lines," *AC*, November 26, 1897; "Union Passenger Depot," *Tifton (GA) Gazette*, November 26,

1897; "New Officers Elected" and "Plant Party," *WH*, November 27, 1897; "Good Showing," *TDTE*, November 27, 1897; "Plant's Programme," *TTr*, November 28, 1897; *OES*, November 29, 1897, 1; unidentified clipping dated December 4, 1897, Loring Chase Scrapbooks, vol. 2, 523, Rollins College Archives and Special Collections, Winter Park, FL; "How to Be Happy," *TTr*, December 4, 1897; "Plant System Officials Elected," *TDTE*, December 4, 1897; "Plant's Party," *TTr*, December 5, 1897; "On Board the Olivette," *TTr*, December 10, 1897; "Winter Festivities Resumed," *LCJ*, December 11, 1897; "Tampa Bay Topics," *TTr*, December 16, 1897; "Florida Season," *AC*, December 17, 1897; "Central Makes Promotions," *SMN*, December 18, 1897; "Will See Who Was to Blame," *SMN*, December 19, 1897; *TTr*, December 21, 1897, 4; "Miss Kerwin Pleased," *TTr*, December 25, 1897.

22. "Cuba to Export Tobacco" and "Cuba's New Government," *NYT*, December 30, 1897; "H. S. Pennington Resigns," *SMN*, December 20, 1897; "Gun and Rod," *BJ*, January 1, 1898; *TTr*, January 9, 1898, 1; *TTr*, January 15, 1898, 4; "Friends of Florida" and "Fish! Fish! Fresh Fish!," *TTr*, January 18, 1898; "Delegates Delighted" and "At the Tampa Bay," *TTr*, January 23, 1898; "Royal Welcome to Tampa's Harbor and River," *TTr*, January 25, 1898; "Cold Wave," *TTr*, February 3, 1898.

23. "New Line to Central America," *BDE*, February 6, 1898; "Back from Florida" and "Kentuckians in Florida," *LCJ*, February 6, 1898; "Plant Line Excursion," *NODP*, February 8, 1898; "Business Ended, Now on Pleasure Bent," *TTr*, February 10, 1898; "Eighteen Miles down Tampa Bay," *Logansport (IN) Times*, February 11, 1898; *TTr*, February 12, 1898, 1; "Praised by H. B. Plant," *TTr*, February 20, 1898; *TTr*, February 15, 1898, 1; Johnson, "Plant's Lieutenants," 385–86; *TTr*, February 20, 1898, 4; "Prominent Visitor," *NOTD*, February 22, 1898; "Railroad News from All Around," *NODP*, February 22, 1898.

24. "Plant Royally Welcomed by People of Polk," *TTr*, March 4, 1898; "Off for Jamaica," *TTr*, March 6, 1898; "Returned from Jamaica," *TTr*, March 16, 1898; Richard Danielson, "Troops Battled Chaos before the War," *St. Petersburg (FL) Times*, April 24, 1998; "Plenty Pertinent Pickings Plucked," *TTr*, March 25, 1898; "Miami Mince Meat," *Miami Metropolis*, April 1, 1898; "Off to Nassau," *TIRA*, April 1, 1898; "Returned from Nassau," *TTr*, April 5, 1898; "Local News," *TIRA*, April 8, 1898.

25. "Rush of the Fleeing Refugees," *TTr*, April 8, 1898; "Americans in Havana Are Threatened," *ACh*, April 9, 1898; "Mr. Plant's Ship," *BS*, April 5, 1898; "Epitome of Spicy Events," *TTr*, April 9, 1898; "Mrs. Plant's Tarpon Catch," *BS*, April 19, 1898; "How a Woman Landed a Bass," *NYS*, April 20, 1898.

26. DeMontravel, *Hero to His Fighting Men*, 415; Schellings, "Advent of the Spanish-American War," 312–19; Cosmas, *Army for Empire*, 90; Johnson, "Plant's Lieutenants," 385–86; F. Q. Brown to My darling Ida, April 22, 1898, Franklin Quimby Brown Papers, 1898, folder April 1898, University of Miami Special Collections; Berner, *Spanish-American War*, 364; "Spain Must Back Down," *BDA*, April 11, 1898; "Tampa, Fla., April 22," *New York American*, April 22, 1898; "Tampa Bay Hotel Taken," *TTr*, April 22, 1898; "Gen. Graham Greeted," *TTr*, April 25, 1898; "Hotel," *TTr*, April 26, 1898; "Social," *CE*, April 28, 1898; "Military Hop," *TTr*, May 1, 1898.

27. "Busy Tampa," *TDTE*, May 5, 1898; "La Grande Duchesse," *Daily Press* (Newport News, VA), May 6, 1898; "Wade's Div., United States Troops," *Army and Navy Journal* (New York, NY), May 7, 1898; "Governor's Banquet," *TTr*, May 19, 1898; *TTr*, May 12, 1898, 4; "Spy Story Exploded," *SFCh*, May 21, 1898; "Our Opportunity," *TTr*, May 28, 1898; "Practice for Dixie's Guns," *NYTr*, May 31, 1898; Morris, *Edith Kermit Roosevelt*, 175–76; Samuels and Samuels, *Teddy Roosevelt at San Juan*, 62–63; Morris, *Rise of Theodore Roosevelt*, 656.

28. "Florida's Great Man," *North Adams (MA) Transcript*, June 4, 1898; "Greatest Man in Florida," 561; "Tall Barber's War Talk," *NYP*, May 25, 1898; "Plant and His Big System," *Daily Telegram* (Adrian, MI), May 27, 1898.

29. "From Tampa and Mobile," *San Antonio (TX) Light*, June 12, 1898; "First Troops in Cuba," *SMN*, June 12, 1898; Robert B. Cramer, "Little Stories of the War," *AC*, September 21, 1898; "Brave Boys in Blue Leaving Home Shores," *BDE*, June 12, 1898; "Embarkation,"

NYEP, June 13, 1898; "Safe at Sea," *TTr*, June 15, 1898; "Pointed for Groton," *BH*, June 18, 1898; "Tampa's Camp to Stay," *NYS*, June 19, 1898; "Why the Troops Could Not Hurry," *NYH*, June 20, 1898; H. B. Plant to The President, June 20, 1898, William McKinley Papers, LC; Robert B. Cramer, "Little Stories of the War," *AC*, September 21, 1898.

30. "In the Railroad World," *SMN*, June 25, 1898; "Mr. Plant Returns," *TTr*, June 26, 1898; *TTr*, June 28, 1898, 4; "New York," *NYH*, July 3, 1898; "Bowling in the Catskills," *CDT*, July 24, 1898; "In the Catskills," *NYH*, August 7, 1898; "Branford News," *BO*, July 30, 1898; "Incidents at Long Beach," *NYTr*, August 7, 1898; John Addison Porter to H. B. Plant, July 4, 14, 1898, H. B. Plant to The President, July 25, 1898, McKinley Papers, LC.

31. "Branford News," *BO*, July 30, 1898; "Along the Water Front," *BP*, July 30, 1898; "Movements of Ocean Vessels," *BDE*, August 9, 1898; J. A. Porter to H. B. Plant, August 26, 1898, McKinley Papers, LC; "An Interesting Assertion," *WES*, August 22, 1898; *SMN*, August 25, 1898, quoted in "Plant's Pet," *TTr*, August 26, 1898; "May Buy Up Cuban Bonds," *ACh*, August 26, 1898; "Telegraphic Notes," *BH*, September 12, 1898; "Branford," *BO*, September 16, 1898.

32. Cosmas, *Army for Empire*, 243–44; "Hospital Ship Olivette Sinks," *NYTr*, September 1, 1898; "No Loss to Government," *BJ*, September 3, 1898; "Wind-Up," *Cleveland (OH) Leader*, September 6, 1898; "Olivette Floats Again," *BH*, September 29, 1898; "Domestic," *BH*, October 16, 1898.

33. "Olivette," *TTr*, January 31, 1899; "Dinner to General Lee," *BS*, October 5, 1898; "Branford," *NHER*, October 21, 1898; "Branford Budget," *NHER*, November 4, 1898; "Notable Event in Chattanooga," *CDE*, October 29, 1898; "Will Arrive on Tuesday," *TTr*, October 30, 1898; "In the Railroad World," *SMN*, October 31, November 8, 1898; "Mr. Plant Passes Through," *OES*, November 1, 1898; "Mr. Plant's Visit," *TTr*, November 2, 1898; "Epitome of Local Events," *TTr*, November 3, 1898; *TTr*, November 5, 1898, 1; "Mr. Plant in Town," *TDTE*, November 6, 1898; "Local Happenings," *TDTE*, November 8, 1898; "Democrats Give Up Hope of Congress," *New York American*, November 8, 1898; "Congress Is Divided," *NYT*, November 9, 1898; "Local News and Views," *OES*, November 9, 1898.

34. "Railroad Magnate Ill," *Jersey Journal* (Jersey City, NJ), November 11, 1898; "H. B. Plant's Illness Short," *NYT*, November 12, 1898; "Illness of Henry B. Plant," *NHER*, November 12, 1898.

35. "Chronique Maritime," *Le Matin* (Paris, France), December 2, 1898; "H. B. Plant Ill Again," *BO*, November 26, 1898; "Personal," *Daily Morning Journal and Courier* (New Haven, CT), November 26, 1898; "Plant Meetings," *TTr*, November 29, 1898; "H. B. Plant Improving," *NYT*, December 8, 1898; "H. B. Plant Well Again," *NYH*, December 13, 1898; "New Books of December," *PT*, December 17, 1898; "Branford," *NHER*, January 6, 1899; "Personal Mention," *Daily Morning Journal and Courier* (New Haven, CT), January 7, 1899.

36. "Henry B. Plant Goes to Tampa," *NYT*, January 17, 1899; "Central's Directors Meet," *SMN*, January 17, 1899; "Epitome of Local Events," *TTr*, January 17, 1899; "About Town," *Branford (CT) Semi-Weekly Record*, January 21, 1899; "Fine Performance," *TTr*, January 22, 1899; "Brilliant," *TTr*, June 26, 1899; "Havana Service" and "Offended," *TTr*, January 28, 1899; "Will Benefit Tampa" and "Olivette," *TTr*, January 31, 1899; "Heard about Town," *NYT*, February 1, 1899; "Judge Harrison Returns," *NHER*, February 2, 1899; *TTr*, February 3, 1899, 1; *CIO*, February 8, 1899, 5.

37. *TTr*, February 25, 1899, 3; "Off for a Cruise," *TTr*, March 2, 1899; "Indianians Take a Practice March," *LCJ*, March 4, 1899; "Dots and Dashes," *Marion (OH) Star*, March 7, 1899; "Growing," *Akron (OH) Beacon Journal*, March 7, 1899; "Upsetting Abner's Schemes," *WMS*, March 14, 1899; "Snap Shots," *Labor World* (Duluth, MN), March 18, 1899.

38. "River Notes" and "Visit to Cuba," *TTr*, March 11, 1899; *TTr*, March 12, 1899, 1; "Windsor Burned; Many Lost" and "McKinleys' Escape," *NYTr*, March 18, 1899; "Fearful Death in Burning Hotel," *PT*, March 18, 1899; "Hotel Holocaust," *Tyrone (PA) Daily Herald*, March 23, 1899; "Human Fragments Found," *Marietta (OH) Daily Leader*, March 25, 1899; "More Bodies Taken Out," *NYTr*, March 25, 1899.

39. "Tribune Timely Topics," *TTr*, March 14, 21, 1899; "Delightful Cuba," *Virginian-Pilot* (Norfolk, VA), March 16, 1899; "Yachting Notes," *NYH*, March 21, 1899; "National Capital," *Indiana State Journal* (Indianapolis, IN), March 22, 1899; "Epitome of Local Events," *TTr*, March 28, 1899; "Smallpox in the Scrub," "Direct Service," and "Docks All Burned Down," *TTr*, March 29, 1899.

40. "Will Plant Get the Property?" *AC*, April 1, 1899; "From Tampa to Charleston," *CNC*, April 4, 1899; "Plant Gets Another Road," *SMN*, April 4, 1899; "Ocala Occurrences," *OES*, April 4, 1899; "Mr. Plant Goes North," *TTr*, April 6, 1899; "Mr. H. B. Plant in Charleston," *CEP*, April 6, 1899; "Mr. Plant in the City," *CNC*, April 7, 1899; "Peace with Spain," *WES*, April 11, 1899; H. B. Plant to Wm. McKinley, April 3, 1899, McKinley Papers, LC; *NHER*, April 22, 1899, 3.

41. *New York Supplement*, 417–25; Reynolds, *Henry Plant*, 185; Henry B. Plant last will and testament, Polk County, FL, Will Records, Wills, 1883–1902, vol. 1–2, 164–74; "New to This Port," *BH*, June 7, 1899; "New Steamer," *BDA*, June 9, 1899.

42. *New York Supplement*, 422–23; "Branford Daily Happenings," *NHER*, June 21, 24, July 5, 1899; "Henry B. Plant Dead," *BO*, June 24, 1899.

43. "Henry B. Plant Dead," *NYT*, June 24, 1899; "Funeral of Henry B. Plant," *NHER*, June 27, 1899.

44. "Hon. H. B. Plant Dead," *North Georgia Citizen* (Dalton, GA), June 29, 1899; "Arp's Heart Is Sad," *ACh*, July 20, 1899.

AFTERWORD

1. Reynolds, *Henry Plant*, 187–204; "Dr. William G. Wood," *NYTr*, May 7, 1890; "Dr. W. G. Wood's Will Probated," *CDT*, May 15, 1890; "They Cannot Have Their Wills," *NYS*, August 5, 1891; "Will Declared Void," *Scranton (PA) Republican*, August 5, 1891; "Will of Henry B. Plant," *NHER*, June 30, 1899; "Henry B. Plant Will," *BO*, July 1, 1899; "Plant Will Contest," *Mount Vernon (NY) Daily Argus*, October 6, 1899; "May Contest Plant Will," *NYTr*, November 14, 1899; "Contest over Plant Will," *NYT*, November 15, 1899; "For Her Rights," *Buffalo (NY) Courier*, December 4, 1899.

2. Swain, *Cravath Firm*, I, 678–86; "M. F. Plant No Schemer," *BH*, May 3, 1900; "Mrs. H. B. Plant May Receive $7,000,000," *NYT*, January 5, 1902; "Mrs. Graves Will Receive $8,000,000," *NYH*, June 12, 1904.

3. "Mrs. H. B. Plant Married," *BS*, January 20, 1904; "Mrs. Robert Graves Back," *NYT*, August 12, 1908; "Mrs. Robt. Graves an Invalid," *NYS*, August 12, 1908; "Robert Graves' Wife Is Dead," *NYH*, May 31, 1909; "Mrs. Robert Graves Dead," *BDE*, May 31, 1909; "Mrs. Robert Graves Dead," *NYT*, May 31, 1909; *Acts of Incorporation, Constitution and By-Laws*, 51.

4. Reynolds, *Henry Plant*, 198–200; "Goodbye Plant System," *TTr*, July 1, 1902; Covington, *Plant's Palace*, 78–79; "Southern Express Co. Today Changes Title," *ACh*, July 1, 1918; "M. J. O'Brien of Express Co. Popular Here," *AC*, September 13, 1909.

Bibliography

PRIMARY SOURCES

Archival Material

Bramson Archive, Miami Beach, FL

Henry Bradley Plant Collection

Church of the Transfiguration, New York, NY

Marriage records, 1873–1877

Connecticut State Library, Hartford

Charles R. Hale Collection
Wills and probate records, 1609–1999

Georgia State Archives, Morrow

John Brown Gordon Records
Richmond County deed records
Richmond County tax digests

Henry B. Plant Museum Archives, Henry B. Plant Museum, Tampa

Henry Bradley Plant Collection

Library of Congress, Washington, DC

Grover Cleveland Papers
William McKinley Papers

National Archives, Washington, DC

Confederate Papers Relating to Citizens or Business Firms, 1861–1865
Internal Revenue Service Tax Assessment Lists, 1862–1918
Passenger Lists of Vessels Arriving at New York, NY, 1820–1897
Records of the Provost Marshal General's Bureau (Civil War), 1863–1865
Registers of Vessels Arriving at the Port of New York from Foreign Ports, 1789–1919
Union Provost Marshals' File of Papers Relating to Individual Civilians
US Passport Applications, 1795–1925

National Society of the Sons of the American Revolution, Louisville, KY

Membership applications

New England Historic Genealogical Society, Boston, MA

Massachusetts death records

New York Municipal Archives, New York, NY

Birth records, 1846–1909
Death records, 1795–1949

P. K. Yonge Library of Florida History, University of Florida, Gainesville

David Levy Yulee Papers
James Edmundson Ingraham Papers

Polk County, FL, Clerk of Court, Polk County Courthouse, Bartow, FL

Will Records

Rollins College Archives and Special Collections, Winter Park, FL

Loring Chase Scrapbooks

University of Miami Special Collections, Miami, FL

Franklin Quimby Brown Papers, 1898

Newspapers and Periodicals

Advertiser and Appeal (Brunswick, GA), 1883–1884
Age-Herald (Birmingham, AL), 1894–1895
Akron (OH) Beacon Journal, 1899
Albany (GA) News, 1879
Albany (GA) Patriot, 1845
Albany (GA) Weekly Herald, 1893
Albany (NY) Argus, 1850
Albany (NY) Evening Journal, 1893
Albany (NY) Times, 1890
Alexandria (VA) Gazette, 1870–1895
American Traveler (Boston, MA), 1868
Americus (GA) Recorder, 1884
Americus (GA) Times-Recorder, 1896
Ancient City (St. Augustine, FL), 1853
Anglo-American Times (London, England), 1873
Army and Navy Journal (New York, NY), 1898
Asheville (NC) Citizen-Times, 1897
Ashtabula (OH) Weekly Telegraph, 1878
Atchison (KS) Daily Champion, 1871
Atlanta Constitution, 1871–1907
Atlanta Daily Herald, 1873
Atlanta Daily Intelligencer, 1867
Atlanta Georgian and News, 1909
Atlanta Weekly Intelligencer, 1854–1867
Auburn (NY) Bulletin, 1888
Auburn (NY) Journal and Advertiser, 1840
Augusta (GA) Chronicle, 1851–1918
Austin (TX) Weekly Statesman, 1875

Bainbridge (GA) Democrat, 1889–1895
Baltimore Gazette and Daily Advertiser, 1832
Bangor (ME) Daily Whig and Courier, 1870
Bar Harbor (ME) Record, 1888–1890
Bartow (FL) Informant, 1883
Black River Democrat (Lowville, NY), 1938
Black River Gazette (Lowville, NY), 1827–1832
Black River Herald (Boonville, NY), 1868
Boston Commercial Gazette, 1840
Boston Courier, 1852
Boston Daily Advertiser, 1832–1899
Boston Daily Bee, 1845
Boston Daily Globe, 1884
Boston Evening Journal, 1873
Boston Evening Transcript, 1846–1849
Boston Herald, 1887–1900
Boston Journal, 1877–1898
Boston Post, 1840–1898
Boston Recorder, 1846
Boston Sunday Globe, 1890–1894
Boston Traveler, 1868–1873
Boston Weekly Globe, 1888
Bradford County Telegraph (Starke, FL), 1895
Branford (CT) Gleaner, 1878–1879
Branford (CT) Opinion, 1896–1900
Branford (CT) Review, 1942
Branford (CT) Review and East Haven News, 1939
Branford (CT) Semi-Weekly Record, 1899
Bristol Mercury (Bristol, England), 1891
Brooklyn (NY) Daily Eagle, 1867–1909
Brooklyn (NY) Evening Star, 1859
Brooklyn (NY) Union-Argus, 1880–1882
Brownlow's Knoxville (TN) Whig, 1865
Buffalo (NY) Courier, 1889
Buffalo (NY) Express, 1881–1893
Charleston (SC) Courier, 1853–1866
Charleston (SC) Daily News, 1867–1872
Charleston (SC) Daily News and Courier, 1875
Charleston (SC) Mercury, 1858–1862
Charleston (SC) News and Courier, 1877–1899
Charlotte (NC) Democrat, 1873
Charlotte (NC) News, 1890–1893
Charlotte (NC) Observer, 1887–1897
Chicago Daily Tribune, 1876–1898
Christian Watchman (Boston, MA), 1850
Cincinnati Commercial Tribune, 1889
Cincinnati Daily Enquirer, 1861
Cincinnati Daily Gazette, 1867–1881
Cincinnati Daily Times, 1875
Cincinnati Enquirer, 1875–1898
Civilian and Gazette (Galveston, TX), 1860
Cleveland (OH) Leader, 1878–1898
Columbia Republican (Hudson, NY), 1889

Columbian Register (New Haven, CT), 1834–1874
Columbus (GA) Daily Enquirer, 1867–1898
Columbus (GA) Daily Enquirer-Sun, 1878–1890
Columbus (IN) Republican, 1873
Commercial Advertiser (New York, NY), 1831–1875
Connecticut Courant (Hartford, CT), 1825–1842, 1876
Connecticut Herald (New Haven, CT), 1819–1825
Connecticut Journal (New Haven, CT), 1819
Constitution (Middletown, CT), 1852–1855
Courier-Informant (Bartow, FL), 1895
Courier-Journal (Louisville, KY), 1866–1898
Courrier des États-Unis (New York, NY), 1864
Critic (Washington, DC), 1888
Daily Albany (NY) Argus, 1832
Daily Alta California (San Francisco, CA), 1858–1871
Daily Atlanta Intelligencer, 1871
Daily Confederation (Montgomery, AL), 1859
Daily Constitution (Middletown, CT), 1875
Daily Constitutionalist (Augusta, GA), 1860–1869
Daily Critic (Washington, DC), 1889
Daily Dispatch (Richmond, VA), 1856
Daily Freeman (Kingston, NY), 1872
Daily Gazette (Niagara Falls, NY), 1859
Daily Gleaner (Kingston, Jamaica), 1890–1897
Daily Herald (New Haven, CT), 1837–1846
Daily Inter Ocean (Chicago, IL), 1876–1891
Daily Ledger (Memphis, TN), 1875
Daily Morning Journal and Courier (New Haven, CT), 1898
Daily Morning News (Savannah, GA), 1853–1861
Daily Nashville (TN) Patriot, 1859
Daily National Intelligencer (Washington, DC), 1851–1864
Daily National Republican (Washington, DC), 1864
Daily News & Herald (Savannah, GA), 1866–1868
Daily News Herald (Jacksonville, FL), 1888
Daily Phoenix (Columbia, SC), 1865–1872
Daily Picayune (New Orleans, LA), 1853–1898
Daily Plainsman (Huron, SD), 1893
Daily Press (Newport News, VA), 1898
Daily Review (Wilmington, NC), 1877–1880
Daily Saratogian (Saratoga Springs, NY), 1875–1890
Daily Sun (Atlanta, GA), 1872–1873
Daily Telegram (Adrian, MI), 1898
Daily Tribune (Salt Lake City, UT), 1878
Daily True Delta (New Orleans, LA), 1858–1861
Dallas Daily Herald, 1880
Dallas Morning News, 1892
Dallas Weekly Herald, 1875
Democrat and Chronicle (Rochester, NY), 1897
Democratic Statesman (Austin, TX), 1875–1876
Dennison Daily Cresset (Dennison, TX), 1875
Dennison Daily News (Dennison, TX), 1875
Detroit Free Press, 1873–1880
Donaldsonville (LA) Chief, 1872

Elyria (OH) Reporter, 1902
Emancipator (New York, NY), 1830–1841
Evening Bulletin (Maysville, KY), 1888
Evening Critic (Washington, DC), 1884
Evening Express (New York, NY), 1866–1879
Evening Post (Charleston, SC), 1895–1899
Evening Post (New York, NY), 1825–1898
Evening Star (Washington, DC), 1854–1899
Evening Telegram (Jacksonville, FL), 1892–1893
Evening Telegram (New York, NY), 1873–1897
Evening Telegraph (Philadelphia, PA), 1869–1870
Evening Times (Washington, DC), 1897
Evening Tribune (San Diego, CA), 1897
Evening World (New York, NY), 1887–1890
Fayetteville (NC) Weekly Observer, 1894
Fitchburg (NY) Sentinel, 1884
Flake's Bulletin (Galveston, TX), 1865
Florida Daily Times (Jacksonville, FL), 1882
Florida Dispatch (Jacksonville, FL), 1882–1886
Florida Herald and Southern Democrat (St. Augustine, FL), 1838
Florida Mirror (Fernandina, FL), 1880–1884
Florida News (Jacksonville, FL), 1856
Florida Republican (Jacksonville, FL), 1856
Florida Star (Titusville, FL), 1889
Florida Times-Union (Jacksonville, FL), 1883–1897
Florida Union (Jacksonville, FL), 1865
Fort Myers Press (Fort Myers, FL), 1897
Frank Leslie's Illustrated Newspaper (New York, NY), 1856–1878
Freeman (Indianapolis, IN), 1902
Freeman's Journal (Dublin, Ireland), 1889
Fremden-Blatt (Vienna, Austria), 1891
Galveston (TX) Daily News, 1872–1895
Galveston (TX) Weekly News, 1882
Geneva (NY) Gazette, 1819–1871
Georgia Weekly Telegraph (Macon, GA), 1861
Gil Blas (Paris, France), 1891
Guardian (London, England), 2005
Halifax (NS) Morning Sun, 1863
Hampshire Gazette (Northampton, MA), 1839
Harrisburg (PA) Telegraph, 1881
Hartford (CT) Daily Courant, 1869
Hawaii Gazette (Honolulu, HI), 1897
Helena (MT) Daily Herald, 1877
Hickory (NC) Press, 1888
Hopkinsville Kentuckian, 1897
Houston Post, 1900
Hudson (NY) Evening Register, 1872
Indiana Herald (Huntington, IN), 1863
Indianapolis Journal, 1889
Indiana State Journal (Indianapolis, IN), 1899
Indian Chieftain (Vinita, OK), 1896
Indian Journal (Muskogee, OK), 1876
Indian River Advocate (Titusville, FL), 1895–1898

Intelligencer (Anderson, SC), 1880
Inter Ocean (Chicago, IL), 1885–1899
Irish Times (Dublin, Ireland), 1864
Jersey Journal (Jersey City, NJ), 1881–1898
Journal and Republican (Lowville, NY), 1877–1908
Kalamazoo (MI) Gazette, 1877
Kansas City (MO) Times, 1887
Keowee Courier (Pickens, SC), 1893
Kissimmee (FL) Valley, 1896
Knoxville (TN) Daily Chronicle, 1872
Knoxville (TN) Journal, 1895
Labor World (Duluth, MN), 1899
Le Gaulois (Paris, France), 1894
Le Matin (Paris, France), 1898
Le Menestrel (Paris, France), 1867
Liberator (Boston, MA), 1840–1861
Liverpool Mail (Merseyside, England), 1873
Liverpool (NS) Transcript, 1863
Lockport (NY) Union-Sun & Journal, 2016
Logansport (IN) Times, 1898
London American Register (London, England), 1873–1894
London Man of the World (London, England), 1894
London Standard (London, England), 1897
Los Angeles Herald, 1891
Louisville (KY) Courier-Journal, 1899
Louisville (KY) Daily Courier, 1849–1861
Lowell (MA) Daily Courier, 1881
Macon (GA) Daily Telegraph, 1865
Macon (GA) Telegraph, 1861–1896
Macon (GA) Weekly Telegraph, 1859, 1867–1892
Manatee River Journal (Bradenton, FL), 1890
Marietta (OH) Daily Leader, 1899
Marion (OH) Star, 1891–1899
McGrawville (NY) Express, 1849
Medina (NY) Tribune, 1871
Memphis Appeal, 1889
Memphis Daily Appeal, 1857–1875
Memphis Daily Avalanche, 1867–1868
Memphis Daily Eagle and Enquirer, 1857
Miami Herald, 1915–1925
Miami Metropolis, 1898
Morganton (NC) Herald, 1895
Morning Courier and New York Enquirer (New York, NY), 1848–1859
Morning Herald (New York, NY), 1840
Morning News (New London, CT), 1845
Morning News (Wilmington, DE), 1891
Morning Post (London, England), 1873
Mount Vernon (NY) Daily Argus, 1899
Musical World (London, England), 1864
Nantucket (RI) Inquirer, 1840
Nashville (TN) Union and American, 1859–1872
National Police Gazette (New York, NY), 1878
National Republican (Washington, DC), 1863–1884

National Tribune (Washington, DC), 1884
Newark Daily Advertiser (Newark, NJ), 1840–1841
Newburyport (MA) Herald, 1841
New Hampshire Patriot and State Gazette (Concord, NH), 1839
New Haven (CT) Evening Register, 1881–1905
New Haven (CT) Palladium, 1863
New London (CT) Daily Chronicle, 1851
New London (CT) Weekly Chronicle, 1861
New National Era (Washington, DC), 1870
New Orleans Bulletin, 1875
New Orleans Crescent, 1869
New Orleans Daily Crescent, 1861–1862
New Orleans Daily Democrat, 1878
New Orleans Item, 1892–1893
New Orleans Republican, 1872
New Orleans Times, 1875
Newport (RI) Daily News, 1875
The News (Frederick, MD), 1888
News and Herald (Winnsboro, NC), 1880
News and Observer (Raleigh, NC), 1886–1900
New York Age, 1890
New York American, 1898
New York Amusement Gazette, 1888–1890
New York Clipper, 1875
New York Daily Graphic, 1873–1878
New York Dramatic Mirror, 1894–1896
New York Evening Express, 1856–1880
New York Express, 1840
New York Herald, 1854–1909
New York Morning Courier, 1830
New York Sun, 1841–1944
New York Times, 1853–1909
New York Times Illustrated Weekly Magazine, 1898
New York Tribune, 1849–1899
New York World, 1862
New Zealand Tablet (Dunedin, New Zealand), 1917
Norfolk Virginian, 1882–1896
North Adams (MA) Transcript, 1898
North American (Philadelphia, PA), 1840–1878
North China Herald (Shanghai, China), 1897
North Georgia Citizen (Dalton, GA), 1899
Norwich (CT) Courier, 1841–1842
Novedades (New York, NY), 1889
Observer (Raleigh, NC), 1877–1879
Ocala (FL) Evening Star, 1895–1899
Olean (NY) Democrat, 1887
Oneida Observer (Utica, NY), March 2, 1830
Ottawa (ON) Journal, 1887
Pacific Commercial Advertiser (Honolulu, HI), 1880–1897
Palatka (FL) Daily News, 1884–1888
People's Advocate (New London, CT), 1845
Philadelphia Inquirer, 1864–1894
Pittsburgh Daily Commercial, 1863

Pittsburgh Daily Post, 1889
Pittsburgh Dispatch, 1890–1892
Pittsburgh Press, 1894
Pittsburgh Weekly Gazette, 1870
Plain Dealer (Cleveland, OH), 1864–1897
Plattsburgh (NY) Republican, 1834
Poughkeepsie (NY) Daily Eagle, 1889
Poughkeepsie (NY) Eagle-News, 1871, 1910
Press (New York, NY), 1889–1898
Press & Tribune (Chicago, IL), 1859
Providence (RI) Evening Press, 1863–1872
Public Ledger (Memphis, TN), 1867–1868
Record of the Times (Wilkes-Barre, PA), 1877
Republican Farmer (Bridgeport, CT), 1865
Richfield Mercury (Richfield Springs, NY)
Richmond (VA) Dispatch, 1855–1896
Richmond (VA) Examiner, 1862
Richmond (VA) Sentinel, 1854
Richmond (VA) Whig, 1873
Roanoke (VA) Times, 1892
Rockland County Messenger (Haverstraw, NY), 1854
Rome (GA) Courier, 1868
Rome (NY) Daily Sentinel, 1891
Royal Gazette (Hamilton, Bermuda), 1863–1879
Sacramento Daily Union, 1871–1878
Salem (MA) Register, 1851–1852
San Antonio (TX) Light, 1898
San Diego (CA) Union, 1897
Sandusky (OH) Register, 1895
San Francisco Bulletin, 1878
San Francisco Call, 1897
San Francisco Chronicle, 1897–1898
Saratoga Sentinel (Saratoga Springs, NY), 1824–1883
Savannah Daily Advertiser, 1871–1872
Savannah Daily Georgian, 1854
Savannah Daily Herald, 1865
Savannah Daily Republican, 1852–1862
Savannah Morning News, 1871–1899
Savannah Tribune, 1889–1900
Scranton (PA) Republican, 1891
Southern Banner (Athens, GA), 1871
Southern Confederacy (Atlanta, GA), 1861
Southern Watchman (Athens, GA), 1871
South Florida Courier (Plant City, FL), 1886
South Side Signal (Babylon, NY), 1892–1897
Spectator (New York, NY), 1832–1848
Springfield (MA) Republican, 1864–1897
Stamford (CT) Advocate, 1876–1888
St. Andrews (FL) Buoy, 1895
State (Columbia, SC), 1891–1893
St. Augustine (FL) Examiner, 1860
St. Louis (MO) Post-Dispatch, 1876–1891
St. Louis (MO) Republic, 1889–1892

St. Petersburg (FL) Times, 1998
Sumter (SC) Banner, 1853
Sun (Baltimore, MD), 1854–1904
Sun and Advertiser (Halifax, NS), 1865
Sunday Herald (Washington, DC), 1890
Sunday Times (Chicago, IL), 1873
Sunland Tribune (Tampa, FL), 1882
Sunny South (Atlanta, GA), 1887
Syracuse (NY) Daily Journal, 1870
Tammany Times (New York, NY), 1898
Tampa Daily Journal, 1890
Tampa Daily Times, 1924
Tampa Guardian, 1886
Tampa Journal, 1889–1890
Tampa Tribune, 1887–1929
Tampa Weekly Journal, 1888
Tampa Weekly Tribune, 1893–1894
Tennessean (Nashville, TN), 1870–1897
Thomasville (GA) Daily Times-Enterprise, 1889–1898
Thomasville (GA) Times, 1879–1888
Thomasville (GA) Weekly Times-Enterprise, 1894
Tifton (GA) Gazette, 1897
Times (Hartford, CT), 1845
Times (London, England), 1882–1891
Times (Philadelphia, PA), 1878–1899
Times (Richmond, VA), 1896
Times-Democrat (New Orleans, LA), 1882–1898
Titusville (PA) Herald, 1870
Topeka (KS) Daily Capital, 1890
Trinity Tripod (Hartford, CT), 1906
Tri-Weekly Commercial (Wilmington, NC), 1851
Tri-Weekly Sentinel (Tallahassee, FL), 1866
Tropical Sun (Juno, FL), 1894–1895
Troy (NY) Daily Whig, 1840
Tyrone (PA) Daily Herald, 1899
Union and Advertiser (Rochester, NY), 1871
Union and Recorder (Milledgeville, GA), 1884
Utica (NY) Daily Press, 1887
Vermont Phoenix (Brattleboro, VT), 1846
Victoria (BC) Daily Colonist, 1887
Virginian-Pilot (Norfolk, VA), 1899
Waco (TX) Daily Examiner, 1875
Washington (PA) Reporter, 1854
Washington Post, 1918
Washington Sentinel (Washington, DC), 1854
Washington Times (Washington, DC), 1896
Watchman and Southron (Sumter, SC), 1892–1894
Watertown (NY) Daily Times, 1928
Waycross (GA) Herald, 1892–1900
Weekly Advertiser-Appeal (Brunswick, GA), 1888
Weekly Atlanta Intelligencer, 1869
Weekly Bee (Gainesville, FL), 1883
Weekly Constitution (Atlanta, GA), 1870

Weekly Democrat (Bainbridge, GA), 1882–1883
Weekly Democratic Statesman (Austin, TX), 1875
Weekly Floridian (Tallahassee, FL), 1882
Weekly Herald (New York, NY), 1852
Weekly Messenger (Boston, MA), 1839
Weekly New Era (Atlanta, GA), 1870
Weekly News and Advertiser (Albany, GA), 1883–1892
Weekly Saratogian (Saratoga Springs, NY), 1892
Weekly Star (Washington, DC), 1892
Weekly Wisconsin (Milwaukee, WI), 1886
Westville (IN) Indicator, 1895
Wilkes-Barre (PA) Record, 1895
Wilkes-Barre (PA) Times Leader, 1889
Wilmington (NC) Journal, 1863
Wilmington (NC) Messenger, 1893
Wilmington (NC) Morning Star, 1874–1899
Worchester (MA) Daily Spy, 1889–1891
World (New York, NY), 1865–1900
Yonkers (NY) Herald-Statesman, 1978
Yorkville (SC) Enquirer, 1880

Published Government Documents

The Acts and Resolutions Adopted by the Legislature of Florida, at Its Eleventh Session, under the Constitution of A. D. 1868. Tallahassee: Charles E. Dyke, State Printer, 1881.

The Acts and Resolutions Adopted by the Legislature of Florida, at Its Twelfth Session, under the Constitution of A. D. 1868. Tallahassee: Charles E. Dyke, State Printer, 1883.

Acts of the Called Session of the General Assembly of Alabama, Held in the City of Montgomery, Commencing on the Second Monday in January, 1861. Montgomery, AL: Shorter & Reid, State Printers, 1861.

Acts of the Seventh Biennial Session of the General Assembly of Alabama, Held in the City of Montgomery, Commencing on the Second Monday in November, 1859. Montgomery, AL: Shorter & Reid, State Printers, 1860.

Annual Report of the Postmaster General of the United States for the Fiscal Year Ending June 30, 1885. Washington, DC: Government Printing Office, 1885.

Annual Report of the Public Utilities Commission of the District of Columbia, 1913. Washington, DC: Public Utilities Commission, 1914.

Annual Report of the Supervising Surgeon-General of the Marine-Hospital Service of the United States for the Fiscal Year 1895. Washington, DC: Government Printing Office, 1896.

Bonds of the State of Tennessee: First Mortgage Liens on Railroads in That State, Opinion of Charles O'Conor, upon Statement of E. L. Andrews, of Counsel. New York: American Book Note, 1879.

Curtis, William Elroy, comp. *Trade and Transportation between the United States and Latin America*. Washington, DC: Government Printing Office, 1890.

The Evidence Taken by the Joint Committee of the Legislature of the State of Georgia, Appointed to Investigate the Management of the State Road, under the Administration of R. B. Bullock and Foster Blodgett. Atlanta, GA: J. Henry Smith, 1872.

Hammond, N. J., comp. *Reports of Cases in Law and Equity, Argued and Determined in the Supreme Court of Georgia, at Atlanta, Parts of December Term, 1869, and June Term, 1870*. Macon, GA: J. W. Burke, 1871.

———. *Reports of Cases in Law and Equity, Argued and Determined in the Supreme Court of*

Georgia, at Milledgeville, Parts of December Term, 1868, and June Term, 1869. Atlanta, GA: Harrison Company, 1913.

Interstate Commerce Commission. *First Annual Report on the Statistics of Express Companies in the United States for the Year Ending June 30, 1909.* Washington, DC: Government Printing Office, 1911.

———. *Report No. 4302, Memphis Freight Bureau et al. v. Adams Express Company et al.* Washington, DC: Government Printing Office, 1913.

Journal of the Congress of the Confederate States of America, 1861–1865. Vol. 1. Washington, DC: Government Printing Office, 1904.

A Journal of the Proceedings of the Assembly of the State of Florida at Its Fifth Session: Begun and Held in the Capitol, in the City of Tallahassee, on Tuesday, January 2, 1872. Tallahassee, FL: Charles H. Walton, State Printer, 1872.

Kennedy, Joseph C. G., comp. *Population of the United States in 1860; Compiled from the Original Returns of the Eighth Census.* Washington, DC: Government Printing Office, 1864.

McClellan, James F., comp. *A Digest of the Laws of the State of Florida, from the Year One Thousand Eight Hundred and Twenty-Two, to the Eleventh Day of March, One Thousand Eight Hundred and Eighty-One, Inclusive.* Tallahassee, FL: Floridian Book and Job Office, 1881.

"Message of the President of the United States, and Accompanying Documents, to the Two Houses of Congress, at the Commencement of the First Session of the Thirty-Ninth Congress: Part III [House Ex. Doc. 1, 39th Congress, 1st Sess.]." Washington, DC: Government Printing Office, 1866.

The New York Supplement. Vol. 74 (*New York State Reporter*, vol. 108), *Containing the Decisions of the Supreme and Lower Courts of Record of New York State: Permanent Edition, February 13–March 27, 1902.* St. Paul, MN: West Publishing, 1902.

N. Y. Supreme Court, William B. Dinsmore et al., Trustees, &c, against Alvin Adams et al.: Arguments on Behalf of Defendants in Support of Motion to Open Decree. New York: Evening Post Steam Presses, 1874.

Otto, William T., comp. *United States Reports, Supreme Court.* Vol. 95, *Cases Argued and Adjudged in the Supreme Court of the United States, October Term, 1877.* Boston: Little, Brown, 1878.

Report of the Joint Committee of the General Assembly of Georgia Appointed to Investigate the Lease of the Western and Atlantic Railroad, 1880–1. Atlanta, GA: Jas. P. Harrison, 1881.

Report of the Postmaster General in Answer to the Resolution of the House of Representatives, of October 13, 1862. Richmond, VA: Confederate States of America, 1862.

Reports of Cases Argued and Determined in the Supreme Court of Tennessee for the Middle Division, December Term, 1880, and for the Western Division, April Term, 1881. Louisville, KY: Fetter Law Book Company, 1902.

Reports of the Secretary of the Navy and of the Postmaster General; Being Part of the Message and Documents Communicated to the Two Houses of Congress at the Beginning of the Second Session of the Forty-Second Congress. Washington, DC: Government Printing Office, 1871.

The Southern Reporter. Vol. 17, *Containing All the Decisions of the Supreme Courts of Alabama, Louisiana, Florida, Mississippi, Permanent Edition, April 10–August 14, 1895.* St. Paul, MN: West Publishing, 1895.

Special Acts and Resolutions Passed by the General Assembly of the State of Connecticut, at the January Session, 1882. Hartford, CT: Case, Lockwood & Brainard, 1882.

Special Acts and Resolutions Passed by the General Assembly of the State of Connecticut, at the January Session, 1893. Hartford, CT: Case, Lockwood & Brainard, 1893.

Supreme Court [for the City and County of New York], General Term. Vol. 51, *May & June 1864.* New York: no publisher, 1864.

Testimony Taken by Committee Appointed to Investigate the Official Conduct of Rufus B. Bullock, Late Governor of Georgia. Atlanta, GA: W. A. Hemphill, State Printer, 1872.

Thomas, Henry W., comp. *Digest of the Railroad Laws of Georgia.* Atlanta, GA: Geo. W. Harrison, State Printer, 1895.

Thomas, Kenneth H., Jr. *The Lapham-Patterson House: A National Historic Landmark, Thomasville, Georgia.* Atlanta, GA: Georgia Department of Natural Resources, 1978.

Walker, Francis A., comp. *Ninth Census.* Vol. 1, *The Statistics of the Population of the United States . . . from the Original Returns of the Ninth Census (June 1, 1870).* Washington, DC: Government Printing Office, 1872.

War of the Rebellion: A Compilation of the Official Records of the Union and Confederate Armies. 128 vols. Washington, DC: Government Printing Office, 1880–1901.

SECONDARY SOURCES

Acts of Incorporation, Constitution and By-Laws, List of Fellows, Honorary Fellows, Benefactors, and Complete List of Fellows from Institution January 6, 1847, to January 1, 1906, of the New York Academy of Medicine. New York: New York Academy of Medicine, 1906.

"The Adams Express Co. and the Baltimore & Ohio Railroad." *Expressman's Monthly* 2 (September 1877): 275–77.

Akin, Edward N. *Flagler: Rockefeller Partner & Florida Baron.* Kent, OH: Kent State University Press, 1988.

"Akron-ic Epidemic." *Expressman's Monthly* 1 (May 1876): 157.

Allman, Timothy D. *Miami, City of the Future.* Rev. ed. Gainesville: University Press of Florida, 2013.

"Alvin Adams." *Friends' Intelligencer* 34 (September 22, 1877): 482–83.

Ambrose, Stephen E. *Nothing Like It in the World: The Men Who Built the Transcontinental Railroad, 1863–1869.* New York: Simon and Schuster, 2000.

Andrews, Alfred. *Genealogical History of Deacon Stephen Hart and His Descendants, 1632–1875.* Hartford, CT: Case, Lockwood & Brainard, 1875.

Andrews, J. Cutler. "The Southern Telegraph Company, 1861–1865: A Chapter in the History of Wartime Communication." *Journal of Southern History* 30 (August 1964): 319–44.

Angevine, Robert G. *The Railroads and the State: War, Politics, and Technology in Nineteenth-Century America.* Stanford, CA: Stanford University Press, 2004.

"Another Important Decision—Southern Express Company vs. Louisville & Nashville Railroad Company." *Expressman's Monthly* 5 (December 1880): 229–30.

Arnold, R. D. "The Identity of Dengue, or Break-Bone Fever, and of Yellow Fever." *Savannah Journal of Medicine* 1 (January 1859): 307–26.

Avery, Isaac Wheeler. *The History of the State of Georgia from 1850 to 1881.* New York: Brown & Derby, 1881.

Ayers, Edward L. *The Promise of the New South: Life after Reconstruction.* New York: Oxford University Press, 1992.

Bacon, Leonard. *Memorial of Elisha Lord Cleaveland.* New Haven, CT: Thomas H. Pease, 1866.

Baker, Ray Stannard. *Woodrow Wilson, Life and Letters: Youth, 1856–1890.* Garden City, NY: Doubleday, Page, 1927.

Balmer, Randall Herbert, and John R. Fitzmier. *The Presbyterians.* Westport, CT: Greenwood Press, 1993.

Baptist, Edward E. *Creating an Old South: Middle Florida's Plantation Frontier before the Civil War.* Chapel Hill: University of North Carolina Press, 2002.

Barber, John W., and Henry Howe. *Historical Collections of the State of New York.* New York: S. Tuttle, 1842.

Barker, Edward Harrison. *France of the French.* New York: Charles Scribner's Sons, 1910.

Barker, Eirlys. "'A Sneaky, Cowardly Enemy': Tampa's Yellow Fever Epidemic of 1887–88." *Tampa Bay History* 8 (Fall/Winter 1986): 4–22.
Barnes, Jay. *Florida's Hurricane History*. Chapel Hill: University of North Carolina Press, 1998.
Barton, Elmer Epenetus. *Historical and Commercial Sketches of Washington and Environs*. Washington, DC: E. E. Barton, 1884.
Bates, David Homer. *Lincoln in the Telegraph Office: Recollections of the United States Military Telegraph Corps during the Civil War*. New York: Century, 1907.
Beck, Lewis C. "Report on Cholera, Made to His Excellency Gov. Throop, August, 1832." In *Transactions of the Medical Society of the State of New York*, vol. 1, *1832–1833*, 348–72. Albany, NY: Webster and Skinners, 1833.
Beecher, Edward C. "Reminiscences of Three Quarters of a Century in New Haven." *Connecticut Magazine* 10 (October–December 1906): 679–91.
Bell, John. *Rebels on the Great Lakes: Confederate Naval Commando Operations Launched from Canada, 1863–1864*. Toronto: Dundurn, 2011.
Benham, J. H. *Benham's* [New Haven] *City Directory, and Annual Advertiser for 1847–8*. New Haven, CT: J. H. Benham, 1847.
Berner, Brad K. *The Spanish-American War: A Historical Dictionary*. Lanham, MD: Scarecrow Press, 1998.
Bernstein, Peter L. *Wedding of the Waters: The Erie Canal and the Making of a Great Nation*. New York: W. W. Norton, 2005.
"Beverly Welford Wrenn." *International Railway Journal* 10 (January 1903): 26.
Biographical Souvenir of the States of Georgia and Florida, Containing Biographical Sketches of the Representative Public, and Many Early Settled Families in These States. Chicago: F. A. Battey, 1889.
Bird, Lawrence. "Aucune Usine au Monde: Dreaming Work in the *Exposition Universelle*, Paris 1878." In *Meet Me at the Fair: A World's Fair Reader*, edited by Laura Hollengreen, Celia Pearce, Rebecca Rouse, and Bobby Schweizer, 299–310. Pittsburgh, PA: ETC Press, 2014.
Bonami, Jean-Paul. *La Diva d'Offenbach: Hortense Schneider, 1833–1920*. Paris, France: Romillat, 2002.
Borchert, Catherine Glennan. "Exscinded! The Schism of 1837 in the Presbyterian Church in the United States of America and the Role of Slavery." PhD diss., Case Western Reserve University, 2009.
Bostaph, Samuel. *Andrew Carnegie: An Economic Biography*. Lanham, MD: Lexington Books, 2015.
Boyle & Chapman's Memphis City Directory . . . for the Years 1872 and 1873. Memphis, TN: Boyle & Chapman, 1872.
Bradlee, Francis B. C. "Blockade Running during the Civil War." *Essex Institute Historical Collections* 63 (January 1927): 42–44.
Brown, Canter, Jr. "The Civil War, 1861–1865." In *The New History of Florida*, edited by Michael Gannon, 231–48. Gainesville: University Press of Florida, 1996.
———. "The Florida, Atlantic and Gulf Central Railroad, 1851–1868." *Florida Historical Quarterly* 69 (April 1991): 411–29.
———. *Florida's Black Public Officials, 1867–1924*. Tuscaloosa: University of Alabama Press, 1998.
———. *Florida's Peace River Frontier*. Orlando: University of Central Florida Press, 1991.
———. *Henry Bradley Plant: The Nineteenth Century "King of Florida."* Tampa, FL: Henry B. Plant Museum, 1999.
———. *In the Midst of All That Makes Life Worth Living: Polk County, Florida, to 1940*. Tallahassee, FL: Sentry Press, 2001.
———. "Tampa and the Coming of the Railroad, 1853–1884." *Sunland Tribune* 17 (November 1991): 13–18.

——. *Tampa in Civil War and Reconstruction*. Tampa, FL: University of Tampa Press, 2000.

Brown, Canter, Jr., and Larry Eugene Rivers. *Mary Edwards Bryan: Her Early Life and Works*. Gainesville: University Press of Florida, 2015.

Brown, C. K. "The Southern Railway Security Company: An Early Instance of the Holding Company." *North Carolina Historical Review* 6 (April 1929): 158–70.

Brown, John Howard, ed. *Lamb's Biographical Dictionary of the United States*. 7 vols. Boston: James H. Lamb, 1900–1903.

Brownell, William Crary. "The Sculpture of Olin Warner." *Scribner's Magazine* 20 (October 1896): 429–41.

Bruce, Wallace. *The Hudson River by Daylight*. New York: Bryant Literary Union, 1884.

Brundage, W. Fitzhugh. *Lynching in the New South: Georgia and Virginia, 1880–1930*. Urbana: University of Illinois Press, 1993.

Bruton, Quintilla Geer, and David E. Bailey Jr. *Plant City: Its Origin and History*. Winston-Salem, NC: Hunter, 1984.

Bullock, C. Seymour. "Perilous Journeys of Some of the First Steamboats in American Waters." *Connecticut Magazine* 16 (October–December 1906): 695–714.

Caffin, Charles H. *American Masters of Sculpture, Being Brief Appreciations of Some American Sculptors and of Some Phases of Sculpture in America*. Garden City, NJ: Doubleday, Page, 1913.

Caldwell, Frank H. "Relief and Hospital Department." *International Journal of Surgery* 10 (January 1897): 22–27.

Campbell, J. P., comp. *The Southern Business Directory and General Commercial Advertiser*. Vol. 1. Charleston, SC: Steam Power Press of Walker & James, 1854.

"A Canal Worker's Legacy: New Haven's First Irish Neighborhood." *The Shanachie* 25 (2013): 1–3.

Carhart, Lucy Ann Morris, comp. *Genealogy of the Morris Family: Descendants of Thomas Morris of Connecticut*. New York: A. S. Barnes, 1911.

Carter, Dan T. *When the War Was Over: The Failure of Self-Reconstruction in the South, 1865–1867*. Baton Rouge: Louisiana State University Press, 1985.

Catalogue of the Officers and Students in the Collegiate and Commercial Institute, New Haven, Conn., for the Term Ending December 23d, 1863. New Haven, CT: Tuttle, Morehouse & Taylor, 1864.

Catalogue of the Officers and Students in the Collegiate and Commercial Institute, New Haven, Conn., for the Two Terms Ending July 27th, 1864. New Haven, CT: Tuttle, Morehouse & Taylor, 1864.

Catalogue of the Officers and Students in the Collegiate and Commercial Institute, New Haven, Conn., for the Two Terms Ending Dec. 21st, 1864. New Haven, CT: Tuttle, Morehouse & Taylor, 1864.

Catalogue of the Officers, Teachers and Students in the Collegiate and Commercial Institute, New Haven, 1876. New Haven, CT: Hodgson & Robinson, 1876.

Chadych, Danielle, and Dominque LeBorgne. *Paris: The Story of a Great City*. New York: Metro Books, 2010.

Churella, Albert J. *The Pennsylvania Railroad*. Vol. 1, *Building an Empire, 1846–1917*. Philadelphia: University of Pennsylvania Press, 2013.

Clark, Judith Freeman. *The Gilded Age*. New York: Infobase Publishing, 2009.

Commemorative Biographical Record of Fairfield County, Connecticut. Chicago: J. H. Beers, 1899.

Commemorative Biographical Record of New Haven County, Connecticut. Chicago: J. H. Beers, 1902.

"Congregational Necrology." *Congregational Quarterly* 69 (January 1876): 63–70.

Connecticut Church Records, Branford Church, 1687–1889. 2 vols. Hartford: Connecticut State Library, 1930.

Connelly, Thomas Lawrence. *Autumn of Glory: The Army of Tennessee, 1862–1865*. Baton Rouge: Louisiana State University Press, 1996.

Cosmas, Graham A. *An Army for Empire: The United States Army in the Spanish-American War*. College Station: Texas A&M University Press, 1994.

Covington, James W. *The Billy Bowlegs War, 1855–1858: The Final Stand of the Seminoles against the Whites*. Chuluota, FL: Mickler House Publishers, 1982.

———. *Plant's Palace: Henry B. Plant and the Tampa Bay Hotel*. Louisville, KY: Harmony House, 1990.

———. *The Story of Southwestern Florida*. 2 vols. New York: Lewis Historical Publishing, 1957.

———. "The Tampa Bay Hotel." *Tequesta* 26 (1966): 3–20.

Crandall, Charles H. *The Season: An Annual Record of Society in New York, Brooklyn, and Vicinity, First Year 1882–1883*. New York: White, Stokes, & Allen, 1883.

Craven, Avery. *The Coming of the Civil War*. 2nd ed. Chicago: University of Chicago Press, 1957.

"The Crest-Fallen." *Journal of the American Temperance Union*, November 1, 1845, 176.

Crist, Linda Lasswell, and Kenneth H. Williams, eds. *The Papers of Jefferson Davis*. Vol. 10, *October 1863–August 1864*. Baton Rouge: Louisiana State University Press, 1999.

Cross, Whitney R. *The Burned-Over District: The Social and Intellectual History of Enthusiastic Religion in Western New York, 1800–1850*. Ithaca, NY: Cornell University Press, 1950.

Culberson, James E., ed. and comp. *Images through the Doors of Time: Photos from the Kroegel Collection*. Melbourne, FL: Sea Bird, 1995.

Cullum, George W. *Biographical Register of the Officers and Graduates of the United States Military Academy . . . 1802–1890*. 3 vols. Boston: Houghton Mifflin, 1891.

Cummins, Joseph. *Anything for a Vote: Dirty Tricks, Cheap Shots, and October Surprises in U.S. Presidential Campaigns*. Rev. ed. Philadelphia: Quirk Books, 2015.

Currie-McDaniel, Ruth. *Carpetbagger of Conscience: A Biography of John Emory Bryant*. New York: Fordham University Press, 1999.

Davis, T. Frederick. *History of Jacksonville, Florida, and Vicinity, 1513 to 1924*. Reprint, Jacksonville, FL: San Marco Bookstore, 1990.

"Death of Mr. A. B. Small." *Expressman's Monthly* 4 (May 1879): 145–46.

De Groff, Isaac. *The Heart of the American Rhine: Illustrated, 1902*. Tarrytown, NY: Tarrytown Press Record, 1902.

Dehler, Gregory J. *Chester Alan Arthur: The Life of a Gilded Age Politician and President*. New York: Nova History Publications, 2007.

DeMontravel, Peter R. *A Hero to His Fighting Men: Nelson A. Miles, 1839–1925*. Kent, OH: Kent State University Press, 1998.

Denby, Elaine. *Grand Hotels: Reality and Illusion*. London: Reaktion Books, 1998.

Denham, James M. *"A Rogue's Paradise": Crime and Punishment in Antebellum Florida, 1821–1861*. Tuscaloosa: University of Alabama Press, 1997.

Dern, J. K. "Recollections of Early Miami." *Tequesta* 9 (1949): 43–60.

Dickens, Charles. *American Notes for General Circulation*. 2 vols. London: Chapman and Hall, 1842.

Dickerman, George Sherwood. *The House of Plant of Macon, Georgia, with Genealogies and Historical Notes*. New Haven, CT: Tuttle, Morehouse, & Taylor, 1900.

Doak, Robin S. *James A. Garfield*. Minneapolis, MN: Compass Point Books, 2003.

Dobson, John. *Bulls, Bears, Boom, and Bust: A Historical Encyclopedia of American Business Concepts*. Santa Barbara, CA: ABC-CLIO, 2007.

Drysdale, William. "Number 100: Frank Howell's Own Account of His Adventure in a Private Car." *Harper's Round Table* 16 (June 18, 1895): 622–24.

Duncan, Russell. *Entrepreneur for Equality: Governor Rufus Bullock, Commerce, and Race in Post–Civil War Georgia*. Athens: University of Georgia Press, 1994.

Dunlap, David W. *From Abyssinian to Zion: A Guide to Manhattan's Houses of Worship*. New York: Columbia University Press, 2004.
Durant, Ghislani. *The Family Physician: A Manual of Domestic Medicine*. New York: Cassell, Pettier, Galpin, 1880.
——. *Hygiene of the Voice: Its Physiology and Anatomy*. New York: F. Schirmer, 1870.
——. *Sea-Bathing: Its Use and Abuse*. New York: Albert Cogswell, 1878.
Dyal, Donald H. *Historical Dictionary of the Spanish American War*. Westport, CT: Greenwood Press, 1996.
Eastman National Business College. *A Start in Business Life: "Teach Your Boys That Which They Will Practice When They Become a Man," 1875–6*. Poughkeepsie, NY: H. G. Eastman, 1875.
Eckert, Ralph Lowell. *John Brown Gordon: Soldier, Southerner, American*. Baton Rouge: Louisiana State University Press, 1989.
Eckford, Henry. "Olin Warner, Sculptor." *Century Magazine* 37 (January 1889): 392–401.
Edwards, H. Sutherland. "The Prima Donna." *Frank Leslie's Popular Monthly* 27 (February 1889): 150–60.
"Elections and Appointments." *Railroad Gazette* 25 (July 7, 1893): 312.
"Elections and Official Changes." *Railway World* 5 (November 29, 1879): 1135–36.
"An Elegant Wedding at Northampton." *Expressman's Monthly* 4 (June 1879): 182–84.
English, Anna Morris. *In Memoriam: James Edward English, March 13, 1812–March 2, 1890*. New Haven, CT: Privately printed, 1891.
"Express Companies." *Weekly Law Gazette* 4 (October 1, 1859): 283–85.
"Expressmen's Aid Society: Seventh Biennial Convention, at Jacksonville, Florida, February 13, 1884." *Express Gazette* 9 (February 29, 1884): 49–60.
Findling, John E., and Frank W. Thackery. *What Happened? An Encyclopedia of Events That Changed America Forever*. Vol. 3, *The Nineteenth Century*. Santa Barbara, CA: ABC-CLIO, 2011.
Finney, Charles Grandison. *Memoirs of Rev. Charles G. Finney, Written by Himself*. New York: Fleming H. Revell, 1876.
"First Annual Report of the Washington Temperance Society, of New Haven, Ct." *Journal of the American Temperance Union* 6 (November 1842): 163–64.
Fishburne, Charles C., Jr. *The Cedar Keys in the 19th Century*. Quincy, FL: Sea Hawk Publications, 1993.
Flayhart, William Henry, III. *The American Line (1871–1902)*. New York: W. W. Norton, 2000.
"Florida—The Means of Entering and Traveling Her Sunny Clime." *Express Gazette* 9 (April 15, 1884): 103–4.
"Florida Project." *Railway World* 36 (June 25, 1892): 617.
Foner, Eric. *Reconstruction: America's Unfinished Revolution, 1863–1877*. New York: Harper & Row, 1988.
Frank, Michael B., and Harriet Elinor Smith, eds. *Mark Twain's Letters*. Vol. 6, *1874–1875*. Berkeley: University of California Press, 2002.
Fraser, Walter J. *Savannah in the Old South*. Athens: University of Georgia Press, 2005.
Gallaudet, Bern B. "Dr. Thomas M. Markoe." *Columbia University Quarterly* 4 (December 1901): 47–50.
Garrett, Franklin M. *Atlanta and Environs: A Chronicle of Its People and Events, 1820s–1870s*. Athens: University of Georgia Press, 1969.
Garrett, William. *Reminiscences of Public Men in Alabama, for Thirty Years*. Atlanta, GA: Plantation Publishing Company's Press, 1872.
Garrison, L. R. "Administrative Problems of the Confederate Post Office Department: II." *Southeastern Historical Quarterly* 19 (January 1916): 232–50.
Genealogical and Biographical Record of New London County, Connecticut. Chicago: J. H. Beers, 1905.

"General Ticket and Passenger Agents." *Railway Age* 3 (March 21, 1878): 155–56.

Geoffrey, Christine, and Richard Sibley. *Going Abroad: Travel, Tourism, and Migration; Cross-Cultural Perspectives on Mobility*. Newcastle, England: Cambridge Scholars, 2007.

Gibson, Carrie. *Empire's Crossroads: A History of the Caribbean from Columbus to the Present Day*. New York: Atlantic Monthly Press, 2014.

Goodrich, Chauncey. "Invasion of New Haven by the British Troops, July 5, 1779." In *Papers of the New Haven Colony Historical Society*, vol. 2, 31–92. New Haven, CT: New Haven Colony Historical Society, 1877.

Gordon, Thomas F. *Gazetteer of the State of New York*. Philadelphia: T. H. and P. G. Collins, 1836.

Graham, Thomas. *Mr. Flagler's St. Augustine*. Gainesville: University Press of Florida, 2014.

"The Greatest Man in Florida." *Brotherhood of Locomotive Engineers' Monthly Journal* 32 (August 1898): 561–62.

"A Great Ship Yard." *Marine Review* 19 (March 30, 1899): 12–23.

Green, J. H. *Twelve Days in the Tombs; or, A Sketch of the Last Eight Years of the Reformed Gambler's Life*. New York: William Taylor, 1850.

Greene, Nelson, ed. *History of the Mohawk Valley: Gateway to the West, 1614–1925*. 2 vols. Chicago: S. J. Clarke, 1925.

Grismer, Karl H. *Tampa: A History of the City of Tampa and the Tampa Bay Region of Florida*. St. Petersburg, FL: St. Petersburg Printing, 1950.

Grossman, Peter Z. "Golden Silence: Why the Express Chose Not to Incorporate." *Business and Economic History* 21 (1992): 300–306.

Hahn, Calvet M. "Adams' Express and Independent Mail." *Collector's Club Philatelist* 69 (May–June 1990): 181–239.

Hall, Henry, ed. *America's Successful Men of Affairs: An Encyclopedia of Contemporaneous Biography*. 2 vols. New York: New York Tribune, 1895–1896.

Hanna, Alfred Jackson. *Flight into Oblivion*. Richmond, VA: Johnson, 1938.

Harlow, Alvin F. *Old Waybills: The Romance of the Express Companies*. New York: D. Appleton-Century, 1934.

Harris, Ruth-Ann Mellish, Donald M. Jacobs, and B. Emer O'Keefe, comps. *The Search for Missing Friends: Irish Immigrant Advertisements Placed in the Boston Pilot, 1866–1870*. Boston: New England Genealogical Society, 1989.

Harrison, Lynde. "James Blackstone and His Family." In *Exercises at the Opening of the James Blackstone Memorial Library, Branford, Conn., June 17, 1896*, 19–26. New Haven, CT: Tuttle, Morehouse & Taylor, 1897.

Hart, Edward Lucas. *Memoranda of the Descendants of Amos Morris, of East Haven, Conn*. New York: A. S. Barnes, 1853.

Hazard, Sharon. *Long Branch in the Golden Age: Tales of Fascinating and Famous People*. Charleston, SC: History Press, 2007.

Henretta, James A., Rebecca Edwards, and Robert O. Self. *America's History*. Vol. 1, *To 1877*. Boston: Bedford/St. Martin's, 2011.

"Henry B. Plant, the King of Florida." *Success* 1 (November 1898): 5–6.

Herndon, Richard, comp. *Men of Progress: Biographical Sketches and Portraits of Leaders in Business and Professional Life in and of the State of Connecticut*. Boston: New England Magazine, 1898.

Hill, Everett G. *A Modern History of New Haven and Eastern New Haven County*. 2 vols. New York: S. J. Clarke, 1918.

Hinshaw, Ward Wade. *Encyclopedia of American Quaker Genealogy*. 6 vols. Reprint, Baltimore: Genealogical Publishing, 1991–1994.

History of Jefferson County, New York, with Illustrations and Biographical Sketches of Some of Its Prominent Men and Pioneers. Philadelphia: L. H. Everts, 1878.

Hoadley, Philemon. "Jamaica Persecutions." *Baptist Magazine* 24 (October 1832): 435.

Hoffman, Glenn. *Building a Great Railroad: A History of the Atlantic Coast Line Railroad Company*. Richmond, VA: CSX, 1998.

Hollengreen, Laura, Celia Pearce, Rebecca Rouse, and Bobby Schweizer, eds. *Meet Me at the Fair: A World's Fair Reader*. Pittsburgh, PA: ETC Press, 2014.

Homberger, Eric. *Mrs. Astor's New York: Money and Social Powers in a Gilded Age*. New Haven, CT: Yale University Press, 2002.

Horwitz, Tony. *Midnight Rising: John Brown and the Raid That Sparked the Civil War*. New York: Henry Holt, 2011.

Hotchkiss, Fanny Winchester. *Winchester Notes*. New Haven, CT: Tuttle, Morehouse & Taylor, 1912.

Hough, Franklin Benjamin. *A History of Lewis County, in the State of New York*. Albany, NY: Munsell and Rowland, 1860.

Howard, Michael. *The Franco-Prussian War: The German Invasion of France, 1870–1871*. New York: Routledge, 2006.

Ingraham, James E. "Sketch of the Life of Mr. Henry B. Plant of Branford, Conn." *Sunland Tribune* 7 (1981): 27–30.

"An Interesting Reminiscence: President Plant's First Express Experience." *Express Gazette* 21 (November 15, 1896): 331.

"Jamaica." *Bulletin of the Pan American Union* 1 (March 1894): 66–69.

Johns, John E. *Florida during the Civil War*. Gainesville: University of Florida Press, 1963.

Johnson, Dudley S. "Early History of the Alabama Midland Railroad Company." *Alabama Review* 21 (October 1968): 276–87.

———. "The Florida Railroad after the Civil War." *Florida Historical Quarterly* 47 (January 1969): 292–309.

———. "Henry Plant and Florida." *Florida Historical Quarterly* 45 (October 1966): 118–31.

———. "Plant's Lieutenants." *Florida Historical Quarterly* 48 (April 1970): 381–91.

———. "The Railroads of Florida." PhD diss., Florida State University, 1965.

———. "The Southern Express Company: A Georgia Corporation." *Georgia Historical Quarterly* 56 (Summer 1972): 224–42.

Johnson, Ludwell H. *Red River Campaign: Politics and Cotton in the Civil War*. Kent, OH: Kent State University Press, 1993.

Johnson, Paul E. *A Shopkeeper's Millennium: Society and Revivals in Rochester, New York, 1815–1837*. New York: Hill and Wang, 2004.

Jolly, Elaine. *The Founding of LePageville: A Legacy to African American Railroad Workers*. Accessed March 12, 2016. www.cvsolarbear.com/LePageville/e%20Jolly%20LeP%20History.pdf.

Jones, Charles C., Jr., and Salem Dutcher. *Memorial History of Augusta, Georgia*. Augusta, GA: D. Mason, 1890.

Jones, John Beauchamp. *A Rebel War Clerk's Diary at the Confederate States Capital*. 2 vols. Philadelphia: J. B. Lippincott, 1866.

Judd, Peter H., ed. *Affection: Ninety Years of Family Letters, 1850s–1930s; Haring, White, Griggs, Judd Families of New York and Waterbury, Connecticut*. 2 vols. Salt Lake City, UT: Family Heritage Publishers, 2006.

Keating, John M. *The Yellow Fever Epidemic of 1878, in Memphis, Tenn*. Memphis: Howard Associates, 1879.

Keehn, David C. *Knights of the Golden Circle: Secret Empire, Southern Secession, Civil War*. Baton Rouge: Louisiana State University Press, 2013.

Kimball, David. "Rev. Charles Finney." *Independent* 20 (May 14, 1868): 6.

King, Moses. *King's Handbook of the City of New York: An Outline History and Description of the American Metropolis*. Boston: Moses King, 1892.

Klein, Herman. *The Reign of Patti*. New York: Century, 1920.

Knetsch, Joe. "Hamilton Disston and the Development of Florida." *Sunland Tribune* 24 (1998): 5–19.

Knetsch, Joe, John Missall, and Mary Lou Missall. *History of the Third Seminole War, 1849–1858*. Philadelphia: Casemate, 2018.

"The Last Roll." *Confederate Veteran* 6 (September 1898): 437–39.

"The Late Henry Sanford." *Express Gazette* 28 (October 15, 1903): 229.

Lauw, Louisa. *Fourteen Years with Adelina Patti: Reminiscences of Louisa Lauw*. New York: Norman L. Munro, 1884.

Leng, Shirie C. "Typhus Syncopalis: An Epidemic in Connecticut in 1823." *Connecticut Medicine* 76 (October 2012): 555–59.

Lepler, Julia. "1837: Anatomy of a Panic." PhD diss., Brandeis University, 2007.

Leslie, Mrs. Frank. "Cuban Bygones." *Frank Leslie's Popular Monthly* 47 (December 1898): 135–43.

Levermore, Charles H. *The Republic of New Haven: A History of Municipal Evolution*. Baltimore: N. Murray, 1886.

Lowville Academy Semi-Centennial Anniversary Celebrated at Lowville, N. Y., July 21st and 22d, 1858. Lowville, NY: Home Committee, 1859.

Mancini, Matthew J. *One Dies, Get Another: Convict Leasing in the American South, 1866–1928*. Columbia: University of South Carolina Press, 1996.

Marchman, Watt P., ed. "The Ingraham Everglades Exploring Expedition, 1892." *Tequesta* 7 (1947): 3–43.

Marden, Orison Swett, ed. *Talks with Great Workers*. New York: Thomas Y. Crowell, 1890.

Martin, Richard A. *The City Makers*. Jacksonville, FL: Convention Press, 1972.

Martin, Sidney Walter. *Florida's Flagler*. Athens: University of Georgia Press, 1949.

———. "Henry Bradley Plant." In *Georgians in Profile*, edited by Horace Montgomery, 261–76. Athens: University of Georgia Press, 1959.

McCabe, James Dabney. *The Lights and Shadows of New York Life; or, The Sights and Sensations of the Great City*. Philadelphia: National Publishing, 1872.

McCaleb, Walter Flavius. "The Organization of the Post-Office Department of the Confederacy." *American Historical Review* 12 (October 1906): 66–74.

McCullough, David. *Brave Companions: Portraits in History*. New York: Simon and Schuster, 1992.

McKay, Donald B. *Pioneer Florida*. 3 vols. Tampa: Southern Publishing, 1959.

McPherson, James M. *Battle Cry of Freedom: The Civil War Era*. New York: Oxford University Press, 1988.

Memorial of Elisha Lord Cleaveland. New Haven, CT: Thomas H. Pease, 1866.

"Memphis, Tenn." *Express Gazette* 21 (September 15, 1896): 266.

Mendelsohn, Joyce. *Touring the Flatiron*. New York: New York Landmarks Conservancy, 1998.

Mesa, Franklin. *Opera: An Encyclopedia of World Premiers and Significant Performances, Singers, Composers, Librettists, Arias and Conductors, 1597–2000*. Jefferson, NC: McFarland, 2007.

Mesic, Harriet Bey. *Cobb's Legion Cavalry: A History and Roster of the Ninth Georgia Volunteers in the Civil War*. Jefferson, NC: McFarland, 2009.

"Metropolitan Trust Company of New York in New Quarters." *Banker's Magazine* 94 (February 1917): 123–72.

"The Middle States." *Express Gazette* 21 (November 15, 1896): 345.

Miller, Vivien M. L. *Crime, Sexual Violence, and Clemency: Florida's Pardon Board and Penal System in the Progressive Era*. Gainesville: University Press of Florida, 2000.

Mintz, Steven. *Moralists and Modernizers: America's Pre-Civil War Reformers*. Baltimore: Johns Hopkins University Press, 1995.

Minutes of the General Assembly of the Presbyterian Church in the United States of America: With an Appendix, A. D. 1828. Philadelphia: Lydia R. Bailey, 1828.

Minutes of the Thirty-Third Annual Meeting of the General Association of Illinois, Held at Quincy, May 23d, 1876. Jacksonville, IL: Office of the Daily Journal, 1876.

Mitchell, William Donald. “Connecticut’s Contribution to Art.” *Connecticut Magazine* 12 (1st Qtr. 1908): 127–28.
Monaghan, Jay. *Diplomat in Carpet Slippers: Abraham Lincoln Deals with Foreign Affairs.* Indianapolis: Bobbs-Merrill, 1945.
Montgomery, Horace, ed. *Georgians in Profile: Historical Essays in Honor of Ellis Merton Coulter.* Athens: University of Georgia Press, 1958.
Moore, J. Hampton. *History of the Five o’Clock Club of Philadelphia.* Philadelphia: Privately published, 1891.
Morford, Henry. *Short-Trip Guide to America.* Philadelphia: J. P. Lippincott, 1874.
Morris, Edmund. *The Rise of Theodore Roosevelt.* New York: Modern Library, 2001.
Morris, Sylvia Jukes. *Edith Kermit Roosevelt: Portrait of a First Lady.* New York: Random House, 2009.
Morrison, John H. *History of American Steam Navigation.* New York: S. F. Sametz, 1903.
Mouheb, Roberta Buckingham. *Yale under God: Roots and Fruits.* Maitland, FL: Xulon Press, 2012.
“Mr. H. B. Plant Buys the Atlantic and Gulf Railroad.” *Expressman’s Monthly* 4 (November 1879): 302–3.
Mueller, Edward A. *Steamships of the Two Henrys: Being an Account of the Maritime Activities of Henry Morrison Flagler and Henry Bradley Plant.* DeLeon Springs, FL: E. O. Painter Printing, 1996.
Nathans, Elizabeth Studley. *Losing the Peace: Georgia Republicans and Reconstruction, 1865–1871.* Baton Rouge: Louisiana State University Press, 1968.
The National Cyclopaedia of American Biography. Vol. 11. New York: James T. White, 1909.
Necrological Reports and Annual Proceedings of the Alumni Association of Princeton Theological Seminary. Vol. 2, *1890–1899.* Princeton, NJ: O. S. Robinson, 1899.
Nelson, Scott Reynolds. *Iron Confederacies: Southern Railways, Klan Violence, and Reconstruction.* Chapel Hill: University of North Carolina Press, 1999.
———. *Nation of Deadbeats: An Uncommon History of America’s Financial Disasters.* New York: Knopf, 2012.
Nelson, Truman John. *The Old Man: John Brown and Harper’s Ferry.* New York: Holt, Rinehart and Winston, 1973.
“New Haven Town Meeting.” *Journal of the American Temperance Union* 8 (February 1844): 20.
Noël, Édouard, and Edmond Stoullig. *Les annales du théatre et de la musique avec une préface par M. Ludovic Halévy de l’Academie française: Seizème année, 1890.* Paris: Bibliothèque-Charpentier, 1891.
———. *Les annales du théatre et de la musique avec une préface par Francisque Sarcey: Vingtième année, 1894.* Paris: Bibliothèque-Charpentier, 1895.
Nolan, David. *Fifty Feet in Paradise: The Booming of Florida.* San Diego, CA: Harcourt Brace Jovanovich, 1984.
North, Frank R., ed. “The Building of the New Tampa Bay Hotel: 1888–1897; Reminiscences of Alexander Browning.” *Sunland Tribune* 25 (1999): 27–36.
Northern Alabama, Historical and Biographical. Birmingham, AL: Smith & DeLand, 1888.
“Notable People of the Day.—No. 8.” *Phrenological Journal and Science of Health* 87 (May 1888): 247–51.
O’Brien, Matthew V. “Only a Messenger.” *Expressman’s Monthly* 1 (October 1876): 295–96.
Offenbach, Jacques. *Offenbach’s Songs from the Great Operettas.* New York: Dover, 1976.
Ogle, Maureen. *Key West: History of an Island of Dreams.* Gainesville: University Press of Florida, 2003.
Olegario, Rowena. *A Culture of Credit: Embedding Trust and Transparency in American Business.* Cambridge, MA: Harvard University Press, 2006.
O’Neill, John P., ed. *American Sculpture in the Metropolitan Museum of Art.* Vol. 1, *A Catalogue of Works by Artists Born before 1865.* New York: Metropolitan Museum of Art, 1999.

Ortiz, Paul. *Emancipation Betrayed: The Hidden History of Black Organizing and White Violence in Florida from Reconstruction to the Bloody Election of 1920*. Berkeley: University of California Press, 2005.

Osterweis, Rollin G. *Three Centuries of New Haven, 1638–1938*. New Haven, CT: Yale University Press, 1953.

Parker, David B. *Alias Bill Arp: Charles Henry Smith and the South's "Goodly Heritage."* Athens: University of Georgia Press, 1991.

Parks, Joseph Howard. *Joseph E. Brown of Georgia*. Baton Rouge: Louisiana State University Press, 1999.

Parsons, Henry. *Parsons Family: Descendants of Cornet Joseph Parsons, Springfield, 1636–Northampton, 1655*. New York: Frank Allaben Genealogical Company, 1912.

Patten, James Madison, comp. *Benham's New Haven City Directory for 1846–7*. New Haven, CT: J. H. Benham, 1846.

———. *Patten's New Haven City Directory for 1845–6*. New Haven, CT: J. H. Benham, 1845.

———. *Patten's New Haven Directory, for the Year 1840*. New Haven, CT: James M. Patten, 1840.

———. *Patten's New Haven Directory for 1844–5*. New Haven, CT: J. H. Benham, 1844.

Peeples, Vernon. *Punta Gorda and the Charlotte Harbor Area: A Pictorial History*. Norfolk, VA: Donning, 1986.

Perdue, Theta. *Race and the Atlanta Cotton States Exposition, 1895*. Athens: University of Georgia Press, 2010.

Pérez, Louis A. *Cuba between Empires, 1878–1902*. Pittsburgh, PA: University of Pittsburgh Press, 1983.

Pettengill, George W., Jr. *The Story of the Florida Railroads, 1834–1903*. Boston: Railway & Locomotive Historical Society, 1952.

Pinkerton, Allan. *The Expressman and the Detective*. Chicago: W. B. Keen, Cooke, 1874.

Plant, Henry Bradley. "The Great Railway Systems of the United States: The South Atlantic Railways." *Cosmopolitan* 13 (October 1892): 677–87.

———. *Reply of H. B. Plant to Misstatements in the Public Document Entitled 'Trade and Transportation between the United States and Spanish America, by William Eleroy Curtis,' concerning the West India Fast Mail via Tampa, Key West and Havana, and the Plant Steamship Line*. New York: Plant Steamship Line, 1889.

Plant, John David, III. *Descendants of John Plant: My Plant Family Ancestors*. Scribd. March 2013. https://www.scribd.com/doc/101283057/Descendants-of-John-Plant-of-Branford-Connecticut.

Plant, W. K. "Increase Cook Plant, 1814–1892." *Roots and Branches: The Official Journal of the Plant Family History Group* 5 (January 1993): 42–45.

"Plant Investment Co." *Travelers' Official Railway Guide for the United States and Canada* 23 (February 1891): xxx.

"Plant of the Plant System: Sketch of the Expressman Who Re-discovered Florida." *Express Gazette* 20 (July 15, 1895): 156.

Poor, Henry V. *Manual of the Railroads of the United States, for 1872–73*. New York: H. V. & H. W. Poor, 1872.

Poore, Benjamin Perley, ed. *The Conspiracy Trial for the Murder of the President, and the Attempt to Overthrow the Government by the Assassination of Its Principal Officers*. Vol. 3. Boston: J. E. Tilton, 1866.

Powell, J. C. *The American Siberia; or, Fourteen Years' Experience in a Southern Convict Camp*. Philadelphia: H. J. Smith, 1891.

Prince, John C. *Cuba Illustrated*. 6th ed. New York: Napoléon Thompson, 1893.

"Proceedings of the Second Annual Convention of the Expressmen's Aid Society, Held at Cincinnati, Ohio, April 12 and 13, 1876." *Expressman's Monthly* 1 (May 1876): 137–44.

"Proceedings of the Third Annual Convention of the Expressmen's Aid Society, Held in the City of Chicago, Ill., April 18 and 19, 1877." *Expressman's Monthly* 2 (May 1877): 150–57.

Pughe, E. H. *Pughe's Directory for the City of Augusta and Its Vicinity, Including Hamburg So. Ca.* Augusta, GA: E. H. Pughe, 1867.
Rable, George C. *The Confederate Republic: A Revolution against Politics.* Chapel Hill: University of North Carolina Press, 1994.
"Railway Projects." *Railway World* 24 (June 10, 1880): 587–90.
Redpath, James. *The Roving Editor; or, Talks with Slaves in the Southern States.* New York: A. B. Burdick, 1859.
Reed, Wallace P. *History of Atlanta, Georgia.* Syracuse, NY: D. Mason, 1889.
Reeves, Thomas C. *Gentleman Boss: The Life and Times of Chester Alan Arthur.* Newtown, CT: American Political Biography Press, 1991.
"Return of Major O'Brien." *Expressman's Monthly* 1 (October 1876): 310.
Reynolds, Cuyler. *Genealogical and Family History of Southern New York and the Hudson River Valley.* 3 vols. New York: Lewis Historical Publishing, 1914.
Reynolds, David S. *John Brown, Abolitionist: The Man Who Killed Slavery, Sparked the Civil War, and Seeded Civil Rights.* New York: Vintage Books, 2006.
Reynolds, Kelly. *Henry Plant: Pioneer Empire Builder.* Cocoa: Florida Historical Society Press, 2003.
Rivers, Larry Eugene. *Slavery in Florida: Territorial Days to Emancipation.* Gainesville: University Press of Florida, 2000.
Rivers, Larry Eugene, Richard Mathews, and Canter Brown Jr., eds. *John Willis Menard: Lays in Summer Lands.* Tampa, FL: University of Tampa Press, 2002.
Rockey, John L. *History of New Haven County, Connecticut.* 2 vols. New York: W. W. Preston, 1892.
Rosenberg, Charles E. *The Cholera Years: The United States in 1832, 1849, and 1866.* Chicago: University of Chicago Press, 1962.
Rutkow, Ira. *James A. Garfield.* New York: Henry Holt, 2006.
Samuels, Peggy, and Harold Samuels. *Teddy Roosevelt at San Juan: The Making of a President.* College Station: Texas A&M University Press, 1997.
Sandage, Scott A. *Born Losers: A History of Failure in America.* Cambridge, MA: Harvard University Press, 2005.
"Savannah, Florida & Western." *Railroad Gazette* 25 (May 12, 1893): 365.
Sawyer, Leicester A. *A Dissertation on Servitude: Embracing an Examination of the Scripture Doctrines on the Subject, and an Inquiry into the Character and Relations of Slavery.* New Haven, CT: Durrie & Peck, 1837.
Schellings, William J. "The Advent of the Spanish-American War in Florida, 1898." *Florida Historical Quarterly* 39 (April 1960): 311–29.
Schoonover, Thomas D., ed. and trans. *Mexican Lobby: Matias Romero in Washington, 1861–1867.* Lexington: University Press of Kentucky, 1986.
Scott, John Anthony, and Robert Alan Scott. *John Brown of Harper's Ferry: With Contemporary Prints, Photographs, and Maps.* New York: Facts on File, 1993.
Second Annual Report of the New-York State Society for the Promotion of Temperance. Albany, NY: Packard & Van Benthuysen, 1831.
Sharpley-Whiting, T. Denean. *Bricktop's Paris: African American Women in Paris between the Two World Wars.* Albany: State University of New York Press, 2015.
Shaw, Ronald E. *Erie Waters West: A History of the Erie Canal, 1792–1854.* Lexington: University of Kentucky Press, 1966.
Shook, John R., ed. *Dictionary of Early American Philosophers.* London: Continuum, 2012.
Simonds, J. Rupert. *A History of the First Church and Society of Branford, Connecticut, 1644–1919.* New Haven, CT: Tuttle, Morehouse & Taylor, 1919.
"Smuggling of Dutiable Goods." *Internal Revenue Record and Customs Journal* 34 (July 16, 1888): 223–24.
Smyth, George Hutchinson. *The Life of Henry Bradley Plant, Founder and President of the*

Plant System of Railroads and Steamships and Also of the Southern Express Company. New York: G. P. Putnam's Sons, 1898.
Society of Colonial Wars in the State of New Hampshire. *List of Officers, Committees and Members: Chronicle for Thirty Years, 1894 to 1924*. Concord, NH: Society of Colonial Wars in the State of New Hampshire, 1924.
"Southern Express Co." *Expressman's Monthly* 1 (March 1876): 86.
"Southern Express Company, Augusta, Ga., July 28." *Expressman's Monthly* 4 (August 1879): 236.
"The Southern Express Company, Memphis, Tenn., December 5, 1870." *Railroad Gazette* 2 (December 10, 1870): 241–42.
"A Southern Express Veteran: Stirring Events in the Life of the Late Capt. Williams, Agent, Athens, Ga." *Express Gazette* 21 (May 15, 1896): 151.
"Southern Florida: Railroad and Express Notes." *Express Gazette* 9 (February 29, 1884): 35.
"Southern News." *Express Gazette* 20 (November 15, 1895): 259.
"South Florida." *Railroad Gazette* 18 (October 1, 1886): 681.
Spann, Joseph E., Jr. "The South Florida Railroad: Polk County's First Railroad, 1880–1893." *Polk County Historical Quarterly* 12 (March 1986): 1–3, 7.
Stampp, Kenneth M. *America in 1857: A Nation on the Brink*. New York: Oxford University Press, 1990.
Stark, James H. *Stark's Jamaica Guide (Illustrated)*. Boston: James H. Stark, 1902.
Starr, Kevin. *California: A History*. New York: Random House, 2005.
Stashower, Daniel. *Hour of Peril: The Secret Plot to Murder Lincoln before the Civil War*. New York: Minotaur Books, 2014.
Steeples, Douglas, and David O. Whitten. *Democracy in Desperation: The Depression of 1893*. Westport, CT: Greenwood Press, 1998.
Sterling, Robin, comp. *Marion County, Alabama, Newspaper Clippings, 1897–1899*. Lulu.com, 2014.
Stiles, T. J. *The First Tycoon: The Epic Life of Cornelius Vanderbilt*. New York: Alfred A. Knopf, 2009.
Stimmell, Gordon. "The Independent Mails." Accessed July 20, 2016. https://www.uspcs.org/stamps-covers/carriers-locals-independent-mails/the-independent-mails/.
Stimson, Alexander Lovett. *History of the Express Business: Including the Origin of the Railway System in America, and the Relation of Both to the Increase of New Settlements and the Prosperity of Cities in the United States*. New York: Baker and Godwin, 1881.
———. *History of the Express Companies and the Origin of American Railroads*. New York: A. L. Stimson, 1858.
Stover, John F. "The Pennsylvania Railroad's Southern Rail Empire." *Pennsylvania Magazine of History and Biography* 81 (January 1957): 28–38.
Strickland, Jeff. "Nativists and Strangers: Yellow Fever and Immigrant Mortality in Antebellum Charleston, South Carolina." In *Death and the American South*, edited by Craig Thompson Friend and Lorri Glover, 131–52. New York: Cambridge University Press, 2015.
Sullivan, G. W. *Early Days in California: The Growth of the Commonwealth under American Rule, with Biographical Sketches of Pioneers*. San Francisco: Enterprise, 1888.
Swaine, Robert T. *The Cravath Firm and Its Predecessors, 1819–1947*. 3 vols. Clark, NJ: Lawbook Exchange, 2007.
Texas Almanac for 1861. Galveston, TX: W. & D. Richardson, 1860.
"The Texas Express Company." *Expressman's Monthly* 1 (March 1876): 86.
Therrell, D. M. "Division One Has Fine Record of Progress." *Southern Telephone News* 8 (May 1920): 2–6, 15.
"Things and Other Things." *Railway Age* 25 (July 4, 1889): 389.
Thomas, Lately. "The Operator and the Emperors." *American Heritage* 15 (April 1964): 4–8, 83–88.

Thompson, Slason, comp. and ed. *The Railway Library, 1910*. Chicago: Gunthorp-Warren, 1911.

Transactions of the American Art Union, for the Year 1849. New York: George F. Nesbitt, 1850.

Trowbridge, Francis Bacon. *The Hoadley Genealogy & History of the Descendants of William Hoadley of Branford, Connecticut, Together with Some Account of Other Families of the Name*. New Haven, CT: Francis Bacon Trowbridge, 1894.

Tucker, Phillip Thomas. *Emily D. West and the "Yellow Rose of Texas" Myth*. Jefferson, NC: MacFarland, 2014.

Turner, Gregg M., and Seth H. Bramson. *The Plant System of Railroads, Steamships and Hotels*. Laurys Station, PA: Garrigues House, 2004.

Twain, Mark, and Charles Dudley Warner. *The Gilded Age: A Tale of To-day*. 3 vols. Hartford, CT: American Publishing, 1873.

"Two Great Sugar Plantations: Properties of the Pedro Fernandez de Castro Sugar Company and Their Able Owner." *South American* 4 (August 1916): 277–80.

Vaill, Dudley L. "Letters from an Old Hair Trunk." *Yale Review* 3 (July 1914): 691–707.

Vanderbilt, Arthur T., II. *Fortune's Children: The Fall of the House of Vanderbilt*. New York: William Morrow, 1989.

Van Slyck, J. D. *New England Manufacturers and Manufactories*. Vol. 1. Boston: Van Slyck, 1879.

Vesa y Fillart, D. Antonio. *Voluntarios de la isla de Cuba: Historial del regimiento caballería de Jaruco y de su estandarte*. Barcelona: José Cunill, 1908.

Victor, Orville James. *The Comprehensive History of the Southern Rebellion and the War for the Union*. New York: James D. Torrey, 1862.

Villard, Oswald Garrison. *John Brown, 1800–1859: A Biography Fifty Years After*. Boston: Houghton, Mifflin, 1910.

Wallace, Irving, Amy Wallace, David Wallechinsky, and Sylvia Wallace. *The Intimate Sex Lives of Famous People*. Port Townsend, WA: Feral House, 2008.

Walther, Eric H. *William Lowndes Yancey and the Coming of the Civil War*. Chapel Hill: University of North Carolina Press, 2006.

"The War of the Express—Adams vs. Union." *Expressman's Monthly* 5 (April 1880): 74–76.

"Washington State Temperance Society of Connecticut." *Journal of the American Temperance Union* 7 (December 1843): 187–88.

Webb, Wanton S., comp. *Webb's Jacksonville and Consolidated Directory of Representative Cities in East and South Florida, 1887*. Jacksonville, FL: Wanton S. Webb, 1887.

"What Young Expressmen Should Do." *Express Gazette* 9 (April 15, 1884): 102.

White, Bill. *America's Fiscal Constitution: Its Triumph and Collapse*. New York: Public Affairs, 2014.

White, Richard. *The Republic for Which It Stands: The United States during Reconstruction and the Gilded Age, 1865–1896*. New York: Oxford University Press, 2007.

Who Was Who in the Theater, 1912–1976: A Biographical Dictionary of Actors, Actresses, Directors, Playwrights, and Producers of the English-Speaking Theater. 4 vols. Detroit: Gale Research, 1978.

Wicker, Elmus. *Banking Panics of the Gilded Age*. New York: Cambridge University Press, 2000.

Williamson, Edward C. *Florida Politics in the Gilded Age, 1877–1893*. Gainesville: University of Florida Press, 1976.

Willis, William Parker. *Dashes at Life with a Free Pencil*. New York: Burgess, Stringer, 1845.

Wilson, Henn, comp. *Trow's New York City Directory for 1853–54*. New York: John F. Trow, 1853.

——. *Trow's New York City Directory for the Year Ending May 1, 1857*. New York: John F. Trow, 1856.

———. *Trow's New York City Directory for the Year Ending May 1, 1865*. New York: John F. Trow, 1865.

———. *Trow's New York City Directory for the Year Ending May 1, 1868*. New York: John F. Trow, 1867.

———. *Trow's New York City Directory for the Year Ending May 1, 1869*. New York: John F. Trow, 1868.

———. *Trow's New York City Directory for the Year Ending May 1, 1871*. New York: John F. Trow, 1870.

———. *Trow's New York City Directory for the Year Ending May 1, 1872*. New York: John F. Trow, 1871.

———. *Trow's New York City Directory for the Year Ending May 1, 1874*. New York: John F. Trow, 1873.

Wilson, Mark. *The Business of Civil War: Military Mobilization and the State, 1861–1865*. Baltimore: Johns Hopkins University Press, 2006.

Winther, Oscar Osburn. *Express and Stagecoach Days in California: From the Gold Rush to the Civil War*. Palo Alto, CA: Stanford University Press, 1936.

Woodward, C. Vann. *Origins of the New South: 1877–1913*. Baton Rouge: Louisiana State University Press, 1971.

Woolf, Joshua D. *Western Union and the Creation of the American Corporate Order, 1845–1893*. New York: Cambridge University Press, 2013.

Ziegler, Vanessa Michelle. "The Revolt of 'the Ever-faithful Isle': The Ten Years' War in Cuba, 1868–1878." PhD diss., University of California, Santa Barbara, 2007.

Index

Page numbers in italics refer to figures.

Abbott, Emma, 153
abolitionism, 19
Academy of Music (NYC), 77, 122
Academy of the Sacred Heart (NYC), 126–27
Adams, Alvin: as express industry pioneer, 33, 35; and Adams Express, 43, 53, 59, 62–63; death of, 144–45; mentioned, 197
Adams, Henry, 223
Adams & Co. *See* Adams Express Co.
Adams Express Co.: origins, 35–36, 47; and California Gold Rush, 46–47; services furnished to US government by, 51; larger headquarters for, 52, 61; expansion into Southeast by, 55–57, 61–62; and organization of as joint stock company, 58–59; and conflict within, 62–63, 68–69; and resentments against in the South, 73, 76–77; political lobbying by, 78–79, 81; civil war planning by, 80; and Confederate government relations, 81–84; post-Civil War actions of and controversies, 104–5, 117–18, 125; postwar reorganization of, 107; offices of at Nathan Mansion, 140; scandal at, 216; mentioned, 43, 96, 112–13. *See also* Alvin Adams and Baltimore Division
Adams Southern Express Co., 83–84. *See* Southern Express Co. (1861)
Agnew, Miss M., 148
Alabama and Florida Railroad Co., 66
Alabama Midland Railroad, 210, 213, 215
Alachua County, FL, 54, 178
Alamo, the, 138
Albany, GA, 155, 180
Albany, NY, 12, 20
Albion Theatre (Havana), 202
Alcazar Hotel (St. Augustine), 196
Aldrich, Thomas Bailey, 196
Alexandria, VA, 56
Alger, Russell A., 248, 253, 255–56
Algeria (steamer), 130
Alicia (yacht), 240, 245
Alligator, FL. *See* Lake City, FL
Allman, Timothy D., 147
Almighty Dollar, The, 141
Ambassadress (yacht), 151
Amelia Island, FL, 66
Amen Corner, 251
American Express Co., 59
American Steamship Co., 130
American Telegraph Co., 105–6
America's Cup, 174, 227, 240
Anclote Key, FL, 170
Anti-Masonic movement, 17, 21
Apalachicola, FL, 155, 172, 238
Apalachicola River, 164, 185
Appomattox, VA, 102
Archduke Karl Hotel (Vienna), 100
Armour, Herman O., 137
Armour, Philip, 224
Arp, Bill. *See* Smith, Charles Henry
Arthur, Chester Alan, 159, 163
Asheville, NC, 252
Asia, 252
Aspinwall, Panama. *See* Colon, Panama
Assembly House Hotel (New Haven), 25
Astor, John Jacob, 153

Astor, William Backhouse, Jr., 151, 153, 155
Atalanta (yacht), 172
Athenaeum (Atlanta), 71
Athens, GA, 87
Atlanta, GA: initial visit to by HBP, 55; express connections with, 60–61, 63, 103; as rail hub, 71, 116; HBP residence at, 71–73; and Cotton States Exposition, 235, 237, 239–41; mentioned, 101, 108–9, 123, 175, 238
Atlanta and LaGrange Railroad, 54, 73
Atlanta and Richmond Air-Line Railroad, 134
Atlanta Cotton Mills, 170
Atlantic and Gulf Railroad, 150–51, 154. *See also* Savannah, Florida and Western Railway Co.
Atlantic Coast Line Railroad, 267
Auburn, NY, 97
Auburndale, FL, 175
Audran, Edmond, 184, 191
Augusta, GA: I. C. Plant at, 54; early visits by HBP to, 55, 57; express connections with, 60, 103; yellow fever at, 60–61, 71; as Adams Express hub, 61–64, 79; rail connections with, 71, 116; as Southern Express headquarters, 83–85, 92–93, 225; Jefferson Davis at, 84; Ellen Blackstone Plant's death and funeral at, 88; national bank at, 102; and Union Republican Party, 109; Ellen Blackstone Plant exhumation at, 231; mentioned, 69–70, 72–73, 77, 81, 99, 122, 138, 151, 176, 200
Augusta (GA), National Bank of, 102
Austin, TX, 138, 142
Austro-Hungarian Empire, 100, 131–32
Avery Hill, Kent, England, 215

Babcock, Isaiah C., 106, 123, 128, 167
Babylon, NY, 221
Bahama Islands, 255–56. *See also* Nassau, Bahamas
Bainbridge, GA, 135, 155, 164, 166–68
Baltimore, MD: express industry origins at, 46, 63; rail access to, 116; and Morton Plant's wedding, 195; W. T. Walters' funeral at, 234; and Henry Bradley Plant Jr.'s birth, 239; mentioned, 68, 167, 180
Baltimore and Ohio Railroad, 178, 246
Baltimore & Potomac Railroad, 116
Baltimore Division (Adams Express), 60, 63, 68, 105
banana train, 207
banks and banking, 102–3. *See also names of individual banks*
Barber of Seville, The (opera), 99, 131
Bar Harbor, ME, 197–98, 206, 208, 210–11
Barker, Jonathan, 10
Barlow, Billy, 110
Barnum, Phineas T., 70
Barnum's Hotel (Baltimore), 116
Bartow, FL, 233, 250
Bates, David Homer, 89
battles: First Battle of Bull Run, 85; Shiloh, 90; Antietam, 91; Vicksburg, 93; Gettysburg, 93
Bayard, Thomas F., 118
Beach, Asa, 79
Beecher, Benjamin, 33–34, 40, 43–44, 48
Beecher, Edward C., 24
Beecher and Company, 36, 44, 46
Belle (early steamboat), 33–36
Belleair, FL, 244, 254, 260
Belleview Hotel (Belleair), 244, 247–48, 254, 267
Bellini, Vincenzo, 115
Belloca, Anna de, 131–32
Benedict, Elias Cornelius, 196
Benedict, Jennie Louise Flagler, 196
Benevolent Empire, 15–17. *See also* Second Great Awakening
Bennett, James Gordon, 32, 35
Berlin, Germany, 131
Bermuda, 94, 96, 154
Bienville (steamer), 120
Billy Bowlegs War. *See* Third Seminole War
Birdsall, George F., 127
Birdsall, Margaret Loughman. *See* Plant, Margaret Loughman Birdsall
Biltmore (Vanderbilt estate), 252
Black River Valley, NY, 12
Blackstone, Ella, 151
Blackstone, Ellen Elizabeth. *See* Plant, Ellen Blackstone
Blackstone, Emily Francis. *See* Freeman, Emily Blackstone
Blackstone, Emily Norton, 37, 151, 174
Blackstone, George William, 8, 86–87
Blackstone, James, 8, 38
Blackstone, James de Trafford, 141, 148, 154
Blackstone, John, 8
Blackstone, Julia Squire, 174
Blackstone, Lorenzo (HBP friend): early career at New Haven of, 25–26; marriage of, 37; as James de Trafford Blackstone's father, 141, 148, 154; as HBP traveling companion, 151–52, 170–71; as PICO director, 167; death of, 199; mentioned, 8, 43, 53, 57, 174
Blackstone, Lorenzo (son of James de Trafford Blackstone), 148
Blackstone, Mary. *See* Plant, Mary Blackstone
Blackstone, Sarah Whitaker. *See* Sondheim, Sarah Whitaker Blackstone
Blackstone, Timothy, 60
Blackstone, Timothy B., 8, 148, 154, 244
Blackstone, William Norton, 174

Blackstone, Wyllis, 73, 146
Blaine, James G., 180
Blake, Arthur. *See* Blake, Henry Arthur
Blake, Asa S., 142
Blake, Henry Arthur, 229, 244
Blatchford, Seward & Griswold (law firm), 88
Block Island, RI, 138, 141, 169
blockade running, 94–96
Blodgett, Foster, 109
Bloxham, William D., 160, 248, 252
Bolivar (early steamboat), 30
Boston, MA: and Adams Express, 33, 35, 53; railroad connections to, 55; and the Pulsifer family, 164; *Olivette* summer runs from, 197–98; steamer service to Halifax from, 220; mentioned, 101, 128, 185, 211, 225–26, 234
Boston Fruit Company, 211
Bradenton, FL, 178
Bradley, Betsey. *See* Hoadley, Betsey Bradley Plant
Bradley, Phineas, 25
Bradley, Levi, 9, 64
Branford, CT: and HBP's childhood, 5–12; HBP marriage at, 38; as problematic refuge, 42, 56–57, 60, 64, 79; and Morton Plant, 148–49; HBP country home at, 153, 173–74, 179, 183, 195, 206, 210, 215, 220, 225–26, 239, 241, 245, 248, 258; Betsey Hoadley's burial at, 187; reburial of Ellen Blackstone Plant at, 231; HBP burial at, 264; mentioned, 53, 91
Branford (CT) Congregational Church, 6–7, 38
Branford, FL, 161–62, 170
Brazil, 207
Breakers Hotel (Palm Beach), 221
Bridgeport, CT, 53, 70, 83, 91, 102, 167
Brighton Beach, NY, 149, 154, 159
Brinckley, Elizabeth, 134–35
Brinckley, Hugh L., 134–35
Bristol, TN, 116
Brooksville, FL, 178
Brougham, John, 52
Brown, Franklin Quincy: as Florida Southern Railway president, 234; Captiva Island development of, 250–51; and friendship with President McKinley, 251; and PICO, 251, 259; Cuban conditions assessed by, 135; and meetings with McKinley, 256; as HBP pallbearer, 264; mentioned, 9–10, 82
Brown, John (abolitionist), 77
Brown, John Calvin, 204
Brown, John Howard, 109
Brown, Joseph E., 119, 122
Browne, Frederick S., 143
Brownell, William Crary, 145
Brunswick, GA, 54, 143, 172, 195, 217, 227, 248
Brunswick and Western Railway, 180, 182
Bryan, Alden Pardee, 11
Bryan, Mary Edwards, 72
Bryan, William Jennings, 248
Buffalo, NY, 226
Buffalo Bill. *See* Cody, William F.
Bull Run, First Battle of, 85
Bullock, C. Seymour, 35
Bullock, Rufus Brown: employed by Adams Express, 73; at 1860 Democratic convention, 79; in charge of Southern Express operations, 91; in New York at war's end, 102; and creation of national banks, 102; as postwar Southern Express general superintendent, 107; and Georgia governorship, 109–11, 113, 117–20, 122–23; as Macon & Augusta Railroad president, 110; railroad sleeping car use by, 119–20; introduction of HBP to W. S. Chisholm by, 150; and the Atlanta Cotton Mills, 170; at Tampa Bay Hotel, 224; and Cotton States Exposition, 235; as HBP pallbearer, 264; mentioned, 136, 148, 175, 212, 222, 245
Bunker Hill (early steamboat), 29–31
Burchard, S. D., 180
Burke, P. B., 33
Burke & Co., 33
Burnt-Over District, 15, 18–19
Burton's Theater (NYC), 51

Caddo Belle (steamer), 170–71
Cahusac, Henri de Roger de (Marquis de Caux), 111
California, 148, 154, 195, 252–53
California Gold Strike (1848), 46
Caloosahatchee River, FL, 244, 250–52
Cameron, James Donald, 121
Cameron, Simon, 117, 119, 121–22
Canada: epidemic outbreaks in, 19; Confederate raids from, 96; collaborative possibilities with Adams Express and Plant System, 128, 224; HBP tour of, 226; mentioned, 195. *See also names of individual places*
Canada-Atlantic and Plant Steamship Company, 224, 232
canal boats, 12
Cape Breton Island, Canada, 226
Cape Fear River, NC, 85, 94
Cape Henry, VA, 240
Cape May, NJ, 149, 154
Capron, Nellie B. *See* Plant, Nellie Capron
Capt. Miller (steamer), 175
Captiva Island, FL, 250–51
Car No. 100, 200, 207, 218, 226
Caribbean. *See* West Indies *and names of individual islands and places*

Carnegie, Andrew: and Adams Express, 63; as Windsor Hotel patron, 137; at Paris exposition, 204; with HBP at Saratoga Springs, 226
Carter, George H., 208
Carter, Gilbert, 255
Casino, The (Tampa Bay Hotel), 244–45, 247–48, 254
Cass, George W., 62–63, 67–68, 70, 121, 124
Cass, Lewis, 63
Castro, Antonio Fernandez de, 233
Castro, Pedro Fernandez de, 181, 188, 232–33, 241
Castro, P. M., 188
Castro, Rafael Fernandez de, 181, 232–33
Catskill Mountains, 125, 211, 258
Caux, Marquis and Marchioness of. *See* Cahusac, Henri de Roger de; Patti, Adelina
Cedar Key, FL: as Gulf railroad terminus, 66, 163–64; and Cuban mail routes, 152; HBP at, 153, 171; and steamers to Cuba, 161–62; hurricane damage at, 169–70, 247; Plant exploratory party at, 170; mentioned, 238
Cedar Keys, FL. *See* Cedar Key, FL
Centennial Exposition of 1876, 131, 153
Central America, 180, 204, 207. *See also names of individual countries and places*
Central American and Tampa Fruit Co., 207
Central National Bank (Columbia, SC), 134
Central Railroad and Banking Company of Georgia, 60, 62
Chapin, Edwin Hubbell, 153
Charles Morand (steamer), 207
Charleston, SC: express connections with, 46, 54, 60, 63, 69, 105; HBP at, 57, 64, 110, 117, 121, 168, 176, 180, 182, 216, 234, 248, 262; hurricane at, 60; yellow fever at, 71, 143; and 1860 Democratic convention, 78–79; visited by HBP and Dinsmore at Civil War outset, 83; Southern Express office burns at, 87; rail connections with, 116, 185; as Charleston and Savannah Railroad headquarters, 167, 171; earthquake at, 190; mentioned, 190, 198, 200, 220
Charleston and Savannah Railroad, 157, 167
Charlotte Harbor, FL, 162, 178, 185, 214, 233, 244, 251
Chattahoochee, FL, 164, 166
Chattahoochee (steamer), 167–68
Chattahoochee and East Pass Railroad, 166, 177
Chattahoochee River, 155, 185
Chattanooga, TN: express connections with, 61, 63; rail connections with, 116; mentioned, 108–9, 152, 225
Chicago, IL: trade routes to, 79, 207–8; HBP at, 109–10, 142, 207, 253; and World's Columbian Exposition, 226–27
Chicago (warship), 215
Chilton, William P.: as Confederate congressman, 81; and Southern Express, 82–84, 86; death of, 120; mentioned, 78
China, 252
Chisholm, Walter Scott: introduced to HBP, 150–51; and Atlantic and Gulf Railroad, 154; and Savannah, Florida and Western Railroad, 154–55, 166; and PICO, 167, 177; in Havana with HBP, 196; and competition to succeed HBP, 198; illness of, 206; death of, 212; mentioned, 197, 201
cholera, 19–21
Christopher, Milton J., 217
Churella, Albert J., 116, 124, 134
cigar industry, 188–89, 231, 241. *See also* Tampa, FL
Cincinnati, OH, 84, 87, 96, 138, 207, 231
Citizen's Line, 33, 36
citrus and citrus industry, 217, 228, 236, 241, 252
City Hotel (Augusta), 91, 95, 103–4
City Hotel (New Orleans), 76
City of Paris (steamer), 204, 206, 216, 235
Civil War, 84–94. *See also* secession crisis
Clearwater, FL, 170, 244, 248
Cleaveland, Elisha Lord, 28, 40–42, 48
Clements, Samuel L. *See* Twain, Mark
Cleveland, Grover: as president, 180, 220, 223, 227–28; in Florida and Cuba, 195–96, 201–3; on *Olivette, 201*; mentioned, 199, 251
Cleveland, OH, 150
Clifton House (Niagara Falls), 76
Cody, William F., 206
Collegiate and Commercial Institute (New Haven). *See* Russell's Military School
Colon, Panama, 215
Colonial Hotel (Nassau), 255
Colt, Samuel, 24
Columbia (yacht), 174
Columbia, SC, 55, 116, 134
Columbia College (NYC), 113
Columbia Exposition, 226–27
Columbus, GA: I. C. Plant at, 54; express connections with, 54, 60, 63, 103; steamer connections with, 167; mentioned, 55, 170
Combs, Sterling Thomas, 61–62
Combs & Co.'s Southern Express, 62, 64
Coney Island, NY, 158, 232
Coney Island Jockey Club, 159
Confederate States of America: organization of, 81; and relocation of its capital, 84; conscription laws of, 92; and raids from Canada by, 96–97; surrender of, 102
Confederate States post office, 81, 84–85, 90
Confederate States treasury, 81, 90, 92
Congregational Church, 28, 42, 131. *See also names of individual churches*
Connecticut River Steamboat Company, 36

convict leasing, 156–57
Cooper, James Fenimore, 174
Cooper, Jim, 25
Corbett, James J. "Gentleman Jim," 229
Corbin, Henry C., 256
Corpus Christi, TX, 135
Cotter, William T., 187, 194, 210
Cottier, Daniel, 145
Cottier & Co., 145
cotton gin, 24
cotton speculation, 91, 103
Cotton Kingdom, 24
Cotton States and International Exposition (1895), 235, 237, 239–41, 244
Coulon, Pauline. *See* Loughman, Pauline Coulon
Courbet, Gustave, 168
Courcillon, Eugene de, 106
Court of Death, The (painting), 42
Covington, James W., 197, 199, 204, 213–14
Cramer, Jennie, 149, 158, 168
Cramp & Sons, 182, 189
Crane, William Lockwood, 43
Crédit Mobilier, 98
Cresson Springs, PA, 232
Crystal Palace (London), 100
Cuba: Phil. Hoadley visit to, 19; cancelled 1860 HBP trip to, 78; HBP in, 120, 152–53, 187–88, 248; US mails to and from, 152, 159, 189–90; *Mascotte*'s first voyage to, 184; *Olivette*'s first voyage to, 195; martial law declared in, 197; Grover Cleveland visit to, 201; possible purchase by US of, 201; revolutionary activities in, 233, 238, 241, 243, 253–54; leadup to war in, 255–56; HBP's postwar plans for, 258, 260–61; mentioned, 2, 57, 203. *See also* Havana, Cuba; Spanish-American War
Cuyler, Richard R., 62

Dallas, TX, 138
Dalton, GA, 71
Damon, Major Seth, 56
Darien, CT, 167
Davis, Jefferson, 81–82, 84, 90, 93, 103
Davis, Richard Harding, 216, 249–50
Davis, Robert W., 2–3
death benefits, 140
Delafield, Edward, 56–57
Delano, Columbus, 122
Della-Sedie, Enrico, 99
Delmonico, Charles, 129, 171, 180
Delmonico's Restaurant (NYC), 129, 180, 183, 220, 259
DeMartin, James, 53–54
Democratic Party, 78–79
Dempsey, Hugh, 72, 264
Denison, TX, 143
Depew, Chauncey, 48
DeWitt Clinton (locomotive), 20, *20*
Díaz, Porfirio, 173
Dickens, Charles, 27
Dinsmore, Augusta Snow, 99, 130–31
Dinsmore, Clarence G., 158
Dinsmore, William Brown: early life and career of, 35, 44, *45*, 46; as HBP mentor, 48–49, 77–78; as Adams Express chief administrator, 59, 65; displaced by G. W. Cass, 63; as Adams Express president, 69, 73, 80, 82–83, 86, 108, 125, 158; and the Maroney scandal, 70, 73, 75; in Florida with HBP, 78, 151–52; as Lincoln Administration ally, 90; with HBP in Paris, 99–100, 130–31; at occupied Charleston and Savannah, 102; and creation of national banks, 102–3; and post–Civil War agreements regarding Southern Express, 105–6, 117–18; and Mexican Express, 106; and postwar Adams Express reorganization, 107; and loan to HBP for Overton Hotel, 111; Fifth Avenue home of, 112–13; as a Western and Atlantic Railroad lessee, 118–19; Hudson River estate of, 122–23, 125; and Alvin Adams's death, 144–45; and PICO, 167, 171, 184; death of, 197; mentioned, 43, 53, 55, 57, 60, 88, 123, 128, 138
disease, 6, 10, 19–20. *See also individual diseases*
Disston, Hamilton, 161, 163, 183
Disston Purchase, 161, 166
Dorsey, Dennis, 87
Double Beach, CT, 232
Drane, Henry M., 160, 166, 176
Dresden, Germany, 131
Drysdale, William, 176, 224
Dublin, Ireland, 131
Ducey, Thomas J., 219–20, 264
Duchess County, NY, 123
Duncan, Russell, 122
Dunham, Bradford, 237, 246, 262, 264
Dupont, GA, 156, 171
Durant, Ghislani: as Margaret Plant's physician, 226, 232; as HBP's physician, 239, 245, 260–62; and HBP's death, 264; and Plant estate litigation, 266–67
Dutch Reformed Church, 28
Duval, Hanson Reiman, 234

Eagle and Phoenix Hotel (Augusta, GA), 64
East Florida Railway Company, 156, 160, 177
East Georgia and Florida Railroad, 189
Eastman National Business College, 109, 113
East Pass, FL, 166
Eclipse (river steamer), 103, 108
École des Beaux-Arts (Paris), 168
economic depressions. *See* Panic (economic)

Edgemere, NY, 267
Edinburgh (steamer), 98
Edwards, H. Sutherland, 111
Eiffel, Gustave, 206
Eiffel Tower (Paris), 206
Eiffel Tower flag, 206, 210, 213
Elliott, David H., 199, 205–6, 210, 220
Elmore, John A., 74, 76, 86
Eltham, England, 215
Emily B. Souder (steamer), 153
employee profit sharing, 221
English, Anna Morris, 27, 68, 139, 182–84, 187–88
English, Caroline Fowler, 138
English, James Edward: early career of, 26–27; as US congressman, 97; and visits HBP in London, 101; at HBP's remarriage, 129; and Texas trip with HBP, 138; as Saratoga Springs promoter, 138–39; in the US Senate, 140–41; and PICO, 167; and Cleveland Administration entrée, 182, 189; married to Anna R. Morris, 182–84; with HBP in Cuba, 187–88; mentioned, 43, 145, 197
Enterprise, FL, 54
Episcopal Church, 9
Era of Good Feelings, 5
Erie (steamer), *176*
Erie Canal, 12, *14*
Erwin, duBignon and Chisholm, 212
Erwin, Robert Gallaudet: as Plant System counsel, 212; drafting of HBP will by, 221–22, 263–64; and South Eastern Investment Co., 225; and Plant estate litigation, 266; mentioned 240
Esther (oratorio), 128
Eufala, AL, 103
Europa (steamer), 101
European travel, 98–101, 109, 115, 118, 130–33, 168–69, 204–6, 215–16, 231, 258–59. *See also names of individual countries and places*
Everglades, 206, 218–19
Exchange Hotel (Montgomery, AL), 82
expositions, 109, 131, 153, 203–6, 226–27, 252. *See also names of individual expositions*
express industry origins, 30–36, 50–51. *See also names of individual companies*
Expressman's Aid Society, 135, 140, 151, 160, 176
Expressman's Mutual Benefit Association. *See* Expressman's Aid Society
expressmen, duties of, 44–45

Fairchild, L. L., 13–14
Fargo, William G., 128
Farmington, CT, 105
Faust e Margherita (opera), 100–101
Fayetteville, NC, 56
Fernandina, FL, 66, 78, 90, 163, 259
Ferry, Orris S., 140
Fifth Avenue (NYC): and William B. Dinsmore, 112–13; fashionable nature of, 113, 135, 151; HBE townhouse on, 129, 136, 141, 146, 169, 183, 195, 206, 217, 245, 260, 264, 267; Windsor Hotel on, 136; and H. M. Flagler, 150; mentioned, 172
Fifth Avenue Hotel (NYC), 140, 163, 220, 231, 251, 257
financial markets and instruments, 26
Finney, Charles Grandison, 15
First National Bank of Augusta (GA), 102
First National Bank of Macon (GA), 103
Fisk, Jim, 125
Fitzgerald, James W.: and *H. B. Plant*, 156; and Savannah River and Gulf coast exploration, 169–70; and Canada-Atlantic and Plant Steamship Co., 232; and *La Grande Duchess*, 240–41; and *Olivette* restoration, 259; mentioned, 165, 226, 256
Flagler, Henry Morrison: as Florida developer, 147; background of, 150; and HBP, 150–52, 185–86, 250; image, *152*; and PICO, 167, 186; married Ida Alice Shourds, 174; at Millionaire's Banquet, 180; at St. Augustine, 174, 182; and South Florida Railroad, 186; St. Augustine plans of, 186–87; with HBP at Tampa, 196, 202; and PICO, 199, 218, 228, 234; and Grover Cleveland visit, 201–2; and extension of rails down Atlantic coast, 219; alliance of with HBP against competition, 219–20; with HBP to Jamaica, 222; and sentiments of regarding Florida politics, 227; and railroad to Palm Beach, 231; Palm Beach tariff conference convened by, 234; Gov. Mitchell's attempted extradition of, 235; at America's Cup races, 240; and HBP's 1896 illness, 245; with HBP in Bahamas, 255; as HBP pallbearer, 264; and purchase of Plant steamship properties, 267; mentioned, 1–2, 183, 204, 216, 221–22, 236, 241, 249
Flagler, Ida Alice Shourds, 174
Flagler, Jennie Louise. *See* Benedict, Jennie Louis Flagler
Flagler, Mary Harkness, 150
Florida: initial HBP visits to, 53–54, 57; described c. 1855, 65; extension of express services to, 106; 1870s need for development in, 147–48; renewed interest in by HBP, 151; tourism in, 159–60; land grants by for railroads, 161, 166, 172–73; impact of Plant railroads on, 188–89; HBP anger at Bourbon government of, 199; and 1889 Paris exposition, 204–5; phosphate discoveries in, 215; sentiments of HBP and H. M. Flagler regarding

politics in, 227; disappointing 1893–94 tourist season in, 230; and attempted Flagler extradition, 235; 1894 freeze in, 235–36; and Great Freeze of 1895, 236–37, 243; renewed optimism about, 253–54. *See names of individual regions and places*
Florida, Atlantic and Gulf Central Railroad, 66
Florida (steamer), 250
Florida Central and Peninsular Railroad, 224, 233–34
Florida Central and Western Railroad, 175
Florida Central Railroad, 163
Florida Constitutional Convention (1885), 228
Florida East Coast Railroad, 241
Florida House of Representatives, 124
Florida Peninsular Railroad, 164
Florida Railroad, 66–67, 161. *See also* Florida Transit Railway; Florida Transit and Peninsular Railroad
Florida Railway and Navigation Co., 177
Florida Southern Railway, 175, 233–34, 244, 250–51
Florida Transit Railway, 161–63
Florida Transit and Peninsular Railroad, 170–72, 176–77. *See also* Florida Railway and Navigation Co.
Florida Yacht Club, 151
Florence, SC, 116
Florence Villa, FL, 248
Folies Bergère (Paris), 231
Forrest, Nathan Bedford, 134
Fort Brooke. *See* Tampa, FL
Fort Dallas. *See* Miami, FL
Fort Donelson, TN, 88
Fort Gates, FL, 195, 203
Fort Henry, TN, 88
Fort Meade, FL, 250
Fort Myers, FL, 214, 218, 244, 248, 256
Fort Myers Steamboat Company, 244
Fortress Monroe, VA, 184
Fort Sumter, SC, 83
Fort Worth, TX, 142–43
Four Hundred, The, 151
Franco-Prussian War, 109, 118, 216
fraternal organizations, 17
Fredericksburg, VA, 55–56
Freeman, Emily Blackstone, 73, 77–78, 120, 146
Freeman, John Morton: early career of, 43–44; relocation to California of, 46–47; rejoined Adams Express, 73; engagement and marriage of, 73, 77–78; impact of wife's death on, 120; death of, 146, 151; mentioned, 52–53, 68
Freeman & Co.'s California Express, 78
freezes, 235–36, 236–37
Frelinghuysen, Frederick, 170
French Riviera, 267
Frieze, Teresa, 38
Frisbee, Joseph, 12
Frisbie, Hannah. *See* Hoadley, Hannah Frisbie
Frisbie, Oliver Libby, 246
Frisbie, Sarah. *See* Plant, Sarah Frisbie
Fulton, Robert, 27

Gainesville, FL, 175, 178, 248
Gaither, Alfred, 135, 145
Galt House (Louisville, KY), 82
Galveston, TX, 71, 80, 117, 138–39, 164, 226
García, Manuel, 233, 253
Garfield, James Abram, 159, 163
Garnier, Charles, 98
Garrett, Franklin, 72
Garrison, L. R., 85
General Ticket and Passenger Agents Convention, 151
George R. Kelsey (steamer). See *Margaret* (steamer)
Georgia: initial visit by HDB to, 54–55; Military Reconstruction in, 108–11; constitutional convention for, 110; mentioned, 66. *See also names of individual places*
Georgia Central Railroad, 180
Germany, 131–32
Gerome, Jean-Léon, 109
Gilded Age, 138
Gilded Age, The (novel), 137–38
Gillett, Timothy Phelps, 7, 10–11, 38, 42
Glasgow, Scotland, 168–69
Globe (steamboat), 35–36
Globe Hotel (Augusta, GA), 67–68
Glogowski, Herman, 214
golf and golf courses, 244, 267
Gómez, Máximo, 233, 253
Gordon, John B., 171, 173
Gould, Jay, 136, 172–73, 180, 182
Gould, Georgie, 224
Gounod, Charles, 100
Governor's Harbor, Bahamas, 255
Grady, Henry W., 196
Graham, Thomas, 174
Grand Hotel de Londres (Paris), 131
Grand Masonic Lodge (NYC), 187
Grand Union Hotel (Saratoga Springs), 138, 142, 221
Grande Duchesse, La (steamer), 235, 239–41, 245, 247–48, *249*, 251, 263
Grande-Duchesse de Gérolstein, La (opera), 109, 153, 210
Granier, Jeanne: Parisian debut of, 132; European career of, 153–54, 168, 216, 231, 239; and *La Grande-Duchesse de Gérolstein*, 210, 245; and HBP interest in, 240, 245, 248

Grant, Lemuel P., 72
Grant, Ulysses S., 87, 102, 122–23, 142
Grant Park (Atlanta), 72
Graves, Robert, 267
Great Depression, 133
Great Freeze of 1895, 236–37, 243
Great Revival of 1831, 18–19
Greeley, Horace, 3
Green, Jonathan Harrington, 48
Greye, Otis, 220
Grito de Yara (Cuban insurrection), 120, 152
Groover, A. H., 237
Grossman, Peter Z., 59
Guiteau, Charles, 163
Gwin, William McKendree, 99

H. B. Plant (steamer), 156, 171, 203, 215
Haile, Charles H., 96, 100
Haines, Henry Stephen: as general superintendent of Savannah, Florida and Western Railway Co., 155, 160–61, 164, 166, 171, 175–76, 184, 197, 212; and Havana hotel plans, 190–92; and competition to succeed HBP, 198; as Plant System manager, 212, 226–27; and South Eastern Investment Co., 225; resignation of, 239–40; as HBP pallbearer, 264; mentioned, 220
Halifax, Nova Scotia, 96, 101, 220, 226, 232
Halifax (steamer), 222
Hall, Richard, 247
Hamilton, Bermuda, 94, 96
Handel, George Frideric, 128
Hanna, Mark, 261
Hansa (steamer), 94
Harlow, Alvin, 114
Harnden, William, 30–31, 33–34
Harnden's Express, 31, 35–36, 53–54, 58–60
Harper's Ferry raid (1859), 77
Harrison, Benjamin, 201, 203, 220, 223
Harrison, Lynde: as HBP's personal attorney, 171, 209, 225, 241, 260, 264; and HBP's will, 262, 266; as HBP pallbearer, 264; mentioned, 184, 220
Harrison, Mary Dimmick, 209
Harrogate, England, 131
Hart, Edward Lucas, 105
Hartford, CT, 43–44, 49
Hart's English and Classical Family School for Boys (Farmington), 105, 109
Haskell, D. H., 47–48
Haskell, E. B., 225
Haussmann, George-Eugène, 98
Havana, Cuba: HBP at, 120, 122, 152–53, 171, 180–82, 184, 187–88, 190, 196, 201–2, 208–9, 215, 221, 229, 250, 254; image of, *121*; and steamer connection with Plant railroads, 171, 173, 199; HBP vision for, 175, 182, 187, 207, 229; construction of piers and warehouses at, 181; and mail service, 189–90; hotel plans for, 190–92, 196, 218–19, 261–62; Grover Cleveland at, 201–2; White Squadron at, 215; *Maine* explosion at, 255; HBP's last visits to, 261; mentioned, 2, 78, 158, 165, 170, 197, 200
Hawaii, 149, 252–53
Hayes, Rutherford B., 144, 159
Hazelhurst, Robert, 54
Hearst, William Randolph, 249–50, 255
Hemingway, Teresa Frieze, 38
Hemingway, Willis, 38
Henry Bradley Plant Company, 263
Hernando County, FL, 178
High Springs, FL, 175, 248
Hill, Benjamin Harvey, 119, 122
Hill, Everett G., 25
Hillsborough River, FL, 193, 195, 197
Hilton, Henry, 48
Hoadley, Amelia, 87
Hoadley, Betsey Bradley Plant: marriage and family with Anderson Plant, 5–6, 9; widowhood of in 1825, 11; second marriage to Philemon Hoadley Jr.,11–12; relocation to Martinsburg, NY, 12–21; resettles at New Haven, 21; Civil War–era visits by HBP to, 92, 97, 101–102; as Margaret Loughman Birdsall employer, 127–28; and HBP's remarriage and honeymoon 129–31, 133; death of, 187; mentioned, 39
Hoadley, George, 12
Hoadley, George Anderson, 18, 25
Hoadley, Hannah Frisbie, 10
Hoadley, Henry Hodges, 11
Hoadley, Horace Philemon: birth of, 21; and relocation to Texas, 80; and wife's death, 87; and PICO, 198; and South Eastern Investment Co., 225; at World Columbian Exposition, 226; death of, 227; mentioned, 119, 141
Hoadley, Orrin, 10
Hoadley, Philemon, Jr.: marriage to Betsey Bradley Plant, 11–12; at Martinsburg, NY, 12–21; religious principles and associations of, 14–19, 40–41, 48; and broken health, Caribbean voyage, and embrace of abolitionism, 19–20; New Haven residence of, 24–25; and clashes with HBP, 28; death of, 92; mentioned, 27, 39, 80
Hoadley, Philemon, Sr., 13
Hoey, John: early life and career of, 35; as HBP companion in New York City, 48–49; and Mexican Express, 106; in Rufus Bullock

traveling party, 123; as matchmaker, 127–28; as Long Branch promoter, 142; and death of Alvin Adams, 145; and PICO, 167, 171; as Adams Express president, 197, 216; death of, 220; mentioned, 43–44, 46–47, 53, 57, 60, 88, 215–16, 220
Hoey, Josephine Shaw Russell, 51–52, 216
Hoey, Sister Margaret, 127
Hoey & Co.'s Charleston, Savannah and Montgomery Express, 46, 58–60
Holt, W. W., 83–84
Honduras, 207, 254–55
Hong Kong., 252
Honolulu, HI, 252
hospitals and health care. *See* Plant System Relief and Hospital Department
Hotel Brunswick (NYC), 174
Hotel del Coronado (near San Diego), 252
Hotel Edgemore (Queens, NY), 240
Hotel Inglaterra (Havana), 192, 254
Hotel Kaaterskill (Catskill Mountains), 211
Hotel Mascotte (Havana), 254
Hotel Pasaje (Havana): appearance of, *181*; Grover Cleveland at, 202; peaceful conditions at, 254; mentioned, 188, 191
Hotel Punta Gorda (FL), 234, 244
Hotel Roma (Havana), 254
hotels: early ownership of by HBP, 91, 110; reluctance of HBP to invest in, 174; H. M. Flagler plans for, 186; and PICO entry into ownership of, 187. *See also names of individual hotels*
Hotel Telegrafo (Havana), 254
Houghton, George H., 128–29
Houston, TX, 138
Howland's Hotel (Long Branch), 144
Hudson River, 12, 27, 123, 125–26, 191
Humphreys, Frederick C., 144
Huntington, Collis P., 136, 239
Hurlbert, Edward, 73, 86, 107, 117
hurricanes: 60, 169–70, 227, 233, 247
Hutchinson (steamer), 171
Hyde Park, NY, 125

Il Barbiere (opera). See *Barber of Seville*
Illinois Central Railroad, 68, 207
Imperial Mexican Express Co., 106
Imperial Opera House (Vienna), 100
Impressionism and Impressionist Art, 100
Indianapolis, IN, 207
Indian River, FL, 203
Indian River Hotel (Rockledge), 230
Industrial Revolution, 26
Ingersoll, Charles Roberts, 140
Ingomar (yacht), 261
Ingraham, James Edmundson: as South Florida Railroad president, 164–66, 175–76, 184, 197, 201; to California with the Plants, 195; observations of on Margaret Plant's health, 211; Everglades expedition of, 218–19
Inman, John, 207
Innocents Abroad, The (novel), 137
International Conference of American States (1889), 207,
International Exposition (Paris): of 1867, 109; of 1889, 204–6
International Fisheries Conference (1898), 254
International Railroad and Steamship Co., 171
Irwinville, GA, 103
Italian Opera (Paris), 131
Italy, 99–100. *See also names of individual places*
Italy, Kingdom of, 99
Ives, Joel, 10

Jack, Doctor F., 212, 220, 240, 251, 264
Jackson, Andrew, 21, 27
Jackson, Arthur C., 205–6
Jackson, MS, 71, 123
Jackson, Thomas, 95–96
Jackson & Sharp Co., 119
Jacksonian Era, 5
Jacksonville, FL: visited by W. B. Dinsmore during Seminole war, 53; HBP at, 54, 57, 122, 175–76, 180, 182, 200, 217, 220, 241, 262; 1854 destruction of by fire, 57; and railroad connections to, 66; express connections, with, 106; yellow fever at, 143, 151, 198; and H. M. Flagler, 150; William B. Astor investments at, 151; tourism at, 160; championship prize fight at, 229; hurricane at, 247; mentioned, 78, 155, 166, 195. *See also* Strawberry Mills, FL
Jacksonville, Pensacola and Mobile Railroad, 164
Jacksonville, Tampa, and Key West Railroad: and purchase of rights regarding Tampa-to-Kissimmee link, 173; standard gauge rails for, 189; purchased by Plant System, 262
Jacksonville and St. John's River Railroad, 262
Jamaica: visited by Philemon Hoadley, 19; steamer service to, 207, 222, 243, 254; HBP plans for, 211, 221, 248, 261; appreciation for Plant at, 227; HBP and Margaret Plant visit, 238, 255; yellow fever in, 253; mentioned, 1, 250
James, D. Willis, 121
Japan, 76, 252–53
Jaruco, Cuba, 253
Jay Cooke & Co., 133
Jefferson County, NY, 18–19
Jennings, Mary. *See* Mary Jennings Loughman

Jersey City, NJ, 260
Jesup, Morris K.: and the Southern Railway Securities Co., 121; and railroad investments of, 154; as PICO director, 167; connections of with Metropolitan Trust Co., 177; and South Eastern Investment Co., 225
Jim Crow discrimination. *See* race and race relations
Johnson, Andrew, 102, 108
Johnson, Dudley S., 162
Johnson, Elijah A., 43–44, 47–48, 52
Johnson's Island, OH, 96
Johnston, Joseph E., 102
joint stock associations, 58–59
Jolie Parfumeuse, La (comic opera), 132
Juarez, Benito, 106
Judson, Curtiss, 49
Judson's Hotel (New York City), 49, 52, 61
Juniata (steamer), 206–7
Jupiter, FL, 202

Kendall, Amos, 31
Key, David M., 152–53, 158–59
Key West, FL: HBP at, 153, 181, 192, 256; major fire at, 188; and mail service to, 189; mentioned, 2, 171, 185, 209
Kimball, David, 16–18
Kimball, Edwin N., 119
Kimball, Hannibal I., 119, 123
Kimball & Ramsey Sleeping Car Co., 119
Kimball House (Atlanta), 119
Kingston, NY, 125
Kingston, Jamaica: Philemon Hoadley at, 19; HBP at, 211, 222, 229, 244, 255; H. M. Flagler at, 222; HBP plans for, 243–44; mentioned, 1, 245
Kinsley & Co.'s Express, 58–59
Kissimmee, FL: construction of South Florida railroad to, 164, 166; HBP at, 165, 175, 177, 182, 248; and Tropical Hotel, 244
Kissimmee Hotel, 244
Knetsch, Joe, 161
Knowles, Francis B., 211
Knoxville, TN, 61, 71, 105, 116
Ku Klux Klan, 122, 124, 134

labor and labor relations, 178–79, 210–11, 213, 215, 221, 242, 246. *See also* strikes
Labor Union Recorder (newspaper), 217
Lafayette, Marquis de (Gilbert du Motier), 8
Lagrange, GA, 61, 63
L'Aimee (painting), 109
Lake City, FL, 66, 155, 175
Lake Erie, 12, 96
Lakeland, FL, 182, 228, 255
Lake Worth, FL, 235
Lancastrian School (New Haven, CT), 21, 25–26
Laurel-in-the-Pines Hotel (Lakewood, NJ), 221–22
Lavaca, TX, 80
Lawn Beach (Flagler estate), 174
Lawrence, E. A., 113
Lee, Fitzhugh, 202, 259
Lee, Robert E., 77, 91, 102, 105
Leesburg, FL, 172
Leffingwell on Hot Coals, or The Victim of Circumstances, 141
Leon County, FL, 65
LePage, Robert, 179
LePageville (Savannah), 179
Leslie, Frank, 187
Leslie, Miriam Florence Squier, 187–88, 204
Leslie's Illustrated Newspaper, 187
L'étoile du Nord (opera), 153
Leventritt, David, 267
Lewis County, NY, 12, 14
Lincoln, Abraham, 79, 83–84, 88, 96, 101–2
Little Church Around the Corner (New York City), 128–29
Little Rock, AK, 138, 180
Live Oak, FL, 122, 156, 161
Live Oak, Tampa & Charlotte Harbor Railroad, 162, 177
Live Oak and Rowland's Bluff Railroad, 161, 169, 171, 177
Liverpool, England, 45, 51, 53, 93, 97–98, 101, 141, 258
Livingston, Winchester & Co.'s Savannah Express, 58–59
Livingston's Philadelphia Express, 58–59
lobbyists and lobbying, 228
Lohengrin (opera), 216
London, England: HBP at, 100–101, 118, 131, 133, 153, 168, 204, 239, 258; mentioned, 99
Long Branch, NJ, 142, 144, 148–49, 154, 163, 258
Long Island Sound, 30, 34, 174, 232, 240
Lookout Mountain, TN, 80
Loughman, Ellen O'Dwyer, 126
Loughman, Freddie, 149
Loughman, Margaret Josephine. *See* Plant, Margaret Loughman Birdsall
Loughman, Martin, 126–29, 241
Loughman, Martin Francis, 127, 149
Loughman, Mary Jennings, 127
Loughman, Pauline Coulon, 127
Loughman, Simon, 126–27, 211, 226
Louisville, KY: express connections with, 69; Adams Express leadership at, 82; as channel to North for HBP and family, 87, 96; yellow fever at, 135
Louisville and Nashville Railroad, 158–60
Loup, C. L., 139

Lovell, John E., 25
Lowville (NY) Academy, 14
lynchings, 227

Maceo, Antonio, 233
Macon, GA: arrival of I. C. Plant at, 54; express business at, 54, 61, 63; initial visits by HBP to, 55, 57; HBP sees Jefferson Davis at, 103; national bank at, 103; mentioned, 64, 70, 220, 238
Macon (GA), National Bank of, 103
Macon & Augusta Railroad, 60, 110
Madame le Diable (opera), 168
Mahoney, John, 176
Maine, M. D., 110
Maine (warship), 120, 255
Maitland, FL, 177
Malvern Hotel (Bar Harbor), 208
Mamaroneck, NY, 174
Manassas Junction, VA, 85
Manatee, FL, 178
Manatee River, FL, 210
Manchester, NC, 56
Manhattan Beach Hotel (Coney Island), 158–59
Manhattanville, NY, 126
Mapleson Opera Festival, 174
March to the Sea, Sherman's, 101
Mardi Gras (New Orleans), 69–70, 113, 117, 128, 238, 255
Margaret (steamer): at Tampa dock, *176*; purchase of, 178; and Pico Park, 232; wreck of, 240; replacement contract for, 241; mentioned, 184–85, 214, 245
Mario, Guiseppe, 99, 111
Marion (steamer), 57
Marion County, FL, 54, 178
Markoe, Thomas M., 56–57
Marks, Matthew R., 170
Maroney, Nathan, 70, 73–75
Marquis and Marchioness de Caux. *See* Cahusac, Henri de Roger de; Patti, Adelina
Martí, José, 233
Martin, S. Walter, 1
Martin, Walter (general), 13
Martinsburg, NY, 12–21
Marveille (opera), 100
Mascotte, La (comic opera), 184
Mascotte (steamer): launched, 183–85; Port Tampa-to-Havana route served by, 187, 189, 192, 209; and service to Honduras, 254–55; mentioned, 194, 238, 244, 255
Matamoras, Mexico, 138
Maximilian I (Mexico), 98, 106
May (steam yacht), 169–70
McCuaig, James Simeon, 96
McDaniel, James E., 86
McInley, Abner, 251, 261–62
McKinley, William: presidential election of, 248; Alger named secretary of war by, 248; and F. Q. Brown friendship, 251; declaration of war issued by, 256; and HBP, 253, 257–58; and Cuban business affairs in postwar era, 261–62
McKeever, James Joseph, 72
McLean, Edward, 143
McPherson, James M., 79
Memminger, Christopher G., 81–82, 92–93, 157
Memphis, TN: express service at, 68–70, 72, 76, 106; surrender to US forces of, 90; rail connections with, 116; yellow fever at, 150; mentioned, 110, 113, 123, 128, 134, 182, 238
Memphis & Charleston Railroad, 67–68
Memphis and Ohio Railroad, 76
Menton, France, 267
Metropolitan Hotel (Washington, DC), 183
Metropolitan Opera (NYC), 240, 245
Metropolitan Trust Co., 177
Mexican Express Co., 106
Mexico: HBP tour of, 200; mentioned, 106–7, 138, 173, 182, 199
Mexico City, Mexico, 199–200
Meyerbeer, Giacomo, 153
Miami, FL: 2, 147, 218–19, 250, 255–56
Miami River, FL, 147
Midland Grant Hotel (London), 131
Midland Railway, 131
Military Reconstruction, 108–11
Milledgeville, GA, 55, 103
Millen, GA, 189
Miller, Vivien M. L., 156
Milliken, James, 103
Millionaire's Banquet, 180
Miolan-Carvalho, Marie-Caroline, 100
Mississippi River, 68, 70
Mitchell, Charles, 229
Mitchell, Edward, 62
Mitchell, Henry L., 175, 228, 235
Mobile, AL: yellow fever at, 71; HBP acquired slave couple at, 87; express connections with, 105; rail connections with, 116–17, 164, 207, 210; and steamer connections with Tampa, 204, 206–7; mentioned 200
Mohawk & Hudson Rail Road, 20
Mohawk River, 12
Monteagle Hotel (Niagara Falls), 76
Montego Bay, Jamaica, 19, 255
Montgomery, AL: express connections with, 54, 61, 63; and the Maroney scandal, 70, 73–76; as Confederate capital, 81–82; litigation at against HBP critics, 86; rail connections with, 116, 180; yellow fever at, 135; mentioned, 55, 200, 225

Montreal, Canada, 19, 93, 96–97, 100, 226
Mora, José M., 171
Morgan, John Tyler, 252
Morgan (steamer), 171
Morgan Steamship Line, 171, 176, 180
Montauk, NY, 259
Morrill, Justin S., 118
Morris, Anna Robinson. *See* English, Anna Morris
Morris, Lucius Smith, 67–68, 183
Morton, Anna Livingston Reade Street, 209
Morton, Levi, 209
Murphy, Lady Mary, 126
Myrtle Bank Hotel (Kingston, Jamaica), 243–44
Mystic Shrine, Ancient Arabic Order of Nobles of the, 187

Naples, Italy, 99
Napoléon III, 98–99
Nashville, TN, 61, 63, 67, 90, 123, 151, 252
Nassau, Bahamas, 96, 152, 184, 222, 255–56
Nast, Thomas, 158
Natchez, MS, 69
Nathan, Benjamin, 140
Nathan Mansion (NYC), 140
national banks, 102–3. *See also* names of banks
National Coast Defense Association, 248
National Republican (Augusta newspaper), 109
Newbern, NC, 105
New Branford, FL. *See* Branford, FL
New Brunswick, Canada, 1, 226
Newcomer, Benjamin F., 121, 157, 167, 171, 177, 264
Newcomer, D. T., 171
New England Spotted Fever, 10
New Guinea (New Haven), 23–24
New Haven, CT: and yellow fever outbreak, 6; described, 22–23; diversity at, 23; shipping, trade, and industry at, 23–24, 26–36; ties to slavery and the South at, 24; temperance movement at, 41, 48; as express industry hub, 46–47; visit to by HBP during Civil War, 92, 101–2; and James E. English remarriage, 184; and International Congress delegates at, 206–7; HBP seeking residence at, 263–64; mentioned 171
New Haven (steamboat), 30
New Haven and Hartford Express, 46
New Haven and New London Railroad, 86
New Haven Steamship Company, 27–28
Newnansville, FL, 175
New Orleans, LA: express connections with, 68–70, 72, 105, 117; HBP affection for, 69–70, 76, 78; opera at, 70; yellow fever at, 71, 135; fruit shipments north from, 79; litigation at against HBP critics, 86; surrender to US forces of, 90; rail connections with, 164, 172, 185, 207; mentioned, 113, 120, 123, 138, 151, 153, 176, 200, 238
Newport, RI, 138
Newport News, VA, 239–41, 245, 247–48
Newport News Ship Building & Dry Dock Co., 239, 248
New School Presbyterians, 28
New York (steamboat), 27–29, *29*, 31–32
New York and Florida Special, 199
New York & New Haven Rail Road, 46–48
New York City, NY: cholera at, 19–20; described c. 1849–50, 49, *50*; rail connections from Deep South to, 55; arrest of Nathan Maroney at, 75; and Adelina Patti debut, 77; HBP residing at during Civil War, 102
New York Custom House, 51
New York Mining Co., 46
Niagara Falls, NY, 76
Nicaragua Canal, 250
Nimrod (steamboat), 32
noces d'Olivette, Les (comic opera), 191
Norfolk, VA, 56, 105, 172
Normandie (steamer), 215
Noroton, CT, 220
North, John T., 215
Northampton, MA, 148
North Congregational Church (New Haven), 28
Northern Pacific Railroad, 133
Norton, Asa, 8–9, 57
Norton, Emily. *See* Blackstone, Emily Norton
Norton, Mary Elizabeth Plant, 53
Norton, Sophia Barker, 9
Norton, William Tyler, 53
Norwich, CT, 141, 146, 167, 199
Nova Scotia, 96, 101, 220, 226, 232
Nuestra Señora del Carmen plantation, 181, 233, 241, 253

O'Brien, Michael J.: employed by Adams Express, 68, 72; as HBP private secretary, 93; as postwar Southern Express assistant superintendent, 106; as Southern Express general superintendent, 110, 113, 123, 138, 144, 151, 158, 213, 225, 253; and HBP's remarriage, 129; as Texas Express superintendent, 139; and PICO, 167, 177, 183–84, 259; expanding influence of, 173; at Havana with HBP, 215, 218–19; as Southern Express president, 268; death of, 268; mentioned, 44–45, 122, 142, 148, 215–16, 220, 240
Ocala, FL., 240–41, 248, 262
Ocala House (Ocala), 240
Ocean View Hotel (Block Island), 138
O'Duyer [O'Dwyer], Ellen. *See* Loughman, Ellen O'Dwyer

Offenbach, Jacques, 109, 132, 239
Ogdensburgh, NY, 19, 21
Oglethorpe, GA, 54
Oglethorpe Hotel (Brunswick), 195
Ohio and Pennsylvania Railroad, 68
Ohio Life Insurance & Trust Co., 69
Ohio River, 105
Okefenokee Swamp, 157, 206
Old School Presbyterians, 28
Olivette (steamer): launch of, 191; initial voyage to Cuba of, 195; summer New England routes of, 197–98, 210; HBP with Grover Cleveland on, *201*, 202; Port Tampa-to-Havana service by, 202, 208–9, 254, 261; at NYC, 216, 227; service to Halifax by, 220; as focus of Hearst attack article, 249–50; sinking and restoration of, 259; mentioned, 194
Oneida (yacht), 196
opera: HBP's beginning love for, 48–49, 70, 77, 100–101, 109. *See also names of individual operas and performers*
Opéra Garnier (Paris), 98, 216
Orange Belt Railroad, 233, 238
Orange Grove Hotel (Tampa), 175
orchestrion, 204
Orlando, FL, 177
Ortiz, Paul, 156
Osborne, Frederick S., 143
Osborne, Nellie, 143
Ottawa, Canada, 226
Overland Contract Company. *See* Southern Railway Security Company
Overlook Mountain House (Catskill Mountains), 125
Overton Hotel (Memphis), 110–11, 128, 182
Owens, Charles D., 169–70, 178, 184, 220, 239

Pacific Ocean, 252–53
Palais des Beaux-Arts (Paris), 100
Palais du Trocadéro (Paris), 153
Palatka, FL, 54, 171, 182, 233, 238
Palm Beach, FL, 221, 231, 234–36, 241, 250
Palmer, John B., 134
Panic (economic): of 1837, 27; of 1857, 69; of 1873, 132–33; of 1893, 222–24, 243
Paris, France: pro-Confederate activities at, 97–99; HBP at, 98–100, 109, 115, 131, 153, 168, 204–6, 209–10, 215–16; and Sisters of the Sacred Heart, 126; Plant System agent posted to, 237; and Margaret Plant Graves illness at, 267
Paris Bourse Crash (1882), 168
Paris Universal Exposition of 1889, 203–6
Parker, Mary, 252
Parsons, Ida Josephine. *See* Plant, Ida Parsons
patriotic societies, 246
Patti, Adelina: New York debut of, 77; performances of, 99–101, 115, 118, 131–32, 153, 168–69; marriage and marital issues of, 111, 118; as Windsor Hotel patron, 137
Payret Theatre (Havana), 188, 192, 254
P. B. Burke & Co., 33
Peace River, FL, 233
Peale, Rembrandt, 42
Peck, Richard, 34
Pemberton's Ferry, FL, 182
Peninsular & Occidental Steamship Company, 267
Pennsylvania (steamer), 130–31, 133
Pennsylvania and Reading Railroad, 222
Pennsylvania Railroad, 115–16, 125, 130, 134, 179
Pensacola, FL, 116, 135, 164
Pensacola and Atlantic Railroad, 164
Pensacola and Georgia Railroad, 66
Pequonnoc Bank, 91, 102
Pequonnoc National Bank, 102
Percival, Wilson, 221
Pérez, Louis A., 232
Perichole, La (opera), 239
Petersburg, VA, 56
Petit Duc, Le (comic opera), 154
Phelps, Charles H., 73
Philadelphia, PA: rail connections from Deep South to, 55; as home of Thomas A. Scott, 117; Hamilton Disston home at, 161; and shipbuilding at, 182–84, 189, 195, 215, 259; mentioned, 28, 43, 130–31
Phillips, Daniel, 101
phosphates and phosphate industry, 215, 217–18, 228
Pickens, F. W., 82–83
PICO Hotel (Sanford, FL), 187, 191, 194
Picolata, FL, 54
Pico Park (Branford, CT), 232
Piedmont Air Line Railroad, 116
Piedmont Park (Atlanta), 240
Pine Island, FL, 214
Pinellas Peninsula, FL, 244
Piney Woods Hotel (Thomasville, Ga.), 191, 195
Pinkerton, Allan, 70, 73–76, 88–89
Pittsburgh, PA, 63, 231
Plandome (schooner), 19
Plant, Anderson, 5–8, 10–11
Plant, Betsey Bradley. *See* Hoadley, Betsey Bradley Plant
Plank, Cyrus S., 72
Plant, David, 6
Plant, Eliza Ann, 8, 10
Plant, Ellen Blackstone: courtship and marriage of, 37–38; image of, *38*; reaction of to son's death and illness, 42, 46; joined HBP at New York City, 49–50; and birth of her sec-

ond son, 50; persistent health problems of, 52, 56–57, 60, 65, 73, 79; Florida rest cure for, 57, 61, 64, 68–69, 73, 81; at Augusta, 63–64, 69–70, 73, 87–88; impact of brother George's death on, 86–87; death of, 88; reburial of, 231; mentioned, 8, 49, 120, 146

Plant, George Henry (son of HBP), 39, 42–43

Plant, George Henry (son of I. C. Plant), 54

Plant, Henry Bradley: family background, birth, and early childhood of, 5–12; religious influences upon, 6–7, 14–21; schooling of, 10–11, 14–15, 25; and remarriage of his mother, 12; relocation to New York of, 12–21; and introduction to steamboat travel, 12; political attitudes of, 17–19; and introduction to railroads, 20; resettlement at New Haven of, 21; and early experiences in steamboats, 28–36; beginning involvement in express industry of, 33, 35–37, 40; as retail merchant, 37, 40–42; first marriage of, 37–38, 40; birth and death of first child of, 39, 40, 42–43; employment of as express messenger, 44–48, 50, *67*; employment of at Adams & Co. headquarters and early residence in New York City, 47–52; birth of second child of, 50; as express courier to Philadelphia mint, 51; as Adams & Co. administrator, 52; initial visits to Southeast of, 53–55, 57, 66; relocation to Augusta by, 60–62, 64–65; expansion plans of, 66–67; and the Maroney scandal, 70; and Atlanta residence, 71–73; and Confederate government relations, 81–85, 91–92; and creation of Southern Express Co., 83–84, 114; Civil War–era criticisms of, 86, 94, 110–11; slave ownership by, 87; trips to North during Civil War by, 86–92; and ties to US intelligence services, 89–91; first hotel purchased by, 91; permanent departure of from Confederate States, 94–96; as representative of Confederate government, 97–98; in Europe during Civil War, 98–101; and Adelina Patti, 77, 99–101, 131–32, 168–69; residence of at New York City late in Civil War, 102; and creation of national banks, 102–3; in the immediate postwar era, 103–7; first steamer commissioned by, 103; and Mexican Express, 106; and postwar Adams Express reorganization, 107; resumed New York City residence of, 110; as principal in Southern Railway Security Co., 115–16, 120–21, 123–25, 133–34; as a Western and Atlantic Railroad lessee, 118–19, 143–44; as Texas Pacific Railroad director, 124; and marriage to Margaret Loughman Birdsall, 128–31, 148; purchase of Fifth Avenue home by, 129, 148, 169; and Jeanne Granier, 132, 168; Panic of 1873 impact on, 133–34, 136; and the Expressman's Aid Society, 135, 140; portrait busts commissioned by, 136, *137*, *142*; and continuing Southern Express business, 138, 142, 151–52; interests of in Texas, 138–39, 142–43; and Alvin Adams's death, 144–45; and Henry M. Flagler, 150–52, 185–86, 234; beginning ownership of railroads and steamboat lines by, 154–58, 213; as Southern Bell director, 155; and convict leasing, 156–57; railroad network envisioned by, 157–58; rail and steamer connections to Havana planned by, 161; and South Florida Railroad control, 164–65, 171, 173, 175–76; and PICO, 167; railroad sleeping car use by, 167, 170, 180, 218; Havana hotel plans of, 190–92, 196, 218–19, 261; and Tampa hotel plans of, 192–93, 195–99; dissatisfaction of, 197–98; and Car No. 100, 200–201, 207; at the Tampa Bay Hotel, 213–15, 218–19, 223–24; and Adams Express scandals, 216; alliance of with Flagler against competition, 219–20; will of, 222, 262; with Flagler to Jamaica, 222; personal holdings reorganized, 225; rail excursion by to Canada and Pacific coast, 226–27; sentiments of regarding Florida politics, 227; at Tampa Bay Hotel, *230*; and Jeanne Granier, 239–40, 245; illness of, 245, 258, 260–61; biography commissioned by, 246; and conflict with W. R. Hearst, 249; with Flagler to Bahamas, 255–56; Spanish-American War criticisms of, 257–58; cartoon of, *259*; biography of published, 260; death and funeral of, 264

Plant, Henry Bradley, II, 239, 263, 266

Plant, Ida Parsons, 148–49

Plant, Increase Cook, 54, 56–57, 64, 70, 103, 220

Plant, Margaret Loughman Birdsall: Catskills rendezvous with HBP, 125; early life and family of, 126–28; and marriage to HBP, 128–31; ambitions of, 134–35; portrait bust of, *142*; personal and family issues of, 148–49, 168; and *Mascotte* launch, 183; tarpon caught by, 202; and Tampa Bay Hotel furnishings, 204; illness of, 211, 217–20, 226, 229, 232, 248, 258; at Tampa Bay Hotel inaugural ball, 213; at Tampa Bay Hotel, 214, *230*, 236; with HBP to Jamaica, 238; and Cotton States Exposition, 239; oil portrait of, *247*; and Plant yellow, 249; as Spanish-American War hostess, 256–57; and *Olivette* restoration, 259; and Plant estate litigation, 266–67; remarriage and death of, 267; mentioned, 167, 194–95, 216

Plant, Mary Blackstone, 8, 121

Plant, Mary Elizabeth. *See* Norton, Mary Elizabeth Plant
Plant, Mary R., 10
Plant, Morton Freeman: birth of, 50; relocation of to Augusta, 64; and Civil War years, 87, 92, 97–98, 102; continuing education of, 105, 109, 113; employed by Southern Express, 113, 122, 128, 195; at Adams Express, 128, 141–42; and his father's honeymoon, 131–32; indiscretions of, 134–35, 141, 143, 148–49, 158; and friction with HBP, 143–44, 195; reconciliation of with HBP, 145; first marriage of, 148–49; and work on river steamers, 168; and Savannah River and Gulf coast exploration by, 169–70; remarriage of, 195; Grover Cleveland hosted by, 203; to Jamaica with HBP, 211–12, 250; as tennis tournament sponsor, 218, 224; and steamship expansion into Canada, 224; and South Eastern Investment Co., 225; as Plant System executive, 238, 240, 259; and *Ingomar* cruise with HBP, 261; and HBP's Cuba plans, 262; sued as HBP estate trustee, 266; HBP estate litigation opposed by, 267; mentioned, 43, 49, 60–61, 68–69, 81, 108, 169, 245
Plant, Nellie Capron, 195
Plant, Samuel, 6, 91
Plant, Samuel Orrin, 6, 8, 121, 177
Plant, Sarah Frisbie, 6, 12, 28, 37
Plant City, FL, 175, 228
Plant Day, 240–41
Plant estate litigation, 266–67
Planter's Hotel (Augusta), 73, 87–88, 110
Plant family, 6
Plant Investment Company (PICO): incorporated, 167; support for expansions from, 171, 199, 218; tour of operations by, 177; consolidation of lines by, 177; financing obtained by, 177, 225, 229, 243; and steamship contracts, 182; and hotels and resorts, 187, 199, 244; and Port Tampa, 193–95; and 1889 Paris exposition, 205–6; mentioned, 174. *See also* Plant System
Plant Steamship Line: service to Central and South America, 180–82, 199–200, 207, 215; HBP takes personal control of, 209; H. S. Haines elevation after W. S. Chisholm's death ratified by, 212; "grand steamship" commissioned by, 239; and wreck of *La Grande Duchesse*, 251; and Spanish-American War, 256, 259; purchase of by H. M. Flagler, 267; mentioned, 178, 191, 193, 206. *See also names of individual ships and places*
Plantsville (Branford), 6
Plant System: vision for, 185; issues of control over, 198; reorganization of, 212–13, 220, 225, 235, 237; negative legacies of Chisholm's administration of, 213; railroad purchases by, 233–34, 238, 262; and employee benefits, 179, 246–47; and Cuban railroad bonds, 258; rail lines of purchased by Atlantic Coast Line Railroad, 267; mentioned, 1
Plant System Relief and Hospital Department, 246–47
Plant yellow, 249–50
Platt, Thomas C., 251, 264
Plaza Hotel (Rockledge), 230
Polk, James K., 46
Polk County, FL, 178, 218, 228, 233, 249–50
Polk County Fair, 255
Ponce de Leon Hotel (St. Augustine): plans for, 186–87; image of, *193*; opening of, 196; HBP at, 196–97, 222, 236; Grover Cleveland at, 202; painting of at 1889 Paris exposition, 206; mentioned, 195, 199
Pope, John, 108
Port Tampa: establishment of, 193–95; improvements at, 199; service to Mobile from, 206; Vice President Morton and First Lady Harrison at, 209; service to Jamaica from, 211, 222, 255; harbor improvements at, 218; and Spanish-American War, 256–58; mentioned, 191, 202, 207, 260
Port Tampa Inn, 194–95, 200, 202
Porter, Horace, 122
Portland, ME, 226
portrait busts, 136, *137*, *142*, 145
Portsmouth, VA, 56
Poughkeepsie, NY, 109
Powell, J. C., 156–57, 169–70
Presbyterian Church, 13, 28
Prescott, Ontario, 21
presidential election: of 1860, 79; of 1876, 143–44; of 1880, 159; of 1884, 180; of 1888, 201; of 1892, 220; of 1896, 248
Puerto Rico, 258, 261
Pullman, George M.: and Car No. 100, 200; at Paris exposition, 204; and PICO, 218; at the Tampa Bay Hotel, 224; mentioned, 119, 136
Pullman, Hattie Sanger, 196
Pullman, Kimball & Ramsey Sleeping Car Co., 119
Pullman palace cars, 119, 200
Pulsifer, Royal M., 164, 177, 199
Punta Gorda, FL, 214, 233–34, 238–39, 244, 248, 250–51
Punta Gorda Hotel. *See* Hotel Punta Gorda
Punta Rassa, FL, 244
Pusey and Jones Co., 215

Quebec, Canada, 19, 226
Queenstown, Ireland, 206

race and race relations, 2, 125–26, 178
railroads and railroading: initial New York development of, 20; early HBP investments in, 91, 104–5; in post-Civil War South, 104–5; and Panic of 1873, 133–34. *See also names of individual rail lines*
Railway Express Agency, 268
Raleigh, NC, 56
Randolph, George W., 92
Reagan, John H., 81, 84–85, 93, 103
Reconstruction Acts (1867), 108. *See also* Military Reconstruction
Red River and Rio Grande Railway, 142
Reed, Edward J., 163–64, 166, 171–73, 176–77, 224
Reed, Henry Wadsworth, 179
Reed, Homer, 224
Reedsville (Waycross), 179
Renaissance Theater (Paris), 153
Reynolds, Frank T., 36, 264–65
Reynolds, Kelly, 27, 82, 187
Reynolds, William Henry, 162, 228
Rhine River, 100
Rice, A. L., 170
Richardson, E. C., 226
Richmond, VA: express connections with, 46, 56, 67, 105; as Confederate capital, 84–85, 92–93
Richmond and Danville System, 189–90
Richmond and West Point Terminal Company, 197
Richmond Terminal Railroad, 207
Rio de Janeiro, Brazil, 207
Robbins, Stephen B., 110, 183
Roblin, Frederick, 226
Rockefeller, John D., 1, 150
Rockledge, FL, 230
Rodriguez, Amelia, 202
Roman Catholic Church, 23, 126, 134, 180
Rome, Italy, 99
Roosevelt, Edith Kermit, 257
Roosevelt, Franklin Delano, 121
Roosevelt, James, 121, 124–25, 128
Roosevelt, Rebecca Howland, 128
Roosevelt, Theodore, 251, 257
Rowland's Bluff, FL. *See* Branford, FL
Royal Italian Opera (London), 168
Royal Palm Hotel (Miami), 250
Royal Poinciana Hotel (Palm Beach), 234–36
Russell, Josephine Shaw. *See* Hoey, Josephine Shaw Russell
Russell, William, 51
Russell's Military School (New Haven), 92, 97–98, 102, 105
Rutkow, Ira, 163

Sacramento, CA, 46
Sacred Heart, Academy of the (New York City), 126–27
Sacred Heart, Society of the, 126
Saint John, New Brunswick, 1, 226
Salamanca y Negrete, Manuel, 202, 208–9
salon des refusés (Paris), 100
San Antonio, TX, 138
Sanchez & Haya (cigars), 189
San Diego, CA, 252
Sanford, Edwards Sewall: association of with Adams & Co., 46; growing familiarity of with HBP, 51; as Adams Express secretary, 63; and the Maroney scandal, 70, 73–75; assistance to HBP by, 72; as censor for Lincoln Administration, 89–90; visits HBP in London, 101; and creation of national banks, 102; as American Telegraph president, 105–6; and Mexican Express, 106; in Rufus Bullock traveling party, 123; and PICO, 167; mentioned, 60, 80, 88, 145
Sanford, FL: PICO construction at 187; railroad access to, 233, 238; mentioned, 175, 177, 182, 191, 217, 237, 248
Sanford, Henry: and the Maroney scandal, 70, 74–76; Civil War experiences of, 80; and creation of Southern Express, 83; as protector of President-Elect Lincoln, 88–89; and postwar Adams Express reorganization, 107; as Adams Express counsel, 114; in Rufus Bullock traveling party, 123; and HBP's remarriage, 129; Texas interests of, 142; and PICO, 167, 183, 198, 218; as Adams Express president, 216; mentioned, 128, 145, 149, 154, 164, 169, 197, 220
Sanford, Henry Shelton, 70, 164
San Francisco, CA, 148
Sanibel Island, FL, 244
San Jacinto (steamer), 152
Santa Fe River, FL, 170, 175
Saratoga Springs, NY: James E. English at, 138–39, 183; HBP at, 138–39, 142, 174, 183, 206, 211, 226; William Percival as headwaiter at, 221
Satan-Revue (burlesque), 231
Satanstoe (Flagler estate), 174
Savannah, Florida and Western Railway Co.: purchased and renamed by HBP, 154, 213; organization of, 145; purchase of Chattahoochee River steamboat line by, 155; prosperity of, 160; completion of Waycross Short

Line by, 160; extensions of, 162, 164, 167, 171–72, 175, 177–78, 218; and possible Savannah hotel investment by, 174; other lines consolidated into by PICO, 177, 180, 189, 225; improvements to, 189; new Savannah depot for, 199; and growing competition, 224, 233; 1894 hurricane damage to, 233; dismissal of union activists by, 246; tidal wave at, 248; mentioned, 203
Savannah, GA: express industry at, 46, 53–54, 60, 105; described c. 1852, 53–54; HBP at, 53–54, 57, 64, 78, 122, 154–55, 167, 176, 182, 187, 215, 217, 220, 225, 234, 238, 241, 248, 262; yellow fever at, 60–61, 71, 143; hurricane at, 61, 227, 247; capture of by Sherman, 102; HBP and H. M. Flagler meet at, 151–52; and *H. B. Plant*, 156; tourism at, 160; as Savannah, Florida and Western Railroad hub, 167, 170–71; LePageville at, 179; new depot for, 199; mentioned, 109, 190, 222
Savannah River, 55, 64, 103
Sawyer, Leicester Ambrose, 21, 28
Schenectady, NY, 20
Schneider, Hortense, 109, 153, 210
Scott, Thomas Alexander: as associate of J. E. Thompson, 63; as Pennsylvania Railroad executive, 115; and the Southern Railway Security Co., 115–16, 123–25, 134; behavior and attitudes of, 124–25, 135; as a lessee of Western and Atlantic Railroad, 118–19; and HBP honeymoon, 130–31
Sebring, Edward, 83–84
secession crisis (1860–1861), 79–81
Second Great Awakening, 15–16. *See also* Benevolent Empire
Second Seminole War, 53
Seddon, James A., 92
Seminole Hotel (Winter Park), 196, 200, 211, 214, 218, 230, 236
Seminole Indians, 66
Sessi, Mathilde, 115
Severn (warship), 120
Seward, Clarence A., 106, 153, 180, 197
Seward, William Henry: as Adams Express counsel, 70, 88, 97, 117; as secretary of state, 88, *89*; intelligence network of, 96–97; 1863 meeting with HBP, 97; new border crossing policy issued by, 101; and Mexican Express, 106
Shafter, William R., 257
Shanghai, China, 252
Shelbourne Hotel (Dublin, Ireland), 131
Sheldon, Lionel A., 118
Shelter Island, NY, 240
Sherman, John, 191
Sherman, TX, 143
Sherman, William Tecumseh, 101–2
ship ownership begun by HBP, 103, 108. *See also names of individual ships and shipping lines*
ships and shipping industry, 8–9, 26–27. *See also individual steamboats, steamboat travel, and names of individual ships and shipping lines*
Shoemaker, Samuel Moor: at Adams Express, 46, 60, 63, 68, 105; as proposed Southern Express director, 123; and PICO, 167; death of, 179; mentioned 145
Shourds, Ida Alice. *See* Flagler, Ida Alice Shourds
Shreveport, LA, 135
Shuter, James: employed by Adams Express, 68, 72, 91, 103; as acting Southern Express president, 93; as Memphis regional superintendent, 106–7; and PICO, 167; mentioned, 148
Sigsbee, Charles Dwight, 255
Simpson, James, 86
slave ownership by HBP, 87
Slevin, Edward, 143
Slidell, John, 97
Slineyville (New Haven, CT), 23–24
Sloan, Sam, 48
Slote, Daniel, 137
Small, Alexander Benson, 107, 138–39
smallpox, 262
Smith, Charles Henry, 5, 265
Smyth, George Hutchinson, 241–42, 246, 260
Snelson, Floyd, 179
Sonnambula, La (opera), 115
Sondheim, Samuel, 148
Sondheim, Sarah Whitaker Blackstone, 141, 145–46, 148, 151, 153
South America, 180, 207, 215. *See also names of individual countries*
Southampton, England, 215
South and West Commercial Congress, 254
South Atlantic and Gulf States Harbor Defense and Improvement Convention, 248
South Carolina, State Bank of, 83
South Carolina Railroad, 60
Southeastern Division. *See* Baltimore Division (Adams Express)
South Eastern Investment Co., 225, 263
Southern Bell Telephone and Telegraph Co., 155
Southern Express, The (1855), 62
Southern Express Co. (1859), 76–78, 81–83
Southern Express Co. (1861): organized, 83–84, 114; criticized as to Southern loyalty, 85–86, 92–93, 110–11; and ties to US intelligence

services, 89–90; Civil War–era business of, 90–91, 101; distribution of wartime profits of, 91, 96; gifts to Confederate officials by, 93; restart following Confederate surrender of, 103; separation contract from Adams Express of, 103–5, 114, 117–18, 125; postwar reorganizations of, 106–7, 110–11; attempts to secure national charter for, 113–14, 117–18, 123; and the Western and Atlantic Railroad, 116–17; and the Texas Express, 138–39; offices of at Nathan Mansion, 139–40; enhanced employee benefit offered by, 140, 143, 149–50; and 1876 presidential election, 144, 159; Union Express as competition for, 158–59; consolidated into Railway Express Agency, 268; mentioned, 198. *See also* Adams Southern Express Co.
Southern Railroad Association, 62, 67, 69
Southern Railway and Steamship Association, 232
Southern Railway Co., 197
Southern Railway Security Co.: organization of, 115–16, 120–21; and HBE support for, 123–25; and growing controversy regarding, 124–25; collapse of during Panic of 1873, 133–43, 142; mentioned, 130, 157
South Florida Railroad: construction to Kissimmee by, 164; and HBP control of, 165, 171, 173; extension to Tampa, 173, 188; inspected by HBP, 175–76; consolidated with Savannah, Florida and Western, 225
Spanish-American War, 256–58
Splendid (steamboat), 29–30
Spooner, Clapp: at Thompson & Co. Express, 43–44; at Adams Express, 60–61, 70, 72, 91, 128, 145, 216; and national bank charters 102; as proposed Southern Express director, 123; and PICO, 167; mentioned, 84, 197
Spooner, Jacob, 72, 84, 86
Springfield, MA, 44
Squire, Julia. *See* Blackstone, Julia Squire
Staatsburg, NY, 123, 125
stagecoach travel, 12–13
Standard Oil Co., 1, 150, 167, 174
Stanton, Edward M., 89
Starkweather, Henry H., 123
Stashower, Daniel, 73
State of Georgia, The (railroad car), 119–20, 123
State of Indiana (steamer), 168
statuary, 136
St. Augustine, FL: HBP visits to, 54, 78, 176, 201, 222, 236; bias against Northerners at, 78, 151; and H. M. Flagler, 174, 182, 185–86; new depot at, 202; mentioned, 2, 122, 152. *See also* Ponce de Leon Hotel (St. Augustine)
St. Charles Hotel (New Orleans), 70, 78, 122, 153
St. Elmo's Inn (Port Tampa), 194–95
St. Johns River, FL: initial HBP visits to, 54, 57; and William B. Astor, 151; and South Florida Railroad, 164; and the *H. B. Plant*, 171; mentioned, 173, 185, 195, 233
St. Leo's Church (NYC), 219
St. Louis, Iron Mountain Railroad and Southern Railway, 180
St. Louis, MO, 69, 110, 180, 207
St. Luke's Hospital (NYC), 267
St. Pancras Station (London), 131
St. Petersburg, FL, 215, 233–34, 238, 262
St. Petersburg, Russia, 216
Strakosch, Maurice, 115
steamboats and steamboat travel, 12, 27, 130–31, 155, 165. *See also names of individual ships and lines*
steamboat war, 35–36
Steeples, Douglas, 223
Stephens, Alexander H., 81, 119
Stiles, T. J., 26
Stimson, Alexander Lovett, 33, 37, 48, 58, 135
Stone, George, 52
Stone, Solomon Bartlett, 29–32, 52
Strawberry Mills, FL, 57, 61, 64, 73, 122
street railways, 185
strikes, 178–79, 210, 215, 217. *See also* labor and labor relations
Stubbeline, Henry, 213
Success (magazine), 2
sugar trade, 232–33
Sullivan, Francis de Chantal, 208
Suwannee River, 161, 169–71, 185
Switzerland, 100
Swoope, Bolling R., 239
Synod of Utica (NY), 28

Tacon Theatre (Havana), 188, 254
Tallahassee, FL, 65–66, 106
Tampa, FL: in 1870s, 147; railroads to, 162, 164–66, 171, 185; Plant exploratory team visit to, 170; HBP at, 175–77, 220, 228, 250; Plant steamship operations at, 178, 184, 204; described subsequent to railroad's arrival, 188–89; cigar industry at, 189; and mail service to and from, 189–90; as port of entry, 192; hotel proposals for, 192–93; yellow fever at, 193–94, 198–99; Grover Cleveland at, 195–96, 201–2; improvements at, 199–200; 1894 hurricane damage at, 233; and Spanish-American War, 256; mentioned, 65, 182, 187, 203, 225. *See also* Port Tampa
Tampa and Havana Steamship Line, 193
Tampa Bay, FL: observed by HBP, 171; excursions on, 175, 224, 262; White Squadron

at, 214–15; improvements at, 218; defense tour of, 248; port defenses at, 255; smallpox quarantine at, 262
Tampa Bay Hotel: purchase of land for, 195–96; planning for and construction of, 196–99, 204; and praise for black laborers at, 204; European furnishings for, 204, 216, 218; painting of at 1889 Paris exposition, 206; construction delays at, 208, 210; laborers strike at, 210; opening of, 213–14; image of, *214*; functions and events at, 215, 248, 254; improvements at, 217, 244–45; black employees at, 221, *230*; purchases for at World Columbian Exposition, 227; 1894 hurricane damage at, 233, 247; 1894–95 season at, 234–35; 1894 freeze damage at, 236; and Great Freeze of 1895, 236–37; and Spanish-American War, 256–57; Abner McKinley at, 262; sold to City of Tampa, 267; mentioned, 217, 228, 238, 246, 248, 254, 260
Tampa Bay Hotel Galop, 214
Tampa Bay Hotel Orchestra, 213
Tampa Bay Lawn Tennis Tournament, 218, 224
Tampa Steamship Co., 170
Tampa Steamship Line, 175
Tampa Tribune (newspaper), 228
tariffs and tariff policy, 232–33
tarpon fishing, 202–3, 250, 252, 256
telegraphy, 73, 136
telephones, 155
temperance and temperance movement, 15–17, 41
Tennessee River, 88
tennis tournaments and championships, 201, 218
Ten Years' War. *See* Grito de Yara
Texas, 107, 138, 142–43
Texas Express Company, 107, 138–39, 142
Texas Pacific Railroad, 124
Théâtre de la Gaîté (Paris), 132
Théâtre des Variétés (Paris), 210, 231, 239
Theatre Royal (London), 153
Théo, Louise, 131
Third Congregational Church (New Haven), 28
Third Seminole War, 66–67
Thomasville, GA, 155, 191, 195
Thompson, J. B., 145
Thompson, J. Edgar, 63
Thompson & Co.'s express line, 43
Thompson, Livingston & Co., 58–59
Thompson's Atlanta Hotel, 71
Thomson, John Stuart, 251
tidal wave, 248
Tilden, Samuel J., 143
Tilley, George Heath: as HBP private secretary, 107, 125, 138; as Southern Express secretary, 148; as Savannah, Florida and Western secretary and director, 154–55; and PICO, 167; and South Eastern Investment Co., 225; and HBP's final days, 264; as HBP pallbearer, 264; sued as HBP estate trustee, 266; mentioned, 197, 220
Titusville, FL, 189
tobacco and tobacco cultivation, 250
Toledo, OH, 56
Tostee, Lucille, 109
tourism industry, vertical integration of, 2
Transfiguration, Episcopal Church of the (New York City), 128–29
Trinidad de Cuba, 19
Tropical Hotel (Kissimmee), 244
Trout House (Atlanta), 71–72
Troy, FL, 170
Tucker, Phillip Thomas, 24
Tupper, J. Nelson, 171
Tuscumbia, AL, 67
Twain, Mark, 137–38
Tybee Island, GA, 156
typhus and typhoid fever, 227. *See also* New England Spotted Fever

Union Express, 158
Union League (New York City), 173
Union Pacific Railroad, 98, 123–24
Union Republican Party of Georgia, 109
United Church on the Green (New Haven, CT), 28
United States Express, 59
United States post office: and the express industry, 30, 37, 43–44, 71; and Cuba, 152, 159, 182. *See also* West Indies; West Indian Fast Mail
Utica, NY, 12, 28

Valkyrie (yacht), 227
Van Buren, Martin, 27
Vance, Zebulon B., 229
Vanderbilt, Cornelius, 26, 29–30, 32, 48
Vanderbilt, George Washington II, 252
Vanderbilt, William R., 136
Venezuela, 238
Venice, Italy, 100
Vera Crux, Mexico, 199
Vicksburg, MS, 69, 71, 123
Vienna, Austria, 100, 131
Vigilant (yacht), 227
Villa Yaddo (Menton, France), 267
Virginia and Tennessee Railroad, 71
Vose Injunction, 161

Wade, James F., 256
Wagner, Richard, 216

Walker, John Grimes, 215
Wallack, John Lester, 52
Wall Street Club, 136
Walters, William T., 121–22, 157, 177, 234
Warner, Charles Dudley, 137–38
Warner, Olin Levi, 136–37, 142, 145
War of 1812, 5
Warrenton, NC, 56
Washington, Booker T., 240
Washington, GA, 103
Washington Artillery (Augusta), 80
Washington Temperance Society (New Haven), 41
Waters, Mary Ann, 18
Watertown, MA,
Watts, Thomas Hill: as Adams Express attorney: 74, 76, 81–82; as Confederate attorney general, 90, 93–94
Waycross, GA, 155, 179, 220, 226, 248
Waycross and Florida Railroad, 156, 160, 177
Waycross Short Line, 156–57, 160
Webb, Washington, 36–37, 41, 43, 47
Webb & Co., 37
Webb & Plant, 37, 40–43
Weldon, NC, 56, 116
Wells Fargo, 59, 128
West End Hotel (Long Branch), 144, 148
West Indian Fast Mail, 189–90, 211, 233
West Indies: trade with at New Haven, 23–24, 41; mail contracts, 182, 189, 211, 233; Plant System links with, 199. *See also names of individual islands and places*
West Point, GA, 103
Western and Atlantic Railroad: lease of, 116–19, 143–44; mentioned, 60
Western and Atlantic Railroad Co., 118–20
Western North Carolina Railroad, 104–5
Westinghouse, George, 196
Whitaker, Sarah A. *See* Sondheim, Sarah Whitaker Blackstone
White Squadron, 214–15
Whitney (steamer), 189
Whitney, Eli, 24
Whitten, David O., 223
Wilcox, Daniel Hand, 100–101
Wildwood, FL, 171–72
William Cramp & Sons. *See* Cramp & Sons
William H. Bunn (sloop), 29
Williams, Jane, 64, 87–88
Williams, William, 64, 87–88
Willis, William Parker, 22–23
Wilmington, DE, 215
Wilmington, NC, 56, 75, 85, 94, 105, 116, 159
Wilmington and Manchester Railroad, 55
Wilmington and Weldon Railroad, 116, 121
Wilmot, Samuel, 91–92
Wilson, James H., 103
Wilson, Joseph R., 88
Wilson, Woodrow, 88
Wilson-Gorman Tariff Act (1894), 232
Winchester, Locke W., 34, 54, 106
Windsor Hotel (Jacksonville, FL), 164
Windsor Hotel (NYC): construction and significance of, 136–38; HBP at, 150; Jim and Anna English honeymoon at, 183; as Abner McKinley residence, 251, 262; destruction of, 262; mentioned, 140
Winter Haven, FL, 248
Winter Park, FL, 177, 196, 200, 211, 214, 217, 225–26, 236
Wood, John A.: background of, 191; and Piney Woods Hotel, 191–92; and Oglethorpe Hotel, 195; as Tampa Bay Hotel architect, 195–97, 199, 204, 210; at Havana, 208, 218
Wood, Mary A., 266
Wood, William G., 266
Woodward, W. T. J., 79
World Columbian Exposition (1893), 226–27
Wrenn, Beverly Welford, 65, 117, 236–37, 264
Wyatt, John W., 124–25

Yale College, 23–24, 28, 113
Yancey, William Lowndes, 74, 76, 78
Ybor, Vicente Martinez, 189
Ybor & Co., 188
Ybor City, FL, 189, 233
yellow fever: in 1819, 6; in 1854, 60–61; in 1858, 71; in 1873, 135; in 1876, 143–44; in 1878–79, 149; in 1887, 193; in 1888, 194, 198–99; in 1893, 227; in 1897
Yokohama, Japan, 252
York, England, 131
Yulee, David Levy, 66, 162–63